AF896376

Islamic Law of the Sea

The doctrine of modern law of the sea is commonly believed to have developed from Renaissance Europe. Often ignored though, is the role of Islamic law of the sea and customary practices at that time. In this book, Hassan S. Khalilieh highlights Islamic legal doctrine regarding freedom of the seas and its implementation in practice. He proves that many of the fundamental principles of the pre-modern international law governing the legal status of the high seas and the territorial sea, though originating in the Mediterranean world, are not a necessarily European creation. Beginning with the commonality of the sea in the Qur'an and legal methods employed to insure the safety, security, and freedom of movement of Muslim and aliens by land and sea, Khalilieh then goes on to examine the concepts of territorial sea and its security premises, as well as issues surrounding piracy and its legal implications as delineated in Islamic law.

Hassan S. Khalilieh is a senior lecturer in the departments of Maritime Civilizations and Multidisciplinary Studies and a senior research fellow in the Leon Recanati Institute for Maritime Studies, Leon H. Charney School of Marine Sciences at the University of Haifa. His publications include *Islamic Maritime Law: An Introduction* (1998) and *Admiralty and Maritime Laws in the Mediterranean Sea (ca. 800–1050): The Kitāb Akriyat al-Sufun and the Nomos Rhodion Nautikos* (2006).

Cambridge Studies in Islamic Civilization

Editorial Board
Chase F. Robinson, *The Graduate Center, The City University of New York (general editor)*

Michael Cook, *Princeton University*
Maribel Fierro, *Spanish National Research Council*
Alan Mikhail, *Yale University*
David O. Morgan, *Professor Emeritus, University of Wisconsin–Madison*
Intisar Rabb, *Harvard University*
Muhammad Qasim Zaman, *Princeton University*

Other titles in the series are listed at the back of the book.

Islamic Law of the Sea

Freedom of Navigation and Passage Rights in Islamic Thought

HASSAN S. KHALILIEH
University of Haifa, Israel

CAMBRIDGE
UNIVERSITY PRESS

CAMBRIDGE
UNIVERSITY PRESS

University Printing House, Cambridge CB2 8BS, United Kingdom

One Liberty Plaza, 20th Floor, New York, NY 10006, USA

477 Williamstown Road, Port Melbourne, VIC 3207, Australia

314–321, 3rd Floor, Plot 3, Splendor Forum, Jasola District Centre, New Delhi – 110025, India

79 Anson Road, #06–04/06, Singapore 079906

Cambridge University Press is part of the University of Cambridge.

It furthers the University's mission by disseminating knowledge in the pursuit of education, learning, and research at the highest international levels of excellence.

www.cambridge.org
Information on this title: www.cambridge.org/9781108481458
DOI: 10.1017/9781108630702

© Hassan S. Khalilieh 2019

This publication is in copyright. Subject to statutory exception and to the provisions of relevant collective licensing agreements, no reproduction of any part may take place without the written permission of Cambridge University Press.

First published 2019

Printed and bound in Great Britain by Clays Ltd, Elcograf S.p.A.

A catalogue record for this publication is available from the British Library.

Library of Congress Cataloging-in-Publication Data
Names: Khalilieh, Hassan Salih, 1965– author.
Title: Islamic law of the sea : freedom of navigation and passage rights in islamic thought / Hassan S. Khalilieh, University of Haifa, Israel.
Description: Cambridge, United Kingdom ; New York, NY, USA : Cambridge University Press, 2019. | Series: Cambridge studies in Islamic civilization | Based on author's thesis (J.S.D. – Saint Thomas University (Miami, Fla.). School of Law, 2014). | Includes bibliographical references and index.
Identifiers: LCCN 2018048308 | ISBN 9781108481458 (hardback)
Subjects: LCSH: Freedom of the seas. | Law – Europe – Islamic influences. | Maritime law (Islamic law)
Classification: LCC KZA1348 .K48 2019 | DDC 341.4/5091767–dc23
LC record available at https://lccn.loc.gov/2018048308

ISBN 978-1-108-48145-8 Hardback

Cambridge University Press has no responsibility for the persistence or accuracy of URLs for external or third-party internet websites referred to in this publication and does not guarantee that any content on such websites is, or will remain, accurate or appropriate.

Contents

Maps

Preface

Legal historians hold that the foundations of the modern law of the sea date to the first decade of the seventeenth century, when the Dutch jurist Hugo Grotius (1583–1645) extracted chapter 12 of his *De Jure Praedae* (*On the Law of Prize and Booty*) and published it in a single treatise titled *Mare Liberum* (*The Free Sea*), which was published anonymously in 1609. To defend and justify the right of other nations to navigate the seas freely, Grotius contended that, with the exception of limited offshore zones, the seas are not susceptible to appropriation by states. Following his contention, contemporaneous European lawyers sparked a legal debate, some challenging and others concurring with his position, leading to further scholarly contribution to the law of the sea. Both advocates and opponents of the freedom of navigation were inspired either by the Natural Law enshrined in the Justinianic *Institutes* and *Corpus Juris Civilis*, or the Hebrew Bible's concept of sovereignty on the open sea. British legal theoretician John Selden (1584–1654) mentions both in his 1635 *Mare Clausum, Sive de Dominio Maris* (*The Closed Sea, or the Dominion of the Sea*). Astoundingly, whether deliberately or accidently, seventeenth-century European legal scholars overlooked contributions by "infidels" (non-Europeans, especially Muslims) to the evolution of the customary law of the sea, giving the impression that the Law of Nature and Nations governing access to the sea is solely a European establishment.

With the advent of Islam in the Mediterranean world in the seventh century CE, the semienclosed sea, which had been called by the Romans "*mare nostrum* (our sea)" for a millennium, ceased to be a Roman lake.

From that time onward, the Mediterranean Sea has continued to be shared by Christians and Muslims, and neither party could consider it to be *mare nostrum*; the eastern, western, and southern shores of the Mediterranean Sea were entirely under Islamic control for several centuries, as have been the Red Sea, the Persian Gulf, and vast littorals of the Indian Ocean until the penetration of the Portuguese into the eastern seas. Eventually, on the eve of the great discoveries, Muslims dominated more than half of the world's maritime possessions. In spite of the importance of the sea in the Qurʾān (mentioned 32 times in comparison to the 13 references made to the land), in hadith literature, in theological, jurisprudential, geographical, and scientific literature, and in the daily life of Muslims throughout history, the theme that this study addresses has failed to attract attention in modern scholarship. For this and other reasons, an attempt will be made to fill the gap left by Renaissance and early modern European lawyers and to explore the Islamic contribution to the development of the customary law of the sea, relying heavily on the Islamic Law of Nature and Nations (*siyar*).

This study comprises three chapters, along with an introduction and a conclusion. The first chapter examines the commonality of the sea in the Qurʾān, legal methods employed to insure the safety, security, and freedom of movement of Muslims and aliens by land and sea, and the historical genesis of the freedom of navigation and its legal implications for Muslim administrations and judicial authorities in the ensuing centuries. The second chapter analyzes the concept of territorial sea and its religious and security premises, describes the right of innocent passage through territorial waters and straits, and explains how legal pluralism could have positive repercussions on the legal protection of individuals and promote local, interregional, and international trade involving subjects of the same and different religious creeds. The third and final chapter deals with piracy and its legal implications, methods employed to combat and reduce sea robbery, punishment, and its socio-economic and cultural impacts on humankind. However, since the time frame of our discussion does not extend beyond the first decades of the sixteenth century, the topic of the Barbary corsairs remains outside the scope of this study.

This book is a revised and expanded version of my JSD dissertation submitted to the School of Law, Saint Thomas University, in Miami, Florida, written under the supervision of Professor John Makdisi, without whose sincere and careful guidance, thoughtful support, and incredible patience this study would never have seen the light. I also extend my deepest appreciation to Professor David F. Forte of Cleveland-Marshall College of Law for his constructive critique and insightful comments, which helped me refine and reshape parts of this manuscript. My heartfelt gratitude and sincere reverence go to two remarkable individuals, Professor Siegfried Wiessner and Haydee Gonzalez, respectively the director and program manager at the Graduate Program in Intercultural Human Rights, Saint Thomas University, for their extraordinary support and encouragement. I also express my sincere gratitude and appreciation to my masters' advisors at Tulane University Law School, Professors Robert Force and Martin Davies, who introduced me to the realm of modern admiralty and maritime law. The Admiralty and Maritime Law Program deeply enriched my legal knowledge and provided me with the academic tools for thoroughly analyzing early and classical jurisprudential literature and international treaties from a wide legal perspective. My sincere appreciation also goes to Professor David Abulafia at Cambridge University and Professor Michael Lobban at the London School of Economics and Political Science for their helpful and invaluable comments on the original draft of the manuscript. I am obliged to express my indebtedness and sincere thanks to the anonymous reviewers, whose thorough reading, insightful observations, and constructive criticism have only strengthened my manuscript. My special thanks go to Professor Chase Robinson, General Editor of the Cambridge Studies in Islamic Civilization, to all the Editorial Board, and to Maria Marsh, Commissioning Editor, Natasha Whelan, Content Manager, Jayavel Radhakrishnan, Senior Project Manager, Integra Software Services, and the publication staff for their efforts to publish this book. I am additionally grateful to Professor François Gipouloux at CNRS, France, and to Dr. Mahmood Kooria and Dr. Sanne Ravensbergen at Leiden University in the Netherlands for inviting me to participate in conferences on trade and law in the Indian Ocean; all of their presentations and discussions shaped my thinking and honed my arguments. My deep sense of gratitude goes to Dr. Helene Furani, Dr. Christina Morris and Cheryl Hutty for their diligent copy-editing and constructive criticism of the manuscript. Warm words of gratitude go to my cousins Doha and Ishraq Khalilieh and to my sincere friends Dirar Bdaiwi and Amer Karkabi for always succeeding in making me feel special. My sincere thanks are also due to the University of Haifa's Research Authority for its cordial assistance and generous financial aid. I am now and will always be indebted to my former advisors and mentors: Professor Michal Artzy at the University of Haifa, and

Professors Abraham Udovitch, Mark Cohen, and William Jordan at Princeton University. Last, but not least, my affectionate gratitude and deep indebtedness are due to my wife Ranin and to our children, Samuel, Mariam, and Awaise, for their understanding, commitment, and emotional support throughout my six-year journey of researching, organizing, and writing this book.

Glossary of Non-English Terms

AH	After the *Hijra*, the migration of the Prophet from Mecca to Medina; the year it occurred, 622 CE, is the base-year of the Muslim era
actio iniuriarum	action for delict, intentional infringement of a personality right
ʿadāla	probity, equality before the law
adat	Malay customary law, probably Persian *ʿādāt*, from the Arabic *ʿādah*
admiral	a term derived from the Arabic words *Amīr al-Baḥr*, literally, "Prince of the Sea," or the Commander in Chief of the Fleet
amān	a temporary safe-conduct, safe passage, promise of assurance of security to be granted to enemies during war, or individual *ḥarbī*, who intend to enter or travel through the Abode of Islam
amir	a prince, also a governor of a province
Amīr al-Muʾminīn	literally, "Commander of the Faithful," Caliph
ʿaqd	pl. **ʿuqūd**, bilateral or unilateral obligations
baghiyy	sedition; sexual relationship outside marriage
bailli	derived from the generic term *bailiff* to mean the king's personal agent or administrative representative
bēt dīn	Jewish rabbinical court
cartaz	a Portuguese word derived from Arabic *qirṭās* or *qarṭās*, which is originally derived from ancient

	Greek χάρτης (*chártēs*), denoting a writing, book, scroll, document, paper cone, or cornet. It is a trading license issued by a Portuguese commissioner or competent authority to ships sailing in the Indian Ocean; a typical *cartaz* contains details regarding the place of origin of cargo, a vessel's destination, types of shipments, identities of crews, shippers, and passengers, etc.
Corpus Juris Civilis	Roman compendium of civil law compiled and promulgated by Justinian I (527–565); it consists of four parts, the Institute, Digest, Code, and Novels
Dār al-ʿAhd	Abode of Covenant/Truce, territories/countries that have treaties of nonaggression or peace with Muslims, agreeing to protect Muslims and their clients in that territory and often including an agreement to pay (receive) tribute
Dār al-Ḥarb	Abode of War, territories/countries that do not have treaties of nonaggression or peace with Muslims and where Islamic law is not in force
Dār al-Islām	Abode of Islam, region of Muslim sovereignty where Islamic law prevails; the Hanafi Law School holds that territory conquered by nonbelievers can remain Abode of Islam so long as the qadi administers Islamic law and Muslims and *dhimmī*s are protected
Dār al-Kufr	Abode of Disbelief, synonymous to the Abode of War where the territory is governed by the laws of infidels and the security is upheld by them
dayyan	literally, a Jewish judge – a well-versed scholar acquainted with rabbinical law, religious rituals, and theology
dhimmī	a Christian, Jew, or Zoroastrian living in the Abode of Islam and acknowledging the domination of Islam
dhirāʿ	a measurement of the arm from the elbow to the tip of the middle finger; i.e., a cubit; also the name given to the instrument for measuring it; *al-dhirāʿ al-sharʿiyya* equals 0.5465 yards/0.49875 meters
faqīh	pl. **fuqahā'**, a jurist or jurisconsult well versed in Islamic theology and jurisprudence

fasād	disturbing peace and spreading evil and mischievous acts on earth; corruption, disorder, turmoil
fatwā	pl. **fatāwā**, an authoritative opinion on a matter of Islamic law
fiqh	knowledge of Islamic law derived through legal reasoning
gabella	an Old Italian word derived from the Arabic *qibālah* denoting duty, tribute, levy; tax paid to the state for goods bought or sold; rent of land; a contract given to somebody who tills the earth for which he pays an annual tax; tax on the transaction of a real estate
geniza	a place for storing unusable books, writings, and ritual objects in order to prevent the desecration of the name of God, which might be found in them, while they await burial in a cemetery
ghazw	a military expedition
ghifāra	a heavy tribute paid to pirates to protect commercial vessels from other piratical attacks
ḥadd	pl. **ḥudūd**, a punishment fixed in the Qur᾽ān and hadith for crimes considered to be against the rights of God
Ḥaram	literally, "protected/inviolable zone"; the Ḥaram signifies the Holy Sanctuary
ḥarbī	a non-Muslim who does not live under the conditions of the *dhimma* (*dhimmī*); if he wants to enter the Abode of Islam, he needs to be equipped with a pledge of *amān*
ḥarīm	an inviolable zone or reserved space, within which access is either prohibited or restricted to prevent the impairment of natural resources and utilities
ḥirāba	brigandage, banditry, highway robbery, or forcible theft; derived from *ḥ.r.b.*, meaning "to contend or wage war"
hostis humani generis	enemies of all humankind; the term may have been first used by the Roman statesman Marcus Cicero (106–43 BCE) "*pirata est hostis humani generis* (a pirate is the common enemy of humankind)." Historically, it applied to persons whose acts

	threatened all societies and took them outside national jurisdiction, such as pirates and slavers.
hudna	a temporary truce or armistice
hunarman	a qadi-like official of the Muslims, who judges according to Islamic *Sharīʿah*
ʿibādāt	performance of religious duties
iḥrām	a state of ritual purity where the Muslim pilgrim dons a special garb consisting of two white unknitted sheets covering the upper and lower parts of the body
imam	an equivalent to Caliph, spiritual and political leadership of the Muslim nation (*ummah*)
imperium	power or dominion; it implies the right of military command and judicial authority; sovereignty of the state over the individual. The term can also be used with a geographical connotation, designating a state's territorial limits.
jihad	literally, "struggle" or "effort"; in Qurʾānic contexts it denotes striving and struggling in the Path of God; technically in law, rules regulating conduct of war and peace treaties
jus ad bellum	a set of criteria that are to be consulted before engaging in war, in order to determine whether entering into war is permissible; that is, justifications for resorting to war
jus gentium	Law of Nations, the body of law, taken to be common to all civilized peoples, and applied in dealing with the relations between Roman citizens and foreigners
jus in bello	rules regulating the conduct of war
jus naturale	Natural Law/Law of Nature, the laws governing men and people in a state of nature, i.e., in advance of organized governments or enacted laws
kharāj	a tax imposed on agrarian/agricultural land
maghāzī	a genre of early biographical writings on the Prophet Muḥammad, or the Prophet's military campaigns
maḥram	pl. **maḥārim**, an unmarriageable male kin
maʾman	a place of safety where a person can feel secure
maẓālim	Court of Appeal; a court that serves as a tribunal of administrative law where the public directly appear

	to the ruler or his deputies against the abuse of or failure to exercise power by other authorities, as well as against decisions made by judges
miḥrās	a watchtower functioning to alert local residents against enemy attack from the sea
mīqāt	pl. **mawāqīt**, a stated place or station at which pilgrims on their way to Mecca are required to purify their souls, don the pilgrim's garb (*iḥrām*), and declare the intention
muʿallim	literally, "shipmaster" or "pilot/navigator of the vessel"; he was responsible for the appropriate fitting of the ship, inspection of the gear, the stores and the supervision of the loading
muḥārib	a predator or a highway plunderer
mujāhid	pl. **mujāhidūn**, a fighter in the Cause of God
mustaʾmin	a recipient/grantee of a pledge of safe-conduct; an enemy-alien merchant who is granted an *amān* pledge to trade and carry out business transactions in the Abode of Islam
naṣṣ	a foundational text, or an explicit textual ruling; the term refers to a text found in either the Qurʾān or hadith
nākhūdha/nakhoda	a Persian term meaning "captain"; derived from *nāv* and *khudā*, meaning "a master of a native vessel," or "Lord of the Ship"
pĕrahu	a large sailing boat carrying 15–20 crew members
praeses	a Roman provincial governor
qadhf	a false accusation of immoral behavior
qaṭʿ al-sabīl	literally, "cut off the highway"; a privately motivated armed robbery
qitāl	literally, "fighting, armed *jihad*"; *qitāl* is viewed as a lesser *jihad*
res communes	joint property of all humankind; things that are common to all, which cannot be owned or appropriated, such as light, air, and the sea
res nullius	things that have no owner/s, or have been abandoned by their owner/s so that their first possessors become their owners; things that are capable of ownership

res publica	public things; originally used for common as opposed to private property; it covers property of the Roman Empire such as highways, inland rivers, and harbors
ribāṭ	literally, "fortified monastery"; a coastal defense system that consists of watch stations along the coastal frontiers
ridda	apostasy, rejection in word or deed of one's former religion by a person who was previously a follower of Islam
Rūm	Byzantines or Italians; in broader contexts, it refers to Europeans
ṣāḥib al-dīwān	a chief financial official
Sharīʿah	God's eternal and immutable will for humanity, as expressed in the Qurʾān and Muḥammad's Sunna, considered binding for all believers; the *Sharīʿah* sometimes applies to all Islamic legislation
shubha	uncertainty about lawfulness in a jurist's view
shuhūd ʿudūl	trustworthy witnesses
sīra(h)	pl. **siyar**, Prophet Muḥammad's life account or biography
stratēgos	a Byzantine governing general
Sufi	a member of an Islamic ascetic and mystical sect, in which the member tries to become united with God through prayer and meditation
ṣulḥ	treaty, reconciliation, or amicable settlement
tanzīmāt	a series of reforms promulgated in the Ottoman Empire between 1839 and 1876; these reforms, heavily influenced by European ideas, were intended to effectuate a fundamental change in the Empire from the old system based on theocratic principles to that of a modern state
terra nullius	a territory not belonging to any particular country
ummah	a common Arabic term denoting a group of people or a nation; it refers to the commitment of the individual to a particular religion and represents a universal world order; the *ummah* comprises all Muslims throughout the world, regardless of ethnic, racial, and regional origins

Transliteration Scheme

1. CONSONANTS

ء	ʾ	ض	ḍ
ب	b	ط	ṭ
ت	t	ظ	ẓ
ث	th	ع	ʿ
ج	j	غ	gh
ح	ḥ	ف	f
خ	kh	ق	q
د	d	ك	k
ذ	dh	ل	l
ر	r	م	m
ز	z	ن	n
س	s	ه	h
ش	sh	و	w
ص	ṣ	ي	y

2. VOWELS

Short vowels		Long vowels	
َ	a	ا	ā
ُ	u	و	ū
ِ	i	ي	ī

To my wife Ranin

And my children

Samuel, Mariam, and Awaise

This Book

Is

Affectionately Dedicated

Introduction

GENERAL

The year 1492 signaled a fundamental turning point in global and, more particularly, maritime history. It marked the expulsion of the Naṣrid dynasty (636–898 AH/1238–1492 CE) from Granada, the last Islamic stronghold in Spain, and the beginning of the great age of Christian maritime discoveries across the two shores of the Atlantic and Indian oceans. On August 3, 1492, Christopher Columbus embarked on a westward voyage to the Indian Ocean in search of alternative maritime routes that would circumvent traditional trade passages through Islamic territories to the Spice Islands. On a similar mission, the Portuguese navigator and explorer Vasco da Gama set sail from Lisbon on July 8, 1497, leading a flotilla of four fully equipped vessels; although, instead of following the steps of Columbus, da Gama sailed southward and circumnavigated Africa. After a lengthy journey with various stops in trading centres on African coasts, da Gama landed at Malindi, Kenya, on April 15, 1498; there he managed to secure a well-versed Arab *mu ʿallim*, who guided the Portuguese fleet across the Arabian Sea, finally arriving in Kappadu (Kappad), near Calicut,[1] on May 20, 1498.[2]

[1] Calicut (Arabic Qāliqūṭ), the modern city of Kozhikode in the province of Kerala, was the premier port on the Malabar Coast during the fifteenth century. Muslim travelers and envoys described Calicut as a large cosmopolitan center and trading hub, which attracted merchants from China, Java, Ceylon, the Maldives, Yemen, and Persia. Ibn Baṭṭūṭa stated that its "port is considered one of the largest in the world." Pepper, ginger, cinnamon, cardamom, tamarind, precious stones, seed pearls, cotton cloths, and porcelain were among its principal exports. See Abū ʿAbd Allāh Muḥammad ibn ʿAbd Allāh ibn Baṭṭūṭa, *Riḥlat Ibn Baṭṭūṭa: Tuḥfat al-Nuẓẓār fī Gharāʾib al-Amṣār wa-ʿAjāʾib al-Asfār* (Beirut: Dār Iḥyāʾ al-ʿUlūm, 1407/1987), 572, 575; Kamāl al-Dīn ʿAbd al-Razzāq ibn Isḥāq al-Samarqandī, *Maṭlaʿ al-Saʿdayn wa-Majmaʿ al-Ba ḥrayn* (*The Dawn of Two Auspicious Planets and the Meeting of the Two Seas*), in *India in the Fifteenth Century: Being a Collection of Voyages to India*, ed. and trans. R. H. Major (London: Hakluyt Society, 1857), 13–14; Anup Mukherjee, "Calicut," *Encyclopedia of World Trade from Ancient Times to the Present*, ed. Cynthia C. Northrup (London: Taylor and Francis, 2015), **1**:137–139; Robert Wolf, "Da Gama's Blundering: Trade Encounters in Africa and Asia during the European 'Age of Discovery,' 1450–1520," *The History Teacher* 31 (1998), 300.

[2] Ḥasan Ṣ. Shihāb, *Al-Nūniyya al-Kubrā maʿ Sitt Qaṣāʾid Ukhrā Naẓm Shihāb al-Dīn Aḥmad Ibn Mājid* (Muscat: Wizārat al-Turāth al-Qawmī wa'l-Thaqāfa, 1413/1993),

The Portuguese circumnavigation of Africa and penetration of the Indian Ocean also marked a new chapter in maritime legal history.[3]

18–21; Abbas Hamadani, "An Islamic Background to the Voyages of Discovery," in *The Legacy of Muslim Spain*, ed. Salma K. Jayyusi (Leiden: E. J. Brill, 1992), 298; R. Sengupta, "History of Oceanography of the Indian Ocean," in *New Trends in Indian Art and Archeology*, ed. B. U. Nayak and N. C. Ghosh (New Delhi: Aditya Prakashan, 1992), 402–403; Ranabir Chakravarti, "An Enchanting Seascape: Through Epigraphic Lens," *Studies in History* 20 (2004), 306.

[3] Aḥmad ibn Mājid (823–914/1421–1509), the famous Arab pilot of the Indian Ocean, witnessed the eventual arrival of the Portuguese in the eastern seas and sensed the beginning of the end of the peaceful oceanic navigation therein. In several places in the Sufāliyya (Sufāla or Sofala, present-day Mozambique) poem he alluded to the prospective serious impacts and adverse effects of the Portuguese on the overseas trade and freedom of navigation, stating:

(27) [And the Franks] arrived at Calicut to acquire profit
in the year nine-hundred and six (AH), even later
(28) There they sold and bought, and displayed their power,
bought off the Zamorin, and oppressed the people
(29) Hatred of Islam came with them
and the people were afraid and anguished
(30) And the land of the Zamorin was snatched away from that of Mecca,
and Guardafui was closed to travelers.

See Shihāb, *Al-Nūniyya al-Kubrā*, 19; Ibrahim Khoury, *As-Sufāliyya: The Poem of Sofala: Arabic Navigation along the East African Coast in the 15th Century* (Coimbra: Junta de Investigações Científicas do Ultramar, 1983), 89–90; Edward A. Alpers, *The Indian Ocean in World History* (New York and Oxford: Oxford University Press, 2014), 69–74; Robert B. Serjeant, *The Portuguese off the South Arabian Coast: Ḥaḍramī Chronicles* (Oxford: Clarendon Press, 1963), 24. Apart from Ibn Mājid's testimony, foreign merchants in Calicut were alarmed at the first appearance of the Portuguese. With the Portuguese arrival in India, Muslims, who had carried out and mastered the transoceanic trade unchallenged for many centuries, felt threatened by the emerging Christian sea power from the Iberian Peninsula. The Muslims' suspicious attitude toward the Portuguese was projected in 1498 before Vasco da Gama himself touched the shores of Calicut. When the Portuguese fleet dropped anchor off the coast of Calicut, the first person ashore was the recent Jewish convert and convict Juao Nomez, the expedition's interpreter, who spoke Spanish, Portuguese, Hebrew, and Arabic. He was taken by two North African merchants from Tunis, who greeted him in Castilian Spanish with the curse: "May the Devil take thee! What brought you hither? They asked what he sought so far away from home, and he told them that we came in search of Christians and of spices." Álvaro Velho, *A Journal of the First Voyage of Vasco da Gama 1497–1499* (London: Hakluyt Society, 1898), 48–49; Bernard S. Cohn, "The Past in the Present: India as Museum of Mankind," *History and Anthropology* 11 (1998), 1; Charles R. Boxer, *The Portuguese Seaborne Empire 1415–1825* (London: Hutchinson and Co., 1969), 37; Ram P. Anand, *Origin and Development of the Law of the Sea* (The Hague: Martinus Nijhoff Publishers, 1982), 47. The Portuguese carried with them a deep antipathy to Islam and Muslims, and apparently the two Tunisian traders predicted the prospective consequences of the Portuguese penetration into the Indian Ocean. They envisioned the Portuguese shifting their colonial strategies and ambitions to the Indian Ocean as they

Contrary to the westward explorations, which revealed to the Spaniards hitherto unknown pre-Columbian cultures, da Gama introduced a new maritime passage to the western European nations, which led to the already known sources of spices and other luxurious commodities from Southeast Asia that previously had made their way to the West solely through the Muslim world. The Portuguese incursion into the Indian Ocean, followed by similar intrusions of other European sea powers, undermined the Muslim-run maritime trading system, disturbed the flow of spices from Calicut to the Red Sea, and produced new forms of naval strategies and powers.[4] Commanded by the viceroy Dom Francisco de Almeida, the Portuguese naval fleet surprised its Egyptian-Ottoman rival and defeated it in Diu on February 3, 1509;[5] this engagement is regarded

had done in Morocco from 1415 onward, when they took control of most of Morocco's Mediterranean and Atlantic ports through a combination of warfare and political and economic incentives offered to local rulers and nobles. For that reason the Maghribī merchants preferred the French and Venetian Christians over the Spaniards and Portuguese, who fueled the spirit of the Crusades in the West and subsequently expelled the Muslims from the Iberian Peninsula. For the Portuguese conquests on the North and Western coasts of Africa, see al-Ḥasan ibn Muḥammad al-Wazzān (Leo Africanus), *Waṣf Ifrīqiya* (Beirut: Dār al-Gharb al-Islāmī, 1983), 309–319; Jocelyn Hendrickson, "Muslim Legal Responses to Portuguese Occupation in Late Fifteenth-Century North Africa," *Journal of Spanish Cultural Studies* 12 (2011), 311–312; Barbara Fuchs and Yuen-Gen Liang, "A Forgotten Empire: The Spanish-North African Borderlands," *Journal of Spanish Cultural Studies* 12 (2011), 261–273.

4 Charles H. Alexandrowicz, "Freitas *versus* Grotius," *British Yearbook of International Law* 35 (1959), 163; Walter J. Fischel, "The Spice Trade in Mamluk Egypt: A Contribution to the Economic History of Medieval Islam," *Journal of the Economic and Social History of the Orient* 2 (1958), 172–174; Frederic C. Lane, "Pepper Prices before Da Gama," *Journal of Economic History* 28 (1968), 590–597; Wan K. Mujani, "Some Notes on the Portuguese and Frankish Pirates during the Mamluk Period (872–922 A.H./1468–1517 A.D.)," *Jurnal Pengajian Umum Asia Tenggara* 8 (2007), 18–20. In addition to the Portuguese naval superiority, the flow of spices, pepper, textiles, sugar, and various luxury goods was partly interrupted by pirate raids carried out by European privateers against commercial fleets sailing to the Near East and Mediterranean countries.

5 Deriving its name from the Sanskrit word "Dvipa" Diu/Div or al-Dyyb/Diyab, in Arabic and Geniza documents, Diu is a leading port lying at the mouth of the Gulf of Cambay in the union territory of Daman and Diu, western India. The city owes its importance to its strategic position on the trade routes of the Arabian Sea in the Indian Ocean. For further details on the role of Diu in domestic and international trade and its military importance, consult Edward D. Ross, "The Portuguese in India and Arabia between 1507 and 1517," *Journal of the Royal Asiatic Society of Great Britain and Ireland* 4 (1921), 547–557; Michael N. Pearson, "Brokers in Western Indian Port Cities: Their Role in Serving Foreign Merchants," *Modern Asian Studies* 22 (1988), 466–468; Ranabir Chakravarti, "Nakhudas and Nauvittakas: Ship-Owning Merchants in the West Coast of India (C. AD 1000–1500)," *Journal of the Economic and Social History of the Orient* 43 (2000), 44–45,

as one of the most decisive naval battles in the maritime and legal history of the Indian Ocean.[6]

The Portuguese penetration into the Indian Ocean ended the system of peaceful oceanic navigation that had been such a notable feature of that arena. Prior to this incursion, merchants at sea feared only pirates and natural hazards. Now, however, they were subject also to the threat of these new intruders, who imported the eastern Atlantic and Mediterranean models of trade and warfare and ended freedom of navigation in the eastern hemisphere. The Portuguese encroachment altered certain of the existing networking systems of maritime trade, as attested to by Sheikh Zayn al-Dīn al-Ma'barī al-Malībārī in 993/1583:

> Now it should be known, that after the Franks had established themselves in Cochin and Cannanore (Kannur) and had settled in those towns, the inhabitants, with all their dependents, became subject to these foreigners, engaged in all the arts of navigation, and in maritime employments, making voyages of trade under the protection of passes from the Franks; every vessel, however small, being provided with a distinct pass, and this with a view to the general security of all. And upon each of these passes a certain fee was fixed, on the payment of which the pass was delivered to the master of the vessel, when about to proceed on his voyage. Now the Franks, in imposing this toll, caused it to appear that it would prove in its consequences a source of advantage to these people, thus to induce them to submit to it; whilst to enforce its payment, if they fell in with any vessel, in which this their letter of marquee, or pass, was not to be found, they would invariably make a seizure both of the ship, its crew, and its cargo.[7]

52, 55; Shelomo D. Goitein and Mordechai A. Friedman, *India Traders of the Middle Ages: Documents from the Cairo Geniza* (Leiden: E. J. Brill, 2008), 316, f. 24.

[6] Mujani, "Some Notes on the Portuguese and Frankish Pirates," 22; Malyn Newitt, *A History of Portuguese Overseas Expansion* (New York: Routledge, 2005), 70; Patricia Risso, *Merchants and Faith: Muslim Commerce and Culture in the Indian Ocean* (Boulder, CO: Westview Press, 1995), 78–80; Kirti N. Chaudhuri, *Trade and Civilization in the Indian Ocean: An Economic History from the Rise of Islam to 1750* (Cambridge: Cambridge University Press, 1985), 68–69; Kirti N. Chaudhuri, "The Portuguese Maritime Empire, Trade, and Society in the Indian Ocean during the Sixteenth Century," *Portuguese Studies* 8 (1992), 57–70; Ross, "The Portuguese in India and Arabia between 1507 and 1517," 545–562; Edward D. Ross, "The Portuguese in India and Arabia between 1517 and 1538," *Journal of the Royal Asiatic Society of Great Britain and Ireland* 4 (1922), 1–18.

[7] Aḥmad ibn 'Abd al-'Aziz ibn Zayn al-Dīn al-Ma'barī al-Malībārī, *Tuḥfat al-Mujāhidīn fī Aḥwāl al-Burtughāliyyīn* (Beirut: Mu'assasat al-Wafā', 1405/1985), 250. The English translation, which preserves the meaning of the original Arabic text, is quoted from Michael N. Pearson, *Merchants and Rulers in Gujarat: The Response to the Portuguese in the Sixteenth Century* (Berkeley: University of California Press, 1976), 40.

Sanctioned by Alexander VI's papal bull *Inter Caetera Divinae* (May 4, 1493),[8] the Portuguese tried to enforce a royal monopoly on trade in the East Indies by patrolling the ocean from strategic points in Hormuz, Goa, Ceylon, and Malacca, and assuming sovereignty over major trunk routes; ships navigating the main shipping lanes between the Indonesian archipelago and the Persian Gulf were required to obtain *cartazes*.[9]

[8] Shortly after the discovery of the new world, the Spanish-born Pope Alexander VI (in office from August 11, 1492 to his death on August 13, 1503), being an instrument in the hands of King Ferdinand and Queen Isabella, promulgated the first bull *Inter Caetera Divinae* granting the Spanish monarchs exclusive jurisdiction over all lands discovered and to be discovered westward. The Spanish–Portuguese diplomatic negotiations over sovereignty of the newly discovered lands outside Europe culminated in the Treaty of Tordesillas (June 7, 1494). For further details, consult H. Vander Linden, "Alexander VI and the Demarcation of the Maritime and Colonial Domains of Spain and Portugal, 1493–1494," *American Historical Review* 22 (1916), 1–20; Carl Schmitt, *The Nomos of the Earth in the International Law of the Jus Publicum Europaeum*, 2nd ed., trans. G. L. Ulmen (New York: Telos Press Publishing, 2006), 88–89; Wilcomb E. Washburn, "The Meaning of 'Discovery' in the Fifteenth and Sixteenth Centuries," *American Historical Review* 68 (1962), 1–21; Alison Reppy, "The Grotian Doctrine of the Freedom of the Sea Reappraised," *Fordham Law Review* 19 (1950), 251–254; Tatiana Waisberg, "The Treaty of Tordesillas and the (re)Invention of International Law in the Age of Discovery," *Journal of Global Studies* 47 (2017), 1–12.

[9] The "protection of passes" described by Zayn al-Dīn al-Malībārī is known in Portuguese as *cartaz*. The word *cartaz* is derived from the Arabic *qirṭās* or *qarṭās*, which is originally derived from ancient Greek χάρτης (*chártēs*) denoting a writing, book, scroll, document, paper cone, or cornet. Some philologists and linguists argue that the word *qirṭās* (Qir-Ṭā-S) was borrowed and Arabicized by Arab sailors from the Hakka Chinese term Chi-Tan-Tsz, signifying paper memo or a merchant's paper/s. The term *qirṭās* occurs respectively twice in the Qur'ān in *sūra* 6. Its seventh verse reads as follows: "وَلَوْ نَزَّلْنَا عَلَيْكَ كِتَاباً فِي قِرْطَاسٍ فَلَمَسُوهُ بِأَيْدِيهِمْ لَقَالَ الَّذِينَ كَفَرُوا إِنْ هَذَا إِلَّا سِحْرٌ مُبِينٌ (If We had sent unto thee a written (Message) on parchment (*qirṭās*), so that they could touch it with their hands, the Unbelievers would have been sure to say 'this is nothing but obvious magic')." Verse 91 of the same *sūra* states: "وَمَا قَدَرُوا اللَّهَ حَقَّ قَدْرِهِ إِذْ قَالُوا مَا أَنزَلَ اللَّهُ عَلَى بَشَرٍ مِنْ شَيْءٍ قُلْ مَنْ أَنزَلَ الْكِتَابَ الَّذِي جَاءَ بِهِ مُوسَى نُوراً وَهُدًى لِلنَّاسِ تَجْعَلُونَهُ قَرَاطِيسَ تُبْدُونَهَا وَتُخْفُونَ كَثِيراً (No just estimate of God do they make when they say: 'Nothing doth God send down to man (by way of revelation),' Say: 'Who then sent down The Book which Moses brought? A light and guidance to man: But ye make it into (separate) sheets (*qarāṭīs*) for show while ye conceal much (of its contents)." Whereas the former refers to an imaginary book sent from Heaven, the latter is mentioned in relation to the scrolls (*qarāṭīs*) of the Jews. On the whole, the word *qirṭās* has always been used for papyrus, parchment, and paper. See Abū Manṣūr Mawhūb ibn Aḥmad ibn Muḥammad al-Jawālīqī, *Al-Mu'arrab min al-Kalām al-A'jamī 'alā Ḥurūf al-Mu'jam* (Damascus: Dār al-Qalam, 1410/1990), 529; Abū al-Faḍl Jamāl al-Dīn Muḥammad ibn Mukarram ibn Manẓūr, *Lisān al-'Arab* (Beirut: Dār Ṣāder, 2003), 12:73–74; Ary A. Roest-Crollius, *The Word in the Experience of Revelation in Qur'ān and Hindu Scriptures* (Rome: Universitá Gregoriana Editrice, 1974), 87; S. Mahdihassan, "Chinese Words in the Holy Koran: Qirtas, Meaning Paper, and Its Synonym, Kagaz," *Journal of the University of Bombay* 24 (1955), 149–151, 161; Federico Corriente, *Dictionary of Arabic and Allied Loanwords: Spanish, Portuguese, Catalan, Gallician and Kindred Dialects* (Leiden:

The Portuguese monopoly not only affected the indigenous peoples and foreigners, both Muslims and non-Muslims, but it also aimed to deprive

E. J. Brill, 2008), 80; Sebastião R. Dalgado, *The Influence of Portuguese Vocables in Asiatic Languages*, trans. Anthony X. Soares (Baroda: Oriental Institute, 1936), 82; Edward W. Lane, *An Arabic–English Lexicon* (Cambridge: Islamic Texts Society Trust, 1984), 2:2517–2518; Benjamin Jokisch, *Islamic Imperial Law: Harun al-Rashid's Codification Project* (Berlin: Walter de Gruyter, 2007), 401.

The *cartaz* was in effect a trading license or navicert issued by the Portuguese commissioner or competent authority to ships sailing in the Indian Ocean in an attempt to control the trade carried out by local people in Asian waters and to finance the Portuguese Empire in Asia. It was used as a means by which a maritime power enforced its jurisdiction and protection of vessels on oceanic routes. According to the Portuguese practice, the process of issuing a ship's *cartaz* by a particular maritime power started with a detailed search of the foreign ship in question. If the inquiry carried out in a harbor was satisfactory and the relevant authority concluded that the ship's intended voyage would be undertaken in good faith, a safe-conduct was granted protecting the vessel from interference on her voyage. Sailing without it gave rise to the risk of being stopped, captured, and deprived of property, freedom, or life. The *cartaz* also served as a navicert, particularly in times of naval warfare in the Indian Ocean and Arabian Sea. A typical *cartaz* contains details regarding the name of the vessel and her tonnage, the place of origin of the cargo, the vessel's destination, types of shipments, identity of crews, shippers, and passengers, the approximate date of departure, the name of the issuing authority and Portuguese writer/s, and the document's date of issue. It should be noted that the *cartaz* was designed solely to protect shippers, crews, and shipowners from the Portuguese themselves, but not from other maritime actors in the Indian Ocean. Charles H. Alexandrowicz, *An Introduction to the History of the Law of Nations in the East Indies (16th, 17th and 18th Centuries)* (Oxford: Clarendon Press, 1967), 71–73; Alexandrowicz, "Freitas *versus* Grotius," 176–180; Anand, *Origin and Development of the Law of the Sea*, 60–62; Heather Sutherland, "Geography as Destiny? The Role of Water in Southeast Asian History," in *A World of Water: Rain, Rivers and Seas in Southeast Asian Histories*, ed. Peter Boomgaard (Leiden: KITLV Press, 2007), 38–39; Pius Malekandathil, *Portuguese Cochin and the Maritime Trade of India, 1500–1663* (New Delhi: Manohar, 2001), 125–126; Pearson, *Merchants and Rulers in Gujarat*, 40–43, 70; Dalgado, *Influence of Portuguese Vocables*, 82; Mohammed H. Salman, "Aspects of Portuguese Rule in the Arabian Gulf, 1521–1622," (PhD diss., University of Hull, 2004), 132–137; Kuzhippalli S. Mathew, "Trade in the Indian Ocean and the Portuguese System of Cartazes," in *The First Portuguese Colonial Empire*, ed. Malyn D. Newitt (Exeter: University of Exeter Press, 1986), 69–84. Nearly a century earlier, King Manuel I (1469–1521) of Portugal promulgated a royal decree ordering the Moors who arrived at and departed from his coastal possessions in Morocco to be equipped with the permission of the Portuguese authorities when traveling by sea. Hendrickson, "Muslim Legal Responses to Portuguese Occupation," 313. It is plausible to hypothesize that the sixteenth-century *cartaz* may possibly owe its legal roots to the thirteenth-century Iberian safe-conduct (*guidaticum*), which apparently emerged from the Islamic *amān*. However, unlike the *amān*, which was free of charge, the Iberian *guidaticum* could be purchased by anyone for a given time, or permanently with an annual fee to ensure the safety of the vessels, their crews, and their shipments. On the basis of legal similarities between the Portuguese *cartaz* and the *guidaticum*, it is sensible to contend that the legal roots of the former might be attributed to the Spanish safe-conduct. Daniel J. Smith, "Heterogeneity and Exchange: Safe-Conducts in Medieval Spain," *Review of Australian Economics* 27 (2014), 190–192.

the newly arrived European Christian merchants from other states of the highly profitable Southeast Asian trade.[10]

The late fifteenth-century papal bull, as mentioned, which partitioned the new world between the Spaniards and the Portuguese, also denied other European nations rights of navigation and access to the newly discovered territories and maritime routes in the Atlantic and Indian oceans. In defence of the seizure of the Portuguese cargo vessel *Santa Catarina* on February 25, 1603, by three ships of the Dutch East India Company (*Vereenigde Oostindische Compagnie, VOC*) in the Singapore Strait,[11] and in response to the unjustified maritime claims of Spain and Portugal, the Dutch lawyer and humanist Hugo Grotius (1583–1645) wrote the *De Jure Praedae* (*On the Law of Prize and Booty*), wherein Chapter 12 deals with the freedom of the seas (*Mare Liberum/The Free Sea*).[12] Relying heavily on the Justinianic *Institutes* and *Corpus Juris Civilis*, from which he derived his legal references,[13] Grotius argued: (a) since the seas are open to all nations by command of the Law of Nations, the Portuguese have no valid title to confine access to the East Indies to themselves;[14] (b) the seas are not subject to appropriation by persons or states but are available to everyone for navigation, and therefore neither Portugal nor other nations can have exclusive rights of navigation whether through seizure, papal grant, prescription, or custom;[15] (c) non-Christians ("infidels" as termed by the author) cannot be divested of public or private rights of ownership merely because they are infidels, whether on grounds of discovery,

[10] Alexandrowicz, "Freitas *versus* Grotius," 178. Save for its monopolistic aspect, the *cartaz* system can be seen as an instrument of the Portuguese jurisdiction assumed in the Indian Ocean under their quasioccupation, and as a navicert assuring safety to vessels at sea during the Portuguese continuous crusade against the Muslim world.

[11] Peter Borschberg, "The Seizure of the *Sta. Catarina* Revisited: The Portuguese Empire in Asia, VOC Politics and the Origins of the Dutch–Johor Alliance (1602–c.1616)," *Journal of Southeast Asian Studies* 33 (2002), 31–36. For a deeper insight into the capture of *Santa Catarina* and the judicial consequences and judicial debates that ensued, refer to Martine J. Van Ittersum, *Profit and Principle: Hugo Grotius, Natural Rights Theories and the Rise of Dutch Power in the East Indies* (Leiden: E. J. Brill, 2006), 1–52.

[12] Hugo Grotius, *The Free Sea*, trans. Richard Hakluyt, ed. David Armitage (Indianapolis: Liberty Fund, 2004); Hugo Grotius, *The Freedom of the Seas, or the Right Which Belongs to the Dutch to Take Part in the East Indian Trade*, ed. and trans. Ralph V. Magoffin (New York: Oxford University Press, 1916).

[13] Robert Fredona, "Angelo degli Ubaldi and the Gulf of the Venetians: Custom, Commerce, and the Control of the Sea before Grotius," in *New Perspectives on the History of Political Economy*, ed. Robert Fredona and Sophus A. Reinert (New York: Palgrave Macmillan, 2018), 30–31.

[14] Grotius, *Freedom of the Seas*, 7–10.

[15] Grotius, *Freedom of the Seas*, 15–60.

papal grant, or war;[16] and (d) no people can acquire a monopoly on commerce with any overseas country.[17] Following Grotius's contention, contemporaneous European lawyers sparked a legal debate, some challenging and others concurring with his position, leading to further scholarly contribution to the law of the sea. Both advocates and opponents of the freedom of navigation were inspired either by the natural law enshrined in the Justinianic *Institutes* and *Corpus Juris Civilis*, or the Hebrew Bible's concept of sovereignty on the open sea. British legal theoretician John Selden mentions both in his 1635 *Mare Clausum, Sive de Dominio Maris* (*The Closed Sea, or the Dominion of the Sea*).[18]

As mentioned earlier, freedom of navigation in the Indian Ocean was common practice until the arrival of the Portuguese in the eastern maritime arena. By the beginning of the seventeenth century and the appearance of the Dutch East India Company the concepts of *mare liberum* and freedom of commerce between littoral countries along the Indian Ocean were no longer confined to locals and Asians. The ocean, which was common to the peoples of Southeast Asia and the Near East, was now shared with the European naval powers, so that in 1615, the Makassarese sultan ʿAlāuddīn Tumenanga ri Gaukanna (1002–1049/1593–1639) asked the Dutch East India Company not to interfere with the ships of the Makassarese Kingdom of Goa on the high seas, declaring, "God made the earth and the sea, has divided the earth among mankind and given the sea in common. It is a thing unheard of that anyone should be forbidden to sail the seas."[19] By this statement, the sultan acknowledged that in

[16] Grotius, *Freedom of the Seas*, 22–44, 65, 66.

[17] Grotius, *Freedom of the Seas*, 69–76; Helen Thornton, "Hugo Grotius and the Freedom of the Seas," *International Journal of Maritime History* 16 (2004), 21–33.

[18] John Selden, *Of the Dominion or Ownership of the Sea* (London: William Du-Gard, 1652); Jonathan Ziskind, "International Law and Ancient Sources: Grotius and Selden," *Review of Politics* 35 (1973), 537–559; Abraham Berkowitz, "John Selden and the Biblical Origins of the Modern International Political System," *Jewish Political Studies Review* 6 (1994): 27–47; Mónica B. Vieira, "Mare Liberum *vs.* Mare Clausum: Grotius, Freitas, and Selden's Debate on Dominion over the Seas," *Journal of the History of Ideas* 64 (2003), 361–377; Charles Leben, "Hebrew Sources in the Doctrine of the Law of Nature and Nations in Early Modern Europe," *European Journal of International Law* 27 (2016), 79–106.

[19] Gertrudes J. Resink, *Indonesia's History between the Myths: Essays in Legal and Historical Theory* (Amsterdam: Royal Tropical Institute, 1968), 45; Leonard Y. Andaya, *The Heritage of Arung Palakka: A History of South Sulawesi (Celebes) in the Seventeenth Century* (The Hague: Martinus Nijhoff, 1981), 45–46; Ram P. Anand, "Maritime Practice in South-East Asia until 1600 A.D. and the Modern Law of the Sea," *The International and Comparative Law Quarterly* 30 (1981), 446; Zakaria M. Yatim, "The Development of the Law of the Sea in Relations to Malaysia," *Malaysian*

contrast to land, Islamic law considers the boundless sea to be the common heritage of mankind. No governing authority or nation could either claim proprietorship over it, or exclusive right of navigation; however, he did not elaborate on how the Islamic Law of Nature entitles human beings to share the sea and enjoy equal rights of exploration and exploitation of its natural resources. It may be assumed that the sultan was referring to the traditional freedom of navigation which had existed in the Indian Ocean on the eve of the European colonial era. Before the appearance of the European navies in the sixteenth century, the polities around the Indian Ocean had enjoyed the natural right to conduct maritime trade and navigate the vast ocean without molestation.

HUMAN RIGHTS AND THE ISLAMIC CUSTOMARY LAW OF THE SEA

Numerous studies have been written on human rights and freedom in Islamic law, few of which have touched on the issue of legal rights and the obligations of shipowners, crews, shippers, and passengers at sea with special reference to private commercial laws.[20] The issue of human rights is best and most succinctly addressed by the fourth Shiite *imam* and Prophet's great-grandson Zayn al-ʿĀbidīn ʿAlī ibn al-Ḥusayn ibn ʿAlī ibn Abū Ṭālib (38–95/659–713) in his *Treatise of Rights* (*Risālat al-Ḥuqūq*).[21] Canonically, Islam does not draw a distinction between

Management Journal 1 (1992), 88; Philip E. Steinberg, *The Social Construction of the Ocean* (Cambridge: Cambridge University Press, 2001), 48; Philip E. Steinberg, "Three Historical Systems of Ocean Governance: A Framework for Analyzing the Law of the Sea," *World Bulletin* 12 (1996), 8; Sutherland, "Geography as Destiny," 27; William Cummings (ed.), *The Makassar Annals* (Leiden: KITLV Press, 2011), 35, 315; William Cummings, "Islam, Empire and Makassarese Historiography in the Reign of Sultan Ala'uddin (1593–1639)," *Journal of Southeast Asian Studies* 38 (2007), 207. Sultan ʿAlāuddīn's declaration was the result of the maritime conflict that took place on Rabi al-Awwal 28, 1024/April 28, 1615, between the VOC and the Makassarese, when the former captured the Malay harbor master Anciq Using and other notables resulting in a long period of simmering hostilities between the two rivals.

20 Hassan S. Khalilieh, *Admiralty and Maritime Laws in the Mediterranean (ca. 800–1050): The Kitāb Akriyat al-Sufun vis-à-vis the Nomos Rhodion Nautikos* (Leiden: E. J. Brill, 2006), 45–84; Hassan S. Khalilieh, *Islamic Maritime Law: An Introduction* (Leiden: E. J. Brill, 1998), 42–57, 162–176; Hassan S. Khalilieh, "Legal Aspects from a Cairo Geniza *Responsum* on the Islamic Law of the Sea," *The Jewish Quarterly Review* 96 (2006), 180–202.

21 Zayn al-ʿĀbidīn ʿAlī ibn al-Ḥusayn ibn ʿAlī ibn Abū Ṭālib, *Risālat al-Ḥuqūq (Treatise of Rights)*, narrated by the prominent Shiite traditionists Abū Jaʿfar Muḥammad ibn ʿAlī ibn al-Ḥusayn ibn Bābawayh, *Man lā Yaḥḍuruhu al-Faqīh* (Qumm: Jamāʿat al-Mudarrisīn fī

rights and obligations on land and at sea, but places them on an equal footing.[22] Human rights, as prescribed by law, are classified into three major categories: the rights of God, the rights of the individual toward himself (*al-nafs*), and the rights of humans or individuals (*ʿibād*); each of the three is further divided into subcategories.

Of interest are the rights of individuals and the community at large that define the relationship between individuals of the same or different religions and nationalities inter se, and those that define the relationship between the individual and the community and state. Among these rights ʿAlī ibn al-Ḥusayn counts the rights of superiors,[23] rights of dependents,[24] rights of relatives,[25] rights based on personal relationships,[26] and most importantly as far as this study is concerned, rights based on financial, judicial, and social relationships; these latter rights cover, among other things, topics associated with the rights of partners, associates, creditors, wealth, claimants, and defendants.[27]

Human rights laws cannot be separated from the customary law of the sea because the two overlap in many ways. One may consider, for instance, the right to life. Since time immemorial, rendering assistance to persons or ships in distress or danger on the high seas or in the territorial sea of a coastal state has been accepted as a common humanitarian norm. Providing assistance to ill-fated individuals at sea is considered by Islamic law to be a moral duty and a religious obligation; the law commands Muslims to render assistance insofar as the rescuers do not compromise their own safety.[28] The rights of individuals apply to the personal safety of

al-Ḥawza al-ʿIlmiyya, 1404/1983), 2:618–625, 3:3–4; Abū Jaʿfar Muḥammad ibn ʿAlī ibn al-Ḥusayn ibn Bābawayh, *Al-Khiṣāl* (Qumm: Jamāʿat al-Mudarrisīn fī al-Ḥawza al-ʿIlmiyya, 1416/1995), 2:564–570. In addition to Ibn Bābawayh's narration, this treatise is also narrated by the fourth-century Shiite traditionist Abū Muḥammad al-Ḥasan ibn ʿAlī ibn al-Ḥusayn ibn Shuʿba al-Ḥarrānī, *Tuḥfat al-ʿUqūl* (Qumm: Jamāʿat al-Mudarris īn fī al-Ḥawza al-ʿIlmiyya, 1404/1983), 255–272.

22 The Umayyad Caliph ʿUmar ibn ʿAbd al-ʿAzīz (99–101/717–720) was quoted as saying, "dry land and sea belong alike to God; He hath subdued them to His servants to seek of His bounty for themselves in both of them." Abū Muḥammad ʿAbd Allāh ibn ʿAbd al-Ḥakam, *Sīrat ʿUmar Ibn ʿAbd al-ʿAzīz ʿalā mā Rawāhu al-Imām Mālik Ibn Anas wa-Aṣḥābihi* (Beirut: ʿĀlam al-Kitāb, 1404/1984), 86–87.

23 Ibn Bābawayh, *Man lā Yaḥḍuruhu al-Faqīh*, 2:620–621.

24 Ibn Bābawayh, *Man lā Yaḥḍuruhu al-Faqīh*, 2:622.

25 Ibn Bābawayh, *Man lā Yaḥḍuruhu al-Faqīh*, 2:621–622.

26 Ibn Bābawayh, *Man lā Yaḥḍuruhu al-Faqīh*, 2:622–623.

27 Ibn Bābawayh, *Man lā Yaḥḍuruhu al-Faqīh*, 2:623–625; 3:2–4.

28 Qurʾān 5:32: "مَن قَتَلَ نَفْسًا بِغَيْرِ نَفْسٍ أَوْ فَسَادٍ فِي الأَرْضِ فَكَأَنَّمَا قَتَلَ النَّاسَ جَمِيعًا وَمَنْ أَحْيَاهَا فَكَأَنَّمَا أَحْيَا النَّاسَ جَمِيعًا (if anyone slew a person – unless it be for murder or for spreading mischief in the land – it would be as if he slew the whole people. And, if anyone saved a life, it would be as if

Muslims and non-Muslims in the Abode of Islam and foreign territories, as they do to foreigners on Islamic soil. Every person is guaranteed safety and protection against physical harm to him and to his property, whether at sea or on land; any person violating these rights is subject to punishment.[29] In the event of robbery or piracy, for instance, jurists hold conflicting opinions with respect to the punishment of a bandit or a pirate who repents prior to being captured. One opinion rules that the rights of God and individuals are forgiven; another states that God's rights are forgiven, as are private rights, unless the act involves injury or death, and a third holds that Divine punishments are forgiven, while private rights pertaining to property, injury, or death are not. According to all opinions, compensation must be paid for the damages incurred by the victim.[30] The state normally carries out the punishment against the offender, irrespective of his creed or nationality.[31]

Other key issues that link the individual, community, and state to the customary law of the sea are the right to justice and equality in justice. Since the standards of justice in the Qur'ān transcend racial, religious, social, and economic considerations, Muslims are commanded to be just at all levels.[32] A Muslim acts more virtuously when he does justice to a party whom he disfavors,[33] or to non-Muslims, as pointed out in Qur'ān 60:8. Here the Qur'ān commands Muslims to deal kindly and equitably

he saved the life of the whole people)"; Khalilieh, *Islamic Maritime Law*, 155–157; Khalilieh, *Admiralty and Maritime Laws*, 206–207, 222; Bernard H. Oxman, "Human Rights and the United Nations Convention on the Law of the Sea," *Columbia Journal of Transnational Law* 36 (1998), 414–415; Tullio Treves, "Human Rights and the Law of the Sea," *Berkeley Journal of International Law* 28 (2010), 3.

29 Qur'ān 5:32–33.

30 Qur'ān 5:32–33; Anver M. Emon, "*Ḥuqūq Allāh* and *Ḥuqūq al-'Ibād*: A Legal Heuristic for a Natural Rights Regime," *Islamic Law and Society* 13 (2006), 373–376. In the case of death, the Qur'ān ordains the judicial authorities to consider crucifixion, or exile from the land. For further details, see Chapter 3, 202–208.

31 Majid Khadduri, "Human Rights in Islam," *American Academy of Political and Social Science* 243 (1946), 78.

32 Qur'ān 4:135: "يَا أَيُّهَا الَّذِينَ آمَنُواْ كُونُواْ قَوَّامِينَ بِالْقِسْطِ شُهَدَاء لِلَّهِ وَلَوْ عَلَى أَنفُسِكُمْ أَوِ الْوَالِدَيْنِ وَالأَقْرَبِينَ إِن يَكُنْ غَنِيًّا أَوْ فَقِيرًا فَاللَّهُ أَوْلَى بِهِمَا فَلاَ تَتَّبِعُواْ الْهَوَى أَن تَعْدِلُواْ وَإِن تَلْوُواْ أَوْ تُعْرِضُواْ فَإِنَّ اللَّهَ كَانَ بِمَا تَعْمَلُونَ خَبِيرًا (O ye who believe! Stand out firmly for justice, as witnesses to God, even as against yourselves, or your parents, or your kin, and whether it be (against) rich or poor: for God can best protect both. Follow not the lusts (of your hearts), lest ye swerve, and if ye distort (justice) or decline to do justice, verily God is well-acquainted with all that ye do)."

33 Qur'ān 5:8: "يَا أَيُّهَا الَّذِينَ آمَنُواْ كُونُواْ قَوَّامِينَ لِلَّهِ شُهَدَاء بِالْقِسْطِ وَلاَ يَجْرِمَنَّكُمْ شَنَآنُ قَوْمٍ عَلَى أَلاَّ تَعْدِلُواْ اعْدِلُواْ هُوَ أَقْرَبُ لِلتَّقْوَى وَاتَّقُواْ اللَّهَ إِنَّ اللَّهَ خَبِيرٌ بِمَا تَعْمَلُونَ (O ye who believe! Stand out firmly for God, as witnesses, to fair dealing, and let not the hatred of others to you make you swerve to wrong and depart from justice. Be just: that is next to Piety: and fear God, for God is well-acquainted with all that ye do)."

with the unbelievers, since this is an inherent right of all human beings under God's law. Notably, as shall be comprehensively explained in Chapter 2, the Qur'ān calls for preservation of the earlier revelations and advises Muslims strongly not to intervene in the judicial affairs of the People of the Book (*Ahl al-Kitāb*), but to grant them legal autonomy to administer justice and to execute judgment pursuant to their own law.[34]

One way to promote trade, improve diplomatic relations with foreign countries, enhance cultural exchange and, most importantly, propagate religion is through the free movement of peoples.[35] Free movement of merchants can enhance trade, create wealth among nations, and improve the living standards of citizens. It is the natural right of human beings to travel within and beyond their countries according to their free will when seeking knowledge, earning a livelihood, or achieving other things.[36] Qur'ān 67:15 rules regarding the freedom of travel that: "It is He Who has made the earth manageable for you, so traverse ye through its tracts and enjoy of the Sustenance which He furnishes: but unto Him is the Resurrection (هُوَ الَّذِي جَعَلَ لَكُمُ الْأَرْضَ ذَلُولًا فَامْشُوا فِي مَنَاكِبِهَا وَكُلُوا مِن رِّزْقِهِ وَإِلَيْهِ النُّشُورُ)." Islamic law mandates that women, who are forbidden to travel alone, always be accompanied by husbands or unmarriageable male kin (*maḥārim*).[37] Additionally, people are strongly advised not to set off if they might be faced by danger.[38]

It is generally recognized by the Law of Nature and the Law of Nations that individuals, communities, and nations have an inherent right to navigate the seas freely and to take advantage of their natural resources. These rights are perhaps best stated in Qur'ān 16:14: "It is He Who has made the sea subject, that ye may eat thereof flesh that is fresh and tender, and that ye may extract therefrom ornaments to wear; and thou seest the ships therein that plough the waves, that ye may seek (thus) of the bounty of God and that ye

[34] Qur'ān 5:42–49.

[35] Michael N. Pearson, *The Indian Ocean* (London: Routledge, 2003), 62–63, 75–78, 81, 101; Michael N. Pearson, "Islamic Trade, Shipping, Port-States and Merchant Communities in the Indian Ocean, Seventh to Sixteenth Centuries," in *The New Cambridge History of Islam: The Eastern Islamic World – Eleventh to Eighteenth Centuries*, ed. David Morgan and Anthony Reid (Cambridge: Cambridge University Press, 2011), 3:329–330, 333–334.

[36] Abdul-Aziz Said, "Precept and Practice of Human Rights in Islam," *Universal Human Rights* 1 (1979), 71–73.

[37] On the travel of Muslim women by sea, consult the article: Hassan S. Khalilieh, "Women at Sea: Modesty, Privacy, and Sexual Misconduct of Passengers and Sailors Aboard Islamic Ships," *Al-Qantara* 37 (2006), 137–153.

[38] Khalilieh, *Admiralty and Maritime Laws*, 121–131.

may be grateful (وَهُوَ الَّذِي سَخَّرَ الْبَحْرَ لِتَأْكُلُواْ مِنْهُ لَحْمًا طَرِيًّا وَتَسْتَخْرِجُواْ مِنْهُ حِلْيَةً تَلْبَسُونَهَا وَتَرَى الْفُلْكَ مَوَاخِرَ فِيهِ وَلِتَبْتَغُواْ مِن فَضْلِهِ وَلَعَلَّكُمْ تَشْكُرُونَ)." With the exception of a limited offshore zone, the high seas and associated assets are among the greatest bounties that God has bestowed on human beings; individuals and nations have the right to use and benefit from them, but that right is not exclusive. Neither the high seas nor their natural resources are subject to dominion and appropriation by one nation or another.[39] Indeed, from the dawn of ancient civilization to the present day, the practices and customary law of the sea, together with Islamic law, are not only about the utilization of the natural resources of the seas and oceans, but also about an individual's rights and liberty to freely navigate and exploit these resources.

CUSTOM AS A SOURCE OF ISLAMIC LAW

Islamic expansion into the former Byzantine and Sassanid territories was not destructive, and so the administrative systems and cultural norms existing in the territories taken over by Muslims were sustained. The early caliphate succeeded by the Umayyad dynasty preserved the governmental system prevailing in the former Byzantine territories along the Mediterranean, and also the Persian administrative counterpart in the eastern provinces of the Islamic Empire. Without the retention of the existing legal, financial, and administrative institutions and practices of the conquered territories, one may surmise that Muslim dominion over a vast, diverse ethnocultural and geographical space would not have survived for such a long period of time.[40] The natural inclination of the peoples who came under Islamic authority or adopted the most recent Divine monotheistic faith, was to maintain the status quo, in their legal relationships, customary practices, and long-standing traditions, and this was merely confirmed and strengthened by the rigidity of *Sharī'ah* provisions.[41]

[39] Said, "Precept and Practice of Human Rights in Islam," 71, 73–75.

[40] Khalilieh, *Admiralty and Maritime Laws*, 18–19.

[41] Wael B. Hallaq, *An Introduction to Islamic Law* (Cambridge: Cambridge University Press, 2009), 8, 11, 61–62; Wael B. Hallaq, *The Origins and Evolution of Islamic Law* (Cambridge: Cambridge University Press, 2005), 4, 24–25, 32–33; Noel J. Coulson, "Muslim Custom and Case-Law," *Die Welt des Islams* 16 (1959), 16–17. The word *Sharī'ah* is derived from the root *sh.r.'a.*, meaning "to start, to enter, or to go"; the noun *shāri'* signifies "road, way, or path"; *shara'a* designates "to introduce, to enact, or to prescribe." *Sharī'ah* also denotes a non-exhaustive water spring, or the path to the water source since the water is considered as the element vital to life, so is the worldly human life, which cannot exist without the path to righteousness (Qur'ān 6:153). If the water is so vital for every living thing, the *Sharī'ah* is, by the same token, the life for souls of

Islamic maritime achievements in the Mediterranean Sea and the Near Eastern seas did not change the material culture of the occupied countries abruptly: instead, there was cultural continuity in various aspects of life for centuries, in spite of the gradual processes of Islamization and Arabization. The non-Muslim subject populations retained their traditional legal institutions, including ecclesiastical and rabbinical tribunals,[42] whereas the jurisdiction of the qadi extended to Muslims and civil cases involving Muslims and non-Muslims. Until the turn of the eighth century, Umayyad qadis gave judgments according to their own discretion (*ra'y*), basing them on Qur'ānic regulations, Prophetic traditions, and customary practices that did not contradict Islamic principles.[43]

With the Islamic expansion in the Mediterranean world and Asia from the seventh century onward came the gradual process of mutual acculturation, by which Muslims absorbed and accommodated to themselves local customs that became an inseparable part of social and legal norms.[44]

Muslims and humanity (Qur'ān 21:107). The *Sharī'ah* in the generic religious context designates the straight path to happiness and good life which Muslims cannot achieve without following the Path of God and the Sunna of His Messenger (Qur'ān 59:7). The *Sharī'ah* is like running water, which remains fresh due to its constant flow. It is dynamic in nature, evolves with human evolution and the changing world, and responds to the challenges and needs not only of the Islamic *ummah*, but also of all mankind across the universe at all times. The *Sharī'ah* comprises the final revelation from God (Qur'ān) and the Prophet's recorded teachings.

42 In addition to their contribution to the development of Islamic naval activity, the *dhimmīs* – mainly native Christians of Syria, Egypt, and North Africa – preserved the maritime laws instituted in the Justinianic Digest, as well as local customs, for centuries to come. With the establishment of the *madhāhib* from the eighth century onward, many canonical regulations and practices were "Islamicized," as long as they did not contradict the sacred law.

43 Joseph Schacht, *An Introduction to Islamic Law* (Oxford: Clarendon Press, 1964), 22–30; Hallaq, *Origins and Evolution of Islamic Law*, 44–45, 53–54, 56; Robert S. Lopez, "Byzantine Law in the Seventh Century and Its Reception by the Germans and the Arabs," *Byzantion* 16 (1942–1943), 451; Shameem Akhtar, "An Inquiry into the Nature, Origin, and Source of Islamic Law of Nations," *Islamic Studies* 10 (1971), 32–33.

44 'Abd al-Raḥmān ibn Khaldūn, *Tārīkh Ibn Khaldūn al-Musammā Kitāb al-'Ibar wa-Dīwān al-Mubtada' wa'l-Khabar fī Ayyām al-'Arab wa'l-'Ajam wa'l-Barbar wa-man 'Āṣarahum min Dhawī al-Sulṭān al-Akbar* (Beirut: Dār al-Kutub al-'Ilmiyyah, 1413/1992), 1:29–30. On the acculturation process he states: "The condition of the world and of nations, their customs and sects, do not persist in the same form or in a constant manner. There are differences according to days and periods, and changes from one condition to another. Such is the case with individuals, times, and cities, and it likewise happens in connection with regions and districts, periods and dynasties. ... The new power, in turn, is taken over by another dynasty, and customs are further mixed with those of the new dynasty. More discrepancies come in, so that the contrast between the

Both Muslim legal and ruling authorities not only retained pre-Islamic customs and traditions, but also adapted and Islamicized laws and customs so long as they were in conformity with the Qurʾān and Sunna.[45] This may explain why jurists and judges often consulted, in the course of resolving specific legal cases, general custom (*ʿurf ʿāmm*), specific custom (*ʿurf khāṣṣ*), jurists' custom (*ʿurf al-fuqahāʾ*), artisans' custom (*ʿurf al-ṣunnāʿ*), merchants' custom (*ʿurf al-tujjār*), etc.[46]

The influence of custom is tangible in Islamic maritime law. In the introductory chapter of *Kitāb Akriyat al-Sufun* (The Treatise on the Leasing of Ships), the author Muḥammad ibn ʿUmar al-Kinānī al-Andalusī al-Iskandarānī (d. 310/923) emphasized the role of local custom and practices in the conclusion of commercial contracts.[47] The jurist went further by claiming that custom could replace and even supersede an

new dynasty and the first one is much greater than that between the second and the first one. Gradual increase in the degree of discrepancy continues. The eventual result is an altogether distinct (set of customs and institutions). As long as there is this continued succession of different races to royal authority and government, changes in customs and institutions will not cease to occur." The English translation, which is compatible with the Arabic text, is quoted from Franz Rosenthal, *The Muqaddimah: An Introduction to History* (Princeton: Princeton University Press, 1967), 25–26; for the electronic version, see: https://asadullahali.files.wordpress.com/2012/10/ibn_khaldun-al_muqaddimah.pdf.

45 The Qurʾān validates customary practices inasmuch as they are consistent with Islamic principles, namely the sacred text and the Prophetic Sunna. Of all the Qurʾānic verses where derivatives of the term *ʿurf* occur, one *āyah* (Qurʾān 7:199) deserves a closer examination: "خُذِ الْعَفْوَ وَأْمُرْ بِالْعُرْفِ وَأَعْرِضْ عَنِ الْجَاهِلِينَ (Hold to forgiveness, enjoin *ʿurf*, but turn away from the ignorant)." The great majority of exegetes argue that the word *ʿurf* is related to the term *maʿrūf*, meaning "good, upright, or beneficial." That is to say, the *ʿurf* cannot be quoted as textual authority for custom as such. Nevertheless, there are some commentators who contend that the term *ʿurf* may also signify "custom" in the true sense of the word, arguing that "what the Muslims deem to be good is good in the sight of God," said ʿAbd Allāh ibn Masʿūd, a prominent Companion of the Prophet. Ayman Shabana, *Custom in Islamic Law and Legal Theory* (New York: Palgrave Macmillan, 2010), 50–58; Wael B. Hallaq, *Authority, Continuity and Change in Islamic Law* (Cambridge: Cambridge University Press, 2004), 215–235; Mohammad H. Kamali, *Principles of Islamic Jurisprudence* (Cambridge: Islamic Texts Society, 1997), 256; Majid Khadduri, "Nature and Sources of Islamic Law," *George Washington Law Review* 22 (1953), 3–4; Taiwo M. Salisu, "*ʿUrf/ʿAdah* (Custom): An Ancillary Mechanism in *Shariʿah*," *Ilorin Journal of Religious Studies* 3 (2013), 137–142; ʿAbdullāh ʿA. Ḥajī-Ḥassan, "Sales and Contracts in Early Islamic Commercial Law," (PhD diss., University of Edinburgh, 1986), 18–20; Gideon Libson, "On the Development of Custom as a Source of Law in Islamic Law," *Islamic Law and Society* 4 (1997), 131–155.

46 Shabana, *Custom in Islamic Law*, 156–157; Salisu, "*ʿUrf/ʿAdah* (Custom)," 135–137.

47 Muṣṭafā A. Ṭāher (ed.), "*Kitāb Akriyat al-Sufun wa'l-Nizāʿ bayna Ahlihā*," *Cahiers de Tunisie* 31 (1983), 6–7, 10–11.

explicit stipulation.[48] Citing the prominent North African jurist Saḥnūn ibn Saʿīd al-Tanūkhī (160–240/776–854), the author of the treatise added that "if hiring arrangements are to be admitted solely on the basis of analogy (*qiyās*), most will be invalidated [only recourse to custom makes them licit]."[49] Accordingly, in the absence of a written contract and explicit stipulations, jurists and judges would normally resort to local custom.[50]

The process of the reception and assimilation of foreign laws, especially Byzantine and Persian laws, is discernible in the realm of Islamic *siyar* (Law of Nations). Early authors of *siyar* literature not only recognized custom as a source of law but also endorsed it as a decisive authority so long as it did not contradict or override the *naṣṣ*.[51] In order to validate custom and make it legally binding, jurists ruled that custom must be: (a) sensible and consistent with the *Sharīʿah*; (b) implicitly or expressly accepted by the Islamic State; (c) dominantly and frequently practiced in interstate relations; and (d) in use before or at the time of the conclusion of an international treaty.[52] To a great degree, the *siyar* share similarities with the Roman *jus gentium*, which regulated relations between Roman citizens and foreigners, with a cardinal difference in that the former addressed legal issues between the *ummah* and non-Islamic states, as shall be elaborated in due course.[53]

PURPOSE, STRUCTURE, AND METHODOLOGY OF THE STUDY

Grotius's reliance on Romano-Byzantine legal codices leaves the impression that the Law of Nature and Law of Nations governing access to the sea are a European establishment. He advertently or inadvertently tended to

[48] Ṭāher, *Akriyat al-Sufun*, 14.

[49] Ṭāher, *Akriyat al-Sufun*, 15; Khalilieh, *Admiralty and Maritime Laws*, 277–278.

[50] Abū al-Qāsim ibn Aḥmad al- Burzulī, *Fatāwā al-Burzulī: Jāmiʿ Masāʾil al-Aḥkām li-mā Nazala min al-Qaḍāyā bil-Muftīn wa'l-Ḥukkām* (Beirut: Dār al-Gharb al-Islāmī, 2002), 3:464.

[51] Anowar Zahid and Rohimi B. Shapiee, "Considering Custom in the Making of *Siyar* (Islamic International Law)," *Journal of East Asia and International Law* 3 (2010), 125, 127; Akhtar, "Nature, Origin, and Source of Islamic Law of Nations," 34.

[52] Zahid and Shapiee, 128–129; Anowar Zahid and Rohimi B. Shapiee, "Customs as a Source of *Siyar* and International Law: A Comparative of the Qualifying Criteria," *International Journal of Civil Society Law* 8 (2010), 44–45.

[53] Muḥammad Ḥamīdullāh, *The Muslim Conduct of State* (Lahore: Sh. Muhammad Ashraf, 1968), 3, 7.

overlook the contribution of the "infidels,"[54] as he called the non-Christian nations and societies, to the development of the customary law of the sea despite his awareness of the long tradition of freedom of navigation that had existed in the Islamic Mediterranean as well as in the Indian Ocean, prior to the intrusion of the European naval powers.[55] In response to the widely accepted legal theory that the doctrine of the freedom of the seas was initiated and promoted by early modern European lawyers, this study aims primarily to achieve an understanding of the theoretical and practical concepts of the Islamic customary law of the sea that are absent not only from the writings of the influential Dutch humanist but also from pre-modern and contemporary Western legal literature.

In order to eliminate any possible confusion on the part of the reader, this study will deal solely with the Islamic concept of the "law of the sea," as opposed to the concept of "maritime law."[56] Despite the fact that the

[54] Grotius (2004), *Free Sea*, 8, 15, 17, 19, 52. He argues that the Portuguese can neither claim exclusive access to the eastern seas by virtue of discovery, nor deprive the infidels, who are partly pagans and partly Muslims, of the right to navigate the sea and carry out commercial transactions.

[55] Ram P. Anand, "The Influence of History on the Literature of International Law," in *The Structure and Process of International Law*, ed. R. St. J. MacDonald and D. M. Johnston (The Hague: Martinus Nijhoff Publishers, 1986), 345–347.

[56] "Maritime law" is a body of private law that governs relationships between parties and private entities engaged in carriage by sea. Among the major areas it encompasses are shipbuilding, hire of crew, charterparties, transport of passengers, carriage of goods, jettison and general average rules, collision, salvage, maritime *qirāḍ* and partnership, and sea loans. One of the oldest treatises, which treats legal aspects of shipping and maritime commerce in the early Islamic Mediterranean, was composed by Muḥammad ibn ʿUmar al-Kinānī al-Andalusī (d. 310/923) and titled: *Kitāb Akriyat al-Sufun wa'l-Nizāʿ bayna Ahlihā (The Treatise on the Leasing of Ships and the Claims between [Contracting] Parties)*, which was edited and published by Muṣṭafā A. Ṭāher in his *Akriyat al-Sufun*; an English translation of the treatise is published in Khalilieh's *Admiralty and Maritime Laws*, 273–330. In addition to the foregoing sources, also consult Khalilieh's *Islamic Maritime Law*, 23–115; Deborah R. Noble, "The Principles of Islamic Maritime Law," (PhD diss., University of London, 1988); Muhammad M. El-Ghirani, "The Law of Charterparty with Particular Reference to Islamic Law," (PhD diss., Glasgow College, 1990); Jamal al-Sumaiti, "The Contribution of Islamic Law to the Maritime Law," (PhD diss., University of Wales, Lampeter, 2004); Muṣṭafā M. Rajab, *Al-Qānūn al-Baḥrī al-Islāmī ka-Maṣdar li-Qawāʿid al-Qānūn al-Baḥrī al-Muʿāṣir* (Alexandria: Al-Maktab al-ʿArabī al-Ḥadīth, 1990); Abraham L. Udovitch, "An Eleventh Century Islamic Treatise on the Law of the Sea," *Annales Islamologiques* 27 (1993), 37–54; ʿAbd al-Raḥmān ibn Fāyiʿ, *Aḥkām al-Baḥr fī al-Fiqh al-Islāmī* (Jeddah: Dār Ibn Ḥazm, 1421/2000); Olivia R. Constable, "The Problem of Jettison in Medieval Mediterranean Maritime Law," *Journal of Medieval History* 20 (1994), 207–220. As regards the Islamic maritime practices

two terms may appear similar to non-experts, they are actually two distinct fields of law with substantially different connotations. This study investigates exclusively the doctrine of the commonality of the seas and freedom of navigation and right of mobility as established by the Islamic Law of Nature and the *siyar*. Gaining a comprehensive understanding of the way that Islamic tradition perceives the high sea and offshore marine spaces, both in theory and practice, requires us to address several key issues: first and foremost, how does the Qur'ān view the legal status of the sea? Did naval supremacy and military expansion empower or entitle a state to claim dominion over the sea? How did the Prophet Muḥammad contribute to the foundations of the Islamic tradition and customary law of the sea despite the fact that he never experienced the sea? Under Islamic law, did vessels enjoy legal immunity while at sea, in ports, or on navigable rivers? What legal measures were employed to protect aliens in the Abode of Islam and at sea, or Muslim subjects in foreign countries? Why does the *Sharīʿah* favor legal pluralism as opposed to a unified judicial system? How did legal pluralism have a significant impact on the exercise of the right to freedom of the seas, ultimately promoting commercial activities? What were the circumstances in which a coastal state could claim jurisdiction over waters adjoining its shoreline? Was that claim exclusive? Did the coastal self-ruling or independent entity have a right to deny access or bar foreign vessels from sailing through its territorial sea? If a ship was exposed to man-made or natural dangers, was she granted permission to seek refuge? What were the legal and practical means employed by authorities to fight, suppress, and even eradicate piracy? What was more meritorious, fighting piracy or launching a war against enemies, and why?

in the Arabian Sea and Indian Ocean, see Liaw Y. Fang, *Undang-undang Melaka (The Laws of Melaka)* (The Hague: Martinus Nijhoff, 1976), 2–7, 33, 38, 40, 48–49, 65, 79, 87, 119, 121, 123, 135; Sir Stamford Raffles, "The Maritime Code of the Malays," *Journal of the Straits Branch of the Royal Asiatic Society* 3 (1879), 62–84; Richard Winstedt and P. E. de Josselin de Jong, "The Maritime Laws of Malacca," *Journal of the Malayan Branch of the Royal Asiatic Society-Singapore* 29 (1956), 22–59; Mardiana Nordin, "Undang-undang Laut Melaka: A Note on Malay Maritime Law in the 15th Century," in *Memory and Knowledge of the Sea in Southeast Asia*, ed. Danny Wong Tze Ken, Institute of Ocean and Earth Sciences Monograph Series 3 (Kuala Lumpur: University of Malaya Press, 2008), 15–21; Badriyyah H. Salleh, "Undang-undang Laut (Melaka Maritime Laws/Code)," in *Southeast Asia: A Historical Encyclopedia from Angkor Wat to East Timor*, ed. Ooi Keat Gin (Santa Barbara: ABC-CLIO, 2004), 1360–1361; Robert B. Serjeant, "Maritime Customary Law off the Arabian Coasts," in *Sociétés et compagnies de commerce en orient et dans l'océan indien*, ed. Michel Mollat (Paris: S. E. V. P. E. N., 1970), 195–207.

Our study does not seek to survey and address Islamic maritime heritage in the western and eastern hemispheres, a subject which has received a fair amount of attention from contemporary scholars.[57] Rather, its aim

[57] The literature on the history of Islamic maritime civilization in the Mediterranean Sea from the seventh to the fifteenth century CE is far too extensive to cite in detail, but consider for example the following selected bibliography: ʿAbd al-ʿAzīz Sālim and Aḥmad ʿAbbādī, *Tārīkh al-Baḥriyya al-Islāmiyya fī al-Maghrib wa'l-Andalus* (Beirut: Dār al-Nahḍa al-ʿArabiyya, 1969); ʿAbd al-ʿAzīz Sālim and Aḥmad ʿAbbādī, *Tārīkh al-Baḥriyya al-Islāmiyya fī Miṣr wa'l-Shām* (Beirut: Dār al-Nahḍa al-ʿArabiyya, 1981); Wilhelm Hoenerbach, *La Marina Arabe del Mar Mediterráneo en Tiempos de Muʿāwiya* (Tetuan: Instituto Muley el-Hasan, 1954); Aḥmad R. Aḥmad, *Tārīkh Fann al-Qitāl al-Baḥrī fī al-Baḥr al-Mutawassiṭ 35–978/655–1571* (Cairo: Wizārat al-Thaqāfa, 1986); Aly M. Fahmy, *Muslim Sea-Power in the Eastern Mediterranean from the Seventh to the Tenth Century A.D.* (Cairo: National Publication and Printing House, 1966); Aly M. Fahmy, *Muslim Naval Organisation in the Eastern Mediterranean from the Seventh to the Tenth Century A.D.* (Cairo: National Publication and Printing House, 1966); Maḥmūd A. ʿAwwād, *Al-Jaysh wa'l-Usṭūl al-Islāmī fī al-ʿAṣr al-Umawī* (Hebron: Al-Adabiyya lil-Ṭibāʿa wa'l-Nashr, 1994); Christophe Picard, *La mer et les musulmans d'Occident au Moyen Âge* (Paris: Presses Universitaires de France, 1997); Christophe Picard, *La mer des califes: Une histoire de la Méditerranée musulmane (VIIe–XIIe siècle)* (Paris: Seuil, 2015); an English version of this book is titled *Sea of the Caliphs: The Mediterranean in the Medieval Islamic World* (Cambridge MA: Harvard University Press, 2018); Archibald Lewis, *Naval Power and Trade in the Mediterranean A.D. 500–1100* (Princeton: Princeton University Press, 1951); Olivia R. Constable, *Trade and Traders in Muslim Spain: The Commercial Realignment of the Iberian Peninsula 900–1500* (Cambridge: Cambridge University Press, 1994); Jorge Lirola Delgado, *El poder naval de Al-Andalus en la época del Califato Omeya* (Granada: Universidad de Granada, 1993); Vassilios Christides, *The Conquest of Crete by the Arabs CA. 824: A Turning Point in the Struggle between Byzantium and Islam* (Athens, 1984); Aziz Ahmad, *A History of Islamic Sicily* (Edinburgh: Edinburgh University Press, 1975); ʿIṣām S. Sī-Sālim, *Juzur al-Andalus al-Mansiyya: Al-Tārīkh al-Islāmī li-Juzur al-Balyār 89–685/708–1287* (Beirut: Dār al-ʿIlm lil-Malāyīn, 1984); Shelomo D. Goitein, *A Mediterranean Society: The Jewish Communities of the Arab World as Portrayed in the Documents of the Cairo Geniza: Economic Foundations* (Berkeley: University of California Press, 1967); Lawrence I. Conrad, "Islam and the Sea: Paradigms and Problematics," *Al-Qanṭara* 23 (2002): 123–154. Concerning the eastern seas, refer generally to George F. Hourani, *Arab Seafaring in the Indian Ocean in Ancient and Early Medieval Times*, 3rd ed. (Princeton: Princeton University Press, 1995); Gerald R. Tibbetts, *Arab Navigation in the Indian Ocean before the Coming of the Portuguese*: Being a Translation of Kitāb al-Fawāʾid fī Uṣūl ʿIlm al-Baḥr wa'l-Qawāʿid of Aḥmad Ibn Mājid al-Najdī (London: Royal Asiatic Society of Great Britain and Ireland, 1971); Janet Abu Lughod, *Before European Hegemony: The World System A.D. 1250–1350* (Oxford: Oxford University Press, 1989); Chaudhuri, *Trade and Civilization in the Indian Ocean*; Roxani E. Margariti, *Aden and the Indian Ocean Trade: 150 Years in the Life of Medieval Arabian Port* (Chapel Hill: University of North Carolina Press, 2007); Risso, *Merchants and Faith*; ʿAbd al-ʿAzīz Sālim, *Al-Baḥr al-Aḥmar fī al-Tārīkh al-Islāmī* (Alexandria: Muʾassasat Shabāb al-Jāmiʿa, 1990); René J. Barendse, *The Arabian Seas: The Indian Ocean World of the Seventeenth Century* (Armonk, NY: M. E. Sharpe, 2002); Pearson, *Indian Ocean*; Pearson, "Islamic Trade,

is twofold. Its primary purpose, as already stated, is to highlight the Islamic legal doctrine regarding freedom of the seas and its implementation in practice, and to divulge how the rights of individuals are protected within and beyond the maritime boundaries and territorial jurisdiction of the state. The second objective is to prove that many of the fundamental principles of the premodern international law governing the legal status of the high seas and the territorial waters originated in the Mediterranean world, though they are not a necessarily European creation. The fading away of the Byzantine maritime hegemony, the Islamic military expansions along the eastern, southern, and western shores of the Mediterranean, and the Christian–Islamic naval rivalries over the Middle Sea, particularly from the second half of the eleventh century onward, undoubtedly gave rise to the introduction of unprecedented legal norms and rules governing the law of the sea.

This work comprises three chapters, with an introduction and a conclusion. Chapter 1 treats the commonality of the sea in the Qurʾān, the genesis of the freedom of navigation, and the immunity of civilian subjects of the Abode of Islam, neutral countries, the Abode of Covenant, and the Abode of War on land and at sea. In addition, it examines the flag state's jurisdiction over national ships, their contents, crew, and passengers. Chapter 2 analyzes the Islamic concept of the territorial sea, its seaward breadth, and the state's sovereignty over offshore zones adjoining the coastal frontiers, with an emphasis on the exclusive jurisdiction over that part of the Red Sea stretching along the coast of the Hijaz (also Ḥijāz/Hejaz). The chapter describes the regime of passage through international straits, which as in the past plays a vital role today in global trade networks; in addition, the chapter investigates the judicial system in Islam and expounds the reasons why the Qurʾān and judicial authorities favor legal pluralism as opposed to a single unified legal system, and the way that the legal theory has been translated into practice. Piracy and its legal, financial, and social implications are treated in Chapter 3; the discussion revolves around the factors fostering piracy and the methods employed to combat and reduce sea robbery.

Shipping, Port-States and Merchant Communities," 3:317–365; Dionisius A. Agius, *Classic Ships of Islam: From Mesopotamia to the Indian Ocean* (Leiden: E. J. Brill, 2008); Abdul Sheriff, *Dhow Cultures of the Indian Ocean: Cosmopolitanism, Commerce, and Islam* (London: Hurst and Company, 2010); Goitein and Friedman, *India Traders*.

Methodologically, coping with the foregoing themes cannot be achieved unless disciplinary boundaries are transcended through an interdisciplinary approach. The primary source upon which this study is based comes from the *Sharī'ah*, which is composed primarily of the Qur'ān and the Prophetic Sunna. Even though the Qur'ān constitutes the cornerstone and foundation of Islamic legislation it should not be approached solely as a book of law,[58] since the majority of it focuses on human moral values and ethics.[59] With regard to the subject matter of this study, however, the Qur'ānic verses analyzed are confined exclusively to the topic of the commonality of the sea highlighting principles of natural and universal laws.[60] The Qur'ānic verses will be quoted in the original Arabic, accompanied by an English translation,[61] in order to maintain their true meaning and avoid depriving the reader of the Divine spirit of the original text. Word-for-word translations of the Qur'ān have traditionally been rejected by Muslim theologians and intellectuals from the eighth century to the present day, the argument being that: (a) the translations could result in a semantic change and therefore ruin the intended meaning; (b) no matter how precise the translation, it can never produce a second original, either in form or in content; (c) the translator's scholarly background of Islamic theology and tradition and linguistic skills in both Arabic and English may directly affect the quality of the translation; a translator who

[58] Classical Muslim jurists and modern intellectuals count some 500 verses with legal prescriptions pertaining to family law, penal law, civil law, constitutional law, jurisdiction and procedure, international relations, and economic and financial order. Abū Ḥāmid Muḥammad ibn Muḥammad al-Ghazālī, *Al-Musṭaṣfā min 'Ilma al-Uṣūl* (Jeddah: Sharikat al-Madīnah al-Munawwara, 1413/1993), 4:6; Wael B. Hallaq, *A History of Islamic Legal Theories* (Cambridge: Cambridge University Press, 1997), 3, 10; Khizr M. Khan, "Juristic Classification of Islamic Law," *Houston Journal of International Law* 6 (1983–1984), 27.

[59] Qur'ān 16:89: "وَنَزَّلْنَا عَلَيْكَ الْكِتَابَ تِبْيَانًا لِّكُلِّ شَيْءٍ وَهُدًى وَرَحْمَةً وَبُشْرَى لِلْمُسْلِمِينَ (and We have sent down to thee a Book explaining all things, a Guide, a Mercy, and Glad Tidings to Muslims)."

[60] For further details on the sea in the Qur'ān refer to Omri Abu Hamad, "The Sea and Marine Environment in the Qur'ān and the Ḥadīth and Their Reflections in the Classical Geographical and Astronomical Sources and Pilot-Books," (PhD diss., University of Haifa, 2014) (Hebrew); Agus S. Djamil and Mulyadhi Kartanegara, "The Philosophy of Oceanic Verses of the Quran and Its Relevance to Indonesian Context," *Analisa* 2 (2017), 103–121; Karen Pinto, "In God's Eyes: The Sacrality of the Seas in the Islamic Cartographic Vision," *Espacio Tiempo y Forma* 5 (2017), 55–79.

[61] The English translation of the quoted Qur'ānic verses relies almost solely on 'Abdullāh Yūsuf 'Alī, *The Meaning of the Holy Qur'ān* (Brentwood: Amana Corporation, 1991), which is considered to be one of the most accurate, authentic, and reliable translations.

lacks the necessary academic background may utterly change the meaning of the verse and provide a totally different translations when the verse itself is very clear; and (d) inaccuracies may occur due to the translator's sectarian and personal biases or sociopolitical interests.[62] All these and other reasons make the English translation interpretive rather than an equivalent text of the original Arabic. As a consequence, the Qur'ān repeatedly asserts why it was revealed to the "Seal of the Prophets (خَاتَمَ النَّبِيِّينَ)"[63] "in the perspicuous Arabic tongue (بِلِسَانٍ عَرَبِيٍّ مُبِينٍ)."[64]

As a supplement to the Qur'ān, the Sunna of the Prophet constitutes the second fundamental and indispensable source of Islamic law.[65]

[62] From the publication of the first English translation of the Qur'ān in 1649 until the present day, more than seventy English versions have seen the light. Alexander Ross, who published the first version, did not translate the Qur'ān from the original Arabic but from the French, thus missing the actual sense of the Divine Words. However, only in 1734 did George Sale translate the Qur'ān directly from the original Arabic, though he was considerably influenced by Marracci's Latin interpretation of the Holy Book. Not until 1905 did Mohammad Abdul Hakim Khan, the first Muslim translator of the Qur'ān, publish his English version, including the Arabic text, in India. Almost all English editions of the Qur'ān are different from each other and vary in wording and quality. Iman N. Khalaf and Zulkifli M. Yusoff, "The *Qur'ān*: Limits of Translatability," *International Journal of Quranic Research* 2 (2012), 73; Ali Y. Aldahesh, "(Un) Translatability of the Qur'ān: A Theoretical Perspective," *International Journal of Linguistics* 6 (2014), 26–30. For a deeper insight into the subject of translatability and untranslatability of the Qur'ān, consult Muḥammad Ṣ. Al-Bundāq, *Al-Mustashriqūn wa-Tarjamat al-Qur'ān al-Karīm* (Beirut: Dār al-Āfāq al-Jadīda, 1403/1983); Hussein Abdul-Raof, *Qur'ān Translation: Discourse, Texture and Exegesis* (Richmond: Curzon Press, 2001); Tariq H. El-Hadary, "Equivalence and Translatability of Qur'ānic Discourse: A Comparative and Analytical Evaluation," (PhD diss., University of Leeds, 2008); Stefan Wild, "Muslim Translators and Translation of the Qur'an into English," *Journal of Qur'ānic Studies* 17 (2015), 158–182; Khaleel Mohammed, "Assessing English Translations of the Qur'an," *Middle East Quarterly* 12 (2005), 58–71; Muhammad T. Saleem, "The English Translations of the Holy Qur'an: A Critique," *Al-Idah* 27 (2013), 77–98.

[63] Qur'ān 33:40.

[64] Qur'ān 26:195; Q 41:3: "كِتَابٌ فُصِّلَتْ آيَاتُهُ قُرْآنًا عَرَبِيًّا لِّقَوْمٍ يَعْلَمُونَ (A Book, whereof the verses are explained in detail – a Qur'ān in Arabic for people who understand)"; Q 43:3: "إِنَّا جَعَلْنَاهُ قُرْآنًا عَرَبِيًّا لَّعَلَّكُمْ تَعْقِلُونَ (We have made a Qur'ān in Arabic that ye may be able to understand and learn wisdom)."

[65] Qur'ān 16:44: "وَأَنزَلْنَا إِلَيْكَ الذِّكْرَ لِتُبَيِّنَ لِلنَّاسِ مَا نُزِّلَ إِلَيْهِمْ وَلَعَلَّهُمْ يَتَفَكَّرُونَ (And We have sent down unto thee (also) the Message; that thou mayest explain clearly to men what is sent for them, and that they may give thought)." It is clearly evident from this verse that the Prophetic tradition can be viewed as an interpretation and explanation of the Qur'ānic injunctions by God's Messenger. Its primary purpose is, therefore, to clarify the meaning of the Qur'ānic verses and remove any probable confusion that may arise from the brevity, ambiguity, and hidden meaning/s of these verses.

Many Qur'ānic verses explicitly equate obedience to God with obedience to His Messenger and command all Muslims to hold tight to his tradition and heritage.[66] Most relevant to our study are specific documents and treaties suggested to have been issued by the Prophet, specifically the 9 AH/630 CE guarantee of protection, which the Prophet granted to Yūḥannā ibn Ru'ba, the Patriarch and governor of the port city of Aylah (present-day 'Aqabah). All of the recorded diplomatic treaties, truces, correspondences, and safe-conducts formulated and endorsed by the Prophet reflect his actual attitude and conduct (*Sīra*),[67] served as the model and basis for later Islamic *siyar*, and were accepted as a customary practice for over a millennium. The vast majority, if not all, of the international treaties concluded in the post-Prophetic era between Muslim central and peripheral authorities on the one hand, and foreign empires, states, and self-ruling entities on the other, seem to have followed the same legal pattern and format introduced by the Prophetic *Sīra*.[68] Historically, being part of Islamic law, the *siyar* was contemporaneously pioneered by early jurists prior to the formation of the *madhāhib*, namely, by Abū 'Amr 'Āmir ibn Sharāḥīl al-Sha'bī (21–103/641–721), Abū Ḥanīfa al-Nu'mān ibn Thābit (80–150/699–767), Ibn Isḥāq (85–151/704–768), 'Abd al-Raḥmān al-Awzā'ī (88–157/707–774), Sufyān al-Thawrī (97–161/716–778), Abū Isḥāq al-Fazārī (d. 186/802), Wāqidī (130–207/747–822), Muḥammad ibn al-Ḥasan al-Shaybānī (131–189/749–805), and Ibn Hishām (d. 218/833).[69] The topics

[66] Qur'ān 3:32, 132; Q 4:13, 59, 69, 80; Q 5:92; Q 8:1, 20, 46; Q 24:52, 54, 56; Q 33:71; Q 47:33; Q 48:17; Q 49:14; Q 58:13; Q 64:12. A good narration attributed to the Prophet states: "I have left behind me two things; if ye maintain will not go astray, the Book of God and my Sunna." Muḥammad Nāṣir al-Dīn al-Albānī, *Al-Ḥadīth Ḥujjatun bi-Nafsihi fī al-'Aqā'id wa'l-Aḥkām* (Riyad: Maktabat al-Ma'ārif lil-Nashr wa'l-Tawzī', 1425/2005), 30–31; Hallaq, *Origins and Evolution of Islamic Law*, 47–49.

[67] *Sīra(h)*, of which the *siyar* is the plural, has two different meanings. First, it signifies a life account or biography; and, second, the behavior and conduct of the ruler during wartime and external and internal affairs of the state. When Muslim jurists use the term *sīra*, they chiefly refer to the conduct of the Prophet and his Rightly Guided Successors (Pious Caliphs) in their wars, and in their relations with foreign states, rules of dealing with rebels, apostates, and non-Muslim citizens and aliens within the Islamic territory.

[68] An analytical treatment of the Prophet Muḥammad's documents – contracts, grants of land, safe-conducts, diplomatic correspondences, and personal letters – is so far best addressed by Sarah Z. Mirza, "Oral Tradition and Scribals Conventions in the Documents Attributed to the Prophet Muḥammad," (PhD diss., University of Michigan, 2010).

[69] Majid Khadduri, *The Islamic Law of Nations: Shaybānī's Siyar* (Baltimore: Johns Hopkins Press, 1966), 22–26; 'Uthmān J. Ḍumayriyya, *Usūl al-'Alāqāt al-Duwaliyya fī*

covered by the *siyar* are best summarized by Muḥammad ibn Aḥmad al-Sarakhsī (d. 490/1096) as follows:

Know that the word *siyar* is the plural form of *sīra(h)*. (*Imam* Muhammad al-Shaybānī) has designated this chapter by it since it describes the *behavior of the Muslims* in dealing with the Associators (non-Muslims) from among the belligerents as well as those of them who have made a pact (with Muslims) and live either as Resident Aliens or as non-Muslim Subjects; in dealing with Apostates who are the worst of infidels, since they abjure after acknowledgement (of Islam); and in dealing with Rebels whose position is less (reprehensible) than that of the Associators, although they be ignorant and in their contention on false ground.[70]

Islamic law covers all areas of human conduct, rules of ritual purification, and rules governing interhuman relations and dealings (*mu'āmalāt*). What matters for this study are two themes that neither the Qur'ān nor the recorded Sunna has treated in straightforward manner: the division of the world, and the sovereign and jurisdictional rights over the Arabian side of the Red Sea, specifically the offshore marine zone adjacent to the Hijaz. Furthermore, the use of early and classical jurisprudential manuals can shed light on the conduct of war, enemy alien merchants and travelers in the Abode of Islam and at sea, the judicial autonomy of non-Muslims and foreigners in Islamic territories, and issues related to piracy.

Surviving international diplomatic and commercial treaties that have come down to us from the pre-Ottoman Mediterranean world contain the most significant legal details and historical facts regarding the legal status of persons, merchant vessels, and property on the high seas, territorial seas, and inland waters. The vast bulk of the Islamic–Christian international treaties cited or quoted in this study deal with the maintenance of peace and security between the contracting parties, the promotion and facilitation of trade, freedom of navigation, protection of persons, vessels, and properties at sea and in inland waters, the suppression and deterrence of piracy, and above all, the implementation of reciprocal interests and mutual respect for state sovereignty and territorial integrity. Moreover,

Fiqh al-Imām Muḥammad Ibn al-Ḥasan al-Shaybānī (Amman: Dār al-Ma'ālī, 1419/1999), 245–254; Labeeb A. Bsoul, "Historical Evolution of Islamic Law of Nations/*Siyar*: Between Memory and Desire," *Digest of Middle East Studies* 17 (2008), 57–61; Anke I. Bouzenita, "The *Siyar* – An Islamic Law of Nations?" *Asian Journal of Social Science* 35 (2007), 22–26; Akhtar, "Nature, Origin, and Source of Islamic Law of Nations," 31–34.

70 Ḥamīdullāh, *Muslim Conduct of State*, 12; for the original Arabic text see Muḥammad ibn Aḥmad ibn Abū Sahl al-Sarakhsī, *Al-Mabsūṭ* (Beirut: Dār al-Ma'rifa, 1409/1989), 10:2.

a thorough scrutiny of these treaties enables us to learn how classical Islam and medieval Europe theorized the concept of the territorial sea and whether sovereignty over a limited marine zone contiguous to the coastal frontier was awarded international recognition. Familiarity with these sources will contribute significantly to our understanding of how the sea is conceived in the Islamic Law of Nature and the Law of Nations.

I

Freedom of the Seas

PRE-ISLAMIC CUSTOMARY LAWS AND PRACTICES

Right of access to the sea has preoccupied ruling authorities and jurisconsults from the dawn of ancient civilization to the present day. The scant legal evidence reaching us from the biblical and ensuing periods suggests that nations bordering the sea – such as those of the Egyptians, Phoenicians, Minoans, Hittites, Philistines, and Assyrians – codified laws regulating navigation in adjacent waters, on rivers, and on the high seas, in addition to establishing regulations pertaining to fishing and access to ports. Despite their military supremacy on land and at sea, ancient Near Eastern empires neither claimed legal dominion over the high seas, in full or in part, nor denied other nations access to them.[1] Dominion over the sea held a symbolic rather

[1] A letter addressed from the King of Tyre to the King of Ugarit from the thirteenth century BCE reports that a Ugaritic ship heading for Egypt had sunk or had been severely damaged in a rainstorm off the coast of Acco (ʿAkkā/Acre). The ship had been unloaded, and her sailors and their belongings sheltered in Acco until the sea had calmed down. The Tyrian king went on to assure the Ugaritic king that the ship's cargo was safe. His letter seems to indicate that the Tyrian king had the concept of territorial waters in mind when he wrote to Ugarit. Regardless of nationality, providing assistance to ships in distress sailing within the territorial waters of a coastal state has always been viewed as a humane duty. Jonathan Ziskind, "The International Legal Status of the Sea in Antiquity," *Acta Orientalia* 35 (1973), 36–40; Oded Tammuz, "*Mare Clausum*: Sailing Seasons in the Mediterranean in Early Antiquity," *Mediterranean Historical Review* 20 (2005), 148–149; Arno Egberts, "The Chronology of 'The Report of Wenamun'," *Journal of Egyptian Archaeology* 77 (1991), 58–61; James H. Breasted, "The Report of Wenamon," *American Journal of Semitic Languages and Literatures* 21 (1905), 103–104; Jan A. Hessbruegge, "The Historical Development of the Doctrines of Attribution and Due Diligence in International Law," *International Law and Politics* 36 (2004), 265–266; Alfred Rubin,

than a formal legal standing; it was *de facto* rather than *de jure* sovereignty. However, access of foreign vessels and merchants to internal waters was restricted, falling under the exclusive sovereignty of coastal states.

Those regulations governing access to the sea, freedom of navigation, and maritime trade on the Great Sea (הַיָּם הַגָּדוֹל)/*ha-yam ha-gadōl*), as expressed in the Bible (Ezekiel 47:20), find far greater documentation in Roman codices. From the beginning of the second century BCE, the Romans, succeeded by the Byzantines, absorbed the independent states of the two Mediterranean basins; they claimed maritime dominion, enforced control with their naval power – which they exercised freely and fully – and came to view the Mediterranean Sea chiefly as their own (*mare nostrum*).[2] Their dominion came to an end only with the appearance of Islam on the shores of the Mediterranean during the middle of the seventh century CE.

As embodied in the *Corpus Juris Civilis* of Justinian I (527–565), Roman law is composed of two parts, *res publica* and *res communes*. *Res publica* addresses the public property of the Roman Empire, such as highways, inland rivers, and harbors, allowing all inhabitants of the empire free use of harbors to navigate, fish, and dock their ships.[3] These structures belonged to the state,

"The Concept of Neutrality in International Law," *Denver Journal of International Law and Policy* 16 (1987–1988), 354–355; Jack Sasson, "Canaanite Maritime Involvement in the Second Millennium B.C.," *Journal of the American Oriental Society* 86 (1966), 131–138; Daniel D. Luckenbill, "Hittite Treaties and Letters," *American Journal of Semitic Languages and Literatures* 37 (1921), 186–187; Robert B. Revere, "'No Man's Coast': Ports of Trade in the Eastern Mediterranean," in *Trade and Market in the Early Empires: Economies in History and Theory*, ed. Karl Polanyi *et al.* (Glencoe, IL: Free Press, 1957), 49–50; Simo Parpola and Kazuko Watanabe, *Neo-Assyrian Treaties and Loyalty Oaths*, State Archives of Assyria (Helsinki: Helsinki University Press, 1988), 2:25; Godfrey R. Driver and John C. Miles, *The Babylonian Laws* (Oxford: Clarendon Press, 1952–1955), 1:427–435, 463–464, 473–475; W. W. Davies, "The Code of Hammurabi," in *Sources of Ancient and Primitive Law*, ed. Albert Kocourek and John Wigmore (Littleton, CO: Fred B. Rothman and Co., 1979), 434–435, 441; Thomas Hodgins, "Ancient Law of Nations Respecting the Sea and Sea-Shore," *Canadian Law Times* 13 (1893), 17–18.

2 For the first two centuries or so of the rise of Islam in the Mediterranean basins, the great majority of learned Muslims and ruling authorities called the Mediterranean Sea "Baḥr al-Rūm" (Sea of the Romans/Byzantines) despite the division of the sea into two distinct entities, Islamic and Christian. Karen C. Pinto, "Ṣūrat Baḥr al-Rūm [Picture of the Sea of Byzantium]: Possible Meanings Underlying the Forms," in *Eastern Mediterranean Cartographies*, ed. George Tolias and Dimitris Loupis (Proceedings of the 18th International Conference on the History of Cartography, Athens, 11–16 July 1999, Athens: Institute for Neohellenic Research, 2004), 223–241; Khalilieh, *Islamic Maritime Law*, 131.

3 Thomas C. Sandars (ed.), *The Institutes of Justinian* (London: Longmans, Green, and Co., 1917), 91, Book 2, Title 1: "The word *publicus* is sometimes used as equivalent to *communis*, but is probably used, as here, for what belongs to the people. Things public belong to a particular people, but may be used and enjoyed by all men.... The particular people or nation in whose territory public things lie may permit all the world to make use of them, but exercises

which enjoyed the right of exclusive jurisdiction. *Res communes*, which some sources refer to as *jus gentium* (the Law of Nations), addressed the common properties that are open to all and cannot be appropriated, such as light, air, running water, the sea, and – in later law – the seashore to the highest level of the winter flood.[4] By law, every Roman citizen or resident was permitted unlimited access to these common endowments.[5] However, unlike the legal status of seashores and navigable rivers, which granted the state appropriation rights and comprehensive jurisdiction,[6] the state's exclusive sovereignty on the high seas was strictly limited to ships flying its flag. Jurisconsults viewed Roman vessels sailing out of sight of the coast as an extension of the land, whereby the imperial law could not be enforced beyond the internal order and human element of the ship since the open sea was legally regarded as *res nullius*.[7] Every person possessed the right to navigate the high seas, to trade,

a special jurisdiction to prevent any one injuring them." In spite of the distinction that Roman law draws between citizens and inhabitants, it mandates that hydrospace is common to all humankind (*res communes*) irrespective of civil status; all people living within the boundaries of the empire should enjoy right of access to hydrospace and draw benefit from it. Pitman B. Potter, *The Freedom of the Seas in History, Law, and Politics* (New York: Longmans, Green, and Co., 1924), 32; William W. Buckland, *A Text-Book of Roman Law from Augustus to Justinian*, 3rd ed., ed. and revised by Peer Stein (Cambridge: Cambridge University Press, 1963), 182–183; Percy T. Fenn, "Justinian and the Freedom of the Sea," *American Journal of International Law* 19 (1925), 723–724; Carol M. Rose, "Romans, Roads, and Romantic Creators: Traditions of Public Property in the Information Age," *Law and Contemporary Problems* 66 (2003), 96–99, 106; Peter Birks, "The Roman Concept of Dominium and the Idea of Absolute Ownership," *Acta Juridica* 31 (1985), 8–10.

4 Samuel P. Scott (ed.), *The Civil Law* (Cincinnati: Central Trust Company, 1932), 3:304, Digest VIII, 4, 13, Domitius Ulpianus (d. 228) rules: "Although a servitude cannot be imposed on the sea by private contract, since by nature it is open to all, still, as the good faith of the contract demands that the conditions of the sale should be observed, the persons in possession or those who succeed to their rights are bound by the provisions of the stipulation or the sale." Identical edicts are established by Islamic law, which considers the big rivers as a common heritage of humankind (*al-anhār al-kibār al-mushtaraka bayna al-nās*), therefore they are not subject to private appropriation. Muḥammad ibn Abū Bakr ibn Qayyim al-Jawziyya, *Zād al-Ma'ād fī Hady Khayr al-'Ibād* (Beirut: Mu'assasat al-Risālah, 1418/1998), 5:709.

5 Potter, *Freedom of the Seas*, 32.

6 Sandars (ed.), *Institutes of Justinian*, 91–92, Book 2, Title 1; foreigners had the right of innocent passage to navigable rivers to reach a different country inasmuch as its laws were observed.

7 Access to the seashore, for instance, was open to all, but no one might build on it. Use of the seashore was connected to use of the sea; one could only erect buildings with the permission of the authorities. Even when the authorities granted such permission, they did not grant ownership of the seashore, but only of the buildings per se. Thus, if a building was ever destroyed, the land would again revert to common ownership. Similarly, nobody could interfere with fishing and navigation on the sea. If a person prevented another from fishing, the latter could obtain an *actio iniuriarum* (action for delict) against the former. The same conditions applied

and to fish at will because the sea is common to all by the Law of Nature (*lex naturalis*). No person should be hindered from exploiting the seas' natural resources, nor should anyone interfere with maritime navigation and seaborne commerce.[8]

During the time the Romans promulgated their civil laws in the Mediterranean, no rival power existed along its shores to dispute or jeopardize Roman hegemony and jurisdiction. Although the Romans dominated the land around the Middle Sea politically, their territorial jurisdiction of the sea itself may not have extended beyond a maritime belt adjacent to their coastal territories, where local authorities could legally regulate and control navigation and carriage. The Romans exercised *imperium* over this belt but never claimed exclusive ownership or usage, because the sea, like the air and running water, belongs to all humankind and nations.[9] The *jus gentium* and *juris civilis* instituted by the Roman *praetors* were designated to protect the welfare of their citizens.[10] Romano-Byzantine dominion over the Mediterranean was a matter of imperial constitutional law and practice,[11]

to navigable rivers, which were regarded as *res nullius* and their use subject to the *jus gentium*. Furthermore, *res communes* were considered an ethical concept. Richard Perruso, "The Development of the Doctrine of *Res Communes* in Medieval and Early Modern Europe," *Tijdschrift voor Rechtsgeschiedenis* 70 (2002), 70–75; Paul W. Gormley, "The Development and Subsequent Influence of the Roman Legal Norm of 'Freedom of the Seas'," *University of Detroit Law Journal* 40 (1963), 578–579; Fenn, "Justinian and the Freedom of the Sea," 717–718, 723–726; Percy T. Fenn, "Origins of the Theory of Territorial Waters," *American Journal of International Law* 20 (1926), 466.

8 Ziskind, "International Law and Ancient Sources," 544. All men have the right to trade and sail the high seas according to their free will; states were not required to protect commercial vessels and traders, particularly those engaged in overseas commerce.

9 Sandars (ed.), *Institutes of Justinian*, 91–92, Book 2, Title 1.1: "By the Law of Nature these things are common to mankind – the air, running water, the sea, and consequently the shores of the sea. No one, therefore, is forbidden to approach the seashore, provided that he respects habitations, monuments, and buildings, which are not, like the sea, subject only to the Law of Nations"; Fenn, "Origins of the Theory," 465–466; Ziskind, "International Law and Ancient Sources," 542; Philip E. Steinberg, "Lines of Division, Lines of Connection: Stewardship in the World Ocean," *Geographical Review* 89 (1999), 259.

10 Gormley, "Roman Legal Norm," 570–571.

11 Potter, *Freedom of the Seas*, 34–35; Aleksandra E. Thurman, "The Justification of the Law of the Sea in Early Modern Europe," (PhD diss., University of Michigan, 2010), 60–61; Fenn, in "Justinian and the Freedom of the Sea," 717, relates phrases regarding the legal status of Roman Mediterranean as follows: "Yet this claim was not expanded into a claim involving any sort of property right in the sea itself, that is, the claim to *imperium* (jurisdiction) was not developed into a claim to *dominium* (possession). Beyond this, positive evidence exists that, in the opinion of men generally, as least during the period of Roman greatness, in other words, at a time when Rome was able to assert effectively the opposite position, the sea, and the fish in it, were open or common to all men, for their use, as to the sea, or for their appropriation, as to the fish."

which began to fade as early as the second third of the seventh century. From that time on, the sea began to no longer be considered a Roman lake, as Muslims introduced a new monotheistic religion, laws, and cultural norms that overturned the notion.

In contrast, the Indian Ocean and its littoral regions never formed a unified or single sociocultural and geopolitical entity. Ethnocultural diversity characterized this area, comprising five major distinct civilizations: Perso-Arabic, African, Hindu, Chinese, and Indonesian, none of which claimed title over the ocean. The Indian Ocean presented no barrier to commercial or cultural interactions among the civilizations and was characterized by indigenous ruling authorities as a *mare liberum*.[12] The empires and political entities along the coasts of the ocean made no attempt to control or monopolize overseas trade, thereby permitting ships of different nationalities to sail unhindered on the high seas and to frequent foreign ports. With the exception of human and natural hazards, all merchants, shippers, and travelers around the Indian littoral enjoyed its bounties, sailed uninterrupted, engaged in commercial transactions, and recognized and honored local laws and customs.[13] In his *Arthashastra*, the most important book on Hindu statecraft, the fourth-century BCE Indian philosopher and royal advisor Kauṭilya emphasizes that international relations are guided strongly by trade considerations but makes no mention of regulation of travel over the ocean.[14] The absence of legal references pertaining to customary law of the sea in the pre-Islamic Indian Ocean undoubtedly reflects the attitudes of the peoples and states toward the free use of the ocean. Furthermore, ancient Hindu and the late fifteenth- and early sixteenth-century Islamic codes include mainly commercial maritime laws.[15]

[12] Yatim, "Development of the Law of the Sea," 87–88.

[13] Hourani, *Arab Seafaring in the Indian Ocean*, 6–46, describes mainly the trade routes; Sheriff, *Dhow Culture*, 15–27; Anand, *Origin and Development of the Law of the Sea*, 10–13; Anand, "Maritime Practice in South-East Asia," 446.

[14] Charles H. Alexandrowicz, "Kautilyan Principles and the Law of Nations," *British Year Book of International Law* 41 (1965–1966), 310–311; Rudrapatnam Shamasastry, *Kautilya's Arthashastra* (Bangalore: Government Press, 1915), 137, https://archive.org/details/Arthasastra_English_Translation, Kauṭilya writes: "The superintendent shall show favor to those who import foreign merchandise: mariners (*návika*) and merchants who import foreign merchandise shall be favored with remission of the trade-taxes, so that they may derive some profit (*áyatikshamam parihåram dadyát*)." He further adds: "Foreigners importing merchandise shall be exempted from being sued for debts unless they are (local) associations and partners."

[15] Shamasastry, *Kautilya's Arthashastra*, 58, 179–182, 255, 418; Raffles, "Maritime Code of the Malays," 62–84; Winstedt and De Jong, "Maritime Laws of Malacca," 22–59; Nordin, "Undang-undang Laut Melaka," 15–21.

LAW OF NATURE: COMMONALITY OF THE SEA IN THE QUR'ĀN

Water is the source of life for every organism and creature. A Qur'ānic verse (21:30) states: "We have made from water every living thing (وَجَعَلْنَا مِنَ الْمَاءِ كُلَّ شَيْءٍ حَيٍّ)," upon which al-Zāhid al-Bukhārī (d. 546/1151) comments: "Water is the source of all drinks and most abundant (on Earth), but the dearest resource when missed."[16] Only when stranded in the desert or at sea can people appreciate the value of fresh water. Since water is an indispensable resource, it has naturally been considered a common good for all creatures on Earth of which no one shall be denied. A tradition attributed to the Prophet Muḥammad states: "Muslims are partners in three things: green pastures, water, and fire."[17] Ibn Qayyim al-Jawziyya (691–751/1292–1349) adds:

> Water is inherently created by God for the common good of all creatures and animals. He assigns water to humans for drinking and watering, without favoring any person in preference to another even if that person settles and constructs a building on the water resource.[18]

It is evident from these statements that fresh water holds a vital position in the Islamic Law of Nature. Equally, except for a narrow strip bordering coastlands, the open sea commands the status of a common heritage for all humankind, whereby no nation, empire, or state may assert proprietary rights over it.

The sea and its assets are among God's bounties that must be kept accessible to and shared by all humankind. Since all human beings on the Earth are born free and equal in dignity and rights, all of them, including slaves,[19] are supposed to enjoy free access to the boundless seas and vast oceans. Such access implies the right to increase knowledge through

16 Muḥammad ibn ʿAbd al-Raḥmān al-Bukhārī, *Maḥāsin al-Islām wa-Sharāʾiʿ al-Islām* (Cairo: Maktabat al-Quds, 1357/1955), 106: (الماءُ اصلُ كل مَشْرُوب وَهو أهوَنُ مَوجودٍ وَأعَزُّ مفقودٍ).

17 Abū ʿAbd Allāh Muḥammad ibn Yazīd ibn Mājah, *Sunan Ibn Mājah* (Cairo: Dār Iḥyāʾ al-Kutub al-ʿArabiyya, 1372/1952), 2:826, hadith no. 2473: (الْمُسْلِمُونَ شُرَكَاءُ فِي ثَلَاثَةٍ: فِي الْمَاءِ وَالْكَلَإِ وَالنَّارِ); Ibn Qayyim al-Jawziyya, *Zād al-Maʿād*, 5:707; Muḥammad Nāṣir al-Dīn al-Albānī, *Irwāʾ al-Ghalīl fī Takhrīj Aḥādīth Manār al-Sabīl* (Beirut: Al-Maktab al-Islāmī, 1405/1985), 6:6–7.

18 Ibn Qayyim al-Jawziyya, *Zād al-Maʿād*, 5:708.

19 Hassan S. Khalilieh, "An Overview of the Slaves' Juridical Status in Roman, Byzantine, and Islamic Admiralty Laws," in *Histories of the Middle East: Studies in Middle Eastern Society, Economy, and Law in Honor of A. L. Udovitch*, ed. Roxani Margariti *et al.* (Leiden: E. J. Brill, 2011), 73–100.

international intercourse, to engage in commercial transactions based on trust, honesty, equity, and mutual respect, and to explore and exploit the sea's natural resources and treasures. The Qur'ān states:

Q 2:164:

Behold! . . . in the sailing of the ships through the ocean for the profit of humankind.

وَالْفُلْكِ الَّتِي تَجْرِي فِي الْبَحْرِ بِمَا يَنفَعُ النَّاسَ

Q 6:97:

It is He Who maketh the stars (as beacons) for you that ye may guide yourselves, with their help, through the dark spaces of land and sea: We detail Our Signs for people who know.

وَهُوَ الَّذِي جَعَلَ لَكُمُ النُّجُومَ لِتَهْتَدُواْ بِهَا فِي ظُلُمَاتِ الْبَرِّ وَالْبَحْرِ قَدْ فَصَّلْنَا الآيَاتِ لِقَوْمٍ يَعْلَمُونَ

Q 10:22:

He it is Who enableth you to traverse through land and sea; till when ye even board ships; they sail with them with a favorable wind, and they rejoice thereat.

هُوَ الَّذِي يُسَيِّرُكُمْ فِي الْبَرِّ وَالْبَحْرِ حَتَّى إِذَا كُنتُمْ فِي الْفُلْكِ وَجَرَيْنَ بِهِم بِرِيحٍ طَيِّبَةٍ وَفَرِحُواْ بِهَا

Q 14:32:

. . . It is He Who hath made the ships subject to you,[20] that they may sail through the sea by His Command; and the rivers (also) hath He made subject to you.

. . . وَسَخَّرَ لَكُمُ الْفُلْكَ لِتَجْرِيَ فِي الْبَحْرِ بِأَمْرِهِ وَسَخَّرَ لَكُمُ الأَنْهَارَ

[20] Regarding the way that God has made ships subservient to humans al-Rāzī explains: "If God did not create trees, iron, and the various tools needed to manufacture ships; if He did not make known to people how to use all of these items; if He did not create water as a running body which allows ships to move on it; if He did not create winds with their powerful movement; and, if He did not widen and deepen rivers enough to allow the movement of ships in them; it would have been impossible to benefit from these ships. He is the Manager (*Mudabbir*) and Subjugator (*Musakhkhir*) of these matters." Abū ʿAbd Allāh Muḥammad ibn ʿUmar ibn al-Ḥusayn al-Rāzī, *Al-Tafsīr al-Kabīr (Mafātīḥ al-Ghayb)* (Beirut: Dār al-Fikr lil-Ṭibāʿa wa'l-Nashr, 1401/1981), 19:130; Sarra Tlili, *Animals in the Qur'ān* (Cambridge: Cambridge University Press, 2012), 96; Robert G. Mourison, "The Portrayal of Nature in a Medieval Qur'ān Commentary," *Studia Islamica* 94 (2002), 127–128, 132.

Q 16:14:
It is He Who has made the sea subject, that ye may eat thereof flesh that is fresh and tender, and that ye may extract therefrom ornaments to wear;[21] and thou seest the ships therein that plough the waves, that ye may seek (thus) of the bounty of God and that ye may be grateful.

وَهُوَ الَّذِي سَخَّرَ الْبَحْرَ لِتَأْكُلُواْ مِنْهُ لَحْمًا طَرِيًّا وَتَسْتَخْرِجُواْ مِنْهُ حِلْيَةً تَلْبَسُونَهَا وَتَرَى الْفُلْكَ مَوَاخِرَ فِيهِ وَلِتَبْتَغُواْ مِن فَضْلِهِ وَلَعَلَّكُمْ تَشْكُرُونَ

Q 17:66:
Your Lord is He That maketh the ship go smoothly for you through the sea, in order that ye may seek of his Bounty.

رَّبُّكُمُ الَّذِي يُزْجِي لَكُمُ الْفُلْكَ فِي الْبَحْرِ لِتَبْتَغُواْ مِن فَضْلِهِ إِنَّهُ كَانَ بِكُمْ رَحِيمًا

Q 17:70:
We have honored dignity on the Children of Adam, provided them with transport on land and sea; given them for sustenance things good and pure; and conferred on them special favors above a great part of Our creation.

وَلَقَدْ كَرَّمْنَا بَنِي آدَمَ وَحَمَلْنَاهُمْ فِي الْبَرِّ وَالْبَحْرِ وَرَزَقْنَاهُم مِّنَ الطَّيِّبَاتِ وَفَضَّلْنَاهُمْ عَلَى كَثِيرٍ مِّمَّنْ خَلَقْنَا تَفْضِيلاً

Q 22:65:
Seest thou not that God has made subject to you (humankind) all that is on the earth, and the ships that sail through the sea by His command?

أَلَمْ تَرَ أَنَّ اللَّهَ سَخَّرَ لَكُم مَّا فِي الأَرْضِ وَالْفُلْكَ تَجْرِي فِي الْبَحْرِ بِأَمْرِهِ . . .

Q 23:22:
And on them, as well as in ships, ye ride.

وَعَلَيْهَا وَعَلَى الْفُلْكِ تُحْمَلُونَ

Q 27:63:
Or, who guides you through the depths of darkness on land and sea, and who sends the winds as heralds of glad tidings, going before His Mercy?

أَمَّن يَهْدِيكُمْ فِي ظُلُمَاتِ الْبَرِّ وَالْبَحْرِ وَمَن يُرْسِلُ الرِّيَاحَ بُشْرًا بَيْنَ يَدَيْ رَحْمَتِهِ أَإِلَهٌ مَّعَ اللَّهِ تَعَالَى اللَّهُ عَمَّا يُشْرِكُونَ

[21] Subjugation of all creatures on the Earth, including marine living resources, as food for humans is also manifested in Genesis 9:2: "וּמוֹרַאֲכֶם וְחִתְּכֶם, יִהְיֶה, עַל כָּל-חַיַּת הָאָרֶץ, וְעַל כָּל-עוֹף הַשָּׁמָיִם; בְּכֹל אֲשֶׁר תִּרְמֹשׂ הָאֲדָמָה וּבְכָל-דְּגֵי הַיָּם, בְּיֶדְכֶם נִתָּנוּ (The fear and dread of you shall fall upon all wild animals on earth, on all birds of heaven, on everything that moves upon the ground and all fish in the sea; they are given into your hands)" http://biblehub.com/genesis/9–2.htm. The Old Testament recognizes the right of humankind to exploit the resources on land and in the sea to satisfy their own needs.

(Can there be another) god besides Allāh? High is Allāh above what they associate with Him!

Q 29:15:

But We saved him, and the Companions of the Ark, and We made the (Ark) a Sign for all Peoples!

فَأَنجَيْنَاهُ وَأَصْحَابَ السَّفِينَةِ وَجَعَلْنَاهَا آيَةً
لِّلْعَالَمِينَ

Q 31:31:

Seest thou not that the ships sail through the ocean by the Grace of God.

أَلَمْ تَرَ أَنَّ الْفُلْكَ تَجْرِي فِي الْبَحْرِ بِنِعْمَتِ اللَّهِ

Q 35:12:

Nor are the two seas alike, the one palatable, sweet, and pleasant to drink, and the other, salt and bitter. Yet from each (kind of water) do ye eat flesh fresh and tender, and ye extract ornaments to wear; and thou seest the ships therein that plough the waves, that ye may seek (thus) of the Bounty of God that ye May be grateful.

وَمَا يَسْتَوِي الْبَحْرَانِ هَٰذَا عَذْبٌ فُرَاتٌ سَائِغٌ
شَرَابُهُ وَهَٰذَا مِلْحٌ أُجَاجٌ وَمِن كُلٍّ تَأْكُلُونَ
لَحْمًا طَرِيًّا وَتَسْتَخْرِجُونَ حِلْيَةً تَلْبَسُونَهَا
وَتَرَى الْفُلْكَ فِيهِ مَوَاخِرَ لِتَبْتَغُوا مِن فَضْلِهِ
وَلَعَلَّكُمْ تَشْكُرُونَ

Q 36:41:

And a Sign for them is that We bore their race (through the Flood) in the loaded Ark.

وَآيَةٌ لَّهُمْ أَنَّا حَمَلْنَا ذُرِّيَّتَهُمْ فِي الْفُلْكِ الْمَشْحُونِ

Q 43:12:

. . . and He has created for you ships and cattle on which ye ride.

. . . وَجَعَلَ لَكُم مِّنَ الْفُلْكِ وَالْأَنْعَامِ مَا تَرْكَبُونَ

Q 45:12:

It is God Who has subjected the sea to you, that ships may sail through it by His command, that ye may seek of His Bounty, and that ye may be grateful.[22]

اللَّهُ الَّذِي سَخَّرَ لَكُمُ الْبَحْرَ لِتَجْرِيَ الْفُلْكُ فِيهِ
بِأَمْرِهِ وَلِتَبْتَغُوا مِن فَضْلِهِ وَلَعَلَّكُمْ تَشْكُرُونَ

---

[22] The English translation of the above verses is quoted from ʿAbdullāh Yūsuf ʿAlī, *Meaning of the Holy Qurʾān; The Holy Qurʾān*, revised and edited by the Presidency of Islamic Researches, Ifta (Al-Madīnah al-Munawwarah, 1410/1989).

The verses above make it evident that the boundless sea neither belongs to any state or nation, nor may it be subject to appropriation because God has subjugated (*sakhkhara*)[23] it just as He has made the sun, the moon,[24] "and all things in the Heaven and on Earth"[25] serviceable to humans and other creatures.[26] This concept of Divine subjugation (*taskhīr*) consists of three components: (a) authority represented by God, Who has meaningful superiority and subjugates things to certain parties; (b) subjugated elements (*musakhkhar*) ranging from angels to inanimate objects; and (c) serviceability (*musakhkhar lahu*), i.e., the party that is being served enjoys the source of the benefit. According to the Qur'ān, God is the sole Creator and Subjugator (*Musakhkhir*) of the cosmic bodies – the sun, moon, and stars – and all that is in Heaven and Earth, including the clouds, mountains, seas, rivers, animals, and birds for His creatures' sake, benefit, and need.[27]

Just as the universe is subjugated for humankind and other creatures, humans, as custodians of the Earth, are subjugated not just to each other and to living things, but to the benefit of Earth as a whole also. Having created humankind, made them His *khalīfah* (vicegerent) on Earth,[28] and

[23] Derived from the root *s.kh.r.*, the verbs *sakhara* and *sakhkhara* mean "to constrain, coerce, subdue, or bring something into service, or to compel something to be of service to something else, or to make something subservient"; *sakhkhara* denotes assigning or charging work to someone without paying compensation or wage. Abū al-Ḥusayn Aḥmad ibn Zakariyyā ibn Fāris, *Mu'jam Maqāyīs al-Lugha* (Beirut: Dār al-Fikr, 1399/1979), 3:144; Ibn Manẓūr, *Lisān al-'Arab*, 7:144–145; Lane, *Arabic–English Lexicon*, 1:1324–1325.

[24] Qur'ān 13:2; Q 14:33; Q 16:12; Q 29:61; Q 31:29; Q 35:13; Q 39:5. Clearly, God has subjugated the sea in the same way He has made the sun and moon subservient to human beings; neither the sun, nor the moon, nor the sea can be commanded by humans, but humans can take advantage of their resources. It is then logically contended that the sea is made available for the benefit of all humans, whom God favors over the rest of His creation, yet definitely not subject to private or national appropriation.

[25] Qur'ān 31:20: (أَلَمْ تَرَوْا أَنَّ اللَّهَ سَخَّرَ لَكُمْ مَا فِي السَّمَاوَاتِ وَمَا فِي الْأَرْضِ وَأَسْبَغَ عَلَيْكُمْ نِعَمَهُ ظَاهِرَةً وَبَاطِنَةً); Q 45:13: (وَسَخَّرَ لَكُمْ مَا فِي السَّمَاوَاتِ وَمَا فِي الْأَرْضِ جَمِيعًا).

[26] Al-Rāzī, *Al-Tafsīr al-Kabīr*, 20:4; 'Adī Setia, "*Taskhīr*, Fine-Tuning, Intelligent Design, and the Scientific Appreciation of Nature," *Islam and Science* 2 (2004), 8–9, 11, 14; Tlili, *Animals in the Qur'ān*, 92–93. Even though God has created human beings in the best of nature and most perfect and intelligent of His creation (Qur'ān 95:4), all created in Heaven and on Earth is not only *musakhkhar* (subjugated) to them, but this right also extends to other creatures, such as animals and birds.

[27] Abū Isḥāq Ibrāhīm ibn al-Sarī al-Zajjāj, *Ma'ānī al-Qur'ān wa-I'rābuh* (Beirut: 'Ālam al-Kitāb, 1408/1988), 3:436–437; 4:200; Setia, "*Taskhīr*," 9–13; Tlili, *Animals in the Qur'ān*, 94–95.

[28] Qur'ān 2:230; Q 38:26; Nomanul Haq, "Islam and Ecology: Toward Retrieval and Reconstruction," *Daedalus* 130 (2001), 147: *khalīfah* signifies a human custodian of the entire natural world.

entrusted them with the Earth, humankind is urged to utilize wealth prudently and manage, develop, and make the Earth prosperous on the condition that God's Laws are observed.[29] Thus, human beings are held accountable for their actions and are required to preserve the environment, not to abuse the living and nonliving resources of the Earth, or to violate the natural rights of others; they are commanded by God to establish a just social order therein.[30] Therefore, powerful peoples and nations do not possess the privilege to conquer or dominate the universe. On the contrary, all human beings should enjoy equal rights, live in harmony with nature, use His natural bounties wisely, and care for the powerless.[31]

Since God has made the seas subservient to all humankind, it follows that every individual should be free to navigate and trade upon them.[32] Religious, political, and military authorities do not have the right to claim

[29] Haq, "Islam and Ecology," 150–151, 153, 155; Mohd Sh. Hanapi, "Development Actors in the Conventional Development Theory: Analysis based on Development Actors according to the Qur'ānic Worldwide," *International Journal of Academic Research in Business and Social Sciences* 7 (2017), 787–788; Seyyed H. Nasr, "Islam, the Contemporary Islamic World, and the Environmental Crisis," in *Islam and Ecology: A Bestowed Trust*, ed. Richard C. Foltz (Cambridge MA: Harvard University Press, 2003), 97–98; Recep Şentürk, "Ādamiyyah 'Ismah: The Contested Relationship between Humanity and Human Rights in Classical Islamic Law," *Islām Araştirmalari Dergisi* 8 (2002), 43–44.

[30] Haq, "Islam and Ecology," 153–154; Mohammad H. Kamali, "Islam and Sustainable Development," *Islam and Civilisational Renewal* 7 (2016), 13–14; Eric Winkel, "Three Relationships," *Islam and Civilisational Renewal* 2 (2011), 397–398; Ida M. Azmi, "Intellectual Property Laws and Islam in Malaysia," (PhD diss., Queen Mary and Westfield College, 1995), 197–198. Balancing the authority humankind enjoys from God, humans are held accountable for their actions – required to preserve the environment and not to abuse the natural resources, as stated in Qur'ān 30:41: "ظَهَرَ الْفَسَادُ فِي الْبَرِّ وَالْبَحْرِ بِمَا كَسَبَتْ أَيْدِي النَّاسِ (Mischief has appeared on land and sea because of (the meed) that the hands of men have earned)"; Omar A. Bakhashab, "Islamic Law and the Environment: Some Basic Principles," *Arab Law Quarterly* 3 (1988), 287–291; Mohammad H. Kamali, "Environmental Care in Islamic Teaching," *Islam and Civilisational Renewal* 3 (2011), especially 264–274.

[31] Qur'ān 31:20: "Do ye not see that God has made serviceable unto you (humans/*sakhkhara lakum*) whatsoever is in the Skies and whatsoever in the Earth"; Zajjāj, *Ma'āni al-Qur'ān*, 3:361.

[32] Abū al-Fidā' Ismā'īl ibn 'Umar ibn Kathīr, *Tafsīr Ibn Kathīr* (Riyad: Dār Ṭība lil-Nashr, 1420/1999), 1:475: "Shaping the sea in this manner, so that it is able to carry ships from one shore to another, so people benefit from what the other region has, and export what they have to them and vice versa"; Abū 'Abd Allāh Muḥammad ibn Aḥmad al-Qurṭubī, *Al-Jāmi' li-Aḥkām al-Qur'ān* (Beirut: Dār al-Fikr lil-Ṭibā'a wa'l-Nashr, 1414/1994), 2:182–184, in reference to the interpretation of Qur'ān 2:164, al-Qurṭubī writes on page 183: "Gabriel ordered Noah to build a ship whose keel resembles the carina of a bird (*ju'ju' al-ṭayr*). Then, Noah, may God's blessing be upon him, fulfilled Gabriel's order and built a ship, which resembles an inverted bird, where the seawater below her is like the air over her." Comparing the sea and the air, the exegete patently denies any exclusive sovereignty of

ownership or exclusive use, or to debar other nations, countries, or groups from using or exploiting the seas' natural resources.[33] Acknowledging this commonality of the seas, governing Muslim authorities have never claimed exclusive dominion or prevented foreign individuals and vessels from navigating the semienclosed Red Sea or Persian Gulf, except in times of external imminent threat to the Holy Sanctuary in Mecca.[34] In fact,

one nation or race over the vast sea. A ship on the sea is like a bird in the sky; just as birds fly freely unhindered in the sky, ships should likewise sail freely over the oceans and seas.

33 Qur'ān 24:42: "وَلِلَّهِ مُلْكُ السَّمَاوَاتِ وَالْأَرْضِ وَإِلَى اللَّهِ الْمَصِيرُ (Yea, to God belongs the dominion of the Heavens and the Earth; and to God is the final goal of all)"; Haq, "Islam and Ecology," 154. Clearly, the Qur'ān does not entitle Muslims to have exclusive dominion over the natural world, but all human beings, as established in this and other verses, have the right to benefit from God's bounties because it is God, "Who will inherit the Earth, and all beings thereon; to Us will they all be returned (إِنَّا نَحْنُ نَرِثُ الْأَرْضَ وَمَنْ عَلَيْهَا وَإِلَيْنَا يُرْجَعُونَ)" (Qur'ān 19:40).

34 Due to the maritime conditions and the difficulty of sailing in the Red Sea, foreign vessels normally did not make their way from the Indian Ocean to the northernmost point of the sea. Ships entering the Red Sea generally sailed only in the southern half and anchored in major ports along the two banks. From there, goods were transshipped aboard local vessels operated by qualified pilots to intermediary ports or to final destinations. Despite the hazardous sailing conditions, caliphs, namely 'Umar ibn al-Khaṭṭāb and Hārūn al-Rashīd (r. 170–193/786–809), opposed the idea of digging a canal connecting the Red Sea with the Mediterranean Sea because such a project would open the way for enemy navies to pass through the canal to the Red Sea, posing a threat to the heart of the Muslim world, Mecca and Medina. In 18/639 'Umar ibn al-Khaṭṭāb, however, approved the cleaning and redigging of the Trajan's canal (Canal of the Pharaohs) connecting the Nile Valley with Qulzum (Clysma) on the Red Sea, which was completed within six months. Indeed, the Crusaders and the Portuguese made unsuccessful attempts to establish a foothold in the Red Sea. With the exception of sporadic major events, Muslim naval powers had exercised uncontested hegemony in the Red Sea from the 830s until the decline of the Ottoman Empire, aimed primarily at safeguarding the holy cities from external intrusion, protecting trunk routes, and maintaining the flow of oriental trade through this semienclosed sea. On the proposed Red Sea–Mediterranean canal and the Nile Valley–Qulzum navigable canal, consult Abū al-Qāsim 'Abd al-Raḥmān ibn 'Abd Allāh ibn 'Abd al-Ḥakam, *Futūḥ Miṣr wa-Akhbāraha* (Cairo: Maktabat Madbouli, 1411/1991), 162–169; Taqiyy al-Dīn Aḥmad ibn 'Alī al-Maqrīzī, *Al-Mawā'iẓ wa'l-I'tibār bi-Dhikr al-Khiṭaṭ wa'l-Āthār* (Cairo: Maktabat Madbouli, 1998), 2:691–702; Sayyed S. Nadavi, "Arab Navigation," *Islamic Culture* 15.4 (1941): 444–445; John P. Cooper, *The Medieval Nile: Route, Navigation, and Landscape in Islamic Egypt* (Cairo: American University Press, 2014), 95–99; John P. Cooper, "Egypt's Nile–Red Sea Canals: Chronology, Location, Seasonality and Function," in *Connected Hinterlands: Proceedings of Red Sea Project IV Held at the University of Southampton September 2008*, ed. L. Blue *et al.*, British Archaeological Reports (Oxford: Archaeopress, 2009), 195–209; Timothy Power, "Red Sea Region during the 'Long' Late Antiquity (AD 500–1000)," (PhD diss., University of Oxford, 2010), 338–344; David Bramoullé, "The Fatimids and the Red Sea (969–1171)," in *Navigated Spaces, Connected Places: Proceedings of Red Sea Project V held at the University of Exeter, September 2010*, ed. Dionisius A. Agius *et al.*, British Archaeological Reports (Oxford: Archaeopress, 2012), 127–136; Sālim, *Al-Baḥr al-Aḥmar fī al-Tārīkh al-Islāmī*, 21–29, 81–97; John L. Meloy, *Imperial Power and Maritime Trade:*

historically, Muslims have deemed it more beneficial to secure maritime traffic and maintain free flow of commerce to the Mediterranean world, and vice versa. Although seaborne commerce between the Indian Ocean and the Mediterranean grew significantly as early as the third century AH/ninth century CE and reached a zenith by the ninth century AH/fifteenth century CE – and despite the Mongol advance in the thirteenth century CE and occurrence of the Black Death in the fourteenth century CE – for over nine centuries the ruling authorities never asserted jurisdictional rights over the semienclosed bodies of water of the Persian Gulf and the Red Sea, despite their location in the heart of the Abode of Islam.[35] The two major threats that occasionally hindered the safe passage of vessels through these waters were piracy and natural perils.

Since "God hath made subject to you (humankind) all that is on the Earth,"[36] then all of humankind possess the right to develop their lives freely,

Mecca and Cairo in the Later Middle Ages (Chicago: University of Chicago, 2010), appendix c, pp. 249–255, lists the number of groups and vessels that visited and anchored in the ports of the Hijaz between 876–944/1471–1537; C. G. Brouwer, "Non-Western Shipping Movements in the Red Sea and Gulf of Aden during the 2nd and 3rd Decades of the 17th Century, According to the Records of the Dutch East India Company," *Die Welt des Islams* 31 (1991), 110–125. With regard to the Crusaders' naval expeditions in the Red Sea, refer to Andrew S. Ehrenkreutz, "The Place of Saladin in the Naval History of the Mediterranean in the Middle Ages," *Journal of the American Oriental Society* 75 (1955), 102–109; Gary L. Leiser, "The Crusader Raid in the Red Sea in 578/1182–83," *Journal of the American Center in Egypt* 14 (1977), 87–100; Douglas Newbold, "The Crusaders in the Red Sea and the Sudan," *Sudan Notes and Records* 26 (1945), 213–227; Muḥsin M. Ḥussein, *Al-Jaysh al-Ayyūbī fī ʿAhd Ṣalāḥ al-Dīn* (Erbil: Dār Tārās lil-Ṭibāʿa, 2002), 219–223. On the Portuguese attempts to establish a foothold in the Strait of Bab el-Mandeb and interrupt the spice trade through the Red Sea, consult Andreu Martínez d'Alòs-Moner, "Conquistadores, Mercenaries, and Missionaries: The Failed Portuguese Dominion of the Red Sea," *Northeast African Studies* (New Series) 12 (2012), 1–28; Charles Boxer, "A Note on Portuguese Reactions to the Revival of the Red Sea Spice Trade and the Rise of Atjeh, 1540–1600," *Journal of Southeast Asian History* 10 (1969), 415–428.

35 On the role of the Red Sea and Persian Gulf in international trade and the presence of foreign vessels and merchants in these waters, consult Agius, *Classic Ships of Islam*, 63–98.

36 Qurʾān 2:65, 164: "profit of humankind"; Q 6:97: "He it is Who has set up for you (humankind)"; Q 10:22: "He it is Who enableth you (humankind)"; Q 14:32: "It is He Who hath made the ships subject to you," etc. However, perhaps the most convincing proof for the indiscriminate subjugation of the sea for all of humankind is established in Qurʾān 17:70: "وَلَقَدْ كَرَّمْنَا بَنِي آدَمَ وَحَمَلْنَاهُمْ فِي الْبَرِّ وَالْبَحْرِ وَرَزَقْنَاهُم مِّنَ الطَّيِّبَاتِ وَفَضَّلْنَاهُمْ عَلَىٰ كَثِيرٍ مِّمَّنْ خَلَقْنَا تَفْضِيلًا (We have honored dignity on the Children of Adam, provided them with transport on land and sea; given them for sustenance things good and pure; and conferred on them special favors above a great part of Our creation)." In the light of this and other Qurʾānic verses, it can safely be argued that God has created the sea with its living creatures to be shared by all humanity irrespective of their religious and ethnic affiliations.

take advantage of His bounties on Earth, and travel into lands and sojourn there insofar as they refrain from deleterious acts.[37] Making no distinction between sea and land, the Qur'ān considers the universe a common whole for all humankind. On this basis, rules regulating free maritime navigation and those governing free movement on land should be made identical but with one cardinal difference: every part and parcel of land can be appropriated and populated,[38] while the sea physically "is not susceptible to human occupation,"[39] though a coastal entity may claim dominion over a limited offshore zone, as shall be discussed in the next chapter.

Moreover, if by the Law of Nature all peoples are the "Children of Adam," then all humans should theoretically enjoy identical rights and receive equal treatment, regardless of national, ethnic, or religious affiliations.[40] They should all feel free to "traverse through the land and

Abū Ja'far Muḥammad ibn Jarīr al-Ṭabarī, *Tafsīr al-Ṭabarī: Jāmi' al-Bayān 'an Ta'wīl Āy al-Qur'ān* (Beirut: Mu'assasat al-Risālah, 1420/2000), 17:501; Abū Bakr Aḥmad ibn 'Alī al-Rāzī al-Jaṣṣāṣ, *Aḥkām al-Qur'ān* (Beirut: Dār Iḥyā' al-Turāth al-'Arabī, 1412/1992), 1:131, humankind enjoys the right to travel by sea as an expeditioner, a trader, or a seeker of different usufructs and benefits, irrespective of their nature; Ḥusayn ibn Mas'ūd al-Baghawī, *Tafsīr al-Baghawī* (Riyad: Dār Ṭība lil-Nashr, 1409/1989), 5:108–109; Qurṭubī, *Al-Jāmi'*, 10:263–264; Abū Ḥayyān Muḥammad ibn Yūsuf ibn 'Alī ibn Yūsuf, *Al-Tafsīr al-Kabīr al-Musammā al-Baḥr al-Muḥīṭ* (Beirut: Dār Iḥyā' al-Turāth al-'Arabī, 1411/1990), 6:61–63; Ibn Kathīr, *Tafsīr*, 5:97–98; also Qur'ān 22:65; Q 27:63.

37 Qur'ān 4:75, 97; Q 16:40; Q 22:57–58; Sami A. Abu Salieh, "The Islamic Conception of Migration," *International Migration Review* 30 (1996), 40–49; Muddathir 'Abd al-Rahim, "Asylum: A Moral and Legal Right in Islam," *Refugee Survey Quarterly* 27 (2008), 17–19; 'Abhara S. 'Āmūdī, "Al-Arḍ fī Ḍaw' al-Qur'ān," (master's thesis, Islamic University, Gaza, 1427/2006), 177–196.

38 Authorities asserted jurisdiction over land routes by constructing caravanserais, *ribāṭ*-fortresses, and watchtowers, official and private, along the coasts and on the overland routes themselves. In addition to armed personnel escorting caravans, soldiers and volunteers manned way stations in order to facilitate the flow of commerce, shelter wayfarers and caravans, and protect merchants and postal systems against highway robbers. Services provided by *ribāṭ*-fortresses to temporary dwellers extended beyond sleeping accommodation to food, water, protection, and assistance in adversity. Officially, the admiral's jurisdiction extended to cover coastal fortifications and territorial waters. Garrisons stationed at *ribāṭs* were instructed to provide assistance in terms of shelter for commercial ships sailing within territorial seas in instances of hostile attack or shipwreck. Abū al-Makārim al-As'ad al-Muhadhdhab ibn Mīnā ibn Zakariyyā ibn Mammātī, *Qawānīn al-Dawāwīn* (Cairo: Maṭba'at Miṣr, 1943), 247–248; Aḥmad ibn 'Abd Allāh al-Qalqashandī, *Ṣubḥ al-A'shā fī Ṣinā'at al-Inshā* (Cairo: Al-Maṭba'a al-Amīriyya, 1338/1919), 14:398–400.

39 Abū Zakariyyā Yaḥyā ibn Sharaf al-Nawawī, *Rawḍat al-Ṭālibīn wa-'Umdat al-Muftīn* (Beirut: Al-Maktab al-Islāmī, 1412/1991), 10:308: "... *li-annahu laysa mawḍi' iqāma.*"

40 Haq, "Islam and Ecology," 154–155; 'Abbās M. al-'Aqqād, *Al-Insān fī al-Qur'ān* (Cairo: Mu'assasat Hindawi Foundation for Education and Culture, 2013), 13–16, 43–48; 'Abd al-Laṭīf S. al-Ghāmidī, *Ḥuqūq al-Insān fī al-Islām* (Riyad: Naif Arab Academy for Security, 1421/2000), 81–106.

sea,"[41] which includes a state's territorial sea, seeking to fulfill their needs and benefit from His bounties. Certainly, the Qur'ān does not exclude any specific nation from navigating the seas or from traveling on land for trade purposes or for any other reason. The world is not the possession of any particular nation. Rather, its two masses – the land and the sea – should be free and accessible to all nations.[42]

[41] Qur'ān 10:22.

[42] Qur'ān 19:40: Haq, "Islam and Ecology," 154; Abū al-Ḥasan Muqātil ibn Sulaymān al-Balkhī, *Tafsīr Muqātil Ibn Sulaymān* (Beirut: Dār Iḥyā' al-Turāth al-'Arabī, 1423/2002), 1:158, 580, 2:234, 407, 461, 540–542, 3:136, 314, 377, 439, 554, 580, 790, 836; Ṭabarī, *Jāmi' al-Bayān*, 11:561–562, 15:51–53, 17:181–182, 496–497, 501, 18:677–678, 19:24, 20:155–156, 449–450; Muḥammad ibn 'Abd Allāh ibn al-'Arabī, *Aḥkām al-Qur'ān* (Beirut: Dār al-Kutub al-'Ilmiyyah, 1424/2003), 3:3–4; Baghawī, *Tafsīr*, 1:177–178, 3:17, 4:353, 5:12–13, 107, 108–109, 398, 415, 16:416–417; Rāzī, *Al-Tafsīr al-Kabīr*, 11:69–74; Abū al-Baqā' 'Abd Allāh ibn al-Ḥussein al-'Ukbarī, *Al-Tibyān fī I'rāb al-Qur'ān* (Beirut: Dār al-Fikr, 1421/2001), 2:7; Qurṭubī, *Al-Jāmi'*, 7:9–10, 8:237–238, 9:31–32, 10:78–82, 260–261, 263–264, 12:86–87, 110–111, 13:73–74, 206–208, 14:299–301; Abū Ḥayyān, *Al-Tafsīr al-Kabīr*, 5:137–138, 471–472, 6:61–62, 401, 7:304–305; Taqiyy al-Dīn Aḥmad ibn 'Abd al-Ḥalīm ibn Taymiyya, *Majmū' Fatāwā Ibn Taymiyya* (Riyad: Majma' al-Malik Fahd, 1416/1995), 11:96–97; Abū al-Fidā' Ismā'īl ibn 'Umar ibn Kathīr, *Al-Bidāya wa'l-Nihāyah* (Damascus: Dār Ibn Kathīr, 1431/2010), 1:41–47; Ibn Kathīr, *Tafsīr*, 1:474–475, 3:303–304, 4:258–259, 511–512 ("He made the sea able to carry these ships in order that travelers can transfer from one area to another to transport goods"), 562–563, 5:95–96, 97–98, 449–450, 470, 6:206, 268, 350–351, 539–540, 579–580, 7:219–220, 265–266; Abū 'Abd Allāh Badr al-Dīn Muḥammad ibn Bahādur al-Zarkashī, *Al-Baḥr al-Muḥīṭ* (Amman: Dār al-Katbī lil-Nashr, 1414/1994), 4:11–12. In support of his advocacy of the freedom of the sea, Hugo Grotius transiently refers to Biblical sources contending that since the natural law is originally derived from the Divine will, the latter must be far more superior than jurist-made law. Since God has bestowed the gifts of His creation upon all human beings collectively, and not particularly, it follows that peoples must have a right of access to all other peoples on Earth. He states: "God himself speaketh this in nature, seeing he will not have all those things, whereof the life of man standeth in need, to be sufficiently ministered by nature in all places and also vouchsafeth some nations to excel others in arts. To what end are these things but that he would maintain human friendship by their mutual wants and plenty, lest everyone thinking themselves sufficient for themselves for this only thing should be made insociable? Now it cometh to pass that one nation should supply the want of another by the appointment of Divine justice, that thereby (as Pliny saith) that which is brought forth anywhere might seem to be bred with all." Grotius, *The Free Sea*, 10. The concept of the nation state is inimical and stands in contrast to the Islamic principles for the Qur'ān, the Prophet, the *fiqh*, the exegetes, and the civil and judicial authorities view Muslims as one nation. Qur'ān 3:110 states: "كُنتُمْ خَيْرَ أُمَّةٍ أُخْرِجَتْ لِلنَّاسِ تَأْمُرُونَ بِالْمَعْرُوفِ وَتَنْهَوْنَ عَنِ الْمُنكَرِ وَتُؤْمِنُونَ بِاللَّهِ (Ye are the best of Peoples, evolved for humankind, enjoining what is right, forbidding what is wrong, and believing in God)"; another verse (Q 49:13) rules: "يَا أَيُّهَا النَّاسُ إِنَّا خَلَقْنَاكُم مِّن ذَكَرٍ وَأُنثَى وَجَعَلْنَاكُمْ شُعُوبًا وَقَبَائِلَ لِتَعَارَفُوا إِنَّ أَكْرَمَكُمْ عِندَ اللَّهِ أَتْقَاكُمْ (O humankind! We created you from a single (pair) of a male and a female, and made you into nations and tribes, that ye may know each other (not that ye may despise each other). Verily the most honored of you in the sight of

To sum up, subjugation of the sea can take two forms: (a) fishing and exploitation of its natural resources for various purposes; and (b) travel by sea for the sake of acquiring knowledge, facilitating socio-cultural and religious interactions, and engaging in overseas trade. The Qur'ān contains no verses bestowing on either Muslims or non-Muslims ownership of the vast seas. On the contrary, it affirms the right of all nations and individuals to exploit the natural resources of the seas and to benefit from free access.[43] The concept of "common heritage of mankind" is deeply enshrined in Islam's Holy Book. No nations, states, or other entities may exercise sovereignty or jurisdiction over the high seas and oceans.

COMMONALITY OF THE SEA UNDER THE ISLAMIC LAW OF NATIONS

The Prophet Muḥammad's Doctrine of the Free Sea

During the time of his prophecy, and particularly following his immigration from Mecca to Yathrib (later named Medina), the Prophet Muḥammad was recognized by local tribal chiefs, regional rulers, and the prevailing international community as *persona jure gentium* (international legal personality). On arrival in Yathrib, the Prophet instituted the

God is (He who is) the most righteous of you)." One of the Prophetic traditions says: "لَا فَضْلَ لِعَرَبِيٍّ عَلَى أَعْجَمِيٍّ وَلَا لِعَجَمِيٍّ عَلَى عَرَبِيٍّ وَلَا لِأَحْمَرَ عَلَى أَسْوَدَ وَلَا أَسْوَدَ عَلَى أَحْمَرَ إِلَّا بِالتَّقْوَى (There is no virtue of an Arab over a foreigner, nor a foreigner over an Arab, and neither white skin over black skin, nor black skin over white skin, except by righteousness)." Under these circumstances, each and every Muslim and non-Muslim resident of the Abode of Islam has the right to liberty of movement and freedom to choose his residence within it excluding, of course, the *dhimmis*' right of taking up permanent residence in the Hijaz. Concerning *ḥarbīs*, they can immigrate to the Abode of Islam provided that they convert to Islam or become *dhimmīs*. On the freedom of movement and religion and the right to immigrate to the Abode of Islam, consult Mohammad H. Kamali, "Citizenship: An Islamic Perspective," *Journal of Islamic Law and Culture* 11 (2009), 121–153; Nawaf A. Salam, "The Emergence of Citizenship in Islamdom," *Arab Law Quarterly* 12 (1997), 125–147; Tazeem Haider, "Universality in the Message of Qur'ān," *Journal of South Asian Studies* 4 (2016), 63–65. For further insight into the Qur'ānic concept of *ummah*, consult Frederick M. Denny, "The Meaning of 'Ummah' in the Qur'ān," *History of Religions* 15 (1975), 34–70.

43 Bakhashab, "Islamic Law and the Environment," 292–294; Ali Ahmad, "Righting Public Wrongs and Enforcing Private Rights: Public Involvement in Islamic Law," in*The New "Public": The Globalization of Public Participation*, ed. Carl Bruch (Washington DC: Environmental Law Institute, 2002), 48–49; Joseph De Somogyi, "Trade in the Qur'ān and Ḥadīth," *The Muslim World* 52 (1962), 110–114.

world's first written constitution (Ṣaḥīfat al-Madīnah/the Constitution of Medina), reconciled the warring Arab tribes of Aws and Khazraj, sent letters through envoys and diplomats to emperors, kings, and other state rulers, waged wars against the idolaters of Mecca, negotiated and concluded dozens of treaties and truces, and granted pledges of safe-conduct.[44] One of the oldest, and the most relevant, comprehensive and succinct pacts (or, more precisely, pledges of safe-conduct) of Islamic heritage that pertains to the law and custom of the sea was granted by the Prophet to Mar Yūḥannā ibn Ru'ba, the governor and bishop of the port city of Aylah (Byzantine Ailanē, ʿAqabah today) on the Red Sea, in Rajab 9 AH/ October 630 CE, shortly after the campaign of Tabūk.

Along with the campaign of Tabūk, a new chapter in Islamic military and legal history unfolded. Leading his first military action on Rajab 10, 9 AH (October 23, 630 CE), the Prophet Muḥammad arrived with the largest Muslim army ever at Tabūk (northwestern Hijaz), and commanded 30,000 combatants against Byzantium, then one of the world's superpowers. Despite outnumbering the Muslims by three to one, the Byzantine army and its northern Arab allies surprisingly opted to avoid confrontation and instead dispersed within their territories. Arguably, the withdrawal of the Byzantines probably constitutes the most brilliant military event in the Prophet's career as a statesman. This campaign enlarged the territorial domain of the nascent Islamic State, secured its northern border, and generated greater political authority in the Arab and international arenas. Some northern Arab tribes immediately embraced Islam, while others pledged to pay a tribute instead. Before returning to Yathrib, the Prophet camped in Tabūk for about twenty days, during which time he contacted frontier rulers inhabiting southern Syria and the northern Hijaz, aiming to conclude treaties of nonaggression with them. He sent envoys to local leaders and other dignitaries in the region around Tabūk, including Maqnā in northwestern Hijaz,[45] and Jarbā',

[44] Mohammad T. Ghunaimi, *The Muslim Conception of International Law and the Western Approach* (The Hague: Martinus Nijhoff, 1968), 31–34; Ḥamīdullāh, *Muslim Conduct of State*, 52–62; Mohd H. Kamal, "International Legal Personality of Prophet Muhammad," *The Sixth Oceanic Conference on International Studies,* University of Melbourne, July 9–11, 2014: http://www.ocis.org.au/files/pdf/full-papers/ocis14final00103.pdf.

[45] The pledge of safe-conduct granted to the Jews of Maqnā contains no reference to the pull tax. However, it does stipulate that one quarter of the farmers' date harvest, of the women's yarn production, and of the fishermen's yield (*rub' mā ṣādat 'urūkukum*) be delivered to the Treasury House in exchange for the security and well-being of the people of Maqnā, as well as for those who travel and sail to the town. Abū 'Abd Allāh

Adhruḥ, and Aylah along the Gulf of ʿAqabah's coast – offering these sovereignties payment of an annual jizya and other taxes as stipulated in the truces in exchange for protection on land and at sea.[46]

Muḥammad ibn ʿUmar Wāqidī, *Al-Maghāzī* (Beirut: ʿĀlam al-Kutub, 1404/1984), 3:1032–1033; Abū ʿAbd Allāh Muḥammad ibn Saʿd ibn Manīʿ, *Al-Ṭabaqāt al-Kubrā* (Cairo: Maktabat al-Khānjī, 1421/2001), 1:251–252; Abū al-ʿAbbās Aḥmad ibn Yaḥyā al-Balādhurī, *Futūḥ al-Buldān* (Beirut: Muʾassasat al-Maʿārif, 1407/1987), 81; Muḥammad Ḥamīdullāh, *Al-Wathāʾiq al-Siyāsiyya lil-ʿAhd al-Nabawī wa'l-Khilāfa al-Rāshida*, 6th ed. (Beirut: Dār al-Nafāʾis, 1407/1987), 115–123; Khalid R. al-Jamīlī, *Aḥkām al-Muʿāhadāt fī al-Sharīʿah al-Islāmiyya: Taḥlīl al-Muʿāhadāt al-Mubrama fī ʿAṣr al-Rasūl* (Baghdad: Markaz al-Buḥūth wa'l-Dirāsāt al-Islāmiyya, 2008), 119, 123; John A. Morrow, *The Covenants of the Prophet Muhammad with Christians of the World* (Kettering, OH: Angelico Press, Sophia Perennis, 2013), 52–55; Moshe Gil, *A History of Palestine 634–1099* (Cambridge: Cambridge University Press, 1992), 29–30.

46 The Prophet addressed a letter to the Governor of Aylah stating: "To Yūḥannā ibn Ruʾba and the chiefs of the people of Aylah. Peace be upon you. Praise be to God, besides whom there is no god. I shall not fight you until I have written to you. Accept Islam or pay the jizya, and obey God and His Prophet and the messengers of the Prophet." The said governor agreed to pay an annual tribute that was fixed at 300 dinars, one dinar per Aylī adult male (*ḥalīm*). In comparison to the city's wealth, the imposition of such an amount was financially insignificant, but symbolically it reflected an act of submission and acknowledgment of Muslim superiority, not only over Aylah and its residents, but also over other cities entering into a treaty with the Prophet. It is not sensible to claim that this annual payment of a protection tax (*ṣulḥ al-jizya*) was intended to fund Muslim military campaigns, or increase revenue for the Treasury House. Instead, this and other pacts were signed to ensure the territorial integrity of the emerging Islamic State from the north, facilitate access of Muslim merchants to Egypt and Greater Syria, and expand Islamic influence beyond the Hijaz. Territories and principalities that never come under direct Muslim rule are viewed as entities and lands that maintain a tributary relationship with the Islamic State. Earlier covenants concluded between the Prophet Muḥammad and the Christians of the world also assured their protection "in the sea and on land," in the same way that the Prophet "protects himself and his Community (*ahl millatī*) among the Muslims." Morrow, *Covenants of the Prophet Muhammad*, 233–234, 238, 297–298; Liyakat Takim, "Peace and War in the Qurʾān and Juridical Literature: A Comparative Perspective," *Journal of Sociology and Social Welfare* 38 (2011), 147–148; Maher Abu Munshar, *Islamic Jerusalem and Its Christians: A History of Tolerance and Tension* (London: Taurus Academic Studies, 2007), 47; ʿAbd-ʿAzīz Duri, "Notes on Taxation in Early Islam," *Journal of the Economic and Social History of the Orient* 17 (1974), 137; Ziauddin Ahmed, "The Concept of Jizya in Early Islam," *Islamic Studies* 14 (1975), 301–302; Fuadah Johari, "The Dynamism in the Implementation of al-Kharaj during the Islamic Rule 634–785," *Sharīʿah Journal* 18 (2010), 631; Mahmood H. al-Denawy, "A Reappraisal of Attitudes to the 'People of the Book' in the Qurʾān and *Ḥadīth*, with Particular Reference to Muslim Fiscal Policy and Covenant of ʿUmar," (PhD diss., University of Durham, 2007), 167.

On this occasion, it should be clearly pointed out that the institution of the poll/head tax, known in Islam as the jizya, has a long history going back as far as the Biblical period. In Exodus 30:12–16, the Lord instructed Moses to tax each male Israelite above the age of twenty a half-shekel: "וְנָתְנוּ אִישׁ כֹּפֶר נַפְשׁוֹ לַיהוָה (then each shall give a ransom for his life to the Lord)." Another Biblical reference, Proverbs 13:8, states: "כֹּפֶר נֶפֶשׁ אִישׁ עָשְׁרוֹ (ransom of a man's life in his wealth)." The payment of head tax continued into the Roman period. It is

Perhaps it was Aylah's strategic geographical location that led the Prophet to grant an unprecedented *amān* to Yuḥannā ibn Ruʾba.[47] This scribal covenant reflects the Prophet's position on access to the sea, freedom of navigation, jurisdiction over a vessel at sea, the legal status of

recorded in the New Testament, Matthew 17:24–27, that every Jewish male over the age of twenty must pay a yearly head tax for the upkeep and maintenance of the Temple. The Roman Empire collected *tributum capitis* in the form of an annual poll tax from Roman subjects but not citizens (Digest L, 15, 3; Digest L, 15, 8, 1–11). Since the institution of poll tax was traditionally one of the major revenues in the Sassanid and Byzantine imperial financial systems, payment of the capitation to the new Muslim lords was easily accepted by the subject nations who enjoyed the status of *dhimmīs*. Brian Sawers, "The Poll Tax before Jim Crow," *American Journal of Legal History* 57 (2017), 168; Adam S. Chodorow, "Biblical Tax Systems and the Case for Progressive Taxation," *Journal of Law and Religion* 23 (2007), 61–65, 79–82; C. F. Balleine, "The Tributum Capitis," *The Classical Review* 20 (1906), 51–53; A. H. M. Jones, "*Capitatio* and *Iugatio*," *Journal of Roman Studies* 47 (1957), 90–94; Alan K. Bowman and Dominic Rathbone, "Cities and Administration in Roman Egypt," *Journal of Roman Studies* 82 (1992), 112–116; Dominic Rathbone, "Egypt, Augustus and Roman Taxation," *Cahiers du Centre Gustave Glotz* 4 (1993), 86–93; Patrick E. Clark, "Taxation and the Formation of the Late Roman Social Contract," (PhD diss., University of California Berkeley, 2017), 9, 45.

47 Aylah's strategic position as a major port connecting the Red and the Mediterranean seas with the hinterland cities of Greater Syria interested the Prophet and his Companions. It stood between the southern and northern Red Sea regions and subsequently served as a way station for Muslim merchants and caravans trading with Egypt and Palestine. In *Aḥsan al-Taqāsīm fī Maʿrifat al-Aqālīm* (Leiden: E. J. Brill, 1906, p. 178), the Jerusalemite geographer Abū ʿAbd Allāh Muḥammad ibn Aḥmad al-Muqaddasī (336–380/947–990), refers to Aylah as "the port of Palestine and the *emporium* of the Hijaz (*furḍat Filasṭīn wa-khazānat al-Ḥijāz*)." Apparently, the Prophet Muḥammad had prophesized that should Muslims embark on military expansion in Palestine they would need to pass through Aylah. Indeed, less than two years after his death, in 13/634 the first Pious Caliph Abū Bakr (r. 11–13/632–634) instructed army commander ʿAmr ibn al-ʿĀṣ "to follow the way of Aylah heading toward Palestine." Balādhurī, *Futūḥ al-Buldān*, 150; Irfān A. Shahīd, *Byzantium and the Arabs in the Sixth-Century* (Washington DC: Dumbarton Oaks Research Library, 2009), 2:24–25, 31–32; Philip Mayerson, "The First Muslim Attacks on Southern Palestine (A.D. 633–634)," *Transactions and Proceedings of the American Philological Association* 95 (1964), 174; Andrew Peterson, *The Towns of Palestine under Muslim Rule AD 600–1600* (Oxford: Archaeopress, 2005), 47–49; Kristoffer Damgaard, "A Palestinian Red Sea Port on the Egyptian Road to Arabia: Early Islamic Aqaba and Its Many Hinterlands," in *Connected Hinterlands: Proceedings of Red Sea Project IV held at the University of Southampton September 2008*, ed. Lucy Blue *et al.* (Oxford: Archaeopress, 2009), 91; Walter E. Kaegi, *Byzantium and the Early Islamic Conquests* (Cambridge: Cambridge University Press, 1992), 67, 82, 86, 92–93; Majid Khadduri, *War and Peace in the Law of Islam* (Baltimore: Johns Hopkins University Press, 1955), 180. Regarding the maritime role played by Aylah in the Red Sea and Indian Ocean prior to the rise of Islam, see Ross L. Thomas, "Maritime Cultures of the Erythraean Sea," (PhD diss., University of Southampton, 2009), 142–171; Abdallah M. Omar, "Towards the Conquest of Islamicjerusalem: The Three Main Practical Steps Taken by Prophet Muhammad," (master's thesis, University of Aberdeen, 2005), 46–50, 54, 70.

subjects aboard national and foreign-flagged ships, and the legal status of commercial vessels sailing on the high seas and in territorial waters. It should be noted that the Prophet had issued this guarantee of protection long before Byzantium lost Greater Syria and Egypt to the Muslims, the Persian Empire faded from the international political map, and the Islamic navy was established. The decree reads as follows:

In the name of God, the Most Gracious, the Most Merciful:	بِسْمِ اللهِ الرَّحْمَنِ الرَّحِيم
This is a guarantee of protection from God and Muḥammad the Prophet, the Messenger of God, to Yūḥannā ibn Ruʾba and the people of Aylah, for their ships, their caravans by land and sea. They and all that are with them, men of Syria and the Yemen, and seamen are under the protection of God and the protection of the Prophet Muḥammad. Should any one of them break the treaty by introducing some new factors, then his wealth shall not save him;	هَذِهِ أَمَنَةٌ مِنَ اللهِ، وَمُحَمَّدٍ النَّبِيِّ رَسُولِ اللهِ لِيُحَنَّةَ بْنِ رُؤْبَةَ وَأَهْلِ أَيْلَةَ، سُفُنُهُمْ وَسَيَّارَتُهُمْ فِي الْبَرِّ وَالْبَحْرِ لَهُمْ ذِمَّةُ اللهِ وَذِمَّةُ مُحَمَّدٍ النَّبِيِّ، وَمَنْ كَانَ مَعَهُمْ مِنْ أَهْلِ الشَّام، وَأَهْلِ الْيَمَنِ، وَأَهْلِ الْبَحْرِ، فَمَنْ أَحْدَثَ مِنْهُمْ حَدَثًا فَإِنَّهُ لَا يَحُولُ مَالُهُ دُونَ نَفْسِهِ. وَإِنَّهُ طَيِّبٌ لِمَنْ أَخَذَهُ مِنَ النَّاسِ. وَإِنَّهُ لَا يَحِلُّ أَنْ يُمْنَعُوا مَاءً يَرِدُونَهُ، وَلَا طَرِيقًا يُرِيدُونَهُ مِنْ بَرٍّ أَوْ بَحْرٍ. هذا كِتاب جُهيم بِن الصَلت وشُرحبيل بن حَسْنَة بِإذنِ رَسُولِ اللهِ صَلّى اللهُ عَلَيهِ وسَلّم.[48]

[48] Muḥammad ibn Isḥāq ibn Yasār, *Al-Sīrah al-Nabawiyyah* (Beirut: Dār al-Kutub al-ʿIlmiyyah, 1424/2004), 604; for the English translation, refer to *The Life of Muhammad: A Translation of Isḥāq's Sīrat Rasūl Allāh*, trans. Alfred Guillaume (Oxford: Oxford University Press, 1955), 607, paragraph no. 902; al-Wāqidī, *Al-Maghāzī*, 3:1031; Abū Muḥammad ʿAbd al-Malik ibn Hishām, *Al-Sīrah al-Nabawiyyah* (Beirut: Dār al-Kitāb al-ʿArabī, 1410/1990), 4:165–166; Ibn Saʿd, *Ṭabaqāt*, 1:250–251; Abū ʿUbyad al-Qāsim ibn Sallām al-Harawī, *Kitāb al-Amwāl* (Beirut: Dār al-Shurūq, 1409/1989), 289; Ḥamīd ibn Mukhlid ibn Qutayba ibn Zanjawayh, *Kitāb al-Amwāl* (Riyad: Markaz al-Malik Faisal lil-Buḥūth wa'l-Dirāsāt al-Islāmiyya, 1406/1986), 463; Abū al-Qāsim ʿAlī ibn al-Ḥasan ibn Hibat Allāh ibn ʿAsākir, *Tārīkh Madīnat Dimashq* (Beirut: Dār al-Fikr, 1415/1995), 2:41–42; Ibn Kathīr, *Al-Bidāya wa'l-Nihāyah*, 4:670; Abū al-Fidāʾ Ismāʿīl ibn ʿUmar ibn Kathīr, *Al-Sīrah al-Nabawiyyah* (Beirut: Dār al-Maʿrifa, 1395/1976), 29–30; for the English translation consult *The Life of the Prophet Muḥammad (Al-Sīrah al-Nabawiyyah)*, trans. Trevor Le Gassick (Reading: Garnet Publishing, 2000), 4:20; Abū al-Fatḥ Muḥammad ibn Muḥammad ibn Sayyid al-Nās al-Yaʿmurī, *ʿUyūn al-Athar fī Funūn al-Maghāzī wa'l-Shamāʾil wa'l-Siyar* (Medina: Maktabat Dār al-Turāth, 1408/1987), 2:297; Ibn Qayyim al-Jawziyya, *Zād al-Maʿād*, 3:470; Taqiyy al-Dīn Aḥmad ibn ʿAlī al-Maqrīzī, *Imtāʿ al-Asmāʿ bimā lil-Nabiyy, Ṣallā Allāh ʿalyh wa-Sallam, min al-Aḥwāl wa'l-Amwāl wa'l-Ḥafadah wa'l-Matāʿ* (Beirut: Dār al-Kutub al-ʿIlmiyyah, 1420/1999), 2:66; Maqrīzī, *Khiṭaṭ*, 1:521; Ḥamīdullāh, *Al-Wathāʾiq al-Siyāsiyya*, 117–118; ʿAwn al-Sharīf Qāsim,

it is the fair prize of him who takes it. It is not permitted that they shall be restrained from going down to their wells or using their roads by land or sea. This treaty is written by Juhaym ibn al-Ṣalt and Shuraḥbīl ibn Ḥasnah on the authority of the Messenger of God – God's blessing and peace be upon him.

Nash'at al-Dawla al-Islāmiyya 'alā 'Ahd Rasūl Allāh (Beirut: Dār al-Jīl, 1411/1991), 123–125, 309–310; ʿAlī al-Aḥmadī al-Miyānjī, *Makātīb al-Rasūl* (Beirut: Dār Ṣaʿb, 2013), 3:97–100; Jamīlī, *Aḥkām al-Muʿāhadāt fī al-Sharīʿah al-Islāmiyya*, 107–113; ʿAbd al-ʿAzīz al-ʿUmarī, *Rasūl Allāh wa-Khātam al-Nabiyyīn* (Riyad: Bīsān lil-Nashr wa'l-Tawzīʿ, 1432/2011), 3:859; Morrow, *Covenants of the Prophet Muhammad*, 54–55; Francis E. Peters, *Muhammad and the Origins of Islam* (Albany: State University of New York, 1994), 241; Ahmed el-Wakil, "Searching for the Covenants: Identifying Authentic Documents of the Prophet based on Scribal Conventions and Textual Analysis," (master's thesis, Hamad bin Khalifa University, 2017), 75. One may question the authenticity of this covenant, especially since the Prophet Muḥammad never experienced life at sea, nor sailing. Even though there is no original copy in existence, this covenant can still be regarded as genuine. It was authenticated by early *sīrah* biographers, historians, and jurists, some of whom were born and lived in the first and second centuries of the Hijra. They include Ibn Isḥāq (85–151/704–768), Wāqidī (130–207/747–822), Ibn Hishām (d. 218/833), Qāsim ibn Sallām (157–224/774–838), and Ibn Zanjawayh (180–251/796–865). Later commentators and jurists reinforced its authenticity, including Ibn Sayyid al-Nās (671–734/1272–1334), Ibn Qayyim al-Jawziyya (691–751/1292–1350), Ibn Kathīr (700–774/1300–1373), and Taqiyy al-Dīn al-Maqrīzī (766–845/1364–1442), who provide a nearly identical form of the deed as that found in the *sīrah* of Ibn Isḥāq. Although one cannot deny the fact that forgeries did take place, this "guarantee of protection" is certainly authentic and can be ascribed to the Prophet Muḥammad. In his *Ṣaḥīḥ*, al-Imam al-Bukhārī twice refers to it as a treaty that the Prophet concluded with the "King of Aylah" allowing him to retain authority over his territory in return for a preestablished collective jizya. Bukhārī substantiates the existence of the treaty but never quotes it in full; however, in his commentary on the *Ṣaḥīḥ Bukhārī*, Ibn Ḥajar al-ʿAsqalānī (773–852/1372–1449), attaches the exact version transmitted by Ibn Isḥāq and others and analyzes it in minute detail. The existence of this Prophetic document is further corroborated by the early Muslim historians Balādhurī (d. 279/892), Ṭabarī (224–310/839–923), and Masʿūdī (282–345/896–956), who highlight its financial ramifications – the imposition of the jizya on able-bodied males of Aylah – but pay no attention to other legal aspects, namely freedom of movement. Ṭabarī reports that the drafter had produced two copies, one of which was retained by the Prophet and the other kept by the "King of Aylah." In view of the foregoing evidence, it is reasonable to infer that the text at our disposal has been preserved in its entirety, matching in language, content, and format the original as dictated by the Prophet in 9 AH/630 CE. Muḥammad ibn Ismāʿīl al-Bukhārī, *Ṣaḥīḥ al-Bukhārī* (Damascus: Dār Ibn Kathīr, 1414/1993), 2:539, hadith no. 1411, 3:1153, hadith no. 2990; Aḥmad Ibn ʿAlī ibn Muḥammad ibn ʿAlī ibn Ḥajar al-

In this scribal pledge, the Prophet gives full recognition to the pacta sunt servanda doctrine, as he does in earlier and later treaties, such as the Treaty of Ḥudaybiyyah (Dhū al-Qiʿdah, 6 AH/March, 628 CE). This pacta bears a Divine nature, which is apparent in the opening line: "This is a guarantee of protection from God and Muḥammad the Prophet, the Messenger of God." God's presence, anthropomorphically conveyed in the conclusion of the covenant, the adherence of Muslims to Qurʾānic principles,[49] and the personal commitment of the Prophet assured the dignitaries of Aylah that he would honor the provisions of the treaty.[50] Yūḥanna ibn Ruʾba and the residents of Aylah likewise committed to compliance with the truce despite the lack of a specified duration.[51]

In order to more fully convey the sacred character attached by the Islamic faith and legal system to personal commitments, safe-conducts, and treaties, a succinct explanation of the lexical meaning and the Qurʾānic significance of the root for the word designating safe-conduct, *a.m.n.* will follow. *A.m.n.* designates calmness, trust, confidence, safety, security, shelter, protection, and faith, signifying the opposite of fear, danger, treachery, disloyalty, and lack of faith. Appearing in numerous Qurʾānic verses in seventeen derivatives,[52] the forms of the word include *amn, amān, amana,* and *āmin,* all of which denote the sense of becoming secure or feeling free from fear or expectation of evil. The verb *ammana* means "to render someone secure or safe from harm by another person." *Istaʾmana* is "to demand safety or its assurance from another." The phrase *dakhala fī*

ʿAsqalānī, *Fatḥ al-Bārī* (Cairo: Dār al-Rayyān lil-Turāth, 1407/1986), 3:402–406; Abū Jaʿfar Muḥammad ibn Jarīr Ṭabarī, *Tārīkh al-Rusul wa'l-Mulūk* (Cairo: Dār al-Maʿārif, 1387/1967), 3:108; Balādhurī, *Futūḥ al-Buldān*, 79, 92; Abū al-Ḥasan ʿAlī ibn al-Ḥusayn ibn ʿAlī al-Masʿūdī, *Al-Tanbīh wa'l-Ishrāf* (Leiden: M. J. de Goeje, 1894), 272; Milka Levy-Rubin, *Non-Muslims in the Early Islamic Empire: From Surrender to Coexistence* (Cambridge: Cambridge University Press, 2011), 33, 38. Although conclusive evidence of the Prophet Muḥammad's traveling by sea has not yet been substantiated, it is reported that he knew how to swim. On the virtues of swimming in the Prophetic tradition, see ʿAbd al-Raḥmān ibn Abū Bakr ibn Muḥammad al-Suyūṭī, *Al-Bāḥa fī Faḍl al-Sibāḥa* (Ṭanṭā: Dār al-Ṣaḥāba lil-Turāth, 1411/1990).

[49] Qurʾān 9:4; Q 16:91; Q 17:34.

[50] A statement attributed to the Prophet rules: "*al-Muslimūn ʿinda shurūṭihim* (Muslims are bound by their stipulations)." Ibn Ḥajar al-ʿAsqalānī, *Fatḥ al-Bārī*, 2:527, hadith no. 2153, 3: 126, hadith no. 4856.

[51] Mirza, "Oral Tradition and Scribals Conventions," 154–155; Sarah Mirza, "*Dhimma* Agreements and Sanctuary Systems at Islamic Origins," *Journal of Near Eastern Studies* 77 (2018), 100, 108–110.

[52] Qurʾān 2:125, 126, 196, 239; Q 3:154; Q 4:83, 91; Q 6:81, 82; Q 7:97, 98, 99; Q 8:11; Q 9:6; Q 12:99, 107; Q 14:35; Q 15:46, 82; Q 16:45, 112; Q 17:68, 69; Q 24:55; Q 26:146; Q 27:89; Q 28:31; Q 29:67; Q 34:18, 37; Q 41:40; Q 44:51, 55; Q 48:27; Q 67:16, 17; Q 70:28; Q 95:3.

amānihi, connotes "he entered within another's pale of protection." The phrase *aʿṭaytahu al-amān*, means that "he granted or gave him promise of security." Finally, *mawḍiʿ āmin* is "a place of safety or security."[53]

The term *amn* ("security" or "safety") conveys two dimensions of sense. The first dimension occurs in the realm of an individual's peace of mind, psychological tranquility, and spiritual satisfaction, whereas the second dimension relates to a people's collective social, political, and economic status. On an international level, *amn* refers to a situation in which superpowers are not supposed to threaten other nations or deprive their residents of their natural rights. In addition, the Qurʾān maintains that foreign affairs should be guided by principle and not by religious or military supremacy.[54] All Children of Adam should enjoy God's bounties equally and not be deprived of inherent natural rights.[55] Furthermore, Islamic law recognizes every individual's right to personal safety against all forms of abuse and aggression.[56] In order to remove any possible ambiguity, the Prophet adopted the principle of reciprocity, guaranteeing the safety of all those heading to or from Aylah in return for assuring Muslims undisturbed passage when passing through or near this port city.

Close examination reveals that this treaty, while being succinct, does concur fully with Qurʾānic principles, addressing various issues related to freedom of navigation and movement of people on land, whether explicitly or implicitly. The Qurʾān does not contain even a single verse excluding members of any particular nation from navigating the seas or from traveling by land for any purpose. Qurʾānic principles maintain that the world belongs to no particular nation; the land and sea should be free and accessible to all. Interestingly, the Prophet did not draw a sharp distinction between adjacent offshore zones and the high seas, but rather appears to regard the entire sea as a common right of all peoples, such that no authority whatsoever may deny access to it or hinder navigation and the exploitation of natural marine resources.

[53] Ibn Fāris, *Muʿjam Maqāyīs al-Lugha*, 1:133–135; Ibn Manẓūr, *Lisān al-ʿArab*, 13:21–27; Jamīlī, *Aḥkām al-Muʿāhadāt fī al-Sharīʿah al-Islāmiyya*, 107–108; Lane, *Arabic-English Lexicon*, 1:100–101; Levy-Rubin, *Non-Muslims in the Early Islamic Empire*, 31–34.

[54] Qurʾān 4:141.

[55] Mohammad Heidarizad *et al.*, "Security from Qurʾān Perspective," *Advances in Environmental Biology* 7 (2013), 3384–3386.

[56] Mohammad H. Kamali, "The Right to Personal Safety and the Principle of Legality in the *Sharīʿah*," *Islamic Studies* 39 (2000), 254–255; Denawy, "'People of the Book' in the Qurʾān and *Ḥadīth*," 11, 50–51, 56, 115–118.

Another Qur'ānic principle is evident in the Prophet's promise not to violate Aylah's territorial integrity. He bound himself to honor the pledge of security and assured protection to the residents of Aylah and all those arriving in or departing from Aylah so long as the provisions of the truce were observed. He promised to protect ships, their crews, passengers, and shipments from Aylah both within and beyond its territorial sovereignty. He pledged not to interfere with the navigation and trade of Aylah's residents and to ensure maintenance of their commercial and diplomatic ties with local and foreign entities as existing prior to the truce. The lack of any reference to the internal governance of a ship can be explained by the Prophet's abstention from interference with the management of a vessel, recognizing her as an extension of her flag state's territory. Thus, as a sovereign principality, Aylah could assert jurisdiction over its flagged vessels, their crews, contents, and passengers, irrespective of nationality, not only within its territorial domain but also while on the high seas and in foreign ports.

The residents of this port city were free to trade with any nation, particularly with the Syrians and Yemenites with whom the local merchants seem to have had strong commercial ties. Notably, the pledge also guarantees the right of foreign individuals to travel to and from Aylah, irrespective of the flag flown by their vessel. Finally, the pledge does not impose any kind of restriction on non-Muslim merchants or voyagers sailing through the Sea of the Hijaz (the Arabian littoral of the Red Sea), whose special legal status would come later.[57] Scribal covenants of the same nature that guaranteed the rights to freedom of religion and liberty of movement and mobility were signed between the Prophet Muḥammad and the Armenian Christians of Jerusalem (4 AH/626 CE),[58] the Monks of Saint Catherine and the Mount of Olives (4 AH/626 CE, renewed in 8 AH/629–30 CE),[59]

[57] Only during the Caliphate of ʿUmar ibn al-Khaṭṭāb has access of non-Muslims to the Province of the Hijaz theoretically been limited.

[58] Ḥamīdullāh, *Al-Wathā'iq al-Siyāsiyya*, 557: "No one of them shall be taken captive, be he on land or at sea"; Morrow, *Covenants of the Prophet Muhammad*, 191; Wakil, "Searching for the Covenants," 61–65, 75–76.

[59] Ḥamīdullāh, *Al-Wathā'iq al-Siyāsiyya*, 561–562, lines 5–19: "That whenever any of the monks in his travels shall happen to settle upon any mountain, hill, village, or other habitable place, on the sea, or in deserts or in any convent, church, or house of prayer, I shall be in the midst of them, as the preserver and protector of them, their goods and effects, with my soul, aid, and protection, jointly with all my national people; because they are a part of my own people, and an honor to me." In lines 30–31 the Prophet declares: "Moreover, neither judges, governors, monks, servants, disciples, or any others depending on them, shall pay any poll-tax, or be molested on that account, because I am their protector, wherever they shall be, either by land or sea, east or west, north or south;

the residents of Maqnā (9 AH/630 CE),[60] and the Christians of the Province of Najrān (10 AH/631 CE).[61]

It should be remembered that the Aylah scribal covenant was promulgated a decade before the establishment of the first Islamic military fleet in the Red Sea.[62] Given the nonexistence of a Muslim naval force, it would seem unreasonable to attribute to the Prophet the intention to offer outright physical security in meeting the pledges of the treaty, such as armed personnel or a naval escort for Aylah-flagged ships. Instead, it seems that the Prophet's "guarantee of protection" meant that Muslims would refrain from harassing, assaulting, or seizing Aylah-flagged vessels or their contents, crews, travelers, or chattels.[63] The absence of reference to any particular jurisdiction verifies the Prophet's abstention from interference with the internal affairs and management a vessel and his recognition that she acts as an extension of her flag state's territory.

The intent of the pledge is closely aligned with Qur'ān 9:6, which states "*ablighhu ma'manahu*," commanding believers to bring, convey, escort,

because both they and all that belong to them are included in this my promissory oath and patent." The English translation, which is compatible with the original Arabic text, is extracted from Akram Zahoor, *Muslim History 570–1950 C.E.* (Gaithersburg, MD, 2000), 167; Morrow, *Covenants of the Prophet Muhammad*, 65–98, 205–212; Wakil, "Searching for the Covenants," 62.

60 Wāqidī, *Al-Maghāzī*, 3:1032–1033; Ḥamīdullāh, *Al-Wathā'iq al-Siyāsiyya*, 119–123; Gil, *History of Palestine*, 29–30; Morrow, *Covenants of the Prophet Muhammad*, 53–54.

61 Ḥamīdullāh, *Al-Wathā'iq al-Siyāsiyya*, 187; for a comprehensive analytical insight into the Covenant of Najrān, refer to Ahmed el-Wakil, "The Prophet's Treaty with the Christians of Najran: An Analytical Study to Determine the Authenticity of the Covenants," *Journal of Islamic Studies* 27 (2016), 273–354; Wakil, "Searching for the Covenants," 76; Morrow, *Covenants of the Prophet Muhammad*, 109–138, 293–311, especially pp. 297–298, 307.

62 Fahmy, *Muslim Sea-Power*, 74. The first maritime campaign in Islamic history was launched in 17 AH/638 CE by al-'Alā' ibn al-Ḥaḍramī, the governor of Bahrain (also al-Baḥrayn), who disobeyed the Caliph's instructions, crossed the Persian Gulf, landed on the coast of Persia, and advanced to Iṣṭakhr (Persepolis). He would have been destroyed had Sa'd ibn Abī Waqqāṣ and 'Utba ibn Ghazwān, the governor of Baṣra, not provided him with reinforcements, which saved him and his army from inevitable defeat. In 20 AH/641 CE, 'Umar ibn al-Khaṭṭāb dispatched 'Alqama ibn al-Mujazziz with a flotilla across the Red Sea toward the Abyssinian coast. With the exception of one vessel, the expedition suffered great losses.

63 As a piece of evidence, the second charter of the Covenant of Najrān states: "وَأَن أَحْرُسَ دِينَهُم وَمِلَّتَهُم أَيْنَ كَانُوا، مِنْ بَرٍّ أَوْ بَحْرٍ، شَرْقاً وَغَرْباً، بِمَا أَحْفَظُ بِهِ نَفْسِي وَخَاصَّتِي، وَأَهْلَ الإِسْلامَ مِنْ مِلَّتِي (I [the Prophet] will protect their religion and their faith wherever they are found, be it on land or at sea, in the East or in the West, with utmost vigilance on my part, whatever belongs to me, and the followers of Islam from my creed)." Ḥamīdullāh, *Al-Wathā'iq al-Siyāsiyya*, 187; Wakil, "The Prophet's Treaty with the Christians of Najran," 277, 316, 337–339; Morrow, *Covenants of the Prophet Muhammad*, 297–298, 307 (Arabic text).

or let a person proceed and attain his ultimate place of safety where he can feel secure.[64] A question may be asked about the geographical range at sea wherein a *musta'min* should feel secure (*ma'man*). In other words, to what extent should a state provide protection to a *musta'min*? *Ma'man* can be defined as a geographical location wherein an alien envoy, trader, or other individual is protected from harm caused by Muslims. *Imam* Mālik ibn Anas (97–179/715–795) and Ibn Nāfiʿ (d. 225/840) both defined *ma'man* as a place at sea where ships cannot be sighted with the naked eye from Islamic coastal frontiers. When an *amān*'s grantee sails to a point at sea where the mountains of his or her native country can be seen with the naked eye, yet the wind drives the ship back to the Islamic port of embarkation, then the pledge remains valid.[65] Ibn al-Mājishūn (d. 212/827) and ʿAbd al-Malik ibn Ḥabīb (174–238/790–853) also held a similar opinion; that even if after sailing on the vastness of the sea, a ship is hurled back to the port from which she departed or the port's vicinity, the decree of safe-conduct remains legally valid with respect to the *musta'min* and his chattels over the high seas until he arrives at a place where he feels secure. However, if a ship is driven into a port or to a coast that is not within the grantor's sovereignty, then the grantee enters "a place without the degree

[64] Qur'ān 9:6 advocates courteous behavior to all, regardless of their religion, and urges Muslims to protect and escort non-Muslims to safety: "إِنْ أَحَدٌ مِّنَ الْمُشْرِكِينَ اسْتَجَارَكَ فَأَجِرْهُ حَتَّىٰ يَسْمَعَ كَلَامَ اللَّهِ ثُمَّ أَبْلِغْهُ مَأْمَنَهُ ذَٰلِكَ بِأَنَّهُمْ قَوْمٌ لَّا يَعْلَمُونَ (If one amongst the Pagans asks thee for asylum, grant it to him so that he may hear the Word of God; and then escort him to where he can be secure, that is because they are men without knowledge)." This verse refers to those polytheists who would like to learn and listen to the Word of God. However, jurists of all law schools, both Sunnis and non-Sunnis, apply it to foreigners visiting or traveling through the Abode of Islam irrespective of the purpose of their travel. They shall be granted safe passage through the Islamic domain and escorted back to a place of safety even if they reject Islam. Asma Afsaruddin, *Striving in the Path of God: Jihad and Martyrdom in Islamic Thought* (Oxford: Oxford University Press, 2013), 88–89. It has been suggested that the place of safety is the position from which the *ḥarbī* had departed to the Abode of Islam; it can be his homeland in the first place; or, secondly, any other area of safety. Ṭabarī, *Tafsīr*, 14:139–140; Baghawī, *Tafsīr*, 4:15–16; Qurṭubī, *Al-Jāmiʿ*, 8:17–18; Abū Ḥayyān, *Al-Tafsīr al-Kabīr*, 5:9–12; Ibn Kathīr, *Tafsīr*, 4:113–114; Ḥamīdullāh, *Muslim Conduct of State*, 210; Qalqashandī, *Ṣubḥ al-Aʿshā*, 13:321; Arafat M. Shoukri, *Refugee Status in Islam: Concepts of Protection in Islamic Tradition and International Law* (London: I. B. Tauris, 2011), 69 (*al-iblāgh – al-taṣyīr ilā muntahā al-ḥadd*/attainment or conveyance means bringing or carrying someone or something to the utmost point), 83.

[65] ʿAbd Allāh ibn ʿAbd al-Raḥmān ibn Abū Zayd al-Qayrawānī, *Al-Nawādir wa'l-Ziyādāt ʿalā mā fī al-Mudawwana min ghayrihā min al-Ummahāt* (Beirut: Dār al-Gharb al-Islāmī, 1999), 3:134–135.

of *amān*."[66] In other words, as a vessel enters the territorial sea of another state, that state is to assert jurisdiction over the ship and her contents, crew, and passengers, regardless of nationality. Moving inward from the outer limits of the other state's territorial sea, an *amān* becomes void and unenforceable, giving way to the jurisdiction of the other state. All jurists dismiss equivocally an *amān*'s application simultaneously with foreign laws, such as when a grantee enters his or her homeland, or a third country's territorial domain.[67] An inquiry with respect to this matter came before the Mālikī jurist Saḥnūn ibn Sa'īd al-Tanūkhī:

Saḥnūn was asked about Byzantine or other subjects who arrive in (Islamic territory) for trade under safe-conduct and then head back to their native country. When are they lawfully subject to capture? At which point at the sea (does their *amān* become void) and can they lawfully be subject to capture? He answered: It is strictly unlawful to capture them until they reach a place at sea where they can feel secure from their enemy and their fear disappears; thus, whenever they reach that point, they can lawfully be taken in possession. People well-versed in naval campaigns and nautical science argue that they are not safe until they reach their native homelands and come out of the sea, because Muslim vessels have multiplied against them and overcome them. For this reason, they can only be subject to capture if they reach a place where they can feel safe, which is when they come out of the sea, as I have elucidated earlier, for God has said: "Make him attain his place of safety." I further asked him: Is it licit to capture a person who has not obtained an *amān* decree but is in the vicinity of our ports, or far off? He replied: Anyone who is regularly engaged in commercial transactions with

[66] Ibn Abū Zayd al-Qayrawānī, *Al-Nawādir wa'l-Ziyādāt*, 3:135. Muslim jurists argued that the salt sea (open sea and ocean) should be treated as non-Islamic territory and beyond the control of any nation. Thus, if a non-Muslim alien subject has weighed anchor from some Islamic territory and, after sailing on the high sea, the wind has driven him to a place other than the point from which he departed or its adjacent area, his permit or safe-conduct certificate is no longer valid and will have to be reissued and retaxed. Moreover, if the sea wind drove the ship to a place outside the grantor's territorial domain, the pledge of *amān* would become null and void. All jurists consensually maintain that the high sea stands beyond the jurisdictional dominion of any ruling authority, belonging neither to Muslims nor to their enemies. Ḥamīdullāh, *Muslim Conduct of State*, 94–95.

[67] Ibn Abū Zayd al-Qayrawānī, *Al-Nawādir wa'l-Ziyādāt*, 3:134; Khalilieh, *Admiralty and Maritime Laws*, 125; Shoukri, *Refugee Status in Islam*, 79, 83; Peter M. Holt, *Early Mamluk Diplomacy (1260–1290)* (Leiden: E. J. Brill, 1995), 47, article 11 of the 667/1269 treaty between al-Ẓāhir Baybars and Lady Isabel of Beirut states: "Provided that if a Frankish merchant goes out from Beirut to the Sultan's territory, he shall be covered by this truce; and if he returns to another place, he shall not be covered by this truce."

Muslims may not be captured if he heads to (us) and seeks *amān* upon approaching or after anchoring in the anchorage. It is strictly impermissible to capture him unless he has arrived in his native homeland or sailed to non-Islamic territories. However, those who are not engaged in trade with Muslims, their capture is licit.[68]

The practices and principles of safe-conduct set by the Prophet are echoed in jurisprudential manuals and official and nonofficial decrees of safe-conduct, as well as in international peace and commercial treaties concluded between Muslim authorities and Christian dignitaries inhabiting the two basins of the Mediterranean.[69] In connection with the expansion of overseas trade, early Muslim jurists advocated in particular the protection of those enemy-alien traders who frequented Islamic ports, even if they did not hold certificates of safe-conduct. Muslims were advised not to seize Christian ships if it had been substantiated without any doubt that they routinely frequented Islamic ports to carry out commercial transactions.[70] As may be expected, the jurists advised that the grantee obtain permission from the *imam* or port superintendent prior to setting sail as an insurance of a safe passage home in spite of the threat that might be posed by Muslim sea raiders.[71]

[68] Abū al-Walīd Muḥammad ibn Aḥmad ibn Rushd, *Al-Bayān wa'l-Taḥṣīl wa'l-Sharḥ wa'l-Tawjīh wa'l-Ta'līl fī Masā'il al-Mustakhraja* (Beirut: Dār al-Gharb al-Islāmī, 1984), 3:60–61; Ibn Abū Zayd al-Qayrawānī, *Al-Nawādir wa'l-Ziyādāt*, 3:132.

[69] For example, the pledge of safe-conduct ʿAmr ibn al-ʿĀṣ granted to the People of Egypt in 20 AH/641 CE is congruent with the 9 AH/630 CE guarantee of protection giving the Copts the right to freedom of movement and navigation: "بِسْمِ اللّٰهِ الرَّحْمَنِ الرَّحِيمِ، هَذَا مَا أَعْطَى عَمْرُو بْنُ الْعَاصِ أَهْلَ مِصْرَ مِنَ الأَمَانِ عَلَى أَنْفُسِهِمْ وَمِلَّتِهِمْ وَأَمْوَالِهِمْ وَكَنَائِسِهِمْ وَصُلُبِهِمْ، وَبَرِّهِمْ وَبَحْرِهِمْ (In the name of God, the Most Merciful, the Most Compassionate. This is the covenant that was granted by ʿAmr ibn al-ʿĀṣ to the People of Egypt concerning security for themselves, their faith, their possessions, churches, and crucifixes, while traveling by land and sea)." Ibn Kathīr, *Al-Bidāya wa'l-Nihāyah*, 7:215; Jamāl al-Dīn Yūsuf ibn al-Amīr Sayf al-Dīn ibn Taghrībirdī, *Al-Nujūm al-Zāhira fī Mulūk Miṣr wa'l-Qāhira* (Cairo: Wizārat al-Thaqāfa, 1383/1963), 1:24; Qalqashandī, *Ṣubḥ al-Aʿshā*, 13:324; Ḥamīdullāh, *Al-Wathā'iq al-Siyāsiyya*, 502–503; Ryan J. Lynch, "Cyprus and Its Legal and Historiographical Significance in Early Islamic History," *Journal of the American Oriental Society* 136 (2016), 546. It is admissible to argue that the term *baḥrihim* applies to the Nile, which is viewed as a sea in the historiographical and documentary sources.

[70] Ibn Abū Zayd al-Qayrawānī, *Al-Nawādir wa'l-Ziyādāt*, 3:132: "If a Byzantine (Rūm) vessel making her way to (an Islamic) port, regardless of whether she is in close proximity to or far away from (the destination), is encountered (by Muslims), if she carries merchants known for having close commercial relations with Muslims, it is unlawful to capture them except if they are found in their homeland or other non-Islamic territories"; Picard, *Sea of the Caliphs*, 105.

[71] Khalilieh, *Admiralty and Maritime Laws*, 42–43.

The Post-Prophetic Era and Muslim Jurists' Division of the World

Any discussion of the freedom of navigation and mobility rights of aliens on the high seas or through Islamic territorial seas and mainland would be incomplete without considering issues related to the geopolitical division of the world and the rules governing international treaties. While such a division exists neither in the Qur'ān nor in the Sunna,[72] by the second century AH/eighth century CE, Muslim jurists had divided the regions of the world into two major entities, Dār al-Islām and Dār al-Ḥarb, and subsequently added the division of Dār al-ʿAhd.[73]

As regards the legal definition of the Abode of Islam, jurists held different positions. One group defined it as encompassing the territories

[72] Qur'ān 6:127 refers to Dār al-Salām but not in the context of worldly life, rather, with regard to the believers' eternal life in the Hereafter: "لَهُمْ دَارُ السَّلَامِ عِندَ رَبِّهِمْ وَهُوَ وَلِيُّهُم بِمَا كَانُوا يَعْمَلُونَ (For them will be a Home of Peace with their Lord; He will be their Friend, because they practiced righteousness)." The Abode of Peace is, thus, associated with the eternal life of the believers, who fulfill their religious duties and moral obligations on Earth in accordance with the Divine teachings and principles.

[73] Jurisprudentially, among the originators of the two major concepts were Muḥammad ibn ʿAbd Allāh ibn al-Ḥasan ibn al-Muḥammad al-Ḥasan ibn ʿAlī ibn Abī Ṭālib, better known as al-Nafs al-Zakiyyah (d. 145/762), who refers on a few occasions to the conduct of war (*siyar*) in Dār al-Ḥarb. Many fragments of his *siyar* survived in the work of Abū ʿAbd Allāh Muḥammad ibn ʿAlī ibn al-Ḥasan al-ʿAlawī (367–445/977–1053), *Al-Jāmiʿ al-Kāfī fī Fiqh al-Zaydiyyah* (Amman: Mu'assasat al-Imām Zayd Ibn ʿAlī, 2014?) www.azzaidiah.com/kotob_mojamaah/feqh/algame_alkafy_fe_fegh_azzaidiah.html. Another early celebrated figure and the founder of the first Law School (*madhhab*) in Islam is Abū Ḥanīfa al-Nuʿmān ibn Thābit (80–150/699–767), who divided the world into two abodes. His opinions are best documented and recorded in the works of his disciple Muḥammad ibn al-Ḥasan al-Shaybānī (131–189/749–805) and others also. And the third renowned jurist, who adopted such a division, is the Syrian jurist and founder of another Sunni School of Fiqh, Abū ʿAmr ʿAbd al-Raḥmān ibn ʿAmr al-Awzāʿī (88–157/707–774), whose *siyar* is preserved by Abū ʿAbd Allāh Muḥammad ibn Idrīs al-Shāfiʿī, *Al-Umm* (Beirut: Dār al-Fikr lil-Ṭibāʿa wa'l-Nashr, 1403/1983), 7:336–369; Abū Yūsuf Yaʿqūb ibn Ibrāhīm al-Anṣārī, *Al-Radd ʿalā Siyar al-Awzāʿī* (Hyderabad: n.p., n.d.). Roy P. Mottahedeh and Ridwan al-Sayyid, "The Idea of the *Jihad* in Islam before the Crusades," in *The Crusades from the Perspective of Byzantium and the Muslim World*, ed. Angeliki E. Laiou and Roy P. Mottahedeh (Washington DC: Dumbarton Oaks Research Library and Collection, 2001), 23–25; Michael Bonner, *Jihad in Islamic History: Doctrines and Practice* (Princeton, NJ: Princeton University Press, 2006), 92–93. To gain a deeper insight into the Islamic conceptual vision of the world, consult Giovanna Calasso and Giuliano Lancioni (ed.), *Dār al-Islām/Dār al-Ḥarb: Territories, People, Identities* (Leiden: E. J. Brill, 2017).

in which Muslims enjoyed peace and security; God's Law is superior and enforced by a Muslim ruler, even if the majority of the population being governed is non-Muslim. A different opinion viewed the Abode of Islam as comprising territories where Muslims practiced their religion freely. A third viewpoint defined it as territory wherein Muslims are protected and cannot be approached by *ḥarbīs*. A fourth view applied the term to territories where Muslims reside and Islamic law prevails. A fifth perspective included any territory where Islamic law prevails. The final legal opinion ruled that the term pertains to any territory where Muslims, whether in the majority or minority, can practice their religious rituals and apply Islamic law free from external intervention.[74]

The Abode of Covenant/Truce pertains to territories ruled by non-Islamic governments who pay a tribute to the Islamic states. Such countries normally maintain long-term commercial and diplomatic accords with the Islamic states and grant Muslims within their domain communal, religious, and juridical autonomy to manage their daily affairs.[75] The Abode of War is the exact opposite of the Abode of Islam, consisting of territories and communities entirely beyond the borders of the abodes of Islam and Covenant. The local authorities of the Abode of War neither have treaties with Dār al-Islām nor enforce the *Sharī'ah*, even if the inhabitants are mostly Muslims; the local Muslim residents have no security in terms of tranquility, peace, and freedom. Although hostilities prevail between the two domains, of the Abode of Islam and the Abode of War, the latter cannot be considered "a no-man's-land." Muslims living both outside and within the Abode of War are obliged to respect the rights of non-Muslims as prescribed by Islamic law.[76] From a legal point of view, neither is the

[74] Manoucher Parvin and Maurie Sommer, "Dar al-Islam: The Evolution of Muslim Territoriality and Its Implications for Conflict Resolution in the Middle East," *International Journal of Middle East Studies* 11 (1980), 4–5; Samy Ayoub, "Territorial Jurisprudence, *Ikhtilaf al-Darayn*: Political Boundaries and Legal Jurisdiction," *Contemporary Islamic Studies* 2 (2012), 4–5, http://dx.doi.org/10.5339/cis.2012.2; Rana S. Othman, "Aḥkām al-Jinsiyya wa'l-Muwāṭana min Manẓūr Islāmī," (master's thesis, An-Najah National University, Nablus, Palestine, 2001), 20–21.

[75] Shoukri, *Refugee Status in Islam*, 50; Parvin and Sommer, "Evolution of Muslim Territoriality," 4; Othman, "Aḥkām al-Jinsiyya wa'l-Muwāṭana," 22–23.

[76] Khadduri, *War and Peace*, 170–171; Ayoub, "Territorial Jurisprudence, *Ikhtilaf al-Darayn*," 5–6; Shoukri, *Refugee Status in Islam*, 46–49; Othman, "Aḥkām al-Jinsiyya wa'l-Muwāṭana," 23–24.

Abode of War necessarily in a permanent state of war with the Abode of Islam, nor are negotiations between them prohibited. Rather, Islamic states are permitted to enter into diplomatic negotiations presaged upon recognizing a sovereign within the enemy territory.[77] Thus, the jurists' division of the world does not denote absolute states of war and peace between the Abode of Islam and other sovereigns, but it does fundamentally underpin and guide international relations between Islamic and foreign entities.

In spite of the jurists' geopolitical division of the world, human factors occasionally interrupted – but did not halt – overseas trade and shipping among the three domains during times of war and political upheaval. Although the right of maritime navigation features in the Qur'ān, in reality, overseas business and the flow of maritime trade would not have thrived and expanded without international diplomatic and commercial treaties having been drawn up between the Abode of Islam and the Abode of War. In the absence of such agreements, *ḥarbī* subjects, in particular, would have been able to sail, travel through, or conduct business in the Islamic territories only on the basis of a decree of safe-conduct.

Amān (*Decree of Safe-Conduct*)

Amān (a decree of safe-conduct) and bilateral or multilateral international treaties and truces have explicitly and implicitly defined the juridical status of subjects when traveling to foreign territories. By definition, *amān* provides temporary safe-conduct, safe passage, or assurance of security to enemies during a time of war, or to individual *ḥarbī*s who intend to enter, travel through, or reside for a fixed period of time in the Abode of Islam.[78]

77 Majid Khadduri, "Islam and the Modern Law of Nations," *American Journal of International Law* 50 (1956), 359–360; Ahmed M. Dawoody, "War in Islamic Law: Justifications and Regulations," (PhD diss., University of Birmingham, 2009), 169.

78 Hassan S. Khalilieh, "*Amān*," *The Encyclopedia of Islam*, 3rd ed. (Leiden: E. J. Brill, 2007), 1:111; ʿAbd al-Karīm Zaydān, *Aḥkām al-Dhimmiyyīn wa'l-Mustaʾminīn fī Dār al-Islām* (Beirut: Muʾassasat al-Risālah, 1402/1982), 39–42; Ahmed M. Masri, "The Classical Conceptions of Treaty, Alliances, and Neutrality in Sunni Islam," (PhD diss., Newcastle University, 1998), 165; Khaled R. Bashir, "Treatment of Foreigners in the Classical Islamic State with Special Focus on Diplomatic Envoys: Al-Shaybānī and *Amān*," in *Islam and International Law: Engaging Self-Centrism from a Plurality of Perspectives*, ed. Marie-Luisa Frick and Andreas Th. Müller (Leiden: Martinus Nijhoff, 2013), 146, 149.

In compliance with the Prophetic tradition,[79] as opposed to *amān ʿāmm* (general safe-conduct),[80] the grantor of *amān khāṣṣ* (particular/private safe-conduct) may be any sane, competent, and mature Muslim, male or female, even if poor, sick, or blind. According to some jurists, the grantor may even be a slave who serves as a soldier in a Muslim army.[81] Such a decree is issued upon request by a specific professional community, merchants, political entity, or diplomatic envoy.[82] The *mustaʾmin* is granted the right to sojourn and stay in the Abode of Islam for a period of at least

79 "الْمُسْلِمُونَ تَتَكَافَأُ دِمَاؤُهُمْ يَسْعَى بِذِمَّتِهِمْ أَدْنَاهُمْ وَيُجِيرُ عَلَيْهِمْ أَقْصَاهُمْ وَهُمْ يَدٌ عَلَى مَنْ سِوَاهُمْ يَرُدُّ مُشِدُّهُمْ عَلَى مُضْعِفِهِمْ وَمُتَسَرِّيهِمْ عَلَى قَاعِدِهِمْ لَا يُقْتَلُ مُؤْمِنٌ بِكَافِرٍ وَلَا ذُو عَهْدٍ فِي عَهْدِهِ (The blood of the Muslims is equal, the lowliest of them can promise protection on their behalf (*bi-dhimmatihim*), and the one residing far away may give protection on behalf of them. They are all united against the others. Those who have quick mounts should return to those who have slow mounts, and those who got out along with a detachment (should return) to those who are stationed. A believer shall not be killed for an unbeliever, nor a confederate within the term of confederation with him)." By saying "the blood of the Muslims is equal," the Prophet distinguishes between Muslims and non-Muslims, thus denying the *dhimmīs*' right to grant *amān* to *ḥarbīs* even if a *dhimmī* was authorized by a Muslim to pledge ***amān***. ***Sunan Abī Dāwūd***, Kitāb al-Jihād, *bāb* 159, no. 2751; Abū al-Ṭayyib Muḥammad Shams al-Ḥaqq Ābādī, *ʿAwn al-Maʿbūd: Sharḥ Sunan Abī Dāwūd* (Beirut: Dār al-Fikr, 1415/1995), 337–338; Abū Bakr Masʿūd ibn Aḥmad al-Kāsānī, *Badāʾiʿ al-Ṣanāʾiʿ fī Tartīb al-Sharāʾiʿ* (Beirut: Dār al-Kutub al-ʿIlmiyyah, 1406/1986), 9:414–416; Khalilieh, "*Amān*," 1:111; Masri, "Classical Conceptions of Treaty, Alliances, and Neutrality," 166–167; Mirza, "*Dhimma* Agreements and Sanctuary Systems at Islamic Origins," 103–105. With reference to the meaning of *dhimmatihim*, it applies to the security of Muslims with respect to non-Muslims and infidels. It signifies that for any Muslim who provides security to an enemy-alien person, any other Muslim is forbidden from bothering him as long as the guarantee still holds.

80 *Amān ʿāmm* is an official pledge whereby the grantor is normally the *imam* or his deputy, authorized to grant it to an unlimited number of *ḥarbīs*, or to a territory within the domain of the Abode of War.

81 Qalqashandī, *Ṣubḥ al-Aʿshā*, 13:322; Zaydān, *Aḥkām al-Dhimmiyyīn wa'l-Mustaʾminīn*, 40–41: "The assurance of safety or protection of the Muslims is one, the most humbled among them is entitled to take it upon himself (*dhimmat al-Muslimīn wāḥida yasʿā bihā adnāhum*)," that is to say, the assurance is binding on all the Muslims; Aharon Ben Shemesh, *Taxation in Islam* (Leiden: E. J. Brill, 1958, 1967, 1969), 3:65–66; Qalqashandī, *Ṣubḥ al-Aʿshā*, 13:321–323; John Wansbrough, "The Safe-Conduct in Muslim Chancery Practice," *Bulletin of the School of Oriental and African Studies* 34 (1971), 26; Ṣobḥī Maḥmaṣṣānī, *Al-Qānūn wa'l-ʿAlāqāt al-Duwaliyya fī al-Islām* (Beirut: Dār al-ʿIlm lil-Malāyīn, 1392/1972), 93–100; Khadduri, *War and Peace*, 164–165; Ḥamīdullāh, *Muslim Conduct of State*, 208–211; Khalilieh, "*Amān*," 1:111; Dawoody, "War in Islamic Law," 240–243; Othman, "Aḥkām al-Jinsiyya wa'l-Muwāṭana," 35–36.

82 Gladys Frantz-Murphy, "Identity and Security in the Mediterranean World ca. AD 640 – ca. 1517," *Proceedings of the Twenty-Fifth International Congress of Papyrology, Ann Arbor 2007*, American Studies in Papyrology (Ann Arbor, 2010), 263–264; Bashir, "Treatment of Foreigners in the Classical Islamic State," 148–149.

four months and up to one lunar year without paying the poll or land tax (*kharāj*).[83]

Certificates of safe-conduct were most commonly issued to ensure the safety of *ḥarbī* commercial vessels, their crew members, and their contents. As a commercial decree, a pledge of *amān* enabled enemy-alien traders to carry on commerce temporarily and in security within the Islamic territorial domain in return for the payment of a trade tax. As with the *dhimmī*, the *musta'min* is allowed to travel freely and visit any place, apart from the Hijaz, where he could sojourn for a limited time under defined conditions.[84] Moreover, he is entitled to protection from physical harm in terms of his person and chattels, and to perform religious rituals, enjoy equal justice, and utilize services of the state. If the grantee violates local laws, commits offensive acts, endangers territorial integrity, arrives at a third state, or returns to his homeland, the decree of *amān* is rescinded.[85] It is worth mentioning that the legal status of the *musta'min* is changed if a female *musta'min* marries a Muslim or a *dhimmī*; if, however, a male *musta'min* marries a female *dhimmī*, he does not become a *dhimmī* but can take his wife to the Abode of War. His status also changes if the *must'amin* stays longer than a year; in this case, he then becomes a *dhimmī* and must pay the jizya. Furthermore, his status changes if he purchases *kharāj* land.[86]

Diplomatic and Commercial Treaties

Under Islamic law, advancing the *ummah*'s welfare, spreading peace, justice, and equity, mitigating insecurity, and averting danger are

83 Qur'ān 9:1–2: "بَرَاءَةٌ مِّنَ اللَّهِ وَرَسُولِهِ إِلَى الَّذِينَ عَاهَدتُّم مِّنَ الْمُشْرِكِينَ فَسِيحُوا فِي الْأَرْضِ أَرْبَعَةَ أَشْهُرٍ (A declaration of immunity from God and His Messenger, to those of the pagans with whom ye have contracted mutual alliances. Go ye, then, for four months, (as ye will), throughout the land)." Law Schools, especially the Hanafi, advocate that although the pledge is limited to a four-month period, the maximum duration should not exceed 355 days. Schacht, *Introduction to Islamic Law*, 131; Hans Theunissen, "Ottoman-Venetian Diplomatics: The *'Ahd-names*: The Historical Background and the Development of a Category of Political-Commercial Instruments together with an Annotated Edition of a Corpus of Relevant Documents," *Electronic Journal of Oriental Studies* 1(2) (1998): 24–26.

84 See Chapter 2, 106–118.

85 Zaydān, *Aḥkām al-Dhimmiyyīn wa'l-Musta'minīn*, 46–47; Frantz-Murphy, "Identity and Security in the Mediterranean World," 254; Bashir, "Treatment of Foreigners in the Classical Islamic State," 148, 154–156; Samuel M. Stern, "Petitions from the Ayyūbid Period," *Bulletin of the School of Oriental and African Studies* 27 (1964), 1–6.

86 Maḥmaṣṣānī, *Al-Qānūn wa'l-'Alāqāt al-Duwaliyya fī al-Islām*, 99–100; Masri, "Classical Conceptions of Treaty, Alliances, and Neutrality," 171–172; Dawoody, "War in Islamic Law," 246–247. The Hanafi and Mālikī jurists argue that even if the *musta'min* is proved to be a spy, he still enjoys the right of protection.

fundamental aims in reaching truces and concluding treaties.[87] As the supreme authority, the *imam* or his deputy is mandated to conclude, ratify, and abrogate treaties on behalf of the *ummah*. A ratified truce or treaty can only be nullified by the *imam* if the other party violates it or commits perfidy, the treaty terms are determined to be contradictory to Islamic law, the other party seizes Islamic lands, or the *imam* is unable on any specific grounds to implement the terms of the treaty. A treaty may be revoked by the mutual consent of both parties. However, if any of the signatories dies or is removed from office, the participating states are still bound by the treaty until it expires. If the treaty is abrogated for any reason, the cancellation does not take effect immediately. Rather, a grace period of several weeks ensues. All foreign travelers and merchants formerly protected by the treaty, along with their chattels, remain safe during that time and may not be prevented from returning to their homelands.[88] As with the Treaty of Ḥudaybiyyah, the time limit

[87] Different Arabic terms are used to denote "treaty": *'ahd/mu'āhada* (commitment of both parties), *hudna* (cessation of hostilities), *muhādana* (conclusion of truce), *muwāda'a* (treaty of protection or agreeing not to fight), *ṣulḥ* (peace treaty), *mīthāq* (covenant or pact), *'aqd* (bond or tie/contract), *ḥilf* (alliance), *musālama* (peacemaking), *mutāraka* (abstention of both parties from hostilities) and *amān* (pledge). 'Uthmān J. Ḍumayriyya, *Al-Mu'āhadāt al-Duwaliyya fī Fiqh al-Imām Muḥammad Ibn al-Ḥasan al-Shaybānī: Dirāsa Muqārana* (Mecca: Rābiṭat al-'Ālam al-Islāmī, 1417/1997), 25–30; Joseph E. B. Lumbard, "Covenant and Covenants in the Qur'an," *Journal of Qur'anic Studies* 17 (2015), 2–4; Mikel de Epalza, "*'Ahd*: Muslim/Mudejar/Morisco Communities and Spanish-Christian Authorities," in *Negotiating Cultures: Bilingual Surrender Treaties in Muslim-Crusader* Spain *under James the Conqueror*, ed. Robert I. Burns and Paul E. Chevedden (Leiden: E. J. Brill, 1999), 195–212. Classical *fuqahā'* set up incentives compatible with those established by the Vienna Convention through the Law of Treaties (1969). Both maintain that international treaties are enacted to settle conflicts and resolve border disputes among states, exchange benefits and utilities, promote cultural and social matters, organize navigation among states, enhance military defense issues, and protect general sovereignty rights. See Masri, "Classical Conceptions of Treaty, Alliances, and Neutrality," 206–208.

[88] Qalqashandī, *Ṣubḥ al-A'shā*, 14:42, 51, 63; Ḥamīdullāh, *Muslim Conduct of State*, 272; Khadduri, *War and Peace*, 220–222; Masri, "Classical Conceptions of Treaty, Alliances, and Neutrality," 209–211, 217; Munir Muhammad, "The Concept of Treaty in Relation to War and Peace in Islam," *Fikro Nazar Urdu Journal* 47 (2009), available at SSRN: http://ssrn.com/abstract=1813024; Holt, *Early Mamluk Diplomacy*, 56–57, article 19 of the treaty of al-Ẓāhir Baybars with the Hospitallers 669/1271; Muḥammad M. Ḥamāda, *Al-Wathā'iq al-Siyāsiyya wa'l-Idāriyya lil-'Aṣr al-Mamlūkī 656-922/1258-1516* (Beirut: Mu'assasat al-Risālah, 1403/1983), 479, the 684/1285 truce between al-Manṣūr Qalāwūn and Hethum II, King of Armenia. All the treaties concluded between the Mamluk sultanate and European principalities and Communes grant a period of forty days' grace.

for a treaty is typically ten lunar years, after which point it is subject to renewal.[89]

Two prominent principles characterize decrees of *amān* and international treaties: (a) the sanctity of the terms of agreement akin to the Roman *pacta sunt servanda*; and (b) the norms of mutuality and reciprocity governing relationships between Muslims and aliens. With respect to the former, the Qur'ānic verses bind all Muslims to keep their promises and pledges with all humans,[90] including infidels, just as if they were made with God.[91] Whereas *'uqūd* (obligations) at times define humankind's spiritual relation to God, including *'ibādāt* and obedience before His commands, this term also conveys worldly obligations regarding all sorts of human material and social dealings – promises, business transactions, international treaties and truces, and an individual's commitments to self, nation, society, community, state, people of the same or different religious affiliation, and aliens from the Abode of Covenant or of War. The Qur'ān considers the fulfillment of all obligations, promises, pledges, truces, and treaties as a solemn religious duty and commands Muslims to abide by them, providing they do not contradict Islamic law.[92]

The compliance of Muslims with agreements concluded with non-Muslim individuals, communities, and states therefore corresponds with the observation of religious obligations. The Qur'ān enjoins state authorities to abide by the terms of a treaty even if the other party breaches those terms.[93] Qur'ān 17:34 states:

89 Ḍumayriyya, *Al-Mu'āhadāt al-Duwaliyya*, 96-97; Holt, *Early Mamluk Diplomacy*, 56, article 18, 87, article 25 (treaty of al-Manṣūr Qalāwūn with the Latin Kingdom 682/1283), 116, article 20 (treaty of al-Manṣūr Qalāwūn with Lady Margaret of Tyre 684/1285), 103, article 3 (treaty of al-Manṣūr Qalāwūn with King Leon III of Lesser Armenia 684/1285), 144 (treaty of al-Manṣūr Qalāwūn with Genoa 689/1290); Ḥamīdullāh, *Muslim Conduct of State*, 269; Khadduri, *Islamic Law of Nations*, 142; Khadduri, *War and Peace*, 219–220, 249–250, 267; Masri, "Classical Conceptions of Treaty, Alliances, and Neutrality," 92, 111, 157.

90 Qur'ān 5:1: "يَا أَيُّهَا الَّذِينَ آمَنُوا أَوْفُوا بِالْعُقُودِ (O ye who believe! Fulfill (all) obligations)"; Q 2:177: "وَالْمُوفُونَ بِعَهْدِهِمْ إِذَا عَاهَدُواْ (and truly pious those who fulfill the contracts which ye have made)"; Q 16:91: "وَأَوْفُواْ بِعَهْدِ اللَّهِ إِذَا عَاهَدتُّمْ (Fulfill the Covenant of God when ye have entered into it)"; Q 23:8: "وَالَّذِينَ هُمْ لِأَمَانَاتِهِمْ وَعَهْدِهِمْ رَاعُونَ (Those who faithfully observe their trusts and their covenants)."

91 Rāzī, *Al-Tafsīr al-Kabīr*, 20:108–109.

92 Ḍumayriyya, *Al-Mu'āhadāt al-Duwaliyya*, 123–127; Lumbard, "Covenant and Covenants in the Qur'an," 3–6; Anowar Zahid and Rohimi Shapiee, "*Pacta Sunt Servanda*: Islamic Perception," *Journal of East Asia and International Law* 3 (2010), 373–379.

93 Rāzī, *Al-Tafsīr al-Kabīr*, 20:109–111.

... and fulfill (every) engagement, for (every) engagement will be enquired into (on the Day of Reckoning).	... وَأَوْفُوا بِالْعَهْدِ إِنَّ الْعَهْدَ كَانَ مَسْؤُولاً
Q 9:4: (But the treaties are) not dissolved with those Pagans with whom ye have entered into alliance and who have not subsequently failed you in aught, nor aided anyone against you. So fulfill your engagements with them to the end of their term: for God loveth the righteous.	إِلَّا الَّذِينَ عَاهَدْتُمْ مِنَ الْمُشْرِكِينَ ثُمَّ لَمْ يَنْقُصُوكُمْ شَيْئًا وَلَمْ يُظَاهِرُوا عَلَيْكُمْ أَحَدًا فَأَتِمُّوا إِلَيْهِمْ عَهْدَهُمْ إِلَى مُدَّتِهِمْ إِنَّ اللَّهَ يُحِبُّ الْمُتَّقِينَ
Q 16:91: Fulfill the Covenant of God when ye have entered into it, and break not your oaths after ye have confirmed them; indeed ye have made.	وَأَوْفُوا بِعَهْدِ اللَّهِ إِذَا عَاهَدتُّمْ وَلَا تَنقُضُوا الْأَيْمَانَ بَعْدَ تَوْكِيدِهَا وَقَدْ جَعَلْتُمُ اللَّهَ عَلَيْكُمْ كَفِيلاً إِنَّ اللَّهَ يَعْلَمُ مَا تَفْعَلُونَ

The Treaty of Ḥudaybiyyah, ratified by the Prophet and the chiefs of Quraysh headed by Suhayl ibn ʿAmr, provides an excellent model of the Islamic *pacta* doctrine. Although it includes clauses unfavorable to Muslims, the Prophet and his Companions honored its terms, observed the *pacta* doctrine, and did not react instantaneously to violations by the Qurayshīs. The treaty was discarded only when the Qurayshīs abrogated the provisions mandating that both parties "lay down the burden of war for ten years" during which "each party shall be safe, and neither shall injure the other; no secret damage shall be inflicted, but uprightness and honor shall prevail between them."[94] It took persecution of the local Meccan Muslim community by the Qurayshīs for the treaty to be fully revoked, after which the Prophet and his followers launched a military campaign that culminated in the liberation of Mecca on Ramadan 20, 8/January 11, 630.[95]

[94] Ibn Hishām, *Al-Sīrah al-Nabawiyyah*, 3:263–264; Qalqashandī, *Ṣubḥ al-Aʿshā*, 14:6; Ḥamīdullāh, *Al-Wathāʾiq al-Siyāsiyya*, 77–80; Hasan al-Karmi, "The Prophet Muḥammad and the Spirit of Compromise," *Islamic Quarterly* 8 (1964), 92; Zahid and Shapiee, "*Pacta Sunt Servanda*: Islamic Perception," 381–382.

[95] Muḥammad ibn Aḥmad al-Sarakhsī, *Sharḥ Kitāb al-Siyar al-Kabīr* (Beirut: Dār al-Kutub al-ʿIlmiyyah, 1417/1997), 1:213–215. The Treaty of Ḥudaybiyyah was not premeditated, but came into being when the Prophet, accompanied by 1,500 unarmed men, decided to perform an *ʿumra* (lesser pilgrimage) to Mecca. In order to explain the Muslims' peaceful mission, he dispatched ʿUthmān ibn ʿAffān as an envoy to convey to the Meccans their intention. In

As did earlier and contemporaneous monotheistic religions and political entities, Islam recognizes the principle of reciprocity and mutual justice, not only among Muslims but also with respect to non-Muslim groups and foreign states and principalities in times of peace and war alike.[96] The application by Islam of this principle is evinced by the overwhelming number of bilateral and multilateral treaties concluded between Muslim and Christian states, within which regulations regarding one state were matched by similar rules vis-à-vis another. States and independent principalities generally proposed treaty terms regarding taxation, exchange of envoys and diplomats, ransoming of captives, fighting piracy, and granting judicial sovereignty to foreign communities, in addition to recognizing a state's jurisdiction over offshore maritime zones and verifying the right to navigate in offshore waters, trade along coasts, and anchor in ports and anchorages in times of duress. In brief, international treaties

response, Suhayl ibn ʿAmr, along with four emissaries, negotiated terms and concluded a treaty with the Prophet. The great majority of Muslim scholars regard this treaty as having served as a model for future diplomatic treaties because: (a) it substantiates the fact that the Islamic State can enter into a relationship and conclude a peace treaty even with sworn enemies; (b) the duration of the treaty was fixed at ten years, a standard duration for subsequent treaties; (c) it defines the rights and obligations of each party to the agreement; (d) as a leader, the Prophet demonstrated concern about the welfare and safety of the Muslim community within his particular jurisdiction; (e) as a statesman, he demonstrated diplomatic ingenuity; and (f) the Prophet displayed utmost respect with regard to his enemy's emissaries. Cherif Bassiouni, "Protection of Diplomats under Islamic Law," *American Society of International Law* 74 (1980), 611; Fiazuddin Shuayb, "Who's Better than God to Rule? An Inquiry into the Formation of the First Islamic State (622–32 C.E.)," (PhD diss., UCLA International Institute, 2012), 420–426; Muhammad-Basheer A. Ismail, "Islamic Diplomatic Law and International Diplomatic Law: A Quest for Compatibility," (PhD diss., University of Hull, 2012), 211–218.

96 Qur'ān 2:194: "فَمَنِ اعْتَدَى عَلَيْكُمْ فَاعْتَدُواْ عَلَيْهِ بِمِثْلِ مَا اعْتَدَى عَلَيْكُمْ (If then any one transgresses the prohibition against you, transgress ye likewise against him)"; Q 9:7: "فَمَا اسْتَقَامُواْ لَكُمْ فَاسْتَقِيمُواْ لَهُمْ (As long as these (Pagans) stand true to you, stand ye true to them)"; Q 16:126: "وَإِنْ عَاقَبْتُمْ فَعَاقِبُواْ بِمِثْلِ مَا عُوقِبْتُم بِهِ وَلَئِن صَبَرْتُمْ لَهُوَ خَيْرٌ لِّلصَّابِرِينَ (And if ye punish, let your punishment be proportionate to the wrong that has been done to you: but if ye show patience, that is indeed the best (course) for those who are patient)"; Q 42:40: "وَجَزَاء سَيِّئَةٍ سَيِّئَةٌ مِّثْلُهَا فَمَنْ عَفَا وَأَصْلَحَ فَأَجْرُهُ عَلَى اللَّهِ إِنَّهُ لا يُحِبُّ الظَّالِمِينَ (The recompense for an injury is an injury equal thereto (in degree): but if a person forgives and makes reconciliation, his reward is due from God: For (God) loveth not those who do wrong)"; Q 55:60: "هَلْ جَزَاء الإِحْسَانِ إِلاَّ الإِحْسَانُ (Is there any Reward for Good – other than Good)"; Gamal M. Badr, "A Survey of Islamic International Law," *American Society of International Law Proceedings* 76 (1982), 59; Ḥamīdullāh, *Muslim Conduct of State*, 34, 125, 138, 151–152, 166; Khadduri, *War and Peace*, 44–45, 278; Khadduri, *Islamic Law of Nations*, 3, 6, 8, 12, 22, 41, 53, 62; Haniff Ahamat, "The Position of *Siyar* on Free Trade: A Historico-Legal Analysis," *Journal of the History of International Law* 12 (2010), 315–316, 319, 324, 326–327.

engendered freedom of movement and navigation, knowledge, and trade activities among nations and sovereigns.

The Contested Sea: Navigational Regimes in the Mediterranean

A significant number of international diplomatic and commercial agreements and truces signed by Christian and Muslim sovereigns and principalities along the Mediterranean contained clauses assuring freedom of navigation on the high seas and along coasts, and of travel on land by foreign civilians, whether shippers, merchants, or voyagers, together with their chattels, in order to enhance interregional and overseas commerce.[97] Articles 5 and 6 of the 667/1269 treaty concluded between al-Ẓāhir Baybars (*r.* 658–676/1260–1277) and Lady Isabel of Beirut (*r.* 1264–1282) stipulate that civilian-subjects, servants, ships, and galleys be considered to fall "under the jurisdiction and obedience" of the respective party to the treaty when traveling by land or sailing the seas and also guarantee "safe and secure (passage) in respect to themselves, their chattels, and their goods."[98]

This freedom of navigation and mutual securing of vessels, crew, traders, voyagers, and their chattels and goods from hostile attacks finds echoes in subsequent commercial and diplomatic treaties. Article 7 of the Treaty of al-Manṣūr Qalāwūn (*r.* 678–689/1279–1290) with Bohemond VII, the prince of Antioch and Tripoli (*r.* 1275–1287) beginning in 680/1281, stipulates that galleys of each party to the agreement shall be safe from interception by the other while at sea.[99] The same sultan signed other treaties with the Latin Kingdom of Acre (682/1283),[100] Lady Margaret of

[97] Dominique Valérian, "Ifrīqiyan Muslim Merchants in the Mediterranean at the End of the Middle Ages," *Mediterranean Historical Review* 14 (1999), 47–66; David Abulafia, "Christian Merchants in the Almohad Cities," *Journal of Medieval Iberian Studies* 2 (2010), 251–257; Holt, *Early Mamluk Diplomacy*, 5. In addition to freedom of navigation, international treaties address: (a) financial aspects of trade – taxation, customs, and port tolls; (b) the application of the law for travelers when on land, which revolves around the implementation of *Sharīʿah* abroad, the judicial autonomy of *dhimmī*s and foreigners, the juridical role of Consuls, and means for appealing to Islamic courts; and (c) the territorial integrity and sovereignty of hosting states.

[98] Holt, *Early Mamluk Diplomacy*, 46–47.

[99] Holt, *Early Mamluk Diplomacy*, 58.

[100] Holt, *Early Mamluk Diplomacy*, 81, article 6: "All this territory and the coastlands as specified in this blessed truce shall be safe from the sultan al-Malik al-Manṣūr and his son al-Malik al-Ṣāliḥ, and safe from their soldiers, their troops and their servants. This territory as set forth above being covered by this blessed truce, whether property or condominium, shall be secure, it and its civilians, all nations of people in it, the residents therein and the wayfarers thereto, of whatever nations and religions, the wayfarers thereto from all the lands of the Franks, the merchants, the travelers and the wayfarers

Tyre (684/1285),[101] Genoa (689/1290),[102] and King Alfonso III of Aragon (*r.* 1285–1291) (689/1290),[103] all of which ensure safety of navigation on the high seas and in coastal waters.

Similar treaties were executed in the western basin of the Mediterranean.[104] On the eve of renewal of the 721/1321 peace treaty originally signed by Sultan Ismāʿīl I of Granada (*r.* 713–725/1314–1325) and Jaime (James) II of Aragon (*r.* 1291–1327), the former's successor, Muḥammad IV (*r.* 725–733/1325–1333), authored (on Jumada al-Thani 11, 726/May 15, 1326) an official letter protesting against an Aragonese

passing to and fro by land and sea, night and day, plain and mountain. They shall be safe in respect of themselves, their chattels, their children, their ships and their beasts of burden, all belonging to them and everything in their possession of whatever kind, from the Sultan, his son, and all under their obedience."

101 Holt, *Early Mamluk Diplomacy*, 114, article 11: "Provided also that ships of either party in passage on the sea shall be safe from the other party, secure at sea and in anchorage, entering and leaving. Every community of the two parties is bound to abstain from damage to the other party."

102 Holt, *Early Mamluk Diplomacy*, 147–148. Articles 2 and 3 concern the personal rights and immunities of Muslim and Genoese subjects in all stages of their journey on land and at sea. Article 3 states: "And that all Genoese will honor, respect and protect all Muslims who come to the territory of our lord the Sultan, and who go out and travel from it by land and sea; they will not interfere with them, or enable any interference with them by wrongful acts, harm or hostility, either to their persons or their chattels, either in coming or going. They shall be safe and secure in respect of their persons and chattels and seafaring from all the Genoese, and from those under the jurisdiction of the Commune of Genoa as stated above." Also Ḥamāda, *Al-Wathāʾiq al-Siyāsiyya wa'l-Idāriyya lil-ʿAṣr al-Mamlūkī*, 482.

103 Holt, *Early Mamluk Diplomacy*, 133–134. The third paragraph of article 3 reads as follows: "Whatever the specified territory and the unspecified provinces contain: the cities, ports, coastlands, harbors, routes by land and sea; departure and arrival, residence and travel of soldiers and troops, Turcomans, Kurds and Arabs, civilians and merchants, galleys, vessels, ships, chattels and beasts; of whatever faiths, persons and nationalities; whatever is possessed of all kinds, chattels, arms, military equipment, property, wares and merchandise; little or much, near or far, by land or sea; shall be safe in respect of persons, people, chattels, women and children, from the King of Aragon and his brothers mentioned above, from their sons, knights, horsemen, allies, fleets and men, and from everyone belonging to them. This regulation shall likewise apply to everything that God shall conquer by the hand of our lord the Sultan al-Malik al-Manṣūr, and by the hand of his sons, soldiery and armies, whether citadels, fortresses, territory or regions."

104 Paul E. Chevedden, "The 1244 Treaty: Arabic Text and Analysis," in *Negotiating Cultures: Bilingual Surrender Treaties in Muslim-Crusader Spain under James the Conqueror*, ed. Robert I. Burns and Paul E. Chevedden (Leiden: E. J. Brill, 1999), 159–160, 164–165. In the 1235 surrender pact of Abū ʿAbd Allāh Muḥammad ibn Hudhayl, known as al-Azraq, to King James I of Aragon and Catalonia, the latter guarantees protection to the Játivans with respect to persons and chattels, while traveling by land and by sea, and within the castles, citadels, cities, towns, coastlands, and harbors under his jurisdiction.

naval raid on Almería – one of the two major port cities of the Emirate of Granada – and the capture of more than a dozen Muslims. In the letter, an appeal was made to the royal envoy of Jaime II, urging him to expedite the release of the hostages and to order his troops to refrain from future attacks on Granadian targets.[105] A few days later, on Jumada al-Thani 15, 726/May 19, 1326, Muḥammad IV dispatched a more detailed letter to Jaime II, reminding him of the terms and provisions of the 721/1321 treaty. He stressed the sanctity of frontiers, of maintaining the territorial integrity of both states, and of freedom of movement of both Muslim and Christian civilian-subjects on land and at sea:

The terms upon which this treaty is established apply to the mainland and the sea. It covers all of our ships that frequent your coastlands, your ships that frequent our coastlands, our civilian-subjects who head for your mainland, and your civilian-subjects who head for our mainland. They shall be safe on land and at sea in respect of their persons and chattels. They shall be safeguarded and secured wherever they arrive and travel. No harm whatsoever shall befall them on land and at sea, secretly or publicly.

Neither our galleys nor yours shall intercept the other party's vessels be they at sea or in port, irrespective of whether they carry subjects of an enemy or a friendly state.

Should your (galleys) capture a Muslim or a Christian vessel not flying our flag and one of our civilian-subjects is on board, or should your (forces) capture a group of Muslims and one of our civilian-subjects is among them, you shall release our detained civilian-subjects with their chattels instantly; reciprocal actions shall be taken on our part in your favor.

(It is also) provided that you shall not target any of our ports irrespective of the identity of the civilian-subjects therein, be they enemy-alien or friendly subjects.

(It is also) provided that your (military) galleys shall not do harm to any vessel mooring in our ports (*marāsīna*) or (along) our country's coastlands (*sawāḥil bilādunā*), or sailing in its territorial sea (*biḥāribā*), regardless of their owners' religious affiliations – Muslims or Christians – and place of origin. Your galleys shall have no right whatsoever to intercept them insofar as the duration of the peace treaty is in force and has not expired.

(If) you shall render any kind of assistance to our Muslim and Christian enemies on land and at sea; reciprocal actions shall be taken on our part to your detriment.[106]

105 Shakīb Arslān, *Al-Ḥulal al-Sundusiyya fī al-Akhbār wa'l-Āthār al-Andalusiyya* (Cairo: Al-Maṭbaʿa al-Raḥmāniyya, 1355/1936), 2:306–308.

106 Arslān, *Al-Ḥulal al-Sundusiyya*, 2:308–309; Muḥammad M. Ḥamāda, *Al-Wathāʾiq al-Siyāsiyya wa'l-Idāriyya fī al-Andalus wa-Shamāliyy Ifrīqiya (64–897/683–1492)* (Beirut: Muʾassasat al-Risālah, 1406/1986), 465–466.

Muḥammad IV reminds Jaime II of their agreement to secure freedom of navigation and movement on land and at sea, and to abide by the principle of extraterritoriality. He argues that both parties had guaranteed the secure passage of civilian-subjects, merchants, and their chattels and ships through both realms, off the coasts, and on the high seas. To further encourage trade, the treaty made no restrictions on the freedom of navigation on the high seas of ships flying Granadian and Aragonese flags, and ordained that the galleys of both parties should refrain from intercepting or hindering those of the other. However, when sailing off the coastal frontiers of either state, or mooring in one of their ports or anchorages, ships were required to comply with local law.

From the birth of Islam in the seventh century up until and throughout the Ottoman period, parties to diplomatic and commercial treaties applied the principle of extraterritorial reciprocity. In the 9 AH/630 CE Prophetic pledge, the grantor declares: "This is a guarantee of protection from God and Muḥammad the Prophet, the Messenger of God, to Yūḥannā ibn Ru'ba and the people of Aylah, for their ships, their caravans by land and sea . . . and all that are with them, men of Syria and the Yemen, and seamen."[107] This statement goes beyond a common pledge of security for the people and property of Aylah because it contains clauses concerning the safety of foreign civilians sailing aboard Aylah-flagged vessels. The Prophet assured that such subjects also would enjoy a legal status akin to that of the people of Aylah, whether at sea or within its territorial sovereignty. By doing so, the Prophet extended the quasiterritorial jurisdiction of the flag state not only to the vessels themselves, but also to all their crew and passengers irrespective of nationality. Thus, when a seagoing vessel ventured outside a state's territorial sovereignty, she and all persons and property on board were subject to the laws of Aylah just as if she were a floating island within the state's jurisdiction.

Concerning the civilian-subjects of Aylah who sailed on board foreign-flagged vessels, they too were covered by this pledge and enjoyed diplomatic protection. This protection remained in force even if the countries to which the ships belonged were hostile or did not maintain diplomatic or commercial relations with the Islamic State. In this case, the doctrine of diplomatic protection with reference to subjects of Aylah aboard alien ships superseded the flag state's quasiterritorial jurisdiction. It is clear that, with respect to the pledge of safe-conduct, both the doctrines of

107 See above p. 45: هَذِهِ أَمَنَةٌ مِنَ اللهِ، ومُحَمَّدٍ النَّبِيِّ رَسُولِ اللهِ لِيُحَنَّةَ بْنِ رُؤْبَةَ وَأَهْلِ أَيْلَةَ، سُفُنُهُمْ وَسَيَّارَتُهُمْ فِي الْبَرِّ وَالْبَحْرِ . . . وَمَنْ كَانَ مَعَهُمْ مِنْ أَهْلِ الشَّامِ، وَأَهْلِ الْيَمَنِ، وَأَهْلِ الْبَحْر.

quasiterritorial jurisdiction and diplomatic protection grant security to Aylah-flagged vessels and all persons and property aboard, as well as to its civilian-subjects sailing on board vessels flying flags of foreign states, even in the absence of relationships with the newly founded Islamic State.

We can identify in later treaties these same principles as set forth by the Prophet in the pledge of 9 AH/630 CE. For instance, article 4 of the treaty signed by al-Manṣūr Qalāwūn and the representatives of Genoa on Jumada al-Awwal 2, 689 AH/May 13, 1290, stipulates:

> And that they will protect all Muslim merchants and others who travel in Genoese and other vessels, going and coming, in all places belonging to the Commune of Genoa and others, the territory of the Franks, the territory of the Greeks and the territory of the Muslims. Every Muslim traveling with them and with others shall be protected, safe and secure; no-one shall ill-treat or wrong them during their journey, their abiding or their residence.
>
> If a Muslim should travel in a vessel other than a Genoese vessel, belonging to the enemies of the Genoese or others, there shall be no interference with any Muslim.
>
> If they [Genoese] take their enemy, the Muslims shall be protected and safe in respect of themselves, their slaves and their slave-girls, in going and coming. The Genoese shall not detain them on any pretext; nor shall they take a Muslim as a hostage, or pursue him for debt or bloodshed, unless he is a guarantor or surety.[108]

The sultan attaches the principle of extraterritoriality to vessels flying the flag of Genoa and those of other states, which under customary law has exclusive jurisdiction over them, not only on the high seas, but also within their territorial seas. However, when merchant vessels moor in foreign ports, local authorities would share jurisdiction over them.[109] Since a flag state asserts jurisdiction over its vessels, it is held liable for conduct occurring on board whether within its territorial domain or on the high

[108] Holt, *Early Mamluk Diplomacy*, 148; Ḥamāda, *Al-Wathā'iq al-Siyāsiyya wa'l-Idāriyya lil-'Aṣr al-Mamlūkī*, 481–482; Michele Amari, *Nuovi Ricordi Arabici su la Storia di Genova* (Genova: Tipografia del R. Istituto sordo-muti, 1873), 19 (Arabic section).

[109] Postclassical jurists attach the principle of extraterritoriality to ships anchoring in foreign ports. The Andalusian jurist Ibn Sirāj (d. 848/1444) "was asked about Muslim captives in the hands of Christians, who, while awaiting ransom on board (enemy vessel) anchoring in one of Islamic anchorages, escaped from captivity." He answered: "Jurisprudentially, it is more likely, may God grant us success, that Muslims shall neither pay ransom nor hand the captives over because the vessels in our days are legally and jurisdictionally akin to their territories and strongholds (*li-anna al-marākib al-yawm tanazzalat manzilat bilādihim wa-ma'āqilihim*)." Abū al-Qāsim Muḥammad ibn Sirāj al-Andalusī, *Fatāwā Qāḍī al-Jamā'a* (Beirut: Dār Ibn Ḥazm, 1427/2006), 223; this *responsum* is fully quoted by Abū al-'Abbās Aḥmad ibn Yaḥyā al-Wansharīsī, *Al-Mi'yār al-Mu'rib wa'l-Jāmi' al-Mughrib 'an Fatāwā Ahl Ifrīqiya wa'l-Andalus wa'l-Maghrib* (Beirut: Dār al-Gharb al-Islāmī, 1981), 2:118.

seas. Genoa is thus responsible for the well-being, safety, and any maltreatment of Muslim subjects and their chattels sailing aboard its vessels when frequenting Genoese territories, as well as aboard vessels sailing under foreign flags, namely Frankish and Byzantine vessels. Should Genoa attack any enemy vessel transporting Muslims, it will be bound to safeguard the Muslims' well-being and to set them free. The lack of reference in this treaty to *dhimmī* citizens should not be interpreted to mean that they were legally distinguished from their Muslim civilian counterparts when traveling abroad. On the contrary, as protected citizens of the Abode of Islam, *dhimmīs*' rights were either explicitly or implicitly embedded in all international agreements signed between Islamic and foreign states. Theoretically and practically, all subjects of the Abode of Islam seemed to have enjoyed the same treatment and rights when at sea and on foreign soil.[110]

Both parties to a treaty or truce were bound not to inflict harm on civilian-subjects of either state, whether traveling by land or sea (*allā yuṭraq aḥad bi-sharr fī barr*[111] *aw baḥr*).[112] Pursuant to the 721/1321

[110] Ḥamīdullāh, Al-Wathā'iq al-Siyāsiyya, 174–193; Muḥammad M. Nashshār, *'Alāqat Mamlakatay Qishtāla wa-Aragon bi-Salṭanat al-Mamālīk 658–741/1260–1341* (Cairo: 'Ein for Human and Social Studies, 1997), 235; Ḥamāda, *Al-Wathā'iq al-Siyāsiyya wa'l-Idāriyya lil-'Aṣr al-Mamlūkī*, 489; Holt, *Early Mamluk Diplomacy*, 53 (treaty of 669/1271, article 8), 135 (treaty of 689/1290 between al-Manṣūr Qalāwūn and King Alfonso III of Aragon, article 9): "if any of the Muslim merchants, the Christians of the territory of our lord the Sultan, or the *dhimmīs* of his territory ... "; Frédéric Bauden, "Due trattati di pace conclusi nel dodicesimo secolo tra i Banū Ġāniya, signori delle isole Baleari, e il commune di Genova," in *Documentos y manuscritos árabes del Occidente musulmán medieval*, ed. Nuria Martínez de Castilla (Madrid: Consejo Superior de Investigaciones Científicas, 2010), 49, articles 12, 13, 16 of the Safar 577/June 1181 Banū Ghāniya–Genoese treaty, and 68–69, articles 8–11 of the 584/1188 Banū Ghāniya–Genoese treaty; Amari, *Nuovi Ricordi Arabici su la Storia di Genova*, 3–5 (Arabic section).

[111] Although the actual meaning of the word *barr* is "land," it could also mean "sailing by cabotage." In an early tenth-century Islamic legal treatise on maritime law we read the following: "*idhā sāfarat al-safīna ma' al-barr al-barr*," meaning: "if the ship sailed by cabotage within the land sight." Ṭāher (ed.), "*Akriyat al-Sufun*," 27; Saḥnūn ibn Sa'īd al-Tanūkhī, *Al-Mudawwanah al-Kubrā* (Beirut: Dār al-Kutub al-'Ilmiyyah, 1415/1994), 4:493, 496; Khalilieh, *Admiralty and Maritime Laws*, 294.

[112] Michele Amari, *I Diplomi Arabi del R. Archivio Fiorentino* (Florence: Dalla Tipografia di Felice le Monnier, 1863), 231–232, 233, 234, the Safar 19, 580/June 1, 1184, bilateral peace treaty (*muṣālaḥa*) and covenant (*mu'āqada*) signed between jurist (*faqīh*) and governor Abū Ibrāhīm Isḥāq ibn Muḥammad ibn 'Alī (r. 551–580/1156–1184), of Banū Ghāniya, of the Balearics, and Siegiero Guccionello Gualandi, the Ambassador of the Republic of Lucca and Pisa, further stipulates that any Pisan and Lucchian subject who sails aboard ships belonging to the enemies of the Balearic Islands shall be treated as an enemy of these islands. Three years earlier (Safar 577/June 1181), the same jurist-

Granadian–Aragonese peace treaty (renewed in 726/1326),[113] and the Ḥafṣīd–Pisa peace treaties of 713/1313, 754/1353, 767/1366, 800/1397, and 817/1414, joined by Florence in 824/1421 and 849/1445, and the Catalan–Mamluk commercial and peace treaty of 1430, the states agreed on their respective: (a) rights to exercise extraterritorial jurisdiction over their flagged ships; and (b) obligations to avoid hindering an individual's freedom of movement and navigation on the high seas. The extraterritorial jurisdiction of Pisa over ships flying its flag was manifested by article 14 of the 713/1313 treaty, renewed in 754/1353, within which the Ḥafṣīd amir expressly affirmed that every foreign merchant sailing on a ship belonging to Pisa was to be treated as if he were a Pisan subject, and to "enjoy rights equal to theirs, and fulfill the same obligations as theirs (*lahu mā lahum, wa-ʿalayhi mā ʿalayhim*)."[114] Apart from the time of berthing in foreign ports, the flag state was entitled to claim jurisdiction over foreign passengers sailing on board its ships.[115] Any unlawful act

governor signed a peace treaty with Genoa containing an express proviso (article 23) considering Genoese subjects to be enemies if captured while sailing aboard vessels of nations unfriendly to Majorca. The institution of diplomatic protection thereby became irrelevant, and Genoa could not assert its own right in its subjects/nationals who violated the terms of the truce (*muhādana*). Bauden, "Due trattati di pace," 50 (articles 23 and 24), 69–70 (articles 16 and 17 of 584/1188 treaty); Amari, *Nuovi Ricordi Arabici su la Storia di Genova*, 1–5 and 6–10 (Arabic section); Amar S. Baaj, "The Struggle for North Africa between Almohads, Ayyubids, and Banū Ghāniya (Late Twelfth to Early Thirteenth Centuries A.D.)," (PhD diss., University of Toronto, 2013), 123–124; Nashshār, *ʿAlāqat Mamlakatay Qishtāla wa-Aragon bi-Salṭanat al-Mamālīk*, 296, "*fī al-barr wa'l-baḥr*"; Mercè Viladrich, "Solving the 'Accursed Riddle' of the Diplomatic Relations between Catalonia and Egypt around 1430," *Al-Masāq* 14 (2002), 26–28.

113 Arslān, *Al-Ḥulal al-Sundusiyya*, 2:309; Ḥamāda, *Al-Wathāʾiq al-Siyasiyya wa'l-Idāriyya*, 466.

114 Amari, *Diplomi Arabi*, 90, 103, 242; Kathryn Reyerson, "Identity in the Medieval Mediterranean World of Merchants and Pirates," *Mediterranean Studies* 20 (2012), 139; Enrica Salvatori, "Corsairs' Crews and Cross-Cultural Interactions: The Case of the Pisan Trapelicinus in the Twelfth Century," *Medieval Encounter* 13 (2007), 34, 41. A similar stipulation appears in the twelfth-century bilateral treaties concluded between Pisa and other Italian Communes. The 1171 Pisa–Florence treaty makes the assurance that the Florentines can enjoy the privilege of sailing, along with their shipments, aboard Pisan-flagged vessels as if they were Pisans. Salvatori maintains that this treaty is perhaps the earliest-known instance of foreigners granted the status of nationals aboard ships. However, her assumption is baseless as, 541 years earlier, the Prophet Muḥammad had already assimilated foreigners sailing aboard Aylah-flagged ships with nationals of Aylah and granted the former complete security for their persons, private belongings, and commercial commodities.

115 Reyerson, "Identity in the Medieval Mediterranean World of Merchants and Pirates," 139–140; David Abulafia, "Crocuses and Crusaders: San Gimignano, Pisa and the Kingdom of Jerusalem," in *Outremer: Studies in the History of the Crusading*

committed en route or in the vessel's home port held the wrongdoer liable for the misconduct; the wrongdoer was punished pursuant to the law of the vessel's flag state.[116] The laws and shipping regulations of the flag state to which a vessel belonged did not exempt alien travelers and shippers from protection; in fact, they may have experienced preferential treatment. The only sensible reason that foreigners may have preferred to sail aboard a vessel flying an alien flag was to take advantage of the protection afforded by the participation of the alien state in bilateral treaties.

The parties to a treaty acknowledged each other's extraterritorial jurisdiction over its own flagged vessels and asserted that crew, shippers, cargoes, and passengers, regardless of citizenship and denomination, were free and safe to sail in its vessels on the high seas, and to moor in ports and anchorages of the contracting parties.[117] Should enemy travelers sail aboard a ship flying the flag of a state that was party to the treaty, upon arrival at its destination the captain would have to notify the port authorities regarding the identities of these enemy travelers and the purposes of their trip.[118] Once the identification process and clearance of the

Kingdom of Jerusalem Presented to Joshua Prawer, ed. B. Z. Kedar, H. E. Mayer, and R. C. Smail (Jerusalem: Yad Izhak Ben-Zvi, 1982), 231–232, describes how the Tuscan merchants posed as Pisans when trading between Acre and Aleppo. These merchants, who were active in the Levant, were instructed to return directly from Syria to Pisa apparently aboard Pisan-flagged vessels.

116 Amari, *Diplomi Arabi*, 145–146, article 19 of the 817/1414 Ḥafṣīd–Pisan treaty: "If one Christian sailing on board a ship belongs to Pisa ... inflicts harm or annoys Muslims, he will personally be treated commensurate with the act he has committed (*yu ʿāmal bi-fi ʿlihi*)."

117 Amari, *Diplomi Arabi*, 22; Ahmed Azzaoui, *Rasāʾil Muwaḥḥidiyya* (Kénitra: Université Ibn Tofayl, 1416/1995), 1:175; Almohads–Pisan long-term treaty (25 years) from Ramadan 1, 582/November 15, 1186, plainly states that "if the fleets of Almohads, may God grant them victory, encounter (Pisan) ships at sea, they shall not inflict harm to them in respect of their persons, chattels, affairs, or anything else"; Baaj, "Struggle for North Africa between Almohads, Ayyubids, and Banū Ghāniya," 123–124; Amari, *Diplomi Arabi*, 131, article 20 of the 800/1397 treaty: "If one of Pisa's vessels or galleys sails on the high sea (*ẓahr al-baḥr*) or anchors in the port of Tūnis or one of its territories and one of the ruler's galleys sights her, the (Ḥafṣīd) galley shall neither block her way nor cause harm to her; all those on board are safe in respect of their persons, chattels, and galleys." This peace treaty (*ṣulḥ*) was originally drawn up between the Ḥafṣīd amir Abū Fāris ʿAbd al-ʿAzīz ibn Aḥmad (r. 796–838/1394–1434) and Pisa, extended in 817/1414, and joined by Florence on Shawwal 7, 824/October 5, 1421.

118 Abū al-Ḥasan ʿAlī ibn ʿUthmān al-Makhzūmī, *Kitāb al-Minhāj fī ʿIlm Kharāj Miṣr*, ed. Claude Cahen and Yūsuf Rāghib (Cairo: Institut Français d'Archéologie Orientale, 1986), 46–49, 57–58; Muḥammad ibn Aḥmad ibn Jubayr, *The Travels of Ibn Jubayr*, ed. and trans. R. J. C. Broadhurst (London: Jonathan Cape, 1952), 301; for this text in

foreigners was completed by the port of call, they and their chattels obtained a guarantee of safety.[119] In the cases of Pisa and Florence, the elders and councilors of the communes expressly guaranteed the protection of all Muslims along with their moveable effects on board vessels flying their flags, and held themselves accountable for pursuing justice and remunerating any ill-fated Muslims exposed to offenses or treacherous acts during the journey. However, if a Muslim preferred to sail on a vessel not flying the flag of the communes, the state in question would assume protection only of those officially permitted to board the vessel.[120]

According to the customary law of the sea, the captain of a vessel holds exclusive jurisdiction over the craft and all those on board when on the high seas, as the vessel is considered a quasiterritory in relation to her nationality or her owner's religious affiliation. However, once a vessel enters a port, she becomes subject to a concurrent jurisdiction; the captain's exclusive jurisdiction gives way to the jurisdiction of the port's superintendent.[121] As the highest-ranking officer on board a vessel, a captain is vested with overriding authority. Apart from being a skillful navigator and professional manager, a captain's duty is to administer the law of his religion or country. The vessel herself, along with all those on board, regardless of their citizenships and religious allegiances, are thereby subject to the laws and regulations of the vessel's flag state. The

Arabic see Muḥammad ibn Aḥmad ibn Jubayr, *Riḥlat Ibn Jubayr* (Beirut: Dār Ṣāder, 1959), 13; Khalilieh, *Islamic Maritime Law*, 83–85.

119 Amari, *Diplomi Arabi*, 178. A sultanate unilateral edict (*rasm*) issued by the Mamluk sultan Qānṣūh al-Ghūrī (r. 906–923/1501–1517) in Dhū al-Qiʿdah 18, 911/April 12, 1506, guarantees protection to the Florentine merchants' guild (*ṭāʾifa*) arriving on Egyptian coastal frontiers aboard non-Florentine-flagged ships; this safe-conduct applies at sea and on land alike. Amari, *Diplomi Arabi*, 216. Under the terms of the 913/1508 treaty between the amir of the port city of Bādis and Venice, he assures (in article 2) through protection for all "vessels sailing under the flag of the Signoria," including their passengers and property. By virtue of quasiterritorial jurisdiction, all passengers, regardless of nationality, are treated as if Venetian subjects when on board Venetian-registered vessels. Article 5 refers to the status of Venetian merchants arriving in Bādis on board non-Venetian-flagged vessels. It assures their protection with respect to their persons and chattels. John Wansbrough, "A Moroccan Amīr's Commercial Treaty with Venice of the Year 913/1508," *Bulletin of the School of Oriental and African Studies* 25 (1962), 455, 459, 460; Pierre Moukarzel, "Venetian Merchants in Thirteenth-Century Alexandria and the Sultans of Egypt: An Analysis of Treaties, Privileges and Intercultural Relations," *Al-Masāq* 28 (2016), 195–196. The Venetian–Mamluk treaty of 1208 guarantees security and protection not only for Venetian subjects, but also for foreign passengers and pilgrims sailing aboard ships flying the Venetian flag heading for the Church of the Holy Sepulchre in Jerusalem or for Alexandria.

120 Amari, *Diplomi Arabi*, 179, article 29 of the 849/1445 peace treaty.

121 Khalilieh, *Islamic Maritime Law*, 143.

jurisdiction of the flag state applies to matters of discipline, the safety of the crew and passengers, and the safe delivery of cargo from the ports of origin to the destinations, unless leasing contracts or treaties stipulate otherwise.[122] For this reason, Muslim jurists discouraged their compatriots from sailing on board foreign-owned vessels, unless: (a) the voyage was being undertaken for religious or educational purposes; (b) the passengers would not be harassed or humiliated during the journey; and (c) the Muslim ruler at the time was sufficiently powerful so as to be held in high regard by the regime governing the ship.[123]

Nationals sailing on foreign-flagged vessels pose problems for the application of the law and the need to assure their protection during an

122 In the second century, Emperor Antoninus Pius (138–161 CE) issued an Imperial Edict adopting the Rhodian Law as the genuine and authoritative reference and an expression of uniformity in maritime law when judging cases and claims arising within Rome's maritime domain and concerning Roman citizens in foreign territories. The Rhodian Sea Law was incorporated in the Romano-Byzantine legal codices, the Digest and the Basilika. Antoninus declared: "I, indeed, am Lord of the world, but the law is lord of the sea. Let it be judged by Rhodian Law, prescribed concerning nautical matters, so far as no one of our laws is opposed." Robert D. Benedict, "The Historical Position of the Rhodian Law," *Yale Law Journal* 18 (1909), 233; Khalilieh, *Admiralty and Maritime Laws*, 70, 73, 78–81; Khalilieh, *Islamic Maritime Law*, 42–45; Khalilieh, "Legal Aspects from a Cairo Geniza *Responsum*," 190–193; Samuel P. Scott (ed.), *Las Siete Partidas* (Philadelphia: University of Pennsylvania Press, 2001), 2:327: "The captains, and all others with him (admiral) in the fleet or the armada, should obey his commands, and acknowledge his superiority, just as they would that of the king."

123 Muḥammad A. Bazzāz, "Ḥawl Naql al-Baḥriyya al-Masīḥiyya li-Ḥujjāj al-Gharb al-Islāmī," in *l'occident musulman et l'occident chrétien au Moyen Âge*, ed. Mohammed Hammam (Rabat: Faculté des lettres et des sciences humaines, Muḥammad al-Khāmis University, 1995), 81–92. Shippers, passengers, and pilgrims of different nationalities and religions eventually realized that they had to abide by the flag-state shipping regulations. Nonetheless, this did not prevent them from sailing aboard European Christian-owned vessels in the Mediterranean arena. The Andalusian judge and traveler Ibn Jubayr (540–614/1145–1217), as an example, embarked on a Genoese vessel in his eastbound and westbound passages. During his westbound passage from ʿAkkā (Acre) to Sicily, he draws attention to the differences between Islamic and Christian maritime traditions and laws in reference to the deceased's property at sea. He reports: "Throughout all these days we had seen no land – may God soon dispel our cares – and two Muslims died – may God have mercy on them. They were thrown into the sea. Of the [Christian] pilgrims two died also, and were followed thereafter by many others. One fell alive into the sea, and the waves carried him off more quickly than a flash of lightning. The captain of the ship inherited the effects of the departed Muslims and Christian pilgrims, for such is their custom for all who die at sea. There is no way for the [true] heir of the deceased to recover his inheritance, and at this we were much astonished." Ibn Jubayr, *Travels*, 329. The European Christian tradition of seizing the deceased's property by the shipmaster is also instituted in their legal codices. Stanley S. Jados, *Consulate of the Sea and Related Documents* (Tuscaloosa: University of Alabama Press, 1975), 66–68, articles 118 and 121.

entire journey. Regarding the application of the law, a captain is regarded as the paramount authority over a vessel and her contents, crew, and travelers while at sea, irrespective of their nationalities and religious affiliations; all must comply with the captain's instructions and with the shipping regulations of his flag state. The flag state exercises jurisdiction not merely over the ship, her own nationals, and their property, but also over foreigners and their property while on board. In the event of unlawful acts being committed on board, the captain has the right to imprison the culprits until the ship reaches the nearest port, or her destination, or returns to her home port. However, the captain is not authorized to act as a judge. Roman law dictates that if legal transgressions occur while en route, then the parties involved must be brought before provincial judicial authorities at the port of destination.[124]

Under Islamic law, if a controversy occurs between a lessee and lessor, local judicial authorities at the destination have the right to prosecute the case on the condition that the qadi be fair and just, and apply Islamic law. However, if a controversy arises among the passengers themselves, it may be settled in any Islamic territory, provided that the judge be evenhanded and the venue be accessible to all parties concerned.[125] If Muslim disputants sail for a foreign country, any lawsuit should be brought before a Muslim qadi. In the absence of an Islamic judicial authority, Muslim disputants may appeal to any Islamic court elsewhere. If a dispute arises between a Muslim party and an alien on board a ship that is heading for her home port or to another foreign country, it must be adjudicated at the destination, or as stipulated within any active treaties.[126]

Human perils – pirates, privateers, or enemy vessels – lurking near ports and major trade routes, could harass commercial ships and prevent them from departing, resulting in financial loss to one or both parties to a shipping contract, and to the relevant state. If a raid were to take place

[124] Scott (ed.), *Civil Law*, 15:168. Maritime traditions of classical Athens, however, establish that the judicial hearing in cases involving disputants of different nationalities is not determined by the national jurisdiction or the flag of convenience, but by the place where the shipping/leasing contracts have been signed. Kathleen M. Atkinson, "Rome and the Rhodian Sea-Law," *Iura* 25 (1974), 58–59.

[125] Burzulī, *Jāmiʿ Masāʾil al-Aḥkām*, 3:654–655; Wansharīsī, *Al-Miʿyār*, 8:304–305; Khalilieh, *Islamic Maritime Law*, 150–151; Khalilieh, *Admiralty and Maritime Laws*, 178–180.

[126] Amari, *Diplomi Arabi*, 127 (article 5 of the Ḥafṣīd–Pisan peace treaty of 800/1397), 141 (article 5 of the Ḥafṣīd–Pisan peace treaty of 817/1414), 155 (article 5 of the 824/1421 multilateral peace treaty concluded between the Ḥafṣīds, Pisa, and Florence).

against a vessel while within a state's inland waters, internal waters, or territorial sea, then that state was held liable for the safety and security of the vessel.[127] In order to minimize financial losses and create favorable conditions for overseas trade, sovereigns and political entities negotiated treaties mandating naval escorts for traders, travelers, and their goods, when traveling between regions party to the treaties. Article 9 of al-Ẓāhir Baybars's treaty with the Hospitallers (669/1271) stipulates:

(It is) provided also that traveling merchants and wayfarers with merchandise from the territories of the Muslims and Christians shall proceed on leaving the harbors specified above under the escort of the two parties without any fee. Nothing shall be accepted on account of the escort as regards themselves until it has brought them out and produced them safe and secure at the land boundaries of al-Marqab.[128]

When merchants arrive from the Sultan's realm at the territory and harbors of al-Marqab, both parties are to organize the escort with the headmen being responsible for guarding the routes both on leaving and arriving, so that they may come to the territory of al-Marqab and the harbors of al-Marqab specified above safe and sound in respect of themselves and their chattels, under escort of both parties as we have set forth.[129]

Uncontested Waters: Navigational Regimes in the Eastern Seas

Whereas, since the advent of Islam, the regime of navigation, mobility rights, and trade relations in the Mediterranean Sea have been regulated by international treaties and the issuance of safe-conduct pledges, Islamic ruling circles seem to have played only a marginal role in administering

127 Samuel M. Stern, "Three Petitions of the Fatimid Period," *Oriens* 15 (1962), 172–178, TS Arabic Box 42, f. 158; Geoffrey Khan, *Arabic Legal and Administrative Documents in the Cambridge Genizah Collections* (Cambridge: Cambridge University Press, 1993), 330–331 [74], TS Arabic 42.158.

128 Built by Muslims in 1061–1062 CE as a coastal fortress, the Castle of al-Marqab, located in Syria, south of the port city of Banyās, lies only 2 kilometers from the Mediterranean. Its strategic position enabled regiments to maintain control over the coastal and offshore routes between Ṭarṭūs and Latakia. In 1104, the Byzantine Admiral Kantakuzenos captured it. From 1116 until its fall in 1285 into Baybars's hands, the castle remained under the control of the Crusaders. Peter M. Holt, "Mamluk-Frankish Diplomatic Relations in the Reign of Qalāwūn (678–89/1279–90)," *Journal of the Royal Asiatic Society* (New Series) 121 (1989), 280, 287.

129 Holt, *Early Mamluk Diplomacy*, 53. Similar clauses can be found in the 682/1283 treaty of al-Manṣūr Qalāwūn with the Latin Kingdom (article 21), and with the 684/1285 treaty between the same sultan and King Leon III of Lesser Armenia (article 4). Both treaties require its signatories to provide escort to merchants and wayfarers to the boundaries of their home territories. Holt, *Early Mamluk Diplomacy*, 86, 99.

navigation in the eastern seas. Instead, they were concerned with creating hospitable environments for facilitating trade locally, regionally, and globally.[130] The navigational rights and freedoms enjoyed in the two semienclosed bodies of water – the Red Sea and the Persian Gulf – paralleled the regime of navigation on the high seas, even though both bodies of water were described as "Islamic lakes." With the ascendancy of the Abbasid dynasty and the establishment of its capital city in Baghdad, the new caliphate embraced a foreign policy less oriented toward the Mediterranean and more toward the eastern world, namely India, Southeast Asia, and China. Major voyages from chief Persian Gulf port cities reached as far as Guangzhou (Canton). The trade routes by sea, or rivers, and over land made the Persian Gulf's warm and shallow waters one of the most vital and active shipping lanes in the world at that time.[131] In order to guard against human threats that existed throughout the Persian Gulf and thereby to enhance the regional, interregional, and overseas trade, generating greater tax and customs revenues, the ruling authorities ceaselessly combatted piracy through a variety of defensive and offensive measures.[132]

A similar maritime policy governed the Red Sea. Following the 358/969 Fatimid conquest of Egypt and the relocation of the capital from al-Mahdiyya in modern-day Tunisia to the newly founded city of Cairo, the Indian Ocean maritime activities gradually shifted from the Persian Gulf to the Red Sea.[133] Expansion of the Fatimids into the Red Sea region

130 Anand, *Origin and Development of the Law of the Sea*, 51.

131 Hourani, *Arab Seafaring*, 61–79; Chaudhuri, *Trade and Civilization in the Indian Ocean*, 44–45, 51; Gerald R. Tibbetts, "Early Muslim Traders in South-East Asia," *Journal of the Malayan Branch of the Royal Asiatic Society* 30 (1957), 1–2, 5–6, 10–11; Alpers, *Indian Ocean*, 41, 48–49, 54, 57–58; Alain George, "Direct Sea Trade between Early Islamic Iraq and Tang China: From the Exchange of Goods to the Transmission of Ideas," *Journal of the Royal Asiatic Society* 25 (2015), 592–599; S. Anas, "In Search of Medieval Asian Seafarers and Islamic World System," *International Journal of South Asian Studies* 5 (2012), 48–49.

132 ʿAbd al-Jabbār Nājī, "Dirāsa Muqārana lil-Aḥwāl al-Tijāriyya li-Mawāniʾ al-Khalīj al-ʿArabī wa'l-Jazīra al-ʿArabiyya fī al-Qarn al-Rābiʿ al-Hijrī," *Majallat Dirāsāt al-Khalīj wa'l-Jazīra al-ʿArabiyya* 14 (1988), 173–198.

133 On the shift of the economic center from Baghdad to Cairo in the late tenth century, the contemporary geographer al-Muqaddasī writes: "Know further that Baghdad was once a magnificent city, but is now fast falling to ruin and decay, and has lost all its splendor, I did not find it a pleasant place or an attractive city; and any eulogy of mine regarding it is merely conventional. The Fusṭāṭ of Miṣr in the present day is like the Baghdad of old; I know of no city in Islam superior to it." Abū ʿAbd Allāh Muḥammad ibn Aḥmad al-Muqaddasī, *Aḥsan al-Taqāsīm fī Maʿrifat al-Aqālīm*, ed. and trans. G. S. A. Ranking and R. F. Azoo (Calcutta: Asiatic Society of Bengal, 1897), 51.

stemmed principally from religious ideologies – namely propagation of the Shiite doctrine – and also economic motivations. By the 1030s, the Fatimids – and after them the Ayyubids and the Mamluks – dominated the African and Arabian coasts of the Red Sea, asserting Egyptian hegemony over the Red Sea region. From the early eleventh century onward, most East–West maritime trade passed through the Red Sea and Nile Valley. No ruling dynasty could allow obstruction of the Red Sea trade, as interruption of the flow of coveted commodities to the eastern Mediterranean would have reduced state tariff income. Therefore, it became an essential Egyptian interest to safeguard merchants, shippers, cargoes, and vessels. Each ruling dynasty maintained naval bases in Aden and other port cities, equipped seagoing vessels with armed personnel, provided naval escorts, and established sites for coastal surveillance and refuge along the Red Sea.[134]

Until the time of Europe's colonial expansion into the eastern hemisphere and its "politicization of oceanic space," a phrase coined by Elizabeth Mancke,[135] the Indian Ocean had been shared by three great and diverse cultural traditions, each of which played a predominant role in the world economy. Islam overlooked the Indian Ocean from the Persian Gulf and the Red Sea; India's influence extended throughout the Indian Ocean; and China bordered the Pacific to the East. Janet Abu Lughod argues persuasively that the boundaries between these major cultures were not established by imperial reach, but by natural forces, namely the monsoon wind patterns that separated the three zones.[136] Supporting Abu Lughod's argument, Françoise Vergès writes:

> From early on, the Indian Ocean presented elements of unity: the role of the monsoon winds, the creation of cosmopolitan port cities with a large degree of

[134] Hassan S. Khalilieh, "The *Ribāṭ* System and Its Role in Coastal Navigation," *Journal of the Economic and Social History of the Orient* 42 (1999), 218–219; Hassan S. Khalilieh, "Security Protection and Naval Escort during the 10th and 12th Centuries in the Islamic Mediterranean," *Graeco-Arabica* 7–8 (2000), 224–225; Sālim, *Al-Baḥr al-Aḥmar fī al-Tārīkh al-Islāmī*, 81–97; Bramoullé, "Fatimids and the Red Sea," 127–136; Geoff Wade, "An Early Age of Commerce in Southeast Asia, 900–1300 CE," *Journal of Southeast Asian Studies* 40 (2009), 232–233; Randall L. Pouwels, "Eastern Africa and the Indian Ocean to 1800: Reviewing Relations in Historical Perspective," *International Journal of African Historical Studies* 35 (2002): 396; Alpers, *Indian Ocean*, 41, 54–55, 58; Pearson, *Indian Ocean*, 96; Margariti, *Aden and the Indian Ocean Trade*, 154; Agius, *Classic Ships of Islam*, 95–98; Anas, "In Search of Medieval Asian Seafarers," 49; Tibbetts, "Early Muslim Traders in South-East Asia," 12–13, 43.

[135] Elizabeth Mancke, "Early Modern Expansion and Politicization of Oceanic Space," *Geographical Review* 89 (1999), 225–236.

[136] Abu Lughod, *Before European Hegemony*, 253; Sebastian R. Prange, "Scholars and the Sea: A Historiography of the Indian Ocean," *History Compass* 6/5 (2008), 1383.

autonomy for their hinterland, the kind of ships that sailed the ocean, transcontinental trade, and piracy. It was a world of encounters and flows between the Islamic world and Africa, Africa and Asia, between Asian and African continents, and the islands of the Ocean.[137]

Ostensibly, as a unique atmospheric phenomenon, the monsoon cycle of the Indian Ocean generated unity along its littoral despite the significant sheer diversity of geography, culture, and religion. Derived from the Arabic *mawsim* (season), the word monsoon identifies a large-scale seasonal wind system, which reverses direction every six months with the change of season, emanating from the southwest in the summer and the northeast in the winter. Both Arab and Persian sailors and traders utilized monsoon routes to establish regular seasonal trade routes. They sailed eastward from their home ports in South Arabia and Persia to all major harbors of South and East Asia from around April to September, and reversed their course westward from October to March.[138]

Aside from its natural uniqueness, the importance of the monsoon lies in its social and economic impacts on the coastal societies along the shores of the Indian Ocean. Near Eastern mariners and merchants had to stay put in their ports of destination for long periods between the two monsoon cycles. These long sojourns emerged as a crucial facilitator of social, commercial, cultural, and personal interactions between visiting merchants and the indigenous populations, transforming the Indian Ocean into a uniquely harmonious space.[139]

137 Françoise Vergès, "Writing on Water: Peripheries, Flows, Capital, and Struggles in the Indian Ocean," *Positions* 11 (2003), 247–248.

138 Brian Fagan, *Beyond the Blue Horizon: How the Earliest Mariners Unlocked the Secrets of the Oceans* (London: Bloomsbury, 2012), 111–116; Eivind H. Seland, "The Indian Ships at Moscha and the Indo-Arabian Trading Circuit," *Proceedings of the Seminar for Arabian Studies* 38 (2008), 284; Agius, *Classic Ships of Islam*, 187–190; P. J. Rivers, "Monsoon Rhythms and Trade Patterns: Ancient Times East of Suez," *Journal of the Malaysian Branch of the Royal Asiatic Society* 77 (2004), 68–71; Gerald R. Tibbetts, "Pre-Islamic Arabia and South-East Asia," *Journal of the Malayan Branch of the Royal Asiatic Society* 29 (1956), 183–191; Philip D. Curtin, *Cross-Cultural Trade in World History* (Cambridge: Cambridge University Press, 1984), 108; Deng Hui and Li Xin, "The Asian Monsoons and Zheng He's Voyages to the Western Ocean," *Journal of Navigation* 64 (2011), 207–218; Sila Tripati and L. N. Raut, "Monsoon Wind and Maritime Trade: A Case Study of Historical Evidence from Orissa, India," *Current Science* 90 (2006), 864–871; Pouwels, "Eastern Africa and the Indian Ocean to 1800," 385–387; Sutherland, "Geography as Destiny," 29–30.

139 Philippe Beaujard, "The Indian Ocean in Eurasian and African World-Systems before the Sixteenth Century," *Journal of World History* 16 (2005), 411; Prange, "Scholars and the Sea," 1384–1385; Sheriff, *Dhow Culture*, 22–23.

During the pre-Islamic period, Near Eastern seafarers and traders already played leading roles in transoceanic commerce. However, beginning with the rise of Islam – or more accurately during the early years of the Abbasid caliphate – Muslims not only influenced transoceanic trade more significantly, but also laid the foundations for profound cultural, socioreligious, and economic changes that would take place throughout the Indian Ocean basin. Burgeoning Muslim commercial activities were accompanied by a gradual spread of the new faith due to the profound growth of Muslim communities in coastal trading centers throughout the Indian subcontinent, Southeast Asia, and East Africa.[140] By the late fifteenth century, transoceanic shipping, trade, and markets in the western Indian Ocean as a whole were dominated by Muslim entrepreneurs.[141] Because of Muslim dominance in overseas shipping and trade and the acute impact of Islam on many cultural zones in the Indian Ocean, contemporary scholars do not hesitate to call it the "Arab Mediterranean,"[142] and the "Muslim lake."[143]

Whereas the spread of Islam in the Mediterranean world was generally due to military campaigns, territorial enlargement, and the efforts of missionaries, expansion into the arena of the Indian Ocean arose largely from the growth and development of commercial networks. The propagation here of Islam occurred through trading contacts, peaceful preaching, and the activities of Sufis and missionaries. These endeavors paved the way for voluntary conversion, or more precisely, for the acceptance and adoption of Islam's doctrine. Diasporic mercantile communities participated actively in the gradual religious conversion to Islam of most of the indigenous coastal populations over the course of a few centuries, from the second half of the seventh century CE onward.[144]

[140] Wade, "Early Age of Commerce in Southeast Asia," 260.

[141] Curtin, *Cross-Cultural Trade*, 106–107; Sanjay Subrahmanyam, "Of Imārat and Tijārat: Asian Merchants and State Power in the Western Indian Ocean, 1400 to 1750," *Comparative Studies in Society and History* 37 (1995), 754.

[142] Muttayil G. S. Narayanan, *Cultural Symbiosis in Kerala* (Trivandrum: Kerala Historical Society, 1972), 65; André Wink, *Al-Hind: The Making of the Indo-Islamic World* (Leiden: E. J. Brill, 1991), 1:65, 2:1; Wade, "Early Age of Commerce in Southeast Asia," 231; M. H. Ilias, "Mappila Muslims and the Cultural Content of Trading Arab Diaspora on the Malabar Coast," *Asian Journal of Social Science* 35 (2007), 441.

[143] Sheriff, *Dhow Culture*, 239; Pearson, *Indian Ocean*, 95; Kenneth McPherson, "Cultural Exchange in the Indian Ocean Region," *Westerly* 4 (1984), 13.

[144] Kenneth McPherson, "Processes of Cultural Interchange in the Indian Ocean Region: An Historical Perspective," *Great Circle* 6 (1984), 82; McPherson, "Cultural Exchange," 10; Curtin, *Cross-Cultural Trade*, 107; Pearson, *Indian Ocean*, 62.

This widespread conversion can be attributed to various factors. First and foremost was the dominance by Muslims of cross-continental trade. Sharing the same faith, the same sacred language (Arabic), and to a great extent many cultural traditions, Muslims controlled almost all ports and trade throughout the littoral of the Indian Ocean. This dominance may explain why a considerable proportion of the populations of port cities adopted the new faith at a faster rate than did those in inland cities and towns. Once a key trading city converted, other port cities and independent polities would quickly follow suit in order to enhance personal ties and install Islamic law to regulate business transactions. Another likely factor contributing to the spread of Islam was its tolerance of local traditions, whereby new converts were not required to cast aside or replace their preexisting customs and beliefs but could simply shift from one defined religion to another. A third driving force for conversion may have stemmed from the egalitarian ethos and universality of Islam. As Islam advocates universal equality among its adherents – regardless of ethnic, racial, geographical, or socioeconomic backgrounds – who comprise a single community (the *ummah*), the religious, social, and economic cohesion of Muslims grew on local, regional, and transregional levels.[145] In summary, by the sixteenth century, the Islamic faith conjoined different oceanic spaces, coastal regions, ethnic groups, cultures, and languages into a unified mercantile system and homogeneous maritime environment.

From a naval perspective, the human and physical unity of the Indian Ocean also owed a significant debt to the relative absence of major naval encounters between the littoral entities within maritime space. In contrast to the Mediterranean world, none of the coastal empires, states, and

[145] McPherson, "Cultural Exchange," 10–12; Pearson, *Indian Ocean*, 62, 76–77; Pearson, "Islamic Trade, Shipping, Port-States and Merchant Communities," 3:328, 329–330, 333–334; Alpers, *Indian Ocean*, 47, 60–61; Ilias, "Mappila Muslims," 442; André Wink, "From the Mediterranean to the Indian Ocean: Medieval History in Geographic Perspective," *Comparative Studies in Society and History* 44 (2002), 436–437; Anas, "In Search of Medieval Asian Seafarers," 44, 47, 50–53; Roxani E. Margariti, "Mercantile Networks, Port Cities, and "Pirate" States: Conflict and Competition in the Indian Ocean World of Trade before the Sixteenth Century," *Journal of the Economic and Social History of the Orient* 51 (2008), 547–549; Risso, *Merchants and Faith*, 18, 51; Vincent J. H. Houben, "Southeast Asia and Islam," *Annals of the American Academy of Political and Social Science* 588 (2003), 153–154; David O. Morgan and Anthony Reid, "Introduction: Islam in a Plural Asia," in *The New Cambridge History of Islam*, ed. David O. Morgan and Anthony Reid (Cambridge: Cambridge University Press, 2010), 3:8–9; Peter Borschberg, "Another Look at Law and Business in the Late Malacca Sultanate, c.1450–1511," in *East Asia Maritime Regional Networks and Port City Societies*, ed. Zheng Yangchang (Taipei: Le Jin Books, 2015), 499.

principalities attempted to control or claim sovereignty over the vast ocean. Nonetheless, historical records highlight sporadic naval conflicts, particularly those involving the thalassocratic Kingdom of Srivijaya, the Cholas, and the early fifteenth-century Chinese Muslim Admiral Zheng He (Cheng Ho), who launched seven spectacular maritime expeditions. Founded around 650 CE in the Palembang area of eastern Sumatra, Srivijaya controlled both the Sunda Strait and the Strait of Malacca in its heyday, despite commanding relatively weak fleets. However, the Srivijayan fleets had not been established to pursue naval ambitions; rather, they primarily provided logistical support to the state's land-based power and suppressed piracy. Most crucially, the fleets maintained a heterogeneous confederation of trade emporia on the island of Sumatra and the Malay Peninsula.[146]

By the early eleventh century, commercial activities in the Indian Ocean became more contentious, in part because of the attempts by the Srivijayan confederation to dominate commercial exchanges conducted within the Strait of Malacca. The Chola (Cōḷa) dynasty of Tamil Nadu in southern India (from the eleventh to the thirteenth centuries) simultaneously became interested in expanding its commercial and political spheres in the Indian Ocean and accessing markets in Song dynasty China. Under the successive leaderships of Rajaraja I (r. 985–1014), Rajendra I (r. 1014–1044), and Rajadhiraja I (r. 1044–1054), Chola forces invaded Sri Lanka and sacked a number of neighboring kingdoms. Between 1017 and 1025, the Chola navy took an interest in the lucrative maritime trade of Southeast Asia and launched unprecedented expeditions against Srivijayan towns, seizing the capital city of Palembang and looting key ports in the Malay Peninsula and Sumatra. Chola's commercially motivated naval campaigns led to the establishment of Tamil-speaking communities in Southern China and Southeast Asia, furnishing the

146 Sebastian R. Prange, "The Contested Sea: Regimes of Maritime Violence in the Pre-Modern Indian Ocean," *Journal of Early Modern History* 17 (2013), 14–15; Derek Heng, "State Formation and the Evolution of Naval Strategies in the Melaka Straits, c. 500–1500 C.E.," *Journal of Southeast Asian Studies* 44 (2013), 383–394, 399; Craig A. Lockard, "'The Sea Common to All'; Maritime Frontiers, Port Cities, and Chinese Traders in the Southeast Asian Age of Commerce, ca. 1400–1750," *Journal of World History* 21 (2010), 226; Craig A. Lockard, "Integrating Southeast Asia into the Framework of World History: The Period before 1500," *History Teacher* 29 (1995), 22–23; Curtin, *Cross-Cultural Trade*, 107; Pearson, *Indian Ocean*, 124. Only around the beginning of the end of the kingdom of Srivijaya, during the latter part of the thirteenth century, did native Sumatrans of the northern part of the island begin adopting the faith of Islam.

Tamil merchants with favorable trading conditions throughout the eastern Indian Ocean.[147]

Another apparent maritime threat emanated from China's Ming dynasty (1368–1644). Commanding 317 ships – manned by 27,870 sailors, soldiers, clerks, interpreters, physicians, scholars, and artisans – in 1405, Admiral Zheng He (1371–1433)[148] unleashed an unparalleled armada on the Indian Ocean. It reached Sri Lanka before turning homeward in 1407. Six subsequent expeditions followed, between 1408 and 1433, setting sail toward Southeast Asia, South Asia, Western Asia, and East Africa. The question of what motivated the Ming dynasty to launch such costly and extensive expeditions over a period of almost three decades (1405–1433) has attracted wide speculation. One theory holds that the first expedition was launched to search for traces of the emperor deposed by Yongle in 1402.[149] However, this would not justify the outfitting and launching of such a massive armada. Another theory suggests that the Ming dynasty intended to outflank and inhibit Tamerlane's army to the east by cultivating friendships and alliances with other countries. A third argument is that these expeditions were aimed at restoring peace and order and suppressing piracy in the Strait of Malacca. A fourth view suggests that the objective was to aggrandize the Ming dynasty's reputation and to exert Chinese influence over foreign countries and nations. A fifth explanation proposes that the expeditions simply intended to promote friendship between China and other countries. A sixth motive could have been to procure "treasure" (tribute) for the Ming court. A seventh

[147] Tansen Sen, "The Military Campaigns of Rajendra Chola and the Chola-Srivijaya-China Triangle," in *Nagapattinam to Suvarnadwipa: Reflections on the Chola Naval Expeditions to Southeast Asia*, ed. Hermann Kulke *et al.* (Singapore: Institute of Southeast Asian Studies, 2009), 61–75; Pearson, *Indian Ocean*, 87–88; Prange, "Contested Sea," 13–16; Wade, "Early Age of Commerce in Southeast Asia," 225, 227, 232–233, 236–238, 246, 251, 255, 262; Heng, "State Formation and the Evolution of Naval Strategies," 385–388, 390, 393; Ramesh C. Majumdar, "The Overseas Expeditions of King Rājendra Cola," *Artibus Asiae* 24 (1961), 338–342; Kenneth R. Hall, "Local and International Trade and Traders in the Straits of Melaka Region: 600–1500," *Journal of the Economic and Social History of the Orient* 47 (2004), 216–218, 220, 224, 244; Risha Lee, "Constructing Community: Tamil Merchant Temples in India and China, 850–1281," (PhD diss., Columbia University, 2012), 17, 19–21, 33, 44, 134.

[148] Zheng He is known in Arabic as Ḥajjī Maḥmūd Shams, and in Southeast Asia as Cheng Ho.

[149] Emperor Yongle was the third emperor of the Ming dynasty. He was born in 1360 and ruled between 1402 and 1424. http://afe.easia.columbia.edu/special/china_1000ce_mingvoyages.htm.

proposed aim involved establishing a Chinese commonwealth, whose goal was to maintain the flow of tribute and to pursue alliances with countries friendly with China. Finally, the expeditions may have served as commercial enterprises, aimed at strengthening government control of overseas trade and commerce, promoting Chinese mercantile networks in Southeast Asia and the Islamic western Indian Ocean.[150] All of these seven expeditions left their mark, not only on Chinese maritime history but also on world history.

Scholars generally acknowledge that Zheng He's maritime missions were peaceful in intent,[151] although some contend that his voyages stemmed from Ming colonial ambitions.[152] Even so, Zheng He's expeditions bear no similarity to Europe's maritime ventures, which resulted in control of the world's oceans from the sixteenth century onward.

[150] Robert Finlay, "The Treasure-Ships of Zheng He: Chinese Maritime Imperialism in the Age of Discovery," *Terrae Incognitae* 23 (1991), 5–6; Tansen Sen, "The Formation of Chinese Maritime Networks to Southern Asia, 1200–1450," *Journal of the Economic and Social History of the Orient* 49 (2006), 422–423, 437, 443, 445; Aurora Roxas-Lim, "Historical and Cultural Significance of Admiral Zheng He's Ocean Voyages," *Asian Studies Journal* 39 (2003), 32, 34; Barbara B. Peterson, "The Ming Voyages of Cheng Ho (Zheng He), 1371–1433," *Great Circle* 16 (1994), 43–51; Sutherland, "Geography as Destiny," 38; Geoff Wade, "Early Expansion in South East Asia, Eighth to Fifteenth Centuries," in *The New Cambridge History of Islam: The Eastern Islamic World – Eleventh to Eighteenth Centuries*, ed. David O. Morgan and Anthony Reid (Cambridge: Cambridge University Press, 2010), 3:391–392; John V. Mills, "Arab and Chinese Navigators in Malaysian Waters in about A.D. 1500," *Journal of the Malaysian Branch of the Royal Asiatic Society* 47 (1974), 8–9; Hyunhee Park, *Mapping the Chinese and Islamic Worlds: Cross-Cultural Exchange in Pre-modern Asia* (Cambridge: Cambridge University Press, 2012), 161–162, 169–180; Su Chung-Jen, "The Expeditions of Cheng Ho to the Western Ocean," (PhD diss., University of Hong Kong, 1964), 118–120, 133–134, 137–142; Haraprasad Ray, "An Analysis of the Chinese Maritime Voyages into the Indian Ocean during Early Ming Dynasty and their *raison d'etre*," *China Report* 23 (1987), 67–73. In addition to Su's dissertation, for comprehensive research wholly dedicated to the expeditions of Zheng He, see Edward L. Dreyer, *Zheng He: China and the Oceans in the Early Ming Dynasty, 1405–1433* (New York: Pearson Longman, 2007); Louise Levathes, *When China Ruled the Seas: The Treasure Fleet of the Dragon Throne, 1405–1433* (New York and Oxford: Oxford University Press, 1994).

[151] Joseph Needham and Colin A. Ronan, *The Shorter Science and Civilisation in China* (Cambridge: Cambridge University Press, 1986), 3:132, characterize the seven expeditions as "fundamentally peaceful"; Joseph Needham, *Science and Civilisation in China* (Cambridge: Cambridge University Press, 1971), 4:479.

[152] Geoff Wade, "The Zheng He Voyages: A Reassessment," *Journal of the Malaysian Branch of the Royal Asiatic Society* 78 (2005), 44–51; Sen, "Formation of Chinese Maritime Networks," 423.

Over the course of three decades, Zheng He journeyed over the western and eastern waters of the Indian Ocean without making any attempt at military conquest. His expeditions never established colonial territories, a fact explaining the abrupt withdrawal of China from the maritime scene shortly after Zheng He's death in 1433. Furthermore, China never showed any interest in imposing its cultural heritage and religious traditions upon foreign sovereigns, including those who came under its influence or joined its commonwealth. Furthermore, the expeditions established no new shipping lanes, nor trading hubs; no existing seaborne commerce was challenged, nor was there any attempt to monopolize regional or international trade, or to enforce global unity, whether by soft diplomacy or the use of force. However, the expeditions did stimulate maritime trade exchanges and establish friendly ties between China and Southeast Asia, the Indian archipelago, and the Muslim world in the western Indian Ocean.[153]

In addition to the peaceful purposes of the Ming expeditions, scholars have suggested that Malacca's conversion to Islam during the Sultanate of Megat Iskandar Shah (r. 817–828/1414–1424)[154] can largely be accredited to Zheng He and his fellow Muslim officers, albeit that Chinese historical records contain no conclusive evidence as to their particular role in spreading the Word of God in the Malay Peninsula. Geostrategic considerations, rather than any personal interest of Zheng He, may have propelled China to encourage elites and common populations to convert to Islam. Established around 1400, the independent Sultanate of Malacca became a pivotal Muslim trade emporium circa 1413. The Ming dynasty supported it with the aim of broadening China's influence in the Strait of Malacca, buttressing a competing power against the Hindus of Java, enhancing the interconnections between China and Southeast Asia, expanding East–West Indian Ocean maritime trade, and combating piracy in the Strait of Malacca.[155]

[153] Anthony Reid, "Flows and Seepages in the Long-Term Chinese Interaction with Southeast Asia," in *Sojourners and Settlers: Histories of Southeast Asia and Chinese in Honour of Jennifer Cushman*, ed. Anthony Reid (St Leonards, NSW: Allen and Unwin, 1996), 26–28; Sutherland, "Geography as Destiny," 30, 38; Lockard, "The Sea Common to All," 227–228; Robert Finlay, "Portuguese and Chinese Maritime Imperialism: Camoes's Lusiads and Luo Maodeng's Voyage of the San Bao Eunuch," *Comparative Studies in Society and History* 34 (1992), 230.

[154] Richard O. Winstedt, "The Malay Founder of Medieval Malacca," *Bulletin of the School of Oriental and African Studies* 12 (1948), 726–729; Fang, *Undang-undang Melaka*, 44, 178.

[155] Kenneth R. Hall, *A History of Early Southeast Asia: Maritime Trade and Societal Development, 100–1500* (Lanham: Rowman and Littlefield Publishers, 2011), 308–309; Alexander Wain, "Chinese Muslims and the Conversion of Melaka to Islam," *International Proceedings of Economics Development and Research* 51 (2012), 35–40;

The support of the Ming dynasty led the humble coastal village of Malacca to become an independent sultanate, rising to regional prominence in the early fifteenth century. Malacca's emergence as one of the most vital entrepôts and commercial emporia on the Strait of Malacca stimulated a group of distinguished *nakhodas* to compile and codify a set of laws known as the *Undang-undang Laut Melaka* (Maritime Codes of Malacca), which regulated commerce, carriage of goods and passengers by water, and navigation on the high seas and into ports.[156] The *Undang-*

Jean G. Taylor, "The Chinese and the Early Centuries of Conversion to Islam in Indonesia," in *Chinese Indonesians: Remembering, Distorting, Forgetting*, ed. Tim Lindsey and Helen Pausacker (Melbourne: Monash University Press, 2005), 149; Wang Gungwu, "The First Three Rulers of Malacca," *Journal of the Malaysian Branch of the Royal Asiatic Society* 41 (1968), 17–22; Tan Ta Sen, *Cheng Ho and Islam in Southeast Asia* (Singapore: Institute of Southeast Asian Studies, 2009), 179, 249–250; Christopher H. Wake, "Malacca's Early Kings and the Reception of Islam," *Journal of Southeast Asian History* 5 (1964), 116–119; Emrys Chew, "Crouching Tiger, Hidden Dragon: The Indian Ocean and the Maritime Balance of Power in Historical Perspective," (Singapore: The S. Rajaratnam School of International Studies, 2007: 2–5, in www.rsis.edu.sg/wp-content/uploads/rsis-pubs/WP144.pdf; Morgan and Reid, "Introduction: Islam in a Plural Asia," 3:8–10; Wade, "Early Expansion in South East Asia," 3:391–392; Mills, "Arab and Chinese Navigators in Malaysian Waters," 8. Mills, who is considered a leading authority on the Chinese maritime history of the fifteenth century, assumes that Admiral Zheng He made at least five visits to Malacca, if not more.

156 "These rules arise from the rules of Patih Harun and Patih Elias and Nakhoda Zainal and Nakhoda Buri [or Dewi] and Nakhoda Isahak. They were the ones who spoke. Then they discussed it with all the *nakhodas*; after they had discussed it, they went to Dato' Bendahara Sri Maharaja [who obtained the sultan's approval] ... Then titles were bestowed on all these *nakhodas* by Seri Paduka Sultan Mahmud Syah ... Nakhoda Zainal was given the title Sang Nayadiraja, and Nakhoda Dewa was given the title Sang Setiadipati, and a third was given the title Sang Utamadiraja." Raffles, "Maritime Code of the Malays," 63; Winstedt and De Josselin de Jong, "Maritime Laws of Malacca," 45–46, 56–57. The English translation is quoted from Anthony Reid, "Hybrid Identities in the Fifteenth-Century Straits of Malacca," *Asia Research Institute Working Paper* no. 67 (Singapore: Asia Research Institute, National University of Singapore, 2006), 30. The surviving digest that has reached us is dated from Sultan Mahmud Shah (r. 1488–1510 and 1513–1528). However, the actual date of the first draft remains uncertain though the generally accepted theory is that these laws were promulgated during the reign of Sultan Muḥammad Shah (r. 1424–1444) and were completed during the reign of Sultan Muzaffar Shah (r. 1445–1458), when Malacca was at the peak of its splendor. Richard O. Winstedt, "The Date of the Malacca Legal Codes," *Journal of the Royal Asiatic Society of Great Britain and Ireland* 1–2 (1953), 32–33; Fang, *Undang-undang Melaka*, 12, 32–33, 36–38, 178; Yatim, "Development of the Law of the Sea," 87; Mohd Nor *et al.*, "From *Undang-undang Melaka* to Federal Constitution: The Dynamics of Multicultural Malaysia," *SpringerPlus* 5 (2016), 5, 8; Borschberg, "Another Look at Law and Business," 492; Nordin, "Undang-undang Laut Melaka," 15–16; Hall, *History of Early Southeast Asia*, 310–314; Ayang U. Yakin, "Le droit musulman dans le monde insulindien du XIVe au XVIIe siècles," (Paris: École des hautes études en sciences sociales, 2005), 53, 58.

undang Laut Melaka addresses a variety of issues related to internal affairs and organization on board ship, including the professional duties of the *nakhoda, mu'allim*, crew members, and behavioral transgressions that could possibly transpire on board a vessel – adultery, theft, murder, slavery, disrespecting an officer, and so forth. The economic and financial clauses of these laws concern activities taking place in the port of Malacca, payment of taxes and customs, and duties of the harbor master. The *Undang-undang Laut Melaka* also clearly reaffirms the primacy of *adat*, some of which dates back to the pre-Islamic era, while accommodating and assimilating *Sharī'ah* principles.[157] Peter Borschberg suggests that while the Islamic legal provisions applied to Muslims, the *adat* rules were intended to apply to all other seafarers and merchants.[158]

Strikingly absent from the Maritime Codes of Malacca is a broad-based discussion of the sea and of the relationship between vessel and sea. Philip E. Steinberg attributes the omission of ocean-specific laws to the perception among the Indian Ocean littoral polities that the sea comprised distances between places, but not territory. As the territory's social space ends at its coastal waters, the sea could not be conceived of "as a space for exercising imperial dominion."[159] However, a ship can be governed, making the universe of governance the conglomerate of all ships on the ocean.[160] Thus the Maritime Codes of Malacca equate a ship with a state or kingdom, whereas her *nakhoda* is assimilated to the "*raja* (king/ruler) at sea."[161]

[157] Richard O. Winstedt, "Old Malay Legal Digests and Malay Customary Law," *Journal of the Royal Asiatic Society of Great Britain and Ireland* 1 (1945), 18–19; Ismail Hamid, "Islamic Influence on Malay Culture in Malaysia and Indonesia," *Islamic Culture* 56 (1982), 277–278; Jamila Hussain, "More than One Law for All: Legal Pluralism in Southeast Asia," *Democracy and Security* 7 (2011), 375, 378–379; Fang, *Undang-undang Melaka*, 65; Manuel Lobato, "'Melaka Is Like a Cropping Field': Trade Management in the Strait of Melaka during the Sultanate and the Portuguese Period," *Journal of Asian History* 46 (2012), 247–248. Already in the early centuries of the advent of Islam in the Mediterranean, North African Mālikī jurists not only validated existing pre-Islamic customs, but upheld that in certain circumstances customs could even supersede explicit contractual stipulations. Normally, customs and practices were admitted so long as they did not contradict Islamic principles. See Ṭāher, "*Akriyat al-Sufun*," 14; Khalilieh, *Admiralty and Maritime Laws*, 19.

[158] Borschberg, "Another Look at Law and Business," 499–500.

[159] Steinberg, *Social Construction of the Ocean*, 51–52.

[160] Steinberg, *Social Construction of the Ocean*, 51.

[161] Raffles, "Maritime Code of the Malays," 63, 64; Winstedt and De Josselin De Jong, "Maritime Laws of Malacca," 51; Fang, *Undang-undang Melaka*, 79; Nordin, "Undang-undang Laut Melaka," 16; Sheriff, *Dhow Culture*, 126–128.

In the absence of clauses addressing the vessel–sea relationship, the Maritime Codes of Malacca draw an analogy between social hierarchies in land-based societies and those on board ship. While at sea, the *nakhoda* corresponds to the "*hakim* (*ḥākim*),"[162] "*imam*,"[163] or "caliph" on land, enjoying undisputed jurisdiction over the vessel, her contents, and all people on board.[164] This exclusive authority is set aside whenever a vessel enters a hostile marine environment. In such circumstances, the *nakhoda* must take counsel with, heed, and even obey advice from experienced crew members in order to escape danger.[165] As a *raja* at sea, the *nakhoda* is the exclusive sovereign, whereas the *pĕrahu* (vessel) is regarded as a floating extension of her home port when outside any harbor. Likewise, her senior officers, from the captain downward, correspond to state officials on land.[166]

Malacca would not have become a prosperous emporium had its port and strait been treated as *mare clausum*.[167] Arab, Persian, Indian, Chinese, and Indonesian merchants and ships frequented its port and markets freely. Offering a welcoming reception, evidence shows that the Sultan of Malacca never levied tolls on foreign vessels passing through the strait, nor did he compel foreign merchant vessels to call at port.[168]

In short, as with the other long-lasting traditions and practices that prevailed across the Indian Ocean at the dawn of the European naval and trade expansion,[169] the *Undang-undang Laut Melaka* reveals a strong

[162] The strict meaning of *hakim*/*ḥākim* is "ruler, governor, or judge."

[163] Muqaddasī, *Aḥsan al-Taqāsīm*, 11. While on the coast of Aden, al-Muqaddasī happened to meet Abū ʿAlī ibn Ḥāzim, a well-versed and prominent captain who, in addition to commanding a commercial fleet of transoceanic vessels, was known at sea as "the chief of merchants (*imām al-tujjār*)." The literal significance of *imam* is ruler, governor, temporal leader of the Islamic community, or worship leader.

[164] Raffles, "Maritime Code of the Malays," 65–66; Fang, *Undang-undang Melaka*, 79.

[165] Fang, *Undang-undang Melaka*, 77, 79; Raffles, "Maritime Code of the Malays," 65: "The *Malim* shall be as a ruler or judge at sea"; Winstedt and De Josselin de Jong, "Maritime Laws of Malacca," 51; Richard O. Winstedt, "Kedah Law," *Journal of the Malayan Branch of the Royal Asiatic Society* 6 (1928), 10–12; Borschberg, "Another Look at Law and Business," 504–505.

[166] Borschberg, "Another Look at Law and Business," 504–505.

[167] Yatim, "Development of the Law of the Sea," 88.

[168] Yatim, "Development of the Law of the Sea," 89.

[169] Shihāb al-Dīn Aḥmad ibn Mājid ibn ʿUmar al-Najdī, *Kitāb al-Fawāʾid fī Uṣūl ʿIlm al-Baḥr wa'l-Qawāʿid* (Damascus: Al-Maṭbaʿa al-Taʿāwuniyya, 1971), 286; K. M. Kurup and K. M. Mathew, *Native Resistance against the Portuguese: The Saga of Kunjali Marakkars* (Calicut: Calicut University Press, 2000), 39; Lakshmi Subramanian, "Of Pirates and Potentates: Maritime Jurisdiction and the Trade Construction of Piracy in the Indian Ocean," in *Cultures of Trade: Indian Ocean Exchanges*, ed. Devleena Ghosh

concept of the high seas. Charles H. Alexandrowicz succinctly articulates the legal status of the vessel at sea as expressed in such codices:

> The reading of these codes brings to our attention the peculiar position of a ship on the high seas beyond the reach of any territorial jurisdiction. She is treated by maritime custom as a piece of quasiterritory sailing in the legally undefined vastness of the sea, which is beyond any Sovereign's control except for the captain's powers on board ship determined by her "nationality."[170]

WARSHIPS AND NONCOMBATANT IMMUNITY

Significant scholarship has addressed the Islamic *jus ad bellum* and *jus in bello*.[171] Consequently, the next short discussion will focus instead on two major issues. The first is an examination of how Muslims were asked to deal with enemy ships when sighting them off Islamic coastal frontiers or encountering them on the high seas. The second is to outline the legal status and treatment of the *musta'mins* on land and at sea.

The Law of Nature and Nations mandates that the sea be treated as common to all humankind and not susceptible to appropriation by one

and Stephen Muecke (Newcastle: Cambridge Scholars Publishing, 2007), 20. A statement ascribed to Sultan Bahadur Shah of Gujarat (r. 1528–1537) states: "Wars by sea are merchants' affairs and of no concern to the prestige of kings." Evidently, there is a close connection between merchants and the customary law of the sea. Basic elements of the law of the sea were originated by the communities of merchants along the Indian Ocean rim that fitted well with the overseas commercial networks. The role played by the ruling authorities and jurists was, on the whole, rather marginal. Thus, it was the merchant who in practice laid down the principles of freedom of navigation. The major contribution of the rulers was in providing a hospitable environment – infrastructure, protection against pirates, and fair treatment – to merchants found within the jurisdictional domain of the port cities.

170 Alexandrowicz, *Law of the Nations in the East Indies*, 64.

171 Examples of the many works that shed a comprehensive light on *jihad* and war in Islamic law include: Yūsuf al-Qarḍāwī, *Fiqh al-Jihād: Dirāsa Muqārana li-Aḥkāmihi wa-Falsafatihi fī Ḍaw' al-Qur'ān wa'l-Sunnah* (Cairo: Maktabat Wahba, 1430/2009), 2 vols.; Muḥammad Kh. Haykal, *Al-Jihād wa'l-Qitāl fī al-Siyāsa al-Shar'iyyah* (Beirut: Dār al-Bayāriq, 1417/1997), 3 vols.; Muḥammad R. 'Uthmān, *Al-Ḥuqūq wa'l-Wājibāt wa'l-'Alāqāt al-Duwaliyya fī al-Islām* (Beirut: Dār Iqra', 1403/1982), 161–211; Khadduri, *War and Peace*, 51–137; Ahmed M. al-Dawoody, *The Islamic Law of War: Justifications and Regulations* (New York: Palgrave Macmillan, 2011); Takim, "Peace and War in the Qur'ān and Juridical Literature," 137–157; Ali R. Naqvi, "Laws of War in Islam," *Islamic Studies* 13 (1974), 25–43; Reuven Firestone, *Jihad: The Origin of Holy War in Islam* (Berkeley: University of California Press, 2005); Bonner, *Jihad in Islamic History*; John Kelsay, "Al-Shaybani and the Islamic Law of War," *Journal of Military Ethics* 2 (2003), 63–75; Hilmi M. Abdul Rahman, "Just War, Peace, and Human Rights under Islamic and International Law," (master's thesis, McGill University, 1997); Khalilieh, *Islamic Maritime Law*, 116–127.

nation or another. Neither Islamic ruling authorities nor jurists could legally claim Islamic dominion over the high seas. Political boundaries and the long-standing enmity between the Abode of Islam and the Abode of War never constituted an obstacle to freedom of navigation; alien merchants frequented Islamic ports, and, in a similar manner, Muslim merchants dropped anchor in enemy territories. In addition to natural hazards, piracy posed a formidable threat to merchant vessels, irrespective of their flag states. Nevertheless, clearing a sea of piracy did not then empower a state with legal dominion over it.

Although divided between Christian and Muslim dominions, the Mediterranean world recovered much of its unity through merchant activity. Neither the Christian North nor the Muslim South could deny freedom of movement to the other.[172] As noted earlier, times of war and political unrest restricted the *ḥarbīs* to visits of only limited duration or certain localities. Neither political issues nor conflicts ever impeded the freedom of movement on land or at sea for individuals or commodities.[173] This freedom owed its workability to three factors. Perhaps the law relating to the person rather than to territory played the most significant role; an individual was judged according to the law of his community, or even his sect, rather than the law of the territory he inhabited at that particular time. In addition, all the countries around the Mediterranean held in common strong and long-standing traditions that had been established centuries before, during the ancient civilizations. Finally, the bourgeois revolution of the eighth and ninth centuries produced a mercantile civilization around the Mediterranean with prominent merchant citizens. It placed a priority on trade, and thus contributed to free movement generally.[174]

Despite the significant social and cultural diversity, the prevailing conditions in the eastern seas – including along the Indian Ocean littoral –

[172] Goitein, *Mediterranean Society*, 1:42–43, describes the Mediterranean as a "*póntos eúxeinos*" (hospitable sea).

[173] Only during wartime and political disturbance were the visits of foreigners limited in time or confined to certain localities. During his visit to ʿAkkā/Acre in 580/1184, the Andalusian qadi and traveler Ibn Jubayr reports: "The Christians impose a tax on the Muslims in their land, which gives them full security; and, likewise, the Christian merchants pay a tax upon their goods in Muslim lands. Agreement exists between them, and there is equal treatment in all cases. The soldiers engage themselves in their war, while the people are at peace and the world goes to him who conquers." Ibn Jubayr, *Travels*, 301; for this text in Arabic see Ibn Jubayr, *Riḥlat Ibn Jubayr*, 260.

[174] Shelomo D. Goitein, *Studies in Islamic History and Institutions* (Leiden: E. J. Brill, 1968), 299–301.

were more hospitable and peaceful even than in the Mediterranean. The carriage of goods by water supplemented the Central Asian caravan routes and created a strong sense of unity. From the ninth century onward, the Abode of Islam constituted far more than just an area of spiritual unity, as its frontiers ran across trade routes. The "Sea of Peace" – the Indian Ocean – experienced free movement of ships, unchecked migration, freedom of trade, and security of merchants and voyagers, motivating merchants and ships to avoid confrontation with commercial rivals, and instead to observe the sanctity of commercial transactions.[175]

Prior to resorting to the use of force, Muslims were required to verify the other party's intentions. If Muslims sighted enemy vessels off Islamic shores and realized that their intention was to harass or plunder commercial ships or to attack coastal targets, the Muslim warships could initiate combat engagement with the enemy forces.[176] Should any doubt arise concerning an enemy's intentions, Muslims were advised to be patient and to avoid making hasty decisions that could lead to unnecessary war or other deleterious consequences.[177] However, during a state of war, Muslims on warships were permitted to engage enemy war vessels on the high seas, as well as ships carrying supplies to enemy belligerents, without the *imam*'s permission. Muslim naval warriors were further advised to seize cargo and vessels rather than set them on fire.[178] If warriors on an enemy warship decided to surrender on the condition of being granted *amān* with respect to their souls and their vessel, Muslims were advised to honor this appeal if it was genuine and sincere.[179]

Before entering the Abode of Islam, every *ḥarbī* had to be equipped with a safe-conduct decree in order to feel secure, receive good treatment, and safeguard any chattels. In the absence of such a decree, the law empowered the *imam* or local governor to determine the status of any illegal-alien merchant as seen fit. Under certain circumstances, if alien merchants without an *amān* were sighted from Islamic shores and halted at sea by a Muslim coastguard, they would be compelled to sail away from

[175] Chaudhuri, *Trade and Civilization in the Indian Ocean*, 21, 34–39, 44; Risso, *Merchants and Faith*, 43–54; Sheriff, *Dhow Culture*, 23–25, 239–258; Park, *Mapping the Chinese and Islamic Worlds*, 159.

[176] Abū Bakr Aḥmad ibn ʿAbd Allāh ibn Mūsā al-Kindī, *Al-Muṣannaf* (Muscat: Wizārat al-Turāth al-Qawmī wa'l-Thaqāfa, 1983), 11:159 (*in thabatū fī al-baḥr ʿalā yaqīn annahum hum al-ladhīn yaghzūn al-muslimīn*).

[177] Kindī, *Muṣannaf*, 11:160 (*inna al-ḥarb idhā lam yurja nafʿuhā turikat*).

[178] Kindī, *Muṣannaf*, 11:158–159.

[179] Sarakhsī, *Sharḥ Kitāb al-Siyar al-Kabīr*, 1:212–213.

the Islamic territorial sea. If an enemy ship were floating adrift along the coast and the merchants on board had no *amān*, they were entitled to be seized as captives (*fay*ʾ). The *imam* would thereby hold exclusive jurisdiction over them. The *imam* held the authority to free such enemy aliens without conditions, order their immediate execution, or release them in exchange for the payment of a ransom.[180]

SUMMARY

The Qurʾān declares that the seas with their natural resources are among the endless bounties that God has bestowed upon humankind. Permission to exploit marine resources and the guarantee of freedom of navigation, trade, and movement are probably best expressed in Qurʾān 16:14,[181] which states that God has subjugated the seas and ships to the benefit of all of humanity. Consequently, no nation or state has the right to debar or exclude others from making use of the seas' natural resources or from plying their waves. Most significantly, the universe's two masses, the seas and the land, are regarded by the Divine Law as one single mass that should be accessible to all nations. However, coastal settlements neighboring the sea are entitled to establish sovereignty over a limited offshore area for the benefit of local residents, as outlined in Qurʾān 7:163.[182]

Although humankind is permitted by the Qurʾān to take full advantage of the bounties God has endowed on His servants through the seas, access to them has, however, been governed by customary laws, bilateral and multilateral treaties, and safe-conduct decrees in regions of struggle over maritime spaces. Even though the Prophet Muḥammad did not personally engage in travel by sea, the 9 AH/630 CE pledge and other documented

[180] Saḥnūn, *Al-Mudawwanah*, 2:10–11; Ibn Abū Zayd al-Qayrawānī, *Al-Nawādir wa'l-Ziyādāt*, 3:130–132; Yūsuf ibn ʿAbd Allāh ibn Muḥammad ibn ʿAbd al-Barr, *Al-Kāfī fī Fiqh Ahl al-Madīna al-Mālikī* (Riyad, 1401/1980), 1:481; Abū al-Walīd Sulaymān ibn Khalaf al-Bājī, *Al-Muntaqā* (Beirut: Dār al-Fikr al-ʿArabī, 1402/1982), 3:187; Abū Zakariyyā Aḥmad ibn Ibrāhīm ibn al-Naḥḥās, *Mashāriʿ al-Ashwāq ilā Maṣāriʿ al-ʿUshshāq wa-Muthīr al-Gharām ilā Dār al-Islām* (Riyad: Dār al-Nashr al-Islāmiyya, 1400/1990), 2:1056; Kindī, *Muṣannaf*, 11:164; Khalilieh, *Islamic Maritime Law*, 125–126.

[181] "وَهُوَ الَّذِي سَخَّرَ الْبَحْرَ لِتَأْكُلُوا مِنْهُ لَحْمًا طَرِيًّا وَتَسْتَخْرِجُوا مِنْهُ حِلْيَةً تَلْبَسُونَهَا وَتَرَى الْفُلْكَ مَوَاخِرَ فِيهِ وَلِتَبْتَغُوا مِن فَضْلِهِ وَلَعَلَّكُمْ تَشْكُرُونَ (It is He Who has made the sea subject, that ye may eat thereof flesh that is fresh and tender, and that ye may extract therefrom ornaments to wear; and thou seest the ships therein that plough the waves, that ye may seek (thus) of the bounty of God and that ye may be grateful)."

[182] "وَاسْأَلْهُمْ عَنِ الْقَرْيَةِ الَّتِي كَانَتْ حَاضِرَةَ الْبَحْرِ (Ask them concerning the town standing close by the sea)."

covenants, truces, and safe-conduct certificates reflect the Muslim authorities' actual position toward freedom of navigation, jurisdiction over ships on the high seas, and the legal status of subjects sailing on board both friend- and enemy-flagged vessels.[183] Equipped with safe-conduct pledges, enemy-alien merchants and travelers could traverse the seas freely, including those surrounded by Islamic-ruled territories, such as the Sea of the Hijaz, which enjoyed a special status in Islamic law from the reign of ʿUmar ibn al-Khaṭṭāb (r. 12–23/634–644) up until the late nineteenth century. In order to ensure the safety and security at sea and in foreign territories of subjects and their chattels, Islamic and foreign sovereigns concluded treaties and truces. Muslims were required by law to assure the safety of all *mustaʾmins* and their property until they reached a place at sea where they felt secure, or arrived at their native country, within the time limits of the relevant pledge. Even during wartime, *ḥarbī*s – unlike combatants – should not be denied free access to the sea.[184]

Whether or not a state of war or peace persisted between states, an *amān* was always issued free of charge and employed as a "sacred peace tool" to reduce hostilities and promote freedom of movement and global interactions among individuals, groups, and nations.[185] It is quite clear that this legal tool contrasted sharply with the Portuguese *cartaz* system, which challenged the concept of the free sea by obliging every Asian commercial vessel to pay customs duties to the Portuguese authorities in return for protection and safe-conduct. This practice significantly altered the character of seaborne trade in the Indian Ocean by creating an unprecedented and unfamiliar practice in the region. In spite of the Muslim naval supremacy over the Red Sea, the

183 God ordains Muslims to comply with the Prophet Muḥammad's tradition. Qurʾān 3:31: "قُلْ إِن كُنتُمْ تُحِبُّونَ اللَّهَ فَاتَّبِعُونِي (Say: If ye do love God, follow me)"; Q 3:32: "قُلْ أَطِيعُواْ اللَّهَ وَالرَّسُولَ (Say: Obey God and His Messenger)"; Q 4:59: "يَا أَيُّهَا الَّذِينَ آمَنُواْ أَطِيعُواْ اللَّهَ وَأَطِيعُواْ الرَّسُولَ (O ye who believe! Obey God, and obey the Messenger)"; Q 4:64: "وَمَا أَرْسَلْنَا مِن رَّسُولٍ إِلَّا لِيُطَاعَ بِإِذْنِ اللَّهِ (We sent not a Messenger, but to be obeyed, in accordance with the will of God)"; Q 24:63: "فَلْيَحْذَرِ الَّذِينَ يُخَالِفُونَ عَنْ أَمْرِهِ (Let those beware who withstand the Messenger's order)"; Q 33:21: "لَقَدْ كَانَ لَكُمْ فِي رَسُولِ اللَّهِ أُسْوَةٌ حَسَنَةٌ (Ye have indeed in the Messenger of God an excellent exemplar)"; Q 33:36: "وَمَا كَانَ لِمُؤْمِنٍ وَلا مُؤْمِنَةٍ إِذَا قَضَى اللَّهُ وَرَسُولُهُ أَمْرًا أَن يَكُونَ لَهُمُ الْخِيَرَةُ مِنْ أَمْرِهِمْ وَمَن يَعْصِ اللَّهَ وَرَسُولَهُ فَقَدْ ضَلَّ ضَلالا مُّبِينًا (It is not fitting for a Believer, man or woman, when a matter has been decided by God and His Messenger, to have any option about their decision; if anyone disobeys God and His Messenger, he is indeed on a clearly wrong Path)."

184 Ibn Jubayr, *Travels*, 301, in his words: "The soldiers engage themselves in their war, while the people are at peace and the world goes to him who conquers."

185 Bashir, "Treatment of Foreigners in the Classical Islamic State," 150–152.

Persian Gulf, the Omani and Yemeni littorals, as well as the Levantine, North African, and Andalusian coasts of the Mediterranean, no state could claim sovereignty or dominion over the open sea, so allowing it to remain common to all.[186]

Also deserving attention is the attribution of certain seas to certain nations, such as Baḥr al-Rūm (Sea of the Romans, i.e., the Mediterranean Sea) to the Romans, Baḥr al-Hind (Indian Sea) to the Indians, Baḥr al-Ṣīn (Chinese Sea) to the Chinese, Baḥr Fāris (Persian Sea/Gulf) to the Persians, Baḥr al-Khazar (Caspian Sea) to the Caspians; as well as to provinces, such as Baḥr al-Yaman (Sea of Yemen) and Baḥr al-Ḥijāz (Sea of the Hijaz); or coastal cities, such as Baḥr al-Qulzum (Sea of Clysma, Suez today), among others. A question arising is whether this attribution might have signaled the appropriation of the sea by a nation or a territorial entity. The Mediterranean Sea can be examined as an example.

With the defeat of the Phoenician colony of Carthage in the Third Punic War (149–146 BCE), the Romans – succeeded by the Byzantines – dominated almost the entire Mediterranean region for over eight centuries and viewed the Great Sea as *mare nostrum*. Rome's hegemony at sea derived from its territorial management and military administrative system, with imperial troops and flotillas posted at strategic positions along the shoreline to preempt piracy.[187] However, from the seventh century CE onward, the Mediterranean ceased to be a Roman lake and became shared by Christians and Muslims.[188] Muslim writers challenged the Byzantines'

[186] The institution of *amān* drew greater attention in regions that generated conflicts among independent political entities. This may explain why the overwhelming majority of the jurisprudential, historical, and documentary sources that describe in minute detail the security and rights of *musta'mins* in various stages of their journeys have reached us from the Mediterranean world. However, the countries around the Indian Ocean rim rarely created conflicts that could hamper overseas trade and freedom of navigation; therefore, the issue of safe-conduct preoccupied jurists and governing authorities to a lesser extent.

[187] Steinberg, *Social Construction of the Ocean*, 65; Steinberg, "Lines of Division, Lines of Connection," 258–259; Khalilieh, *Admiralty and Maritime Laws*, 5–6.

[188] Ibn Khaldūn, *Al-Muqaddimah*, 1:267: "When God revealed the religion of Islam and His religion has overcome other religions, the Roman/Byzantine Empire had already dominated the two shores of the Roman/Byzantine (Mediterranean) Sea. In the beginning, Muslim took by force all of its southern shores – Syria, Egypt, Ifrīqiya, and the Maghrib – crossed the Bay of Tangier and took possession of all Andalusia (Spain) from the Goths and Galicians. ... (The Muslims) took possession of all the islands that lie in the Rūm Sea, which the Romans had dominated, such as Sicily, Majorca, and Dénia and its sisters ... ." The author acknowledges that the entire Mediterranean was a Roman/ Byzantine possession, which ended with the advent of Islam, whose followers gained control militarily over the largest part of it for several centuries. From the seventh

sovereignty over the Mediterranean Sea, noting: (a) the sea lies along the coastal frontier lines (*thughūr*), so that what is beyond it is the Land of the *Rūm*; (b) Muslim naval powers, particularly in the Maghrib, rivaled Byzantine maritime supremacy; (c) ships arriving in Islamic ports from Christian Europe were identified as "*Rūm*'s ships," bearing Byzantine sovereignty; and (d) by the early tenth century the Mediterranean came to have other names, including Baḥr al-Shām (the Sea of Greater Syria) and Baḥr al-Maghrib (the Sea of the Islamic West).[189] The Mediterranean was considered a frontier in relation to all the populations residing along its shores. The same point could be made about all the other seas around the world.[190]

Freedom of the high seas, as enshrined in article 87 of the United Nations Convention on the Law of the Sea (UNCLOS), aligns with Qur'ānic principles and with the Islamic Law of Nations. It reads:

1. The high seas are open to all states, whether coastal or landlocked. Freedom of the high seas is exercised under the conditions laid down

century onward, the Mediterranean has been divided between the Christian north and Islamic south. Despite the military dominance over the high sea, Ibn Khaldūn does not view the Mediterranean as an "Islamic lake," meaning that the high sea is not susceptible to appropriation.

189 Tarek Kahlaoui, "The Depiction of the Mediterranean in Islamic Cartography," (PhD diss., University of Pennsylvania, 2008), 40–48. The author draws our attention to the fact that the word Rūm has more than a meaning. When conjoined with *baḥr*, i.e., Baḥr al-Rūm (Byzantines/Greeks Sea), the word would purposely signify the "Land of the Byzantines/Greeks." However, whenever it is thought of as the Mediterranean, then the word Rūm would roughly mean "Europe."

190 Ibn Kathīr, *Al-Bidāyah wa'l-Nihāyah*, 1:46: "The seas that branch off from the Western, Eastern, Southern, and Northern Surrounding Seas/Oceans (*muḥīṭ*) are numerous, some of which are isolated (without exit to other seas). Some of the seas' names are attributed to the countries bordering their shores such as the Sea of Qulzum (Clysma), a small town situated on its coast and in the vicinity of Aylah, the Sea of Fāris (Persia), Khazar (Caspian) Sea, Warank (Varangian) Sea, Rūm (Roman/Byzantine) Sea, Banṭash (Black) Sea, Azraq (Blue) Sea, named after a city on its coast, is also called al-Qarm (Crimea) Sea, which flows in a narrow straits called the Gulf of Constantinople Gulf, to the Rūm (Mediterranean) Sea, south of Constantinople"; Qalqashandī, *Ṣubḥ al-A'shā*, 3:234–242: "Baḥr al-Rūm aka al-Baḥr al-Rūmī is attributed to the Rūm (Romans/ Byzantines) because their nations live to its north. It could be called al-Baḥr al-Shāmī (Syrian Sea) too because of the Syrian (Shām) coasts in its eastern part"; Kahlaoui, "Depiction of the Mediterranean in Islamic Cartography," 47; Predrag Matvejević, *Mediterranean: A Cultural Landscape*, trans. Michael Heim (Berkeley: University of California Press, 1999), 139–146; Douglas M. Dunlop, "Baḥr al-Rūm," in *Encyclopaedia of Islam*, 2nd ed., ed. P. Bearman *et al.* (Brill Online, 2012) http://brillonline.nl/entries/encyclopaedia-of-islam-2/bahr-al-rum-SIM_1065.

by this Convention and by other rules of international law. It comprises, inter alia, both for coastal and landlocked states:
(a) freedom of navigation;
(b) freedom of overflight;
(c) freedom to lay submarine cables and pipelines, subject to Part VI;
(d) freedom to construct artificial islands and other installations permitted under international law, subject to Part VI;
(e) freedom of fishing, subject to the conditions laid down in section 2;
(f) freedom of scientific research, subject to Parts VI and XIII.
2. These freedoms shall be exercised by all states with due regard for the interests of other states in their exercise of the freedom of the high seas, and also with due regard for the rights under this Convention with respect to activities in the Area.[191]

Similarly, article 89 states: "No state may validly purport to subject any part of the high seas to its sovereignty." Other articles of UNCLOS assert that every state, even if landlocked, has the right to send its ships across the high seas unimpeded by other states. As access to the sea and freedom of navigation are enshrined in the Qur'ān, one would be right to infer that Muslim merchants and seafarers, in the first place, and ruling circles and jurisconsults, in the second place, heavily influenced the development of the doctrine of freedom of the seas. However, Muslims were certainly not the first to introduce laws of the free sea. Earlier monotheistic religions and cultures enshrined free access to the sea as a natural right and defended it by initiating regulations and concluding diplomatic and commercial agreements. On the account of the above, one may justifiably ask: did the doctrine of freedom of the seas extend to offshore belts adjacent to coastal states and principalities?

[191] www.un.org/depts/los/convention_agreements/texts/unclos/part7.htm.

2

Offshore Sovereignty and the Territorial Sea

Article 2 of the 1982 United Nations Convention on the Law of the Sea (UNCLOS) defines territorial waters as follows:

1. The sovereignty of a coastal state extends, beyond its land territory and internal waters and, in the case of an archipelagic state, its archipelagic waters, to an adjacent belt of sea, described as the territorial sea.
2. This sovereignty extends to the air space over the territorial sea as well as to its bed and subsoil.
3. The sovereignty over the territorial sea is exercised subject to this Convention and to other rules of international law.

As concerns the outer limits of the territorial sea, article 3 rules:

> Every state has the right to establish the breadth of its territorial sea up to a limit not exceeding 12 nautical miles [22 kilometers], measured from baselines determined in accordance with this Convention.[1]

This article establishes that coastal states have the right to claim and exercise sovereignty over a defined maritime belt adjacent to their shores extending seaward up to 12 nautical miles (22 kilometers). It grants such states exclusive rights to explore, exploit, manage, and conserve both living and nonliving natural resources found within this zone.[2] Under the regime of innocent passage, a coastal state may regulate navigation through its territorial sea and access to its ports. The territorial sea is thus

[1] http://www.un.org/depts/los/convention_agreements/texts/unclos/part2.htm.
[2] UNCLOS, article 56.

considered an inseparable part of the *terra* (land) of a coastal state over which it possesses full sovereignty.

Whereas UNCLOS clearly establishes a standard seaward breadth for a territorial sea, the international community had previously failed to do so, either at the Hague Convention (1930) or the Geneva Conventions (1958 and 1970). Indeed, prior to the twentieth century, every nation held a different view regarding the juridical nature and seaward breadth of a territorial sea.[3] In the following discussion, an attempt will be made to: (a) trace the Islamic genesis of the concept of territorial sea and its juridical ramifications; and (b) examine the motives behind the ultimate establishment of an offshore maritime belt. Before proceeding with the Islamic territorial jurisdiction over offshore marine zones, the Roman and medieval European claims over coastal waters is examined briefly.

THE CONCEPT OF THE TERRITORIAL SEA IN MEDIEVAL EUROPE

Legal scholars have suggested that claims to jurisdiction, sovereignty, or *dominium* (absolute ownership) over nearshore waters emerged in the latter part of the fifth century with the dissolution of the Western Roman Empire and the rise of the Gothic tribes.[4] However, this hypothesis finds no basis in legal documents. Within a century of the final collapse of the western half, the two parts of the Roman Empire were reunited during Justinian's reign,[5] yet no solid legislative action appropriating waters adjacent to coasts exists in the sixth century *Corpus Juris Civilis*, or in the later Byzantine codices.[6] However, the absence of such a codified law from the Romano-Byzantine digests does not preclude the possibility that ancient, classical, and medieval coastal states asserted jurisdiction over

[3] Jesse S. Reeves, "The Codification of the Law of Territorial Waters," *American Journal of International Law* 24 (1930), 486–499; Robin R. Churchill and Alan V. Lowe, *The Law of the Sea*, 3rd ed. (Manchester: Manchester University Press, 1999), 71–81.

[4] Michael J. Feakes, "Formative Influences on the Evolution of International Law: A Case Study of Territorial Waters (1550–1650)," (PhD diss., University of Hull, 1994), 44; William L. Schachte, "The History of the Territorial Sea from a National Security Perspective," *Territorial Sea Journal* 1 (1990), 144–145; Bowen L. Florsheim, "Territorial Sea – 3000 Year Old Question," *Journal of Air Law and Commerce* 36 (1970), 76.

[5] M. Stuart Madden, "Paths of Western Law after Justinian," *London Law Review* 1 (2005), 368–378.

[6] Fenn, "Origins of the Theory of Territorial Waters," 470; Thurman, "Law of the Sea in Early Modern Europe," 60; Steinberg, "Lines of Division, Lines of Connection," 259.

offshore maritime belts.[7] On the contrary, economic and security considerations in particular motivated states to claim property rights in gulfs, bays, and indentations adjacent to their lands, and to exercise some degree of jurisdiction over them; however, documents describing the precise seaward breadths of such extensions of sovereignty have not been found.[8]

7 Domenico A. Azuni, *The Maritime Law of Europe* (New York: George Forman, 1806), 1: 186–190; Ziskind, "International Legal Status of the Sea in Antiquity," 36–37; Egberts, "Chronology of 'The Report of Wenamun'," 58–61; Breasted, "Report of Wenamon," 103–104; Hessbruegge, "Historical Development of the Doctrines of Attribution," 265–266; Rubin, "Neutrality in International Law," 354–355; Sasson, "Canaanite Maritime Involvement in the Second Millennium B.C.," 131–138; Tammuz, "*Mare Clausum*," 148–149. A letter addressed from the King of Tyre to the King of Ugarit from the thirteenth century BCE reports that a Ugaritic ship heading for Egypt had sunk or was severely damaged in a rainstorm off the coast of Acco/Akko (Acre). The ship was unloaded and her sailors and their belongings sheltered in Acco until the sea had calmed down. The Tyrian King went on to assure the King of Ugarit that the cargo was safe. This turn of phase would seem to indicate that the Tyrian King had the concept of territorial waters in mind when he wrote to Ugarit. Providing assistance to ships in distress, regardless of nationality, sailing within the territorial sea of a coastal state was and remained a humane duty. Parpola and Watanabe, *Neo-Assyrian Treaties and Loyalty Oaths*, 2:25, articles 15–17 of the treaty concluded between Esarhaddon, King of Assyria (681–669 BCE) and Baʿal, King of Tyre (680–660 BCE), state: "If there is a ship of Baʿal or the people of Tyre that is shipwrecked off the land of the Philistines or within Assyrian territory, everything that is on the ship belongs to Esarhaddon, King of Assyria; however, one must not do any harm to any person on board the ship but one must return them all to their country."

8 *Institutes of Justinian*, Book 2, Title 1.5: "Of things that are common to all any one may take such a portion as he pleases. Thus a man may inhale the air, or float his ship on any part of the sea. As long as he occupies any portion, his occupation is respected; but directly his occupation ceases, the thing occupied again becomes common to all. The sea-shore, that is, the shore as far as the waves go at furthest, was considered to belong to all men. For the purposes of self-defense any nation had a right to occupy the shore and to repel strangers. Individuals, if they built on it, by means of piles or otherwise, were secured in exclusive enjoyment of the portion occupied; but if the building was taken away, their occupancy was at an end, and the spot on which the building stood again became common." By virtue of natural law, air, rivers, sea, and seashores are *res communes* and unsuited for private ownership, meaning they are *res nullius*. Despite their commonality, one may acquire ownership and build on the shore to the extent that this act does not interfere with public use. Sandars (ed.), *Institutes of Justinian*, 158; Digest I, 8, 2, 1; Digest I, 8, 4; Fenn, "Origins of the Theory of Territorial Waters," 469, 471; Thomas W. Fulton, *The Sovereignty of the Sea: An Historical Account of the Claims of England to the Dominion of the British Seas, and of the Evolution of the Territorial Waters, with Special Reference to the Rights of Fishing and the Naval Salute* (Edinburgh: William Blackwood and Sons, 1911), 538; F. S. Ruddy, "*Res Nullius* and Occupation in Roman and International Law," *University of Missouri (Kansas City) Law Review* 36 (1968), 274–277; Ziskind, "International Law and Ancient Sources," 558–559. Talmudic texts show that Jewish rabbis maintain that the state boundaries are drawn to include part of the sea and the zone lying between the coastline and the state's offshore islands; Alexandrowicz, "Kautilyan Principles and the Law of Nations," 310–311.

Whereas Roman law expressly states that by the Law of Nature the sea is common to all humankind (*communes omnium naturali jure*),[9] medieval Italian post-Glossators challenged the public nature of the sea. They argued that parts of the sea can be claimed by applying laws that pertain to land to those waters adjacent to a coast, either by recognizing long-standing custom (*per longam consuetudinem*),[10] or acquisition through possession or use for a fixed time (*longi temporis praescriptio*),[11] or by imposing naval supremacy to subdue piracy and secure shipping lanes. As the feudal system arose in Europe, public authority became fragmented and decentralized, leading to the emergence of local entities. Lawyers of that period applied land laws to the adjacent coastal waters and granted feudal barons the right to retain territorial jurisdiction, not only over their own coastal estates, but also over the span between them and any neighboring islands. The feudal barons asserted wide jurisdiction by granting, restricting, or preventing access to fishing, coastal installations, and ports, through regulating navigation and commerce, and by imposing or exempting from duties people sailing through their waters. Such royal rights (*jura regalia*) and practices led to assertions of sovereignty and the gradual creation of territorial waters.[12]

Although rights of navigation and exploitation of the seas' natural resources are objective features of natural law, the post-Glossators argued that humans can alter these rights through sea power and treaties, which ultimately establish jurisdiction. Even if the power of a state fades such that it can no longer sustain a claim to sovereignty by military means, recognition of its dominion by other nations remains.[13] On a domestic level – contrary to Digest I, 8 – air, flowing water, sea, seashores, rivers,

[9] Digest I, 8, 2, 1; Digest I, 8, 3; Digest I, 8, 4; Sandars (ed.), *Institutes of Justinian*, 159, Book 2, Title 1.5; Sayer A. Swarztrauber, "The Three-Mile Limit of Territorial Seas: A Brief History," (PhD diss., American University, Washington DC, 1970), 20; Schachte, "History of the Territorial Sea," 144; Thurman, "Law of the Sea in Early Modern Europe," 60–61; Guillaume Calafat, "Une mer jalousie: jurisdictions maritimes, ports francs et regulation du commerce en Méditerranée (1590–1740)," (PhD diss., Université Paris 1 Panthéon-Sorbonne, 2013), 29–30.

[10] Sebastian I. Sobecki, *The Sea and Medieval English Literature* (Cambridge: D. S. Brewer, 2008), 142.

[11] Fredona, "Angelo degli Ubaldi and the Gulf of the Venetians," 41, 46.

[12] Fenn, "Origins of the Theory of Territorial Waters," 467, 469, 472–473; Sobecki, *Sea and Medieval English Literature*, 142–143; Beatrice Heuser, "*Regina Maris* and the Command of the Sea: The Sixteenth Century Origins of Modern Maritime Strategy," *Journal of Strategic Studies* 40 (2017), 227–233.

[13] Fulton, *Sovereignty of the Sea*, 4; Fenn, "Origins of the Theory of Territorial Waters," 466; Ryan M. Greenwood, "Law and War in Late Medieval Italy: The *Jus Commune* on

fisheries, and other marine resources are common to all by *jus naturale*. They can neither be possessed nor monopolized by individuals,[14] nor may access to these areas and resources be denied or limited, even to bays, gulfs, or coastal indentations claimed as feudal areas, or fall under the exclusive jurisdiction of maritime empires in adherence to long-standing custom.[15]

Late medieval and Renaissance European jurists justified a state's jurisdictional claims over a portion of the sea by reason of naval supremacy. The eminent fourteenth-century Italian jurist Bartolus of Sassoferrato (1314–1357) – founder of the post-Glossator school and considered to be "the father of territorial sea in legal history"[16] – advocated that a coastal state was entitled to assert *imperium* over waters and islands within a distance of up to 100 nautical miles (185 kilometers), provided that this could be traversed within two days' travel by sea. Baldus de Ubaldis (1327–1400), a student of Bartolus of Sassoferrato, concurred with this principle of proprietary rights, but disagreed with the breadth possible for a territorial sea, arguing that it should not extend beyond a day's journey and not exceed a distance of 60 nautical miles (110 kilometers) from the coast.[17] The positions held by these jurists were

War and its Application in Florence, c. 1150–1450," (PhD diss., University of Toronto, 2011), 13.

14 As regards the juridical status and the exploitation of the sea's natural resources in Roman legal thought, consult Annalisa Marzano, *Harvesting the Sea: The Exploitation of Marine Resources in the Roman Mediterranean* (Oxford: Oxford University Press, 2013), 236–267.

15 Sandars (ed.), *Institutes of Justinian*, 155–159, Book 2, Title 1.1–5; Fulton, *Sovereignty of the Sea*, 4–8; Fenn, "Origins of the Theory of Territorial Waters," 467; Sobecki, *Sea and Medieval English Literature*, 142; Perruso, "Development of the Doctrine of *Res Communes*," 81.

16 Sobecki, *Sea and Medieval English Literature*, 143.

17 Azuni, *Maritime Law of Europe*, 1:196–197; Fenn, "Origins of the Theory of Territorial Waters," 472; Fulton, *Sovereignty of the Sea*, 539–540; Schmitt, *Nomos of the Earth*, 89; Schachte, "History of the Territorial Sea," 145; Sobecki, *Sea and Medieval English Literature*, 144; Fredona, "Angelo degli Ubaldi and the Gulf of the Venetians," 51–52, 53–56; Swarztrauber, "Three-Mile Limit of Territorial Seas," 22; Augusto P. Miceli, "Forum Juridicum: Bartolus of Sassoferrato," *Louisiana Law Review* 37 (1977), 1033–1034; Feakes, "Formative Influences on the Evolution of International Law," 57–58; Greenwood, "Law and War in Late Medieval Italy," 6–7: Bartolus contends that city-states can claim de facto sovereignty at sea in the same way that classical Roman emperors asserted de jure jurisdiction over the Mediterranean Sea. In his *On the Rights of War and Peace*, Book 2, Title 3, Capitula 13, 2, Grotius defines the furthest seaward limit of the territorial sea as the space that a man could command from the land. He writes: "The empire of a portion of the sea is, it would seem, acquired in the same way as other lordship; that is, as above stated, as belonging to a person, or as

promulgated during a time when Christian powers were dominant in the naval arena. With its naval superiority, Venice established sovereignty over the Adriatic Sea and parts of the Aegean and eastern Mediterranean, became a dominant commercial power, and played a pivotal role in seaborne trade between the European and Near Eastern markets. In order to maintain peace in these seas, Venice needed to strengthen its dominance of trunk routes by eliminating piracy wherever possible.[18] Naval endeavors culminated in Venice claiming jurisdiction over the waters under its control. Pope Alexander III (papacy 1159–1181) subsequently sanctioned this sovereignty in the 1177 Peace of Venice.[19]

Documentation from 1269 reveals that ships sailing through Venetian waters in the Adriatic and Aegean seas had to pay *gabellas*[20] and taxes at its ports.[21] After Genoa had claimed the sea as its own, similar naval conditions prevailed in the Ligurian Sea. Following naval victories over the Pisans, Venetians, and Muslims, and having eliminated pirates from strategic

belonging to a territory: belonging to a person, when he has a fleet which commands that part of the sea; belonging to a territory, in so far as those who sail in that part of the sea can be compelled from the shore as if they were on land." Hugo Grotius, *On the Rights of War and Peace: An Abridged Translation*, trans. William Whewell (Cambridge: Cambridge University Press, 1853), 81; Hodgins, "Ancient Law of Nations Respecting the Sea," 15, 17; Thornton, "Hugo Grotius and the Freedom of the Seas," 28.

18 Fenn, "Origins of the Theory of Territorial Waters," 473; Frederic C. Lane, *Venice: A Maritime Republic* (Baltimore: Johns Hopkins University Press, 1973), 23–29; Calafat, "Mer jalousie," 45–51.

19 Selden, *Of the Dominion or Ownership of the Sea*, 99–107; Fulton, *Sovereignty of the Sea*, 341; Filippo de Vivo, "Historical Justifications of Venetian Power in the Adriatic," *Journal of the History of Ideas* 64 (2003), 159–176, especially 163–167; Greenwood, "Law and War in Late Medieval Italy," 13; Feakes, "Formative Influences on the Evolution of International Law," 55–56.

20 *Gabella* (*cabella, cabbella*) is a word transmitted from Norman Sicily derived from the Arabic *qibālah* to denote duty, tribute, levy, or tax paid to the state on goods brought or sold, rent of land, or tax on a real estate transaction. By extension, the term *gabelou* means a tax collector (*employé d'octroi*). See Albert Dauzat, *Dictionnaire étymologique de la langue française* (Paris: Larousse, 1938), 349; Fulton, *Sovereignty of the Sea*, 361; Dionisius A. Agius, *Siculo Arabic* (New York: Routledge, 2010), 115, 250; Khaled Abou el-Fadl, "Tax Farming in Islamic Law (*Qibālah* and *Ḍamān* of *Kharāj*): A Search for a Concept," *Islamic Studies* 31 (1992), 5–8.

21 Azuni, *Maritime Law of Europe*, 1:76–82, 194; Ruth Schilling, "Asserting the Boundaries: Defining the City and Its Territory by Political Ritual," in *Imagining the City*, ed. Christian Emden and David Midgley (Bern: Peter Lang – International Academic Publisher, 2006), 90–99; Maria P. Pedani, "Beyond the Frontier: The Ottoman–Venetian Border in the Adriatic Context from the Sixteenth to the Eighteenth Centuries," in *Zones of Fracture in Modern Europe: The Baltic Countries, the Balkans, and Northern Italy*, ed. Almut Bues (Wiesbaden: Harrassowitz, 2005), 50–51; Feakes, "Formative Influences on the Evolution of International Law," 55.

maritime positions, Genoa also asserted sovereignty over shipping lanes in the Mediterranean, Aegean, and Black seas, regulated passage through them, granted or refused ships permission to sail, and demanded fees from vessels using its ports or navigating the sea-lanes it claimed.[22]

The *Amiratus* (Admiral of the Sea) arose as a special position within these new jurisdictions.[23] In addition to possessing juridical, administrative, and organizational powers, the *Amiratus* was charged with maintaining good order and securing coastal frontiers, guarding against external intrusions, driving pirates off the sea, and launching military campaigns against enemy targets. As the highest authority at sea, the *Amiratus* also claimed the right to exercise jurisdiction over newly captured territories and properties seized with or without force.[24]

In the late thirteenth century, when Muslim naval power began deteriorating in parts of the central and western Mediterranean and on the eastern shores of the Atlantic Ocean, Christian European admirals roamed the seas and took over from the infidels (i.e., Muslims) strategic positions and islands. In 1295, shortly after the conquest of Jerba (Djerba) and the Kerkennah islands off the Tunisian coast (in 1284), Pope Boniface

[22] Azuni, *Maritime Law of Europe*, 1:83–85; Fulton, *Sovereignty of the Sea*, 361; Feakes, "Formative Influences on the Evolution of International Law," 55–56; Greenwood, "Law and War in Late Medieval Italy," 104–110; Emily S. Tai, "Piracy and Law in Medieval Genoa: The *Consilia* of Bartolomeo Bosco," *Medieval Encounters* 9 (2003), 260, 279; George P. Smith, "The Concept of Free Seas: Shaping Modern Maritime Policy within a Vector of Historical Influence," *International Lawyer* 11 (1977), 356; Marina V. Žužul, "The Law of the Sea in the Mediterranean throughout the History," *Miscellanea Hadriatica et Mediterranea* 4 (2017), 58–59.

[23] Agius, *Siculo Arabic*, 115, 248. The term "admiral" is derived from the Arabic words *Amīr al-Baḥr*, literally, "Prince of the Sea," or "Commander of the Fleet." According to the *Oxford English Dictionary*, the word *amiratus* was first found during the second half of the eleventh century in the kingdom of Norman Sicily. It applied to the highest ranking naval officer, the commander of the fleet. Its earliest use was in 1178 as *admiratus stolii*. This title was also used in 1194 by Margaritus of Brindisi, whose fame at the time helped consolidate naval associations. Other forms of the word have also been recorded, e.g., *admiralis*. As a number of native Genoese men commanded the fleet in Sicily from the end of the twelfth century onward, the title *amiratus* was taken to Genoa in the first half of the thirteenth century and spread further from there. The first Englishman recorded as being referred to as admiral is William of Leybourne in 1295. *Oxford English Dictionary*, http://www.oed.com/view/Entry/2558; Frederic R. Sanborn, *Origins of the Early English Maritime and Commercial Law* (New York: Century Co., 1930), 278–279; Reginald G. Marsden (ed.), *Select Pleas in the Court of Admiralty* (London: Bernard Quaritch 1894), 1:xiv–xv.

[24] Scott (ed.), *Las Siete Partidas*, 2:326–327; Fulton, *Sovereignty of the Sea*, 544; Fenn, "Origins of the Theory of Territorial Waters," 473, 476; Sanborn, *Early English Maritime and Commercial Law*, 278–282; Feakes, "Formative Influences on the Evolution of International Law," 45; Sobecki, *Sea and Medieval English Literature*, 150.

VIII (d. 1303) bestowed them as a fiefdom to the Aragonese conquistador and admiral Roger de Lauria.[25] This papal donation was perhaps the first assertion of jurisdiction by Christian authorities over non-European territories. The fief in question may subsequently have served as a legal precedent for establishing ownership over territory within the high seas. Fifty years later, in 1344, Pope Clement VI (d. 1352) granted Castilian Prince Luis de la Cerda temporal jurisdiction over the Canary Islands off the Moroccan coast in return for an annual payment of 400 florins to the Vatican. If the prince had violated the papal bull, he would have faced excommunication and the Church of Rome would have reasserted ownership of the islands.[26]

The discussion so far succinctly traces the origins of the territorial sea from a European perspective until the 1648 Peace of Westphalia. Prior to this point, Rome had attained hegemony over the Mediterranean Sea,[27] but had never claimed exclusive proprietorship over it: "The claim to *imperium* was not developed into a claim of *dominium*."[28] Roman authorities, legislators, and jurists, and their Byzantine successors, did not deny access to the sea in either their codices or legal writings; instead, they uniformly stressed its commonality to all nations and the right of all humans to exploit and use the sea without any interference. Only internal waters, lagoons, and small coastal indentations could be claimed by sovereigns.[29] Therefore, European legal precedents for appropriation of the sea derived from Venice's claims to hegemony over the Adriatic, the papal donation of the Canary Islands, and the 1494 Treaty of Tordesillas between Spain and Portugal that divided the non-Christian world into two zones of influence.[30]

[25] David Abulafia, *A Mediterranean Emporium: The Catalan Kingdom of Majorca* (Cambridge: Cambridge University Press, 1994), 145, f. 77; Mariarosaria Salerno, "Relations, Politics, and Economic Choices in the Mediterranean: The Kingdom of Naples and Tunisia between the Thirteenth and the Fourteenth Centuries," in *People and Goods on the Move: Merchants, Networks and Communication Routes in the Medieval and Early Modern Mediterranean*, ed. Özlem Çaykent and Luca Zavagno (Fisciano: ICSR Mediterranean Knowledge, 2016), 70–71.

[26] Joseph F. O'Callaghan, "Castile, Portugal, and the Canary Islands: Claims and Counterclaims, 1344–1479," *Viator* 24 (1993), 289–291; Thurman, "Law of the Sea in Early Modern Europe," 67–68; Feakes, "Formative Influences on the Evolution of International Law," 82.

[27] Steinberg, *Social Construction of the Ocean*, 64–67.

[28] Florsheim, "Territorial Sea – 3000 Year Old Question," 76; Douglas M. Johnston, *The Theory and History of Ocean Boundary-Making* (Kingston: McGill-Queen's University Press, 1988), 321, f. 10.

[29] Marzano, *Harvesting the Sea*, 236–237.

[30] Thurman, "Law of the Sea in Early Modern Europe," 64; Feakes, "Formative Influences on the Evolution of International Law," 89–90.

With the ascendancy of the Italian commercial empires and the subsequent birth of nation states, the post-Glossators limited access to maritime spaces adjoining the coastline. Although Bartolus fixed the seaward breadth of a territorial sea to a maritime journey of two days, Baldus established that it extended to one day's sail from a coastal state.[31] Both jurists contended that a state may claim a territorial sea on the grounds of naval supremacy, long-established custom, or *regalia* (donation or grant of a privilege), with no differentiation between the laws of land and those of the sea, especially regarding the use of force.[32]

When Bartolus wrote his *Commentaria in Corpus Juris Civilis* (*Commentary on the Civil Law*) in the first half of the fourteenth century, the Mediterranean Sea was not exclusively Christian, but shared between Christians and Muslims. Surprisingly, the non-Roman concept of territorial sea was overlooked by the post-Glossators as if the Mediterranean Sea were still a Roman lake. Relying almost exclusively on the writings of the post-Glossators, the overwhelming majority of contemporary scholars accept as a historical fact that the modern conception of the territorial sea originated in late medieval Christian Europe, thereby disregarding contributions by other nations.

THE ISLAMIC CONCEPT OF THE TERRITORIAL SEA

Prior to 1492, Muslim ruling authorities, jurists, captains, navigators, crew members, experienced sea travelers, merchants engaged in overseas trade, and coastal residents observed a distinction between the high seas and the territorial sea.[33] The celebrated Arab *mu'allim* Aḥmad ibn Mājid writes in the fifteenth century:

[31] Calafat, "Mer jalousie," 50–51. [32] Calafat, "Mer jalousie," 55–56, 86–87.

[33] Muslims have left an indelible stamp upon many branches of science, including nautical science and the art of navigation. From the ninth century onward, at a time when captains and navigators relied largely on their personal expertise from memory and perhaps personal notes, captains (*mu'allims*) and navigators (*rubbāns*) from the Muslim world and Indian Ocean carried with them instruments, such as the angle measure (*qiyās*), *bussola*/compass (*ḥuqqa* or *dīra*), lodestone (*ḥajar*), lot (*buld*), lantern (*fānūs*), measurement instrument (*kamāl*), astrolabes, and most importantly portolan charts (*qunbāṣ*, *ṣaḥīfah*, or *daftar*/booklet) depicting coastlines, bays, capes, shallows, ports of call, and provisioning places. As Ibn Mājid writes, through the use of sophisticated nautical instruments in conjunction with portolan charts and mathematical tables, an experienced and learned captain and navigator was expected to be able to establish his global position in relation to his course and distance to his destination; Arab navigators in the Indian Ocean measured the distance by the *zām* method, a three-hour watch corresponding roughly to 12 nautical miles. This notation suggests that navigators knew precisely the

Know, o seeker, that every man knows his own coast best; the Chinese, China; the people of Sufāla, Sufāla (also Sofala, Mozambique); the Indians, India; the people

point at which they moved from the high seas into the maritime frontiers of their own or foreign entities. Describing the portolan charts in use in the fourteenth-century Mediterranean, Ibn Khaldūn writes: "The countries situated on the two shores of the Mediterranean are noted on a chart (*ṣaḥīfa*) which indicates the true facts regarding them and gives their positions along the coast in the proper order. The various winds and their paths are likewise put down on the chart. This chart is called the 'compass'. It is on this (compass) that (sailors) rely on their voyages." Ibn Khaldūn, *Al-Muqaddimah*, 1:58; the English translation is quoted from Franz Rosenthal, *The Muqaddimah*, https://asadullahali.files.wordpress.com/2012/10/ibn_khaldun-al_muqaddimah.pdf; Shahāb al-Dīn Aḥmad ibn Yaḥyā ibn Faḍl Allāh al-ʿUmarī, *Masālik al-Abṣār fī Mamālik al-Amṣār* (Beirut: Dār al-Kutub al-ʿIlmiyyah, 2010), 2:190, states that sailors in the Mediterranean Sea (al-Baḥr al-Shāmī) use these manuals (*qanābis*/nautical charts) for their voyages; Kahlaoui, "Depiction of the Mediterranean in Islamic Cartography," 102, 110–111, 133, 160–163, 283; Tarek Kahlaoui, "The Maghrib's Medieval Mariners and Sea Maps: The *Muqaddimah* as a Primary Source," *Journal of Historical Sociology* 30 (2017), 43–56; Jeremy F. Ledger, "Mapping Mediterranean Geographies: Geographic and Cartographic Encounters between the Islamic World and Europe, c. 1100–1600," (PhD diss., University of Michigan, 2016), 184–188; ʿAlī ibn Aḥmad ibn Muḥammad al-Sharafī al-Ṣifāqsī, *Sea Atlas Made by ʿAlī Ibn Muḥammad al-Sharafī al-Ṣifāqsi*, Manuscript (1551 CE), Arabe 2278, Bibliothèque nationale de France; Mónica Herrera-Casais, "The Nautical Atlases of ʿAlī al-Sharafī," *Suhayl* 8 (2008), 247–251; Mónica Herrera-Casais, "The 1413–14 Sea Chart of Aḥmad al-Ṭanjī," in *A Shared Legacy: Islamic Science East and West – Homage to Prof. J. M. Millàs Vallicrosa*, ed. E. Calvo *et al.* (Barcelona: Universitat de Barcelona, 2008), 284–285, 292–297. Concerning the eastern seas, Muqaddasī, *Aḥsan al-Taqāsīm*, 10, corroborates that during the first half of the tenth century CE, shipmasters and pilots in the Arabian Sea had already used nautical charts and sailing manuals, "which they constantly study and follow with implicit confidence," for their voyages: ("*wa-raʿayt(u) maʿhum dafātir fī dhālik yatadārasūnahā wa-yaʿūlūn(a) ʿalayhā wa-yaʿmalūna bimā fīhā*"); Tibbetts, in *Arab Navigation in the Indian Ocean*, 6, argues that by 400 AH/1009 CE, Arab navigational practice had already been documented; Gerald R. Tibbetts, "The Role of Charts in Islamic Navigation in the Indian Ocean," in *The History of Cartography*, ed. J. B. Harley and David Woodward (Chicago: University of Chicago Press, 1992), 2:256–262, especially p. 258; A. Arunachalam, "Technology of Indian Ocean Navigation (c. 1200–c. 1800)," *Medieval History Journal* 11 (2008), 222–226; Agius, *Classic Ships of Islam*, 196–202; Anwar ʿAbd al-ʿAleem, *Al-Milāḥa wa-ʿUlūm al-Biḥār ʿind al-ʿArab* (Kuwait, 1979), 153–173; Marina Tolmacheva, "The Indian Ocean in Arab Geography: Transmission of Knowledge between Formal and Informal Geographical Traditions," *Terra Brasilis* 6 (2015), 7–8; Naeem M. al-Hosani, "Arab Wayfinding on Land and at Sea: An Historical Comparison of Traditional Navigation Techniques," (master's thesis, University of Kansas, 2005), 7–40, 59; Bryan D. Averbuch, "From Siraf to Sumatra: Seafaring and Spices in the Islamicate Indo-Pacific, Ninth–Eleventh Centuries C.E.," (PhD diss., Harvard University, 2013), 214, 235–237. The Chinese Muslim Admiral Zheng He equipped his fleet with nautical charts, a magnetic compass, hourglass, and other navigational instruments that enabled him to fix the direction and define the position of his vessel in the vast sea. This fact necessarily signifies that skillful navigators could measure the completed and remaining distance to their destination. J. Ding *et al.*, "An Important Waypoint on Passage of Navigation History: Zheng He's Sailing to West

of Hijaz, Hijaz; the Syrians, Syria; but the sea is not peculiar to anyone of these peoples, and when you are out of sight of the coasts, you have only your own knowledge of the stars and guides to rely on.[34]

In saying that the sea "is not peculiar to anyone of these people," Ibn Mājid plainly precluded the right of any political authority or nation to claim possession of any part of the high seas. He further clearly defined the borders between the high seas and the offshore zones, although he did not delineate the extent of a state's territorial sea. One may interpret Ibn Mājid's assertion "that every man knows his own coast best" as bestowing on coastal states exclusive jurisdictional rights over limited maritime belts, the width of which may extend for a limited distance from coastal frontiers.[35] When sailing by cabotage (within sight of land), ships normally do not hug the shoreline closely, but sail at a visible distance from the coast in order to avoid manmade and natural dangers.[36] Muslim jurists and geographers defined that relatively small part of the sea adjacent to a coastal state – which the Sailors' Union (*baḥriyyūn*) of Bajjāna (Pechina, Spain) established over limited marine space off the coast of Andalusia[37] – as a "place of safety (*ma'man*),"

Ocean," *International Journal on Marine Navigation and Safety of Sea Transportation* 1 (2007), 289–291.

34 Tibbetts, *Arab Navigation in the Indian Ocean*, 215. For the original text in Arabic, consult Ibn Mājid, *Kitāb al-Fawā'id*, 286. In support of Ibn Mājid's claim, Brauer writes: "Sea frontiers, unlike most other kinds, were recognized as sharply defined borders. For this reason the experiences of travelers arriving by ship provide an appropriate basis for comparison with experiences associated with the crossing of zone type boundaries on land. Cargo and passengers carried on ships entering port from stations outside the jurisdiction of a given ruler were inevitably assumed to be coming from abroad." Ralph W. Brauer, "Boundaries and Frontiers in Medieval Muslim Geography," *Transactions of the American Philosophical Society* (New Series) 85 (1995), 33. In fact, boundaries on land are not necessarily fixed and can be relocated and adjusted by military or peaceful means since land can be possessed and inhabited, whereas the sea is not susceptible to ownership and habitation, as asserted by Nawawī, *Rawḍat al-Ṭālibīn*, 10:308: "*li-annahu laysa mawḍi' iqāma.*"

35 Qalqashandī, *Ṣubḥ al-A'shā*, 14:41. Defining the territorial sovereignty of the Egyptian Kingdom (al-Mamlaka al-Miṣriyya) in the thirteenth century, al-Qalqashandī includes within its boundaries the state land and the maritime domain. Its sovereignty extends over the external frontiers and the fortresses, provinces, cities, coasts, mainland, territorial sea (*baḥrihā*), and citizens within them.

36 Sailing across the high sea was occasionally preferred since hugging the coast could lead to dangerous encounters with pirates, natural hazards, port tolls, and longer routes.

37 Iḥsān 'Abbās, "Ittiḥād al-Baḥriyyīn fī Bajjāna bil-Andalus," *Al-Abḥāth* 23 (1970), 3–14; Lirola Delgado, *El poder naval de Al-Andalus en la época del Calefato Omeya*, 390; Picard, *La mer et les musulmans d'Occident au Moyen Âge*, 16–19, 23; Picard, *Sea of the Caliphs*, 119, 122–124, 252, 254; Khalilieh, *Islamic Maritime Law*, 139–140.

wherein the holders of safe-conduct were to feel secure within the sovereignty of the particular coastal entity.[38]

If experienced seafarers and maritime voyagers recognized the offshore sovereignty of coastal states, how then has Islamic law deemed the legal status of coastal maritime belts? This question raises a host of component questions: Did early and classical Islamic governments exercise de facto or de jure authority over limited maritime zones adjacent to coastal frontiers, and if so, according to what demarcation? Did states recognize other states' sovereignty over offshore zones, and what legal justification was there for such claims? Has Islamic law regarded the territorial sea as a *res communes* or *res nullius*? Does Islamic law grant authorities the right to impose taxes and tolls over the use of sea-lanes within a territorial sea? Addressing these and other questions may enable us to gain a better understanding of the religious, juridical, and practical bases for Islamic claims of territorial seas.

Religious Premises of Offshore Proprietorship: The Sea of Hijaz

Jurisprudentially, the Abode of Islam divides into three regions: the Ḥaram, the Hijaz, and all other territories. Non-Muslims have limited rights in the Hijaz, and *dhimmī*s and unbelievers presumably are not allowed to ingress the Ḥaram proper, although the status of the environs of Mecca has remained controversial.[39] While non-Muslims are explicitly prohibited from dwelling in the Hijaz, jurists and theologians all agree that they have the right to sojourn there for up to three nights. Muḥammad ibn Idrīs al-Shāfiʿī (150–204/767–820), eponymous founder of the classical Shāfiʿī School, ruled at length on the judicial and legal statuses of the Ḥaram and the Hijaz:

The seaward distance fixed by the *baḥriyyūn* was recognized by foreign shippers and shipowners sailing off the coast of Pechina. The territorial sea was particular to that semi-independent coastal colony. The central government of Islamic Spain authorized the *baḥriyyūn* to treat the offshore zone as part and parcel of the colony's maritime frontiers for the purposes of exploitation of marine resources and security.

[38] Ibn Rushd (al-Jadd), *Al-Bayān wa'l-Taḥṣīl*, 3:60–61.

[39] Abū al-Ḥasan ʿAlī ibn Muḥammad ibn Ḥabīb al-Māwardī, *The Ordinances of Government (Al-Aḥkām al-Sulṭāniyya wa'l-Wilāyāt al-Dīniyya)*, trans. Asadullah Yate (London: Ta-Ha, 1996), 227; Maḥmaṣṣānī, *Al-Qānūn wa'l-ʿAlāqāt al-Duwaliyya fī al-Islām*, 77; Arthur S. Tritton, *The Caliphs and Their Non-Muslim Subjects: A Critical Study of the Covenant of ʿUmar* (London: F. Cass, 1930), 175–176. This topic is best addressed and analyzed by Harry Munt, "'No Two Religions': Non-Muslims in the Early Islamic Ḥijāz," *Bulletin of the School of Oriental and African Studies* 78 (2015), 249–269.

God, be He Blessed and Exalted, has said: "The polytheists are impure" (Qur'ān 9:28). I have heard some of the people of knowledge saying that al-Masjid al-Ḥarām (Holy Sanctuary at Mecca) is an inviolate zone.

(Al-Shāfi'ī said): I was told, however, that the Messenger of God – God's blessing and peace be upon him – has said: "A Muslim shall not pay the land tax (*kharāj*), and a polytheist shall not enter into the Ḥaram." Also, he said: I heard a number of renowned scholars narrating in the *maghāzī* (a genre of Prophetic biography) that in a message attributed to the Prophet – God's blessing and peace be upon him – says: "A Muslim and a polytheist shall not convene (to perform pilgrimage) in the Ḥaram after this year of theirs." However, if some *jizya* payer seeks permission to enter freely into the Ḥaram, the *imam* shall neither admit him nor allow him to sojourn in the Ḥaram under no circumstance – be he a physician, an artisan, a professional builder, and so forth – due to God's, the Almighty and Majestic, forbiddance of the polytheists from entering al-Masjid al-Ḥarām, an act which was subsequently observed by His Messenger. If a *jizya* payer pays the tribute on the condition to take up permanent residence, he shall not be permitted to live in the Hijaz, Mecca, Medina, al-Yamāmah, and their villages; allowing them to live in the Hijaz is abrogated. However, the Prophet – God's blessing and peace be upon him – made a contract with the Jews of Khaybar, ruled them out, and said: "We allow you (to stay in your land) as long as God allows you." Other than that, God's Messenger – God's blessing and peace be upon him – has ordered to exile them from the Hijaz. It is absolutely impermissible to allow a *dhimmī* to live in the Hijaz.

(Al-Shāfi'ī) – may God Almighty have mercy upon him – said: "It is preferable to me not to allow a polytheist to enter into the Hijaz at all, as I have clarified as commanded by the Prophet – God's blessing and peace be upon him. He added: It is not evident to me to deny access for a *dhimmī* to travel through the Hijaz if his stay, as a sojourner, in any of its towns is no longer than three nights, which is the sojourner's length of stay; the likelihood is that of the Prophet – God's blessing and peace be upon him – ordered their evacuation and forbade their permanent residence therein. Probably, if it is proven that he said: "Let there not be two religions in Arabia," then two religions shall not coexist and remain there. If it were not 'Umar, who was officially appointed by the Prophet – God's blessing and peace be upon him – to collect the *kharāj* tax from a *dhimmī* merchant arriving in (the Hijaz), and who accorded them to stay in for no longer than three (nights), it would seem to me not to allow them to enter into (the Hijaz), be it as it may. (Al-Shāfi'ī), may God Almighty have mercy upon him, said: A *dhimmī* shall neither take up residence in the Hijaz nor be permitted to enter into it except if he travels through it on condition that he is given permission; this account is attributed to Yaḥyā ibn Sulaym ascribed to 'Ubayd Allāh ibn 'Umar from Nāfi' on the authority of Ibn 'Umar relates from 'Umar ibn al-Khaṭṭāb.

(Al-Shāfi'ī), may God Almighty have mercy upon him, said: If they are given permission to enter into the Hijaz but their money is taken away (from them), or are offered to carry out business transactions, they have to commission Muslims at their wish as their agents, but they have to be driven out and not stay in longer than three (nights). Concerning Mecca, no one shall enter into the Ḥaram at all, regardless of whether or not they have money there. If one of their men is left unwatched, enters into Mecca and falls ill, he shall be expelled therefrom in his present state of illness. Furthermore, if he dies, his corpse shall be transferred elsewhere, but not be laid to rest therein. If someone of them dies in some place (in the Hijaz) other than Mecca, the deceased shall be buried wherever he had died. If he is critically ill so that the (patient's) transport will result in the deterioration and escalation of his illness, he shall be left there until the transport becomes bearable; afterwards, he must be deported. If the *imam* reconciles a *dhimmī* on something to be delivered by the year's end, as I have mentioned, such an amicable settlement is forbidden provided that whatever has been paid is a nonrefundable right; by so doing he has fulfilled the covenant between (the *imam*) and (the *dhimmī*). If, after a half year has elapsed, (the *imam*) realizes that the covenant is unlawful, he shall throw it back to them; you should know that their truce is impermissible. He added that (the *imam* must say to them): If you are satisfied with a lawful truce, I will renew for you. However, if you are unsatisfied with it, I will collect from you the dues as established by law, that is, half of the annual tax for which you have completed, whereby I return the remainder to you. If they concluded a truce on the condition that they lend him something in advance for a couple of years, he must return to them everything except for the dues corresponding to their stay; he shall throw the remainder to them. I do not know of any *dhimmī* from Yemen who has been evacuated from there. *Dhimmī*s have been there, but not in the Hijaz. Therefore, no one has the right to expel them from Yemen, and there is no harm in concluding a truce allowing their stay in Yemen.

As regards to all other territories, with the exception of the Hijaz, it is unobjectionable to conclude a truce arranging their stay therein. However, if there is a due belonging to a *dhimmī* in the Hijaz, he shall authorize a (Muslim) agent (to collect it); I, furthermore, disfavor letting him into (the Hijaz) under any circumstances. He shall not be allowed to enter into it for the benefit of its residents or any other reasons like trade, of which part of its profits goes to charity, or have the right to rent from a Muslim, and so forth. If an evacuation order is issued against him, he shall be prevented from returning back to the place from which he has been turned away. If he observes this rule, he will not be held accountable. *If that were the case, they shall evidently not be prevented from sailing in the Sea of Hijaz; they shall, however, be prevented from taking up (permanent) residence on its coasts. Equally, if there are islands and mountains in the Sea of Hijaz that can sustain human habitation, (dhimmīs) shall be prevented from taking up (permanent) residence on them because all of them are part of the Hijazi territory.*[40] However, if one of them entered into the Hijaz and headed toward (the Ḥaram) under this state, he shall be punished and expelled. If he has not entered into it (Ḥaram), he shall not be punished but expelled only. And, if he returns back, he shall be punished. If one of them dies in Mecca, in such a case the body shall be taken-out from the Ḥaram and buried in the Ḥill; it shall not be buried in the Ḥaram under any circumstance because God, the Almighty and Majestic, has

40 Emphasis is mine. The Arabic text reads as follows: "وَإِذَا كَانَ هَذَا هَكَذَا فَلَا يَتَبَيَّنُ أَنْ يُمْنَعُوا رُكُوبَ بَحْرِ الْحِجَازِ وَيُمْنَعُونَ الْمُقَامَ فِي سَوَاحِلِهِ، وَكَذَلِكَ إِنْ كَانَتْ فِي بَحْرِ الْحِجَازِ جَزَائِرُ وَجِبَالٌ تُسْكَنُ مُنِعُوا سُكْنَاهَا; لِأَنَّهَا مِنْ أَرْضِ الْحِجَازِ."

commanded that polytheists shall not approach al-Masjid al-Ḥarām. If the body starts to decay, it shall be taken-out of the Ḥaram. Were it buried (in the Ḥaram), the grave must be uncovered and the body removed to the degree that it remains intact. If he falls sick in the Ḥaram, he must be taken-out. If he falls sick in the Hijaz, he must be granted some delay until travel becomes bearable; in this case, he must be taken-out. He said: As I have described what taxes shall be levied on their commodities upon their arrival at the Hijaz. May God guide me to the right path. I prefer that they shall not be allowed to carry-out commercial transactions or the like in the Hijaz.[41]

This exegesis generates more questions than answers regarding the way Islamic law has defined the "Sea of Hijaz." First and foremost, does the term apply to the entire Red Sea, or only to offshore areas adjacent to the coasts of Arabia and its islands? Which parts of the Sea of Hijaz have been considered by jurists to be sacred? How have these sacred parts been delimited? Were alien sea travelers able to enjoy innocent passage through these sacred passages? What regulations have governed such passage? Have non-Muslim shipowners, seafarers, shippers, and carriers recognized the sovereign right of the Islamic State over the offshore zones of the Red Sea adjacent to the coast of the Hijaz? Have Islamic governments

[41] Shāfiʿī, *Al-Umm*, 4:187–188 (my translation). I have chosen to quote al-Shāfiʿī's judicial viewpoint in its entirety as it is one of the oldest and most comprehensive written opinions ever presented by a founder of a Law School. However, earlier jurists such as Abū Ḥanīfa and Mālik also expressed relevant legal positions, cited by contemporaneous and succeeding theologians and jurists, but these are not as thorough as al-Shāfiʿī's exegesis. For gaining a deeper insight into the leading scholars' positions on the temporary presence of non-Muslims in the region of the Hijaz and its maritime domain, consult Ibn Qayyim al-Jawziyya, *Aḥkām Ahl al-Dhimma*, 370–408; Abū al-Ḥasan ʿAlī ibn Muḥammad ibn Ḥabīb al-Māwardī, *Al-Aḥkām al-Sulṭāniyya* (Bonn: Adolphum Marcum, 1269/1853), 291–292; Abū al-Ḥasan ʿAlī ibn Muḥammad ibn Ḥabīb al-Māwardī, *Al-Ḥāwī al-Kabīr fī Fiqh Madhhab al-Imām al-Shāfiʿī* (Beirut: Dār al-Kutub al-ʿIlmiyyah, 1419/1999), 14: 337–339; Muwaffaq al-Dīn Abd Allāh ibn Aḥmad ibn Qudāma al-Maqdisī, *Al-Mughnī* (Beirut: Dār Iḥyāʾ al-Turāth al-ʿArabī, 1405/1985), 9:286–287; Badr al-Dīn Abū Muḥammad ibn Maḥmūd ibn Aḥmad al-ʿAynī, *ʿUmdat al-Qāriʾ Sharḥ Ṣaḥīḥ al-Bukhārī* (Beirut: Dār al-Fikr al-Muʿāṣir, 1418/1998), 14:297–300; Nawawī, *Rawḍat al-Ṭālibīn*, 10:308–309; Abū Zakariyyā Yaḥyā ibn Sharaf al-Nawawī, *Al-Majmūʿ* (Jeddah: Maktabat al-Irshād, 1405/1984), 21:354–358; Shihāb al-Dīn Abū al-ʿAbbās ibn Muḥammad ibn Ḥajar al-Haythamī, *Tuḥfat al-Muḥtāj li-Sharḥ al-Minhāj* (Cairo: Al-Maktaba al-Tijāriyya al-Kubrā, 1357/1938), 9:280–283; Abū Isḥāq Burhān al-Dīn Ibrāhīm ibn Muḥammad ibn ʿAbd Allāh, *Al-Mubdiʿ fī Sharḥ al-Muqniʿ* (Beirut: Al-Maktab al-Islāmī, 1421/2000), 3:424–426; Muḥammad ibn Abū al-ʿAbbās Aḥmad ibn Shihāb al-Dīn al-Ramlī, *Nihāyat al-Muḥtāj ilā Sharḥ al-Minhāj* (Beirut: Dār al-Fikr lil-Ṭibāʿa, 1404/1984), 8:89–91; Jamāl al-Dīn al-Ḥasan ibn Yūsuf al-Ḥillī, *Taḥrīr al-Aḥkām* (Qumm: Muʾassasat al-Imām al-Ṣādiq, 1420/1999), 2:213; ʿAbd Allāh ibn al-Shaykh Ḥasan al-Kawhajī, *Zād al-Muḥtāj bi-Sharḥ al-Minhāj* (Doha: Al-Shuʾūn al-Dīniyya, 1402/1982), 4:340–343.

or judicial authorities ever claimed proprietorship over these zones? Finally, would it be correct to presume that contemporary elements governing the regime of innocent passage of foreign vessels in the territorial sea originated in the Red Sea shortly after the Prophet's death? In order to address these questions, it is first necessary to understand how the Hijaz and the geographical domain of the Ḥaram have been defined.

Located in the western Arabian Peninsula, the Hijaz consists of the coastal region bordering the Red Sea, extending from the uplands of the Najd plateau to the low-lying coastal plain called Tihāmah. Abdullah al-Wohaibi argues that classical Muslim geographers differ in their opinions regarding the demarcation of the Hijaz, some of them even confusing the Hijaz with Najd. Wohaibi's conclusion is compatible with that of ʿAbd Allāh ibn ʿAbbās (618/9–687 CE), who defines the Hijaz as comprising the mountain range called al-Sarāh, which stretches from the borders of Yemen in the south to the Syrian steppes in the north.[42] He further demarcates the Hijaz as extending to the north of Mecca as far as Surāgh and Aylah and includes the regions between the Red Sea and Dhāt ʿIrq (al-Ḍarībah), Khaybar, Wādī al-Qurā, Taimāʾ, and Tabūk. With regard to southern Hijaz, Wohaibi accepts al-Hamdānī's definition as the most reliable authority on the political boundary between the Yemen and the Hijaz in the tenth century CE, that is, as stretching from al-Hujairah in the east to Tathlīth, the valley of Jurash, Kutnah, and then Umm Jaḥdam in Tihāmah in the west.[43] Some authors refer to the Hijaz as "Arab land," thus explaining the expulsion of the *dhimmī*s, beginning with the expulsion of the Jews in 21/642 by the caliph ʿUmar ibn al-Khaṭṭāb (see Map 1).[44]

Within the Hijaz, the Ḥaram consists not only of the central shrine of the Kaaba (Kaʿba; Sacred House), but also of the area lying within the five fixed places (*mawāqīt*) on the routes leading to it. When en route to the holy sites, pilgrims must stop by one of the *mawāqīt* to purify their souls,

[42] Abdullah al-Wohaibi, *The Northern Hijaz in the Writings of the Arab* Geographers *800–1150* (Beirut: Al-Risalah, 1973), 18–20; Mohammed Bin A. Rashed al-Thenayian, "An Archaeological Study of the Yemeni Highland Pilgrim Route between Ṣanʿāʾ and Mecca," (PhD diss., Durham University, 1993), 10.

[43] Ḥasan ibn Aḥmad ibn Yaʿqūb al-Hamdānī, *Ṣifat Jazīrat al-ʿArab* (Sana'a: Maktabat al-Irshād, 1410/1990), 83–90; Wohaibi, *Northern Hijaz*, 26–27; Thenayian, "Archaeological Study of the Yemeni Highland Pilgrim Route," 13; Eldon Rutter, "The Hejaz," *Geographical Journal* 77 (1931), 97; Meloy, *Imperial Power and Maritime Trade*, 40–41.

[44] Wohaibi, *Northern Hijaz*, 27–28; Munt, "Non-Muslims in the Early Islamic Ḥijāz," 261–264.

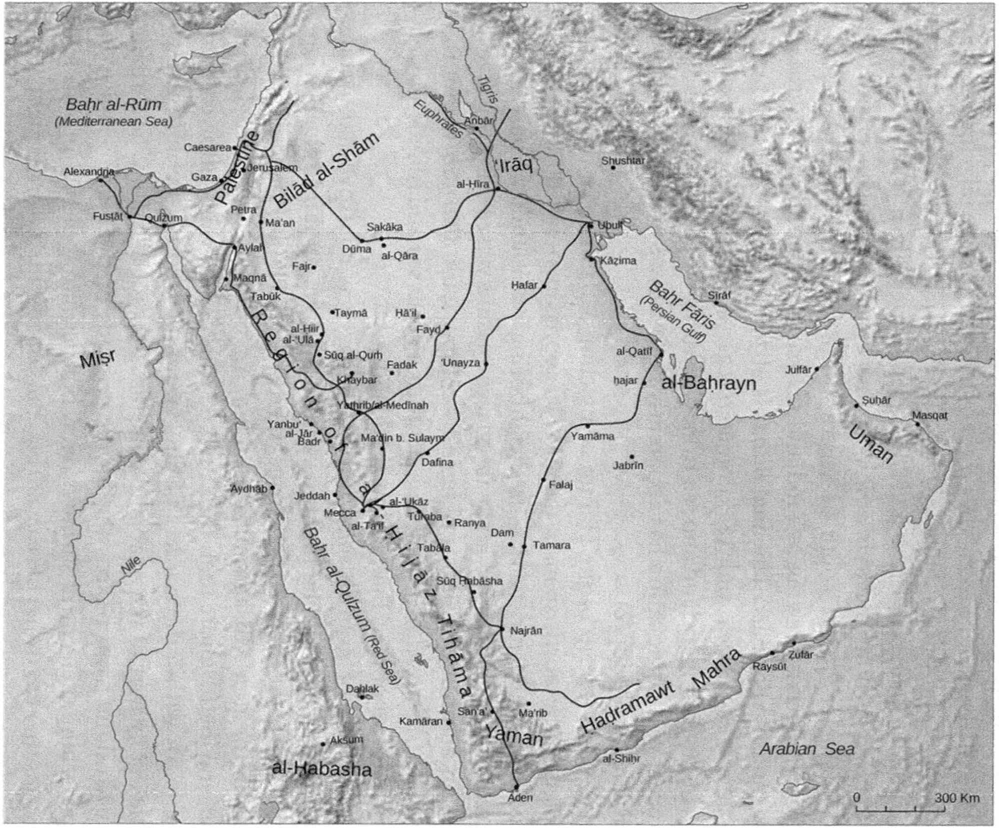

MAP 1: The Arabian Peninsula during the Prophetic and early Islamic periods.

don the pilgrim's garb (*iḥrām*), and declare the intention to reach the Kaaba. Three of the *mawāqīt* can be reached only by land, while the other two sites can also be accessed by sea. Dhul Ḥulaifa (commonly known as Masjid al-Shajarah or Ābār 'Alī), located about 10 kilometers from the Masjid of the Prophet in Medina and 420 kilometers from Mecca to the north, is the *mīqāt* serving residents of Medina. Situated about 100 kilometers from Mecca, the *mīqāt* of Dhāt 'Irq serves pilgrims coming from Iraq. The third inland *mīqāt*, called Qarn al-Manāzil, is situated about 80 kilometers to the east of Mecca and serves pilgrims arriving from Yemen. Regarding the *mawāqīt* near the coast, Yalamlam is situated 120 kilometers to the south of Mecca and a few miles from the coast. It serves pilgrims arriving by land and sea from Yemen, India, Southeast Asia, and the Far East. The final *mīqāt* is al-Juḥfah, lying 180 kilometers northwest of Mecca and 18 kilometers east of the Red Sea. It serves pilgrims traveling by land and sea from Greater Syria and Egypt, although in recent years its location has apparently been moved to the coastal town of Rābigh (see Map 2).

The coastal strip of the Ḥaram connecting Yalamlam in the south to Rābigh in the north spans a distance of approximately 300 kilometers. Theologians and jurists view its neighboring sea-islands as part of the sacred zone and thereby inviolate places of safety (see Map 2). Every Muslim and non-Muslim is obliged to comply with *Sharī'ah* within the region of the *mawāqīt*, which includes the adjacent sea and islands, as well as the littoral of the Hijaz and its mainland.

Ingression of non-Muslims into the Hijaz was controversial among classical jurists. Abū Ḥanīfa allowed them to enter even into the Ḥaram, but he forbade them from setting there.[45] Ibn Ḥanbal sanctioned the entering of non-Muslims into the Hijaz to trade, but he barred them from staying for more than three nights (four days). Mālik allowed them to sojourn within the borders of the Ḥaram, but did not permit them to settle in any part of the Arabian Peninsula.[46] As for al-Shāfi'ī, he forbade non-Muslims from trespassing on the grounds of the Ḥaram and from approaching the central shrine proper, but permitted them a provisional stay in the environs of the shrine no longer than three nights for

[45] Māwardī, *Ordinances of Government*, 240; Munt, "Non-Muslims in the Early Islamic Ḥijāz," 258.

[46] Munt, "Non-Muslims in the Early Islamic Ḥijāz," 258; Ze'ev Maghen, "'They Shall not Draw Nigh': The Access of Unbelievers to Sacred Space in Islamic and Jewish Law," *Journal of Arabic and Islamic Studies* 7 (2007), 104, 107–108.

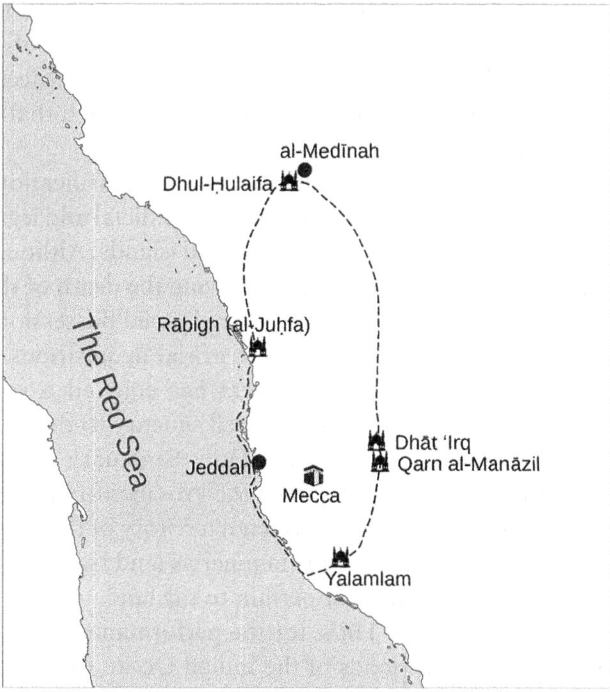

MAP 2: *Mawāqīt* geographical demarcation.

commercial purposes; this included the Sea of Hijaz and its islands. As a rule, non-Muslims are barred from taking up residence in the Hijaz; however, jurists commonly permitted them to trade in the region of Mecca and to stay no more than three nights in a given place, after which time they were required to leave voluntarily or else would be expelled.[47]

Abū Zakariyyā Yaḥyā ibn Sharaf al-Nawawī (631–676/1234–1277) decreed that, if granted the *imam*'s permission, a non-Muslim could enter the Hijaz provided that his ingression would benefit Muslims, such as through conveying a message, signing a truce or a treaty, or carrying indispensable goods.[48] However, if his purpose was to trade in goods

[47] Māwardī, *Ordinances of Government*, 240; Qalqashandī, *Ṣubḥ al-A'shā*, 13:361: "*wa-yumna'ūn min al-iqāma fī Baḥr al-Ḥijāz, bi-khilāf rukūbihi lil-safar* (they [*dhimmīs*] are forbidden from taking up permanent residence within the Sea of Hijaz, except for sailing through it)."

[48] Nawawī, *Rawḍat al-Ṭālibīn*, 10:309–311. The Holy Sanctuary is situated in a hot, arid, and uncultivatable valley as stated in Qur'ān 14:37: "رَبَّنَا إِنِّي أَسْكَنتُ مِن ذُرِّيَّتِي بِوَادٍ غَيْرِ ذِي زَرْعٍ

dispensable to Muslims, he was to be barred; that is, unless some part of his merchandise had been taken from him.[49] In the case of death, the corpses of non-Muslims were to be transferred outside of Mecca because burial there would amount to a continued presence, such that "they had become residents."[50]

Given the discrepancies in these juristic opinions, clarification is needed of the position of Islamic law with respect to the judicial and legal status of non-Muslims on the Sea of Hijaz, its coasts, and islands. Although the Red Sea was denoted an Islamic inland sea following the death of the Prophet Muḥammad in 10/632, his successors never claimed possession either on the grounds of military supremacy or territorial acquisitions. Spanning some 1,126 kilometers, the Hijazi littoral has enjoyed a special legal status. Jurists and theologians have attached sanctity to the Arabian side of the Red Sea, associating it with the Holy Sanctuary in Mecca, and thereby considering it an integral part of the Province of Hijaz. So, as the Sea of Hijaz has been designated a sovereign territory of the state, then sea travelers are to be treated in the same manner as land travelers, simply by applying to the sea those laws that pertain to the land.

When sailing in the Sea of Hijaz for the performance of hajj, pilgrims arrive from Yemen and the lands of the Indian Ocean rim on the coastal *mawāqīt* of Yalamlam or al-Juḥfah/Rābigh. When sailing for the purpose of performing hajj, it is not obligatory to don pilgrims' garb before the ship reaches a sea point adjacent to either one of the two *mawāqīt*. On his way to perform hajj by sea in 1854, the Malayan writer Munshi Abdullah (1796–1854) reported that he and the other pilgrims had to don the *iḥrām* outfit when the ship drew parallel to the *mīqāt* of Lamlam (Yalamlam).[51] In the same way, pilgrims coming by sea from Egypt and Greater Syria

عِندَ بَيْتِكَ الْمُحَرَّمِ رَبَّنَا لِيُقِيمُواْ الصَّلاَةَ فَاجْعَلْ أَفْئِدَةً مِّنَ النَّاسِ تَهْوِي إِلَيْهِمْ وَارْزُقْهُم مِّنَ الثَّمَرَاتِ لَعَلَّهُمْ يَشْكُرُونَ (O our Lord! I have made some of my offspring to dwell in a valley without cultivation, by Thy Sacred House; in order, O our Lord, that they may establish regular Prayer: so fill the hearts of some among men with love toward them, and feed them with fruits: so that they may give thanks)." For this reason, pilgrims and local residents have to rely upon food imports from outside the Hijaz through indigenous or foreign proxies, Muslims and non-Muslims alike. Jurists generally tended to grant access to non-Muslims to engage in trade of indispensable goods in Mecca and its surroundings. During the caliphate of al-Walīd ibn ʿAbd al-Malik (r. 86–96/705–715), Byzantine Christian artisans were recruited to perform restorations in the Prophet's Mosque in Medina. Munt, "Non-Muslims in the Early Islamic Ḥijāz," 260.

49 Nawawī, *Rawḍat al-Ṭālibīn*, 10:309–310.

50 Nawawī, *Rawḍat al-Ṭālibīn*, 10:310–311; Māwardī, *Ordinances of Government*, 241.

51 Raimy Ché-Ross, "Munshi Abdullah's Voyage to Mecca: A Preliminary Introduction and Annotated Translation," *Indonesia and the Malay World* 28 (2000), 197.

have to don their *iḥrām* when the vessel is adjacent to the *mīqāt* of al-Ju ḥfah/Rābigh. They may either disembark on a nearby island, or else don the *iḥrām* on board ship if there is sufficient space and privacy to do so. For these reasons, the coastal strip between the two *mawāqīt* – extending over 260 kilometers – its adjacent waters and offshore islands became part of the sanctified zone (see Map 2).

The most relevant point al-Shāfiʿī addresses with reference to the law of the sea is the status of the Sea of Hijaz in the Islamic legal tradition. The Islamic Law of Nature denotes the sea as being common to all nations, with the exception of offshore security and the fishing zone. However, contrary to the Law of Nature, on the basis of religious considerations, Muslims have claimed exclusive de facto and de jure proprietorship of the offshore belt off the Hijazi coast. Similar to the regulations for the *mawāqīt*, the law does not forbid non-Muslims from sailing within this maritime zone, nor from carrying out commercial transactions. Right of passage and free access to ports are regularly granted to foreign ships either at their request, through diplomatic channels – via treaties or general or private *amān*[52] – or when they are experiencing distress. Passage of ships in the Sea of Hijaz has always been free of charge and not associated with the payment of *qibālah* (tribute), in contrast to the Venetian practice (*gabella*) in the Adriatic Sea. Pursuant to general maritime custom, it is morally obligatory to provide safety and security for all ships sailing through the territorial sea of the Hijaz, irrespective of nationality.

As long as a foreign ship does not moor in port, the captain enjoys exclusive jurisdiction over her, her human element, and her contents. As non-Muslims have been permitted to engage in trade in the region of Mecca, it should go without saying that the law would grant them the right to fish for personal consumption in the Sea of Hijaz. The fact that prominent jurists have not addressed this issue perhaps indicates that there is indeed no prohibition against exploitation of the living natural

[52] The earliest, as well as most reliable, evidence of the de facto existence of the right of foreign vessels to innocent passage in the Sea of Hijaz is the 9 AH/630 CE guarantee of protection given by the Prophet Muḥammad to Yūḥannā ibn Ruʾba, the governor and bishop of the port city of Aylah, which deems foreign vessels floating territorial units. The Prophet granted Aylah's governing authorities the right to apply the territoriality principle not only to vessels flying its flag, but also to its nationals even when sailing aboard non-national vessels. For further details, consult the previous chapter. On the *amān* granted to Chinese and Indian traders in the Red Sea region during the Mamluk period, see Qalqashandī, *Ṣubḥ al-Aʿshā*, 13:339–342; Ḥamāda, *Al-Wathāʾiq al-Siyāsiyya wa'l-Idāriyya lil-ʿAṣr al-Mamlūkī*, 504–507.

resources of the Sea of Hijaz, at least for private consumption. Finally, regarding the death of a non-Muslim within the maritime domain of the Hijaz, the corpse may be laid to rest at sea, on one of the islets, or on the coast, in order to avoid the spread of disease and possible damage to cargo from decomposition and associated smells. Alternatively, the shipmaster may retain the corpse until either the ship's destination or the nearest port is reached.[53]

Extending 2,250 kilometers from Bab el-Mandeb to Suez with a breadth ranging 30–355 kilometers, the Red Sea has been surrounded on all sides by Islamic territories from as early as the second half of the seventh century. Despite a topology that permits it to be viewed as an inland sea, the Prophet, caliphs, and sultans never assumed proprietorship, nor referred to the Red Sea as *mare nostrum*. Pursuant to Qur'ān 14:32[54] and 45:12,[55] the earth and its natural resources are common to all humankind; all nations may enjoy free access to the seas, including the Sea of Hijaz, regardless of its sanctity, and by virtue of the fact that the seas are not susceptible to human occupation.[56] Only habitable zones may be claimed as a private or communal possession.

Like many natural resources, the seas cannot become the property of any particular nation. However, contrary to other seas around the world, the Sea of Hijaz has been characterized as the "*ḥarīm*," whereby access is either restricted or prohibited outright for *ḥarbī*s and for subjects of countries without commercial or diplomatic truces with the Abode of Islam. However, foreign ships and ships owned or operated by non-Muslim entrepreneurs are not barred outright from sailing through it, or anchoring in any port located on the sanctified coastal zone of Mecca (the zone between the *mawāqīt* of Yalamlam and Rābigh). Central and provincial governments even encouraged and promoted overseas trade by granting commercial privileges, fighting piracy, and establishing an autonomous judicial system for

[53] Khalilieh, *Islamic Maritime Law*, 168–171.

[54] "وَسَخَّرَ لَكُمُ الْفُلْكَ لِتَجْرِيَ فِي الْبَحْرِ بِأَمْرِهِ (He Who hath made the ships subject to you (humankind) that they may sail through the sea by His Command)."

[55] "اللَّهُ الَّذِي سَخَّرَ لَكُمُ الْبَحْرَ لِتَجْرِيَ الْفُلْكُ فِيهِ بِأَمْرِهِ وَلِتَبْتَغُوا مِن فَضْلِهِ وَلَعَلَّكُمْ تَشْكُرُونَ (It is God Who has subjected the sea to you (humankind) that the ships may sail through it by His command, that ye may seek of His Bounty, and that ye may be grateful)."

[56] Nawawī, *Rawḍat al-Ṭālibīn*, 10:308: " … they are not prevented from sailing in the Sea of Hijaz because (the sea) is not susceptible to human occupation (*li-annahu laysa mawḍi' iqāma*)."

dhimmīs and non-Muslim foreign subjects.[57] The "maritime *ḥarīm*" of the Hijaz, equivalent to the present-day territorial sea, can be defined as a belt of the sea adjacent to the Hijazi coast, the breadth of which extends to its farthest island and the length of which extends from Tihāmah in the south to the Syrian steppes in the north. One may argue that, in fact, the northernmost point of the *ḥarīm* falls within the offshore space opposite Tabūk, the point of the Prophet Muḥammad's most distant expedition in northern Arabia, an area from which non-Muslims were presumably expelled by the second caliph, ʿUmar ibn al-Khaṭṭāb.

It should be emphasized that the concept of religious sovereignty over an offshore zone adjacent to the littoral zone of the Hijaz is universally unique and has no equivalent in legal history. However, despite the religious merits of Palestine in Islam and the geographical proximity of the third Holy Shrine (Al-Aqṣā Mosque) to the contested Mediterranean, Muslim jurists did not attach sanctity to the Palestinian territorial sea. Essentially, extension of the state's jurisdiction over a limited offshore

[57] Documentary and literary evidence corroborate the fact that *dhimmīs* persisted in the region of Mecca and invested in business dealings through their Muslim agents or partners, especially during the pilgrimage season. The ninth-century Radhanite Jewish merchants used the west Arabian ports of al-Jār and Jeddah on their route from Qulzum down the Red Sea. Correspondingly, Indian, Chinese, and Southeast Asian traders frequented the Red Sea ports on the coast of Arabia. Describing the port city of Jār, port of Medina, as a colony of foreign merchants and one of the major ports for foreign flag vessels departing for the Hijaz, Yāqūt writes: "it is a port-city (*furḍa*), which is frequented by ships arriving from Ethiopia, Egypt, Aden, China, and the rest of the Lands of India." Yāqūt ibn ʿAbd Allāh al-Ḥamawī, *Muʿjam al-Buldān* (Beirut: Dār Ṣāder, 1986), 2:92–93; Abū al-Qāsim ʿUbayd Allāh ibn ʿAbd Allāh ibn Khurdādhbih, *Al-Masālik wa'l-Mamālik* (Leiden, 1889), 153–154; Goitein, *Mediterranean Society*, 1:177, 200; Moshe Gil, *In the Kingdom of Ishmael: Texts from the Cairo Geniza* (Tel Aviv: Tel Aviv University Press, 1997), 2:485–490, docs. TS 8.12, l. 10 and DK 246 a-b, l. 21; Moshe Gil, "The Rādhānite Merchants and the Land of Rādhān," *Journal of the Economic and Social History of the Orient* 17 (1974), 308–309; Munt, "Non-Muslims in the Early Islamic Ḥijāz," 260; Agius, *Classic Ships of Islam*, 96; Hikoichi Yajima, "Maritime Activities of the Arab Gulf People and the Indian Ocean World in the Eleventh and Twelfth Centuries," *Journal of Asian and African Studies* 14 (1977), 199, 201; Patrick Wing, "Indian Ocean Trade and Sultanic Authority: The *Nāẓir* of Jeddah and the Mamluk Political Economy," *Journal of the Economic and Social History of the Orient* 57 (2014), 66, describes two Chinese vessels transporting a cargo of porcelain, musk, and silk that could not anchor in Aden, and therefore they made their way to the port of Jeddah after obtaining permission from the Mamluk sultan al-Ashraf Barsbāy (r.825–841/1422–1438). On the maritime traffic between Jeddah and the Indian Ocean and Red Sea ports in the late fifteenth and early sixteenth centuries, consult Meloy, *Imperial Power and Maritime Trade*, 66–80, 249–255.

zone sought to protect the fishing and economic rights, and interests of the locals, and to defend the coastal frontiers from external raids.

Civil Justifications of Offshore Claims: The *Ḥarīm* Zone

Ḥarīm denotes an inviolable zone within which development is prohibited or restricted to prevent the impairment of: (a) natural resources, such as water – seas, lakes, rivers, wells, springs, and waterways; trees growing on barren lands (*mawāt*: unused or dead land); woodlands; and other natural resources indispensable to the welfare of a community; and (b) utilities, such as streets, open spaces alongside streets; open areas around markets; artificial waterways and channels; resting places for travelers; and other public spaces crucial to public welfare.[58] The creation of *ḥarīms* around natural resources was aimed at saving these from overexploitation, damage, abuse, or misuse.

The Prophet placed great importance on conserving, safeguarding, and rehabilitating the natural environment by designating spaces as inviolable in order to protect natural resources. A tradition attributed to the Prophet rules that "every land has its appurtenance forbidden/*ḥarīm* (to other than the proprietor) (لِكُلّ أرْضٍ حَرِيمًا)."[59] Following this principle, to which the Prophet and his successors abided, spaces adjacent to water sources have been declared as *ḥarīm*. The *ḥarīm* boundaries of public and private wells were fixed at a 40-cubit (*dhirāʿ*) radius (21.86 yards/20 meters);[60] for natural springs, the *ḥarīm* area extended to a radius of 500 cubits (273.25 yards/250 meters).[61] With respect to rivers, the authority of Abū Ḥanīfa

[58] Māwardī, *Ordinances of Government*, 265; Lutfallah Gari, "A History of the *Ḥimā* Conservation System," *Environment and History* 12 (2006), 213–215; Abubakr A. Bagader *et al.*, *Environmental Protection in Islam* (Gland, Switzerland: IUCN Commission on Environmental Law, 1994), 26–27; Ben Shemesh, *Taxation in Islam*, 1: 72–74; 2:63–64, 122–124, 127; 3:121; Ibn Fāyiʿ, *Aḥkām al-Baḥr fī al-Fiqh al-Islāmī*, 683–684; Aḥmad A. Ḥasan, *Qānūn al-Biḥār wa'l-Anhār al-Duwaliyya fī al-Islām* (Cairo: Maʿhad al-Buḥūth wa'l-Dirāsāt al-ʿArabiyya, 1988), 19–22.

[59] Kāsānī, *Badāʾiʿ al-Ṣanāʾiʿ*, 6:195; the English translation is quoted from Ḥamīdullāh, *Muslim Conduct of State*, 95.

[60] Ben Shemesh, *Taxation in Islam*, 1:72–74; 2:63–64; Māwardī, *Ordinances of Government*, 260–261. Jurists argued that the reserved area of a well differs from one well to another. A new well maintains a reserved space of twenty-five cubits (13.66 yards/ 12.5 meters) on all sides, whereas an ancient well is fixed at fifty cubits (27.32 yards/25 meters). As for an agricultural well, it assumes an inviolable zone of three hundred cubits (163.93 yards/150 meters) on all sides.

[61] Ben Shemesh, *Taxation in Islam*, 1:73–74; 2:63, 123–124; Māwardī, *Ordinances of Government*, 261–262.

stated that "there is no reserved public space for rivers" because all people are partners in the water of great rivers. However, other jurists maintained that lands along the riverbanks should be reserved for the maintenance of water and for other activities and so no one may claim these spaces as private property.[62] All jurists agreed that the great rivers are akin to public highways and must be traversable, clear, and unobstructed on all sides. The governing authorities had to ensure the removal of any construction, private and public, which may have caused damage or affected the safe passage of vessels. Any person who built a structure which caused damage to rivercraft, their contents, or their human element was held liable for any losses.[63]

Whether or not the seas should have *ḥarīm* zones was also dealt with in the early jurisprudential compendia. The Mālikī jurist Ashhab ibn ʿAbd

[62] Ben Shemesh, *Taxation in Islam*, 2:60, 64; 3:127; Ibn Qayyim al-Jawziyya, *Zād al-Maʿād*, 5:709: "the great rivers are common to all people (*al-anhār al-kibār al-mushtaraka bayna al-nās*)"; Ḥasan, *Qānūn al-Biḥār wa'l-Anhār*, 22–24.

[63] Ben Shemesh, *Taxation in Islam*, 3:128; ʿAlī ibn Aḥmad ibn Saʿīd ibn Ḥazm, *Al-Muḥallā* (Amman: International Ideas Home, 1424/2003), 880, answer to question no. 969: "There is no difference between sea coast and river banks in religion; there is no preference for one coast over another (*lā farq bayn sāḥil baḥr wa-sāḥil nahr fī al-dīn, wa-lā faḍl li-shayʾ min dhālik*)." The Qurʾān does not distinguish between the banks of great rivers and the sea coast. For instance, the Nile is frequently referred to as *yam* (sea), as in classical Arabic sources and documents from the Cairo Geniza. Respecting the birth of Moses, Qurʾān 20:39 states: "أَنِ اقْذِفِيهِ فِي التَّابُوتِ فَاقْذِفِيهِ فِي الْيَمِّ فَلْيُلْقِهِ الْيَمُّ بِالسَّاحِلِ يَأْخُذْهُ عَدُوٌّ لِي وَعَدُوٌّ لَهُ (Throw [the child] into the chest, and throw [the chest] into the sea [Nile], so the sea [river] will cast him up on the shore [river bank], and he will be taken up by one who is an enemy to me and an enemy to him)." For further details on the description and importance of the Nile in Islamic tradition, consult Ahmad Nazmi, "The Nile River in Islamic Geographical Sources," *Studia Arabistyczne i Islamistyczne* 12 (2004), 28–54. Legally, inland and internal waters were recognized as being under state sovereignty and proprietorship. The government in charge of regulating navigation on rivers and in harbors was held responsible for embanking the rivers and prohibiting private construction within a specific distance from the riverbanks. A space of 200–500 ells/yards (100–250 meters) from the banks of a river was to be kept clear of all buildings. Ibn ʿAbdūn reports that the local governor of a port city "has to be very vigilant against any enterprise that might have a harmful effect on the port, and that the superintendent of the port is under obligation not to permit selling plots of lands in the port." Muḥammad ibn Aḥmad ibn ʿAbdūn al-Tujībī, *Séville Musulmane au début du XIIe Siècle, le Traité d'Ibn ʿAbdūn*, ed. Évariste Levi-Provençal (Paris: G. P. Maisonneuve, 1947), 60, 64–65; Évariste Levi-Provençal (ed.), *Thalāth Rasāʾil Andalusiyya fī Ādāb al-Ḥisba wa'l-Muḥtasib* (Cairo: L'Institut Français d'archéologie orientale, 1955), 29–30; ʿAbd al-Raḥmān ibn Abū Bakr ibn Muḥammad al-Suyūṭī, *Al-Ḥāwī lil-Fatāwī* (Cairo: Al-Ṭibāʿa al-Munīriyya, 1352/1933), 1:133–143; Khamīs ibn Saʿīd al-Shiqṣī, *Manhaj al-Ṭālibīn wa-Balāgh al-Rāshidīn* (Muscat: Wizārat al-Awqāf wa'l-Shuʾūn al-Dīniyya, 1403/1983), 13:6–7; Ṣafāʾ ʿAbd al-Fattāḥ, *Al-Mawāniʾ wa'l-Thughūr al-Miṣriyya min al-Fatḥ al-Islāmī ḥattā al-ʿAṣr al-Fāṭimī* (Cairo: Dār al-Fikr al-ʿArabī, 1986), 103–111.

al-ʿAzīz al-Qaysī (140–204/757–820) made a clear distinction between property rights on land as distinct to those pertaining to maritime spaces, arguing that – contrary to the sea – land can be occupied. The inquiry reads as follows:

Ashhab was asked about a group of voluntary guards, who arrived in some town, set up boundary lines, and settled therein for the performance of garrison duty (*ribāṭ*); a woodland area separated their settlement from the sea. Along the coast there were deserted towns occupied by *ribāṭ* practitioners, too. Since these were exposed to immediate threat and frequent raids of the Byzantines (Rūm), governors refused the practitioners' appeal to extend their boundaries. Their living conditions have improved in due course and, as a result, they have expanded their woodland zone so that their territorial rights extended to the seacoast. Are they entitled to do so? Do you think that the sea should have a *ḥarīm* zone on the pretext of repulsing Byzantine (maritime) threat? Or, can their zone be expanded under the pretense of feeding their animals?

He answered: They shall not be forbidden from developing their woodlands as much as they wish, provided that their territorial extension should not get close to populated areas and cause harm to local residents. If that were to happen, they shall be forbidden from doing so. I do not think that the sea should have its own inviolable zone.[64]

As the Prophetic tradition maintains that every land has its *ḥarīm*, by extension, the coast must also have its *ḥarīm* to include part of the maritime space along the shoreline. However, Ashhab offers a different interpretation. As land, the coast can have *ḥarīm* extending over a limited and clearly visible seaward distance. However, the sea itself does not have *ḥarīm*. Thus, the sea bordering the coast can be an appurtenant to the coastland, but not vice versa.[65] This legal opinion does not suggest that nonlocal residents may exploit marine natural resources off coastal settlements, *ribāṭs*, or installations other than their own according to their free will. Contrary to the open sea, which is common and openly accessible to all, maritime zones contiguous to populated coastal frontiers enjoy a different legal status, although they still may not be subject to private ownership. Dwellers in coastal settlements, garrisoned warriors, and volunteers at *ribāṭs* could claim exclusive fishing rights, restrict access, or exclude outsiders from exploiting marine resources.[66] Even so, they still

[64] Abū Zayd al-Qayrawānī, *Al-Nawādir wa'l-Ziyādāt*, 10:521: "*wa-lā arā lil-baḥr(i) ḥarīm(an).*"

[65] Ḥamīdullāh, *Muslim Conduct of State*, 93–94.

[66] An extraordinary example is documented in a royal decree issued by the Fatimid caliph al-Ḥāfiẓ (r. 525–544/1131–1149) on Rajab 21, 528 /May 17, 1134. According to this caliphal decree, access to Lake Burullus, laying to the west of Rosetta on the Mediterranean, was

could not prevent nonthreatening vessels from freely navigating these waters.

Historians have affirmed that *ribāṭ* occupants made a living from gathering hay, collecting wood, producing salt, and catching fish.[67] Tunisian jurist Abū al-Ḥasan Muḥammad ibn Khalaf al-Qābisī (324–403/935–1012) was asked about fish vendors purchasing fish from garrisons at the Ribāṭ of Monastir (Tunisia) and selling them in different towns. He responded with concern that this activity could negatively affect the economy of the *ribāṭ*:

In my view, fishing in (Monastir's Sea) is like collecting hay and wood from its woodland areas; outsiders cannot exploit them, except if harm is not caused to them, or its occupants do not yield benefits from leaving it (marine species) unfished. It is not something attainable, like collecting hay and wood in land, which are always within reach. This means that any resident of Monastir who catches fish in this sea has to sell them in its market; whoever wishes may buy (fish) provided that he neither pays a very low price to the seller nor fixes the rate of sale. They must, however, be sold in conformity with what God has assigned to him at that time, regardless of whether they fetch a greater or lesser price. Whatever is left over from the purchase for the consumption of the residents of Monastir, the catcher (*al-ṣā'id*) can dispose of and sell (them) as he wishes and at his own free well.

If the catcher intends to fish in this sea with the intention of selling them in the local market, then no one is eligible to buy the fish at the gateway to the sea, or when heading for the market; they must, however, be sold at the marketplace. Merchants who take-up residence in these strongholds are associates of other occupants. Nevertheless, if they inflict harm on occupants, their affiliation will

exclusively restricted to local residents and the *ḍāmin* (tax-farmer), who normally paid a sum determined in advance to the treasury in return for keeping tax revenues for himself from a defined district or area, including a limited offshore zone. Save for local residents and the *ḍāmin*(s), outsiders were denied access to fishing in Lake Burullus and its adjacent Mediterranean waters. Nonlocals and aliens were required to abide by the rules and regulations of fisheries in every province and coastal zone. The decree reads: "Fishermen from outside of this province living in the province of al-Gharbiyya are fishing along the shores of the Lake (of Burullus) in the said province and all this is causing damage to the *ḍāmins* and to the finances of the *dīwān* (custom house). … (It enjoins) the prevention of whomsoever of those who are not their tenants encroaches upon the shores of their province. … Let the Chosen *Amīr*, the diligent representative of its *dīwān* – may God save him (and all the *amīrs*, governors, and employees) ensure that all the commands and prohibitions contained in this decree are carried out; let him stand within the bounds of his office in loyalty and absolute obedience." Geoffrey Khan, "A Copy of a Decree from the Archives of the Fāṭimīd Chancery in Egypt," *Bulletin of the School of Oriental and African Studies* 49 (1986), 441–443.

[67] Néji Djelloul, *Al-Ribāṭāt al-Baḥriyya bi-Ifrīqiya fī al-'Aṣr al-Wasīṭ* (Tunis: Markaz al-Dirāsāt wa'l-Buḥūth al-Iqtiṣādiyya wa'l-Ijtimā'iyya, 1999), 88, 111, 114–115, 118, 119–120, 137, 139, 150, 168, 177, 194, 202–203.

be terminated and their residence revoked because they are disqualified from meeting the *ribāṭ*'s religious duties and conditions. Their way of earning a livelihood is equivalent to that of shopkeepers (*ahl al-aswāq*); therefore, they must be forbidden from residing due to the harm they may inflict. Those who inflict harm in one way or another on practitioners of the strongholds must be expelled. Any merchant who arrives in this place for fishing therein with the purpose of trading them in various places other than Monastir must not be permitted to do so because he inflicts harm on those who fish in Monastir. However, if the residents of Monastir have taken what is sufficient to supply their want, there is no harm, if God wills, in transporting what they caught from this sea on the condition that such an action neither inflicts harm nor straitens their conditions; this is because sea fishing is dissimilar to land hunting, where the land prey (is easier to attain). If someone inclines to leave them unexploited in that place, I do not see any reason why local people be prevented from reaping benefit from fishing! This is what seems to me (is happening) in the case of the Sea of Monastir. May God grant us success![68]

A number of legal inferences can be gleaned from this *responsum*. First, and consistent with the Prophetic tradition, being part of the land, every coast has its own *ḥarīm*. Second, local residents of coastal settlements enjoyed exclusive rights to exploit marine resources available within a specified distance from the coast. Therefore, access to any offshore *ḥarīm* was either conditional or denied outright to outsiders. Third, although exact boundaries for the maritime *ḥarīm*s were not fixed, it is reasonable to assume that they ranged up to the seaward distance at which a vessel could be sighted from the coast. Fourth, exploitation of natural resources in the "protected maritime zones" – if such a term is appropriate – required prior approval from local, and at times peripheral, governing authorities. Fifth, in order to conserve the marine ecosystem and not to affect the economies and livelihoods of the local residents, both native and foreign fishermen alike were obliged not to overfish and deplete the resources, since the needs of the community held precedence over those of the individual. Sixth, even though the sea is considered to be the property of no particular person but instead common to all, and although fishermen could freely set sail for any destination, they were not licensed to fish unrestrained within sighting distance of populated coastal areas other than those of their own hometowns. In other words, the maritime spaces bordering coastal settlements may be considered to have had the status of *res communes*, whereby local residents held exclusive rights over – but could not deny nonlocal vessels from passing through – these

[68] Wansharīsī, *Al-Mi'yār*, 2:5–6.

natural resources. In sum, while non-Muslims and non-native Muslims were permitted to sail freely through the Sea of Hijaz, it is clear that they were not entitled to exploit its natural resources for commercial purposes.

With the installation of the *ribāṭ* system along the coastal frontiers and the associated increasing number of garrisoned volunteers, the governing authorities and jurists needed to develop regulations providing for the communal and sustainable use of marine resources. In order to encourage people to move to the maritime frontiers as an impediment against enemy raids, the state allocated large tracts of unused land for cultivation and mandated that they be cultivated by *ribāṭ* practitioners. The state also created *ḥarīm* zones for protecting natural resources from abuse, misuse, and exploitation by outsiders. Perhaps when Ashhab ruled that the sea could have no *ḥarīm*, he relied on the absence from Prophetic tradition of such a reference. He may also have relied on the fact that not all of the sea is within sight from the shore, that the sea is not susceptible to occupation,[69] or that it cannot be subject to private ownership. The notion of a "protected maritime zone" was common to the Mediterranean polities for many centuries prior to, and certainly after, the advent of Islam.[70] Since Islamic expansion did not abruptly change the material culture of the indigenous populations, it is plausible to assume that many of the prevailing legal elements survived and were incorporated into early and classical Islamic jurisprudence.[71] Despite such influences, the state held exclusive sovereignty over the maritime spaces adjacent to the coast.

Military and Security Justifications of Offshore Jurisdiction

Unlike the Roman *praeses* and the Byzantine *stratēgos*, both of whom enjoyed supreme authority over their subjects and properties at sea, the *Amīr al-Baḥr*'s (Admiral's) authority was superior.[72] His jurisdiction

[69] Nawawī, *Rawḍat al-Ṭālibīn*, 10:308: "(*li-annahu laysa mawḍiʿ iqāma*)."

[70] Ephraim Lytle, "Η θάλασσακοινή: Fishermen, the Sea, and the Limits of Ancient Greek Regulatory Reach," *Classical Antiquity* 31 (2012), 1–55.

[71] Jokisch, *Islamic Imperial Law*, 134, 136, 241–242.

[72] Fahmy, *Muslim Naval Organization*, 92; Rana M. Mikati, "The Creation of Early Islamic Beirut: The Sea, Scholars, Jihad and the Sacred," (PhD diss., University of Chicago, 2013), draws our attention to the fact that classical Arabic sources use different names and titles to denote "admiral": 42, f. 65 (*ṣāḥib al-thughūr al-baḥriyya*/commander of the maritime frontiers); 45, f. 73 (*ʿalā al-baḥr*/governorship of the sea); 47, f. 79 (*ṣāḥib al-baḥr*/commander of the sea/fleet); 49, f. 85 (*wilāyat ghāziyat al-baḥr*/governor of maritime expeditions); 57, f. 108 (*wilāyat thaghr al-baḥr*/governor of the maritime

extended not only to Muslim subjects and properties at sea, but also to the coastal frontiers and adjacent waters of the state.[73] Upon his appointment as admiral, Qudāma ibn Jaʿfar (d. 337/948) writes that the Commander of the Faithful (*Amīr al-Muʾminīn*/caliph) must select for this role a person with distinctive traits. First and foremost, he must fear God, obey Him, be aware of His punishment, please Him, seek justice; keep away from Satan's path, purify his soul and heart from spiritual sins, and be exemplary in his conduct. As the highest-ranking officer in the navy, the admiral is required to recruit worthy, trusted, and experienced officers, soldiers, seafarers, spies, policemen, shipwrights, and artisans, and provide them with arms, equipment, and nourishment. The admiral must also be well-versed in naval war tactics, knowing how best to maneuver his fleet during naval combat. The fortification of coastal towns and settlements, and establishment of fortresses, watchtowers, and shipyards (*dār al-ṣināʿa*/arsenal) were among the most important military duties of the admiral. Since his authority extended to all people traveling along the coast or sailing through the territorial sea, he asserted jurisdiction over these spaces and was authorized to intervene in disputes involving local residents and foreigners, provided that he took a rigorous stance against suspicious individuals.[74]

As the fundamental principle underlying a territorial sea is the protection of the coastal frontiers against enemy and pirate raids, the commonality of these areas was not affected by the advent of the office of *Amīr al-Baḥr*. As they possessed no navy that could match Christian sea powers, and in view of the *mujāhidūn*'s land-based culture during the early years of Islam in the Mediterranean, Muslim army commanders and rulers took defensive positions.[75] They erected *ribāṭ*-fortresses

frontier); 57, f. 107 (*amīr al-sāḥil*/governor of the coast); 167, f. 22 (*ṣāḥib ghazw al-baḥr*/commander of maritime expeditions).

[73] Ibn Mammātī, *Qawānīn al-Dawāwīn*, 247–248.

[74] Qudāma ibn Jaʿfar ibn Ziyād al-Baghdādī, *Al-Kharāj wa-Ṣināʿat al-Kitāba* (Baghdad: Dār al-Rashīd lil-Nashr, 1981), 47–51. Also, H. Idris Bell and Frederic G. Kenyon, *Greek Papyri in the British Museum* (London: British Museum, 1893–1917), 4:64–67, Pap. 1392, Pap. 1393; Jaser Abu Safieh, *Bardiyyāt Qurra Ibn Sharīk al-ʿAbsī* (Riyad: Markaz al-Malik Faiṣal lil-Buḥūth wa'l-Dirāsāt al-Islāmiyya, 2004), 259, Pap. 1354; 266–269, Pap. 1392, Pap. 1393; Fahmy, *Muslim Naval Organization*, 107–109; Saif Sh. al-Muraikhi, "Imārat al-Baḥr fī ʿAṣr al-Khulafāʾ al-Rāshidīn wa'l-Umawiyyīn (11–131/632–748)," *Majallat Kulliyyat al-Insāniyyāt wa'l-ʿUlūm al-Ijtimāʿiyya* 23 (2000), 22–26; Picard, *Sea of the Caliphs*, 81–82.

[75] Hussain Mones, *Tārīkh al-Muslimīn fī al-Baḥr al-Mutawassiṭ: Al-Awḍāʿ al-Siyāsiyya, wa'l-Iqtiṣādiyya, wa'l-Ijtimāʿiyya* (Cairo: Al-Dār al-Miṣriyya al-Lubnāniyya, 1413/1993), 57–60.

and *miḥrās*es along the coast,[76] a practice already widespread within the Roman-Byzantine world.[77] This system sought not only to defend the coast from external attacks, but also to maintain peace, safeguard trade routes on land, and secure navigation channels within the territorial sea.[78] Reporting on the *ribāṭ* system along the coastal strip of Palestine from Gaza in the south to Arsūf in the north, the Palestinian geographer al-Muqaddasī (al-Maqdisī) (336–380/947–990) provides the following description:

Along the seacoast of the capital [Ramla] are watch-stations [*ribāṭ*s], from which the summons to arms is given. The warships and the galleys [*shalandiyyāt* and *shawānī*] of the Greeks come into these ports, bringing aboard them the captives taken from Muslims; these they offer for ransom three for a hundred *dīnār*s. And in each of these stations there are men who know the Greek tongue, for they have missions to the Greeks, and trade with them in provisions of all kinds. At the stations, whenever a Greek vessel appears, they give the alarm by lighting a beacon on the tower of the station if it be night or, if it be day, by making a great smoke. From every watch-station on the coast up to the capital [Ramla] are built, at intervals, high towers, in each of which is stationed a company of men. As soon as they perceive the beacon on the tower of the coast station, the men of the next tower above it kindle their own, and then on, one after another; so that hardly has an hour elapsed before the trumpets are sounding in the capital, and drums are beating from the city tower, calling the people down to that watch-station by the sea; and they hurry-out in force, with their arms, and the young men of the villages gather together. Then the ransoming begins. One prisoner will be given in exchange for another, or money and jewels will be offered; until at length all the prisoners who are in the Greek ships have been set free. And the *ribāṭ*s of this District [Palestine] where this ransoming of captives takes place are: Gaza, Mīmās [Maiuma of Gaza], ʿAsqalān, Māḥūz [the port of] Azdūd, [the port of] Yubnā, Yāfā, and Arsūf.[79]

Muqaddasī does not specify an exact seaward distance at which a vessel can be discerned from the shore, apparently due to variations in regional topography. However, in light of his "whenever a Greek vessel appears,"

[76] *Ribāṭ* derives from an Arabic root (*r.b.ṭ.*) meaning "to tie up an animal or bring a horse into a defense position against an enemy." *Murābaṭa* signifies a fighter stationed either in a frontier fort or watchtower, or in an exposed area. *Miḥrās* derives from the Arabic root (*ḥ.r.s.*) meaning "to watch." The difference between calling an installation *ribāṭ* or *miḥrās* lay in the structure's physical size and in the number of warriors stationed there. *Miḥrās* simply referred to a fortified area containing a small garrison and a watchtower. A *ribāṭ* was several times larger. Ibn Manẓūr, *Lisān al-ʿArab*, 6:48–49 (*ḥ.r.s.*); 7:302–303 (*r.b.ṭ.*).

[77] Chester G. Starr, "Coastal Defense in the Roman World," *American Journal of Philology* 64 (1943), 56–70.

[78] Aḥmad ibn Yaḥyā al-Balādhurī, *Futūḥ al-Buldān* (Leiden: E. J. Brill, 1968), 163–164; Khalilieh, "*Ribāṭ* System and Its Role in Coastal Navigation," 212–225; Khalilieh, "Security Protection and Naval Escort," 221–232.

[79] Muqaddasī (1897), *Aḥsan al-Taqāsīm*, 291.

it is justifiable to infer that the breadth of the territorial sea was considered to be the distance at which the top of a vessel's masts could be sighted from the land. Whenever enemy warships were observed from watch-stations and towers, those prepared to fight the enemy were alerted.[80] So far, with the exception of a single reference, classical Islamic literature is silent concerning the exact distance from the shore – should an enemy ship be observed sailing there – that would prompt the alerting of local residents. Describing the Maghrib in 549/1154, Abū ʿAbd Allāh Muḥammad ibn Muḥammad al-Idrīsī (493–560/1100–1164) uniquely reports: "In the village of Bajānis (Bajañi, Andalusia) . . . there is a stone tower in which a fire is kindled when the enemy is seen approaching by sea from a distance of six miles [10 kilometers]."[81] From this, one can infer that the Andalusian maritime sovereignty extended at this time to about 10 kilometers offshore.

The Andalusians seem to have maintained sovereignty over limited bodies of water along their Mediterranean frontiers. Coastguards were authorized to inspect ships and to interrogate crew members and passengers sailing within a distance of 10 kilometers offshore. Coastguards commonly escorted commercial vessels into Islamic harbors or along the shores.[82] As a rule, a ship's captain was required to present documentation indicating the purpose of the journey, the contents of the shipment, and the personal identity and citizenship of each passenger.[83] If the relevant documents were lacking, the ship would be escorted into port and her crew and passengers summoned before the authorities.[84] Furthermore, the vessel had to be presented with an official endorsement permitting

[80] Muqaddasī (1897), *Aḥsan al-Taqāsīm*, 291; Maqrīzī, *Khiṭaṭ*, 1:324; Qalqashandī, *Ṣubḥ al-Aʿshā*, 14:398–399; Évariste Lévi-Provençal (ed.), "Un nouveau texte d'histoire mérinide, le Musnad d'Ibn Marzūq," *Hespéris* 5 (1925), 30–31; Hannah Baader and Gerhard Wolf, "A Sea-to-Shore Perspective: Littoral and Liminal Spaces of the Medieval and Early Modern Mediterranean," *Mitteilungen des Kunsthistorischen Institutes in Florenz* 56 (2014), 12–13.

[81] Abū ʿAbd Allāh Muḥammad ibn Muḥammad al-Idrīsī, *Nuzhat al-Mushtāq fī Ikhtirāq al-Āfāq* (Cairo: Maktabat al-Thaqāfa al-Dīniyya, 1422/2002), 2:563: "*wa-ʿalayhi burj mabnī bil-ḥijāra maṣnūʿ li-waqīd al-nār fīhi ʿind ẓuhūr al-ʿaduw fī al-baḥr sittat amyāl.*"

[82] Jamāl al-Dīn Abū al-Fatḥ Yūsuf ibn al-Mujāwir, *Ṣifat Bilād al-Yaman wa-Makkah wa-ba ʿẓ al-Ḥijāz al-Musammā Taʾrīkh al-Mustabṣir* (Cairo: Maktabat al-Thaqāfa al-Dīniyya, 1996) 1:157–158; Nājī, "Mawāniʾ al-Khalīj al-ʿArabī wa'l-Jazīra al-ʿArabiyya," 177.

[83] Ibn Jubayr, *Riḥlat Ibn Jubayr*, 13.

[84] Ibn Rushd (al-Jadd), *Al-Bayān wa'l-Taḥṣīl*, 3:56, 62–63; Shelomo D. Goitein, *Letters of Medieval Jewish Traders* (Princeton: Princeton University Press, 1973), 339; Majid Khadduri, *The Law of War and Peace in Islam* (London: Luzac and Co., 1941), 78–79.

departure.[85] These measures were painstakingly elaborated by the Andalusian geographer Muḥammad ibn ʿAbd al-Munʿim al-Ḥimyarī (d. 866/1462):

The motive behind allowing the (Yemeni) sailors (*baḥriyyūn*) to reside in Bajjāna (Pechina) was as follows: when Banū Idrīs (Idrisid dynasty 172–363/788–974) became powerful in the Maghrib, the Umayyad caliphs (of Andalusia) ordered the control and fortification of the coasts so that no vessel could sail at sea without a permit and supervision. No vessel could sail out of Andalusia without official documents; likewise, no-one could enter the country from the sea without identifying himself, the country he came from, and the purpose of his journey. In addition, no vessel could sail off (the Andalusian) shore unless she was inspected and her crew investigated. Whenever a vessel sat in the water, her length should not exceed twelve ells, otherwise it would be put ashore unless she would follow the standard (regulation size of ships).[86]

Al-Ḥimyarī's description substantiates the political and legal sovereignty of the state over a limited zone at sea. Among the rules was the adoption by the Andalusians of the ancient custom of regulating the size of vessels sailing off the coasts. The Sailors' Union of Bajjāna had imposed a requirement that local shipwrights build vessels that did not "exceed twelve ells." This regulation helped local coastguards to identify foreign vessels entering their territorial sea.[87]

Similar coastal observation systems also existed along the eastern seas. They served as precautionary guides for captains sailing in coastal waters,[88] as military strongholds protecting vessels against hostile raids,[89] and as observation points for monitoring the movement of ships

85 ʿAbbās, "Ittiḥād al-Baḥriyyīn fī Bajjāna," 6; Picard, *La mer et les musulmans d'Occident au Moyen Âge*, 16–19.

86 Muḥammad ibn ʿAbd al-Munʿim al-Ḥimyarī, *Al-Rawḍ al-Miʿṭār fī Khabar al-Aqṭār* (Beirut: Maktabat Lubnān, 1984), 80; Khalilieh, *Islamic Maritime Law*, 139; Lirola Delgado, *El poder naval de Al-Andalus en la época del Calefato Omeya*, 390; Picard, *La mer et les musulmans d'Occident au Moyen Âge*, 17–18; Picard, *Sea of the Caliphs*, 252, 254.

87 Similar conditions existed in classical Greece. An agreement concluded between Athens and Sparta stipulated that the latter may not sail along the Greek coasts in vessels exceeding 12 ells. Khalilieh, *Islamic Maritime Law*, 140.

88 Muqaddasī, *Aḥsan al-Taqāsīm*, 12. He describes stockades/watchtowers (*khashabāt*) being constructed in the vicinity of the port city of Baṣra in order to guide coastal ships and avoid them being grounded.

89 Nāṣīr-ī Khosraw, *Book of Travels (Safarnāma)* (New York: State University of New York Press, 1986), 96, describes how watchtowers (*khashabāt*) rising 18 meters above sea level stretched along the coast between Baṣra and ʿAbbādān. Also see Edmund Bosworth, "The Nomenclature of the Persian Gulf," *Iranian Studies* 30 (1997), 84–85. Muslim and Christian sovereigns concluded treaties addressing the legal status of Christian merchants

at sea. Ibn al-Mujāwir (601–691/1204–1291) reports governmental observers stationed in watchtowers on hills along the coast tracking commercial vessels sailing near the coasts of Aden. Upon sighting a vessel offshore, the watchmen transmitted a message by shouting from one station to the next until news of the sighting reached the customs officials at the port. As a ship approached the port, the governor sent officials to meet the vessel at sea and to register all details regarding her port of origin, the type, quantity, and purchase price of her shipments, and the name and citizenship of each passenger.[90]

Although the Islamic law deems the sea common to all nations, a state can claim sovereignty over a belt of water off its coastline in order to secure and protect the coastal frontiers. Indeed, security is perhaps among the most significant raison d'être for a coastal state to claim sovereignty over the portion of sea adjacent to its shoreline.[91] Such sovereignty inherently aligned with a coastal defense system, which tracked the movements of the enemy and pirate seacraft, transmitted warnings of hostile intent, and guided friendly ships to avoid dangerous reefs and shallow waters. When necessary, ships could stop at coastal installations for a rest, to undertake minor repairs, or to take on basic supplies, such as food and water. While al-Idrīsī implied that the breadth of a territorial sea is six

sailing within sight of Islamic coasts. They included articles wherein Muslim authorities pledged to capture and try indigenous and foreign pirates who plundered ships within the Islamic maritime domain. In the case of an emergency, these ships could seek refuge in one of the coastal fortresses. Muslims had to then provide them with whatever assistance they needed to repel the enemy. Likewise, Muslims had to render assistance to commercial vessels in the event of enemy attack, inclement weather, or technical problems. A thorough examination of authentic documents patently confirms that foreign governments recognized Islamic sovereignty over coastal waters. Khalilieh, "*Ribāṭ* System and Its Role in Coastal Navigation," 214–218; Khalilieh, *Islamic Maritime Law*, 140–141; Nājī, "Mawāni' al-Khalīj al-ʿArabī wa'l-Jazīra al-ʿArabiyya," 177; Amari, *Diplomi Arabi*, 8; John Wansbrough, "Venice and Florence in the Mamluk Commercial Privileges," *Bulletin of the School of Oriental and African Studies* 28 (1965), 501 (article 12), 505 (article 24); Wansbrough, "A Moroccan Amīr's Commercial Treaty," 454, 460 (Article 5); Wansbrough, "Safe-Conduct in Muslim Chancery Practice," 32–33.

90 Ibn al-Mujāwir, *Ṣifat Bilād al-Yaman*, 157–158; Khalilieh, *Islamic Maritime Law*, 83; Himanshu P. Ray, "Writings on the Maritime History of Ancient India," in *Approaches to History: Essays in Indian Historiography*, ed. Sabyasachi Bhattacharya (New Delhi: Indian Council of Historical Research, 2011), 34.

91 Michael A. Furtado, "Islands of Castile: Artistic, Literary, and Legal Perception of the Sea in Castile-Leon, 1248–1450," (PhD diss., University of Oregon, 2011), 188–190. The Castilian *Siete Partidas*, likewise, grants the king de facto power over coastal indentations and a limited breadth of the sea for defending his maritime frontiers against external raids, and for launching wars. Nevertheless, no part of the sea was subject to ownership as it belongs "to the creatures of the world."

miles (10 kilometers), the exact distance remained vague and dependent upon the range of vision from the shore, which would vary naturally with regional topography and climatic fluctuations.

THE RIGHT OF PASSAGE UNDER INTERNATIONAL TREATIES

Offshore Passage

Treaties often expressed the agreements of states concerning rules pertaining to territorial claims over offshore marine zones. Privileges were normally granted to one city or state, and often brought with them exclusive rights of trade and navigation. During the twelfth and thirteenth centuries, the Almohads (r. 515–668/1121–1269) made a series of diplomatic and commercial treaties with Pisa recognizing each other's sovereign rights over a belt of water adjacent to the shoreline of the respective state, albeit that the outer boundaries remained unspecified. An official letter from the governor of Tūnis Abū Zayd ʿAbd al-Raḥmān ibn Abū Ḥafṣ (r. 583–588 or 590/1187–1192 or 1194) to the merchants of Pisa guarantees them personal safety and security be they in Ifrīqiya's "strongholds (*maʿāqilihā*), coastlands (*sawāḥilihā*), mainland (*barrihā*), and territorial sea (*baḥrihā*)."[92] A close examination of the word *baḥrihā* undoubtedly designates the offshore zone off the coastal frontiers of Ifrīqiya. Similarly, the 721/1321 Granadian–Aragonese treaty patently distinguished between inland waters – harbors and anchorages – and the territorial sea, giving the coastal state full jurisdiction over a limited offshore zone:

> Provided that your (military) galleys shall not do harm to any vessel mooring in our ports/anchorages (*marāsīna*) or our country's coastlands (*sawāḥil bilādunā*), or sailing in its territorial waters (*biḥārihā*), regardless of their owners' religious affiliations – Muslims or Christians – and place of origin.[93]

Bilateral and multilateral treaties permitted states and self-ruling entities to exercise jurisdiction beyond the territories of their land and internal waters to include a defined offshore zone adjacent to the shoreline.[94]

[92] Amari, *Diplomi Arabi*, 30; Azzaoui, *Rasāʾil Muwaḥḥidiyya*, 1:177.

[93] Arslān, *Al-Ḥulal al-Sundusiyya*, 2:306–308; Ḥamāda, *Al-Wathāʾiq al-Siyāsiyya wa'l-Idāriyya*, 465–466.

[94] K. E. F. Thomson, "Relations between the Fatimid and Byzantine Empires during the Reign of the Caliph al-Mustansir bi'llah, 1036–1094/427–487," *Byzantine and Modern*

Additionally, treaties also recognized territorial integrity and sovereignty over internal and inland waters, including ports, anchorages, rivers, and artificial channels, and allowed states to deny access by alien citizens and ships to any of their sovereign waters.[95] Through signing a treaty on Rabi al Thani 13, 689/April 24, 1290, al-Manṣūr Qalāwūn and King Alfonso III of Aragon committed themselves not only to observing each state's existing boundaries and territorial integrity, but also to provide aid in terms of defending each other in the event of external aggression.[96] This inclusion in the treaty of an obligation to provide mutual defense likely contributed to a regional reduction in conflicts and expansion of commercial relations.

Coasting was essential to international and interregional trade as vessels had no choice but to hug the coast and make frequent stopovers. An extraordinary example of coasting can be found in trade treaties signed between the Mamluks and various states from the thirteenth century onward. Article 15 of the 682/1283 treaty signed between the Sultan al-Manṣūr Qalāwūn and the Latin Kingdom of Acre stipulates, "if the galleys of the Sultan and his son are commissioned and set sail, they shall not cause harm to the coastlands to which this truce applies."[97] This provision makes clear that innocent passage can be defined as navigation

Greek Studies 32 (2008), 57. As a clear indication of asserting the sovereign rights of a state over offshore marine zones adjacent to its coastal frontiers, in 444/1053 the Fatimid Caliph al-Mustanṣir dispatched sailors from the Syrian navy to escort the envoy of the Byzantine Emperor Constantine IX Monomachus (r. 1042–1055) from Cairo to Jaffa so that he could pray at the Church of the Holy Sepulchre in Jerusalem.

95 Bauden, "Due trattati di pace," 49, articles 12–20 of the Safar 577/June 1181 treaty; on p. 68 the author presents the Jumada al-Thani, 585/August 1188 Banū Ghāniya–Genoese truce, in which articles 14–16 refer to the Balearic Islands' territorial integrity.

96 Nashshār, *'Alāqat Mamlakatay Qishtāla wa-Aragon bi-Salṭanat al-Mamālīk*, 232–234; Holt, *Early Mamluk Diplomacy*, 133–135, articles 3–6. For instance, article 5 rules: "Provided also that the King of Aragon and his brothers shall be the friends of him who is friendly to our lord the Sultan al-Malik al-Manṣūr and of the kings his sons, and the enemies of all who are hostile to him, whether Frankish kings or otherwise. If the Pope of Rome, or one of the rulers of the Franks, crowned or uncrowned, great or small, or of the Genoese, or of the Venetians, or of any nation, whether Franks, Greeks, or the Orders, the Orders of the Brethren the Templars and the Hospitallers, or all the nations of the Christians, should seek to harm our lord the Sultan by warfare or wrongful act, the King of Aragon and his brothers shall prevent and repulse them, shall commission their galleys and vessels, proceed against their territory, and distract them personally from seeking harm to the territory of our lord the Sultan, his harbors, coastlands and ports, whether specified or unspecified. They shall fight them by land and sea with their galleys, fleets, knights, horsemen and foot-soldiers."

97 Holt, *Early Mamluk Diplomacy*, 84.

through a maritime belt adjacent to the shoreline of a coastal entity in which vessels do not threaten, cause harm, or violate the coastal state's laws. This treaty also stipulates that if a Mamluk galley is heading through the territorial sea toward a destination other than the kingdom's places, then it shall not be granted permission to stop ashore and be provisioned, that is, unless she is bound for one of the kingdom's allies and suffers damage while en route. Under such a circumstance, the *bailli* and the masters in Acre will have to guard the vessel, enable the crew to obtain provisions, repair the wreck, and return the vessel to Islamic territory.[98]

Even though it was considered a custom of the sea, a civil duty, and a moral duty to render assistance to vessels in distress caused by force majeure, technical difficulties, or hostile attack, this practice was also enshrined in international treaties.[99] Granting entry to a distressed vessel was generally to save the ship, her crew, passengers, cargoes, and equipment, and prevent plundering.[100] Beyond the moral obligation, providing assistance to distressed vessels may have led to strengthened commercial and diplomatic ties among states. Article 13 of this treaty stipulates:

[98] Holt, *Early Mamluk Diplomacy*, 84.

[99] Azzaoui, *Rasāʾil Muwaḥḥidiyya*, 1:173–174, Almohads–Pisan treaty from Ramadan 1, 582/November 15, 1186.

[100] Abulafia, "Christian Merchants in the Almohad Cities," 254–255; M. E. Martin, "The Venetian–Seljuk Treaty of 1220," *English Historical Review* 95 (1980), 328; Alauddin Samarrai, "Medieval Commerce and Diplomacy: Islam and Europe, A.D. 850–1300," *Canadian Journal of History* 15 (1980), 15; Maria P. Pedani, *The Ottoman–Venetian Border (15th–18th Centuries)* (Venice: Università Ca' Foscari Venezia, 2017), 89–90. International treaties could contain clauses restricting access to certain ports and confining the movements of foreigners, commercial transactions, and lodging to specific places. For instance, the 582/1186 Almohads–Pisan peace treaty limited free access for nationals of Pisa to four major port cities, Sebta (Ceuta), Wahrān (Oran), Béjaïa (Bougie), and Tūnis, except in the event of a ship in distress. A Pisan-flagged vessel could seek shelter under conditions of rough seas, inclement weather, or technical problems, and anchor in any Islamic port or anchorage. Free access would then be granted to her crew and passengers in the nearest designated port on the condition not "to sell or purchase anything, or even speak to or make contact with the local inhabitants (*lam yubaḥ lahum al-nuzūl bi-ghayrihā wa-lā al-iḥtilāl bi-siwāhā illā li-ḍarūrat(in) min ṣuʿūbat al-baḥr tuljiʾhum ilā al-irsāʾ bi-sāḥil min al-sawāḥil dūn an yabīʿū fīhi shayʾ(an) aw-yashtarūh aw yukallimū aḥad(an) min ahlihi fī dhālik aw yukhāṭibūh*)." See Azzaoui, *Rasāʾil Muwaḥḥidiyya*, 1:174. Indeed, not all Islamic ports were accessible to foreign-flagged vessels. Access to distressed foreign-flagged ships was usually granted only through treaties between Muslim and Christian sovereigns, as this treaty exemplifies. It not only specifies the places of refuge for distressed Pisan vessels, but also forbids any commercial activities within the four designated port cities. It prescribes the guidelines and rules to which ill-fated Pisans were to abide while their ship was undergoing repairs.

Provided also that if a ship of the merchants of the Sultan and his son, to which this truce applies, or of their subjects, whether Muslims or otherwise, of whatever nations and religions, be wrecked in the harbor of Acre, its coasts or the coastlands to which this truce applies; everyone in it shall be safe in respect of themselves, their chattels, their followers and their stock-in-trade. If the owners of these wrecked ships are found, their ships and chattels shall be delivered to them. If they are missing through death, drowning or absence, their possessions shall be kept, and delivered to the representatives of the Sultan and his son.

Likewise for the ships belonging to the Franks, and sailing from these coastlands to which this truce applies, the same procedure shall be followed in the territory of the Sultan and his son. Their possessions shall be kept in the absence of their owner until they are delivered to the *Bailli* of the kingdom in Acre or the Master.[101]

This article provides clear and valuable evidence for our discussion. For one, it explicitly recognizes the coastal sovereigns claiming some ownership rights in maritime zones adjacent to their coastal frontiers. In addition, neither this article, nor similar articles in other treaties and truces, nor any sort of diplomatic correspondences shed light on the exact seaward breadth of such zones. Ultimately, it is rightly assumed that the extent of such a maritime zone was limited to the furthest distance at which a ship can be spotted from the coast. This article also answers the question as to what jurisdiction and laws applied to jetsam, flotsam, and salvage found in a territorial sea. Regardless of sovereignty over offshore waters, this article entitled the flag state to exercise diplomatic protection on behalf of a wrecked vessel. The hosting coastal state did not have legal standing to seize the wreck, her contents, or any unfortunate surviving crew members and voyagers, irrespective of their religious affiliations, nationalities, or citizenships. In short, whereas the coastal state enjoyed exclusive jurisdiction over its adjacent sea, the flag state still retained control and jurisdiction over intact vessels, and wreckage from ships formerly flying its flag.[102]

101 Holt, *Early Mamluk Diplomacy*, 83–84; Ḥamāda, *Al-Wathā'iq al-Siyāsiyya wa'l-Idāriyya lil-'Aṣr al-Mamlūkī*, 477, 489; Moukarzel, "Venetian Merchants," 195, the 1238 treaty stipulates that in case of shipwreck within the Mamluk territorial and maritime domains, the sultan guarantees to restore the Venetians' goods; Nashshār, *'Alāqat Mamlakatay Qishtāla wa-Aragon bi-Salṭanat al-Mamālīk*, 234–235, the 689/1290 treaty between Sultan al-Manṣūr Qalāwūn and King Alfonso III of Aragon.

102 Martin, "Venetian–Seljuk Treaty of 1220," 327–329. Comparable provisions coexisted in the Christian world. Apparently, it was common practice among the Christian ruling authorities to include salvage provisions in their diplomatic and commercial treaties. In principle, ill-fated proprietors had a priority right to retain their salvaged goods and personal belongings inasmuch as they did not voluntarily relinquish them, provided that they pay a fixed percentage to the salvager as established by the bilateral treaty of their mother state. The Russo-Byzantine treaties of 911 and 944, for instance, declared that if

Further legal evidence demonstrating the prevalence of this arrangement comes from the 684/1285 treaty signed by the same sultan and Lady Margaret of Tyre. The treaty decrees that when a ship of either party is wrecked, should she belong to a Muslim, then she will be delivered to the rightful owner, if the owner can be located, or else to the sultan's delegates. If the wrecked ship belonged to a Christian (*dhimmī*) from the sultan's territory, then the same process would take place as in the case of a Muslim. If, on the other hand, the rightful owner was a subject of the Lady of Tyre, then the chattels were to be delivered to that owner, if found, or else to the Lady of Tyre's administration.[103]

Maritime property found in Islamic or foreign territorial sea or on coasts was not considered derelict unless the real owners voluntarily relinquished it, or if they failed to claim it during the period designated by international treaties, local custom, or religious law. Civil authorities frequently delivered items that had been salvaged from jetsam or flotsam within their territorial sea to the rightful owners in person.[104] In other cases, if it was established with certainty that salvaged maritime property belonged to an alien merchant, the authorities would transfer it to a consul from the owner's flag state, who would then return the property to the rightful owner.[105] Despite the lack of written evidence from earlier times,

a Greek ship was cast ashore in the land of Rus, it was to remain safe and inviolate. Should it be plundered, the violator would be liable for the legal consequences. For further details, refer to Daphne Penna, *The Byzantine Imperial Acts to Venice, Pisa and Genoa, 10th–12th Centuries: A Comparative Legal Study* (Groningen: Eleven International Publishing, 2012), 108, 149, 153, 156, 232, 241–253, 280.

103 Peter M. Holt, "The Treaties of the Early Mamluk Sultans with the Frankish States," *Bulletin of the School of Oriental and African Studies* 43 (1980), 75. An identical provision is stipulated in the treaty signed between Sultan Qalāwūn and King Leon III of Lesser Armenia in 684/1285. Holt, *Early Mamluk Diplomacy*, 84, article 12; Amari, *Diplomi Arabi*, 89, article 7 of the 713/1313 Ḥafṣīd–Pisan treaty stipulates that if a ship is wrecked off the coast of Ifrīqiya, local residents will guard and protect her and her crew, passengers, and contents until she is repaired and again seaworthy.

104 According to the custom of the sea in the Indian Ocean and the Mediterranean Sea, goods driven ashore by tempest or other force must be delivered to their true owners. An edict attributed to Maharaja Ganapati (1199–1262) assures the safety of foreign sea traders whose vessels are wrecked on his coasts. Alexandrowicz, *Law of the Nations in the East Indies*, 78; Khalilieh, *Islamic Maritime Law*, 136.

105 Louis Mas Latrie, *Traité de paix et de commerce et documents divers concernant les relations des chrétiens avec les Arabes de l'Afrique septentrionale au Moyen Âge* (Paris: Henri Plon, 1866), 2:97–98; Amari, *Diplomi Arabi*, 7–13, 17–22, 29–35, 45–47, 70–71, 86–111, 123–164, 169–180, 184–209, 214–217, 221–236; Wansbrough, "Safe-Conduct in Muslim Chancery Practice," 20–35; Wansbrough, "A Moroccan Amīr's Commercial Treaty," 455–456, 458–461; Khalilieh, *Islamic Maritime Law*, 136; Angeliki E. Laiou, "Byzantine Trade with Christian and Muslims and Crusades," in

it is not unreasonable to propose the existence of prior treaties of the same nature between the Christian and Muslim worlds.

Strait Passage

The right of a state to exercise sovereignty over its inland seas is also attested to in international treaties. Consider, for instance, the 659/1261 and 680/1281 treaties signed between the Egyptian sultan al-Manṣūr Qalāwūn and the Byzantine emperor Michael VIII Palaeologus. In order to secure the inflow of Crimean slaves of both genders, especially males for military conscription, the sultan was compelled to circumvent an embargo imposed by the Ilkhanate dynasty (654–736/1256–1335) – which primarily ruled regions of Persia and neighboring territories in present-day central Turkey – by signing two agreements with Byzantium.[106] Article 6 of the 680/1281 treaty states:

> The ambassadors sent from our realm to the land of Berke and his sons, their territory and those parts, the Sea of Sūdāq (Sudak/Soladia)[107] and its mainland, shall be absolutely safe and secure. They shall pass through the territory of the realm of the Emperor, Lord Michael, from end to end without let or hindrance. They shall be sent by land and by sea to our realm according to the exigency of the time. They shall proceed to where we shall dispatch them in that territory, and

The Crusades from the Perspective of Byzantium and the Muslim World, ed. Angeliki E. Laiou and Roy P. Mottahedeh (Washington DC: Dumbarton Oaks Research Library, 2001), 180–187; Samarrai, "Medieval Commerce and Diplomacy," 13–14; Bauden, "Due trattati di pace," 50, articles 24 and 25; 69, articles 10 and 11.

106 Reuven Amitai, "Diplomacy and the Slave Trade in the Eastern Mediterranean: A Re-Examination of the Mamluk–Byzantine–Genoese Triangle in the Late Thirteenth Century in Light of the Existing Early Correspondence," *Oriente Moderno* 88 (2008), 364–365; Dimitri A. Korobeinikov, "Diplomatic Correspondence between Byzantium and the Mamlūk Sultanate in the Fourteenth Century," *Al-Masaq* 16 (2010), 64.

107 The "Sea of Sūdāq" most surely refers to a defined maritime belt on the Black Sea adjacent to the port city of Sūdāq. In modern legal terms, the "Sea of Sūdāq" most likely refers to the territorial sea of Sūdāq, over which the local government enjoyed exclusive dominion and so was able to restrict access to non-residents and foreign individuals and convoys, and forbid or impose restrictions on the exploitation of natural resources. When sailing offshore or approaching a coastal or port city, experienced merchants, voyagers, and sailors normally attached the word *baḥr* to the nearest place by saying, for instance, al-Baḥr al-Mālībārī (Sea of Malabar), or Baḥr ʿAydhāb (or ʿAydhab, on the west coast of the Red Sea), or Baḥr Berbera (in Somalia), or Baḥr al-Mahdiyya (Sea of al-Mahdiyya) and Baḥr al-Monastir (Sea of Monastir), in Tunisia. In so saying, there is every reason to assume that they were referring to the territorial sea of the coastal city and its offshore jurisdictional claim. Wansharīsī, *Al-Miʿyār*, 2:5; Ṭāher (ed.), "*Akriyat al-Sufun*," 36; Khalilieh, *Admiralty and Maritime Laws*, 308, f. 132; Goitein and Friedman, *India Traders*, 7, f. 18; 599, f. 29.

likewise return to our realm, safely, securely, and without impediment, together with any ambassadors of those parts or elsewhere who may come with them, and all the slaves, slave-girls and others accompanying them.[108]

The treaty contains two clauses granting the people of Sūdāq and Egyptian vessels permission to transport slaves through extensive inland Byzantine maritime domain stretching from the Black Sea in the north to the Mediterranean in the south, passing through the straits of Bosporus and Dardanelles (Çanakkale), the Sea of Marmara, and the Aegean Sea. From its early days as the ancient city of Byzantium (later renamed Constantinople and then Istanbul), its strategic geographical position provided an undisputed sovereignty over vital bodies of water. Byzantium could suspend passage at will through both the straits of Bosporus and Dardanelles when public peace, good order, and territorial integrity were threatened, or else to bar political entities that had no diplomatic or commercial treaties with the Byzantine Empire. Therefore, in order to secure freedom of passage for ships coming from the Black Sea laden with young slaves, the Egyptian sultan negotiated with the Byzantine emperor the terms of transit for cargo and ambassadors. Article 7 of the treaty states:

If merchants come from the territory of Sūdāq, and wish to travel to his Majesty's territory, they shall not be hindered in our territory, but their transit and return shall be without let or hindrance after they have paid the due charge on their wares in our territory. Likewise, if merchants from the people of his Majesty's territory appear, and wish to cross to the territory of Sūdāq, they shall cross from our territory without let or hindrance, and likewise if they return; all this after paying the due charge. If these merchants from the people of his Majesty's territory and from the people of Sūdāq are accompanied by slaves and slave-girls, they may pass with them to his Majesty's territory without let or hindrance, unless they [the slaves] are Christians, for our law and religious code do not allow us this in the case of Christians.[109]

Article 8 further stipulates:

Any merchants coming from Sūdāq or elsewhere with slaves and slave-girls shall be enabled by the Emperor, Lord Michael, to proceed with them to our realm without hindrance.[110]

Until the late eighteenth and early nineteenth century, the Ottoman Empire could deny access to ships through the straits of Bosporus and

[108] Qalqashandī, *Ṣubḥ al-Aʿshā*, 14:73–74; Holt, *Early Mamluk Diplomacy*, 127; Ḥamāda, *Al-Wathāʾiq al-Siyāsiyya wa'l-Idāriyya lil-ʿAṣr al-Mamlūkī*, 498–501.
[109] Qalqashandī, *Ṣubḥ al-Aʿshā*, 14:73–74; Holt, *Early Mamluk Diplomacy*, 123–124.
[110] Holt, *Early Mamluk Diplomacy*, 127.

Dardanelles because the right of passage had not yet been established as a customary rule. Only vessels whose countries maintained bilateral agreements with the Ottoman government enjoyed free passage through these bodies of water.[111] This situation explains why the right of transit passage was vested in the 659/1261 and 680/1281 Mamluk–Byzantine treaties. Slaves and other commodities that were in high demand could not be transported from Crimea to Egypt by sea without passing through the inland waters of Byzantium, which extended over 740 kilometers from Constantinople to the southernmost limits of the Aegean Sea.[112] Both parties agreed to pay retribution for damage or loss caused by pirates or privateers to subjects of the emperor or sultan whether sea travelers, shippers, or shipowners.[113]

The question that arises is whether or not the same regime of passage also applied within the Abode of Islam? In fact, until the Portuguese

111 Nihan Ünlü, *The Legal Regime of the Turkish Straits* (The Hague: Kluwer Law International, 2002), 23–25; Glen Plant, "Navigation Regime in the Turkish Straits for Merchant Ships in Peacetime: Safety, Environmental Protection and High Politics," *Marine Policy* 20 (1995), 15–17. Procopius of Caesarea (500–565 CE) draws our attention to the customhouses established on the Bosporus and Dardanelles during Justinian's reign to collect passage tolls and taxes from ships sailing through the straits. He writes: "There are two straits on either side of Constantinople: one in the Hellespont between Sestos and Abydus, the other at the mouth of the Euxine Sea, where the Church of the Holy Mother is situated. Now in the Hellespontine Strait there had been no customhouse, though an officer was stationed by the Emperor at Abydus, to see that no ship carrying a cargo of arms should pass to Constantinople without orders from the Emperor, and that no one should set sail from Constantinople without papers signed by the proper officials; for no ship was allowed to leave Constantinople without permission of the bureau of the Master of Offices. The toll extracted from the shipowners, however, had been inconsequential. The officer stationed at the other strait received a regular salary from the Emperor, and his duty was exactly the same, to see that nothing was transported to the barbarians dwelling beyond the Euxine that was not permitted to be sent from Roman to hostile territory; but he was not allowed to collect any duties from navigators at this point." Procopius of Caesarea, *Secret History*, or *Anecdota*, trans. Richard Atwater (Chicago: P. Covici, 1927), paragraph no. 25, "How He Robbed His Own Official"; C. Richard Baker, "Administrative and Accounting Practices in the Byzantine Empire," *Accounting History* 18 (2013), 222; Azuni, *Maritime Law of Europe*, 1:226–232, reports that imposing tolls on foreign ships sailing across the straits located within the state's territorial jurisdiction was a common practice among earlier and contemporaneous states.

112 Virgil Ciocîltan, *The Mongols and the Black Sea Trade in the Thirteenth and Fourteenth Centuries* (Leiden: E. J. Brill, 2012), 153–154; Amitai, "Diplomacy and the Slave Trade," 365–366. The length of passage from the entrance to the Dardanelles on the Aegean Sea to the exit of the Bosporus on the Black Sea is 164 nautical miles (300 kilometers).

113 Holt, *Early Mamluk Diplomacy*, 124–125, 127.

penetration into the Indian Ocean arena in the sixteenth century, the straits of Hormuz and Bab el-Mandeb played a far more significant role in East–West maritime trade than did the straits of Bosporus and Dardanelles. Interstate trade and the economy of individual states were far more dependent upon the transit passage through these straits, which connect the high sea (Arabian Sea) and inland seas, the Persian Gulf and the Red Sea; historically, all of these seas have been entirely surrounded by Islamic-ruled territories, the access of which to the Mediterranean Sea was by land alone until 1869 when the Suez Canal was officially opened.

Situated at the entrance to the Persian Gulf, the Strait of Hormuz attained great importance as a convenient natural entry point for sea trade between India, Southeast Asia, and the Far East with the Islamic Near East, particularly the Persian Gulf provinces of Iraq, and Greater Syria. From the fall of Baghdad to the Ilkhanate Mongol forces in 656/1258 until its capture in 913/1507 by the Portuguese conquistador Afonso de Albuquerque (1453–1515), the Kingdom of Hormuz ruled over strategic positions in the Persian Gulf and vital sea-lanes for over 200 years; it became a powerful emporium of commerce controlling trade coming from the Indian Ocean.[114] In order to hold sway over domestic and international trade and to manage marine resources efficiently, Hormuz kings and viziers promulgated regulations prohibiting sea travel, trade, and local pearl fishing without an official permit. Weaker sheikhs in the Persian Gulf complied with this unprecedented regime of navigation and trade laws. They were reluctant to defend their right to free navigation and trade and officially succumbed to the new reality, although they passively resisted the new restrictions. However, some of them sought ways to bypass the regulations. For instance, Omani traders opted to develop new commercial hubs and ports in Zhufār (Dhofar) and Mirbāṭ (Mirbat) on the southwest coast of Oman so that by the end of the

[114] Thomas M. Ricks, "Persian Gulf Seafaring and East Africa: Ninth–Twelfth Centuries," *African Historical Studies* 3 (1970), 354: "The prince of the port of Hormuz . . . was able to take-over the sea power of the former dominions of this part of the Persian Gulf [between Kish and the Strait of Hormuz] and develop his own sphere of influence in the regions of Bahrain and Oman, even to the coasts of Zanzibar"; Bosworth, "Nomenclature of the Persian Gulf," 84–87; Ralph Kauz and Roderich Ptak, "Hormuz in Yuan and Ming Sources," *Bulletin de l'Ecole française d'Extrême-Orient* 88 (2001), 29–30; Salman, "Aspects of Portuguese Rule in the Arabian Gulf," 21, 38, 49–50; René J. Barendse, "Trade and State in the Arabian Seas: A Survey from the Fifteenth to the Eighteenth Century," *Journal of World History* 11 (2000), 182, 187, 192.

fifteenth century they had gained sufficient power to revolt against the Kingdom of Hormuz.[115]

The unilateral restriction by Hormuz of access only to licensed shippers, shipowners, and traders and their agents through the straits stood in sharp contradiction to the Islamic custom of the sea. Prior to the fall of the Abbasid dynasty and the fragmentation of the empire into independent political entities, the governing authorities in Hormuz were required to facilitate seaborne trade and were prohibited from taking any action that could hamper freedom of navigation and flow of commodities through the straits. During that time, therefore, *musta'min*s and subjects of the Abode of Covenant could sail unhampered through this strategic waterway. That no references are made in pre-thirteenth century Arabic sources to any imposition of restrictions on transit passage may imply that national and foreign vessels enjoyed free access through the Strait of Hormuz so long as public peace, good order, and territorial integrity remained inviolate.[116]

As a pivotal passageway for Asian pilgrims traveling by sea and the shortest and fastest waterway for East–West commercial networks, the Strait of Bab el-Mandeb was obviously more vital to the economy of the Red Sea and Mediterranean countries than the Strait of Hormuz. Before the circumnavigation of Africa and discovery of the Cape of Good Hope, the large volume of spices and other luxury items from the East Indies reached Mediterranean and European markets through the Strait of Bab el-Mandeb. Cargo heading for the Mediterranean and European markets had to be transported along overland caravan routes within the Egyptian and Syrian territories. The commercial centrality of Egypt may explain why its rulers attributed great strategic significance to the water passage running through the country. The rulers maintained naval centers and flotillas in major port cities and along trunk routes to protect vessels against pirates, or even to escort them, in order to assure

[115] Ibrāhīm Khoury and Aḥmad J. Tadmurī, *Salṭanat Hormuz al-'Arabiyya* (Ras al-Khaimah: Documentaries and Studies Center, 1421/2000), 1:339–342; Salman, "Aspects of Portuguese Rule in the Arabian Gulf," 60–61. The author argues that the Portuguese copied the "trade license" in their *cartaz* system, in that an equivalent system already existed in the Persian Gulf's trade routes prior to the Portuguese arrival. However, as argued in the Introduction (p. 5, f. 9), it is more appropriate to assume that the *cartaz* institution might have been developed from the Spanish *guidaticum* rather than the Islamic *amān*, although the latter surely owes its origins to the Islamic pledge of security. The Latin word *guidaticum* (Aragonese *guyage*, Catalan *guiatge*) is derived from the Arabic Maghribi *widād*, meaning "a bond of friendship, love, and affection." Chevedden, "The 1244 Treaty," 169–170, f. 8.

[116] Khoury and Tadmurī, *Salṭanat Hormuz al-'Arabiyya*, 2:115–134.

the flow of trade to and from the Red Sea, and to enable unimpeded access through the strait.[117] Even so, as the use of force against human threats was not always effective, merchants and shipowners had to pay tribute in exchange for safe navigation and free passage.[118]

In an attempt to monopolize the supply of fine spices from the East Indies, to drive Muslim trade from the Indian Ocean, and to control the entrance to the Red Sea, in 919/1513 Afonso de Albuquerque launched two attacks on the port city of Aden.[119] These attacks were unsuccessful, as were raids that he launched against other targets on the Red Sea.[120] In spite of these regular efforts to block the Strait of Bab el-Mandeb, Muslim pilgrims and goods from the Indian Ocean countries made their way through the strait to the Hijazi and African littorals of the Red Sea. At times, the Portuguese temporarily disrupted the Muslims' communication patterns, not to mention their *cartaz* system and naval presence, but never seriously affected the passage of domestic and foreign vessels through the Strait of Bab el-Mandeb.[121] Save for a single reference from the second quarter of the sixteenth-century Ottoman Yemen,[122] it appears that ships had been accorded free passage through the Bab el-Mandeb from a time prior to the advent of Islam until later periods.

Maintaining freedom of navigation through the straits of Hormuz and Bab el-Mandeb was an essential Islamic interest. Major port cities located in the vicinity of the two straits prospered as ports of call and intermediate waypoints. Trading vessels coming from the Indian Ocean regularly anchored in major ports located at the entrances to the Red Sea and

[117] Qalqashandī, *Ṣubḥ al-Aʿshā*, 3:524; Sālim, *Al-Baḥr al-Aḥmar fī al-Tārīkh al-Islāmī*, 24–29; Ross, "The Portuguese in India and Arabia between 1507 and 1517," 553–559; also Chapter 3, 191–192.

[118] Power, "Red Sea Region during the 'Long' Late Antiquity," (PhD diss., University of Oxford, 2010), 296–297. For further details, see Chapter 3, 189 –191.

[119] Al-Ṭayyib ibn ʿAbd Allāh Abū Aḥmad Abū Makhrama, *Tārīkh Thaghr ʿAden* (Beirut: Dār al-Jīl, 1408/1987), 24–25.

[120] Venetia-Ann Porter, "The History and Monuments of the Tahirid Dynasty of the Yemen 858–923/1454–1517," (PhD diss., Durham University, 1992), 96–133; D'Alòs-Moner, "Conquistadores, Mercenaries, and Missionaries," 3–12; Salman, "Aspects of Portuguese Rule in the Arabian Gulf," 184–185, f. 55; Mujani, "Some Notes on the Portuguese and Frankish Pirates," 22–23.

[121] D'Alòs-Moner, "Conquistadores, Mercenaries, and Missionaries," 16–17; Salman, "Aspects of Portuguese Rule in the Arabian Gulf," 109–110; Meloy, *Imperial Power and Maritime Trade*, 249–254 (Appendix C).

[122] Giancarlo Casale, *The Ottoman Age of Exploration* (Oxford: Oxford University Press, 2010), 44. The Ottomans established a permanent naval base and a customs house on Kamarān, the largest Yemen-controlled island in the Red Sea, so that all ships arriving from India "would be required to stop and pay a transit fee."

Persian Gulf. From these locales, goods were either transshipped aboard different vessels or transported by the same vessels to different destinations along the relevant littoral. Most of the cargo was then carried by overland caravans to ports on the Mediterranean Sea.

Even though the ruler of Dahlak seems to have first introduced the payment of tolls, the Kingdom of Hormuz – and following them the Ottoman governor of Kamarān – collected tolls in exchange for the safe passage of ships through the straits. One must be careful not to assume that these historic impositions of tolls were justified by Islamic law. On the contrary, Islamic law grants all commercial ships, irrespective of their nationalities, the right to sail through the Near Eastern straits free of charge. Such freedom had been economically vital both for the Abode of Islam and for other nations. Free passage increased the volume of shipping, created job opportunities, and enhanced economic and social developments. Indeed, it can reasonably be assumed that as long as ships sailed directly to Red Sea destinations without anchoring in any of the ports in the straits, then no taxes were due to be paid at the customs houses located at the mouth of the relevant straits.[123]

PERSONALITY, TERRITORIALITY, AND EXTRATERRITORIALITY

Trade activity, especially long-distance, could involve persons and parties from different territories, nationalities, religions, and sects. In order to secure smooth relations, give impetus to domestic and overseas trade, avoid legal altercations whenever possible, and to protect the rights of all those engaged in commercial transactions, an effective legal mechanism had to be established. While emerging city-states in medieval Europe constituted an impenetrable obstacle to forming common supraterritorial regulations, until the rise of the Ottoman *tanzīmāt* in the middle of the nineteenth century, Muslim administrative authorities granted *dhimmī*s and foreign merchants the judicial freedom to adjudicate lawsuits involving parties from the same community, "nationality," or religion.[124] Two cardinal questions must be addressed here. First, why

[123] Gerald R. Tibbetts, "Arab Navigation in the Red Sea," *Geographical Journal* 127 (1961), 329.

[124] The Qur'ān, the Prophetic tradition, and the writings of eminent scholars all imply that diversity is a natural law for humankind, they endorse pluralism and encourage coexistence among all segments of society irrespective of ethnic, racial, cultural, and religious backgrounds. This perception of juridical sovereignty, which sanctions a pluralistic legal

does Islamic law grant judicial autonomy to *dhimmī*s and aliens? And second, how does legal pluralism enhance freedom of movement, navigation, and the expansion of domestic and overseas trade? To find answers to these and other questions, it is necessary to examine the administration of justice in the Abode of Islam and the position that Islamic law holds on the judicial status of Muslims, *dhimmī*s, and foreign subjects within the territorial sovereignty of a state.

Muslims' Judicial Status within and beyond the Abode of Islam

As a universal religion, Islam identifies its affiliates around the world, irrespective of their territorial, cultural, ethnic, and linguistic backgrounds, as belonging to one *ummah*.[125] Muslims uniformly believe that Islam is the last monotheistic religion, acknowledge the oneness of God and the unity of humankind, and share many other tenets of faith.[126] Islam considers the judicial status of a subject as stemming from his/her religious allegiance, regardless of his/her residence in any particular society. In other words, the personal allegiance of an individual to religious doctrine, rather than the principle of territoriality, determines the law by which he/she is to be governed. Membership in the *ummah* signifies that all believers are bound to observe Islamic principles even if they happen to reside in the Abodes of War (*Ḥarb*), Peace (*Ṣulḥ*), or Truce (*'Ahd*).[127] However, the concept of territoriality can still be implemented under certain circumstances for *dhimmī*s and aliens living within the *imam*'s jurisdiction.[128] Therefore the application of the law within and outside the Abode of Islam needs to be examined.

system and grants various religious groups extensive communal autonomy, is undeniably alien to the present-day nation-state judicial system.

125 Qur'ān 2:213; Q 12:45; Q 16:120; Q 21:9; Q 23:52 states: "وَإِنَّ هَٰذِهِۦٓ أُمَّتُكُمْ أُمَّةً وَاحِدَةً وَأَنَا۠ رَبُّكُمْ فَاتَّقُونِ (And verily this *Ummah* of yours is a single *Ummah* and I am your Lord and Cherisher; therefore, fear Me and no other)." The term *ummah* is mentioned forty-nine times in the Qur'ān, some of which define it as "religion," "community of believers," "nation" (not in racial terms), "brotherhood," and "way of life."

126 Muhittin Ataman, "Islamic Perspective on Ethnicity and Nationalism," *Journal of Muslim Minority Affairs* 23 (2003), 89–92.

127 Herbert J. Liebesny, "Comparative Legal History: Its Role in the Analysis of Islamic and Modern Near Eastern Legal Institutions," *American Journal of Comparative Law* 20 (1972), 38–39; Herbert J. Liebesny, "Religious Law and Westernization in the Moslem Near East," *American Journal of Comparative Law* 2 (1953), 495–496; Parvin and Sommer, "Evolution of Muslim Territoriality," 3–4.

128 Abdur Rahim, *The Principles of Muhammadan Jurisprudence according to the Hanafi, Maliki, Shafi'i and Hanbali Schools* (London: Luzac and Co., 1911), 59.

Except for under limited circumstances, *Sharīʿah* provisions must prevail in the Islamic territorial domain and exclusively be enforced on all Muslims regardless of their adherence to one denominational school or another. All controversies involving Muslim litigants that take place within the Islamic maritime dominion, including in ports and along navigable rivers, must be heard before the qadi.[129] However, legal disputes arising among Muslims sailing for foreign countries might be tried in either Islamic or in foreign territories on the condition that the presiding judge is Muslim, evenhanded, impartial, and well-versed in Islamic theology and jurisprudence. For this reason, central and peripheral authorities concluded diplomatic and commercial treaties with foreign countries granting Muslims a degree of independence in administering justice. These treaties stipulated that Muslims could set up their own courts in those port-cities most frequented by Muslims so as to expedite judicial proceedings and prevent unreasonable delays.

In spite of the sectarian division and religious differences between Sunnis and Shiites, Muslim mercantile communities saw themselves as part of the global Muslim nation (*ummah*), which contributed to the cohesiveness of diasporic communities of merchants at local, regional, and transregional levels. For instance, writing around 237 AH/851 CE, the Merchant Sulaymān (Sulaymān al-Tājir) reports that at Khānfū

[129] Burzulī, *Jāmiʿ Masāʾil al-Aḥkām*, 3:654–655; Wansharīsī, *Al-Miʿyār*, 8:304–305; Hady R. Idris, "Commerce maritime et *kirāḍ* en berberie orientale d'après un recueil inédit *fatwās* médievales," *Journal of the Economic and Social History of the Orient* 4 (1961), 238; Khalilieh, *Islamic Maritime Law*, 149–150. For example, disputes between lessees and lessors, irrespective of their affiliation with a particular school of law, as a rule, must be tried upon arrival at their destination so long as the qadi is reasonably just. Otherwise, the trial shall be held in any Islamic territory wherein the qadi is fair and just and the location is fairly accessible to all parties. A Geniza document dated September 30, 1030 penned by Khallūf ibn Zakariyyā al-Ashqar, the agent in the port city of Alexandria, and addressed to his master-merchant Joseph ibn Jacob ibn ʿAwkal in Fusṭāṭ, reports on a payment dispute that arose at a journey's end between shippers and the agent of a Tunisian ship proprietor (*wakīl al-maqrūḍ*, lit. "agent of the loaned person"). The Alexandrian qadi, whom I presume was affiliated with the Shāfiʿī Law School, initiated in rem proceedings and ruled in favor of the shippers. He required the agent to sell the vessel for 300 dinars. The ship's proprietor appealed to the Mālikī qadi of Qayrawān, ʿAbd al-Raḥmān ibn Muḥammad ibn ʿAbd Allāh ibn Hāshim (in office 397–425/1006–1033), seeking a repeal of the judgment, but to no avail. TS 13 J 17, f. 11; Menahem Ben-Sasson, *The Jews of Sicily 825–1068: Documents and Sources* (Jerusalem: Ben-Zvi Institute, 1991), 226–229; Shelomo D. Goitein, "Jewish Trade in the Mediterranean at the Beginning of the Eleventh Century," *Tarbiz* 36.1 (1967), 387–389; Shlomo Simonsohn, *The Jews in Sicily: 383–1300* (Leiden: E. J. Brill, 1997), 1: 77–79.

(Canton, present-day Guangzhou) – a rendezvous port for Muslim merchants – the appointed Muslim judge was charged with maintaining order and presiding over cases involving his coreligionists, regardless of their sectarian differences.[130] A century later, when Abū Zayd al-Sīrāfī (died after 330 AH/941 CE) arrived at Khānfū, the office of the qadi continued to exist. He states in his *Travel Account* that "the merchants of Iraq cannot arise against (the judge's) decisions" since "he acts with justice in conformity with God's Book (Qur'ān) and the precepts of Islamic law."[131] Indian rulers also sanctioned the handling by Muslim merchants and communities of their own civil and religious affairs, the administering of justice and settling of their own disputes in accordance with the *Sharī'ah* insofar as their actions did not impinge on the peace and order of the state.[132] The *hunarman* was selected solely by the community of Muslim merchants and officially recognized as the chief judicial authority, compelling all Muslim litigants to comply with his

[130] Sulaymān al-Tājir, *'Ajā'ib al-Dunyā wa-Qiyās al-Buldān*, ed. Saif Sh. al-Muraikhi (Al-'Ayn: Markaz Zāyid lil-Turāth wa'l-Tārīkh, 1426/2005), 36; for the French version, see Gabriel Ferrand, *Voyage du marchand arabe Sulaymān en Inde et en Chine rédigé en 851* (Paris: Éditions Bossard, 1922), 38–39.

[131] Abū Zayd Ḥasan ibn Yazīd al-Sīrāfī, *Riḥlat al-Sīrāfī* (Abu Dhabi: Al-Majma' al-Thaqāfī, 1999), 24; Eusèbe Renaudot, *Ancient Accounts of India and China by Two Mohammedan Travellers Who Went to those Parts in the 9th Century* (London: S. Harding, 1733), 7–8; Ḥamīdullāh, *Muslim Conduct of State*, 122–123; John Chaffee, "Diasporic Identities in the Historical Development of the Maritime Muslim Communities of Song–Yuan China," *Journal of the Economic and Social History of the Orient* 49 (2006), 403–408, 416; John Anderson, "Chinese Mohammedans," *Journal of the Anthropological Institute of Great Britain and Ireland* 1 (1872), 149, 160; Mi Shoujiang and You Jia, *Islam in China*, trans. Min Chang (Beijing: China Intercontinental Press, 2005), 24–27; Albert E. Dien, "The Tomb of the Sogdian Master Shi: Insights into the Life of a *Sabao*," *Silk Road* 7 (2009), 47–48; Albert E. Dien, "The Sa-pao Problem Re-Examined," *Journal of the American Oriental Society* 82 (1962), 340–341; Alain George, "Direct Sea Trade between Early Islamic Iraq and Tang China," 601–603; Hee-Soo Lee, "The Spread of Islamic Culture to the East Asia before the Era of Modern European Hegemony," *Islām Araştirmalari Dergisi* 7 (2002), 68–69; Ma Jianzhao, "The Role of Islam in the Formation of the Culture and Economy of the Hui Community in Guangzhou," *Journal of Muslim Minority Affairs* 16 (1996), 31–32; Fan Ke, "Maritime Muslims and Hui Identity: A South Fujian Case," *Journal of Muslim Minority Affairs* 21 (2001), 310–311; Park, *Mapping the Chinese and Islamic Worlds*, 66–67, 155.

[132] Ḥamīdullah, *Muslim Conduct of State*, 122–123, 146; Anand, *Origin and Development of the Law of the Sea*, 33; Alpers, *Indian Ocean*, 47; Mehrdad Shokoohy, "The Town of Cochin and Its Muslim Heritage on the Malabar Coast, South India," *Journal of the Royal Asiatic Society of Great Britain and Ireland* 8 (1998), 391–392; Noble, "Principles of Islamic Maritime Law," 90–92; Derryl N. MacLean, *Religion and Society in Arab Sind* (Leiden: E. J. Brill, 1989), 71.

decisions.[133] In the early years of the sixteenth century, the Portuguese traveler and official Duarte Barbosa (1480–1521) observed that the Muslim community of Calicut comprised two groups, the locals (known as Mapillas) and the foreigners or Pardesīs, Muslims who came from various places including the Red Sea region, Cairo, Arabian Peninsula, Iraq, Persia, Khurasan (or Khorasan), and Asia Minor. Regardless of their religious, sectarian, and juridical school affiliations, Muslims administered their judicial affairs before the same judge according to *Sharīʿah* without interference from the local ruler. Barbosa describes the Moors as great merchants, who "possess in this place wives and children, and ships for sailing to all parts with all kinds of goods. They have among them a Moorish governor who rules over and chastises them, without the king meddling with them."[134] The fact that both the Chinese and Indian authorities had granted Muslim communities permission to arbitrate and resolve disputes and legal cases amongst their coreligionists is a conclusive indication of the extraterritorial application of Islamic law outside the Abode of Islam.[135]

International treaties concluded between Muslim and Christian sovereigns called upon each party not to interfere in the judicial affairs of foreign merchants of the other denomination, but rather to let them administer lawsuits autonomously and in compliance with civil and religious laws of their homeland. Article 7 of the 665/1267 treaty signed between al-Ẓāhir Baybars and the Hospitallers stipulates that inter-Islamic legal disputes occurring in the territory of the latter shall be summoned before the sultan's representative for judgment in conformity

[133] Buzurg ibn Shahriyār, *The Book of Wonders of India* (London: East-West Publication, 1981), 94; for the text in Arabic, see Buzurg ibn Shahriyār, *ʿAjāʾib al-Hind*, ed. Yousef al-Sharouni (London: Riad El-Rayyes Books, 1990), 133, Ibn Shahriyār refers to this office as *hunarman al-Muslimīn*; Suhanna Shafiq, "The Maritime Culture in the *Kitāb ʿAjāʾib al-Hind* (The Book of the Marvels of India) by Buzurg Ibn Shahriyār (d. 399/1009)," (master's thesis, University of Exeter, 2011), 76, 147; Park, *Mapping the Chinese and Islamic Worlds*, 151. A similar autonomous judicial system existed in the course of the twelfth century in the port city of Broach, northwest India. Jewish traders set up therein an ad hoc court system to adjudicate disputes arising among their coreligionists. See Goitein and Friedman, *India Traders*, 714.

[134] Duarte Barbosa, A Description of the Coasts of East Africa and Malabar in the Beginning of the Sixteenth Century, trans. Henry E. Stanley (London: Hakluyt Society, 1866), 147; Sanjay Subrahmanyam, *The Political Economy of Commerce Southern India 1500–1650* (Cambridge: Cambridge University Press, 1990), 117–118; Pearson, Indian Ocean, 75–76, 101; Stephen F. Dale, "Trade, Conversion and the Growth of the Islamic Community of Kerala, South India," *Studia Islamica* 71 (1990), 157–159.

[135] George, "Direct Sea Trade between Early Islamic Iraq and Tang China," 601.

with the "Holy Law of Islam." Correspondingly, the Hospitaller's representatives were designated as presiding over cases involving affiliates of Krak des Chevaliers within the sultan's territory, that they may judge them according to the "regime of Ḥiṣn al-Akrād."[136]

This charter finds echoes in later Mamluk treaties. An identical provision was placed in al-Manṣūr Qalāwūn's 684/1285 treaty with Lady Margaret of Tyre granting the sultan's representative authorization to implement Islamic penal law in the Lady's domain if both the victim and accused are Muslim subjects. Equally, if in the sultan's domain the perpetrator and victim were both Christian subjects of Tyre, the Lady's representative was authorized to proceed with judgment in accordance with Tyre's penal laws. Both parties to the treaty were required to restore the chattels and private belongings of any slain subject from the other's dominion and to pay a wergild if the perpetrator was not found. If the victim's booty was not found, "there shall be 40 days of grace for the investigation of the matter," and, if no information came to light, an equivalent value of the booty was to be paid.[137] Article 10 of the 682/1283 treaty concluded between Qalāwūn and the Latin Kingdom similarly grants the two political entities judicial autonomy in all fields of law to try cases between their citizens regarding disputes arising on foreign soil.[138]

Similar international diplomatic treaties signed between North African Islamic sovereigns and their Christian European counterparts consist of charters empowering each of the contracting parties to apply its religious or statutory laws to its citizens when in foreign territories. Any person arriving in Islamic domains had a duty to obey the laws of his home country and to avoid violating the local laws and interests of the country of sojourn.[139] Article 9 of the Ḥafṣīd-Pisan treaty (dated September 14, 1313) rules that if a controversy arises between a Muslim and a Christian, or between two Christian affiliates from different countries, Islamic law shall prevail; whereas article 36 stipulates that if the disputants are both Pisan citizens, the case shall be settled by the Pisan Consul.[140] If a Pisan inflicted harm on a Muslim found within the territorial jurisdiction of Pisa, the Pisan Governor, Elders, and Consuls were required to "do justice

[136] Holt, *Early Mamluk Diplomacy*, 35. [137] Holt, *Early Mamluk Diplomacy*, 115.
[138] Holt, *Early Mamluk Diplomacy*, 82.
[139] Amari, *Diplomi Arabi*, 89; 102, article 10 of May 16, 1353 treaty.
[140] Amari, *Diplomi Arabi*, 94; 102, article 36 of the 1353 treaty; 126, article 5 of the treaty from December 14, 1397; 172, article 5 of the 1445 Covenant; 188–189, 192–193, articles 5 and 10 of the Royal Decree addressed by the Mamluk sultan Qāitbāy to the Doge of Firenze from February 22, 1496.

to him" – take all necessary legal measures to punish the perpetrator severely and to return any stolen property to the rightful owner.[141] Appeal to the *maẓālim* by one of the litigants, even if alien, could take place if he believed that justice had not been served in the lower court.[142]

The admissibility of judicial authority from outside the Abode of Islam to the courts within it – decrees and testimonies from qadis, muftis, notaries, and trustworthy witnesses – inspired debates among classical jurists, especially after the loss of Islamic Mediterranean territories to Christian powers from the mid-eleventh century onward. The prominent jurist al-Māzarī (453–536/1061–1141) was asked about the validity of judicial decisions handed down by the chief qadi of Norman Sicily as well as the disposition of trustworthy witnesses (*shuhūd ʿudūl*) from the island in the Abode of Islam. He ruled that although the trustworthiness of the Sicilian chief qadi was diminished as he lives in the Abode of War, his judgments and legal opinions remain valid provided that he is professionally qualified and his legal probity, expertise, education, and methodology are beyond question. Al-Māzarī adds that five criteria may justify the legitimacy of the qadi. He first explained the value of the qadi's continued presence by noting that his absence could delegitimize the entire Muslim community of the island and jeopardize its members' practice of Islam. Second, he noted that, despite the qadi's illegal investiture by an infidel ruler, the Muslim community needs some form of leadership to represent it before the authorities, rendering an appointed leader better than no Muslim representative. Third, as the chief Muslim judicial authority, the qadi can preside over cases engaging local Muslim merchants and those who sojourn in Dār al-Ḥarb. Fourth, his authority should be obeyed as if he had been appointed by a Muslim amir; his appointment by a Sicilian king was equally valid to that by a Muslim sovereign (*kamā law kāna wallāhu sulṭān Muslim*). Finally, the qadi could engage in ransoming prisoners and guiding people away from error.[143] Not far from Sicily, the Muslim community in Lucera (northern Apulia, Italy)

141 Amari, *Diplomi Arabi*, 94, article 34; 107, article 34 of the 1353 treaty.

142 Amari, *Diplomi Arabi*, 126–127, articles 5 and 6 of the treaty from December 14, 1397; 140–141, articles 3 and 5 of December 14, 1414 treaty; 154–155, articles 3 and 5 of the 1421 treaty.

143 Abū ʿAbd Allāh Muḥammad ibn ʿAlī ibn ʿUmar al-Māzarī, *Fatāwā al-Māzarī* (Qayrawān: Al-Dār al-Tūnisiyya lil-Nashr, 1994), 365–366; Abū al-ʿAbbās Aḥmad ibn Yaḥyā al-Wansharīsī, "*Asnā al-Matājir fī Bayān Aḥkām Man Ghalaba ʿalā Waṭanihi al-Naṣārā wa-lam Yuhājir*," ed. Ḥusayn Muʾnis, *Revista del Instituto Egipcio de Estudios Islamicos en Madrid* 5 (1957), 174–177; Wansharīsī, *Al-Miʿyār*, 2: 133–134, 10:107–109; Abdel-Magid Turki, "Consultation juridique d'al-Imam al-

was granted judicial autonomy and the right to practice the Sunna of Muḥammad's religion on Christian soil, "so that the *qāḍī* is their leader (*adeo quod primates ipsorum qui Alchadi dicuntur*)."[144]

Islamic judicial sovereignty in non-Muslim domains was revisited during the Spanish Reconquista.[145] In both Sicily and Spain, the new

Mazari sur le cas des musulmans vivant en Sicile sous l'autorité des Normands," *Mélanges de l'Université St-Joseph* 50 (1980), 697–704; Michael Brett, "Muslim Justice under Infidel Rule: The Normans in Ifriqiya 517–555/1123–1160 A.D.," *Cahiers de Tunisie* 33 (1991), 330–332; Abu Salieh, "Islamic Conception of Migration," 46; Jocelyn N. Hendrickson, "The Islamic Obligation to Emigrate: Al-Wansharīsī's *Asnā al-Matājir* Reconsidered," (PhD diss., Emory University, 2009), 374–376; Sarah Davis-Secord, "Muslims in Norman Sicily: The Evidence of Imām al-Māzarī's Fatwās," *Mediterranean Studies* 16 (2007), 56–59; John Tolan, "Identité et statut minoritaire dans les traditions légales: Deux exemples (XIIe-XIIIe siècles)," in *Identitats: Reunió Científica, XIX Curs d'Estiu Comtat d'Urgell*, Universitat de Lleida (2012), 100–102; Jean-Pierre Molénat, "Le problème de la permanence des musulmans dans les territoires conquis par les chrétiens, dupoint de vue de la loi islamique," *Arabica* 48 (2001), 395–396; Sami A. Abu-Sahlieh, "The Islamic Conception of Migration," *International Migration Review* 30 (1996), 45–46.

144 Julie A. Taylor, "Freedom and Bondage among Muslims in Southern Italy during the Thirteenth Century," *Journal of Muslim Minority Affairs* 27 (2007), 71–77; Julie A. Taylor, *Muslims in Medieval Italy: The Colony at Lucera* (Lanham: Lexington Books, 2003), 83–86; Alexander Harper, "Patronage in the re-Christianized Landscape of Angevin Apulia: the Rebuilding of *Luceria sarracenorum* into *Civitas Sanctae Mariae*," (PhD diss., University of Toronto, 2014), 34–35. The qadi in late thirteenth-century Lucera was not only the chief judge, but also represented his community in the royal court. Similarly, Christian authorities in the Balearics granted Muslim communities the right to judge lawsuits between them in accordance with Islamic law. Elena Lourie, "Free Moslems in the Balearics under Christian Rule in the Thirteenth Century," *Speculum* 45 (1970), 646.

145 With reference to the juridical discourse on Muslim residence in Dār al-Ḥarb, Abou el Fadl and others have demonstrated that jurists expressed diverse opinions, although the majority maintains that Muslims' presence is permissible inasmuch as their security and freedom of religion are protected. This subject goes well beyond the scope of this discussion. For a deeper treatment, see Khaled Abou el Fadl, "Islamic Law and Muslim Minorities: The Juristic Discourse on Muslim Minorities from the Second/Eighth to the Eleventh/Seventeenth Centuries," *Islamic Law and Society* 1 (1994), 141–187; Khaled Abou el Fadl, "Legal Debate on Muslim Minorities: Between Rejection and Accommodation," *Journal of Religious Ethics* 22 (1994), 127–162; Muhammad K. Masud, "Being Muslim in a non-Muslim Polity: Three Alternate Models," *Journal of Muslim Minority Affairs* 10 (1989), 118–128; Bernard Lewis, "Legal and Historical Reflections on the Position of Muslim Populations under non-Muslim Rule," *Journal of Muslim Minority Affairs* 13 (1992), 1–16; Kathryn A. Miller, "Muslim Minorities and the Obligation to Emigrate to Islamic Territory: Two Fatwās from Fifteenth-Century Granada," *Islamic Law and Society* 7 (2000), 256–288; Abu-Sahlieh, "Islamic Conception of Migration," 46–49; Molénat, "Le problème de la permanence des musulmans dans les territoires conquis par les chrétiens," 392–400; Tauseef A. Parray, "The Legal Methodology of 'Fiqh al-

Christian sovereigns borrowed the Islamic tradition of *dhimmī* and applied this pattern of governance generally to Muslim minorities until the late fifteenth century. Christian officials recognized the exclusive jurisdiction of Muslims in the judicial sphere,[146] in the same way that the Islamic administration had acknowledged the continuing validity of Jewish and Christian judicial sovereignty under the Islamic expansion in Spain.[147] Articles 1, 4, and 5 of the 641/1244 surrender treaty of Játiva between James I the Conqueror, King of Aragon and Catalonia (1208–1278) and Abū Bakr Muḥammad ibn Yaḥyā, commander of the Castle of Játiva (1237–1278) grants Muslims religious freedom and enables them to preserve their judicial institutions in the full sense of the word. Qadis acted in the name of and under the immediate control of the Christian king, in order to ensure that their decisions were duly executed.[148] Muslims were granted the right to administer justice according to *çuna* (Sunna, which could mean Prophetic tradition, or Muslims' local customary law, or both) and *xara* (*Sharīʿah*).[149]

Aqalliyyat' and Its Critics: An Analytical Study," *Journal of Muslim Minority Affairs* 32 (2012), 88–107; Hendrickson, "Islamic Obligation to Emigrate."

146 The 508/1115 capitulation treaty signed between the Muslims of Tudela and Alfonso el Batallador (1073/4–1134) stipulates that Muslims not only retain their own criminal courts and judges, but they also have ultimate jurisdiction over Muslims even in cases involving Christians. It states that "(Muslims) be and remain in their litigations and trials under the jurisdiction of their qadi and his lieutenants, just as in the days of Muslim rule. And if a Muslim shall have litigation with a Christian, or a Christian with a Muslim, the Muslim qadi shall render judgment to the Muslim, according to Islamic law, and the Christian judge to the Christian, according to [Christian] law." John Boswell, *The Royal Treasure: Muslim Communities under the Crown of Aragon in the Fourteenth Century* (New Haven: Yale University Press, 1977), 108.

147 Antoine Fattal, "How *Dhimmīs* were Judged in the Islamic World," in *Muslims and Others in Early Islamic Society*, ed. Robert Hoyland (Burlington, VT: Ashgate, 2002), 87–88, the Christian magistrate was known as *qāḍī al-naṣārā* or *qāḍī al-ʿajam*, and in Latin, *censor*.

148 Chevedden, "The 1244 Treaty," 159–160, 164–165, 168–169, 172–173.

149 Mark D. Meyerson, *The Muslims of Valencia in the Age of Fernando and Isabel: Between co-Existence and Crusade* (Berkeley: University of California Press, 1991), 185; Robert I. Burns, *Islam under the Crusaders: Colonial Survival in the Thirteenth-Century Kingdom of Valencia* (Princeton: Princeton University Press, 1973), 223–231; Robert I. Burns, "The *Guidaticum* Safe-Conduct in Medieval Arago-Catalonia: A Mini-Institution for Muslims, Christians, and Jews," *Medieval Encounters* 1 (1995), 107–108, concerns a safe-conduct granted to the Muslim residents of Zaragoza (December 8, 1276), which guarantees justice according to "the *Sunnah* of the Saracens." On p. 111, a safe-conduct from Valencia dated June 22, 1279 assures that Muslims administer their cases in accordance with the Sunna "under the control of their *ṣāḥib al-aḥkām*." Being a deputy magistrate, *ṣāḥib al-aḥkām* was inferior in prestige to the qadi and subordinate to the former's jurisdiction. He was authorized to adjudicate

Islamic courts outside the Abode of Islam enjoyed exclusive jurisdiction over cases involving solely Muslims, including in the areas of family law,[150] criminal offenses (*ḥadd*),[151] property rights, and commercial transactions.[152] Christian sovereigns granted Muslims the authority to independently administer their own legal system with its own courts, qadis, codes, practices, precedents, and judicial procedures.[153] However, Christian magistrates would exercise jurisdiction upon a qadi's request in order to execute sentences, if some members of the disputing parties were

civil disputes, preside over criminal cases, and provide legal advice to all members of the Muslim community. Maribel Fierro, "The *Qāḍī* as Ruler," in *Saber religioso y poder político en el Islam: actas del Simposio Internacional (Granada, 15–18 octubre 1991)* (Madrid: Agencia Española de Cooperación Internacional, 1994), 74, f. 14; 84–85, f. 53; Rachid Amro, "Le '*ṣāḥib al-aḥkām*' à l'époque almoravide," *Al-Andalus Maghreb: Estudios árabes e islámicos* 8–9 (2000–2001), 51–55.

150 Marriage, divorce, succession, breach of contract, and guardianship of minors.

151 Illicit sexual intercourse – premarital sex and adultery – slanderous accusations of unchastity, theft, wine drinking, and armed robbery.

152 Burns, *Islam under the Crusaders*, 224.

153 Islamic judicial and community institutions presided in eastern Christian countries beginning in the early centuries following the advent of Islam. Tenth-century Arabic sources report that the oldest *masjid* (mosque) in Constantinople was erected at the demand of the Umayyad prince Maslamah ibn 'Abd al-Malik (66–121/685–738) as a condition for lifting the 717–718 siege from the city. Located in the Imperial precinct (*praitōrion*), the Islamic colony (Dār al-Balāṭ) in Constantinople, which was under the governor's personal protection and care, served as a *mitaton* (dwelling), a place of worship, a detention center for high-ranking Muslim captives, and a courthouse, wherein a qualified qadi presided over cases involving Muslim litigants. Abū Bakr Aḥmad ibn Muḥammad ibn al-Faqīh al-Hamadhānī, *Mukhtaṣar Kitāb al-Buldān* (Leiden: E. J. Brill, 1302/1885), 145; Muqaddasī, *Aḥsan al-Taqāsīm*, 147–148; Stephen W. Reinert, "The Muslim Presence in Constantinople, 9th–15th Centuries: Some Preliminary Observations," in *Studies on the Internal Diaspora of the Byzantine Empire*, ed. Hélène Ahrweiler and Angeliki E. Laiou (Washington DC: Dumbarton Oaks Research Library and Collection, 1998), 125–150; Paul Magdalino, "The Maritime Neighborhoods of Constantinople: Commercial and Residential Functions, Sixth to Twelfth Centuries," *Dumbarton Oaks Papers* 54 (2000), 220–222; Olivia R. Constable, *Housing the Stranger in the Mediterranean World: Lodging, Trade, and Travel in Late Antiquity and the Middle Ages* (Cambridge: Cambridge University Press, 2003), 147–150; Glaire D. Anderson, "Islamic Spaces and Diplomacy in Constantinople (Tenth to Thirteenth Centuries C.E.)," *Medieval Encounters* 15 (2009), 86–98. Similar colonies existed in major trading cities, such as in Thessaloniki and along the eastern Byzantine frontiers until the fall of the empire in the fifteenth century. For instance, in the northern Syrian port town of Laodikeia/ Laodicea, local Muslims had their own qadi. Catherine Holmes, "Treaties between Byzantium and the Islamic World," in *War and Peace in Ancient and Medieval History*, ed. Philip de Souza and John France (Cambridge: Cambridge University Press, 2008), 150; David Jacoby, "Foreigners and the Urban Economy in Thessalonike, ca. 1150–ca. 1450," *Dumbarton Oaks Papers* 57 (2003), 121–122; Penna, *Byzantine Imperial Acts to Venice, Pisa and Genoa*, 204.

affiliates of other religions, or if one of the parties appealed to the civil court. Finally, as was tradition in the Islamic State, the principle of personality continued to override the principle of territoriality. Qadis heard and judged cases according to *Sharīʿah* so long as both disputing parties were Muslims.[154]

Judicial Autonomy of *Dhimmīs*

The Qurʾān calls for recognition of the legislative autonomy of *dhimmī* communities, commanding the Prophet and his fellow Muslims to safeguard and preserve God's older revelations, which had been corrupted over the course of centuries. As the last Word of God, the Qurʾān contains the true teachings of all prior Holy Books, which nonetheless remain holy. Therefore, it is advised that there be no intervention in the judicial affairs of the followers of these Scriptures, but rather they be granted full judicial autonomy to administer justice according to their religions, customs, and civil laws.[155] The Qurʾān, Prophetic traditions, theologians, and jurists all discouraged *dhimmī* litigants from appealing to Islamic courts, advising the Islamic judicial authorities to avoid presiding over cases involving solely non-Muslims. Verses 42–49 of the fifth chapter of the Qurʾān (*Al-Māʾida*) represent the clearest Qurʾānic explanation as to why *dhimmīs* should be granted an independent judicial system and how it should be put into practice:

(They are found of) listening to falsehood, of devouring anything forbidden. If they do come to thee, either judge between them, or decline to interfere. If thou decline, they cannot hurt thee in the least. If thou judge, judge in equity between them. For God loveth those who judge in equity (42) But why do they come to thee for decision, when they have (their own) Torah before them? Therein is the (plain) Command of God; yet even after that, they would turn away. For they are not (really) People of Faith (43) It was We who revealed the Torah (to Moses): therein was

سَمَّاعُونَ لِلْكَذِبِ أَكَّالُونَ لِلسُّحْتِ فَإِن
جَاؤُوكَ فَاحْكُم بَيْنَهُم أَوْ أَعْرِضْ
عَنْهُمْ وَإِن تُعْرِضْ عَنْهُمْ فَلَن
يَضُرُّوكَ شَيْئًا وَإِنْ حَكَمْتَ فَاحْكُم
بَيْنَهُمْ بِالْقِسْطِ إِنَّ اللَّهَ يُحِبُّ
الْمُقْسِطِينَ (42) وَكَيْفَ يُحَكِّمُونَكَ
وَعِندَهُمُ التَّوْرَاةُ فِيهَا حُكْمُ اللَّهِ ثُمَّ
يَتَوَلَّوْنَ مِن بَعْدِ ذَلِكَ وَمَا أُوْلَئِكَ
بِالْمُؤْمِنِينَ (43) إِنَّا أَنزَلْنَا التَّوْرَاةَ
فِيهَا هُدًى وَنُورٌ يَحْكُمُ بِهَا النَّبِيُّونَ

[154] Burns, *Islam under the Crusaders*, 228–229; Boswell, *Muslim Communities under the Crown of Aragon*, 108–112; Meyerson, *Muslims of Valencia*, 189–201.
[155] Hallaq, *History of Islamic Legal Theories*, 4–5.

guidance and light. By its standard have been judged the Jews, by the Prophets who bowed (as in Islam) to God's Will, by the Rabbis and the Doctors of Law: for to them was entrusted the protection of God's Book, and they were witnesses thereto: therefore fear not men, but fear Me, and sell not My Signs for a miserable price. If any do fail to judge by what God hath revealed, they are Unbelievers (44)

We ordained therein for them: "life for life, eye for eye, nose for nose, ear for ear, tooth for tooth, and wounds equal for equal." But if anyone remits the retaliation by way of charity, it is an act of atonement for himself. And if any fail to judge by what God hath revealed, they are wrongdoers (45) And in their footsteps We sent Jesus the son of Mary, confirming the Torah that had come before him: We sent him the Gospel: therein was guidance and light, and confirmation of the Torah that had come before him: a guidance and an admonition to those who fear God (46) Let the People of the Gospel judge by what God hath revealed therein. If any do fail to judge by what God hath revealed, they are those who rebel (47) To thee We sent the Scripture in truth, confirming the scripture that came before it, and guarding it in safety: so judge between them by what God hath revealed, and follow not their vain desires, diverging from the Truth that hath come to thee. To each among you have We prescribed a Law and an Open Way if God had so willed, He would have made you a single People, but (His Plan is) to test you in what He hath given you; so strive as in a race in all virtues.

The goal of you all is to God; it is He that will show you the truth of the matters in which ye dispute (48) And this (He commands) judge thou between them by what God hath revealed, and follow not their vain desires, but beware of them lest they beguile thee from any of that (teaching) which God hath sent down to thee. And if they turn away, be assured that for some of their crimes it is God's purpose to punish them. And truly most men are rebellious (49)

الَّذِينَ أَسْلَمُواْ لِلَّذِينَ هَادُواْ
وَالرَّبَّانِيُّونَ وَالأَحْبَارُ بِمَا اسْتُحْفِظُواْ
مِن كِتَابِ اللّهِ وَكَانُواْ عَلَيْهِ شُهَدَاء
فَلاَ تَخْشَوُاْ النَّاسَ وَاخْشَوْنِ وَلاَ
تَشْتَرُواْ بِآيَاتِي ثَمَنًا قَلِيلاً وَمَن لَّمْ
يَحْكُم بِمَا أَنزَلَ اللّهُ فَأُولَئِكَ هُمُ
الْكَافِرُونَ (44) وَكَتَبْنَا عَلَيْهِمْ فِيهَا
أَنَّ النَّفْسَ بِالنَّفْسِ وَالْعَيْنَ بِالْعَيْنِ
وَالأَنفَ بِالأَنفِ وَالأُذُنَ بِالأُذُنِ
وَالسِّنَّ بِالسِّنِّ وَالْجُرُوحَ قِصَاصٌ
فَمَن تَصَدَّقَ بِهِ فَهُوَ كَفَّارَةٌ لَّهُ وَمَن
لَّمْ يَحْكُم بِمَا أنزَلَ اللّهُ فَأُولَئِكَ هُمُ
الظَّالِمُونَ (45) وَقَفَّيْنَا عَلَى آثَارِهِم
بِعَيسَى ابْنِ مَرْيَمَ مُصَدِّقًا لِّمَا بَيْنَ
يَدَيْهِ مِنَ التَّوْرَاةِ وَآتَيْنَاهُ الإِنجِيلَ
فِيهِ هُدًى وَنُورٌ وَمُصَدِّقًا لِّمَ ابَيْنَ
يَدَيْهِ مِنَ التَّوْرَاةِ وَهُدًى وَمَوْعِظَةً
لِّلْمُتَّقِينَ (46) وَلْيَحْكُمْ أَهْلُ
الإِنجِيلِ بِمَا أَنزَلَ اللّهُ فِيهِ وَمَن لَّمْ
يَحْكُم بِمَا أَنزَلَ اللّهُ فَأُولَئِكَ هُمُ
الْفَاسِقُونَ (47) وَأَنزَلْنَا إِلَيْكَ
الْكِتَابَ بِالْحَقِّ مُصَدِّقًا لِّمَا بَيْنَ يَدَيْهِ
مِنَ الْكِتَابِ وَمُهَيْمِنًا عَلَيْهِ فَاحْكُم
بَيْنَهُم بِمَا أَنزَلَ اللّهُ وَلاَ تَتَّبِعْ
أَهْوَاءهُمْ عَمَّا جَاءَكَ مِنَ الْحَقِّ لِكُلٍّ
جَعَلْنَا مِنكُمْ شِرْعَةً وَمِنْهَاجًا وَلَوْ
شَاء اللّهُ لَجَعَلَكُمْ أُمَّةً وَاحِدَةً وَلَكِن
لِّيَبْلُوَكُمْ فِي مَا آتَاكُم فَاسْتَبِقُوا
الْخَيْرَاتِ إِلَى الله مَرْجِعُكُمْ جَمِيعًا
فَيُنَبِّئُكُم بِمَا كُنتُمْ فِيهِ تَخْتَلِفُونَ
(48) وَأَنِ احْكُم بَيْنَهُم بِمَا أَنزَلَ
اللّهُ وَلاَ تَتَّبِعْ أَهْوَاءهُمْ وَاحْذَرْهُمْ
أَن يَفْتِنُوكَ عَن بَعْضِ مَا أَنزَلَ اللّهُ
إِلَيْكَ فَإِن تَوَلَّوْا فَاعْلَمْ أَنَّمَا يُرِيدُ
اللّهُ أَن يُصِيبَهُم بِبَعْضِ ذُنُوبِهِمْ وَإِنَّ
كَثِيرًا مِّنَ النَّاسِ لَفَاسِقُونَ
(49)

Out of respect for older Divine Revelations, the Qurʾān patently sanctions legal diversity and calls for a pluralistic judicial system within the Abode of Islam, in keeping with recognizing other monotheistic religions as separate nations. In verse 42, God commands the Prophet to refrain from interfering in the judicial affairs of non-Muslims. However, if the parties insist on seeking the Prophet's justice, he is required not to pervert justice or make any concessions in its implementation, but to judge the parties equitably and in compliance with *Sharīʿah*.[156] God next (verse 43) praises the Torah, which He revealed to Moses asking: why should they (Jews) come to you when they have their own Law (Torah), which consists of the commands of God (*fīhā ḥukm Allāh*)? None of these prophets had deviated from the law of the Torah, changed or altered it. Rabbis and renowned religious scholars continued to find in it guidance to higher realms of the spirit. The Qurʾān further declares that whosoever fails to judge by what God has revealed are unbelievers (verse 44) and unjust (verse 45).

Regarding the People of the Gospel, the Qurʾān clearly stresses that later prophets confirmed the messages of their predecessors and sought to promote the same sacred mission. God did not reveal any of the Books in order to repudiate previous ones, rather each confirmed and supported those preceding it. Similar to the Islamic judicio-religious attitude toward the Jews, Muslims are also instructed not to intervene in the judicial affairs of *dhimmī* Christians, who should administer justice among themselves according to what God has revealed.[157] Those who counter God's Law are unbelievers, transgressors, and wrongdoers (verse 47).

In those cases when Christians call upon the authority of Muḥammad, they must accept that his judgment will be made in accordance with the principles of Islam (verses 48 and 49). Since the Qurʾān commands against

[156] Qurʾān 4:141: "وَلَن يَجعَلَ ٱللَّهُ لِلكَٰفِرِينَ عَلَى ٱلْمُؤمِنِينَ سَبِيلًا (And never will God grant to the Unbelievers a way to triumph over the Believers)"; Māwardī, *Al-Ḥāwī al-Kabīr*, 14:277: "*Al-Islām yaʿlū wa-lā yuʿlā ʿalayhi* (Islam dominates and is not dominated)"; Mark R. Cohen, "Defending Jewish Judicial Autonomy in the Islamic Middle Ages," in *Law and Religious Minorities in Medieval Societies: Between Theory and Praxis*, ed. Ana Echevarria *et al.* (Turnhout: Brepols Publishers, 2016), 14–17; Richard R. Rose, "Islam and the Development of Personal Status Laws among Christian Dhimmis: Motives, Sources, Consequences," *Muslim World* 72 (1982), 165–168.

[157] The reliance of Christians and Jews on the Islamic judiciary is best addressed by Uriel Simonsohn, *A Common Justice: The Legal Allegiances of Christians and Jews under Early Islam* (Philadelphia: University of Pennsylvania Press, 2011).

a compulsion to embrace Islam,[158] it follows that it would be optional for non-Muslims to seek justice in Islamic courts and this would take place only if the disputing coreligionists voluntarily chose to bring their lawsuit before the qadi. Before proceeding, the qadi is obliged to ensure that the case had not previously been brought before an ecclesiastical court and to inform the parties that they will be treated like Muslims and judged pursuant to Islamic law.[159]

Christians

For many centuries, Christians made up the majority of residents in the countries of the Islamic Mediterranean. Islamic military victories did not abruptly change the material culture of the occupied countries. Cultural continuity persisted in various aspects of life for centuries, despite the gradual processes of Arabization and Islamization. Perhaps one of the wisest decisions made by the Arabs shortly after their military advent in the former Byzantine territories and the Sassanid Empire was to retain the prevailing administrative framework and ecclesiastical organizations and tribunals as established by Canon VI of the Nestorian synod of Mar George I, which took place in 57 AH/676 CE.[160] This canon is generally echoed in the text of the Pact of ʿUmar (*al-ʿUhda/al-Shurūṭ al-ʿUmariyya*), the terms of which presumably were laid down by the Christian leaders of Greater Syria immediately following its fall.[161] For over a millennium, the

[158] Qurʾān 2:256: "لا إِكْرَاهَ فِي الدِّينِ قَدْ تَبَيَّنَ الرُّشْدُ مِنْ الغَيِّ (Let there be no compulsion in religion: truth stands out clear from error)."

[159] Fattal, "How *Dhimmīs* were Judged in the Islamic World," 92; Ahmad Yousif, "Islam, Minorities, and Religious Freedom: A Challenge to Modern Theory of Pluralism," *Journal of Muslim Minority Affairs* 20 (2000), 35–38; Rose, "Personal Status Laws among Christian Dhimmis," 163; Ṣāliḥ ʿA. al-Zayd, *Aḥkām ʿAqd al-Amān wa'l-Mustaʾminīn fī al-Islām* (Riyad: Al-Dār al-Waṭaniyya, 1406/1985), 107–109.

[160] Fattal, "How *Dhimmīs* were Judged in the Islamic World," 84–85: "Trials and disputes between Christians must be judged within the Church. They must not be public. . . . They must be judged in the presence of magistrates, designated by the bishop and consented to by the community, chosen among the priests known for their love of truth and their fear of God, with wisdom and sufficient knowledge of the cases. . . . Christians should not follow their impetuous consciences in taking their discussions outside of the Church. If there is something that must be concealed from those designated for the position of judge, they should present their case before the bishop. . . . No believer can . . . have the authority to appoint himself to the function of a judge of the faithful, without the order of the bishop and the consent of the community, as long as he is not obliged by the order of the authorities."

[161] Mark R. Cohen, *Under Crescent and Cross: The Jews in the Middle Ages* (Princeton: Princeton University Press, 1994), 54–57; Mark R. Cohen, "What was the Pact of ʿUmar? A Literary-Historical Study," *Jerusalem Studies in Arabic and Islam* 23

pact regulated the Christians' legal status, not only in this particular province, but also across the Islamic world. A thorough scrutiny of the pact reveals that the Muslim governing and religious authorities did not attempt to impose a new legal system upon the Christians. On the contrary – perhaps remarkably – they granted the Christian *dhimmīs* freedom of religion and authorized them to continue abiding by their own laws free from external intervention.[162]

Prior to the Islamic expansion in Egypt throughout the fourteenth century, or even later, Alexandria was not only the seat of the Church Patriarch, but also a vital commercial center where the Church maintained dockyards, operated commercial fleets that sailed as far as India to the east and Marseilles to the west, hired sailors, and, above all, regulated river and sea navigation.[163] The promulgation of the Christian Arabic *Ecloga*, an Arabic version of the Greek *Ecloga* – which came into existence in the

(1999), 100–116; Denawy, "People of the Book in the Qur'ān and *Ḥadīth*," 230–254, presents the thirteen *asānīd* (sing. *isnād*/chain of transmitters) of the covenant.

162 Fattal, "How *Dhimmīs* were Judged in the Islamic World, 86; Tritton, *The Caliphs and Their Non-Muslim Subjects*, 38–39, 100–101; Milka Levy-Rubin, "*Shurūṭ 'Umar* and Its Alternatives: The Legal Debate on the Status of the *Dhimmīs*," *Jerusalem Studies in Arabic and Islam* 30 (2005), 185–186, 193; Aibek S. Ahmedov, "Origins of Law of Religious Minorities in Islam: Evolution of Concept of *Dhimmī* as Portrayed in Early Sources," *Journal of Islamic State Practices in International Law* 3 (2007), 33–46; Denawy, "People of the Book in the Qur'ān and *Ḥadīth*," 116–118, 155, 171, 205, 228. Several centuries later, Ibn Faḍl Allāh al-'Umarī (700–749/1301–1349) wrote on the investiture and jurisdictional privileges that Muslim sovereigns granted to Christian religious leaders: "He is the leader of the members of his community and their judge, for as long as he lives. He tells them what is permitted and what is forbidden and who judges them, according to the principles laid down in the Torah and not repealed by the Gospel. … Before dispensing justice among them, he must attempt to reconcile the parties, since a compromise is the best of judgments, and the religion of the Messiah, like that of Muḥammad, being based in peace." Shihāb al-Dīn Aḥmad ibn Yaḥyā ibn Faḍl Allāh al-'Umarī, *Al-Ta'rīf bil-Muṣṭalaḥ al-Sharīf* (Beirut: Dār al-Kutub al-'Ilmiyyah, 1408/1988), 182–183; the English translation of the Arabic text is quoted from Fattal, "How *Dhimmīs* were Judged in the Islamic World," 87.

163 George R. Monks, "The Church of Alexandria and the City's Economic Life in the Sixth Century," *Speculum* 28 (1953), 355–362; Roger S. Bagnall, *Egypt in Late Antiquity* (Princeton: Princeton University Press, 1993), 289–293; Michael Hollerich, "The Alexandrian Bishops and the Grain Trade: Ecclesiastical Commerce in Late Roman Egypt," *Journal of the Economic and Social History of the Orient* 25 (1982), 187–207; Charles P. Sherman, "The Roman Administrative Marine," in *Studi in onore di Salvatore Riccobono nel XL anno del suo insegnamento*, ed. Salvatore Riccobono and Giovanni Baviera (Palermo: Arti grafiche G. Castiglia, 1936), 2:65–76; Raphael Taubenschlag, *The Law of Greco-Roman Egypt in the Light of the Papyri 332 B.C.–640 A.D.* (New York: Herald Square Press, 1944–1948), 2:91–93; Mostafa el Abbadi, "A Code of Navigation on the Nile in Greco-Roman Egypt," *Graeco-Arabica* 4 (1991), 157–162; Dimitrios G. Letsios, "Sea Trade as Illustrated in the 'Rhodian Sea

twelfth century during the patriarchate of Gabriel ibn Turaik (70th Patriarch of the Church of Alexandria 1135–1145 CE) – appears to attest that, for many centuries of the Islamic State, Christians managed their own communal and religious affairs unhampered by either local or central authorities.[164]

The judicial autonomy enjoyed by the Church of Alexandria did not differ from the judicial privileges of Jewish communities. Both "nations" (Scriptuaries/*Ahl al-Kitāb* or *Kitābiyyūn*) were commanded by the Qur'ān to be treated on an equal footing. While cases involving parties from different religions were to be presided over by qadis and judged in conformity with Islamic law, intracommunal disputes were to be judged by magistrates of the same affiliation as the litigants.[165] Christian clergy, monks, and other judicial authorities did not favor seeking justice in Islamic courts for religious and communal considerations.[166] Nevertheless, Christians turned to Islamic courts when one party was a Muslim, for cases involving *dhimmīs* from different faiths, at the request of one of the parties, or for crimes committed on Islamic territory by one *dhimmī* against another that could lead to public disorder (*fasād fī al-arḍ*).[167] Despite such occasional appeals, Muslim administrations through history gave preference to the principle of personal affiliation by principally emphasizing, in particular, the religious character of the law.[168] Therefore, Christians were almost exclusively governed by

Law' with Special Reference to the Reception of Its Norms in the Arabic *Ecloga*," *Graeco-Arabica* 6 (1995), 209–225.

164 Stefen Leder, *Die arabische Ecloga* (Frankfurt: Forschungen zur byzantinischen Rechtsgeschichte, 1985), 114–119. On the economic and judicial roles played by the Church in overseas trade during the medieval period, refer to R. F. Wright, "The High Seas and the Church in the Middle Ages," *Mariner's Mirror* 53 (1967), 3–31, 115–135.

165 Personal status matters – marriage, divorce, adoption, inheritance, and oaths – and matters Islamic law does not recognize, such as commercial transactions involving swine among Christians and usury among Jews, were almost exclusively left to rabbinical and ecclesiastical tribunals.

166 U. Simonsohn, *Common Justice*, 157; Uriel Simonsohn, "Seeking Justice among the 'Outsiders': Christian Recourse to Non-Ecclesiastical Judicial Systems under Early Islam," *Church History and Religious Culture* 89 (2009), 198–202.

167 Fattal, "How *Dhimmīs* were Judged in the Islamic World," 89–90.

168 Runciman notes that the Ottoman military expansion and capture of Constantinople consolidated the Greek Orthodox Church's legal system and jurisdiction. He writes: "The integrity of the Orthodox *millet* was guaranteed by the new powers accorded to the Patriarch. The Muslim conquest had not resulted in the disestablishment of the Church. On the contrary, it was firmly established with new powers of jurisdiction that it had never enjoyed in Byzantine times. With the conquest of the capital and the subsequent conquest of other districts, practically the whole of the Patriarchal territory

ecclesiastical code, even though the concept of territoriality was generally applied to *dhimmīs* and foreigners in the area of penal law.

Jews

In the spring of 1058 CE, two Jewish merchants, Moshe bar Yehuda ha-Ḥazan of Palermo and al-Ḥasan ha-Cohen ben Salmān of Alexandria, concluded three different commercial contracts at the Jewish courthouse of Fusṭāṭ, which provided that the former would escort the shipments and sell them in Sicily. Accompanied by his cousin and another Jew, Moshe bar Yehuda then sailed aboard an Islamic-owned vessel to his hometown of Palermo. While en route he fell ill, died, and his corpse was thrown overboard, following the proper performance of Jewish funerary rituals. In the absence of a rightful heir on board the vessel, the captain – as Islamic law dictates – became the temporary depositary of the deceased's property. The vessel had intended to sail directly from Alexandria to Palermo, but for an unknown reason, perhaps technical, the captain diverted course following Bar Yehuda's death and docked at the port-city of Tripoli. In adherence to Islamic maritime law, the captain turned the deceased's property over to the qadi, who – upon verifying that no Muslim party was engaged in the transaction and that both parties were Jewish – passed the case on to the Jewish judicial authority of Tripoli. Through his agent, the Egyptian merchant Ben Salmān tried to recover his property, but the Jewish court (*bēt dīn*) in Tripoli refused to deliver it without a fully-fledged lawsuit between the merchant and representatives of the trader's widow and orphan. To assist their compatriot, the rabbinical court in Old Cairo appealed to the Jewish high court in Jerusalem on the premise that: (a) the Cairene rabbinical court cannot overrule decisions of another court

was united one more, and, though there was an alien power superimposed, it was its own master. … The integrity of the Church had been preserved, and with it the integrity of the Greek people." Steven Runciman, *The Great Church in Captivity: A Study of the Patriarchate of Constantinople* (Cambridge: Cambridge University Press, 1968), 181–182. Similarly, Inalcik and Merlino argue that the Ottomans unified all Christians living within the empire's domain – Arabs, Albanians, Romanians, Greeks, Bulgarians, Georgians, and Serbs – under a single *millet* (Arabic *milla*, confessional community). While the patriarchs of Alexandria, Jerusalem, Antioch, the Serbian Church, and the Bulgarian Church, lost autonomy to some degree, they retained a measure of independence under the new administrative system and the Patriarchate of Istanbul. The ecumenical patriarch was not just a religious leader, but he was also the temporal leader of the empire's Orthodox population. Halil Inalcik, "The Status of the Greek Orthodox Patriarch under the Ottomans," *Turcica* 21–23 (1991), 413–418; Mark Merlino, "The Post-Byzantine Legal Tradition in Theory and Practice," (master's thesis, Bilkent University, 2004), 34–55.

of equivalent authority, and (b) further delay in returning the goods of the Egyptian merchant might lead to their confiscation by the Muslim authorities of Tripoli. In his inquiries to Daniel ben ʿAzarya, head of the Yeshiva of Palestine, the appellant points out that the Tripolitanian *dayyan* (judge) ruled in favor of the widow and her orphaned daughter, fearing that the governor would confiscate the merchandise under the pretense that its owner was absent, or that part of it belonged to a minor. In so doing, the *dayyan* at the *bēt dīn* of Tripoli disregarded the written contracts that had been drafted by a notary and signed by both merchants at the courthouse of Fusṭāṭ. Ben Salmān's appeal to the Jewish high court (*bēt dīn ha-gadōl*) in Jerusalem was accepted and the gaon instructed the elders of the Jewish community of Palermo to advocate the acceleration of the judicial process in Tripoli and the release of the property to the Egyptian merchant.[169]

Eventually, the gaon had the final word in this particular case, as well as in other lawsuits involving the extraterritorial application of Jewish law within and outside the Abode of Islam. Non-Muslim coreligious subjects clearly enjoyed judicial privileges and had the right to administer lawsuits freely in accordance with their own religious code, even if they did not reside in the same territory. Territorial affiliation never constituted an impediment because sovereignty was dictated by religious law in accordance with the religion of each subject.

We find perhaps the most eloquent evidence of freedom of movement via judicial sovereignty as practiced up until the late eleventh century CE in the juristic correspondence between Jewish communities in the diaspora and the three leading yeshivas of Pumbedita and Sura in Iraq, and the Palestinian in Jerusalem. Jews around the world posed countless questions to the gaons seeking appropriate halachic judgment on matters related to faith and civil affairs.[170] Many responsa were produced, addressing queries from Jewish merchants, agents, shippers, and, to a lesser extent, shipowners.[171]

[169] Khalilieh, "Legal Aspects from a Cairo Geniza *Responsum*," 180–183, doc. Bodl. MS Heb. a 3 (Cat. 2873). The Hebrew version of this document has been published by Simcha Assaf, *Gaonic Responsa from Geniza Manuscripts* (Jerusalem: Darom Publishing, 1970), 125–127; Moshe Gil, *Palestine during the First Muslim Period 654–1099* (Tel Aviv: Tel Aviv University and the Ministry of Defense Publishing House, 1983), 2:728–732; Ben-Sasson, *Jews of Sicily*, 166–169.

[170] Goitein, *Mediterranean Society*, 1:65, 66. Such relationships among all parts of the Jewish diaspora never posed "an infringement on (the states') sovereignty," since a person's legal standing derived from his religious affiliation.

[171] Steven F. Friedell, "Admiralty and the Sea of Jewish Law," *Journal of Maritime Law and Commerce* 27 (1996), 647–660; Stephen M. Passamaneck, "A Particular Analysis of

As a rule, Jewish litigants were to be judged in accordance with the "Law of the Torah," or "Law of Moses and Israel," or "of and for the Jews," or "of the Jews" alone.[172] Nevertheless, prior to the rise of Islam, Jewish halacha did not prohibit Jewish litigants from appearing before non-Jewish courts, but rather expressed some flexibility toward such adjudications. The Babylonian Talmud, Gittin, 9b states: "All deeds which appear in legal courts of the heathen ones, although those who sign them are the heathens, are valid, except for bills of divorce and manumission of slaves."[173] Except for the last two categories, Jewish law allows Jews to appear in gentile courts and to engage in business agreements – commenda, partnership, *suftaja* (banking), sale, lease, transport, and so forth – according to the law of the gentiles.[174]

At times, the Jews turned to the Islamic courts for adjudication in cases when: (a) the Jewish *bēt dīn* was limited in enforcing verdicts;[175] (b) the Islamic court was better able to ensure the claiming of debts;[176] (c) the dispute was interreligious;[177] (d) contracts clearly stipulated Islamic authority for enforcement (ex ante);[178] (e) one or both parties refused to appear before the Jewish court,[179] such as when recognizing the Islamic

General Average," *Journal of Jewish Studies* 25 (1974): 155–168; Stephen M. Passamaneck, "Two Aspects of Rabbinical Maritime Law," *The Journal of Jewish Studies* 22 (1971), 53–67; Stephen M. Passamaneck, "Traces of Rabbinical Maritime Law and Custom," *Revue d'Histoire du Droit* 34 (1966), 525–551. On the pre-Gaonic period Jewish maritime tradition and practice, consult Raphael Patai, "Ancient Jewish Seafaring and Riverfaring Laws," in *By Study and Also By Faith: Essays in Honor of Hugh W. Nibley*, ed. John M. Lundquist and Stephen D. Ricks (Salt Lake City: Desert Book Company, 1990), 389–416; Daniel Sperber, *Nautica Talmudica* (Leiden: E. J. Brill, 1986).

172 Goitein, *Mediterranean Society*, 2:327; Rose, "Personal Status Laws among Christian Dhimmis," 169.

173 Uriel Simonsohn, "Communal Boundaries Reconsidered: Jews and Christians Appealing to Muslim Authorities in the Medieval Near East," *Jewish Studies Quarterly* 14 (2007), 335.

174 Goitein, *Mediterranean Society*, 2:328; Zaydān, *Aḥkām al-Dhimmiyyīn wa'l-Musta'minīn*, 467–469.

175 U. Simonsohn, "Communal Boundaries," 338; U. Simonsohn, *Common Justice*, 177, 185.

176 U. Simonsohn, "Communal Boundaries," 339; U. Simonsohn, *Common Justice*, 177–178; Goitein, *Mediterranean Society*, 2:395.

177 U. Simonsohn, "Communal Boundaries," 340; Timur Kuran, "The Economic Ascent of the Middle East's Religious Minorities: The Role of Islamic Legal Pluralism," *The Journal of Legal Studies* 33 (2004), 485.

178 U. Simonsohn, "Communal Boundaries," 340; Kuran, "Economic Ascent of the Middle East's Religious Minorities," 485.

179 U. Simonsohn, "Communal Boundaries," 341–342; U. Simonsohn, *Common Justice*, 177.

court as more advantageous;[180] (f) a litigant had lost a previous lawsuit in a Jewish court;[181] or (g) Islamic courts seemed to offer more expedient judicial proceedings to resolve disputes and legal cases than Jewish and Christian courts.[182]

It should be noted that appeal by Scriptuaries to the Islamic judicial courts is not favored in the Qurʾān or by prominent scholars. Qadis, therefore, tried not to interfere in the judicial affairs of non-Muslims and avoided hearing cases before first referring them to their Jewish colleagues.[183] In order to prevent Jews from appealing to Islamic courts, four methods were employed: (a) proclaiming the litigants excommunicated; (b) resolving disputes by arbitration; (c) the paying of one's debt;[184] and most interestingly, (d) gaons attempted to offer juristic solutions similar to those promulgated by Muslim *fuqahāʾ*.[185] Furthermore, decisions of the Islamic court were final. They could not be appealed or submitted to judicial review, except in cases in which an appellant established beyond the slightest doubt before the *maẓālim* or other superior court that a manifest injustice had occurred.[186]

It is observable from Ben Salmān's 1058 CE appeal to the Palestinian Yeshiva that although both parties to the lawsuit were from different territories, the qadi in the port-city of Tripoli disregarded the principle of territoriality to enforce the personal law of both litigants. Once it had been established with certainty that the case was exclusively Jewish, the qadi transferred jurisdiction to the local Jewish *dayyan*. Indeed, judicial precedents and religious writings by prominent scholars were universally applicable to all Jewish communities around the world, including in Christian Europe. Jews in the Abode of Islam and in foreign countries were judged according to the "Law of Moses and Israel," although particular communities chose to follow either the Babylonian or the Palestinian Talmud.

Consuls and Their Fellow Nationals

One of the earliest documents to establish the consular institution dates from 1082 CE, when Venice was privileged by the Emperor Alexios

[180] U. Simonsohn, "Communal Boundaries," 346; U. Simonsohn, *Common Justice*, 180.
[181] U. Simonsohn, "Communal Boundaries," 354.
[182] U. Simonsohn, *Common Justice*, 198.
[183] Goitein, *Mediterranean Society*, 2:396, 398.
[184] U. Simonsohn, "Communal Boundaries," 356.
[185] U. Simonsohn, "Communal Boundaries," 358; U. Simonsohn, *Common Justice*, 196.
[186] David Powers, "On Judicial Review in Islamic Law," *Law and Society Review* 26 (1992), 316–317.

I Komnenos (r. 1081–1118) to create mercantile headquarters in Constantinople and extend its customary laws (*usus*) to its nationals residing in the territorial domain of the empire.[187] Elected in the early stages of their history by a majority vote of traders, the primary function of the consuls was to stimulate international business between the eastern and western basins of the Mediterranean and to protect Venetian interests in Byzantium. By the turn of the twelfth century, the maritime republics of Christian Europe on the Middle Sea had installed their own consuls and vice-consuls across the Islamic and Byzantine Mediterranean.[188]

As commissioner of a foreign independent political entity, the consul had to be endorsed by local authorities. He performed a dual role of both political representative and commercial agent. On the political level, he acted as a mediator between his sovereign and the local ruler, protected national interests, and negotiated and enforced commercial treaties.[189]

[187] Penna, *Byzantine Imperial Acts to Venice, Pisa and Genoa*, 26; Vsevolod Slessarev, "Ecclesiae Mercatorum and the Rise of Merchant Colonies," *Business History Review* 41 (1967), 182–183; Nasim M. Soosa, "The Historical Interpretation of the Origin of the Capitulations in the Ottoman Empire," *Temple Law Quarterly* 4 (1929–1930), 360–361.

[188] The judicial privileges and jurisdictional rights of the Communes' consuls in the Byzantine Empire during the eleventh and twelfth centuries are best addressed by Penna, *Byzantine Imperial Acts to Venice, Pisa and Genoa*; Daphne Penna, "Venetian Judges and their Jurisdiction in Constantinople in the 12th Century: Some Observations based on Information Drawn from the Chrysobull of Alexios III Angelos to Venice in 1198," *Subseciva Groningana, Studies in Roman and Byzantine Law* 8 (2009), 135–146. In 1198, Emperor Alexios III Angelos (r. 1195–1203) granted Venetian magistrates the right not only to settle disputes between Venetian nationals, but also to grant them the privilege to preside over mixed cases involving subjects of the empire and Venetian citizens, namely when the plaintiff is Byzantine and the defendant is Venetian. However, in cases of criminal law, the criterion of the severity of the crime determines the jurisdiction and venue. Cases involving homicide and severe wounding were brought ordinarily before the office of the *logothetēs tou dromou* (acting as the "Minister of Foreign Affairs"), or other competent judicial authority in the absence of the former. For further details on the office of the *logothetēs tou dromou*, consult the article of Dean A. Miller, "The Logothete of the Drome in the Middle Byzantine Period," *Byzantion* 36 (1966), 438–470, especially 439. In reference to similar concessions that had already been awarded to Amalfi (1056), Genoa (1098), and Pisa (1110), see Julius I. Puente, "The Nature of the Consular Establishment," *University of Pennsylvania Law Review and American Law Register* 78 (1930), 323–325; David Abulafia, "Pisan Commercial Colonies and Consulates in Twelfth-Century Sicily," *English Historical Review* 93 (1978), 68–69. For later periods, consult Lucius E. Thayer, "The Capitulations of the Ottoman Empire and the Question of their Abrogation as It Affects the United States," *American Journal of International Law* 17 (1923), 208–210; Soosa, "Origin of the Capitulations in the Ottoman Empire," 362–363.

[189] Julius I. Puente, "Functions and Powers of the Foreign Consulate: A Study in Medieval Legal History," *New York University Law Quarterly Review* 20 (1944), 57–60;

As a commercial agent, he held vast executive and judicial powers, and was charged with assisting, claiming, and defending the rights, status, and privileges of his fellow nationals before local authorities.[190] He was held responsible for their conduct, protected them and their properties from harm, assisted them in all matters at the customs house, granted special immunity to honorable nationals, ordered the arrest of sailors and fugitives, reported on foreign laws affecting his nationals, and met with the sultan once a month in order to foster friendly relations between states and to further develop commercial ties.[191] Concerning the administration of justice, the consul represented his fellow compatriots before local courts, maintained discipline, adjudicated disputes arising among his own nationals, and enforced on his subjects his own nation's rule of law, as well as that of the host country.[192]

Prior to the establishment of the consular institution, churches – as monastic hospices – functioned as centers for foreign merchants trading far from home.[193] It appears that foreigners were not then able to adjudicate their controversies in accordance with customary practices and prescribed laws of their native countries, but had to submit to the ecclesiastical judicial system, as well as to local regulations and traditions.

Travers Twiss, "The Exterritoriality of Public Ships of War in Foreign Waters," *Law Magazine and Review* 3 (1876), 204–205; Moukarzel, "Venetian Merchants," 198–199.

190 Puente, "Functions and Powers of the Foreign Consulate," 61–62.

191 Mas Latrie, *Traité de paix et de commerce et documents*, 2:86–87; Constable, *Housing the Stranger*, 116, 282–285; Georg Christ, *Trading Conflicts: Venetian Merchants and Mamluk Officials in Late Medieval Alexandria* (Leiden: E. J. Brill, 2012), 67–69; Soosa, "Origin of the Capitulations in the Ottoman Empire," 361, 364; Michael E. Mallett, "The Sea Consuls of Florence in the Fifteenth Century," *Papers of the British School at Rome* 27 (1959), 160–163; Robert S. Smith, "The Early History of the Spanish Sea Consulate," *Politica* 3 (1935), 318–324; Puente, "Functions and Powers of the Foreign Consulate," 63–64. Every one of the maritime trading empires of medieval Christian Europe – Venice, Genoa, Amalfi, Florence, Valencia, and Catalonia, for example – had its own colony in major Islamic trading centers, namely the port cities on the Mediterranean. In these cities, each foreign Christian community maintained its own guest complex (*fondaco, funduq*), thereby segregating travelers from the local residents. Each complex contained storehouses, facilities for beasts of burden, living spaces, places intended for commercial activities, and offices for the consul, notaries, and other officials. There the consul or his deputy were available to handle administrative and judicial affairs.

192 Mas Latrie, *Traité de paix et de commerce et documents*, 87; Mallett, "Sea Consuls of Florence," 161; R. Smith, "Early History of the Spanish Sea Consulate," 316–317. Respecting the Pisan consuls' judicial role in the Levant during the Crusaders, refer to Abulafia, "Crocuses and Crusaders," 235–239.

193 Slessarev, "Ecclesiae Mercatorum," 177–182.

However, with the formation of the consular post, which was made possible by the mutual agreement of both sovereigns, the custom of extraterritoriality became applicable to all persons of the same nation. Did the political entities of the Islamic Mediterranean thereby voluntarily give up their territorial sovereignty? Put another way, is the principle of extraterritoriality represented by the consul institution compatible or incompatible with Islamic law?

Islamic law rules that the rights and obligations of an individual are to be determined on the basis of personal religious law. Until the twelfth century, in places where *dhimmīs* maintained their own religious identity and judicial autonomy, Christian and Jewish *musta'mins* appear to have settled their controversies before ecclesiastical and rabbinical tribunals.[194] However, once the consular post was founded, through international diplomatic and commercial treaties, sultans and rulers around the Islamic Mediterranean granted European governments – including the Crusaders – judicial privileges authorizing their consular representatives to extend their nations' jurisdiction to merchants, passengers, masters of vessels, sailors, and others, be they nationals of the accrediting sovereign, or nationals of another state, or nationals of the admitting sovereign.[195] A recalcitrant refusing to comply with the jurisdiction of the consul could instead be tried in the local court.[196]

Typically, Islamic law prevailed on Islamic soil when controversies arose among Muslim disputants, between Muslims and non-Muslims, or between Christians of different sovereigns.[197] However, with the

194 Rose, "Personal Status Laws among Christian Dhimmis," 173–174.

195 Moukarzel, "Venetian Merchants," 198–199; Puente, "Functions and Powers of the Foreign Consulate," 70–73; Holt, *Early Mamluk Diplomacy*, 82: article 10 of the 682/1283 treaty concluded between al-Manṣūr Qalāwūn and the Latin Kingdom states that "the *Bailli* (bailiff/king's administrative representative) of the kingdom in Acre and the Masters shall have jurisdiction over their subjects who leave their territory as covered by this truce." On reciprocal, "the Sultan and his son shall have jurisdiction over any of his subjects, of whatever religions and nations, who leave their territory"; Samīr al-Khādim, *Al-Sharq al-Islāmī wa'l-Gharb al-Masīḥī 'abr al-'Alāqāt bayna al-Mudun al-Īṭāliyya wa-Sharqiyy al-Baḥr al-Mutawassiṭ 1450–1517* (Beirut: Mu'assasat al-Rīḥānī, 1989), 239, article 14 of the Florentine–Mamluk treaty of 894/1489.

196 Puente, "Functions and Powers of the Foreign Consulate," 76; Yadira González de Lara, "The Secret of Venetian Success: A Public-order, Reputation-based Institution," *European Review of Economic History* 12 (2008), 266, 268.

197 Amari, *Diplomi Arabi*, 89, 102, article 9 of the 713/1313 treaty and article 10 of the 754/1353 treaty: "*matā kāna khiṣām bayna Muslim wa-Naṣrānī aw bayna Naṣrāniyyayn, ujriyā 'alā la-ḥaqq*"; 172, article 5 of the 849/1445 treaty concluded between the Ḥafṣīd amir Abū 'Umar 'Uthmān ibn Muḥammad al-Manṣūr and Pisa and Florence stipulates that any legal dispute arising with Muslims, or between these states' subjects and other

advent of the consul, cases involving subjects of different nations entailed further consideration. The judicial sovereignty of the consul depended on whether his fellow national was the plaintiff or defendant in a case. The 689/1290 treaty between al-Manṣūr Qalāwūn and Genoa ruled quite clearly that the Genoese consul was to preside over cases in which the plaintiff was a Muslim or a local Christian and the defendant was Genoese. By contrast, should the plaintiff be a subject of Genoa and the defendant a local resident, the case was to be heard in the customs house before the finance officer (*milus*).[198] Clauses with an identical wording are inserted in the 713/1313,[199] 754/1353, 800/1397,[200] 817/1414,[201] and 824/1421[202] Ḥafṣīd–Pisan treaties. These treaties provided that the Pisan

Christian nationals shall be tried exclusively by *ṣāḥib al-dīwān* and no one may intervene in the matter. Concerning the eastern Islamic countries on the Mediterranean, article 26 of the 833/1430 Florentine–Mamluk treaty decrees: "When there is within the Florentine nation a dispute or quarrel, or one of them has a claim against another of his nation, no one of the viceroys or magistrates [Muslim officers] or merchants shall adjudicate between them except the consul of their nation according to their custom." Constable, *Housing the Stranger*, 283; John Wansbrough, "A Mamluk Commercial Treaty Concluded with the Republic of Florence, 894/1489," in *Documents from Islamic Chanceries*, ed. Samuel M. Stern (Oxford: Bruno Cassirer, 1965), 68. Article 5 of a letter (*mukātaba*) sent by Sultan Qaitbay (r. 872–901/1468–1496) to the Doge of Firenze in Jumāda II 7, 901/February 22, 1496 decrees that "where a litigation, a dispute, or an action for money and other things such as a Muslim against a Venetian, or a Venetian against a Muslim, the adjudication should be brought before the noble portals (*al-Abwāb al-Sharīfa*/high ranking aides of the sultan) if they happened to be in Cairo, or their viceroy, or chamberlain or officials of that province if they (disputants) happened to be in the frontiers." Amari, *Diplomi Arabi*, 188–189; Wansbrough, "Venice and Florence in the Mamluk Commercial Privileges," 499, 512, article 34 of the 902/1497 treaty between the Republic of Florence and the Mamluk sultan al-Nāṣir Muḥammad (r. 901–903/1496–1498) used identical wording; Frantz-Murphy, "Identity and Security in the Mediterranean World," 254, 261, 264; Moukarzel, "Venetian Merchants," 198–199; Victor O. Pita, "Commercial Litigation across Religious Borders: Rendering Justice for Valencian Merchants in Fifteenth-Century North Africa and Granada," *Comparative Legal History* 5 (2017), 95, 100, 102–103; Louis Sicking, "Introduction: Maritime Conflict Management, Diplomacy and International Law, 1100–1800," *Comparative Legal History* 5 (2017), 9–10; Rose, "Personal Status Laws among Christian Dhimmis," 165–168; Cohen, "Defending Jewish Judicial Autonomy in the Islamic Middle Ages," 14–17.

198 Holt, *Early Mamluk Diplomacy*, 145; Pita, "Commercial Litigation across Religious Borders," 100. Early fourteenth-century Catalan consuls in the Islamic West (Maghrib) could preside over mixed cases when the defendant was a fellow-national, whereas the plaintiff was a local or foreign Muslim.

199 Amari, *Diplomi Arabi*, 94, article 34; 107, article 34 states that if a Muslim subject inflicts harm in a foreign territory party to the agreement, the plaintiff shall bring his lawsuit before the Elders and consuls "to do justice to him (*inṣāf*)."

200 Amari, *Diplomi Arabi*, 127, article 5.

201 Amari, *Diplomi Arabi*, 141, article 5.

202 Amari, *Diplomi Arabi*, 155, article 5.

Consul preside over lawsuits engaging a Muslim and a Pisan party regarding controversies taking place in the territorial domain of Pisa. On the other hand, the same lawsuit was to be judged in accordance with Islamic Holy Law if arising in Ḥafṣīd territory. However, if the consul showed bias to one party over another, inflicted injustice on his fellow national or anyone else, or neglected his judicial duty, then the *ṣāḥib al-dīwān* was to usurp jurisdiction over the case. Put another way, if one of the litigants was not satisfied with the consul's decision, he could appeal to the *maẓālim*.[203] Occasionally, some intercolonial lawsuits originating in Islamic territories ended up in the homeland courts of the disputants.[204]

The consul enjoyed exclusive jurisdiction over his fellow compatriots in the host country.[205] However, when cases involved multinational parties, the jurisdiction of the consul depended on whether his fellow national was the plaintiff or defendant. Should the plaintiff be a subject of a third state, the consul could not preside over the case unless this had been stipulated in the bilateral treaty establishing his authority. It was also outside the consul's judicial capacity to preside over cases where the defendant was the subject of a third state, unless the stranger's own government endorsed such judicial procedures. In such cases, the courts had to administer justice within a reasonable time.[206] Ultimately, the consul's sovereignty extended over vessels flying his sovereign's flag, whether on the high seas or in ports, including over their crew and passengers – even if nationals of different states – their cargoes, wreckage, salvaged properties, and estates of the deceased.[207]

203 Amari, *Diplomi Arabi*, 126, article 3; Christ, *Venetian Merchants and Mamluk Officials*, 54; Wansbrough, "Venice and Florence in the Mamluk Commercial Privileges," 507, 522, article 31 of the 902/1497 Mamluk–Florentine treaty; Constable, *Housing the Stranger*, 283.

204 Christ, *Venetian Merchants and Mamluk Officials*, 69; Pita, "Commercial Litigation across Religious Borders," 91, 95, 102.

205 Amari, *Diplomi Arabi*, 94, article 36 (713/1313); 107, article 10 (754/1353); 127, article 5 (800/1397); Holt, *Early Mamluk Diplomacy*, 35, article 7 of the 665/1267 treaty concluded between al-Ẓāhir Baybars and the Hospitallers); 115, article 13 of the 684/1285 treaty between al-Manṣūr Qalāwūn and the Lady Margaret of Tyre; 145, al-Manṣūr Qalāwūn–Genoa Treaty of 689/1290; Frantz-Murphy, "Identity and Security in the Mediterranean World," 259.

206 Puente, "Functions and Powers of the Foreign Consulate," 76–79; Constable, *Housing the Stranger*, 283. Small claims involving parties from different nationalities were generally brought before one of the consuls unless one of the parties chose to appeal to the Islamic courts.

207 Puente, "Functions and Powers of the Foreign Consulate," 81–86.

As exclusive judicial authority vested in the consul for adjudicating disputes between his nationals, the Muslim judicial and civil authorities were reluctant to interfere in the consul's judicial affairs. However, local tribunals could try cases of a commercial nature if foreign nationals of the same country had concluded their business deal on Islamic soil.[208] Furthermore, *musta'mins* were entitled to appeal to higher local courts – or even the *maẓālim* tribunal – if dissatisfied with their consul's verdict. In sum, it appears that the significant degree of judicial autonomy enjoyed by foreign consuls in the Abode of Islam did not disturb the territorial integrity of the state nor affect its sovereign jurisdiction and the pluralistic legal system.

SUMMARY

The concept of extending the sovereignty of a coastal state over the maritime spaces off its coasts is not a modern notion, but derives from a long history that extends as far back as the dawn of ancient maritime civilizations. However, legal historians tend to date the doctrine of the territorial sea to late medieval Europe, associating its formulation with the rise of the feudal system and naval supremacy of Italian Communes. These historians are strongly inclined to regard the post-Glossators, who espoused the Roman *Corpus Juris Civilis*, as the first to institute the theoretical foundations of the relevant concept in their legal writings and commentaries, paying no heed to contemporaneous non-European practices around the heterogeneous Mediterranean world. This omission likely follows from that of distinguished legal theorists, such as Bartolus of Sassoferrato and his disciple Baldus de Ubaldis, who similarly fail to mention application of the doctrine of the territorial sea in non-European sovereigns in the Mediterranean Sea, starting from the second half of the seventh century. This lack of reference maybe derived from a lack of awareness on the part of the jurists of similar practices in non-European maritime traditions, a lack of access to non-Romance legal writings, or an intentional overlooking of the role of non-Christian cultures in formulating this doctrine.

Early and classical jurists categorically divided the Abode of Islam into three geographical domains: the Ḥaram, the Hijaz, and all other territories. Unlike any other place on Earth, Muslim jurists and theologians

[208] Sawsan G. Kanj, "Aḥkām Mukhāṣamāt al-Musta'minīn fī al-Fiqh al-Islāmī," (master's thesis, Āl al-Bayt University, 2004), 38–39.

attach sanctity to the Hijaz and its littoral, and forbid *dhimmīs* and non-Muslim aliens from taking up permanent residence and exploiting the natural resources found there. However, non-Muslims are allowed to sojourn in the land, sail through the maritime domain, and carry on trade, provided that their stay does not extend beyond three nights in any given place. It seems that non-Muslims also enjoyed the right of transit passage through the Sea of Hijaz so long as good order, public peace, and sanctity of the holy sites were not infringed upon. Although the seaward breadth of the Hijazi territorial sea has never been specifically defined in units of measurement, its width extends from the shoreline of the mainland to the outermost points of the islands and islets off the Hijazi side of the Red Sea, and its length extends from northwestern Yemen to the coastal point parallel to Tabūk. Although Muslims claim exclusive de facto and de jure proprietorship over the Sea of Hijaz due to religious considerations, nonetheless, they never regard it as *mare nostrum*. Significantly, the proprietorial rights of Muslims over the Arabian side of the Red Sea, which rest solely on religious premises, have never been challenged, but rather are acknowledged by foreign powers. From the early years of Islam until the present day, Muslims have charged no tolls for passage through the Sea of Hijaz.

Pursuant to Qur'ān 20:9 and the Prophetic tradition that "every land has its appurtenance forbidden (to other than the proprietor)," each and every coast has its own *ḥarīm*, conferring upon local residents priority rights to exploit marine natural resources off their coastlands. Even so, they may not impede the free use of offshore waters for navigation. In addition, *ḥarbīs* equipped with *amān* pledges enjoyed the right of passage through maritime *ḥarīms* of coastal settlements.

The need to protect coastal frontiers from intrusion, provide lodging for caravan traffic, and shelter imperiled vessels, including enemy warships in distress, made sailing in sight of the coast a fundamental factor inducing admirals and governing authorities to exercise sovereignty over limited offshore zones.[209] Save for Idrīsī's unique fixing of the maritime sovereignty of the coastal village of Bajānis at six miles (10 kilometers), the breadth of a territorial sea varies from one place to another due to topographical differences. Ships sailing within the maritime domain of a coastal city could be subject to inspection, and her crew and passengers

[209] Maqrīzī, *Khiṭaṭ*, 1:49. During the Fatimid period, the Gulf of Aylah and the Gulf of Suez were an inseparable part of the internal waters of Egypt, over which Egypt held exclusive sovereignty.

had to present their property and documentation indicating the purposes of their journey, personal identity, and citizenship.[210]

States recognized each other's exclusive rights in their adjoining seas through bilateral and multilateral commercial and diplomatic treaties. A sample of Islamic–Christian treaties concluded from the tenth to the early sixteenth centuries demonstrates that part of the neighboring sea can be subject to the exclusive dominion of a coastal state. As already pointed out, the treaties remain silent as to the seaward breadth of the offshore zone, leading to the assumption that each zone must have been uniquely determined according to the relevant range of vision. Within these narrow bands, states enjoyed absolute sovereignty over resources, mainly fisheries, wrecks, and salvage. They also had the right to regulate passage, protect commercial vessels from hostile and piratical raids, provide aid to distressed vessels, and grant them permission to obtain food supply and drink.

It can safely be deduced that the modern concept of the territorial sea is duly compatible with the Islamic tradition, given that its seaward breadth does not encroach upon the high sea and state sovereignty is limited to a breadth of several miles. Foreign commercial vessels, even those flying the flag of enemy countries, retain the right of innocent passage through territorial seas without the state levying charges upon them. The same right applies to passage through the straits located within the Abode of Islam. When exposed to force majeure or man-made dangers, the local ruling authorities should render assistance to any person or vessel. In the case of a shipwreck, the property cannot be considered derelict and the rightful owners or their heirs enjoy sole salvage rights to wrecks and their contents inasmuch as they do not voluntarily relinquish them. Implicitly, local residents, in the first place, and nationals, in the second, have exclusive rights to fish and exploit the natural resources within the territorial sea.

By contrast, the European doctrine – which was formulated by the post-Glossator commentators – associates sovereignty of the territorial sea with naval supremacy. Eminent Renaissance and early modern legal theorists such as Hugo Grotius (1583–1645), Samuel von Pufendorf (1632–1694), Cornelius van Bynkershoek (1673–1743), and Emer de Vattel (1714–1767) advocate that a coastal state can assert jurisdictional claims over a narrow maritime band adjacent to its coastlands provided that it does not extend beyond the sight of

[210] Khalilieh, *Islamic Maritime Law*, 83–85.

land,[211] a doctrine which is in line with the principle introduced by early and classical Muslim governing authorities, admirals, and jurists. Beyond the offshore maritime belt, the vast ocean/sea is viewed in Islamic jurisprudential, geographical, military literature, and international and interregional treaties and truces as *nullius territorium*,[212] as termed by Travers Twiss,[213] being accessible to free navigation and the trade of all nations.

The absence of a formal international legal system never constituted an obstacle to the development of domestic and overseas transactions. On the contrary, domestic and overseas trade would not have prospered significantly had legal pluralism not existed. Until the rise of nation states in early Renaissance Europe, subjects of the Abode of Islam, at the very least, were identified by their own religion, each and every denomination having its independent legal system. The office of consul, which emerged at the beginning of the twelfth century, functioned as a judicial institution for subjects of the same nationality. Parties to a transaction always had the right to choose the application of a particular jurisdiction through contract; however, if they failed contractually to select the law, then the state law would become applicable. The local judicial authorities would then exercise the principle of territoriality over foreign actors if one of the litigants sought recourse to local courts. With the exception of family and personal related matters – marriage, divorce, inheritance, custody, adoption, slavery, and oath – and transactions that Islamic law does not recognize, which were almost exclusively handled by the denominational courts, *dhimmīs* and *musta'mins* were entitled to appeal to Islamic courts on the condition that the lawsuit was not brought before the arbitration of the ecclesiastical or consular court. Nevertheless, recourse by minorities to the Islamic courts could stem from contractual obligations, personal and financial considerations, and enforcement of judgments. However, once the non-Muslim plaintiff and the defendant moved the case out of their denominational court of their own free will, they became subject

[211] Grotius, *On the Rights of War and Peace*, 79–82; Samuel von Pufendorf, *Of the Law of Nature and Nations*, 4th ed., trans. Basil Kennett (London, 1729), 381–383; Emer de Vattel, *The Law of Nations*, ed. Béla Kapossy and Richard Whatmore (Indianapolis: Liberty Fund, 2008), 252–253; Cornelius van Bynkershoek, *Questions of Public Law*, trans. Tenney Frank, available at: http://www.constitution.org/bynk/bynk.htm (accessed February 14, 2014); Travers Twiss, *Law of Nations Considered as Political Communities: On the Rights and Duties of in Time of Peace* (Oxford: Clarendon Press, 1884), 293–294.

[212] *Terra nullius* signifies a territory not belonging to any particular country.

[213] Twiss, *Law of Nations*, 285.

ultimately to Islamic law. Similarly, Muslim minorities and colonies enjoyed comparable legal privileges in the Christian kingdoms along the Mediterranean Sea and the Indian Ocean littorals; minority communities were normally privileged to choose between two different tribunals, state or denominational. In both situations the principle of personality applied to all actors; this included *dhimmī*s and *musta'min*s, to whom, in certain cases, the territoriality principle pertained.

3

Piracy and Its Legal Implications

DEFINITION

From the dawn of ancient seafaring, maritime piracy has continually undermined seaborne commerce, affecting shippers, shipowners, and carriers. Ever since it arose, the subject of piracy has preoccupied jurists around the globe. Roman jurisprudents deemed pirates "*hostis humani generis* (enemies of all mankind)"[1] and included piracy, along with fire and shipwreck, as the three cardinal adversities that could befall a vessel.[2] With reference to current legal discourse, article 101 of the United Nations Convention on the Law of the Sea (UNCLOS) (1982) defines piracy as follows:

(a) Any illegal acts of violence or detention, or any act of depredation, committed for private ends by the crew or the passengers of a private ship or a private aircraft, and directed:
   (i) *on the high seas*, against another ship or aircraft, or against persons or property on board such ship or aircraft;
   (ii) against a ship, aircraft, persons or property in a place outside the jurisdiction of any state;

[1] Alfred P. Rubin, "The Law of Piracy," *Denver Journal of International Law and Policy* 15 (1986–1987), 187.

[2] Clyde Pharr *et al.* (ed.), *Theodosian Code and Novels and the Sirmondian Constitutions* (Princeton: Princeton University Press, 1952), 98, CTh 4.20.1; Scott (ed.), *Civil Law*, 3:136, Digest IV, 9, 3, 1; 4:185, Digest XIII, 6, 18; Walter Ashburner, *The Rhodian Sea Law* (Oxford: Clarendon Press, 1909), 87, article III:9; Edwin H. Freshfield, *A Manual of Later Roman Law: The Ecloga* (Cambridge: Cambridge University Press, 1927), 197; Emily S. Tai, "Honor among Thieves: Piracy, Restitution, and Reprisal in Genoa, Venice, and the Crown of Catalonia-Aragon," (PhD diss., Harvard University, 1996), 73.

(b) any act of voluntary participation in the operation of a ship or of an aircraft with knowledge of facts making it a pirate ship or aircraft;
(c) any act of inciting or of intentionally facilitating an act described in subparagraph (a) or (b).

Piracy is thereby defined as encompassing offences taking place on the high seas, outside the territorial sea of any state. This convention grants judicial rights that extend the sovereignty of a state over pirates if they are captured by its emissaries or citizens on the high seas. No reference is made to such attacks occurring on a territorial sea or within internal navigable waters.[3] The International Maritime Bureau (IMB) articulates a broader definition of piracy: "An act of boarding or attempting to board any ship with the apparent intent to commit theft or any other crime and with the apparent intent or capability to use force in furtherance of that act."[4] Thus, irrespective of location, whether within or outside a state's territorial jurisdiction, all acts of piracy are to be treated on an equal footing. The question here is – which of the two legal definitions is more compatible with Islamic law?

The most common colloquial Arabic word for maritime piracy is *qarṣana*.[5] Etymologically, this word derives from a mispronunciation of *kursāliyya* (corsair),[6] a corrupt Arabic form of the Italian *corsale* (Old

3 Article 105 of UNCLOS refers to pirates operating within or from the territorial waters of a state, forbidding other states from pursuing pirates into the territorial sea of that state without its expressed permission. Therefore, the limits prescribed by article 101 aim to avoid legal and political chaos among present-day states and to enhance multilateral cooperation in combating piracy by leaving the coastal state responsible for fighting piracy within its maritime jurisdiction.

4 William M. Davis, "Analysis of the Strategy to Combat Maritime Piracy," (master's thesis, Fort Leavenworth, Kansas, 2009), 5. In Moore's *Digest of International Law*, a pirate is defined as "one who, without legal authority from any state, attacks a ship with intention to appropriate what belongs to it. The pirate is a sea brigand. He has no right to any flag and is justiciable by all." John B. Moore, *A Digest of International Law as Embodied in Diplomatic Discussions, Treaties and other International Agreements, International Awards, Decisions of Municipal Courts and the Writings of Jurists* (Washington DC: Government Printing Office, 1906), 2:953.

5 The two terms *qurṣān* and *qarṣana* are explicitly stated in article 26 of the peace treaties (*ṣulḥ*) concluded between the Ḥafṣīd amir Abū Fāris ʿAbd al-ʿAzīz al-Mutawakkil (r. 797–838/1394–1434) and Pisa on Rabīʿ I 23, 800/December 14, 1397; article 26 on Jumādā II, 817/September 1414; and article 26 of the treaty that the amir concluded with Pisa and Florence on Shawwal 7, 824/October 5, 1421. Similarly, the words *qurṣān* and *qarṣana* appear in articles 8, 22, and 23 of the peace treaty signed between the Ḥafṣīd amir Abū ʿUmar ʿUthmān ibn Muḥammad al-Manṣūr (r. 840–893/1436–1488) and Pisa and Florence on Muḥarram 15, 849/April 23, 1445. Amari, *Diplomi Arabi*, 133–134, 147–149, 161–163, 173, 177.

6 Qalqashandī, *Ṣubḥ al-Aʿshā*, 14:74, 77, the 680/1281 Mamluk–Byzantine treaty concluded between al-Manṣūr Qalāwūn and Michael VIII Palaeologus, article 11 of the

Italian *corsaro*), which itself stems from the medieval Latin *cursārius*, a derivative of the verb *currō*, meaning "to run."[7] Another term identifying pirates in international treaties is *ḥarāmiyyat al-baḥr* (literally, "sea thieves or robbers").[8] The two terms *kursāliyya* and *ḥarāmiyya* ostensibly appear synonymous. However, sophisticated international treaties drafted by experienced and learned scribes draw a clear distinction between *kursāliyya* (corsairs) and *ḥarāmiyya* (thieves).[9]

Jurisprudential inquiries, compendia, and official and private documents use different terms for highway robbery on land compared with that at sea, without drawing any distinctions on the basis of whether or not the crime includes homicide. Highway robbers are generally referred to as *luṣūṣ* (sing. *liṣṣ*/thief).[10] In order to distinguish such criminals from maritime robbers, the word *baḥr* (sea) was appended: *luṣūṣ al-baḥr*.[11] For

Arabic version of that treaty refers to licensed sea robbers as *kursāliyya*. Similarly, article 11 of the treaty of al-Manṣūr Qalāwūn with King Alfonso III of Aragon 689/1290 states: "Provided also that the King of Aragon shall not enable pirates (*al-ḥarāmiyya*) or corsairs (*al-kursāliyya*)." Holt, *Early Mamluk Diplomacy*, 136; Ḥamāda, *Al-Wathā'iq al-Siy āsiyya wa'l-Idāriyya lil-'Aṣr al-Mamlūkī*, 500; Nashshār, *'Alāqat Mamlakatay Qishtāla wa-Aragon bi-Salṭanat al-Mamālīk*, 235.

7 Ch. Pellat *et al.*, "Ḳurṣān," in *Encyclopaedia of Islam*, 2nd ed., ed. P. Bearman *et al.* (Brill Online, 2012) http://referenceworks.brillonline.com/entries/encyclopaedia-of-islam-2/kursan-COM_0546.

8 Article 18 of the 682/1283 truce concluded between al-Manṣūr Qalāwūn with the *bailli* of the kingdom of Acre and its Masters stipulates that "pirates (*ḥarāmiyyat al-baḥr*) shall not be enabled to obtain provisions or take on water from them (Crusaders)." Holt, *Early Mamluk Diplomacy*, 85; Peter M. Holt, "Qalāwūn's Treaty with Acre in 1283," *English Historical Review* 91 (1976), 807; Qalqashandī, *Ṣubḥ al-A'shā*, 8:125, 14:60 (*ḥarāmiyyat al-baḥr*).

9 Article 11 of the 689/1290 treaty between al-Manṣūr Qalāwūn and King Alfonso III of Aragon states: "Provided also that the King of Aragon shall not enable pirates (*al-ḥarāmiyya*) or corsairs (*al-kursāliyya*) to obtain provisions or take on water from his territory." Legally, the *kursāliyya* were officially licensed corsairs/privateers whose sponsoring state/s shared the prizes with them. The *ḥarāmiyya*, on the other hand, operated outside the law, launching their attacks indiscriminately against domestic and foreign targets. Consult Holt, *Early Mamluk Diplomacy*, 136. An earlier reference to *kursāliyya* is mentioned in article 11 of the 680/1281 Mamluk–Byzantine treaty. Holt, *Early Mamluk Diplomacy*, 124; Ḥamāda, *Al-Wathā'iq al-Siyāsiyya wa'l-Idāriyya lil-'Aṣr al-Mamlūkī*, 512; Nashshār, *'Alāqat Mamlakatay Qishtāla wa-Aragon bi-Salṭanat al-Mamālīk*, 235.

10 Ṭāher (ed.), "*Akriyat al-Sufun*," 22; Ibn Rushd (al-Jadd), *Al-Bayān wa'l-Taḥṣīl*, 9:148–150; Abū 'Abd Allāh Muḥammad al-Raṣṣā', *Sharḥ Ḥudūd Ibn 'Arafa* (Beirut: Dār al-Gharb al-Islāmī, 1993), 2:525. Some Geniza documents use the term *liṣṣ* to prescribe piracy: Bodl. Ms Heb. D 66 6 (Cat. 2878), l. 12; TS 8 265, l. 13; TS 8 J 24 f. 4, l. 14; TS Arabic Box 43 200, l. 7; Averbuch, "From Siraf to Sumatra," 193, 218.

11 Wansharīsī, *Al-Mi'yār*, 8:302 (*luṣūṣ al-baḥr*/sea robbers); Abū Isḥāq Ibrāhīm ibn Muḥammad al-Iṣṭakhrī, *Kitāb Masālik al-Mamālik* (Leiden: E. J. Brill, 1870), 33, calls them *mutalaṣṣiṣat al-baḥr* (sea rovers/thieves); Saif Sh. al-Muraikhi, "Al-Qarṣana fī al-Khalīj al-'Arabī wa'l-Baḥr al-Aḥmar wa'l-Muḥīṭ al-Hindī fī al-'Uṣūr al-Islāmiyya al-

pirates on the Indian Ocean and the eastern seas, the terms *bawārij al-Hunūd* (pirate ships of the Indians),[12] *bawārij al-Hind* (pirate ships of India) are given, [13] which along with *luṣūṣ al-bawārij* (buccaneers),[14] are the most frequently cited terms in classical primary sources. The *bawārij* (sing. *bārija*) first meant "pirate ships," but in time became synonymous with pirates.[15] Similarly, letters of merchants found in the Cairo Geniza call them *aṣḥāb al-shawānī* (sailors of the *shīnī*s).[16]

Making no distinction in terms of category between land and sea, the Qur'ān refers implicitly to piracy alternatively as *qaṭ' al-sabīl* (cutting the highway/highway robbery),[17] *ḥirāba* (brigandage), and *fasād* (disturbing peace and spreading evil on earth). In one instance, the latter two terms

'Ūlā min Qiyām al-Dawla al-'Arabiyya al-Islāmiyya wa-ḥatā Muntaṣaf al-Qarn al-Thālith al-Hijrī," *Bulletin of the Faculty of Arts* [University of Alexandria] 58 (2008), 159.

12 Kindī, *Muṣannaf*, 11:158–164; Alpers, *Indian Ocean*, 66.

13 Yāqūt ibn 'Abd Allāh al-Ḥamawī, *Mu'jam al-Buldān* (Beirut: Dār Iḥyā' al-Turāth al-'Arabī, 1979), 3:227.

14 Abū al-Rayḥān Muḥammad ibn Aḥmad al-Bīrūnī, *Taḥqīq mā lil-Hind min Maqūla Maqbūla fī al-'Aql aw Mardhūla* (Beirut: 'Ālam al-Kutub, 1403/1983), 148.

15 Agius, *Classic Ships of Islam*, 328–329; Averbuch, "From Siraf to Sumatra," 157–158, 168, 182. It is reported that the pirates' raids were not confined to ships, but also extended to coastal targets. Muqaddasī writes: "The island of Usquṭrah [Socotra] rises like a tower in the dark sea; it is a refuge for the pirates, who are the terror of sailing ships in these parts; and not till the island is cleared do they cease to be a cause of fear." Muqaddasī, *Aḥsan al-Taqāsīm*, 14. *Shīnī, shīniyya*, or *shānī* is the model for the Byzantine *dromon*. It is a type of Islamic galley or warship used in the Mediterranean with a watchtower placed next to the main sail; it is propelled by lateen sails – originally two and later three – and oars, and can carry up to 165 sailors. Vassilios Christides, "Shīnī, Shīniyya, Shānī," in *Encyclopaedia of Islam*, 2nd ed., ed. P. Bearman *et al.* (Brill Online, 2012) http://referenceworks.brillonline.com/entries/encyclopaedia-of-islam-2/shini-shiniyya-shani-SIM_6949.

16 Goitein and Friedman, *India Traders*, 142, 760; on the attack of the King of Kīsh (Arabic: Qays) on the port of Aden, see pp. 437–450; in a few instances, pirates are referred to as *surrāq* (brigands or thieves), see p. 370. Ibn al-Mujāwir portrays the pirates who operated during the eleventh century in the vicinity of Kīsh, a small island in the lower Persian Gulf, as *surrāq* (highway robbery at sea). Ibn al-Mujāwir, *Ṣifat Bilād al-Yaman*, 160–161, 329; Prange, "Contested Sea," 17–20. On Kīsh's role in naval history and maritime trade during the tenth and thirteenth centuries, consult David Whitehouse, "Maritime Trade in the Gulf: The 11th and 12th Centuries," *World Archaeology* 14 (1983), 328–334; Daniel T. Potts, "Persian Gulf: Kish Island," *Circle of Ancient Iranian Studies*, www.cais-soas.com/CAIS/Geography/persian.gulf/kish_island.htm; Ricks, "Persian Gulf Seafaring and East Africa," 352–357; Margariti, "Mercantile Networks, Port Cities, and 'Pirate' States," 556–561.

17 Amari, *Diplomi Arabi*, 193–195, sections 11 and 13 of sultan Qaitbay's (r. 872–901/1468–1496) letter to the Doge of Florence (Jumādā II 7, 901/February 22, 1496) refers to piracy as "*qaṭ' al-ṭarīq* (sea highway robbery)"; Schacht, *Introduction to Islamic Law*, 9, 175, 180. Most often commentators and jurists used the term *qaṭ' al-ṭarīq*, which is equivalent to *qaṭ' al-sabīl*.

appear in the same verse and context. Qurʾān 29:29 decries those who openly and publicly "cut[ting] the highway" (*taqṭaʿūn al-sabīl*) and commit horrible crimes such that they fear neither shame nor God. It states:

Q 29:29:	
Do ye indeed approach men, and cut off the highway? And practice wickedness (even) in your councils? But his people gave no answer but this: They said: Bring us the Wrath of God if thou tellest the truth (29)	أَئِنَّكُمْ لَتَأْتُونَ الرِّجَالَ وَتَقْطَعُونَ السَّبِيلَ وَتَأْتُونَ فِي نَادِيكُمُ الْمُنكَرَ فَمَا كَانَ جَوَابَ قَوْمِهِ إِلَّا أَنْ قَالُوا ائْتِنَا بِعَذَابِ اللَّهِ إِنْ كُنتَ مِنَ الصَّادِقِينَ (29)

Armed robbery and the penalties for it are addressed thoroughly in the verse of *Ḥirāba* in the Chapter of *Al-Māʾida* (The Table, Q 5),[18] which states:

Q 5:33–34:	
The punishment of those who wage war (*yuḥāribūna*) against God and His Messenger, and strive with might and main for mischief through the land is: execution, or crucifixion, or the cutting off of hands and feet from opposite sides, or exile from the land: that is their disgrace in this world, and a heavy punishment is theirs in the Hereafter (33) Except for those who repent before they fall into your Power: in that case, know that God is Oft-forgiving, Most Merciful (34)	إِنَّمَا جَزَاءُ الَّذِينَ يُحَارِبُونَ اللَّهَ وَرَسُولَهُ وَيَسْعَوْنَ فِي الأَرْضِ فَسَاداً أَنْ يُقَتَّلُوا أَوْ يُصَلَّبُوا أَوْ تُقَطَّعَ أَيْدِيهِمْ وَأَرْجُلُهُمْ مِنْ خِلافٍ أَوْ يُنفَوْا مِنْ الأَرْضِ ذَلِكَ لَهُمْ خِزْيٌ فِي الدُّنيَا وَلَهُمْ فِي الآخِرَةِ عَذَابٌ عَظِيمٌ (33) إِلَّا الَّذِينَ تَابُوا مِنْ قَبْلِ أَنْ تَقْدِرُوا عَلَيْهِمْ فَاعْلَمُوا أَنَّ اللَّهَ غَفُورٌ رَحِيمٌ (34)

[18] *Al-Māʾida* is the only Qurʾānic Chapter revealed in two different cities. Most of its verses were revealed in Medina, whereas the remainder was revealed in Mecca shortly after the Prophet's Farewell Pilgrimage on Dhū al-Ḥijja 9, 10 AH/March 6, 632 CE. The final revelations of the Qurʾān coincided with the establishment of the Islamic State by the Prophet Muḥammad: "الْيَوْمَ أَكْمَلْتُ لَكُمْ دِينَكُمْ وَأَتْمَمْتُ عَلَيْكُمْ نِعْمَتِي وَرَضِيتُ لَكُمُ الإِسْلامَ دِيناً (This day I have perfected your religion for you, completed my favor upon you, and I have chosen for you Islam as your religion)" (Qurʾān 5:3). All of *Al-Māʾida*'s verses revolve around the principles of lawful (*ḥalāl*) and forbidden (*ḥarām*) deeds in worldly life with reference to (a) food, drink, and slaughter; (b) family and marriage; (c) faith and expiations (*kaffārāt*/repentance for an unlawful act); (d) principles of worship, verdicts, judiciary rules, testimonies, and the realization of justice; and (e) organizing Muslim relations with other religions, namely with the Jews and Christians. This chapter urges Muslims to be kind to their wives, to the weak, and to all mankind: "وَتَعَاوَنُوا عَلَى الْبِرِّ وَالتَّقْوَى وَلا تَعَاوَنُوا عَلَى الإِثْمِ وَالْعُدْوَانِ (...help ye one another in righteousness and piety, but help ye not one another in sin and rancour)" (Qurʾān 5:2). It is the only *sūra* in the Qurʾān that includes the five Islamic legal intents: the protection of religion (Q 5:54), soul (Q 5:32), mind (Q 5:90), honor (Q 5:5), and money (Q 5:38).

Classical exegetical traditions provide six distinctive commentaries on *Ḥirāba*,[19] with the overwhelming majority arguing that the intended subject is highway robbery. Etymologically, the term *yuḥāribūn*, as it appears in the original Qur'ānic text, is the present progressive of *ḥāraba*, derived from the root *ḥ.r.b.* meaning "to contend or wage war." *Ḥarb* (pl. *ḥurūb*) means "war," "fight," and "battle." *Ḥarāba* indicates the wealth or property despoiled or plundered, as well as "forcible theft," "highway robbery," "brigandage," and "banditry," all involving the use of a deadly weapon. The *muḥārib* (pl. *muḥāribūn* or *ḥarrāba*/a troop of plunderers)[20] is a person whose life is protected prior to committing *ḥirāba*, whether Muslim or *dhimmī*, free or a slave, who brandishes a weapon, disturbs free passage on the street and commits robbery, dispossession of property, murder, and intimidation, rendering it unsafe for people to travel.[21]

In interpreting the Qur'ānic excerpt: "الَّذِينَ يُحَارِبُونَ اللَّهَ وَرَسُولَهُ (those who wage war (*yuḥāribūna*) against God)," one should consider the metaphorical meaning of the words rather than the literal and metaphysical senses alone. Humankind stands powerless before God and is incapable of fighting Him physically. Man can, however, violate or disobey Divine Revelations by spreading *fasād*, by infringing the Divine and worldly rights of others, including those of his own coreligionists.[22] For

[19] Exegetes hold different positions, alternatively associating this verse's revelation with: (a) the People of the Book (Jews and Christians), who had concluded a truce but then abrogated it, causing the spread of corruption on earth; (b) Banū Hilāl, who broke their covenant with the Prophet; (c) the punishment to be inflicted on unrepentant idolaters defeated in battle; (d) the Children of Israel; (e) the Ḥārūriyya (Khārijites); and (f) highway robbery. Khaled Abou el-Fadl, *Rebellion and Violence in Islamic Law* (Cambridge: Cambridge University Press, 2001), 49–51.

[20] Lane, *Arabic–English Lexicon*, 1:540–541.

[21] Abū 'Umar Yūsuf ibn 'Abd Allāh ibn 'Abd al-Barr, *Al-Kāfī fī Fiqh Ahl al-Madīnah al-Mālikī* (Beirut: Dār al-Kutub al-'Ilmiyyah, 1997), 582–583; Zakaria I. al-Zumayli and Kā'ināt M. 'Idwān, "Al-I'jāz al-Tashrī'ī fī Ḥadday al-Sariqa wa'l-Ḥirāba," *Majallat al-Jāmi'a al-Islāmiyya* 14 (2006), 100; Sherman A. Jackson, "Domestic Terrorism in the Islamic Legal Tradition," *Muslim World* 91 (2001), 295; Abdelwahab Bouhdiba and Muḥammad M. Dawālībī, *The Different Aspects of Islamic Culture: The Individual and Society in Islam* (Paris: Presses Universitaires de France, 1998), 309–310; Mohd F. Sharif, "The Concept of *Jihād* and *Baghy* in Islamic Law with Special Reference to Ibn Taymiyya," (PhD diss., University of Edinburgh, 2006), 163–167.

[22] Qur'ān 18:29: "وَقُلْ الْحَقُّ مِنْ رَبِّكُمْ فَمَنْ شَاءَ فَلْيُؤْمِنْ وَمَنْ شَاءَ فَلْيَكْفُرْ إِنَّا أَعْتَدْنَا لِلظَّالِمِينَ نَاراً (Say, 'The Truth is from your Lord; let him who will believe, and let him who will reject (it), for the wrongdoers We have prepared a Fire)."

brigandage, evildoers shall be tried in this life and in the Hereafter, and the earth will testify against them.[23]

Derivatives of the term *f.s.d.* (corruption/disorder) occur fifty times in the Qur'ān, including twice in *Al-Mā'ida*. In order that they may avoid committing mischief and disruption, Muslims are ordered to obey God's commands and to maintain high moral standards, ethics, religious values, and norms of behavior.[24] They are required, inter alia, to fight against those who wage war against humanity – who seek to spread mischief on earth and destabilize society.

Close examination of the term *fasād* in the Qur'ān reveals that this act can take many forms to encompass: committing disobedience, vices, and forbidden deeds;[25] causing the destruction of nations;[26] harming the environment resulting in a loss of water and a decrease in cultivated fields;[27] practicing magic;[28] taking lives;[29] and perpetrating highway robbery against innocent victims. As already noted, the Qur'ān associates mischief with the *ḥirāba*, phrasing both terms in one verse for the same purpose: "those who wage war (*yuḥāribūn*) against God and His Messenger, and strive with might and main for mischief through the land (*wa-yas'awna fī al-arḍi fasādan*)." A further link of mischief to brigandage appears in the immediately preceding verse:

Q 5:32: if anyone slew a person – unless it be for murder or for spreading mischief in the land – it would be as if he slew the whole people	مَنْ قَتَلَ نَفْسًا بِغَيْرِ نَفْسٍ أَوْ فَسَادٍ فِي الْأَرْضِ فَكَأَنَّمَا قَتَلَ النَّاسَ جَمِيعًا

[23] For whatever a person has done in his life on earth, he is accountable before God. In addition to the traditional commentaries on Qur'ān 99 (*Al-Zalzala*/The Earthquake) some commentators say that the earth will cast out her treasures, precious minerals, and every kind of wealth lying hidden in her belly and man will see it and realize how he thirsted for these things in the world. The earth will testify against every evildoer who committed murder, theft, piracy, usurped the rights of others, waged war, or devastated populations. On that Day all that will lie heaped up before him, yet of no avail, but will rather become a means of punishment for him.

[24] Qur'ān 28:77: "وَلَا تَبْغِ الْفَسَادَ فِي الْأَرْضِ إِنَّ اللَّهَ لَا يُحِبُّ الْمُفْسِدِينَ (but do thou good, as God has been good to thee, and seek not (occasions for) mischief in the land: for God loves not those who do mischief)." A sound Prophetic tradition narrated by al-Bukhārī, Muslim, al-Nisā'ī, and Aḥmad states: "There is a *ṣadaqa* (charity) due on every Muslim; if he cannot give because he has no money, let him work then he can support himself and give charity; if he is unable to work, then let him help someone in need of his help; if he does not do that, let him adjoin good; if he does not do that, then he should not do evil or harm others: it will be written for him as a *ṣadaqa*." Bukhārī, *Ṣaḥīḥ*, 2:524, hadith no. 1376.

[25] Qur'ān 2:11, 60; Q 7:56, 74, 85; Q 47:22. [26] Qur'ān 17:4; Q 21:22; Q 23:71.

[27] Qur'ān 30:41. [28] Qur'ān 10:81. [29] Qur'ān 7:127; Q 40:26; Q 18:94.

Q 2:205: When he turns his back, his aim everywhere is to spread mischief through the earth and destroy crops and progeny. But Allah loveth not mischief	وَإِذَا تَوَلَّىٰ سَعَىٰ فِي ٱلْأَرْضِ لِيُفْسِدَ فِيهَا وَيُهْلِكَ ٱلْحَرْثَ وَٱلنَّسْلَ وَٱللَّهُ لَا يُحِبُّ ٱلْفَسَادَ

Thus, *ḥirāba, fasād*, and *qaṭ' al-ṭarīq* (*sabīl* in the Qur'ān) can all be defined as privately motivated armed robbery directed against innocent commercial vessels, their contents, crews, and passengers, and against coastal installations and targets, thereby posing a threat to the public peace for the sole purpose of looting movable property for private gain. As robbers who roam various bodies of water to spread evil and cause corruption (*fasād*) on the earth, *muḥāribūn* can be seafarers, passengers, or organized brigands from the Abode of Islam, who commit forcible theft within or outside Islamic territorial jurisdiction, on land or at sea.[30] Ibn Rushd's/Averroës's (520–595/1126–1198) legal definition of *ḥirāba*, which considers all legal opinions of the founders of the four main Islamic Law Schools (*madhāhib*), provides conclusive evidence of *Sharī'ah* applying banditry law to piracy at sea. He writes:

They agreed that *ḥirāba* is a show of armed force and the obstruction of the highways outside the city. They disagreed about the brigands inside the city. Mālik said that they are the same inside and outside the city. Al-Shāfi'ī stipulated power (*shawka*), though he did not stipulate numbers. The meaning of *shawka*, according to him, is the strength to overpower, because of which he stipulated remoteness from settlements, as overpowering is usually from outside the settlements. Likewise, al-Shāfi'ī maintained that if (the political) authority weakens and domination by another is found in the city, it amounts to *muḥāraba*. In cases other than this, according to him, it amounts to misappropriation. Abū Ḥanīfa said that *muḥāraba* does not take place within a city.[31]

[30] Abū al-Walīd Muḥammad ibn Aḥmad ibn Muḥammad Ibn Rushd, *Sharḥ Bidāyat al-Mujtahid wa-Nihāyat al-Muqtaṣid* (Cairo: Dār al-Salām, 1416/1995), 4:2279; Haykal, *Al-Jihād wa'l-Qitāl*, 1:73; Abou el-Fadl, *Rebellion and Violence*, 143–144; Khaled Abou el-Fadl, "The Death Penalty, Mercy, and Islam: A Call for Retrospection," in *Religion and the Death Penalty: A Call for Reckoning*, ed. Erik C. Owens *et al.* (Michigan: William B. Eerdmans, 2004), 80.

[31] Abū al-Walīd Muḥammad ibn Aḥmad ibn Muḥammad ibn Rushd, *The Distinguished Jurist's Primer*, trans. Imran Nyazee (London: Garnet Publishing, 2002), 2:547; for the Arabic text, refer to *Sharḥ Bidāyat al-Mujtahid wa-Nihāyat al-Muqtaṣid* (Cairo: Dār al-Salām, 1416/1995), 4:2279.

From the discussion above it can be deduced that a pirate is simply a "maritime *muḥārib.*" To be labeled a "maritime *muḥārib,*" the perpetrator must be a subject of the Abode of Islam, a Muslim subject of a foreign territory, or a *dhimmī*, who commits armed robbery indiscriminately against innocent targets on the high seas, or at coastal installations, or in inland waters – ports, rivers, and artificial waterways. A *musta'min* found guilty of maritime *ḥirāba* bears a different legal status from that of domestic actor, although jurists hold diverse opinions on this matter.[32] The term "innocent targets" refers to private movable and immovable property owned by Muslims, *dhimmī*s, *musta'min*s, and subjects of those states who hold treaties with central or peripheral Islamic authorities, or are the subjects of states not at war with the Abode of Islam.[33]

"Combating highway robbers is a religious duty," says *imam* Mālik,[34] who goes on to explain:

> Combating (highway robbers) is the best type of religious duty (*jihad*) and the most rewarding . . . more preferable to me than launching religious war against the Byzantines. The Prophet, God's blessing and peace be upon him, said: Whoever is killed defending his wealth is a martyr. Therefore, if someone is killed defending his own and/or Muslims' wealth, he will be granted a greater reward.[35]

Unless a perpetrator of piracy repents prior to arrest, those penalties prescribed in the Qur'ān for forcible theft must be enforced. A *muḥārib* must be pursued by the authorities, whether he travels on board ship, rides on horseback, or resides in a port, an impregnable bastion, or an unreachable area. Consider a case in which a *muḥārib* sought refuge in a Byzantine castle, which was under siege by Muslims, and then the occupants asked for safe-conduct (*amān*). The jurists decreed that, except for the *muḥārib*,

[32] Zaydān, *Aḥkām al-Dhimmiyyīn wa'l-Musta'minīn*, 190–193.

[33] Ibn Rushd (al-Jadd), *Al-Bayān wa'l-Taḥṣīl*, 16:373; Ibn Rushd (Averroës), *Bidāyat al-Mujtahid*, 4:2279–2280; Burzulī, *Jāmi' Masā'il al-Aḥkām*, 6:174–176; Haykal, *Al-Jihād wa'l-Qitāl*, 73; Mahmood Kooria, "An Abode of Islam under a Hindu King: Circuitous Imagination of Kingdoms among Muslims of Sixteenth-Century Malabar," *Journal of Indian Ocean World Studies* (2017), 97–98. In his *Qaṣīdat al-Jihādiyya* (Poem in Praise of *Jihad*), Muḥy al-Dīn Māla denounces piracy and warns his fellow Muslim warriors, who participated in the war against the Portuguese, not to engage in sea robbery, which stands in contradiction with the Qur'ānic principles. A legal opinion attributed to him states that when drinking water is scarce, it should be given to animals rather than to pirates.

[34] Saḥnūn, *Al-Mudawwanah*, 4:556, writes: "*jihāduhum jihād*"; Ibn Abū Zayd al-Qayraw ānī, *Al-Nawādir wa'l-Ziyādāt*, 14:472; Sharif, "Concept of *Jihād* and *Baghy* in Islamic Law," 164.

[35] Ibn Abū Zayd Qayrawānī, *Al-Nawādir wa'l-Ziyādāt*, 14:472.

all of the occupants of the castle were eligible for *amān*. It was considered invalid for an army commander to grant *amān* to a *muḥārib* as it would contradict the Divine ordained laws of God duly prescribed in the Qur'ān.[36] The jurists further added that, even if the armed robbery were committed to collect money to redeem Muslim captives, the punishment should nevertheless be carried out because God alone, not a sultan, an *imam*, or other earthly authority, is empowered to revoke the right of protection from theft.[37]

A pirate is therefore a *muḥārib* who commits armed robbery and spreads evil, and violates the "primordial order and logic existence"[38] set by the Divine Text. Islamic jurisprudence defines a pirate as a predator who targets: (a) subjects of the Abode of Islam – Muslims and *dhimmīs* and their movable properties regardless of their either fixed or varying locations; (b) *musta'mins*, holders of a pledge of safe-conduct; (c) subjects of states that are parties to treaties with the Abode of Islam; (d) subjects of states not at war with the Abode of Islam. If an attack does not fall within any of these categories, then it may be assumed that it does not constitute piracy. Even so, this issue remains controversial among contemporary legal scholars. What one group regards as piracy others may view as a legally justified raid. Furthermore, unlike the law of medieval Europe, Islamic law makes no categorical distinction between piracy and privateering.[39]

36 Ibn Abū Zayd Qayrawānī, *Al-Nawādir wa'l-Ziyādāt*, 14:473–474; Wansharīsī, *Al-Mi 'yār*, 2:434–435.

37 Wansharīsī, *Al-Mi'yār*, 2:322–323, 434 "*li-annahu ḥaqq li-Allāh ta'ālā*."

38 Abou el-Fadl, "Death Penalty, Mercy, and Islam," 80.

39 Medieval Europe knew two forms of sea robbery, piracy and privateering, although the two terms have occasionally been used interchangeably. Practically, both terms delineate marine rovers and prizetakers overtly employing threats and violent means to deprive by force their victims of their personal valuables and mercantile commodities, at times also seizing vessels and passengers, at sea, on coasts or on rivers. Theoretically, the two differences between piracy and privateering rest on legitimacy and the division of looted movable property. Pirates operated fully outside the law and solely for their own personal profit, as well as choosing targets indiscriminately, irrespective of religious or ethnic affiliations or maritime venue. By contrast, privateers were raiders commissioned by a sovereign state according to its laws. This sort of commission was known in medieval Europe as a "*letter of marque* (letter of reprisal)." It was a legal instrument by which a private individual injured by a foreign power or its subjects was authorized to retaliate for his loss. Privateers could pass beyond the state's frontiers to retaliate for damage done to individuals and domestic commercial vessels and cargo. Concerning a domestic search, a *letter of marque* did not empower a privateer to exceed the authority granted him, except under certain circumstances. Irene B. Katele, "Piracy and the Venetian State: The Dilemma of Maritime Defense in the Fourteenth Century," *Speculum* 63 (1988),

PIRACY AND THE MISCONCEPTION OF MARITIME *JIHAD*

A group of Western scholars maintains that independent groups of Muslim pirates randomly organized and undertook many of the major Islamic naval expeditions in the Mediterranean world. Certain of these scholars have further emphasized this viewpoint by describing the Islamic Mediterranean territories as having been a haven for pirates.[40] In doing so, scholars have confused the concept of *ḥirāba* (piracy/robbery of sea highways) with *jihad* (striving "in the Cause of God"), *ghazw* (military expedition), and *qitāl* (military engagement). It is possible that this misconception arose out of a number of factors, including prejudice, an exclusive reliance on non-Arabic sources, a misunderstanding of Arabic terms denoting piracy, a misinterpretation of the relevant Qur'ānic verses

874, f. 59; Tai, "Piracy and Law in Medieval Genoa," 264; Sybil Jack, "Piracy: An Elemental Way of Life," *Arts: The Journal of the Sydney University Arts Association* 18 (1996), 110; Bryan D. Dick, "Framing 'Piracy': Restitution at Sea in the Later Middle Ages," (PhD diss., University of Glasgow, 2010), 84–129.

[40] For example, the reader's attention is drawn to the publication of an article by Travis Bruce, "Piracy as Statecraft: The Mediterranean Policies of the Fifth/Eleventh-Century Taifa of Denia," *Al-Masaq* 22 (2010), 235–248. Bruce attempts to portray the governor of Dénia and Majorca and founder of the 'Āmirī dynasty, Mujāhid ibn Yūsuf ibn 'Alī al-'Āmirī (349–436/960–1044), as a sponsor of piracy in the western basin of the Mediterranean in the fifth/eleventh century, claiming, "Both Latin and Arabic sources emphasize [Dénia's] practice of piracy on a grand scale" (p. 238). The author relies heavily on modern Western scholarship and overlooks primary Arabic sources as well as the pioneering and classical work of Clelia Sarnelli Cerqua, *Mujāhid al-'Āmirī Qā'id al-Usṭūl al-'Arabī fī Gharbiyy al-Baḥr al-Mutawassiṭ fī al-Qarn al-Khāmis al-Hijrī* (Cairo: Maktabat al-Qāhira al-Ḥadītha, 1961). It should be borne in mind that what one person may regard as piracy another will regard as an act undertaken to "strive in the Cause of God." Mujāhid al-'Āmirī emerged as the strongest *ṭā'ifa* kingdom at sea at a time when Islamic naval power began losing ground to the rising Italian city-states. However, it is undeniable that, like their Christian counterparts, Muslims practiced piracy across the Mediterranean Sea and constituted an immediate threat to seaborne carriage undertaken by Muslims, non-Muslims, and Europeans alike. Nevertheless, associating Mujāhid al-'Āmiri's naval operations with privateering or the sponsoring of piracy is a distortion of his genuine legacy. The analysis here is compatible with Christides's theory, arguing that since Islamic law bans piracy, the booty of pirates is illegal, and therefore one-fifth (20 percent) of it cannot be transferred to the House of Treasury and accepted as the spoils of war. This is certainly not applicable to the governor of Dénia, who distributed the spoils of war among the warriors leaving one-fifth to the *imam*. Had Bruce drawn on the Islamic legal definition of piracy he would have been able to categorize al-'Āmirī's naval activities accurately as *jihad*. Vassilios Christides, "Piracy, Privateering and Maritime Violent Actions: Maritime Violent Activities of the Taifa of Denia in Spain (11th c.) *vs.* the Arab Maritime *Jihād* in the Eastern Mediterranean from the Middle of the 7th to 11th Century," in *Seeraub im Mittelmeerraum: Piraterie, Korsarentum und maritime Gewalt von der Antike bis zur Neuzeit*, ed. Mihran Dabag *et al.* (Brussels: Ferdinand Schöningh, 2013), 204–205.

and Prophetic traditions, and a lack of familiarity with the exegetical literature and jurisprudential inquiries.

While the issue of *jihad* is beyond the current scope,[41] a clarification of the doctrine of maritime *jihad* may allow amelioration of any confusion and misconception regarding the misinterpretation of *jihad* at sea as piracy. The root *j.h.d.* and cognate words occur forty-one times in the Qur'ān and can be expressed in personal,[42] verbal,[43] and physical forms. This root frequently appears in the idiomatic expression "striving (*jihad*) in the Cause of God."[44] Suffice to say that the Qur'ān sets forth in detail clear objectives and benefits of *jihad*, directly stating that it does not encompass causing harm to innocent people, even if during a fight against the Abode of War,[45] or the enforcing of Islamic conversion by coercive means.[46]

Notably, hundreds of transmitted hadiths detail the virtues of *jihad*.[47] Those hadiths that are related to military maritime *jihad* and *ghazw*

41 Many classical monographs discuss the theological significance of *jihad*. Among the most notable are: Abū Bakr Aḥmad ibn'Amr ibn Abī 'Āṣim al-Ḍaḥḥāk, *Kitāb al-Jihād* (Damascus: Dār al-Qalam, 1409/1989); Abū al-Qāsim 'Alī ibn al-Ḥasan ibn Hibat Allāh ibn 'Asākir, *Al-Arba'ūn fī al-Ḥathth 'Alā al-Jihād* (Kuwait: Dār al-Khulafā' lil-Kitāb al-Islāmī, 1404/1984); 'Izz al-Dīn ibn 'Abd al-Salām al-Sulaymī, *Aḥkām al-Jihād wa-Faḍā'ilihi* (Damascus: Dār al-Fikr, 1417/1996); Taqiyy al-Dīn Aḥmad ibn Taymiyya, *Fiqh al-Jihād* (Beirut: Dār al-Fikr al-'Arabī, 1412/1992); Ibn al-Naḥḥās, *Mashāri' al-Ashwāq*.

42 A hadith attributed to the Prophet Muḥammad states: "The best *jihad* (struggle) is (by) the one who struggles against his own soul for the sake of God." Ibn Ḥajar al-'Asqalānī, *Fatḥ al-Bārī*, 2:5, hadith no. 2630: "Struggle against the soul (*jihād al-nafs*)" is the most virtuous form of *jihad* and falls under the greater (inner) struggle (*al-jihād al-kabīr*) by which one must struggle between the two competing powers of evil and good desires. He who fails in this struggle will be consigned to the legions of the devil. In nine out of forty-one Qur'ānic verses that mention *jihad* in some form, it is specified that Muslims who sincerely strive in the Path of God must sacrifice two beloved things, life/soul (*nafs*) and a portion of their wealth (*māl*). No Muslim is superior to one who properly and earnestly fulfills the duty of *jihad*. Qur'ān 4:95; Q 6:11; Q 9:20, 41, 44, 81, 88; Q 8:72; Q 49:15.

43 When the Prophet Muḥammad was asked: "What kind of *jihad* is better?" he replied: "A word of truth in front of an oppressive ruler (*afḍal al-jihād kalimat ḥaqq 'inda sulṭān jā'ir*)." Abū Dāwūd Sulaymān ibn al-Ash'ath, *Sunan Abū Dāwūd* (Beirut: Dār al-Ḥadīth, 1388–1394/1968–1974), hadith no. 4344; Muḥammad ibn 'Īsā al-Tirmidhī, *Sunan al-Tirmidhī* (Beirut: Dār al-Kutub al-'Ilmiyyah, 1408/1987), *hadīth* no. 2174.

44 This idiomatic expression appears in twenty-six of forty-one Qur'ānic verses in which derivatives of the word *j.h.d.* appear. A Latin equivalent to the Islamic *jihad* is *bellum sanctum* (holy war/crusade), a term that emerged in medieval Europe with the advent of the Crusaders. However, neither the Qur'ān nor the Prophetic tradition mentions the term "*ḥarb muqaddasa* (holy war)." The affiliation of *jihad* with holy war is a Western misconception and mistranslation.

45 Qur'ān 5:8. 46 Qur'ān 2:256.

47 For instance, *Ṣaḥīḥ al-Bukhārī* consists of 282 hadiths under the title of *jihad*, whereas *Ṣaḥīḥ Muslim* consists of 220 on the same topic.

emphasize the merits of naval campaigns and the Divine rewards granted to those who survive them, or suffer from seasickness, or die "in the Cause of God."[48] Obviously, God alone knows the inner intentions of fighters as they join up for naval expeditions. One Prophetic tradition asserts:

> Whoever participates in a military expedition at sea in God's Cause, and God knows better who really strives for His Cause (*wa-Allāh a'lam bi-man yujāhidu fī sabīlihi*), is like a person who has fully subjugated himself and made himself obedient to God, searched for himself the Paradise from everywhere, and sought refuge for himself from the punishment of the Hell-fire.[49]

Every *mujāhid* must comply with military discipline and the laws of war as established by the Qur'ān,[50] Sunna, military command, and juristic and governmental authorities. He is required to perform his duty in the best possible manner by refraining from committing evil acts such as shedding blood, plundering, destroying public or private property, or acting independently to achieve personal worldly goals. Violation of these laws and regulations warrants the application of Islamic penal laws,[51] such as for the crime of armed highway robbery committed in a foreign territory, whether on land or at sea.

Close examination of the hadith literature affirms without the slightest doubt that there is not even a single Prophetic hadith, whether *ṣaḥīḥ* (sound/authentic), *ḥasan* (good), or even *ḍa'īf* (weak), that relates highway robbery to *jihad*. Rather, the Qur'ān and hadith employ the term *jihad* to denote striving "in the Path of God," along with *ghazw* and *qitāl*, all of which are generally conjoined to the phrase "in the Cause of God." Furthermore, the two foremost sources of Islamic law, the Qur'ān and the Sunna, never use the word *ḥ.r.b.* and its derivatives to designate fighting "in the Path of God." In the four Qur'ānic verses where it does appear, *ḥarb* has no bearing on the concept of *jihad*.[52] Therefore, someone who engages in a religious war is normally referred to as *mujāhid*, and less

48 Ibn al-Ḍaḥḥāk, *Kitāb al-Jihād*, 2: 654–669, hadiths 279–291; Ibn al-Naḥḥās, *Mashāri' al-Ashwāq*, 244–262, hadiths 290–327; Abū Muḥāmmad 'Abd al-'Azīm ibn 'Abd al-Qawiyy al-Mundhirī, *Al-Targhīb wa'l-Tarhīb min al-Ḥadīth al-Sharīf* (Beirut: Dār al-Kutub al-'Ilmiyyah, 1417/1998), 2:198–200, hadiths 2089–2093.

49 Abū al-Qāsim Sulaymān ibn Aḥmad ibn Ayyūb al-Ṭabarānī, *Al-Mu'jam al-Kabīr* (Mosul: Maktabat al-'Ulūm wa'l-Ḥikam, 1404/1983), 18:54; Mundhirī, *Al-Targhīb wa'l-Tarhīb*, 2:199.

50 Qur'ān 4:59: "يَا أَيُّهَا الَّذِينَ آمَنُوا أَطِيعُوا اللَّهَ وَأَطِيعُوا الرَّسُولَ وَأُولِي الْأَمْرِ مِنكُمْ (O ye who believe! Obey God and obey the Messenger and those charged with authority among you)."

51 Khadduri, *Islamic Law of Nations*, 95–105; Haykal, *Al-Jihād wa'l-Qitāl*, 1095–1108.

52 Qur'ān 2:279; Q 5:64; Q 8:57; Q 47:4.

frequently as *muqātil* (fighter) or *ghāzī* (raider), but certainly never as *muḥārib*, a term bearing the connotation of evil, mischief, and treachery.

After clarifying the meanings attributed to *jihad* and *mujāhid*, it is prudent to discuss the legal significance of the word "pirate" in Islamic jurisprudence. Of foremost importance, Islamic penal law does not differentiate between criminal acts committed on land and at sea. When jurists encountered acts of piracy with no legal precedent, they simply applied land laws to the sea. On many occasions the jurists issued rulings solely on the basis of analogy (*qiyās*), comparing a ship to a camel, and carriage by sea to carriage on land.[53] Similarly, in cases of forcible theft at sea, jurists depended on drawing analogies to laws governing land *ḥirāba*.[54]

Given, then, that there is a clear distinction between *jihad* and *ḥirāba*, how were Muslim maritime adventurers portrayed by Byzantine hagiographies and European historical sources? A plausible answer is provided in the erudite article by Vassilios Christides, in which a differentiation is made between maritime *jihad*, violence, and piracy during the Byzantine–Islamic struggles for supremacy over the Mediterranean. Christides contests that the series of Arab raids that took place in the eastern Mediterranean from the middle of the seventh through until the eleventh century were not razzias who launched their campaigns to plunder, but instead the raids constituted acts of naval warfare between two naval powers. The fact that contemporary European academics consider the naval activities of Muslims to be "aimless sea raids" with no purpose other than to plunder is both prejudiced and without foundation.[55] With the conquest of Crete and the establishment of the Arab emirate on the island, trade relations and activities between Byzantium and the Muslim world were strengthened. Equipped with *amān* pledges, a large number of Byzantine and Islamic commercial vessels reciprocally frequented each other's ports.[56] For the purpose of maintaining commercial ties and unhindered business transactions with the Abode of War, the Cretan Arabs rarely carried out attacks against Byzantine merchant vessels on the high seas.[57] Coastal installations and maritime trade were affected and exposed to violence only during times of warfare.[58] On the basis of the sporadic historical data presented here, the labelling of Muslim naval

[53] Khalilieh, *Admiralty and Maritime Laws*, 252; Ṭāher (ed.), "*Akriyat al-Sufun*," 15.
[54] Khalilieh, *Islamic Maritime Law*, 157–160, 162.
[55] Christides, "Piracy, Privateering and Maritime Violent Actions," 200.
[56] Christides, "Piracy, Privateering and Maritime Violent Actions," 203.
[57] Christides, "Piracy, Privateering and Maritime Violent Actions," 204–205.
[58] Christides, "Piracy, Privateering and Maritime Violent Actions," 206.

activities by Byzantine hagiographical sources as acts of piracy and privateering is a "false accusation"[59] and "should be taken into consideration with special care."[60] From the early twelfth century onward, Muslim–Christian commercial and diplomatic treaties contained provisions aimed not only at combating and reducing piracy and enhancing overseas trade, but also at empowering the contracting parties to prosecute offenders and pirates, irrespective of their religious and national affiliations, as shall be discussed.

MARITIME VENUES AND FACTORS FOSTERING PIRACY

Despite maintaining exclusive dominance over the two semienclosed inland seas, the Red Sea and the Persian Gulf, and the coastal frontiers along the Arabian and the Mediterranean seas, neither the central nor provincial Islamic authorities ever claimed to have wiped out the threat of piracy within their littoral and maritime sovereignty. Organized groups and independent communities of marauders never ceased to rove over the various bodies of water, including navigable rivers,[61] arteries, and artificial waterways,[62] or to target coastal ports, anchorages,[63] settlements,[64]

59 Christides, "Piracy, Privateering and Maritime Violent Actions," 205; Picard, *Sea of the Caliphs*, 220–223.

60 Christides, "Piracy, Privateering and Maritime Violent Actions," 201; Picard, *Sea of the Caliphs*, 71, 121–122.

61 Ibn Rushd (al-Jadd), *Al-Bayān wa'l-Taḥṣīl*, 9:63–64, 82–83; ʿAbd al-Laṭīf al-Baghdādī, *Al-Ifāda wa'l-Iʿtibār fī al-Umūr al-Mushāhada wa'l-Ḥawādith al-Muʿāyana bi-Arḍ Miṣr*, ed. and trans. Kamal Zand *et al.* (London: George Allen and Unwin, 1965), 240–241; Abū Bakr Muḥammad ibn Muḥammad ibn ʿĀṣim, *Tuḥfat al-Ḥukkām fī Nukat al-ʿUqūd wa'l-Aḥkām* (Beirut: Dār al-Kutub al-ʿIlmiyyah, 1415/1994), 580–581; Stern, "Three Petitions of the Fatimid Period," 172–178, doc. TS Arabic 42, f. 158; Khan, *Arabic Legal and Administrative Documents*, 330–331.

62 Ṭāher (ed.) "*Akriyat al-Sufun*," 16–17, 21, 42, 48–49; Ibn Abū Zayd al-Qayrawānī, *Al-Nawadir wa'l-Ziyādāt*, 7:100–102, 109; Ibn Rushd (al-Jadd), *Al-Bayan wa'l-Taḥṣīl*, 9:63–65; Shihāb al-Dīn Abū al-ʿAbbās Ibn Idrīs Qarāfī, *Al-Dhakhīra* (Beirut: Dār al-Gharb al-Islāmī, 1994), 5:485–486; Abu Safieh, *Bardiyyāt Qurra Ibn Sharīk*, 258, Pap. 1353, l. 6.

63 Goitein, *Letters*, 322–323 [letter no. 73], TS 8 J 24, f. 21; Ben-Sasson, *Jews of Sicily*, 588–592; Gil, *In the Kingdom of Ishmael*, 4:194–197. A mid-eleventh century letter describes a violent pirate attack on the port of Alexandria, one of the hubs most vital to the Mediterranean economies.

64 Agius, *Classic Ships of Islam*, 328–329; Wink, *Al-Hind*, 3:111. The *bawārij* (pirate ships) of Sind planted fear in the hearts of people such that the residents of the Islamic coastal frontiers were on constant alert. The *bawārij* sailed up the Red Sea to the ports of Jeddah (for Mecca) and al-Jār (for Medina), harassing shippers and pilgrims and posing an immediate threat to the two holiest cities of Islam.

or vital sea-lanes[65] in the quest of booty, paying no heed to explicit Divine prohibitions and the severe penalties meted out for forcible theft.

Piracy prospered as the Islamic world fragmented politically into a number of smaller self-ruling dynasties. Local dynasties, former army commanders, and organized groups took advantage of the auspicious political climate to declare autonomy and independence from central governments.[66] Another factor fostering piracy, no less important than political instability, was the proliferation of maritime venues where piracy was conducted. Pirates normally operated in rich and busy shipping lanes, in the vicinity of ports, offshore routes, and vital straits, and rarely operated far out to sea.[67] A third key criterion for fostering piracy was socioethnic affiliation. Organized groups of pirates broadly shared the same cultural heritage, values, beliefs, social norms, and language.[68]

The separation into territories for security reasons of the sea region contiguous to the shores was common practice among garrison commanders and governors of the Islamic coastal provinces. However, with the growth of coastal and port cities, the expansion of trade, and the fragmentation of the empire especially from the tenth century onward, the territorialization of adjacent waters and remote sea-lanes by independent and autonomous local principalities also became a major instrument of fiscal policy.[69] In the middle of the eleventh century, Jabbāra ibn Mukhtār

[65] Burzulī, *Jāmiʿ Masāʾil al-Aḥkām*, 3:650–651; Raṣṣāʿ, *Sharḥ Ḥudūd Ibn ʿArafa*, 2:525; Qalqashandī, *Ṣubḥ al-Aʿshā*, 3:524; Muqaddasī, *Aḥsan al-Taqāsīm*, 14; Sālim and ʿAbbādī, *Tārīkh al-Baḥriyya al-Islāmiyya fī Miṣr wa'l-Shām*, 157–158; Sālim, *Al-Baḥr al-Aḥmar fī al-Tārīkh al-Islāmī*, 27–29, 44; Muraikhi, "Al-Qarṣana fī al-Khalīj al-ʿArabī wa'l-Baḥr al-Aḥmar wa'l-Muḥīṭ al-Hindī," 159–161; Ricks, "Persian Gulf Seafaring and East Africa," 342, 353; Wink, *Al-Hind*, 1:164, 3:111; Shawqī ʿA. ʿUthmān, *Tijārat al-Muḥīṭ al-Hindī fī ʿAṣr al-Siyāda al-Islāmiyya (41–904/661–1498)* (Kuwait: Al-Majlis al-Waṭanī lil-Thaqāfa, 1990), 77–78. Cautioning against sailing in the pirate-infested sea off the Malabar Coast, the southwestern shoreline of the mainland of the Indian subcontinent, the well-known Arab *muʿallim* Aḥmad ibn Mājid, writes: "Beware of the al-Kābkūr in these places (around Calicut), for they come here sometimes, although their original habitat is between *Kōshī* (Cochin) and *Kūlam* (Quilon) where there is a large bay. They are a people ruled by their own rulers and number about 1,000 men and a people of both land and sea with small boats." Sebastian R. Prange, "A Trade of No Dishonor: Piracy, Commerce, and Community in the Western Indian Ocean – Twelfth to Sixteenth Century," *American Historical Review* 116 (2011), 1274, his translation is cited from Tibbetts, *Arab Navigation in the Indian Ocean*, 202.

[66] Prange, "Trade of No Dishonor," 1270.

[67] Prange, "Trade of No Dishonor," 1291–1292.

[68] Prange, "Trade of No Dishonor," 1273.

[69] Ḥimyarī, *Al-Rawḍ al-Miʿṭār*, 80; ʿAbbās, "Ittiḥād al-Baḥriyyīn fī Bajjāna," 3–14; Sālim and ʿAbbādī, *Tārīkh al-Baḥriyya al-Islāmiyya fī al-Maghrib wa'l-Andalus*, 167–171; Muṣṭafā Aḥmad, *Al-Qabāʾil al-ʿArabiyya fī al-Andalus ḥattā Suqūṭ al-Khilāfa al-*

al-ʿArabī, the governor of Barqa (Libya), became perhaps one of the most notorious "privateers" (in European judicial terms) in the history of the Islamic Mediterranean.[70]

Strange as it may seem, maritime predation was common in the semi-enclosed seas located in the heart of the Islamic East. Neither the sanctity of the Hijaz nor Divine prohibition against forcible theft were sufficient deterrents to predators,[71] who were indiscriminately targeting convoys of pilgrims, shippers, carriers, and voyagers sailing in all regions of the Red Sea, including the territorial sea of the Hijaz. As the sole artery for East–West maritime trade, through which vast quantities of lucrative manufactured products and spices flowed to and from the Mediterranean world, the Red Sea was littered with pirate communities, especially the islands and coasts across the Strait of Bab el-Mandeb.[72]

Umawiyya (91–422/710–1031) (Casablanca: Dār al-Nashr al-Maghribiyya, 1983), 470–471; Khalilieh, *Islamic Maritime Law*, 8–9, 139–140. Contemporaries to Pechina, a group of Andalusian pirates founded the port city of Ténès in northern Algeria around 875 CE on the ruins of the ancient Roman colony of Catenna, which maintained long-standing contact with the motherland. Constable, *Trade and Traders in Muslim Spain*, 34; T. Lewicki, "Les voies maritimes de la Méditerranée dans le haut Moyen Âge d'aprè le sources arabes," in *La navigazione mediterranea nell'alto medioevo* (Spoleto: Presso la sede del Centro, 1978), 460.

70 Goitein, *Mediterranean Society*, 1:327–328, docs. TS 16.13*v*, ll. 22–24; Bodl. MS Heb. a3 (Cat. 2873), f. 26*v*, l. 28; Ben-Sasson, *Jews of Sicily*, 350–358; Khalilieh, *Islamic Maritime Law*, 72. In addition to his engagement in the shipping business between Barqa and Tunisia, he levied a heavy tribute (*ghifāra*) on nonresident shipowners, shippers, and sea voyagers, irrespective of their nationality, ethnicity, and religious allegiances, and served as protector against the forcible theft he engendered, but not necessarily against other pirates lurking along the coastal strip between the two port cities. Thus, for people willing to pay tribute, the governor served as a protector against potential violence from him, but not always against that threatened by others.

71 In addition to the two holy cities of Mecca and Medina and sanctuaries located therein, the Hijaz comprises territory extending from the Gulf of ʿAqabah to Jazān, in northwestern Yemen, as well as the maritime zone adjacent to the land. Khaleda A. Yaseen, "Mawqif al-Rasūl min Yahūd al-Ḥijāz," (master's thesis, An-Najah National University, Nablus, 2009), 21–26. The Sea of Hijaz is legally viewed as part of the sanctity of the region so that non-Muslims can sail through it, but they are not allowed to sojourn for longer than three nights, or to take up residence. This sanctity inspires the question: If the *iḥrām* (state of ritual purity) of a Muslim pilgrim traveling by sea is to be performed once his ship enters the Sea of Hijaz, how could Muslim pirates apparently overlook this sanctity? Did their pursuit of an easy profit so surpass the relevant human and religious values? On the sanctity of the Sea of Hijaz consult al-Shāfiʿī, *Al-Umm*, 4:187–188; for the English translation, see Chapter 2, 107–109.

72 For instance, over the two-and-a-half centuries of the sultanate of Dahlak only a handful of its rulers seemed to have sponsored piracy. However, archeological remains reveal that the Sultan Bahā' al-Dīn Abū al-Fāḍil al-Mālik ibn Yaḥyā ibn Abī al-Sadād (d. 567/1172) was known to have "acquired the unenviable reputation of a pirate." Margariti, "Mercantile

In summary, in their pursuit of easy profits, pirates recognized no territorial restrictions, nor religious prohibitions, nor mercy. They lurked in busy shipping lanes, in the vicinity of ports, on inland rivers and waterways, and even in the territorial sea of the Hijaz, despite its sanctity to all Muslims. Organizationally and communally, these pirates shared common social, ethnic, and religious affiliations.

METHODS EMPLOYED TO COMBAT AND REDUCE PIRACY

In response to the question as to why central and provincial governments must combat highway robbery and maritime piracy, the celebrated philosopher and ethnologist Ibn Khaldūn (732–808/1332–1406) explains in his classic *Muqaddimah*:

It should be known that attacks on people's property remove the incentive to acquire and gain property. People, then, become of the opinion that the purpose and ultimate destiny of (acquiring property) is to have it taken away from them. When the incentive to acquire and obtain property is gone, people no longer make efforts to acquire any. The extent and degree to which property rights are infringed upon determines the extent and degree to which the efforts of the subjects to acquire property slacken. When attacks (on property) are extensive and general, extending to all means of making a livelihood, business inactivity, too, becomes (general), because the general extent of (such attacks upon property) means a general destruction of the incentive (to do business). If the attacks upon property are but light, the stoppage of gainful activity is correspondingly slight. Civilization and its well-being as well as business prosperity depend on productivity and people's efforts in all directions in their own interest and profit.

Network, Port Cities, and 'Pirate' States," 563, n. 66; Shelomo D. Goitein, "Portrait of a Medieval India Trader: Three Letters from the Cairo Geniza," *Bulletin of the School of Oriental and African Studies* 50 (1987), 458, n. 38: Dahlak is "also as the seat of a petty ruler engaged in piracy"; Goitein, *Studies in Islamic History and Institutions*, 356, describes one of Dahlak's rulers as "a dangerous pirate"; Power, "Red Sea Region during the 'Long' Late Antiquity," 296–297. Further evidence of the violation of Islamic maritime laws on salvage was attested to by al-Maqrīzī, who reported that on Safar 11, 662 (December 13, 1263) the Mamluk sultan al-Ẓāhir Baybars dispatched one of his courtiers to the rulers of the islands of Suwākin (Suakin) and Dahlak, reprimanding them for "targeting the capitals of those merchants who died (within their territories) for such actions are disapproved." Taqiyy al-Dīn Aḥmad ibn ʿAlī al-Maqrīzī, *Al-Sulūk li-Maʿrifat Duwal al-Mulūk* (Beirut: Dār al-Kutub al-ʿIlmiyyah, 1997), 2:5. Baybars's appeal to both rulers attempted to reinforce the Islamic regulations and customary practices on maritime salvage that forbid the confiscation of salvaged properties from the sea inasmuch as the rightful owner or his heir has not voluntarily relinquished his title to them. By custom, salvaged properties holding a high monetary value were retained by the salvager or authorities for one lunar year. However, lower-priced articles that did not exceed twenty dinars had to be retained only for a few days. Khalilieh, *Islamic Maritime Law*, 109–115.

> When people no longer do business in order to make a living, and when they cease all gainful activity, the business of civilization slumps and everything decays. People scatter everywhere in search of sustenance, to places outside the jurisdiction of their present government. The population of the particular region becomes light. The settlements there become empty. The cities lie in ruins. The disintegration of (civilization) causes the disintegration of the status of dynasty and ruler, because (their peculiar status) constitutes the form of civilization and the form necessarily decays when its matter (in this case, civilization) decays.[73]

In addition to the physical and psychological effects on victims of highway robbery and piracy, Ibn Khaldūn emphasizes the direct destructive impact on domestic and global commerce and the disruption of social norms and public peace, which, in turn, could trigger the decay of civilization. Ibn Khaldūn also suggests that these negative impacts can certainly be curtailed if people defend themselves against them "according to both the religious and the political law."[74] He goes on to add that a highway robber's greatest asset "is merely an ability to cause fear," which facilitates his usurping of the property of others.[75] In other words, Ibn Khaldūn claims that the fear planted by pirates in the hearts of seafarers, entrepreneurs, travelers, and coastal communities can undoubtedly be contained. People can – and should – protect themselves on an individual and communal level and involve the political authorities in any effort to combat and reduce piracy.

Individual and Communal Initiatives

Vigilance

As does its Christian counterpart, Islamic law forbids its followers from taking the risk of setting sail during inclement weather or in perilous conditions of security, such as when enemies and pirates are lurking en route, as the "Prophet has ordained against risk-taking."[76] Neither captains nor venturers may divert the course of a ship toward a known pirate-infested region. A fundamental point of law arises here as to the liability of a party to a contract who insists upon taking risks and departs when conditions are not safe. A shipowner is held liable for any losses if he, or

[73] Ibn Khaldūn, *The Muqaddimah*, 238. For the Arabic text refer to *Al-Muqaddimah*, 1:302.

[74] Ibn Khaldūn, *Al-Muqaddimah*, 1:303. [75] Ibn Khaldūn, *Al-Muqaddimah*.

[76] Ṭāher (ed.), "*Akriyat al-Sufun*," 20: "*wa-qad nahā rasūl Allāh ʿan al-gharar*"; Qarāfī, *Al-Dhakhīra*, 10:378; Burzulī, *Jāmiʿ Masāʾil al-Aḥkām*, 3:646; Wansharīsī, *Al-Miʿyār*, 8:299.

the captain, jeopardizes the vessel and her contents by sailing in risky situations despite the protests from apprehensive passengers. Equally, if the voyagers and shippers are adamant that they set sail in the face of a tangible threat of pirate attack, then they must bear the financial losses incurred by the shipowner if pirates do in fact seize the vessel. However, if a vessel is exposed to a pirate attack while docked, the captain can justifiably exercise jurisdiction over the craft and her contents. The captain is authorized by both custom and law to sail without delay in order to save the property of passengers and lessee merchants. Anyone who had disembarked and was abandoned by the captain may attempt to file suit, but such a complaint would bear no validity if the captain had acted reasonably in response to an emergency situation. The shipowner is held liable for losses only when acting independently without obtaining the consent of shippers and voyagers so long as there had been sufficient time for proper consultation.[77] Therefore, by law, it is better to risk a little profit by delaying departure or even missing the season of navigation, rather than lose a whole ship with her contents, crew, and passengers. As the Danish proverb says, "better lose the anchor than the whole ship."[78]

Bribery and Extortion of Tribute

Paying tribute in return for sailing unmolested through certain shipping lanes provided another means of reducing piracy, even though such tributes were deemed to be submission to "protectors," which could both directly and indirectly foster further piracy. Such arrangements indeed stand in diametric opposition to Islamic principles even if undertaken by shippers, merchants, and shipowners on personal or communal levels. The Mālikī jurist ʿAbd al-Malik ibn Ḥabīb emphatically forbade the payment of tribute to highway robbers, even an insignificant amount.

[77] Ṭāher (ed.), "*Akriyat al-Sufun*," 19–20, 22; ʿAlī ibn Yaḥyā al-Jazīrī, *Al-Maqṣad al-Maḥmūd fī Talkhīṣ al-ʿUqūd* (Madrid: Consejo Superior de Investigaciones Científicas, 1998), 228; Raṣṣāʿ, *Sharḥ Ḥudūd Ibn ʿArafa*, 2:525; Khalilieh, *Admiralty and Maritime Laws*, 72–73, 83, 100, 115, 117, 123–125; Khalilieh, *Islamic Maritime Law*, 70–72; Ashburner, *Rhodian Sea Law*, 83, 87, article III:4; 95–96, article III:15; Freshfield, *Manual of Later Roman Law*, 196; Michael McCormick, *Origins of the European Economy: Communications and Commerce A.D. 300–900* (Cambridge: Cambridge University Press, 2001), 428–429, describes how crews and passengers reached a consensus about diverting the ship's course for fear of Arab ships lying in wait for Byzantine commercial vessels somewhere en route.

[78] Jon R. Stone, *The Routledge Book of World Proverbs* (New York: Routledge, 2006), 266.

Paying tribute "will be considered a sign of weakness, submissiveness of Islam, and uncertainty regarding the validity of the religious principles."[79] Pirates could not be trusted to guard people's wealth, nor be exempt from punishment, nor be granted a pledge of *amān*.[80]

Despite this explicit prohibition, financial and commercial considerations seem to have adapted to the callous reality dictated by pirate communities. Records from the Cairo Geniza reveal that shippers and shipowners unwillingly overlooked the law and paid protection tribute as a necessary means for conducting commerce. This capitulation meant that their cargoes and ships were left alone, so the number of piracy victims was reduced. The privateer Jabbāra ibn Mukhtār al-ʿArabī offered his protection services for a heavy tribute levied on travelers, shippers, and shipowners when sailing in coastal waters between the port cities of Barqa and Tunis. Both parties to a contract of carriage had to bear protection expenses, which might be referred to as "regional protection,"[81] or "sea/ocean regionalism," as termed by Lauren Benton.[82]

"Regional protection" services provided by local pirate communities were also well known to the shipping industry in the eastern seas. For example, in the interest of Jewish merchants, the head of the Jewish communities in Yemen (*raʾīs al-yahūd* or *nagīd*, in Hebrew) – one of the most powerful juridical dioceses of the time – known as "the trustee of all lords of the sea and the deserts," concluded agreements with sovereigns of maritime domains, including pirates, so that his coreligionists and their cargo ships traveled unmolested. He also negotiated with tribal chiefs along the southern Arabian coast, and perhaps along the

[79] Ibn Abū Zayd al-Qayrawānī, *Al-Nawādir wa'l-Ziyādāt*, 14:474.

[80] Ibn Abū Zayd al-Qayrawānī, *Al-Nawādir wa'l-Ziyādāt*, 14:472–473.

[81] Goitein, *Mediterranean Society*, 1:327–328, docs. TS 16.13*v*, ll. 22–24; Bodl. MS Heb. a3 (Cat. 2873), f. 26*v*, l. 28; Ben-Sasson, *Jews of Sicily*, 350–358; Khalilieh, *Islamic Maritime Law*, 72; Khalilieh, *Admiralty and Maritime Laws*, 109–110; Gil, *In the Kingdom of Ishmael*, 3:169 [354], TS K 2.32, i, l. 4. In a lengthy account from 1055, Barhūn ben Mūsā Tāhertī makes a clear distinction between the freightage and protection: "He had to pay for the freightage and protection in order to sail (from Sfax) for al-Mahdiyya (*wa-ʿalayhi mā yalzamuhu kirāʾ wa-ghifāra ilā al-Mahdiyya*)"; 4:86 [629], TS 8 J 26, f. 4*r*., l. 18: "deducting the freightage, protection, and brokerage"; 4:171–172, TS 16.13, ll. 22–24. The writer Haim ben ʿAmmār Madīnī (i.e., of Palermo) reports to Joseph ben Mūsā Tāhertī of selling two of his own bales of flax to pay tribute to the Jabbāra ben Mukhtār and save the remaining shipment.

[82] Lauren Benton, "Legal Spaces of Empire: Piracy and the Origins of Ocean Regionalism," *Comparative Studies in Society and History* 47 (2005), 722.

Hijaz route, in whose territory caravans, Jews, and their goods travelled.[83]

Defensive Measures

"How similar today is to yesterday," says the Arabic maxim. In spite of sophisticated technologies, the 86th Session of the International Maritime Organization's (IMO) Maritime Safety Committee (2009) advises shipping companies to employ on vessels the services of licensed armed security officers and to seek a military escort when traversing pirate-infested waters.[84] These two defensive methods have been used by seafarers since the dawn of maritime civilization.[85]

Armed Personnel and Naval Escorts

While this issue has been explored in detail in an earlier study,[86] it is useful to touch briefly upon some key points. Ships sailed in concert for mutual assistance to safeguard against natural or human perils. Carriers and shippers generally had to find their own means of protection. Almost all able-bodied men carried personal arms when on board ship, ready to defend themselves and their wealth against imminent threat.[87] To ensure greater security, lessors commonly hired the services of professional warriors known in sailors' jargon as "maritime warriors (*ʿasākir al-baḥriyya*)" or "ships' warriors (*ʿasākir al-marākib*)."[88] Referring to Arab merchant

[83] Shelomo D. Goitein, "From the Mediterranean to India: Documents on the Trade to India, South Arabia, and East Africa from the Eleventh and Twelfth Centuries," *Speculum* 29 (1954),189–190, 191 n. 16; Goitein, *Mediterranean Society*, 2:26, 95; Shelomo D. Goitein, *The Yemenites: History, Communal Organization, Spiritual Life*, ed. M. Ben-Sasson (Jerusalem: Ben-Zvi Institute, 1983), 79; Goitein and Friedman, *India Traders*, 397, Letter from the Court to the Community of Dhū Jibla in defense of Maḍmūn, doc. JNUL 4° 557.2/15, ll. 11–12: "rulers who are overseas and those who are in the desert"; Wink, *Al-Hind*, 3:102.

[84] Ademun Odeke, "Somali Piracy – Effects on Oceanborne Commerce and Regional Security and Challenges to International Law and World Order," *Australian and New Zealand Maritime Law Journal* 25 (2011), 138, 143–144, 147.

[85] Grotius, *The Free Sea*, 35, reports that Roman vessels carried cohorts of archers as protection against pirates; Lionel Casson, *Ships and Seamanship in the Ancient World* (Baltimore: Johns Hopkins University Press, 1995), 320–321; McCormick, *Origins of the European Economy*, 409–415, 428–430.

[86] Khalilieh, "Security Protection and Naval Escort," 221–232.

[87] Kindī, *Muṣannaf*, 18:55–56. In the absence of armed personnel, the sailors were required to defend the ship against assaults by enemies and pirates.

[88] Lein O. Schuman, *Political History of the Yemen at the Beginning of the 16th Century* (Amsterdam: Djambatan, 1961), 71.

vessels sailing in sight of the Omani coast, al-Muqaddasī reports that they all "are compelled to carry for protection a body of fighting men and throwers of *naphtha* (a flammable liquid mixture of hydrocarbons)."[89] Naturally, defending a ship against piratical raids was in the common interest of all consignees and passengers.

The most effective, yet costly, instrument of deterrence was naval escort, hired to convey convoys of merchant vessels on treacherous sea highways.[90] Tangible evidence of such use of armed protection is documented in a 1025 CE merchant letter:

> The ships, my lord, are in the last stage of preparations. Not a single soldier charged with their protection has remained on land. They have already loaded their water and provisions and are waiting now for the completion of the warships; they will set it afloat and sail, and the boats (of the merchants) will sail with (the soldiers). The day after the writing of this letter the galleys (*qaṭāʾiʿ*) will be set afloat, for today they have completed their repair.[91]

Naval escorts were used in this way in the eastern seas. For instance, the Rasūlīd dynasty (626–858/1229–1454) of Yemen provided naval galleys and guards known as galley escorts and crossbow bearers (*ghilmān al-shawānī wa'l-jarrakhiyya*) to escort ships sailing on the trunk routes between Aden and western India.[92] Frequently, shipowners, shippers,

[89] Muqaddasī, *Aḥsan al-Taqāsīm*, 12; Abū ʿAbd Allāh Muḥammad ibn ʿAbd Allāh ibn Baṭṭūṭa, *Travels in Asia and Africa*, trans. and selected H. A. R. Gibb (London: Broadway House, 1929), 229–230. It should be pointed out that neither the Rhodian Sea Law, nor the *Kitāb Akriyat al-Sufun*, nor early *fatāwā* inquiries include articles demanding that shipowners provide armed protection against pirates and hostile raids, although Byzantine and Muslim jurists warn in their digests and legal literature against sailing in pirate-infested waters. By hiring onboard armed guards, vessels aimed to achieve a safer environment and to attract shippers, although documentary evidence shows that both shippers and voyagers had to pay extra fees for this service. Khalilieh, *Admiralty and Maritime Laws*, 124; Nājī, "Mawāniʾ al-Khalīj al-ʿArabī wa'l-Jazīra al-ʿArabiyya," 177; Ibn Baṭṭūṭa, *Riḥlat Ibn Baṭṭūṭa*, 563–564, the vessel he travelled on carried fifty archers and fifty Abyssinian warriors to protect them from Hindu pirates and infidels at sea; Marco Polo, *The Travels of Marco Polo*, trans. John Frampton (New York: Macmillan, 1937), 115–116; Risso, *Merchants and Faith*, 52–53; Edward A. Alpers, "Piracy and Indian Ocean," *Journal of African Development* 13 (2011), 19–21; Alpers, *Indian Ocean*, 66–67; Agius, *Classic Ships of Islam*, 235–236.

[90] Abraham L. Udovitch, "Time, the Sea and Society: Duration of Commercial Voyages on the Southern Shores of the Mediterranean during the High Middle Ages," in *La navigazione mediterranea nell'alto medioevo* (Spoleto: Presso la sede del Centro, 1978), 539–540.

[91] Goitein, *Letters*, 312, doc. TS 13 J 17, f. 3.

[92] Muḥammad ʿA. Jāzim (ed.), *Nūr al-Maʿārif fī Nuzum wa-Qawānīn wa-Aʿrāf al-Yaman fī al-ʿAhd al-Muzaffarī al-Wārif* (Sana'a: Centre français d'archéologie et de sciences sociales, 2003), 176.

and travelers took the initiative and hired private mercenaries to protect themselves and their shipments against piracy.[93]

In response to the relentless raids of pirates on Kārimī merchant vessels, the Fatimids assembled a flotilla at the naval base of ʿAydhāb for escorting commercial vessels and preventing acts of piracy.[94] Al-Qalqashandī (756–821/1355–1418) writes:

> The Fatimids deployed a flotilla of warships at the naval base of ʿAydhāb to escort and protect the Kārimī commercial vessels traversing the sea lanes between ʿAydhāb, Sawākin, and the surrounding areas, against pirate communities lurking in some islands and attacking these vessels in the Qulzum (Red) Sea. The flotilla which at the beginning consisted of five warships decreased to three. The governor of Qūṣ or some other courtier who was in charge of the flotilla, had to provide it with armaments and provisions for this purpose.[95]

By all accounts, with the advent of escorting missions, those engaged in maritime commerce enjoyed safer voyages. Naval escorts may indeed have been the most efficient method of defense against piracy, significantly contributing to a steady flow of East–West and interprovincial maritime commerce.[96] Some treaties concluded between the Mamluks and the Crusader kingdoms contain clauses imposing upon both parties the obligation to escort vessels and assure their security, free of any charge, when entering and leaving the territories of the treaty parties.[97]

[93] Goitein and Friedman, *India Traders*, 475. Sometimes paying an additional fee to the lessor does not necessarily guarantee the safety of travelers and shipments against piratical attacks. This is what is reflected in a business letter written around 1145 CE from Mangalore, India, by a Jewish merchant called Maḥrūz ibn Jacob al-ʿAdanī to his master Abū Zikrī Kohen, which describes how the soldiers escorting merchant vessels stood helpless against the seizure of a ship by pirates: "(9) I wish to inform you, my lord, that I had previously written to you (10) at Tāna. Meanwhile, the boat escorting the ship arrived, (11) and its soldiers told us that the ship (12) in which your excellency, my lord, traveled had been seized by pirates, (13) and I was very sad about this"; Prange, "Contested Sea," 20–24.

[94] Sālim and ʿAbbādī, *Tārīkh al-Baḥriyya al-Islāmiyya fī Miṣr wa'l-Shām*, 157–158; Sālim, *Al-Baḥr al-Aḥmar fī al-Tārīkh al-Islāmī*, 27–29; Ṣubḥī Labīb, "Al-Tujār al-Kārimiyya wa-Tijārat Miṣr fī al-ʿUṣūr al-Wusṭā," *Al-Majalla al-Tārīkhiyya al-Miṣriyya* 4 (1952), 7, 18; Margariti, "Mercantile Networks, Port Cities, and 'Pirate' States," 568. The Ayyūbīds in Yemen protected vessels from pirates (*surrāq*) through a patrolling force, which was funded by levying heavy taxes on the merchants in the port of Aden.

[95] Qalqashandī, *Ṣubḥ al-Aʿshā*, 3:524.

[96] Jāzim (ed.), *Nūr al-Maʿārif fī Nuzum wa-Qawānīn*, 176; Prange, "Contested Sea," 22–24; Eric Vallet, "Yemeni 'Oceanic Policy' at the End of the 13th Century," *Proceedings of the Seminar for Arabian Studies* 36 (2006), 289–296; Alpers, *Indian Ocean*, 66–67.

[97] Holt, *Early Mamluk Diplomacy*, 53, article 9 of the treaty concluded between al-Ẓāhir and the Hospitallers 669/1271; 86, article 21 of al-Manṣūr Qalāwūn's treaty with the Latin Kingdom of Acre, 682/1283; 99, article 4 of al-Manṣūr Qalāwūn's treaty with King

Coastal Surveillance, Protection, and Refuge

Even though the Romans physically dominated the Mediterranean Sea to a far greater degree than any other state in antiquity, they certainly had no love for the sea. Their dominion consisted largely of territorial management, with imperial troops and flotillas posted at close distances along the shoreline as a preemptive measure against piracy. To maintain their dominion over the sea, the Romans forbade local inhabitants from assembling their own fleets, and over time succeeded in wiping out piracy in nearly all Mediterranean waters, with the exception of the far western region. With piracy largely disappearing from the Mediterranean, trade routes became safe. Pirates could not sail from or land on Roman soil garrisoned by imperial squadrons and naval warriors, who together fought any approaching pirate ships.[98]

It is of note that Muslims employed a similar defensive approach known as *ribāṭ* or *murābaṭa*, to protect coastal frontiers, thwart intrusions, provide lodging for caravan traffic, and shelter imperiled vessels.[99] The Abbasid Caliphate in the East erected watchtowers and lighthouses along the shores as guides for ships and to secure maritime routes.[100] The Persian poet, theologian, philosopher, and traveler Nāṣīr-ī Khosraw (395–481/1004–1088) describes the architectural features and purposes of the watchtowers situated between Baṣra and ʿAbādān:

> At dawn something like a small bird could be seen on the sea. The closer we approached, the larger it appeared. When it was about one *parasang* to our left,[101]

Leon III of Lesser Armenia, 684/1285; 116, article 20 of the treaty that the same sultan signed with Lady Margaret of Tyre, 684/1285; "Qalāwūn's Treaty with Acre in 1283," 811.

98 Starr, "Coastal Defense in the Roman World," 56–70; Chester G. Starr, *The Roman Imperial Navy 31 B.C.–A.D. 324* (Chicago: Ares Publishers, 1993), 1–8; Henry A. Ormerod, *Piracy in the Ancient World* (Liverpool; Liverpool University Press, 1924), 248–259; Philip de Souza, *Piracy in the Graeco-Roman World* (Cambridge: Cambridge University Press, 1999), 206; Ellen C. Semple, "Pirate Coasts of the Mediterranean Sea,"*Geographical Review* 2 (1916), 136; Brent D. Shaw, "Bandits in the Roman Empire," *Past and Present* 105 (1984), 33–34.

99 Khalilieh, "*Ribāṭ* System," 212–225.

100 Doris Behrens-Abouseif, "The Islamic History of the Lighthouse of Alexandria," *Muqarnas* 23 (2006), 10–12; T. M. P. Duggan and Aykan Akçay, "On the Missing Navigational Markers – Beacon Towers – Pharos of Antiquity – and Notice of Two Extant Small Marker Beacon Towers of the Roman Late 1st c. B.C. – Early 1st c. A.D. Anemorium," *Cedrus* 2 (2014), 401, f. 143.

101 The *parasang* or *farsakh* is a measure of distance used in the eastern provinces of the Caliphate. It was regarded as the equivalent of three miles, as used in the former Byzantine provinces. The mile, of four-thousand cubits, is estimated at about two kilometers.

an adverse wind came up so they dropped anchor and took down the sail. I asked what that thing was and was told that it was called a "*khashshāb*" (stockades). It consisted of four enormous wooden posts made of teak and was shaped something like a war machine, squarish, wide at the base and narrow at the top. It was about forty ells above the surface of the water and had tile and stone on top held together by wood so as to form a kind of ceiling. On top of that were four arched openings where a sentinel could be stationed. Some said this *khashshāb* had been constructed by a rich merchant, others that a king had it made. It served two functions: first, that area was being silted and the sea consequently becoming shallow so that if a large ship chanced to pass, it would strike the bottom. At night lamps encased in glass (so that the wind would not blow them out) were lit for people to see from afar and take precaution, since there was no possibility of rescue. Second, one could know the extent of the land and, if there were thieves, steer a ship away. When the *khashshāb* was no longer visible, another one of the same shape came into view; but this one did not have the watchtower on top, as though it had not been finished.[102]

*Ribāṭ*s and *miḥrās*es (watchtowers) functioned as observation points for ships sailing off the Islamic coastal frontiers. In a Geniza letter written in late June or early July in the 1060s, a consignor names merchant vessels commuting between Egypt and the Maghrib and identifies the observation points from which they were sighted.[103] In addition to functioning as places of refuge from potential threats, certain observations accommodated vessels for rest, minor repairs, and taking on basic supplies such as food and

[102] Nāṣir-ī Khosraw, *Book of Travels (Safarnāma)*, 96; Duggan and Akçay, "On the Missing Navigational Markers," 420. Describing the stockades (*khashabāt*) near the port city of Baṣra, Muqaddasī reports: "This is by far the greatest evil, a strait and a shallow combined. Here small huts have been erected on palm trunks set in the sea, and people stationed therein to keep a fine lighted at night, as a warning to ships to steer clear of this shallow place." Muqaddasī, *Aḥsan al-Taqāsīm*, 12. Similar regulations were in force in Roman law. The Justinian Digest warns provincial governors against hindering coastal navigation and warns them to secure the coastal trunk routes and prevent fishermen from showing lights at night, which might mislead seafarers and endanger a ship with her cargo. Scott (ed.), *Civil Law*, 10:305, Digest XLVII, 9, 10.

[103] Udovitch, "Time, the Sea and Society," 542–543: "From these letters which I have received and from the passengers on the barge [that has just arrived], it has been confirmed that the following ships have safely moved farther from the coast: Ibn al-Iskander, Ibn Labad, al-Qāḍī Bū Ṭālib, al-Mufaḍḍal, the vessel of Ibn Madhkūr, the vessel of al-Tarājima and that of al-Jiljilānī; ... the barge of al-Ghazzāl was sighted at Suhat Barqa; at Ḥirāsat al-Qāḍī, the ships of Ṣadaqa ibn al-Ṣafrāwī, Ibn Raḥmān and Ibn al-ʿŪdī [were sighted] at Raʾs Tīn, the ships of Ṣabī ibn Shiblūn and al-Zaffāt were sighted. At Shaqqāt al-Waʿr, to the west of Tobruk, the ships of al-Lakkī, al-Mursī and Ibn Shabih [were sighted]. The second ship of Ibn Madhkūr and those of Ibn al-Shubnī and ʿAbbās Ashnas, and the vessel of Amīr and of Ibn Abū Qashsh were sighted at Milḥā."

water.[104] Furthermore, regardless of whether a *ribāṭ* was a state-run or private establishment, it was subject to the jurisdiction of the state. Formally, the admiral's jurisdiction extended over the length of the coastal frontiers and territorial waters; he was responsible for managing the security arrangements and reinforcing the coasts with an array of fortresses and watchtowers.[105] Garrisons stationed at *ribāṭ*s were instructed to assist and shelter commercial ships sailing by cabotage when encountering hostile threat or suffering damage, including alien vessels that had entered the Abode of Islam under *amān*.[106]

Bilateral treaties and truces concluded between Islamic and Christian entities contained provisions on the need of merchant vessels to seek shelter from pirates in foreign coastal fortresses. Each party to an agreement gave an assurance that whenever ships sought refuge from pirates in any coastal fortress and port, its garrisoned forces and occupants would provide assistance and attempt to repel the pirates. In order to avoid troublesome incidents, the parties to a treaty guaranteed that when ships approached and departed their maritime domain, the local naval forces would be obliged to escort foreign ships and assure their safety since pirate ships tended to lurk near busy ports. Both parties also pledged to bring captured native and foreign pirates to justice.[107]

International Collaboration

Treaties addressing piracy invariably addressed both the domestic and international dimensions. On the domestic level, insofar as a crime of

[104] Khalilieh, "*Ribāṭ* System and Its Role in Coastal Navigation," 214–215.

[105] Jalāl al-Din Muḥammad ibn Maḥmūd ibn Mankalī, *Al-Adilla al-Rasmiyya fī al-Taʿābī al-Ḥarbiyya*, ed. Maḥmūd Sh. Khaṭṭāb (Baghdad: Al-Majmaʿ al-ʿIlmī al-ʿIrāqī, 1988), 241–254; Khalilieh, *Admiralty and Maritime Laws*, 18; Duggan and Akçay, "On the Missing Navigational Markers," 405, 414.

[106] Wansharīsī, *Al-Miʿyār*, 8:207–208. A responsum attributed to the Sicilian jurist Muḥammad ibn ʿAlī al-Māzarī illustrates how a shipowner, acting as a *tractator* (labor-investor), was forced to seek protection in an Islamic *ḥiṣn/ribāṭ* due to an unanticipated hostile attack.

[107] For example, article 15 of Qalāwūn's treaty with the Latin Kingdom of Acre in 682/1283 requires garrisons in the Latin and Islamic frontiers to protect and guard wrecked vessels, enable the crew to have provisions, repair the wreck, and return the vessel to its territory. Holt, *Early Mamluk Diplomacy*, 84; Holt, "Qalāwūn's Treaty with Acre in 1283," 811. Similar conditions were stipulated in bilateral treaties concluded between North African Islamic entities and their European Christian counterparts. See, for instance, article 7 of the treaty of 14/9/1313 between Pisa and the Ḥafṣid sultan Abū Yaḥyā Zakariyyā ibn Yaḥyā al-Liḥyānī. Amari, *Diplomi Arabi*, 89.

piracy was committed within the territorial sovereignty of a state or the victims were its nationals in foreign or international waters, the state bore the natural right to prosecute the offenders. However, legal challenges and jurisdictional issues potentially could arise in the following scenarios: (a) the pirates were subjects of state A, conducted a raid on their conationals or coreligionists and fled or sought refuge in state B, which was either in a state of peace (*ṣulḥ*), temporary truce (*hudna*), or at war (*ḥarb*) with state A; or (b) the act of piracy involved multinational parties, for instance, pirates of state A attacked nationals of state B then fled to state C, which had a peace treaty with A, but was in state of war or temporary truce with state B.

International maritime trade could not have prospered without the legal framework for combating piracy provided by diplomatic and commercial treaties. Islamic–Christian treaties and correspondence show that both societies abided by these treaties and protected foreign nationals against piracy within their own territories, as well as guaranteed the safety and restitution of any redeemed people or chattels plundered by pirates, as these people were their subjects regardless of where the incidents occurred.[108] The parties to the treaties also committed to preventing pirates of all nationalities from anchoring in or departing from their territorial domains, as well as from obtaining provisions. If Muslim or Christian captives were found on their ships, then the authorities must release them and prosecute the thieves.[109] However, the contracting

[108] Holt, *Early Mamluk Diplomacy*, 129, article 9 of the 680/1281 Mamluk–Byzantine treaty between al-Manṣūr Qalāwūn and Michael VIII Palaeologus; Baaj, "Struggle for North Africa between Almohads, Ayyubids, and Banū Ghāniya," 119–120.

[109] Holt, *Early Mamluk Diplomacy*, 124–125, article 11. Identical rules were incorporated in the Byzantine–Genoese treaties from the twelfth century. The Treaty of Nymphaeum from March 13, 1261 concluded between Michael VIII Palaeologus and Genoa dictated that the empire is under an obligation to protect Genoese vessels and nationals against piracy and prosecute pirates according to the law if caught in Byzantine waters. The same emperor ratified another treaty with Genoa in 1272 holding the Genoese *podestà* (chief magistrate of the city-state) liable for damage caused by Genoese pirates to Byzantine nationals at sea. If the culprit was not caught, the Genoese authority had to undertake an investigation and pay reparation to the victim from the aggressor's property. In the case that the Genoese *podestà* fails to take measures against the Genoese pirates, the emperor would apply collective liability against the Genoese merchant community in Constantinople. Such a practice of reprisal was adopted by independent and autonomous principalities across the Mediterranean. Daphne Penna, "Piracy and Reprisal in Byzantine Waters: Resolving a Maritime Conflict between Byzantines and Genoese at the End of the Twelfth Century," *Comparative Legal History* 5 (2017), 42, 48–49; Sicking, "Maritime Conflict Management," 7.

parties did not take responsibility for piratical actions committed by foreign nationals on the high seas.[110]

The peace treaty (*ṣulḥ*) concluded between the Ḥafṣīd amir Abū Fāris ʿAbd al-ʿAzīz ibn Aḥmad and Pisa deserves special mention. It was initially signed as a bilateral treaty between the Ḥafṣīds of Tunis and Pisa in Rabīʿ I 23, 800/December 14, 1397 and renewed in Jumādā II, 817/September, 1414, with Florence being added to make the treaty multilateral on Shawwal 7, 824/October 5, 1421. Article 26 reads:

If a vessel departs from Pisa or its territories for causing harm and committing robberies against the Muslims, the Pisan authorities shall have to capture the vessel, execute the robbers, and take away their chattels, if they happened to be in Pisa or its territories, and be handed over to the custom-house (in Tunis). However, if they cannot catch the robbers, the Pisans will only have to deliver the chattels to the mentioned custom-house. If the ships of the esteemed Caliph in the lofty Tunis are equipped for pursuing pirates, the Pisans shall likewise have to outfit theirs with arms, provide assistance, and sail with their naval force wherever they are instructed for the duration of the whole pursuit. If a Pisan or any person living within Pisa's territory equips his vessel with arms, he shall cause no harm whatsoever to Tunisian Muslim subjects or others residing within the Caliph's dominion. Similarly, a Muslim traveler departing from the lofty capital (Tunis) or other territory of the caliphate shall not be harmed by any Pisan. And, if a Pisan enemy arrives in the port of the lofty capital (of Tunis) or any territory within the caliphate's domain, those Pisans residing in the lofty capital are required to assist Muslims and get together with them to fight their enemy. When Muslims travel for the Pisan territories as they habitually do, they all shall be guaranteed protection for their souls, chattels, and vessels; they, likewise, shall be protected and honored in all of their matters and affairs.[111]

This multilateral treaty was extended in 849/1445, appending an article holding the governments of both Communes liable for losses resulting from corsairs who were either nationals or else had departed from their sovereign territories for committing "evil purposes" against Muslim subjects and territories. Article 8 of the same treaty dictates:

If any of their vessels departs from their cities or provinces for evil purposes against Muslims, or enters one of the Islamic anchorages/ports with the intent of mischievous acts, they (Florence and Pisa) have to capture all men on board the vessel, deprive them of their rights, and execute them. If they (Florentines and

[110] Holt, *Early Mamluk Diplomacy*, 136, article 11 of the treaty of al-Manṣūr Qalāwūn with King Alfonso III of Aragon, 689/1290; Nashshār, *ʿAlāqat Mamlakatay Qishtāla wa-Aragon bi-Salṭanat al-Mamālīk*, 106, 235.

[111] Amari, *Diplomi Arabi*, 132–133, 147–149, 161–163.

Pisans) neither find the corsairs nor being able to reach them, they have to confiscate their properties and deliver the restitution to the lofty capital, Tunis.[112]

Perhaps one of the most interesting issues is the integration of provisions authorizing the parties to the agreement to pursue pirates into the territorial waters of another contracting state. Article 3 of the 849/1445 treaty stipulates that if an Islamic vessel pursues a Christian vessel – whose flag state is not party to the treaty – into the territorial and internal waters of either one of the two city-states, such pursuit shall face no interference. By the same token, the Ḥafṣīds authorize both city-states to chase enemies and pirates into Islamic territorial seas and internal waters.[113]

Clearly, in the absence of a universal legal regime to prevent disorder at sea, political entities employed diplomatic mechanisms to enforce bilateral and multilateral treaty terms on nationals and subjects of foreign sovereigns. According to the treaties, state members were held liable for the piratical actions of their subjects, and occasionally of foreign nationals, if committed at sea or against coastal targets of other parties. Furthermore, the state was responsible for restituting the injured party regardless of whether the corsairs were captured or still at large. When caught, pirates were to be brought to justice by judicial authorities and put to death.[114] Notably, their long-standing and oft-renewed treaty commanded Pisans and Florentines found on Islamic soil to fit out their vessels, join local naval forces, and pursue and fight their corsair nationals "for the duration of the whole pursuit," had they targeted Islamic maritime installations and properties. Likewise, Pisa was bound to protect Muslim subjects against local corsairs within their territories,[115] and prevent the sale of stolen goods captured by pirates on its territories.[116]

That we do not find a similar commitment to combatting piracy in other treaties and truces concluded with Islamic sovereigns can be explained by three factors: (a) the explicit Qur'ānic prohibition against legitimizing brigandage; (b) the safety of foreigners and their chattels was

112 Amari, *Diplomi Arabi*, 172–173. 113 Amari, *Diplomi Arabi*, 172.

114 Azzaoui, *Rasā'il Muwaḥḥidiyya*, 1:174–175; Abulafia, "Christian Merchants in the Almohad Cities," 254–256; Salerno, "Relations, Politics, and Economic Choices in the Mediterranean," 66.

115 Amari, *Diplomi Arabi*, 324.

116 Amari, *Diplomi Arabi*, 94, treaty of 1313, article 35; 107, treaty of 1353, article 35. In order to target the income sources of pirates and discourage their actions, article 22 of the 1445 treaty stipulates that a buyer who purchases a vessel that was known to have engaged in piracy must pay a tax of 10 percent of her purchase price. Amari, *Diplomi Arabi*, 177.

already embodied in the pledge of *amān*; and (c) European piracy was probably far more threatening than the Islamic in the Mediterranean arena, especially during times when most of the European Mediterranean political entities fostered the so-called privateering.[117]

The sea was not a lawless domain, as some academics appear to assume.[118] Combating piracy in the pre-Renaissance era was made possible by a complex of continental and intercontinental treaties. Certainly, Islamic law was territorially enforced on limited offshore zones for security purposes (except for the Hijaz), and on Muslim subjects, their assets, and their vessels, irrespective of geographical location, national affiliation, and the ethnic origin of passengers and crew.

Military Subjugation

Only as a last resort did Muslim central governments tend to use military might to subjugate pirates' dens and eradicate piracy from vital sea-lanes. Two incidents in early Islamic history deserve our attention – the Abyssinian and the Sindhi piratical attacks in the seventh and eighth centuries CE. With reference to the former, it was reported that during the reign of the third caliph ʿUthmān ibn ʿAffān (r. 23–35/644–656), Abyssinian sea robbers attacked Islamic targets on the Red Sea, robbing and enslaving many Muslims. The caliph was profoundly disturbed and consulted some of the Companions about launching a counterattack against Abyssinia. The Companions advised him to be patient and withhold any punitive military campaign until learning from the Abyssinian

[117] A remarkable piece of evidence is found in a 689/1290 treaty, renewed in 692/1293. Concluded by Alfonso III the Liberal of Aragon and al-Manṣūr Qalāwūn, this treaty was signed at a time when Muslim naval forces had weakened in the Mediterranean arena, but had flourished in the Syro-Palestinian littoral. European naval powers, privateers, and pirates infested the waters of the eastern basin of the Mediterranean and created a hostile environment for domestic and international trade, which harmed the Mamluk economy. For that reason, it was in the Mamluks' interest to sign and renew the treaty, in which the Catalans pledged to prevent raids on Islamic vessels, fight piracy, and bring sea robbers to justice irrespective of their national affiliation. Most Europeans expressed great disdain for the two treaties, which lifted the papal embargo on trade with the Mamluks and enabled both political entities to cooperate closely on counter-piracy. Holt, *Early Mamluk Diplomacy*, 136; Albrecht Fuess, "Rotting Ships and Razed Harbors: The Naval Policy of the Mamluks," *Mamluk Studies Review* 5 (2001), 61–62.

[118] Nicholas M. Rodger, "The Naval Service of the Cinque Ports," *English Historical Review* 111 (1996), 646: "The word piracy has to be applied with caution in the medieval context, when the sea was widely perceived as a lawless realm beyond the frontiers of all nations, where neither law nor truce nor treaty ran."

king about the circumstances that had motivated the pirates. If he learned that the assault had been executed in compliance with the king's instructions, then the Muslims could launch a military expedition against Abyssinia. If the caliph were able to establish with certainty that the king was unaware of that assault and its circumstances, the caliph should relinquish the military expedition and prepare to reinforce coastal frontiers against future attacks. The caliph sent Muḥammad ibn Maslama al-Anṣārī (d. 43/663),[119] a Companion of the Prophet, to the Abyssinian king, who vigorously denied having any awareness of the assault. He further denounced the raid and ordered his men to bring him the Muslim captives and deliver them to the caliph's envoy.[120]

Another extraordinary event was the military expansion in Sind (Sindh). Islam spread throughout the western region of the Indian subcontinent in part due to perpetual pirate attacks against commercial vessels sailing off the coasts. Al-Balādhurī (d. 297/892) relates the following revealing tale. The king of Ceylon wanted to send by sea the orphaned daughters and widows of some Muslim merchants – who had died in Ceylon – back to their homeland. He wrote a message to al-Ḥajjāj ibn Yūsuf al-Thaqafī, then the Umayyad governor of Iraq, informing him that he was sending the girls and women home by ship. The ship was captured by Indian pirates operating off the shores of Debal and the orphaned girls and widowed women were captured. When the news reached al-Ḥajjāj, he became infuriated and sent for Dāhir, the king of Sind, demanding that he set the captives free immediately. The latter mocked al-Ḥajjāj's request and refused to release them, claiming he had no control over pirates at sea. Enraged by the king's refusal, al-Ḥajjāj appealed to Caliph al-Walīd ibn 'Abd al-Malik, who reluctantly sanctioned a military expedition against Sind. After two defeats, on the third attempt in 92/711, under the command of Muḥammad ibn al-Qāsīm al-Thaqafī, al-Ḥajjāj's nephew and son-in-law, the Islamic fleet succeeded in subjugating the pirates and capturing the western territories of the Indian subcontinent as an additional prize.[121]

Four subtle legal insights can be gleaned from these incidents. First, hostile acts involving international actors required the parties concerned

[119] Muḥammad ibn Aḥmad ibn 'Uthmān al-Dhahabī, *Siyar A'lām al-Nubalā'* (Beirut: Mu'assasat al-Risālah, 1422/2001), 2:372–373.

[120] Abū Muḥammad Aḥmad ibn A'tham al-Kūfī, *Kitāb al-Futūḥ* (Beirut: Dār al-Aḍwā' lil-Ṭibā'a wa'l-Nashr, 1411/1991), 2:347.

[121] Balādhurī, *Futūḥ al-Buldān*, 611–612, 616–622.

to undertake a thorough investigation before states could launch reprisals with possibly irreparable consequences. Second, in order to avoid unnecessary escalation, central and provincial governments were strongly advised to dispatch emissaries to resolve such issues peacefully. Third, the state was only held responsible for actions committed by its nationals if it had been proven without doubt that the state had been aware of its nationals' nefarious acts. Finally, historically, Muslims resorted to military force for combating piracy only when all other means had failed.

PUNISHMENT

Sharīʿah identifies seven major offences that call for severe punishment in the earthly life and the Hereafter: (a) highway robbery/piracy (*muḥāraba*) and spreading malevolence and disorder (*fasād*); (b) murder and injury; (c) theft; (d) adultery; (e) false accusation of immorality (*qadhf*); (f) apostasy (*ridda*); and (g) sedition (*baghy*). Of interest here are the worldly punishments for the crimes of *ḥirāba* and *fasād* as mentioned in Qurʾān 5:33, which have at times been deemed applicable to all highway robbery and piracy regardless of the gender, age, socioeconomic status, or political, ethnic, or religious allegiance of the actors. However, the great majority of exegetes and jurists argued that this verse is subject to various interpretations, thereby raising two fundamental questions. First, shall punishments be applied indiscriminately to all spectrums of society? Second, is there any relationship between the seriousness of the crime and the severity of the punishment?

To clarify, the jurists stipulated that culpability for an armed robbery or piracy could only legally be established by meeting the following legal requirements. The offender must be an adult and sane, the legal qualifications to stand trial. The judge must determine that the offender acted voluntarily and knowledgeably, and had in his possession the lethal weapons used to commit the armed robbery. An additional criterion is *mujāhara* – the brigandage was committed in public and overtly challenged the system of justice. Another factor pertains to the location of the offense. Some scholars suggested that brigandage can only take place in open spaces away from urban centers or residential areas, whereas others argued that, according to the Qurʾān, the crime carries the same legal weight regardless of location. The final element is the identity, religious affiliation, and citizenship of the actor; in other words, he should be

Muslim.[122] This requirement raises the question as to what law applies to non-Muslim actors, to *dhimmīs* and aliens, who victimize residents of an Islamic state, or commit piracy within the Abode of Islam?

Islamic law regards piracy as a heinous crime, an act against God and His Messenger. In fact, Qur'ān 5:33 ordains the judiciary to consider the "execution, or crucifixion, or the cutting off of hands and feet from opposite sides, or exile from the land" as punishment for offenders. This verse gives the judicial system flexibility to administer punishments commensurate with the nature, severity, and circumstances of the offense.[123] A punishment can only be lessened if the accused repents prior to arrest (Qur'ān 5:34). The death penalty or crucifixion is specified as a punishment for crimes in which the offender kills his victims and absconds with their property. If the offender only commits murder but does not take property, he is to be decapitated, not hanged. If he only steals property, but kills no one, the offender's opposite hand and leg must be amputated (i.e., right hand and left leg, or right leg and left hand).[124] If he terrorizes his victims but does not kill them, nor usurps their property, then the offender is to be exiled for a fixed period.[125] Jurists defended

[122] Muḥammad Ṭ. Qādirī, "Punishments in Islam: Their Classification and Philosophy," (PhD diss., Punjab University, Lahore, 1984), 342–343; Mohamed S. el-Awa, *Punishment in Islamic Law* (Plainfield: American Trust Publication, 2000), 9–10; Hisham Ramadan, "Larceny Offenses in Islamic Law," *Michigan State Law Review* 1609 (2006): 1634–1636; Jackson, "Domestic Terrorism in the Islamic Legal Tradition," 295–296; Zumayli and 'Idwān, "Al-I'jāz al-Tashrī'ī fī Ḥadday al-Sariqa wa'l-Ḥirāba," 102–103; Sharif, "Concept of *Jihād* and *Baghy* in Islamic Law," 166.

[123] Bouhdiba and Dawālībī, *Different Aspects of Islamic Culture*, 309–310.

[124] Qādirī, "Punishments in Islām," 343–346; Awa, *Punishment in Islamic Law*, 9–10; Ramadan, "Larceny Offenses in Islamic Law," 1636–1637; Ḥamīdullāh, *Muslim Conduct of State*, 186–189; Jackson, "Domestic Terrorism in the Islamic Legal Tradition," 299–301; Zumayli and 'Idwān, "Al-I'jāz al-Tashrī'ī fī Ḥadday al-Sariqa wa'l-Ḥirāba," 103–106; Rudolph Peters, *Crime and Punishment in Islamic Law: Theory and Practice from the Sixteenth to the Twenty-First Century* (Cambridge: Cambridge University Press, 2005), 30–38.

[125] A controversy prevailed among scholars regarding the concept of banishment. Abū Ḥanīfa interpreted it as imprisonment by arguing that the brigand must be kept behind bars within the territory where the act of forcible theft had taken place. By sending him to isolation in jail, local people will feel safer from criminal acts that might be caused should the offender be merely banished. The great majority of the Mālikī jurists claimed that the bandit must be exiled from his hometown to a different place. The majority of Shāfi'ī jurists and exegetes contended that exile is applicable to Muslim *muḥāribs* only, who complied with the corporal punishment but subsequently escaped from the Abode of Islam. The Hanbalis and Ẓāhirīs held that Qur'ān 5:33 refers to banishment and expulsion of the *muḥārib* from all Islamic soil. Some Shāfi'ī scholars authorized the

employment of these harsh punishments both as a deterrent to potential repeat offenders and to dissuade others so as to maintain social and economic order and foster security for the individual and the public.[126]

Despite meting out strict corporal punishment, the law keeps the door open for repentance for those offenders "who repent before they fall into your power" (Qur'ān 5:34). This possibility raises three questions. First, is the *ḥadd* for highway robbery and piracy abolished by repentance? Second, would the repentant brigand or pirate be absolved from liability for shedding blood and usurping property? Third, what conditions are required to render repentance legally valid?

In principle, pre-arrest repentance revokes the *ḥadd* for highway robbery and piracy, but does not absolve the offender from liability if the victims or their heirs seek justice.[127] Interestingly, the Shāfiʿīs hold controversial opinions respecting punishment for a repentant bandit who repents prior to capture. One opinion states that all rights of God and individuals are waved, whereas another position maintains that God's rights fall away with respect to theft but not murder or assault, and all private rights remain. A final view holds that all Divine punishments are waved but private rights are not. The Mālikī, Hanbali, and some Shafiʿi jurists add yet another position, maintaining that repentant pirates are not subject to punishment, but must pay damages for any injuries sustained by the victim.[128] In all cases, whoever commits piracy must surrender the

judicial authorities to mitigate the penalty to discretionary punishment (*taʿzīr*) as a substitute for imprisonment and expulsion, which could take one of the following forms: admonition, reprimand, threat, boycott, public disclosure, fine and seizure of property, imprisonment, flogging, or the death penalty in extreme cases. Others as well as learned ancestors approved of an offender's banishment from his hometown to another at his own discretion on the condition that he promised not to repeat the offense. The banishment was to remain in effect until the offender's righteousness and sincere repentance became manifest and apparent. Abū ʿAbd Allāh Muḥammad ibn Idrīs al-Sh āfiʿī, *Aḥkām al-Qurʾān* (Cairo: Maktabat al-Khānjī, 1414/1994), 1:313–318; Muḥammad Juraywī, *Al-Sijn wa-Mūjibātuhu fī al-Sharīʿah al-Islāmiyya: Muqāranan bi-Niẓām al-Sijn wa'l-Tawqīf fī al-Mamlaka al-ʿArabiyya al-Saʿūdiyya* (Riyad: Idārat al-Thaqāfa wa'l-Nashr, 1990), 616–632; Sharif, "Concept of *Jihād* and *Baghy* in Islamic Law," 164–166; Ahmad S. Z. Hemeidah, "Repentance as a Legal Concept," (master's thesis, University of Arizona, 2011), 35–38; Awa, *Punishment in Islamic Law*, 12–13, for the *taʿzīr* see pp. 100–110. The island of Dahlak was a place of exile during the Umayyad and Abbasid periods. Power, "Red Sea Region during the 'Long' Late Antiquity," 149.

126 Ramadan, "Larceny Offenses in Islamic Law," 1640.

127 Hemeidah, "Repentance as a Legal Concept," 35–38.

128 Emon, "*Ḥuqūq Allāh* and *Ḥuqūq al-ʿIbād*," 373–376.

usurped property to the rightful owner or heirs, who hold the right to either sue or pardon the accused.[129]

The punishments prescribed for piracy might make Islamic penal law appear excessively cruel. However, to avoid making undue assumptions, we must consider the historical contexts, noting that the punitive laws prescribed by the Qurʾān were prevalent also in the ancient Near East and early modern European societies. In his excellent essay, which traces the origins of punitive practices outside the Islamic framework, Andrew Marsham argues that beheading and crucifixion were common practices for public prosecution across the pre-Islamic Near East. Exile, as a substitute for execution and the amputation of limbs, was codified in the Roman and Sassanid legal digests. Identical punitive practices are also attested to in the Hebrew Bible and Judaic tradition.[130]

Documentary evidence from sixteenth-century England sheds light on the punishment there for piracy. A convicted pirate was hanged on a riverbank or seashore so that his toes "well-nigh" touched the water.[131] As regards the practice of banishment, it was commonplace for European empires to exile convicts, including dissidents, rebels, political prisoners, and disgraced officials, in addition to criminals, to "penal colonies" located at the distant reaches of the imperial jurisdiction. Great Britain would transport convicts on board "convict ships" to colonies and

[129] Hemeidah, "Repentance as a Legal Concept," 14–17, 33, 53–54, 61, 64, 82; Abou el-Fadl, *Rebellion and Violence*, 144.

[130] Andrew Marsham, "Public Execution in the Umayyad Period: Early Islamic Punitive Practice and Its Late Antique Context," *Journal of Arabic and Islamic Studies* 11 (2011), 101–126. Categorizing pirates as *hostis humani generis* induced Roman jurists to sanction the most savage penalties against them in order to deter others from performing similar acts. For instance, capital punishment consisted of exposure to beasts, being burnt alive, crucifixion, and beheading. Shaw, "Bandits in the Roman Empire," 20–21; Ormerod, *Piracy in the Ancient World*, 54–55. However, a slave who acted under the orders of his master was exonerated from punishment for the reason that he was only an agent of his master. William A. Hunter, *A Systematic and Historical Exposition of Roman Law* (London: William Maxwell and Son, 1885), 168.

[131] Ormerod, *Piracy in the Ancient World*, 54; Clive M. Senior, "An Investigation of the Activities and Importance of English Pirates 1603–40," (PhD diss., University of Bristol, 1972), 30–31, 35; William M. E. Pitcaithly, "Pirates, Robbers and other Malefactors: The Role Played by Violence at Sea in Relations between England and the Hanse Towns, 1385–1420," (PhD diss., University of Exeter, 2011), 23; Shaw, "Bandits in the Roman Empire," 21. Public execution in England was procedurally similar to the Roman practice, whereby bandits' bodies were impaled on forked stakes at the location where the robbery had been committed.

exploit their labor for public projects.[132] Other examples include that of France, using Devil's Island (French Guiana) as a penal colony from 1852 to 1946,[133] and the Dutch East India Company's penal colony on the Cape of Good Hope.[134]

As far as *dhimmīs* who engaged in piracy are concerned, their willingness to live under an Islamic regime meant that they were subject to the social, ethical, and legal principles of the Qur'ān. Therefore, the great majority of legal scholars contended that if a *dhimmī* offender committed piracy, the punishments had to be strictly enforced just as if the offender were Muslim. A *dhimmī muḥārib* committing aggravated robbery and violence for financial gains violates God's primordial covenant with all humanity,[135] spreads disorder, and breaches his covenant with the Islamic State.[136] However, as *dhimmī* communities maintained autonomous judicial systems and institutions, they may have been granted the right to adjudicate court cases pursuant to their own religious laws if both the brigands and victims were their coreligionists. Therefore, a *dhimmī* brigand who targeted his coreligionists was likely to be tried by a Christian ecumenical council or a Jewish court, even though most Muslim jurists and exegetes maintained that Qur'ān 5:33 is applicable to all human beings irrespective of religious allegiances. Thus, the case of every offender found on Islamic soil was generally adjudicated in the Islamic courts, except for that of a *musta'min.*

If a *musta'min* committed armed robbery or piracy, he was not to be punished pursuant to the *ḥudūd* penalties prescribed in the Qur'ān. The intellectual legal debate that took place between Abū Ḥanīfa al-Nu 'mān, founder of the Hanafi Law School, and his disciple Abū Yūsuf al-Shaybānī may constitute one of the earliest binding precedents for subsequent rulings and juristic decisions on this matter. Abū Yūsuf writes:

132 Sue Ballyn, "The British Invasion of Australia – Convicts: Exile and Dislocation," in *Lives in Migration: Rupture and Continuity*, ed. Martin Renes, http://www.ub.edu/dpfilsa/0renes.pdf. To be specific, Great Britain transported 165,000 convicts to Australia during the period from 1787 to 1867. http://landing.ancestry.co.uk/intl/au/convict/.

133 Michel Foucault, *Discipline and Punish: The Birth of the Prison*, trans. Alan Sheridan (New York: Vintage Books, 1979), 293.

134 Kerry Ward, *Networks of Empire: Forced Migration in the Dutch East India Company* (Cambridge: Cambridge University Press, 2009), 179–180.

135 Qur'ān 5:7: "وَاذْكُرُوا نِعْمَةَ اللَّهِ عَلَيْكُمْ وَمِيثَاقَهُ الَّذِي وَاثَقَكُمْ بِهِ (And call in remembrance the favor of God unto you, and His covenant, which He ratified with you)"; Marsham, "Public Execution," 111.

136 Zaydān, *Aḥkām al-Dhimmiyyīn wa'l-Musta'minīn*, 229–230; Labeeb A. Bsoul, *International Treaties (Mu'āhadāt) in Islam* (Lanham: University Press of America, 2008), 64; Masri, "Classical Conceptions of Treaty, Alliances, and Neutrality," 172.

I (ABŪ YŪSUF) ASKED:	If one (of the *musta'mins*) commits fornication or theft in the Dār al-Islām, do you think that we should apply the *ḥudūd* penalties to him?
HE (ABŪ ḤANĪFA) REPLIED:	No.
I ASKED:	Why?
HE REPLIED:	Because they (the persons from the Dār al-Ḥarb) had made neither a peace treaty (with us) nor had they become *dhimmīs*. Thus, Muslim rulings would not apply to them. However, I should make them responsible for any property they might steal, but I should not impose on them the penalty of amputation (of the hand for theft).
I ASKED:	If one of them killed a Muslim or a *dhimmī* – intentionally or unintentionally – would his case be judged (by Muslim *qāḍī*)?
HE REPLIED:	Yes.
I ASKED:	How do the *ḥudūd* penalties differ from the latter penalties?
HE REPLIED:	The *ḥudūd* penalties are prescribed for (the right of) God, whereas the case in question involves the rights of Muslims and *dhimmīs*; therefore, they should be procured in their favor.[137]

The legal rationale behind Abū Ḥanīfa's opinion is that the *musta'min* is not a permanent resident of the Abode of Islam. His residence for only a fixed period of time does not require him to comply with the right of God, only to civil and criminal law; the rights of individuals, whether Muslims, *dhimmīs*, and other subjects, remain inviolable. Thus, victims are entitled to sue non-Muslim alien offenders in civil courts and enforce the domestic rule of law against them; the financial penalty for piracy still stands, but corporal punishment is explicitly forbidden. A *musta'min* offender must pay wergild to his victims or heirs in the event of injury or death, and return any stolen property, or else property of identical quality and quantity or of equivalent value. The Shāfiʿī School of Law approves of the ruling of the Hanafis as it stands, whereas al-Awzāʿī's doctrine sanctions administering the

[137] Khadduri, *Islamic Law of Nations*, 172.

ḥudūd penalties for a *musta'min* just as if he were a Muslim or a *dhimmī* actor.[138]

The adjudication of cases of piracy was embodied in international treaties and diplomatic correspondence. As a rule, a coastal state was authorized to adjudicate cases of foreign piracy pursuant to the domestic rule of law whenever such acts occurred within its territory or maritime domain. Article 11 of the 689/1290 Mamluk–Catalan treaty stipulates that both parties to it must take legal actions against pirates: "(The Catalan King) shall take any pirate who falls into his power, and deal duly with him." Reciprocally, the Mamluk sultan is committed to trying any pirate who enters his territory in accordance with his domestic penal codes.[139]

Although judicial procedures for trying accused pirates follow the religious code and require due process of law, some international treaties contained provisions demanding the capturing state to execute pirates instantly upon capture, on the orders of the flotilla commander. Article 26 of the 800/1397 Ḥafṣīd–Pisan/Florentine treaty, renewed in 817/1414 and again in 824/1421, requires the two Italian city-states to immediately put captured pirates to death and to return any stolen chattels and property to the customs house in Tunis, providing that the pirate attack had originated from the state's territories and had launched attacks against Islamic ships. If the pirates escaped capture, Pisa and Florence would have to pay retribution to the victims.[140] Such field trials were aimed at apprehending pirates and so reducing armed robbery at sea.

FINANCIAL RAMIFICATIONS

Encounters with pirates gave rise to legal and financial claims. Three different kinds of scenarios bore distinct financial consequences: (a) a potentially threatened vessel succeeds in evading pirates lurking on the horizon; (b) a vessel's captain orders that all or part of the cargo be jettisoned so that pirates are less tempted to attack the vessel; and (c) pirates seize a vessel, her cargo, or both.

138 Zaydān, *Aḥkām al-Dhimmiyyīn wa'l-Musta'minīn*, 231–233; Bsoul, *International Treaties*, 77–78; Masri, "Classical Conceptions of Treaty, Alliances, and Neutrality," 173–175.

139 Holt, *Early Mamluk Diplomacy*, 136; Fuess, "Rotting Ships and Razed Harbors," 61–62.

140 Amari, *Diplomi Arabi*, 133, 147–148, 161–162.

Neither legal codices nor customary practices call on captains and voyagers to set sail under perilous conditions, such as when enemy or pirate ships are known to be lurking near the ports of call or en route. Both parties to a contract, the lessee and lessor, are advised to wait until the threat has dissipated, on the condition that the delay is not indefinite. Should such a delay appear indefinite, the parties are eligible to seek cancellation of the contract of carriage, in congruence with the Prophetic tradition that "there shall be no harming of one man by another."[141] Under such circumstances, both parties must appraise and justly divide any losses.[142] Should any loss or damage be caused by pirates to a ship, her contents, or both, it is to be borne by the negligent party.[143]

Incidents of piracy can always occur once a vessel is underway. The best scenario would involve evading pirates and escaping unharmed, while diverting from the original planned course – which may have financial repercussions for the parties to the contract of carriage. Whereas the maritime laws of Rhodes entitle the shipowner to retain one half of the shipping charges paid in advance if the vessel cannot proceed to the port of destination due to pirates, Islamic law introduced unprecedented methods for calculating the freight charges. If, after covering a part of the distance of a voyage, a vessel encounters extreme human peril that causes her to divert course and moor in a region where the shipper cannot profit from the hire, the shipper will be absolved from paying shipping fees. However, if the vessel anchors in a safely guarded place near the port of embarkation, the shipowner is entitled to collect the full shipping charges. If she sails beyond the destination, the shipper will have to pay an additional comparable fee for the increased distance.[144]

Some jurists provide further detail with respect to this issue by decreeing that if the shipowner returns to the port of origin at the passengers' request, then they must pay the freight charges. The only two circumstances in which passengers are exempt from paying transport costs are: (a) when the shipowner voluntarily hastens back to the embarkation point

[141] Khalilieh, *Admiralty and Maritime Laws*, 146–147 (*lā ḍarar wa-lā ḍirār*). The only – but nevertheless significant – difference between Islamic law and the Justinian Digest on this matter relates to the sum payable. While Muslim jurists did not entitle the shipowner or carrier to collect freight charges until after the ship had departed, Byzantine jurists provided leeway for him to charge the shipper "in accordance with the contract."

[142] Khalilieh, *Islamic Maritime Law*, 76–77.

[143] Khalilieh, *Islamic Maritime Law*, 77–78; Kindī, *Muṣannaf*, 21:154–155; Ashburner, *Rhodian Sea Law*, 106–107, articles 3:28 and 29; Freshfield, *Manual of Later Roman Law*, 201–202.

[144] Khalilieh, *Admiralty and Maritime Laws*, 130–131.

against their will; and (b) when danger is imminent and unavoidable and either or both parties call for sailing back to the port of origin. These rules are valid so long as the shippers/consignors do not reap any benefits from their journey. Under such circumstances, when the ship's manager cannot head to the final destination or return to the home port, but instead finds shelter in a third location where the shippers can nonetheless sell their commodities, the shippers must compensate the carrier commensurate with the profits made. However, those who opt not to disembark and return with their cargoes to the port of origin must pay shipping fees commensurate with the distance covered in the outward-bound and return trips. If the shipowner prevents the shippers from unloading their cargoes at the first stopover, then the shippers are exempt from any shipping fees.[145]

Contention may arise between shippers and carriers when the whole or part of the cargo is jettisoned overboard to evade an encounter with pirates. Jettisoning all or part of a ship's contents will make her a less tempting target for pirates, also lighter, and therefore more maneuverable, thus improving the chances of escaping attack. A relevant incident took place toward the end of the first half of the twelfth century. A business letter addressed by the Adenese mercantile representative Maḍmūn ibn Ḥasan to the Tunisian merchant Abraham ben Yījū describes the arrival of imports from India, the jettisoning of part of the cargo en route to avoid a piratical raid, and the distribution of losses among the parties engaged in the venture. An excerpt of the letter reads as follows:

> I, your servant, took notice (6) of what you – may God preserve your well-being! – wrote (7) concerning the shipment of 15 *bahār*s of standard (*rasmī* – legal or official) iron (8) and seven *bahār*s of belts (?) of eggs. This is to inform you that the sailors (9) jettisoned some of the 'eggs' when the pirates (*al-surrāq*) [approached] (10) the gulf Fam al-Khawr (alt. translation: on the mouth of the gulf). But I, your servant, already distributed it (the loss) (11) according to the freight of the ship, and I collected this for you.[146]

From this account it can be inferred that piracy in the classical Islamic world gave rise to claims for general average – pro rata – contributions from all parties concerned where the remedy was deemed applicable.[147] Like their Roman and Byzantine counterparts, Muslim jurists decreed that the general average rules cannot be enforced unless the sacrifice in

145 Khalilieh, *Admiralty and Maritime Laws*, 131.
146 Goitein and Friedman, *India Traders*, 370.
147 Khalilieh, *Admiralty and Maritime Laws*, 150–151.

question was made, or the expenditure incurred, for the common safety and common good – in order to save the ship, cargo, crew, and passengers. The captain, shippers, and their agents, and passengers on board, who used their combined reasoning to escape potentially dire consequences, shared an understanding that they were all bound by law to contribute proportionately to the value of the goods jettisoned.

The instances where pirates seized the cargo but freed the ship, captured the vessel but released the cargo, or seized the craft with all her contents comprised the most intricate cases, often requiring proceedings in rem. These claims were brought by those who forfeited properties of a greater relative value than did others sailing on board the same ship. The Justinianic Digest ruled that when a commercial ship was captured by pirates, everyone on board had to pay a contribution toward ransoming the ship. However, only the cargo owners had to bear the loss of any property seized by the pirates, and whoever ransomed his own goods could not claim a contribution from other shippers.[148] By contrast, Islamic law distinguishes between cases where the ship is redeemed and those in which a shipper redeems his own goods. In the first situation the travelers are obliged to contribute, while in the second, each cargo owner had to personally bear the entire expense of redeeming his commodities. Islamic law further rules that if pirates capture cargo but release the vessel, the cargo owners are to pay the freight costs, nonetheless. On the other hand, if the vessel is seized, they are exempt from paying such costs.[149] These principles were implemented on condition that the threat of pirates could not have been anticipated and that the ship traversed standard shipping lanes without deviating from course.[150]

[148] Scott (ed.), *Civil Law*, 4:209, Digest XIV, 2, 2, 3; Ashburner, *Rhodian Sea Law*, 87, article III:9.

[149] Raṣṣāʿ, *Sharḥ Ḥudūd Ibn ʿArafa*, 2:525. A comparable rule, with just a slight difference, is instituted in the Castilian's *Las Siete Partidas*, compiled during the reign of Alfonso X (r. 1252–1284). Title 9, Law 12 rules that if the pirates or corsairs captured a ship along with her human element and property on board, and subsequently they were ransomed by peaceful means, whatever is paid shall be proportionately divided among all, each paying his share according to the value and amount of property with him on board. Likewise, persons who have nothing with them on board the ship have to contribute. However, if the pirates captured some property of a certain consignee, liability for the loss is laid solely upon the actual owner. That is to say, other consignees and voyagers whose cargoes remained safe do not have to contribute toward the looted cargo. Scott (ed.), *Las Siete Partidas*, 4:1081.

[150] Jazīrī, *Al-Maqṣad al-Maḥmūd*, 224–225; Raṣṣāʿ, *Sharḥ Ḥudūd Ibn ʿArafa*, 2:525; Wansharīsī, *Al-Miʿyār*, 8:302; Ashburner, *Rhodian Sea Law*, 83, article III:4 of the maritime code of Rhodes, which rules that if the captain steers his vessel into a place

Pirate raids occurred most frequently in the vicinity of ports and anchorages. If a vessel arrived at her destination but could not dock due to the presence of hostile warships or pirates, the ship's manager could divert course to a safer harbor nearby, anchoring there until the threat had dissipated, provided that the contract with the shippers would remain valid. A shipper is at liberty to discharge his cargo upon paying the shipping charges to the carrier. However, the original contract remains valid for shippers intending to wait out the threat and unload their cargo in the original port, owing no additional charges to the carrier.[151]

Once cargo is placed on a ship and entrusted to the captain, the owners become involuntary partners, such that in the event of loss or damage due to human perils, all the shippers become active partners in conveying any remaining shipments. Ill-fated parties can proceed in rem against the remaining cargo and the vessel herself to seek remuneration for the looted property. The judicial authorities can impound the vessel with her contents until losses are calculated and divided proportionately among all the shippers.

SUMMARY

As a formidable threat to vessels, piracy has preoccupied jurists over the course of history up until the present day, when Somali pirates threaten safe navigation in Bab el-Mandeb, still a vital and busy strait for East–West shipping. Whereas Roman jurisprudents deemed pirates *hostis humani generis*, their Muslim counterparts viewed maritime *ḥirāba* as an immediate threat to Islamic civilization, culture, and economy, as well as to all of humanity. The founders of all four schools of Islamic law hold

infested by pirates after being informed of the danger thereof by the passengers and thereupon they happen to be spoiled (robbed), the captain shall make good the loss. However, if the passengers bring the ship to a dangerous place in spite of the captain's protests and any mischief happens, they shall sustain the damage.

Jurists distinguish between piracy on inland waterways and at sea. For attacks on rivers, a ship's captain has to bring his claims before the sultan, who is in charge of providing security and protection to vessels sailing on rivers and waterways within his jurisdiction. Therefore, if a captain fails to bring the case to the local authorities, he must personally indemnify the shipper for his loss. Ibn Rushd (al-Jadd), *Al-Bayān wa'l-Taḥṣīl*, 9:63–64; Stern, "Three Petitions of the Fāṭimīd Period," 172–178, TS Arabic Box 42, f. 158; Khan, *Arabic Legal and Administrative Documents*, 330–331 [74], TS Arabic 42.158.

151 Ṭāher (ed.), "*Akriyat al-Sufun*," 20; Raṣṣā', *Sharḥ Ḥudūd Ibn 'Arafa*, 2:526; Abū Isḥāq Ibrāhīm ibn Ḥasan al-Rafī', *Mu'īn al-Ḥukkām 'alā al-Qaḍāyā wa'l-Aḥkām* (Beirut: Dār al-Gharb al-Islāmī, 1989), 2:526; Wansharīsī, *Al-Mi'yār*, 8:302–305.

that combating *ḥirāba* is the highest form of *jihad*, more meritorious than launching wars against ordinary enemies in the Abode of War. Even if a pirate participated in a military expedition along with ordinary troops, the Qur'ān prescribes that punishment must be carried out once the perpetrator has been identified. However, the Qur'ān keeps the door open for repentance prior to apprehension and evasion of corporal punishment.

Conclusion

Contemporary scholars universally regard renowned Dutch philosopher and legal scholar Hugo Grotius, one of the founding fathers of modern international law, as first propounding the doctrine of freedom of the seas at the dawn of the seventeenth century. However, documentary, legal, and literary evidence reveals that this doctrine had already been deeply rooted in non-European cultures and nations.[1] Strikingly, none of Grotius's contemporaneous or succeeding European thinkers who had commented on this doctrine – British legal theoretician John Selden, the German jurist and philosopher Samuel von Pufendorf, and the Swiss diplomat and philosopher Emer de Vattel – took into account the contributions by non-European such as Muslims who, by the time the European states ventured into overseas explorations, controlled over 60 percent of the world's shorelines.

During that period, the Abode of Islam stretched from the Indonesian archipelago in Southeast Asia to the Canary Islands in the eastern Atlantic Ocean. Muslim and Arab merchants established colonies along the coastlands from the Horn of Africa to Mozambique

[1] Hodgins, "Ancient Law of Nations Respecting the Sea," 14–21; Jesse S. Reeves, "Two Conceptions of the Freedom of the Seas," *American Historical Review* 22 (1917), 535–543; Potter, *Freedom of the Seas*, 12–35; Fenn, "Justinian and the Freedom of the Sea," 716–727; Ziskind, "International Legal Status of the Sea in Antiquity," 35–49; Ziskind, "International Law and Ancient Sources," 537–559; Benjamin Straumann, "Is Modern Liberty Ancient? Roman Remedies and Natural Rights in Hugo Grotius's Early Works on Natural Law," *Law and History Review* 2009 (27): 55–85; Benjamin Straumann, "'Ancient Caesarian Lawyers' in a State of Nature: Roman Tradition and Natural Rights in Hugo Grotius's *De iure praedae*," *Political Theory* 34 (2006), 328–350.

(Sufāla) and Madagascar.[2] As early as the tenth century CE, Muslim merchants had reached the Wāqwāq (Wakoku/UoKuok) territories of present-day Japan.[3] The advent of extensive trade networks across the globe owes its success to the religious tolerance of Muslims towards non-Muslims, advanced trade techniques (such as commenda and partnership),[4] commercial maritime laws that regulated and encouraged trade and shipping,[5] the development of nautical science and the art of navigation, and diplomatic and commercial relationships among foreign countries.[6] In this inviting atmosphere, merchants and seafarers could freely navigate the seas and arrived at foreign destinations hindered only by unanticipated man-made and natural hazards.

According to the Islamic Law of Nature, the commonality of the sea must not be disputed. God has bestowed the boundless sea on all humankind – to transact business, seek knowledge, and to exploit its natural resources. As all humans are by Divine law the Children of Adam, members of all races and religions should enjoy equal rights of access to the seas for their own benefit, insofar as they inflict no harm. Nowhere does the Qur'ān assert Muslims' proprietorship over the sea, neither the high seas nor even those located in the heart of Muslim territory. The Abode of Islam's two semienclosed bodies of water, the Persian Gulf and the Red

[2] Ibn Mājid, *Al-Fawā'id*, 286; Abdulaziz Lodhi, "Muslims in Eastern Africa: Their Past and Present," *Nordic Journal of African Studies* 3 (1994), 88–89.

[3] Shawkat M. Toorawa, "Wāq al-Wāq: Fabulous, Fabular, Indian Ocean (?) Island(s) ...." *Emergences* 10 (2000), 389–391; Akira Mizuguchi, "From Ancient to Modern Times: A Retrospective of Japan's Relationship with the Middle East," *Asia-Pacific Review* 9 (2002), 94–95.

[4] Abraham L. Udovitch, *Partnership and Profit in Medieval Islam* (Princeton: Princeton University Press, 1970).

[5] This subject is comprehensively covered in Khalilieh's *Admiralty and Maritime Laws*.

[6] For a thorough insight into the diplomatic relations of Islamic West with Western and Northwestern Europe, consult 'Abd al-Raḥmān 'Alī al-Ḥajjī, *Al-'Alāqāt al-Diblūmāsiyya al-Andalusiyya ma' Urūbbā al-Gharbiyya khilāl al-Mudda al-Amawiyya (138–366/755–976): Dirāsa Tārīkhiyya* (Abu Dhabi: Al-Majma' al-Thaqāfī, 1424/2004); for the English translation see ' Abd al-Raḥmān 'Alī al-Ḥajjī, *Andalusian Diplomatic Relations with Western Europe during the Umayyad Period (A.H. 138–366/A.D. 755–976): An Historical Survey* (Beirut: Dār al-Irshād, 1970);' Abd al-Ra ḥmān 'Alī al-Ḥajjī, "Andalusian Diplomatic Relations with the Franks during the Umayyad Period," *Islamic Studies* 30 (1991), 241–262; Nicholas Drocourt, "Christian–Muslim Diplomatic Relations: An Overview of the Main Sources and Themes of Encounter (600–1000)," in *Christian–Muslim Relations: A Bibliographical History*, ed. David Thomas and Alex Mallet (Leiden: E. J. Brill, 2010), 2:29–72; Elsa R. F. Cardoso, "Diplomacy and Oriental Influence in the Court of Cordoba (9th–10th Centuries)," (master's thesis, University of Lisbon, 2015).

Sea, were fully accessible to all nations provided that the Islamic holy sites in Arabia were not exposed to imminent military threats such as Raynald of Châtillon's Red Sea campaign in 1183, and Afonso de Albuquerque's unsuccessful attempt in 1513 to gain a foothold in the Red Sea. When Christian naval powers posed serious threats to the Noble Sanctuaries in Arabia, access to the Red Sea by European merchants was limited and the flow of commerce through this vital artery between the Far East and Southeast Asia and the Mediterranean sphere was temporarily disrupted.

Documentary evidence undisputedly demonstrates how the Islamic customary law of the sea derived from the Prophet Muḥammad's words and deeds through his Sunna generally and most directly through the 9 AH/630 CE pledge of security granted to the Patriarch and the governor of the port city of Aylah.[7] The importance of this pledge rests on several facets: (a) it does not draw a clear-cut distinction between coastal waters and the high seas, but treats all equally; (b) it assures freedom of navigation to those heading for or departing from Aylah, regardless of nationality; (c) it asserts Aylah's jurisdiction over its flagged ships and all crew and passengers, both while at sea and in ports;[8] and (d) along with others of the Prophet's practices, it formed a basis for the advent of safe-conducts, treaties, and truces between Muslim foreign authorities.

Moreover, this decree paved the way for entry by alien merchants, albeit for a limited time and scope, even during times of diplomatic crisis and outright war. Freedom of movement at sea and on land was facilitated for non-Muslims by safe-conduct pledges, which temporarily guaranteed protection of persons and chattels to enemy-alien merchants within the Abode of Islam. This institution overrode political boundaries as an

[7] Morrow, *Covenants of the Prophet Muhammad*, 233, 238, 297–298. The concept of freedom of navigation is enshrined in the Islamic Law of Nations as far back as the Prophet Muḥammad's early years in Yathrib (Medina). The Prophet's covenant with Christians of the World from the last day of Rabi al-Thani, 4 AH/October 10, 625 CE, stresses Christians' rights of mobility on land and the freedom to navigate the seas: "I grant security to their churches, their places of pilgrimage (*siyāḥa*) wherever they are and wherever they may be found, be they in the mountains or the valleys, in the caves or the inhabited regions, in the plains or the desert, or in buildings; and that I protect their religion and their property wherever they are and wherever they may be found in land or at sea, in the East or West, the same way that I protect myself, my Companions (*khillatī*), and the People of my Community (*ahl millatī*) among the Believers and the Muslims."

[8] As in this particular case, the 754/1353 Ḥafṣīd–Pisan treaty rules that "every foreign merchant, who sails aboard ships belonging to Pisa will 'enjoy equal rights as theirs, and fulfill the same obligations as theirs (*lahu mā lahum, wa-'alayhi mā 'alayhim*)'." Amari, *Diplomi Arabi*, 90, 103, 242.

obstacle to foreign nationals' freedom of movement and mobility right on land and at sea.

Whereas the open sea may not be appropriated, security and economic considerations could dictate that states exercise some degree of sovereign jurisdiction over limited offshore maritime zones, including bays, gulfs, indentations, islands, and islets. However, most significant to global legal history was the introduction by Islamic law of unprecedented principles to jurisprudence respecting that part of the Red Sea adjacent to the Hijazi coast. Following the *dhimmīs*' expulsion from the Hijaz by the second Pious Caliph ʿUmar ibn al-Khaṭṭāb, the Muslim authorities categorically divided the Abode of Islam into three geographical domains: the Ḥaram (Sharīf Sanctuary), the Hijaz, and all other territories. Non-Muslims had been forbidden from taking up permanent residence in the Ḥaram and the Hijaz, including the islands and islets of the Sea of Hijaz. The Hijaz's maritime domain extends from northwestern Yemen in the south to a point parallel to Tabūk in the north, with its seaward breadth extending from the coast to the outermost points of the islands and islets of the Sea of Hijaz.

In many ways, UNCLOS III establishes legal features for territorial seas akin to those that classical Muslim theologians and jurists ascribed to the Hijaz, by asserting de jure and de facto possessory control over a large portion of the Red Sea bordering Arabia. Non-Muslims, including Hindus and Buddhists,[9] enjoyed the right of innocent passage through the Hijazi territorial waters and access to ports, through treaties, general or private *amān*, or when exposed to distress, provided that the rule of law remained inviolate. However, they were not granted the right to take up permanent residence, or to exploit the waters' natural resources other than for the purpose of personal sustenance. Elsewhere in the Abode of Islam, marine areas adjacent to coastal frontiers enjoyed a different legal status. Central and provincial governing authorities claimed de facto proprietorship over a limited offshore zone, not exceeding a few miles from the shoreline, in order to defend their frontiers from seaborne raids, secure coastal

[9] Although Chinese vessels rarely made their way to the Red Sea ports, historical records highlight two visits. The first was in 1414, when the Chinese fleet under the command of the Admiral Zheng anchored in the port city of Jeddah, whereas the second took place in 1433, when the Chinese envoys sailing with Indian ships of the Calicut Kingdom anchored in the port of Jeddah. The two incidents show that the port of Jeddah was not exclusively reserved for Muslims only, but was also opened to non-Muslims. Wing, "Indian Ocean Trade and Sultanic Authority," 65–66; Meloy, *Imperial Power and Maritime Trade*, 66–80, 249–255.

navigation and trade, collect customs and taxes, and protect the fishing rights of local residents.

Even within the same state, province, or region people may have different languages, customs, habits, ideologies, cultural traditions, social norms, religions, denominations, and so forth. Such factors may constitute major obstacles to the unification of societies embodying people of different backgrounds. The Qur'ān does not classify human affiliation on the basis of nationality or ethnicity, but in accordance with religious conviction. Religion conjoins Muslims around the world as a powerful unifying instrument, with *Sharī'ah* applying to all Muslims irrespective of their denominational schools, whether within or outside Islam's territorial domain. *Sharī'ah* thus constitutes a uniform flexible legal system with judges primarily trying cases between Muslim disputants in conformity with the sacred law of Islam. Islam grants a parallel legal status to other monotheistic religions. Jews are an *ummah* based on the Torah, divinely revealed to Moses, and the Christians another *ummah* based on the Gospel of Jesus Christ. International treaties concluded between Muslim ruling dynasts and foreign principalities empowered the former to apply *Sharī'ah* to Muslim subjects even when in foreign territories.

Respecting previously ordained Divine laws, the Qur'ān enjoins Muslim ruling and judicial authorities not to intervene in *dhimmī*s' judicial affairs. Qur'ān 5:42–48 sanctions outright the coexistence of a pluralistic judicial system for the *dhimmī*s. However, if *dhimmī* litigants choose to bring a case before a Muslim qadi, he should apply the Islamic legal principles, since he must adjudicate according to "what Allāh has revealed." Regarding *ḥarbī*s, their lawsuits historically came before denominational courts until the rise of the consular office at the beginning of the twelfth century, which functioned as a judicial institution. A consul presided over cases involving only his fellow nationals, except for when a governing treaty stipulated otherwise.[10]

In the concluding remarks of Chapter 2, the advantages of legal pluralism to international trade have been outlined. One important advantage is individuals' familiarity with their own religious law and their essential equality before the court. Individual rights could be infringed by an Islamic court decision running counter to litigants' religious law, constituting another reason why the Qur'ān strongly urges qadis to avoid

[10] For instance, the 689/1290 treaty signed by the Mamluk sultan al-Manṣūr Qalāwūn and Genoa authorizes the Genoese consul to administer cases involving disputes between Genoese and Muslim parties. See Holt, *Early Mamluk Diplomacy*, 145.

presiding over lawsuits involving non-Muslim coreligionists. Freedom and equality constitute fundamental rights in Islamic law, which come into practice in the Qurʾān's sanctions of a pluralistic judicial system.

The final chapter is devoted to examining the legal implications of piracy in Islamic law. From the dawn of ancient civilization to the present day, piracy has posed a formidable threat to freedom of navigation and movement. The Qurʾān, exegetical literature, and jurisprudential sources eliminate ambiguities between *jihad* and piracy and essentially define the latter as a privately motivated armed robbery, directed against innocent commercial vessels, their contents, crews, and passengers, or against coastal targets, posing a threat to the public peace for the sole purpose of looting properties for private gain.[11] Designating pirates as common enemies of all humankind, jurists urged their fellow Muslims to exercise no tolerance toward their actions. In fact, they commended combating piracy as even more meritorious than fighting in the Cause of God (*jihad*). A pirate taking part in *jihad* would not mitigate his Divine punishments or abrogate his victim's rights. However, jurists held conflicting opinions regarding repentance prior to capture, which for some nullified a pirate's illegal acts. On the question as to why governments must combat piracy, Ibn Khaldūn emphasized its destructive impacts on the domestic and global economy; it could even precipitate the "decay of civilization."[12] Fighting piracy required a multidimensional domestic and international approach. An overwhelming majority of Islamic–Christian diplomatic and commercial treaties held authorities responsible for the safety of persons and chattels captured by their nationals. In principle, a state party to an agreement was held legally accountable for the personal safety of captives, even if their captors were still at large. Piracy would have proliferated unabated had states not employed military force against nests of pirates, built coastal surveillances, provided armed personal and naval escorts to commercial vessels, paid bribes to pirates, or imposed severe punishments on perpetrators.

At this point, two fundamental questions should be addressed: where did the foundations for the pre-Renaissance European law of the sea find footing? Is the precolonial law of the sea an exclusively European product as many scholars claim? To address the first question, it is incumbent on us to uncover when and how the late antiquity and early medieval empires, states, and principalities de facto exercised the principles underlying the customary international law of the sea. To give a simple answer, naval

[11] See Chapter 3, 177. [12] Ibn Khaldūn, *Muqaddimah*, 1:302.

rivalries and wars largely induced the international law of the sea, without which it would have been superfluous.[13] In other words, the precolonial international law of the sea likely owed its inception to Islam's rise in the Mediterranean arena toward the end of the first half of the seventh century, when the Romano-Byzantine *mare nostrum* ceased to exist. As the Mediterranean world's political unity fractured into two competing powers, Byzantium and Islam, overseas trade depended upon international diplomatic and economic agreements, and the issuance of private and general safe-conducts. A large number of diplomatic and commercial treaties concluded between Christian and Islamic political entities between the seventh and fifteenth centuries contain provisions governing the freedom of navigation on the high seas and innocent passage through the territorial seas and straits, as well as regulating the status of Christian and Muslim subjects in the various stages of their overland and maritime ventures.[14] It is here in the contested Mediterranean world where the foundations of the early modern law of the sea were laid down. At the dawn of the sixteenth century, European naval rivalries penetrated into

[13] Anand, *Origin and Development of the Law of the Sea*, 160. Most significant to the development of the international law of the sea were operations involving naval blockade, economic warfare, and papal embargoes, pioneered by the Latin West and the Crusades as tools for undermining Islamic independent and semi-independent entities along the Mediterranean littoral. Such naval strategies – also effectively implemented by the Portuguese in the Indian Ocean and Arabian Sea at the beginning of the sixteenth century – were anchored in European legal codices. Carl J. Kulsrud, *Maritime Neutrality to 1780: A History of the Main Principles Governing Neutrality and Belligerency to 1780* (Boston: Little, Brown, and Company, 1936), 212, 217, 221. On the enforcement of naval blockades and commercial embargo in the medieval Mediterranean, consult Sophia Menache, "Papal Attempts at a Commercial Boycott of the Muslims in the Crusader Period," *Journal of Ecclesiastical History* 63 (2012), 236–259; Stefan K. Stantchev, *Spiritual Rationality: Papal Embargo as Cultural Practice* (Oxford: Oxford University Press, 2014); Stefan K. Stantchev, "The Medieval Origins of Embargo as a Policy Tool," *History of Political Thought* 33 (2012), 373–399; Stefan K. Stantchev, "Embargo: The Origins on an Idea and the Implications of a Policy in Europe and the Mediterranean, ca. 1100–ca. 1500," (PhD diss., University of Michigan, 2009).

[14] Nahed Samour, "Is There a Role for Islamic International Law in the History of International Law?" *European Journal of International Law* 25 (2014), 315–316; Maurits Berger, "Islamic Views on International Law," in *Culture and International Law*, ed. Paul Meerts (The Hague: Hague Academic Press, 2008), 107–109. The diplomatic treaties and commercial agreements concluded by the Fatimids, Mamluks, and North African dynasts and Byzantium, Italian city-states, and the Crusades from the eleventh century onward reflect the actual attitudes of Muslim and Christian political entities toward use of the high seas for commercial purposes and the operational and legal tools employed to thwart piracy.

the Indian Ocean and transferred with them the Mediterranean model of freedom of the seas.

Unlike in the Mediterranean world, the Indian Ocean of the pre-European era afforded a more hospitable environment for overseas trade. Until the thirteenth century, the Indian Ocean's space was divided geographically and culturally into three realms without physical boundaries: the westernmost, connecting the Persian Gulf and the Red Sea with the western coast of India, inhabited by the Arabs and Persians; the middle or Hindu–Buddhist region, stretching from the south Indian coast to the Strait of Malacca, Java, and other Indonesian archipelago; and the easternmost or the Chinese realm.[15] For centuries before the rise of Islam, Arab and Persian merchants had uncontestably dominated the trade and shipping in this peaceful ocean. With the founding of the Abbasid Caliphate, the capital's transfer from Damascus to Baghdad, and the Arabs' and the Persians' conversion to the new faith, maritime commerce burgeoned between the Abode of Islam and India, China, and Southeast Asia. Luxury and other commodities from India, Southeast Asia, and the Far East could only reach Christian Europe through Muslim and Jewish merchants.

With the Arabian Peninsula's Islamization, the Hadrami Arab merchants, who already dominated Indian Ocean trade, carried the new Divine faith by sea to the western coasts of India. The gradual and peaceful spread of Islam across the western coastal strip of the Indian subcontinent derived from trade expansion and Islam's tolerance of local traditions. Here conversion to Islam did not signify a sudden change in the social order or an abandonment of existing cosmology. Michael Pearson argues to the contrary, that converted indigenous populations maintained existing beliefs by attributing Islamic traits to them.[16] Rather than being "substantive," change was "additive," with converts preserving local traditions.[17] Muslim dominance over the Indian Ocean trade network further resulted from Muslim traders' structure of commerce. In the Muslim-majority regions, rulers, jurists, and qadis recognized a plurality of legal systems and allowed local communities to govern themselves in accordance with their own *adat* (traditions and customs).[18]

[15] Abu Lughod, *Before European Hegemony*, 251–253.

[16] It may be assumed that this hypothesis holds true so long as any *muḥarramāt* (forbidden matters) were annulled.

[17] Pearson, *Indian Ocean*, 62, 76–77, 95; Pearson, "Islamic Trade, Shipping, Port-states and Merchant Communities," 3:328.

[18] Barendse, *Arabian Seas*, 87.

During a time when the Mediterranean Sea was a theatre of ongoing naval conflicts between Christian and Muslim powers from the middle of the seventh century onward, use of force in the Indian Ocean, especially the westernmost circuit, was hardly ever recorded. Except for the major overseas expeditions of Rājendra Cola/Chola (1014–1044) and the Ming dynasty's seven impressive naval expeditions commanded by the Muslim Chinese Admiral Zheng He between 1405 and 1433, armed interventions amounted to sporadic episodes with none aimed at dominating the vast expanse of the oceanic waters. The absence of large-scale naval conflicts contributed to the profusion of regional and international overseas trade, developed by traders without governmental intervention. Indigenous rulers cordially welcomed merchants who traveled freely among sovereign states and principalities without passports. This condition may explain why international commercial and diplomatic treaties did not appear along the shorelines of the Indian Ocean until the Portuguese intrusion into the eastern hemisphere. In support of this hypothesis, a statement attributed to Sultan Bahadur Shah of Gujarat (r. 1528–1537) rules that "wars by sea are merchant's affairs and of no concern to the prestige of kings."[19] Eventually, the rules governing the freedom of navigation and mobility rights in the Indian Ocean were not laid down by coastal sovereigns and empires, but by merchants and seafarers, who plied freely these peaceful waters hindered only by man-made dangers and unfavorable natural and climatic conditions. However, from the early sixteenth century onward, freedom of navigation carried a different connotation for European naval powers.[20]

As this monograph comes to a close, I am reminded of the letter of apology addressed by the prominent Palestinian rhetorician, counsellor, and head of Saladin's chancery ʿAbd al-Raḥīm ibn ʿAli al-Baysānī al-ʿAsqalānī, known as al-Qāḍī al-Fāḍil (529–596/1135–1200), to ʿImād al-Dīn al-Iṣfahānī (519–597/1125–1201), a renowned rhetorician and counsellor in Saladin's court, by which he hoped to calm tensions and

[19] Kurup and Mathew, *Native Resistance against the Portuguese*, 39; Subramanian, "Of Pirates and Potentates," 20.

[20] Anand, "Maritime Practice in South-East Asia until 1600," 451–452: "Freedom of the seas was used not only for the perfectly legitimate purpose of navigation, but more often than not it was interpreted by the militarily strong European Powers as permitting them to move across the wide open sea to threaten small states for their own ends, or to subjugate and colonize them. ... Freedom of the high seas also came to be transformed into a license to overfish, especially near the coasts of other countries, triggering numerous fishery disputes. ... Freedom of the seas has always meant unequal freedom or freedom for the few."

settle disagreements that had arisen between them. A paragraph of al-Qāḍī al-Fāḍil's letter reads as follows:

> Something occurred to me, and I do not know whether you have encountered as such, or not! I hereby describe it to you. I have noticed that no one writes a letter (*kitāb*) on the day before, then on the next day says: "If it were amended, it would have been more effective; if it were expanded, it would have been more desirable; if it were prefaced, it would have been more appropriate; and if this were left unchanged, it would have been more aesthetic." This is a meaningful example of how the sense of imperfection captures the entirety of humankind.[21]

This study has begun to grapple with the evolution of the Islamic customary law of the sea and its contribution to the development of international law and relations at a time when Arabic was the world's *lingua franca*. While it takes some first steps in filling this gap in Islamic legal history, as yet undiscovered legal texts, treaties, and other documentary evidence may unearth additional and more valuable information offering deeper insights into the way that Islamic law treats the legal status of the high seas and offshore maritime zones. By all indications, congruent with contributions of Muslims to the art of navigation and nautical science, jurists, scholars, *siyar* authors, pilots, seafarers, central and provincial ruling authorities, and, above all, merchants engaged in regional and overseas trade activities have also left indelible imprints on the development and formation of the customary law of the sea.

[21] Al-Murtaḍā Muḥammad ibn Muḥammad al-Zabīdī, *Itḥāf al-Sāda al-Muttaqīn bi-Sharḥ Iḥyā' 'Ulūm al-Dīn* (Beirut: Mu'assasat al-Tārīkh al-'Arabī, 1414/1994), 1:3; Ṣiddīq ibn Ḥasan al-Qannūjī, *Abjad al-'Ulūm: Al-Washy al-Marqūm fī Bayān Aḥwāl al-'Ulūm* (Damascus: Wizārat al-Thaqāfa wa'l-Irshād al-Qawmī, 1978), 1:71.

Bibliography

The Meaning of the Holy Qur'ān. Translated by 'Abdullāh Yūsuf 'Alī. Brentwood: Amana Corporation, 1991.

The Holy Qur'ān. Revised and edited by the Presidency of Islamic Researches, IFTA. Medina: King Fahd Glorious Qur'ān Printing Complex, 1410/1989.

PRIMARY ARABIC SOURCES

Abū Dāwūd, Sulaymān ibn al-Ash'ath (202–275/817–889). *Sunan Abū Dāwūd*. Beirut: Dār al-Ḥadīth, 1388–1394/1968–1974.

Abū Ḥayyān, Muḥammad ibn Yūsuf ibn 'Alī ibn Yūsuf (654–745/1256–1344). *Al-Tafsīr al-Kabīr al-Musammā al-Baḥr al-Muḥīṭ*. 8 vols. Beirut: Dār Iḥyā' al-Turāth al-'Arabī, 1411/1990.

Abū Makhrama, Al-Ṭayyib ibn 'Abd Allāh Abū Aḥmad (d. 947/1540). *Tārīkh Thaghr 'Aden*. Beirut: Dār al-Jīl, 1408/1987.

'Alawī, Abū 'Abd Allāh Muḥammad ibn 'Alī ibn al-Ḥasan (367–445/977–1053). *Al-Jāmi' al-Kāfī fī Fiqh al-Zaydiyyah* (Amman: Mu'assasat al-Imām Zayd ibn 'Alī) www.azzaidiah.com/kotob_mojamaah/feqh/algame_alkafy_fe_fegh_azzaidiah.html.

Albānī, Muḥammad Nāṣir al-Dīn. *Al-Ḥadīth Ḥujjatun bi-Nafsihi fī al-'Aqā'id wa'l-Aḥkām*. Riyad: Maktabat al-Ma'ārif lil-Nashr wa'l-Tawzī', 1425/2005.

Ghāyat al-Marām fī Takhrīj Aḥādīth al-Ḥalāl wa'l-Ḥarām. 3rd ed. Beirut: Al-Maktab al-Islāmī, 1405/1985.

Irwā' al-Ghalīl fī Takhrīj Aḥādīth Manār al-Sabīl. 8 vols. Beirut: Al-Maktab al-Islāmī, 1405/1985.

Anṣārī, Abū Yūsuf Ya'qūb ibn Ibrāhīm (113–182/731–798). *Al-Radd 'alā Siyar al-Awzā'ī*. Hyderabad: n.p., n.d.

'Aynī, Badr al-Dīn Abū Muḥammad ibn Maḥmūd ibn Aḥmad (762–855/1360–1453). *'Umdat al-Qārī' Sharḥ Ṣaḥīḥ al-Bukhārī*. 25 vols. Beirut: Dār al-Fikr al-Mu'āṣir, 1418/1998.

Baghawī, Ḥusayn ibn Mas'ūd (d. 510/1117). *Tafsīr al-Baghawī*. 8 vols. Riyad: Dār Ṭība lil-Nashr, 1409/1989.

Baghdādī, 'Abd al-Laṭīf (557–629/1162–1231). *Al-Ifāda wa'l-I'tibār fī al-Umūr al-Mushāhada wa'l-Ḥawādith al-Mu'āyana bi-Arḍ Miṣr*. Edited and translated by K. H. Zand, J. A. Videan, and I. E. Videan. London: George Allen and Unwin, 1965.

Bājī, Abū al-Walīd Sulaymān ibn Khalaf ibn Sa'd ibn Ayyūb (403–494/1012–1100). *Al-Muntaqā*. 7 vols. Beirut: Dār al-Fikr al-'Arabī, 1402/1982.

Balādhurī, Abū al-'Abbās Aḥmad ibn Yaḥyā (d. 279/892). *Futūḥ al-Buldān*. Leiden: E. J. Brill, 1968.

Balkhī, Abū al-Ḥasan Muqātil ibn Sulaymān (d. 150/767). *Tafsīr Muqātil Ibn Sulaymān*. 5 vols. Beirut: Dār Iḥyā' al-Turāth al-'Arabī, 1423/2002.

Ben Shemesh, Aharon. *Taxation in Islam*. 3 vols. Leiden: E. J. Brill, 1958, 1967, 1969.

Bīrūnī, Abū al-Rayḥān Muḥammad ibn Aḥmad. *Taḥqīq mā lil-Hind min Maqūla Maqbūla fī al-'Aql aw Mardhūla*. Beirut: 'Ālam al-Kutub, 1403/1983.

Bukhārī, Muḥammad ibn 'Abd al-Raḥmān (d. 546/1151). *Maḥāsin al-Islām wa-Sharā'i' al-Islām*. Cairo: Maktabat al-Quds, 1357/1955.

Bukhārī, Muḥammad ibn Ismā'īl (194–256/810–870). *Ṣaḥīḥ al-Bukhārī*. 7 vols. Damascus: Dār Ibn Kathīr, 1414/1993.

Burzulī, Abū al-Qāsim ibn Aḥmad (d. 841/1438). *Fatāwā al-Burzulī: Jāmi' Masā'il al-Aḥkām li-mā Nazala min al-Qaḍāyā bil-Muftīn wa'l-Ḥukkām*. 7 vols. Beirut: Dār al-Gharb al-Islāmī, 2002.

Ḍaḥḥāk, Abū Bakr Aḥmad Ibn'Amr ibn Abī 'Āṣim (206–287/821–900). *Kitāb al-Jihād*. Damascus: Dār al-Qalam, 1409/1989.

Dhahabī, Muḥammad ibn Aḥmad ibn 'Uthmān (673–748/1274–1348). *Siyar A'lām al-Nubalā'*. 24 vols. Beirut: Mu'assasat al-Risālah, 1422/2001.

Ghazālī, Abū Ḥāmid Muḥammad ibn Muḥammad (450–505/1058–1111). *Al-Mustaṣfā min 'Ilma al-Uṣūl*. 4 vols. Jeddah: Sharikat al-Madīnah al-Munawwara, 1413/1993.

Ḥamawī, Yāqūt ibn 'Abd Allāh (575–627/1179–1229). *Mu'jam al-Buldān*. 5 vols. Beirut: Dār Ṣāder, 1986.

Hamdānī, Ḥasan ibn Aḥmad ibn Ya'qūb (280–336/893–947). *Ṣifat Jazīrat al-'Arab*. Sana'a: Maktabat al-Irshād, 1410/1990.

Ḥillī, Jamāl al-Dīn al-Ḥasan ibn Yūsuf (648–726/1250–1325). *Taḥrīr al-Aḥkām*. 2 vols. Qumm: Mu'assasat al-Imām al-Ṣādiq, 1420/1999.

Ḥimyarī, Muḥammad ibn 'Abd al-Mun'im (d. 866/1462). *Al-Rawḍ al-Mi'ṭār fī Khabar al-Aqṭār*. Beirut: Maktabat Lubnān, 1984.

Ibn 'Abd Allāh, Abū Isḥāq Burhān al-Dīn Ibrāhīm ibn Muḥammad (d. 884/1479). *Al-Mubdi' fī Sharḥ al-Muqni'*. 10 vols. Beirut: Al-Maktab al-Islāmī, 1421/2000.

Ibn 'Abd al-Barr, Yūsuf ibn 'Abd Allāh ibn Muḥammad al-Qurṭubī (368–464/978–1071). *Al-Kāfī fī Fiqh Ahl al-Madīnah al-Mālikī*. 2 vols. Riyad: n.p., 1401/1980. See also Beirut edition: Dār al-Kutub al-'Ilmiyyah, 1997.

Ibn 'Abd al-Ḥakam, Abū Muḥammad 'Abd Allāh (155–214/772–829). *Sīrat 'Umar Ibn 'Abd al-'Azīz 'alā mā Rawāhu al-Imām Mālik Ibn Anas wa-Aṣḥābihi*. Beirut: 'Ālam al-Kitāb, 1404/1984.

Ibn ʿAbd al-Ḥakam, Abū al-Qāsim ʿAbd al-Raḥmān ibn ʿAbd Allāh (187–214/803–871). *Futūḥ Miṣr wa-Akhbārahā*. Cairo: Maktabat Madbouli, 1411/1991.

Ibn Abū Zayd Qayrawānī, ʿAbd Allāh ibn ʿAbd al-Raḥmān (310–386/922–996). *Al-Nawādir wa'l-Ziyādāt ʿalā mā fī al-Mudawwana min ghayrihā min al-Ummahāt*. 15 vols. Beirut: Dār al-Gharb al-Islāmī, 1999.

Ibn al-ʿArabī, Muḥammad ibn ʿAbd Allāh (468–543/1075–1148). *Aḥkām al-Qur'ān*. 4 vols. Beirut: Dār al-Kutub al-ʿIlmiyyah, 1424/2003.

Ibn ʿAsākir, Abū al-Qāsim ʿAlī ibn al-Ḥasan ibn Hibat Allāh (499–571/1106–1176). *Al-Arbaʿūn fī al-Ḥathth ʿAlā al-Jihād*. Kuwait: Dār al-Khulafā' lil-Kitāb al-Isl āmī, 1404/1984.

Tārīkh Madīnat Dimashq. 80 vols. Beirut: Dār al-Fikr, 1415/1995.

Ibn ʿĀṣim, Abū Bakr Muḥammad ibn Muḥammad (760–830/1358–1426). *Tuḥfat al-Ḥukkām fī Nukat al-ʿUqūd wa'l-Aḥkām*. Beirut: Dār al-Kutub al-ʿIlmiyyah, 1415/1994.

Ibn Aʿtham, Abū Muḥammad Aḥmad al-Kūfī (d. 314/926). *Kitāb al-Futūḥ*. 5 vols. Beirut: Dār al-Aḍwā' lil-Ṭibāʿa wa'l-Nashr, 1411/1991.

Ibn Bābawayh, Abū Jaʿfar Muḥammad ibn ʿAlī ibn al-Ḥusayn (310–381/923–991). *Al-Khiṣāl*. 2 vols. Qumm: Jamāʿat al-Mudarrisīn fī al-Ḥawza al-ʿIlmiyya, 1416/1995.

Man lā Yaḥḍuruhu al-Faqīh. 4 vols. Qumm: Jamāʿat al-Mudarrisīn fī al-Ḥawza al-ʿIlmiyya, 1404/1983.

Ibn Baṭṭūṭa, Abū ʿAbd Allāh Muḥammad ibn ʿAbd Allāh (703–779/1304–1377). *Travels in Asia and Africa*. Translated and selected by H. A. R. Gibb. London: Broadway House, 1929.

Riḥlat Ibn Baṭṭūṭa: Tuḥfat al-Nuẓẓār fī Gharā'ib al-Amṣār wa-ʿAjā'ib al-Asfār. Beirut: Dār Iḥyāj al-ʿUlūm, 1407/1987.

Ibn Faḍl Allāh al-ʿUmarī, Shihāb al-Dīn Aḥmad ibn Yaḥyā (701–749/1301–1348). *Masālik al-Abṣār fī Mamālik al-Amṣār*. 27 vols. Beirut: Dār al-Kutub al-ʿIlmiyyah, 2010.

Al-Taʿrīf bil-Muṣṭalaḥ al-Sharīf. Beirut: Dār al-Kutub al-ʿIlmiyyah, 1408/1988.

Ibn al-Faqīh, Abū Bakr Aḥmad ibn Muḥammad al-Hamadhānī (d. after 290/903). *Mukhtaṣar Kitāb al-Buldān*. Leiden: E. J. Brill, 1302/1885.

Ibn Fāris, Abū al-Ḥusayn Aḥmad ibn Zakariyyā (d. 395/1004). *Muʿjam Maqāyīs al-Lugha*. 6 vols. Beirut: Dār al-Fikr, 1399/1979.

Ibn Ḥajar ʿAsqalānī, Aḥmad Ibn ʿAlī ibn Muḥammad ibn ʿAlī (773–852/1372–1449). *Fatḥ al-Bārī*. 13 vols. Cairo: Dār al-Rayyān lil-Turāth, 1407/1986.

Ibn Ḥajar al-Haythamī, Shihāb al-Dīn Abū al-ʿAbbās ibn Muḥammad (909–974/1503–1566). *Tuḥfat al-Muḥtāj li-Sharḥ al-Minhāj*. 10 vols. Cairo: Al-Maktaba al-Tijāriyya al-Kubrā, 1357/1938.

Ibn Ḥazm, ʿAlī ibn Aḥmad ibn Saʿīd (384–456/994–1064). *Al-Muḥallā*. Amman: International Ideas Home, 1424/2003.

Ibn Hishām, Abū Muḥammad ʿAbd al-Malik (d. 212/828 or 218/833). *Al-Sīrah al-Nabawiyyah*. 4 vols. Beirut: Dār al-Kitāb al-ʿArabī, 1410/1990.

Ibn Isḥāq, Muḥammad ibn Yasār (85–151/704–768). *Al-Sīrah al-Nabawiyyah*. Beirut: Dār al-Kutub al-ʿIlmiyyah, 1424/2004. For the English translation, refer to: *The Life of Muhammad*: A Translation of Isḥāq's *Sīrat Rasūl Allāh*. Translated by Alfred Guillaume. Oxford: Oxford University Press, 1955.

Ibn Ja'far ibn Ziyād al-Baghdādī, Qudāma (d. 337/948). *Al-Kharāj wa-Ṣinā'at al-Kitāba*. Baghdad: Dār al-Rashīd lil-Nashr, 1981.

Ibn Jubayr, Muḥammad ibn Aḥmad (539–614/1144–1217). *The Travels of Ibn Jubayr*. Edited and translated by R. J. C. Broadhurst. London: Jonathan Cape, 1952.

Riḥlat Ibn Jubayr. Beirut: Dār Ṣāder, 1379/1959.

Ibn Kathīr, Abū al-Fidā' Ismā'īl ibn 'Umar al-Qurashī al-Dimashqī (700–774/1300–1373). *Al-Bidāya wa'l-Nihāyah*. 20 vols. Damascus: Dār Ibn Kathīr, 1431/2010.

Tafsīr Ibn Kathīr. 8 vols. Riyad: Dār Ṭība lil-Nashr, 1420/1999.

Al-Sīrah al-Nabawiyyah. 4 vols. Beirut: Dār al-Ma'rifa, 1395/1976. For the English translation, see *The Life of the Prophet Muḥammad (Al-Sīrah al-Nabawiyyah)*. Translated by Trevor Le Gassick. Reading: Garnet Publishing, 2000.

Ibn Khaldūn, 'Abd al-Raḥmān (732–808/1332–1406). *Kitāb al-'Ibar wa-Dīwān al-Mubtada' wa'l-Khabar fī Ayyām al-'Arab wa'l-'Ajam wa'l-Barbar wa-man 'Āṣarahum min Dhawī al-Sulṭān al-Akbar*. 7 vols. Beirut: Dār al-Kutub al-'Ilmiyyah, 1413/1992. For the English translation, see *The Muqaddimah: An Introduction to History*. Translated by Franz Rosenthal. Princeton: Princeton University Press, 1967. For the electronic version visit: https://asadullahali.files.wordpress.com/2012/10/ibn_khaldun-al_muqaddimah.pdf.

Ibn Khurdādhbih, Abū al-Qāsim 'Ubayd Allāh ibn 'Abd Allāh (205–300/820–912). *Al-Masālik wa'l-Mamālik*. Leiden, 1889.

Ibn Mājah, Abū 'Abd Allāh Muḥammad ibn Yazīd (209–273/824–886). *Sunan Ibn Mājah*. 2 vols. Cairo: Dār Iḥyā' al-Kutub al-'Arabiyya, 1372/1952.

Ibn Mājid, Shihāb al-Dīn Aḥmad ibn Mājid ibn 'Umar al-Najdī (823–914/1421–1509). *Kitāb al-Fawā'id fī Uṣūl 'Ilm al-Baḥr wa'l-Qawā'id*. Damascus: Al-Maṭba'a al-Ta'āwuniyya, 1971. For the English translation, see Gerald R. Tibbetts, *Arab Navigation in the Indian Ocean before the Coming of the Portuguese: Being a Translation of Kitāb al-Fawā'id fī Uṣūl 'Ilm al-Baḥr wa'l-Qawā'id of Aḥmad Ibn Mājid al-Najdī*. London: Royal Asiatic Society of Great Britain and Ireland, 1971.

Ibn Mammātī, Abū al-Makārim al-As'ad ibn al-Muhadhdhab ibn Mīnā ibn Zakariyyā (544–606/1149–1209). *Qawānīn al-Dawāwīn*. Cairo: Maṭba'at Miṣr, 1943.

Ibn Mankalī, Jalāl al-Dīm Muḥammad ibn Maḥmūd (d. 784/1382). *Al-Adilla al-Rasmiyya fī al-Ta'ābī al-Ḥarbiyya*. Edited by Maḥmūd Sh. Khaṭṭāb. Baghdad: Al-Majma' al-'Ilmī al-'Irāqī, 1988.

Ibn Manẓūr, Muḥammad ibn Mukarram ibn 'Alī (630–711/1232–1311). *Lisān al-'Arab*. 15 vols. Beirut: Dār Ṣāder, 2003.

Ibn al-Mujāwir, Jamāl al-Dīn Abū al-Fatḥ Yūsuf ibn Ya'qūb (601–691/1204–1291). *Ṣifat Bilād al-Yaman, wa-Makkah wa-ba'ẓ al-Ḥijāz al-Musammā Ta'rīkh al-Mustabṣir*. 2 vols. Cairo: Maktabat al-Thaqāfa al-Dīniyya, 1996.

Ibn al-Naḥḥās, Abū Zakariyyā Aḥmad ibn Ibrāhīm ibn Muḥammad al-Dimashqī (d. 814/1411). *Mashāri' al-Ashwāq ilā Maṣāri' al-'Ushshāq wa-Muthīr al-*

Gharām ilā Dār al-Islām. 2 vols. Riyad: Dār al-Nashr al-Islāmiyya, 1400/1990.

Ibn Qayyim al-Jawziyya, Muḥammad ibn Abū Bakr ibn Ayyūb ibn Sa'd (691–751/1292–1349). *Aḥkām Ahl al-Dhimma*. Al-Dammām: Ramādī lil-Nashr, 1418/1997.

Zād al-Ma'ād fī Hady Khayr al-'Ibād. 5 vols. Beirut: Mu'assasat al-Risālah, 1418/1998.

Ibn Qudāma, Muwaffaq al-Dīn Abd Allāh ibn Aḥmad al-Maqdisī (541–620/1147–1223). *Al-Mughnī*. 10 vols. Beirut: Dār Iḥyā' al-Turāth al-'Arabī, 1405/1985.

Ibn Rushd (al-Jadd/Grandfather), Abū al-Walīd Muḥammad ibn Aḥmad (450–520/1058–1126). *Al-Bayān wa'l-Taḥṣīl wa'l-Sharḥ wa'l-Tawjīh wa'l-Ta'līl fī Masā'il al Mustakhraja*. 20 vols. Beirut: Dār al-Gharb al-Isl āmī, 1984.

Ibn Rushd (Averroës), Abū al-Walīd Muḥammad ibn Aḥmad ibn Muḥammad (520–595/1126–1198). *The Distinguished Jurist's Primer*. Translated by Imran Nyazee. 2 vols. London: Garnet Publishing, 2002. Arabic text: *Sharḥ Bidāyat al-Mujtahid wa-Nihāyat al-Muqtaṣid. 4 vols*. Cairo: Dār al-Salām, 1416/1995.

Ibn Sa'd, Abū 'Abd Allāh Muḥammad ibn Manī' (168–230/784–845). *Al-Ṭabaqāt al-Kubrā*. 11 vols. Cairo: Maktabat al-Khānjī, 1421/2001.

Ibn Sallām, Abū 'Ubyad al-Qāsim al-Harawī (157–224/774–838). *Kitāb al-Amw āl*. Beirut: Dār al-Shurūq, 1409/1989.

Ibn Shahriyār, Buzurg (d. 399/1009). *The Book of Wonders of India*. Edited and translated by G. S. P. Freeman-Grenville. London: East–West Publication, 1981. For the text in Arabic, see *'Ajā'ib al-Hind*. Edited by Yousef al-Sharouni. London: Riad El-Rayyes Books, 1990.

Ibn Shu'ba al-Ḥarrānī, Abū Muḥammad al-Ḥasan ibn 'Alī ibn al-Ḥusayn (4th century AH/10th century CE). *Tuḥfat al-'Uqūl*. Qumm: Jamā'at al-Mudarris īn fī al-Ḥawza al-'Ilmiyya, 1404/1983.

Ibn Sirāj al-Andalusī, Abū al-Qāsim Muḥammad ibn Muḥammad (d. 848/1444). *Fatāwā Qāḍī al-Jamā'a*. Beirut: Dār Ibn Ḥazm, 1427/2006.

Ibn Taghrībirdī, Jamāl al-Dīn Yūsuf ibn al-Amīr Sayf al-Dīn (813–874/1410–1470). *Al-Nujūm al-Zāhira fī Mulūk Miṣr wa'l-Qāhira*. 16 vols. Cairo: Wizārat al-Thaqāfa, 1383/1963.

Ibn Taymiyya, Taqiyy al-Dīn Aḥmad ibn 'Abd al-Ḥalīm (663–728/1263–1328). *Majmū' Fatāwā Ibn Taymiyya*. 37 vols. Riyad: Majma' al-Malik Fahd, 1416/1995.

Fiqh al-Jihād. Beirut: Dār al-Fikr al-'Arabī, 1412/1992.

Ibn Zanjawayh, Ḥamīd ibn Mukhlid ibn Qutayba (180–251/796–865). *Kitāb al-Amwāl*. Edited by S. D. Fayyāḍ. Riyad: Markaz al-Malik Faisal lil-Buḥūth wa'l-Dirāsāt al-Islāmiyya, 1406/1986.

Idrīsī, Abū 'Abd Allāh Muḥammad ibn Muḥammad (493–560/1100–1164). *Nuzhat al-Mushtāq fī Ikhtirāq al-Āfāq*. 2 vols. Cairo: Maktabat al-Thaqāfa al-Dīniyya, 1422/2002.

Iṣṭakhrī, Abū Isḥāq Ibrāhīm ibn Muḥammad (d. 346/957). *Kitāb Masālik al-Mam ālik*. Leiden: E. J. Brill, 1870.

Jaṣṣāṣ, Abū Bakr Aḥmad ibn ʿAlī al-Rāzī (305–370/917–980). *Aḥkām al-Qurʾān*. 5 vols. Beirut: Dār Iḥyāʾ al-Turāth al-ʿArabī, 1412/1992.

Jawālīqī, Abū Manṣūr Mawhūb ibn Aḥmad ibn Muḥammad (465–540/1074–1144). *Al-Muʿarrab min al-Kalām al-Aʿjamī ʿalā Ḥurūf al-Muʿjam*. Damascus: Dār al-Qalam, 1410/1990.

Jāzim, Muḥammad ʿA. (ed.), *Nūr al-Maʿārif fī Nuzum wa-Qawānīn wa-Aʿrāf al-Yaman fī al-ʿAhd al-Muẓaffarī al-Wārif*. Sana'a: Centre français d'archéologie et de sciences sociales, 2003.

Jazīrī, ʿAlī ibn Yaḥyā (d. 585/1189). *Al-Maqṣad al-Maḥmūd fī Talkhīṣ al-ʿUqūd*. Madrid: Consejo Superior de Investigaciones Científicas, 1998.

Kāsānī, Abū Bakr Masʿūd ibn Aḥmad (d. 587/1191). *Badāʾiʿ al-Ṣanāʾiʿ fī Tartīb al-Sharāʾiʿ*. 7 vols. Beirut: Dār al-Kutub al-ʿIlmiyyah, 1406/1986.

Kawhajī, ʿAbd Allāh ibn al-Shaykh Ḥasan. *Zād al-Muḥtāj bi-Sharḥ al-Minhāj*. Doha: Al-Shuʾūn al-Dīniyya, 1402/1982.

Khosraw, Abū Muʿīn Ḥāmid al-Dīn Nāṣir-ī (395–481/1004–1088). *Book of Travels (Safarnāma)*. New York: State University of New York Press, 1986.

Kindī, Abū Bakr Aḥmad ibn ʿAbd Allāh ibn Mūsā (d. 557/1162). *Al-Muṣannaf*. 36 vols. Muscat: Wizārat al-Turāth al-Qawmī wa'l-Thaqāfa, 1983.

Makhzūmī, Abū al-Ḥasan ʿAlī ibn ʿUthmān (d. 585/1189). *Kitāb al-Minhāj fī ʿIlm Kharāj Miṣr*. Edited by Claude Cahen and Yūsuf Rāghib. Cairo: Institut Français d'Archéologie Orientale, 1986.

Malībārī, Aḥmad ibn ʿAbd al-ʿAziz ibn Zayn al-Dīn al-Maʿbarī (d. after 993/1585). *Tuḥfat al-Mujāhidīn fī Aḥwāl al-Burtughāliyyīn*. Beirut: Muʾassasat al-Wafāʾ, 1405/1985.

Maqrīzī, Taqiyy al-Dīn Aḥmad ibn ʿAlī (766–845/1364–1442). *Al-Mawāʿiz wa'l-Iʿtibār bi-Dhikr al-Khiṭaṭ wa'l-Āthār*. 3 vols. Cairo: Maktabat Madbouli, 1998.

Al-Sulūk li-Maʿrifat Duwal al-Mulūk. 8 vols. Beirut: Dār al-Kutub al-ʿIlmiyyah, 1418/1997.

Imtāʿ al-Asmāʿ bimā lil-Nabiyy Ṣallā Allāh ʿalyh wa-Sallam min al-Aḥwāl wa'l-Amwāl wa'l-Ḥafadah wa'l-Matāʿ. 15 vols. Beirut: Dār al-Kutub al-ʿIlmiyyah, 1420/1999.

Masʿūdī, Abū al-Ḥasan ʿAlī ibn al-Ḥusayn ibn ʿAlī (282–345/896–956). *Al-Tanb īh wa'l-Ishrāf*. Leiden: M. J. de Goeje, 1894.

Māwardī, Abū al-Ḥasan ʿAlī ibn Muḥammad ibn Ḥabīb (362–450/972–1058). *Al-Aḥkām al-Sulṭāniyya*. Bonn: Adolphum Marcum, 1269/1853.

The Ordinances of Government (Al-Aḥkām al-Sulṭāniyya wa'l-Wilāyāt al-Dīniyya). Translated by Asadullah Yate. London: Ta-Ha, 1996.

Al-Ḥāwī al-Kabīr fī Fiqh Madhhab al-Imām al-Shāfiʿī. 18 vols. Beirut: Dār al-Kutub al-ʿIlmiyyah, 1419/1999.

Māzarī, Abū ʿAbd Allāh Muḥammad ibn ʿAlī ibn ʿUmar (453–536/1061–1141). *Īḍāḥ al-Maḥṣūl min Burhān al-Uṣūl*. Beirut: Dār al-Gharb al-Islāmī, 1421/2001.

Fatāwā al-Māzarī. Qayrawān: Al-Dār al-Tūnisiyya lil-Nashr, 1994.

Mundhirī, Abū Muḥāmmad ʿAbd al-ʿAzīm ibn ʿAbd al-Qawiyy (581–656/1185–1258). *Al-Targhīb wa'l-Tarhīb min al-Ḥadīth al-Sharīf*. 4 vols. Beirut: Dār al-Kutub al-ʿIlmiyyah, 1417/1998.

Muqaddasī, Abū ʿAbd Allāh Muḥammad ibn Aḥmad (336–380/947–990). *Aḥsan al-Taqāsīm fī Maʿrifat al-Aqālīm*. Leiden: E. J. Brill, 1906. For the English translation, see *Aḥsan al-Taqāsīm fī Maʿrifat al-Aqālīm*, edited and translated by G. S. A. Ranking and R. F. Azoo. Calcutta: Asiatic Society of Bengal, 1897.

Nawawī, Abū Zakariyyā Yaḥyā ibn Sharaf (631–676/1233–1277). *Rawḍat al-Ṭālibīn wa-ʿUmdat al-Muftīn*. 12 vols. Beirut: Al-Maktab al-Islāmī, 1412/1991.

Al-Majmūʿ. 23 vols. Jeddah: Maktabat al-Irshād, 1405/1984.

Qalqashandī, Aḥmad ibn ʿAlī (765–821/1355–1418). *Ṣubḥ al-Aʿshā fī Ṣināʿat al-Inshā*. 14 vols. Cairo: Al-Maṭbaʿa al-Amīriyya, 1338/1919.

Qarāfī, Shihāb al-Dīn Abū al-ʿAbbās ibn Idrīs (626–684/1229–1285). *Al-Dhakhīra*. 14 vols. Beirut: Dār al-Gharb al-Islāmī, 1415/1994.

Qurṭubī, Abū ʿAbd Allāh Muḥammad ibn Aḥmad (d. 671/1273). *Al-Jāmiʿ li-Aḥkām al-Qurʾān*. 20 vols. Beirut: Dār al-Fikr lil-Ṭibāʿa wa'l-Nashr, 1414/1994.

Rafīʿ, Abū Isḥāq Ibrāhīm ibn Ḥasan (639–733/1241–1333). *Muʿīn al-Ḥukkām ʿalā al-Qaḍāyā wa'l-Aḥkām*. 2 vols. Beirut: Dār al-Gharb al-Islāmī, 1989.

Ramlī, Muḥammad ibn Abū al-ʿAbbās Aḥmad ibn Shihāb al-Dīn (d. 1004/1595). *Nihāyat al-Muḥtāj ilā Sharḥ al-Minhāj*. 8 vols. Beirut: Dār al-Fikr lil-Ṭibāʿa, 1404/1984.

Raṣṣāʿ, Abū ʿAbd Allāh Muḥammad (d. 894/1489). *Sharḥ Ḥudūd Ibn ʿArafa*. 2 vols. Beirut: Dār al-Gharb al-Islāmī, 1993.

Rāzī, Abū ʿAbd Allāh Muḥammad ibn ʿUmar ibn al-Ḥusayn (543–606/1148–1209). *Al-Tafsīr al-Kabīr (Mafātīḥ al-Ghayb)*. 32 vols. Beirut: Dār al-Fikr lil-Ṭibāʿa wa'l-Nashr, 1401/1981.

Samarqandī, Kamāl al-Dīn ʿAbd al-Razzāq ibn Isḥāq (816–887/1413–1482). *Maṭlaʿ al-Saʿdayn wa-Majmaʿ al-Baḥrayn* (*The Dawn of Two Auspicious Planets and the Meeting of the Two Seas*). In *India in the Fifteenth Century: Being a Collection of Voyages to India*. Edited and translated by R. H. Major. London: Hakluyt Society, 1857.

Sarakhsī, Muḥammad ibn Aḥmad ibn Abī Sahl (d. 490/1097). *Sharḥ Kitāb al-Siyar al-Kabīr*. 5 vols. Beirut: Dār al-Kutub al-ʿIlmiyyah, 1417/1997.

Al-Mabsūṭ. 30 vols. Beirut: Dār al-Maʿrifa, 1409/1989.

Shāfiʿī, Abū ʿAbd Allāh Muḥammad ibn Idrīs (150–204/767–820). *Al-Umm*. 8 vols. Beirut: Dār al-Fikr lil-Ṭibāʿa wa'l-Nashr, 1403/1983.

Aḥkām al-Qurʾān. 2 vols. Cairo: Maktabat al-Khānjī, 1414/1994.

Sharafī, ʿAlī ibn Aḥmad ibn Muḥammad al-Ṣifāqsī (fl. 1551–1579). *Sea Atlas Made by ʿAlī Ibn Muḥammad al-Sharafī al-Ṣifāqsi*. Manuscript (1551 CE), Arabe 2278, Bibliothèque nationale de France.

Shiqṣī, Khamīs ibn Saʿīd (17th century). *Manhaj al-Ṭālibīn wa-Balāgh al-Rāshidīn*. 16 vols. Muscat: Wizārat al-Awqāf wa'l-Shuʾūn al-Dīniyya, 1403/1983.

Sīrāfī, Abū Zayd Ḥasan ibn Yazīd (d. after 330/941). *Riḥlat al-Sīrāfī*. Abu Dhabī: Al-Majmaʿ al-Thaqāfī, 1999.

Sulaymān al-Tājir (3rd century AH/9th century CE). *ʿAjāʾib al-Dunyā wa-Qiyās al-Buldān* (composed in 237 AH/851 CE). Edited by Saif Sh. al-Muraikhi. Al-

'Ayn: Markaz Zāyid lil-Turāth wa'l-Tārīkh, 1426/2005. For the French edition, see Ferrand, Gabriel. *Voyage du marchand arabe Sulaymān en Inde et en Chine rédigé en 851*. Paris: Éditions Bossard, 1922.

Sulaymī, 'Izz al-Dīn ibn 'Abd al-Salām (d. 660/1262). *Aḥkām al-Jihād wa-Fa ḍā'ilihi*. Damascus: Dār al-Fikr, 1417/1996.

Suyūṭī, 'Abd al-Raḥmān ibn Abū Bakr ibn Muḥammad (849–911/1445–1505). *Al-Bāḥa fī Faḍl al-Sibāḥa*. Ṭanṭā: Dār al-Ṣaḥāba lil-Turāth, 1411/1990.

Al-Ḥāwī lil-Fatāwī. 2 vols. Cairo: Al-Ṭibā'a al-Munīriyya, 1352/1933.

Ṭabarānī, Abū al-Qāsim Sulaymān ibn Aḥmad ibn Ayyūb (260–360/821–920). *Al-Mu'jam al-Kabīr*. 20 vols. Mosul: Maktabat al-'Ulūm wa'l-Ḥikam, 1404/ 1983.

Ṭabarī, Abū Ja'far Muḥammad ibn Jarīr (224–310/839–923). *Tafsīr al-Ṭabarī: Jāmi' al-Bayān 'an Ta'wīl Āy al-Qur'ān*. 24 vols. Beirut: Mu'assasat al-Ris ālah, 1420/2000.

Tārīkh al-Rusul wa'l-Mulūk. 11 vols. Cairo: Dār al-Ma'ārif, 1387/1967.

Ṭāher, Muṣṭafā A. (ed.). "*Kitāb Akriyat al-Sufun wa'l-Nizā' bayna Ahlihā*." *Cahiers de Tunisie* 31 (1983): 5–54.

Tanūkhī, Saḥnūn ibn Sa'īd (160–240/776–854). *Al-Mudawwanah al-Kubrā*. 4 vols. Beirut: Dār al-Kutub al-'Ilmiyyah, 1415/1994.

Tirmidhī, Abū 'Īsā Muḥammad ibn 'Īsā (209–279/824–892). *Sunan al-Tirmidhī*. Beirut: Dār al-Kutub al-'Ilmiyyah, 1408/1987.

Tujībī, Muḥāmmad ibn Aḥmad ibn 'Abdūn (12th century CE). *Séville Musulmane au début du XIIe Siècle, le Traité d'Ibn 'Abdūn*. Edited by Évariste Levi-Provençal. Paris: G. P. Maisonneuve, 1947.

'Ukbarī, Abū al-Baqā' 'Abd Allāh ibn al-Ḥussein (538–616/1143–1219). *Al-Tiby ān fī I'rāb al-Qur'ān*. 2 vols. Beirut: Dār al-Fikr, 1421/2001.

Wansharīsī, Abū al-'Abbās Aḥmad ibn Yaḥyā (834–914/1430–1508). *Al-Mi'yār al-Mu'rib wa'l-Jāmi' al-Mughrib 'an Fatāwā Ahl Ifrīqiya wa'l-Andalus wa'l-Maghrib*. 13 vols. Beirut: Dār al-Gharb al-Islāmī, 1981.

"Asnā al-Matājir fī Bayān Aḥkām Man Ghalaba 'alā Waṭanihi al-Naṣārā wa-lam Yuhājir." Edited by Ḥusayn Mu'nis. Revista del Instituto Egipcio de Estudios Islamicos en Madrid 5 (1957): 1–63 (also numbered 129–191).

Wāqidī, Abū 'Abd Allāh Muḥammad ibn 'Umar (130–207/747–822). *Al-Magh āzī*. 3 vols. Beirut: 'Ālam al-Kutub, 1404/1984.

Wazzān, al-Ḥasan ibn Muḥammad/Leo Africanus (888–957/1483–1550?). *Waṣf Ifrīqiya*. Beirut: Dār al-Gharb al-Islāmī, 1983.

Ya'murī, Abū al-Fatḥ Muḥammad ibn Muḥammad ibn Sayyid al-Nās (671–734/1272–1334). *Uyūn al-Athar fī Funūn al-Maghāzī wa'l-Shamā'il wa'l-Siyar*. 2 vols. Medina: Maktabat Dār al-Turāth, 1408/1987.

Yāqūt, Shihāb al-Dīn Abū 'Abd Allāh ibn 'Abd Allāh al-Ḥamawī (574–626/1179–1229). *Mu'jam al-Buldān*. 5 vols. Beirut: Dār Ṣāder, 1986.

Zabīdī, al-Murtaḍā Muḥammad ibn Muḥammad (1145–1205/1732–1790). *Itḥāf al-Sāda al-Muttaqīn bi-Sharḥ Iḥyā' 'Ulūm al-Dīn*. 10 vols. Beirut: Mu'assasat al-Tārīkh al-'Arabī, 1414/1994.

Zajjāj, Abū Isḥāq Ibrāhīm ibn al-Sarī (241–311/855–923). *Ma'āni al-Qur'ān wa-I'rābuh*. 5 vols. Beirut: 'Ālam al-Kitāb, 1408/1988.

Zarkashī, Abū 'Abd Allāh Badr al-Dīn Muḥammad ibn Bahadur (745–794/1344–1392). *Al-Baḥr al-Muḥīṭ*. 8 vols. Amman: Dar al-Katbī lil-Nashr, 1414/1994.

CLASSICAL, RENAISSANCE, AND EARLY MODERN EUROPEAN LEGAL WORKS AND LITERATURE TO C.1900

Ashburner, Walter. *The Rhodian Sea Law*. Oxford: Clarendon Press, 1909.

Azuni, Domenico A. (1749–1827). *The Maritime Law of Europe*. 2 vols. New York: George Forman, 1806.

Barbosa, Duarte (1480–1521). *A Description of the Coasts of East Africa and Malabar in the Beginning of the Sixteenth Century*. Translated by Henry E. Stanley. London: Hakluyt Society, 1866.

Buckland, William W. *A Text-Book of Roman Law from Augustus to Justinian*. 3rd ed. Edited and revised by Peer Stein. Cambridge: Cambridge University Press, 1963.

Driver, Godfrey R. and Miles, John C. *The Babylonian Laws*. 2 vols. Oxford: Clarendon Press, 1952–1955.

Fulton, Thomas W. *The Sovereignty of the Sea: An Historical Account of the Claims of England to the Dominion of the British Seas, and of the Evolution of the Territorial Waters, with Special Reference to the Rights of Fishing and the Naval Salute*. Edinburgh: William Blackwood and Sons, 1911.

Freshfield, Edwin H. *A Manual of Later Roman Law: The Ecloga*. Cambridge: Cambridge University Press, 1927.

Grotius, Hugo (1583–1645). *The Free Sea*. Translated by Richard Hakluyt, edited and with an Introduction by David Armitage. Indianapolis: Liberty Fund, 2004.

The Freedom of the Seas, or the Right Which Belongs to the Dutch to Take Part in the East Indian Trade. Edited and translated by Ralph V. Magoffin. New York: Oxford University Press, 1916.

On the Rights of War and Peace: An Abridged Translation. Translated by William Whewell. Cambridge: Cambridge University Press, 1853.

Hunter, William A. (1844–1898). *A Systematic and Historical Exposition of Roman Law*. London: William Maxwell and Son, 1885.

Justice, Alexander. *A General Treatise of the Dominion of the Sea*. London: n.p., 1724.

Letsios, Dimitrios G. *Nomos Rhodion Nautikos-Das Seegesetz der Rhodier: Untersuchungen zu Seerecht und Handelsschiffahrt in Byzanz*. Rhodes: Institouto Aigaiou tou Dikaiou tes Thalassas kai tou Nautikou Diakiou, 1996.

Marsden, Reginald G. (ed.). *Select Pleas in the Court of Admiralty*. 2 vols. London: Bernard Quaritch, 1894–1897.

Pharr, Clyde, Davidson, Theresa S., and Pharr, Mary B. (ed.). *Theodosian Code and Novels and the Sirmondian Constitutions*. Princeton: Princeton University Press, 1952.

Polo, Marco (1254–1327). *The Travels of Marco Polo*. Translated by John Frampton. New York: Macmillan, 1937.

Procopius of Caesarea (500–565 CE). *Secret History*, or *Anecdota*. Translated by Richard Atwater. Chicago: P. Covici, 1927.
Renaudot, Eusèbe. *Ancient Accounts of India and China by Two Mohammedan Travellers Who Went to Those Parts in the 9th Century*. London: S. Harding, 1733.
Sandars, Thomas C. (ed.). *The Institutes of Justinian*. London: Longmans, Green and Co., 1917.
Schomberg, Alexander C. (1756–1792). *A Treatise on the Maritime Laws of Rhodes*. Oxford: n.p., 1786.
Scott, Samuel P. (ed.). *Las Siete Partidas*. 5 vols. Philadelphia: University of Pennsylvania Press, 2001.
(ed.). *The Civil Law*. 17 vols. Cincinnati: Central Trust Company, 1932.
Selden, John (1584–1654). *Of the Dominion or Ownership of the Sea*. London: William Du-Gard, 1652.
Shamasastry, Rudrapatnam (ed.). *Kautilya's Arthashastra*. Bangalore: Government Press, 1915). https://archive.org/details/Arthasastra_English_Translation.
Twiss, Travers (1809–1897). *Law of Nations Considered as Political Communities: On the Rights and Duties of in Time of Peace*. Oxford: Clarendon Press, 1884.
"The Exterritoriality of Public Ships of War in Foreign Waters." *Law Magazine and Review* 3 (1876): 201–234.
Van Bynkershoek, Cornelius (1673–1743). Questions of Public Law. Translated by Tenney Frank. www.constitution.org/bynk/bynk.htm.
Vattel, Emer de (1714–1767). *The Law of Nations*. Edited by Béla Kapossy and Richard Whatmore. Indianapolis: Liberty Fund, 2008.
Velho, Álvaro (15th–16th century). *A Journal of the First Voyage of Vasco da Gama 1497–1499*. London: Hakluyt Society, 1898.
Von Pufendorf, Samuel (1632–1694). *Of the Law of Nature and Nations*. 4th ed. Translated by Basil Kennett. London, 1729.

TREATIES, LETTERS, AND DOCUMENTARY EVIDENCE

Abu Safieh, Jaser. *Bardiyyāt Qurra Ibn Sharīk al-ʿAbsī*. Riyad: Markaz al-Malik Faiṣal lil-Buḥūth wa'l-Dirāsāt al-Islāmiyya, 1425/2004.
Amari, Michele. *Nuovi Ricordi Arabici su la Storia di Genova*. Genova: Tipografia del R. Istituto sordo-muti, 1873.
I Diplomi Arabi del R. Archivio Fiorentino. Florence: Dalla Tipografia di Felice le Monnier, 1863.
Assaf, Simcha. *Gaonic Responsa from Geniza Manuscripts*. Jerusalem: Darom Publishing, 1970 (Hebrew).
Azzaoui, Ahmed. *Rasāʾil Muwaḥḥidiyya*. 2 vols. Kénitra: Université Ibn Tofayl, 1416/1995.
Bauden, Frédéric. "Due trattati di pace conclusi nel dodicesimo secolo tra i Banū Ġāniya, signori delle isole Baleari, e il commune di Genova." In *Documentos y manuscritos árabes del Occidente musulmán medieval*. Edited by Nuria

Martínez de Castilla. Madrid: Consejo Superior de Investigaciones Científicas, 2010: 33–86.

Bell, H. Idris and Kenyon, Frederic G. *Greek Papyri in the British Museum*. 5 vols. London: British Museum, 1893–1917.

Ben-Sasson, Menahem. *The Jews of Sicily 825–1068: Documents and Sources*. Jerusalem: Ben-Zvi Institute, 1991 (Hebrew).

Burns, Robert I. *Islam under the Crusaders: Colonial Survival in the Thirteenth-Century Kingdom of Valencia*. Princeton: Princeton University Press, 1973.

"The *Guidaticum* Safe-Conduct in Medieval Arago-Catalonia: A Mini-Institution for Muslims, Christians, and Jews." *Medieval Encounters* 1 (1995): 51–113.

Chevedden, Paul E. "The 1244 Treaty: Arabic Text and Analysis." In *Negotiating Cultures: Bilingual Surrender Treaties in Muslim-Crusader Spain under James the Conqueror*. Edited by Robert I. Burns and Paul E. Chevedden. Leiden: E. J. Brill, 1999: 158–194.

De Epalza, Mikel. "*ʿAhd*: Muslim/Mudejar/Morisco Communities and Spanish-Christian Authorities." In *Negotiating Cultures: Bilingual Surrender Treaties in Muslim-Crusader Spain under James the Conqueror*. Edited by Robert I. Burns and Paul E. Chevedden. Leiden: E. J. Brill, 1999: 195–212.

Gil, Moshe. *In the Kingdom of Ishmael: Texts from the Cairo Geniza*. 4 vols. Tel Aviv: Tel Aviv University Press, 1997 (Hebrew).

A History of Palestine 634–1099. Cambridge: Cambridge University Press, 1992.

Palestine during the First Muslim Period 654–1099. 3 vols. Tel Aviv: Tel Aviv University and the Ministry of Defense Publishing House, 1983 (Hebrew). For the English translation of the historical part, see *A History of Palestine 634–1099*. Cambridge: Cambridge University Press, 1992.

"The Rādhānite Merchants and the Land of Rādhān." *Journal of the Economic and Social History of the Orient* 17 (1974): 299–328.

Goitein, Shelomo D. *A Mediterranean Society: The Jewish Communities of the Arab World as Portrayed in the Documents of the Cairo Geniza*. 6 vols. Berkeley: University of California, 1967–1993.

"Portrait of a Medieval India Trader: Three Letters from the Cairo Geniza." *Bulletin of the School of Oriental and African Studies* 50 (1987): 449–464.

The Yemenites: History Communal Organization, Spiritual Life. Edited by Menahem Ben Sasson. Jerusalem: Ben Zvi Institute, 1983 (Hebrew).

Letters of Medieval Jewish Traders. Princeton: Princeton University Press, 1973.

Studies in Islamic History and Institutions. Leiden: E. J. Brill, 1968.

"Jewish Trade in the Mediterranean at the Beginning of the Eleventh Century." *Tarbiz* 36.1 (1967): 366–395; 36.2: 48–77; 36.3: 158–190 (Hebrew).

"From the Mediterranean to India: Documents on the Trade to India, South Arabia, and East Africa from the Eleventh and Twelfth Centuries." *Speculum* 29 (1954): 181–197.

Goitein, Shelomo D. and Friedman, Mordechai A. *India Traders of the Middle Ages: Documents from the Cairo Geniza*. Leiden: E. J. Brill, 2008.

Ḥamāda, Muḥammad M. *Al-Wathāʾiq al-Siyāsiyya wa'l-Idāriyya fī al-Andalus wa-Shamāliyy Ifrīqiya* (64–897/683–1492). Beirut: Muʾassasat al-Risālah, 1406/1986.

Al-Wathā'iq al-Siyāsiyya wa'l-Idāriyya lil-'Aṣr al-Mamlūkī (656–922/1258–1516). Beirut: Mu'assasat al-Risālah, 1403/1983.

Ḥamīdullāh, Muḥammad. *Al-Wathā'iq al-Siyāsiyya lil-'Ahd al-Nabawī wa'l-Khilāfa al-Rāshida*. 6th ed. Beirut: Dār al-Nafā'is, 1407/1987.

The Muslim Conduct of State. 5th ed. Lahore: Sh. Muhammad Ashraf, 1968.

Holmes, Catherine. "Treaties between Byzantium and the Islamic World." In *War and Peace in Ancient and Medieval History*. Edited by Philip de Souza and John France. Cambridge: Cambridge University Press, 2008: 141–157.

Holt, Peter M. *Early Mamluk Diplomacy* (1260–1290). Leiden: E. J. Brill, 1995.

"Mamluk-Frankish Diplomatic Relations in the Reign of Qalāwūn (678–89/1279–90)." *Journal of the Royal Asiatic Society* (New Series) 121 (1989): 278–289.

"The Treaties of the Early Mamluk Sultans with the Frankish States." *Bulletin of the School of Oriental and African Studies* 43 (1980): 67–76.

"Qalāwūn's Treaty with Acre in 1283." *English Historical Review* 91 (1976): 802–812.

Jamīlī, Khalid R. *Aḥkām al-Mu'āhadāt fī al-Sharī'ah al-Islāmiyya: Taḥlīl al-Mu 'āhadāt al-Mubrama fī 'Aṣr al-Rasūl*. Baghdad: Markaz al-Buḥūth wa'l-Dirāsāt al-Islāmiyya, 2008.

Khan, Geoffrey. *Arabic Legal and Administrative Documents in the Cambridge Genizah Collections*. Cambridge: Cambridge University Press, 1993.

"A Copy of a Decree from the Archives of the Fāṭimīd Chancery in Egypt." *Bulletin of the School of Oriental and African Studies* 49 (1986): 439–453.

Korobeinikov, Dimitri A. "Diplomatic Correspondence between Byzantium and the Mamlūk Sultanate in the Fourteenth Century." *Al-Masaq* 16 (2010): 53–74.

Luckenbill, Daniel D. "Hittite Treaties and Letters." *American Journal of Semitic Languages and Literatures* 37 (1921): 161–211.

Martin, M. E. "The Venetian–Seljuk Treaty of 1220." *English Historical Review* 95 (1980): 321–330.

Mas Latrie, Louis. *Traité de paix et de commerce et documents divers concernant les relations des chrétiens avec les Arabes de l'Afrique septentrionale au Moyen Âge*. 2 vols. Paris: Henri Plon, 1866.

Miyānjī, 'Alī al-Aḥmadī. *Makātīb al-Rasūl*. 3 vols. Beirut: Dār Ṣa'b, 2013.

Morrow, John A. *The Covenants of the Prophet Muhammad with Christians of the World*. Kettering, OH: Angelico Press, Sophia Perennis, 2013.

Moukarzel, Pierre. "Venetian Merchants in Thirteenth-Century Alexandria and the Sultans of Egypt: An Analysis of Treaties, Privileges and Intercultural Relations." *Al-Masāq* 28 (2016): 187–205.

Parpola, Simo and Watanabe, Kazuko. *Neo-Assyrian Treaties and Loyalty Oaths, State Archives of Assyria*. Helsinki: Helsinki University Press, 1988.

Penna, Daphne. *The Byzantine Imperial Acts to Venice, Pisa and Genoa, 10th–12th Centuries: A Comparative Legal Study*. Groningen: Eleven International Publishing, 2012.

"Piracy and Reprisal in Byzantine Waters: Resolving a Maritime Conflict between Byzantines and Genoese at the End of the Twelfth Century." *Comparative Legal History* 5 (2017): 36–52.

"Venetian Judges and Their Jurisdiction in Constantinople in the 12th Century: Some Observations based on Information Drawn from the Chrysobull of Alexios III Angelos to Venice in 1198." *Subseciva Groningana, Studies in Roman and Byzantine Law* 8 (2009): 135–146.

Stern, Samuel M. "Petitions from the Ayyūbid Period." *Bulletin of the School of Oriental and African Studies* 27 (1964): 1–32.

"Three Petitions of the Fāṭimīd Period." *Oriens* 15 (1962): 172–209.

Theunissen, Hans. "Ottoman-Venetian Diplomatics: The *ʿAhd-names*: The Historical Background and the Development of a Category of Political-Commercial Instruments Together with an Annotated Edition of a Corpus of Relevant Documents." *Electronic Journal of Oriental Studies* 1 (2) (1998): 1–698.

Viladrich, Mercè. "Solving the 'Accursed Riddle' of the Diplomatic Relations between Catalonia and Egypt around 1430." *Al-Masāq* 14 (2002): 25–31.

Wakil, Ahmed. "The Prophet's Treaty with the Christians of Najran: An Analytical Study to Determine the Authenticity of the Covenants." *Journal of Islamic Studies* 27 (2016): 273–354.

Wansbrough, John. "The Safe-Conduct in Muslim Chancery Practice." *Bulletin of the School of Oriental and African Studies* 34 (1971): 20–35.

"A Mamluk Commercial Treaty Concluded with the Republic of Florence, 894/1489." In *Documents from Islamic Chanceries*. Edited by Samuel M. Stern. Oxford: Bruno Cassirer, 1965: 39–79.

"Venice and Florence in the Mamluk Commercial Privileges." *Bulletin of the School of Oriental and African Studies* 28 (1965): 483–523.

"A Moroccan Amīr's Commercial Treaty with Venice of the Year 913/1508." *Bulletin of the School of Oriental and African Studies* 25 (1962): 449–471.

"A Mamluk Letter of 877/1473." *Bulletin of the School of Oriental and African Studies* 24 (1961): 200–213.

SECONDARY LITERATURE

Ābādī, Abū al-Ṭayyib Muḥammad Shams al-Ḥaqq. *ʿAwn al-Maʿbūd: Sharḥ Sunan Abī Dāwūd*. Beirut: Dār al-Fikr, 1415/1995.

Abbadi, Mostafa. "A Code of Navigation on the Nile in Greco-Roman Egypt." *Graeco-Arabica* 4 (1991): 157–162.

ʿAbbās, Iḥsān. "Ittiḥād al-Baḥriyyīn fī Bajjāna bil-Andalus." *Al-Abḥāth* 23 (1970): 3–14.

ʿAbd al-ʿAleem, Anwar. *Al-Milāḥa wa-ʿUlūm al-Biḥār ʿind al-ʿArab*. Kuwait: Al-Majlis al-Waṭanī lil-Thaqāfa, 1979.

ʿAbd al-Fattāḥ, Ṣafāʾ. *Al-Mawāniʾ wa'l-Thughūr al-Miṣriyya min al-Fatḥ al-Isl āmī ḥattā al-ʿAṣr al-Fāṭimī*. Cairo: Dār al-Fikr al-ʿArabī, 1986.

ʿAbd al-Rahim, Muddathir. "Asylum: A Moral and Legal Right in Islam." *Refugee Survey Quarterly* 27 (2008): 15–23.

Abdul-Raof, Hussein. *Qur'an Translation: Discourse, Texture and Exegesis*. Richmond: Curzon Press, 2001.

Abou el-Fadl, Khaled. *Rebellion and Violence in Islamic Law*. Cambridge: Cambridge University Press, 2001.

"The Death Penalty, Mercy, and Islam: A Call for Retrospection." In *Religion and the Death Penalty: A Call for Reckoning*. Edited by Erik C. Owens, John D. Carlson, and Eric P. Elshtain. Michigan: William B. Eerdmans, 2004: 73–105.

"Islamic Law and Muslim Minorities: The Juristic Discourse on Muslim Minorities from the Second/Eighth to the Eleventh/Seventeenth Centuries." *Islamic Law and Society* 1 (1994): 141–187.

"Legal Debate on Muslim Minorities: Between Rejection and Accommodation." *Journal of Religious Ethics* 22 (1994): 127–162.

"Tax Farming in Islamic Law (*Qibālah* and *Ḍamān* of *Kharāj*): A Search for a Concept." *Islamic Studies* 31 (1992): 5–32.

Abu Lughod, Janet. *Before European Hegemony: The World System A.D. 1250–1350*. Oxford: Oxford University Press, 1989.

Abu Munshar, Maher. *Islamic Jerusalem and Its Christians: A History of Tolerance and Tension*. London: Taurus Academic Studies, 2007.

Abu Salieh, Sami A. "The Islamic Conception of Migration." *International Migration Review* 30 (1996): 37–57.

Abulafia, David. *A Mediterranean Emporium: The Catalan Kingdom of Majorca*. Cambridge: Cambridge University Press, 1994.

"Christian Merchants in the Almohad Cities." *Journal of Medieval Iberian Studies* 2 (2010): 251–257.

"Crocuses and Crusaders: San Gimignano, Pisa and the Kingdom of Jerusalem." In: *Outremer: Studies in the History of the Crusading Kingdom of Jerusalem Presented to Joshua Prawer*. Edited by B. Z. Kedar, H. E. Mayer, and R. C. Smail. Jerusalem: Yad Izhak Ben-Zvi, 1982: 227–243.

"Pisan Commercial Colonies and Consulates in Twelfth-Century Sicily." *English Historical Review* 93 (1978): 68–81.

Abu-Sahlieh, Sami A. "The Islamic Conception of Migration." *International Migration Review* 30 (1996): 37–57.

Afsaruddin, Asma. *Striving in the Path of God: Jihad and Martyrdom in Islamic Thought*. Oxford: Oxford University Press, 2013.

Agius, Dionisius A. *Siculo Arabic*. New York: Routledge, 2010.

Classic Ships of Islam: From Mesopotamia to the Indian Ocean. Leiden: E. J. Brill, 2008.

Ahamat, Haniff. "The Position of *Siyar* on Free Trade: A Historico-Legal Analysis." *Journal of the History of International Law* 12 (2010): 307–327.

Aḥmad, Aḥmad R. *Tārīkh Fann al-Qitāl al-Baḥrī fī al-Baḥr al-Mutawassiṭ 35–978/655–1571*. Cairo: Wizārat al-Thaqāfa, 1986.

Ahmad, Ali. "Righting Public Wrongs and Enforcing Private Rights: Public Involvement in Islamic Law." In *The New "Public": The Globalization of Public Participation*. Edited by Carl Bruch. Washington DC: Environmental Law Institute, 2002: 39–52.

Ahmad, Aziz. *A History of Islamic Sicily*. Edinburgh: Edinburgh University Press, 1975.

Aḥmad, Muṣṭafā. *Al-Qabā'il al-'Arabiyya fī al-Andalus ḥattā Suqūṭ al-Khilāfa al-Umawiyya* (91–422/710–1031). Casablanca: Dār al-Nashr al-Maghribiyya, 1983.

Ahmed, Ziauddin. "The Concept of Jizya in Early Islam." *Islamic Studies* 14 (1975): 293–305.

Ahmedov, Aibek S. "Origins of Law of Religious Minorities in Islam: Evolution of Concept of *Dhimmī* as Portrayed in Early Sources." *Journal of Islamic State Practices in International Law* 3 (2007): 23–47.

Akhtar, Shameem. "An Inquiry into the Nature, Origin, and Source of Islamic Law of Nations." *Islamic Studies* 10 (1971): 23–37.

Aldahesh, Ali Y. "(Un)Translatability of the Qur'ān: A Theoretical Perspective." *International Journal of Linguistics* 6 (2014): 23–45.

Alexandrowicz, Charles H. *An Introduction to the History of the Law of the Nations in the East Indies (16th, 17th and 18th Centuries)*. Oxford: Clarendon Press, 1967.

"Kautilyan Principles and the Law of Nations." *British Year Book of International Law* 41 (1965–1966): 301–320.

"Freitas *versus* Grotius." *British Yearbook of International Law* 35 (1959): 162–182.

Alpers, Edward A. *The Indian Ocean in World History*. New York and Oxford: Oxford University Press, 2014.

"Piracy and Indian Ocean." *Journal of African Development* 13 (2011): 17–38.

Amitai, Reuven. "Diplomacy and the Slave Trade in the Eastern Mediterranean: A Re-Examination of the Mamluk–Byzantine–Genoese Triangle in the Late Thirteenth Century in Light of the Existing Early Correspondence." *Oriente Moderno* 88 (2008): 349–368.

Amro, Rachid. "Le '*ṣāḥib al-aḥkām*' à l'époque almoravide." *Al-Andalus Maghreb: Estudios árabes e islámicos* 8–9 (2000–2001): 49–64.

Anand, Ram P. *Origin and Development of the Law of the Sea*. The Hague: Martinus Nijhoff. 1982.

"The Influence of History on the Literature of International Law." In *The Structure and Process of International Law*. 2nd ed. Edited by R. St. J. MacDonald and D. M. Johnston. The Hague: Martinus Nijhoff Publishers, 1986: 341–380.

"Maritime Practice in South-East Asia until 1600 A.D. and the Modern Law of the Sea." *International and Comparative Law Quarterly* 30 (1981): 440–454.

Anas, S. "In Search of Medieval Asian Seafarers and Islamic World System." *International Journal of South Asian Studies* 5 (2012): 42–56.

Andaya, Leonard Y. *The Heritage of Arung Palakka: A History of South Sulawesi (Celebes) in the Seventeenth Century*. The Hague: Martinus Nijhoff, 1981.

Anderson, Glaire D. "Islamic Spaces and Diplomacy in Constantinople (Tenth to Thirteenth Centuries C.E.)." *Medieval Encounters* 15 (2009): 86–113.

Anderson, John. "Chinese Mohammedans." *Journal of the Anthropological Institute of Great Britain and Ireland* 1 (1872): 147–162.

ʿAqqād, ʿAbbās M. *Al-Insān fī al-Qur'ān*. Cairo: Mu'assasat Hindawi Foundation for Education and Culture, 2013.

Arslān, Shakīb. *Al-Ḥulal al-Sundusiyya fī al-Akhbār wa'l-Āthār al-Andalusiyya*. 2 vols. Cairo: Al-Maṭbaʿa al-Raḥmāniyya, 1355/1936.

Arunachalam, A. "Technology of Indian Ocean Navigation (c. 1200-c. 1800)." *Medieval History Journal* 11 (2008): 187–227.
Ataman, Muhittin. "Islamic Perspective on Ethnicity and Nationalism." *Journal of Muslim Minority Affairs* 23 (2003): 89–102.
Atkinson, Kathleen M. "Rome and the Rhodian Sea-Law." *Iura* 25 (1974): 46–98.
Awa, Mohamed S. *Punishment in Islamic Law*. Plainfield: American Trust Publication, 2000.
ʿAwwād, Maḥmūd A. *Al-Jaysh wa'l-Usṭūl al-Islāmī fī al-ʿAṣr al-Umawī*. Hebron: Al-Adabiyya lil-Ṭibāʿa wa'l-Nashr, 1994.
Ayoub, Samy. "Territorial Jurisprudence, *Ikhtilaf al-Darayn*: Political Boundaries and Legal Jurisdiction." *Contemporary Islamic Studies* 2 (2012), 1–14. Available at: http://dx.doi.org/10.5339/cis.2012.2.
Baader, Hannah and Wolf, Gerhard. "A Sea-to-Shore Perspective: Littoral and Liminal Spaces of the Medieval and Early Modern Mediterranean." *Mitteilungen des Kunsthistorischen Institutes in Florenz* 56 (2014): 2–15.
Badr, Gamal M. "A Survey of Islamic International Law." *American Society of International Law Proceedings* 76 (1982): 56–61.
Bagader, Abubakr, el-Sabbagh, Abdullatif, al-Glayand, Mohamad, and Samarrai, Mawil. *Environmental Protection in Islam*. Gland, Switzerland: IUCN Commission on Environmental Law, 1994.
Bagnall, Roger S. *Egypt in Late Antiquity*. Princeton: Princeton University Press, 1993.
Baker, C. Richard. "Administrative and Accounting Practices in the Byzantine Empire." *Accounting History* 18 (2013): 211–227.
Bakhashab, Omar A. "Islamic Law and the Environment: Some Basic Principles." *Arab Law Quarterly* 3 (1988): 287–298.
Balleine, C. F. "The Tributum Capitis." *The Classical Review* 20 (1906): 51–53.
Ballyn, Sue. "The British Invasion of Australia – Convicts: Exile and Dislocation." In *Lives in Migration: Rupture and Continuity*. Edited by Martin Renes. Available at: www.ub.edu/dpfilsa/0renes.pdf.
Barendse, René J. *The Arabian Seas: The Indian Ocean World of the Seventeenth Century*. Armonk, NY: M. E. Sharpe, 2002.
"Trade and State in the Arabian Seas: A Survey from the Fifteenth to the Eighteenth Century." *Journal of World History* 11 (2000): 173–225.
Bashir, Khaled R. "Treatment of Foreigners in the Classical Islamic State with Special Focus on Diplomatic Envoys: Al-Shaybānī and *Amān*." In *Islam and International Law: Engaging Self-Centrism from a Plurality of Perspectives*. Edited by Marie-Luisa Frick and Andreas Th. Müller. Leiden: Martinus Nijhoff, 2013: 146–160.
Bassiouni, Cherif. "Protection of Diplomats under Islamic Law." *American Society of International Law* 74 (1980): 609–633.
Bazzāz, Muḥammad A. "Ḥawl Naql al-Baḥriyya al-Masīḥiyya li-Ḥujjāj al-Gharb al-Islāmī." In *l'occident musulman et l'occident chrétien au Moyen Âge*. Edited by Mohammed Hammam. Rabat: Faculté des lettres et des sciences humaines, Muḥammad al-Khāmis University, 1995: 81–92.

Beaujard, Philippe. "The Indian Ocean in Eurasian and African World-Systems before the Sixteenth Century." *Journal of World History* 16 (2005): 411–465.

Behrens-Abouseif, Doris. "The Islamic History of the Lighthouse of Alexandria." *Muqarnas* 23 (2006): 1–14.

Benedict, Robert D. "The Historical Position of the Rhodian Law." *Yale Law Journal* 18 (1909): 223–242.

Benton, Lauren. "Legal Spaces of Empire: Piracy and the Origins of Ocean Regionalism." *Comparative Studies in Society and History* 47 (2005): 700–724.

Berger, Maurits. "Islamic Views on International Law." In *Culture and International Law*. Edited by Paul Meerts. The Hague: Hague Academic Press, 2008: 105–117.

Berkowitz, Abraham. "John Selden and the Biblical Origins of the Modern International Political System." *Jewish Political Studies Review* 6 (1994): 27–47.

Birks, Peter. "The Roman Concept of Dominium and the Idea of Absolute Ownership." *Acta Juridica* 31 (1985): 1–37.

Bonner, Michael. *Jihad in Islamic History: Doctrines and Practice*. Princeton: Princeton University Press, 2006.

Borschberg, Peter. "Another Look at Law and Business in the Late Malacca Sultanate, c.1450–1511." In East Asia Maritime Regional Networks and Port City Societies. Edited by Zheng Yangchang. Taipei: Le Jin Books, 2015: 485–528.

"The Seizure of the *Sta. Catarina* Revisited: The Portuguese Empire in Asia, VOC Politics and the Origins of the Dutch–Johor Alliance (1602–c.1616)." *Journal of Southeast Asian Studies* 33 (2002): 31–62.

Boswell, John. *The Royal Treasure: Muslim Communities under the Crown of Aragon in the Fourteenth Century*. New Haven: Yale University Press, 1977.

Bosworth, Edmund. "The Nomenclature of the Persian Gulf." *Iranian Studies* 30 (1997): 77–94.

Bosworth, Michael L. "The Rise and Fall of 15th Century Chinese Sea." https://militaryrevolution.s3.amazonaws.com/Primary%20sources/china.pdf.

Bouhdiba, Abdelwahab and Dawālībī, Muḥammad M. *The Different Aspects of Islamic Culture: The Individual and Society in Islam*. Paris: Presses Universitaires de France, 1998.

Bouzenita, Anke I. "The *Siyar* – An Islamic Law of Nations?" *Asian Journal of Social Science* 35 (2007): 19–46.

Bowman, Alan K. and Rathbone, Dominic. "Cities and Administration in Roman Egypt." *Journal of Roman Studies* 82 (1992): 107–127.

Boxer, Charles R. *The Portuguese Seaborne Empire 1415–1825*. London: Hutchinson and Co., 1969.

"A Note on Portuguese Reactions to the Revival of the Red Sea Spice Trade and the Rise of Atjeh, 1540–1600." *Journal of Southeast Asian History* 10 (1969): 415–428.

Bramoullé, David. "The Fatimids and the Red Sea (969–1171)." In *Navigated Spaces, Connected Places: Proceedings of Red Sea Project V Held at the*

University of Exeter, September 2010. Edited by Dionisius A. Agius, John P. Cooper, Athena Trakadas, and Chiara Zazzaro. British Archaeological Reports. Oxford: Archaeopress, 2012: 127–136.

Brauer, Ralph W. "Boundaries and Frontiers in Medieval Muslim Geography." *Transactions of the American Philosophical Society* (New Series) 85 (1995): 1–73.

Breasted, James H. "The Report of Wenamon." *American Journal of Semitic Languages and Literatures* 21 (1905): 100–109.

Brett, Michael. "Muslim Justice under Infidel Rule: The Normans in Ifriqiya 517–555/1123–1160 A.D." *Cahiers de Tunisie* 33 (1991): 325–368.

Brouwer, C. G. "Non-Western Shipping Movements in the Red Sea and Gulf of Aden during the 2nd and 3rd Decades of the 17th Century, According to the Records of the Dutch East India Company." *Die Welt des Islams* 31 (1991): 105–167.

Bruce, Travis. "Piracy as Statecraft: The Mediterranean Policies of the Fifth/Eleventh-Century Taifa of Denia." *Al-Masaq* 22 (2010): 235–248.

Bsoul, Labeeb A. *International Treaties (Muʿāhadāt) in Islam*. Lanham: University Press of America, 2008.

"Historical Evolution of Islamic Law of Nations/*Siyar*: Between Memory and Desire." *Digest of Middle East Studies* 17 (2008): 48–67.

Bundāq, Muḥammad Ṣ. *Al-Mustashriqūn wa-Tarjamat al-Qurʾān al-Karīm*. Beirut: Dār al-Āfāq al-Jadīda, 1403/1983.

Calasso, Giovanna and Lancioni, Giuliano (ed.). *Dār al-Islām/Dār al-Ḥarb: Territories, People, Identities*. Leiden: E. J. Brill, 2017.

Casale, Giancarlo. *The Ottoman Age of Exploration*. Oxford: Oxford University Press, 2010.

Casson, Lionel. *Ships and Seamanship in the Ancient World*. Baltimore: Johns Hopkins University Press, 1995.

Cerqua, Clelia S. *Mujāhid al-ʿĀmirī Qāʾid al-Usṭūl al-ʿArabī fī Gharbiyy al-Baḥr al-Mutawassiṭ fī al-Qarn al-Khāmis al-Hijrī*. Cairo: Maktabat al-Qāhira al-Ḥadītha, 1961.

Chaffee, John. "Diasporic Identities in the Historical Development of the Maritime Muslim Communities of Song–Yuan China." *Journal of the Economic and Social History of the Orient* 49 (2006): 395–420.

Chakravarti, Ranabir. "An Enchanting Seascape: Through Epigraphic Lens." *Studies in History* 20 (2004): 305–315.

"Nakhudas and Nauvittakas: Ship-Owning Merchants in the West Coast of India (C. AD 1000–1500)." *Journal of the Economic and Social History of the Orient* 43 (2000): 34–64.

Chaudhuri, Kirti N. *Trade and Civilization in the Indian Ocean: An Economic History from the Rise of Islam to 1750*. Cambridge: Cambridge University Press, 1985.

"The Portuguese Maritime Empire, Trade, and Society in the Indian Ocean during the Sixteenth Century." *Portuguese Studies* 8 (1992): 57–70.

Ché-Ross, Raimy. "Munshi Abdullah's Voyage to Mecca: A Preliminary Introduction and Annotated Translation." *Indonesia and the Malay World* 28 (2000): 173–213.

Chew, Emrys. "Crouching Tiger, Hidden Dragon: The Indian Ocean and the Maritime Balance of Power in Historical Perspective." Singapore: S. Rajaratnam School of International Studies, 2007: 1–21. www.rsis.edu.sg/wp-content/uploads/rsis-pubs/WP144.pdf.

Chodorow, Adam S. "Biblical Tax Systems and the Case for Progressive Taxation." *Journal of Law and Religion* 23 (2007): 51–96.

Christ, Georg. *Trading Conflicts: Venetian Merchants and Mamluk Officials in Late Medieval Alexandria*. Leiden: E. J. Brill, 2012.

Christides, Vassilios. *The Conquest of Crete by the Arabs CA. 824: A Turning Point in the Struggle between Byzantium and Islam*. Athens: n.p., 1984.

"Shīnī, Shīniyya, Shānī." In *Encyclopaedia of Islam*, 2nd ed. Edited by P. Bearman, Th. Bianquis, C. E. Bosworth, E. van Donzel, and W. P. Heinrichs. Brill Online, 2012: http://referenceworks.brillonline.com/entries/encyclopaedia-of-islam-2/shini-shiniyya-shani-SIM_6949.

"Piracy, Privateering and Maritime Violent Actions: Maritime Violent Activities of the Taifa of Denia in Spain (11th c.) *vs.* the Arab Maritime *Jihād* in the Eastern Mediterranean from the Middle of the 7th to 11th Century." In *Seeraub im Mittelmeerraum: Piraterie, Korsarentum und maritime Gewalt von der Antike bis zur Neuzeit*. Edited by Mihran Dabag, Dieter Haller, Nikolas Jaspert, and Achim Lichtenberger. Brussels: Ferdinand Schöningh, 2013: 199–208.

Churchill, Robin R. and Lowe, Alan V. *The Law of the Sea*. 3rd ed. Manchester: Manchester University Press, 1999.

Ciocîltan, Virgil. *The Mongols and the Black Sea Trade in the Thirteenth and Fourteenth Centuries*. Leiden: E. J. Brill, 2012.

Cohen, Mark R. *Under Crescent and Cross: The Jews in the Middle Ages*. Princeton: Princeton University Press, 1994.

"Defending Jewish Judicial Autonomy in the Islamic Middle Ages." In *Law and Religious Minorities in Medieval Societies: Between* Theory *and* Praxis. Edited by Ana Echevarria, Juan P. Monferrer-Sala, and John Tolan. Turnhout: Brepols Publishers, 2016: 13–33.

"What Was the Pact of ʿUmar? A Literary-Historical Study." *Jerusalem Studies in Arabic and Islam* 23 (1999): 100–157.

Cohn, Bernard S. "The Past in the Present: India as Museum of Mankind." *History and Anthropology* 11 (1998): 1–38.

Conrad, Lawrence I. "Islam and the Sea: Paradigms and Problematics." *Al-Qanṭara* 23 (2002): 123–154.

Constable, Olivia R. *Housing the Stranger in the Mediterranean World: Lodging, Trade, and Travel in Late Antiquity and the Middle Ages*. Cambridge: Cambridge University Press, 2003.

Trade and Traders in Muslim Spain: The Commercial Realignment of the Iberian Peninsula 900–1500. Cambridge: Cambridge University Press, 1994.

"The Problem of Jettison in Medieval Mediterranean Maritime Law." *Journal of Medieval History* 20 (1994): 207–220.

Cooper, John P. *The Medieval Nile: Route, Navigation, and Landscape in Islamic Egypt*. Cairo: American University Press, 2014.

"Egypt's Nile-Red Sea Canals: Chronology, Location, Seasonality and Function." In *Connected Hinterlands: Proceedings of Red Sea Project IV Held at the University of Southampton September 2008*. Edited by Lucy Blue, John Cooper, Ross Thomas, and Julian Whitewright. British Archaeological Reports. Oxford: Archaeopress, 2009: 195–209.

Corriente, Federico. *Dictionary of Arabic and Allied Loanwords: Spanish, Portuguese, Catalan, Gallician and Kindred Dialects*. Leiden: E. J. Brill, 2008.

Coulson, Noel J. "Muslim Custom and Case-Law." *Die Welt des Islams* 16 (1959): 13–24.

Cummings, William (ed.). *The Makassar Annals*. Leiden: KITLV Press, 2011.

"Islam, Empire and Makassarese Historiography in the Reign of Sultan Ala'uddin (1593–1639)." *Journal of Southeast Asian Studies* 38 (2007): 197–214.

Curtin, Philip D. *Cross-Cultural Trade in World History*. Cambridge: Cambridge University Press, 1984.

Dale, Stephen F. "Trade, Conversion and the Growth of the Islamic Community of Kerala, South India." *Studia Islamica* 71 (1990): 155–175.

Dalgado, Sebastião R. *The Influence of Portuguese Vocables in Asiatic Languages*. Translated by Anthony X. Soares. Baroda: Oriental Institute, 1936.

D'Alòs-Moner, Andreu Martínez. "Conquistadores, Mercenaries, and Missionaries: The Failed Portuguese Dominion of the Red Sea." *Northeast African Studies* (New Series) 12 (2012): 1–28.

Damgaard, Kristoffer. "A Palestinian Red Sea Port on the Egyptian Road to Arabia: Early Islamic Aqaba and Its Many Hinterlands." In *Connected Hinterlands: Proceedings of Red Sea Project IV Held at the University of Southampton September 2008*. Edited by Lucy Blue, John Cooper, Ross Thomas, and Julian Whitewright. Oxford: Archaeopress, 2009: 85–97.

Dauzat, Albert. *Dictionnaire étymologique de la langue française*. Paris: Larousse, 1938.

Davis-Secord, Sarah. "Muslims in Norman Sicily: The Evidence of Imām al-Māzarī's Fatwās." *Mediterranean Studies* 16 (2007): 46–66.

Davies, W. W. "The Code of Hammurabi." In *Sources of Ancient and Primitive Law*. Edited by Albert Kocourek and John Wigmore. Littleton, CO: Fred B. Rothman and Co., 1979: 387–442.

Dawoody, Ahmed. *The Islamic Law of War: Justifications and Regulations*. New York: Palgrave Macmillan, 2011. This book is based on his PhD diss. titled "War in Islamic Law: Justifications and Regulations." Department of Theology and Religion, University of Birmingham, 2009.

De Lara, Yadira González. "The Secret of Venetian Success: A Public-order, Reputation-based Institution." *European Review of Economic History* 12 (2008): 247–285.

Deng, Hui and Li, Xin. "The Asian Monsoons and Zheng He's Voyages to the Western Ocean." *Journal of Navigation* 64 (2011): 207–218.

Denny, Frederick M. "The Meaning of 'Ummah' in the Qur'ān." *History of Religions* 15 (1975): 34–70.

De Somogyi, Joseph. "Trade in the Qur'ān and Ḥadīth." *The Muslim World* 52 (1962): 110–114.

De Souza, Philip. *Piracy in the Graeco-Roman World*. Cambridge: Cambridge University Press, 1999.

De Vivo, Filippo. "Historical Justifications of Venetian Power in the Adriatic." *Journal of the History of Ideas* 64 (2003): 159–176.

Deveney, Patrick. "Title, Jus Publicum, and the Public Trust: An Historical Analysis." *Sea Grant Law Journal* 13 (1976): 13–81.

Dien, Albert E. "The Tomb of the Sogdian Master Shi: Insights into the Life of a *Sabao*." *Silk Road* 7 (2009): 42–50.

"The Sa-pao Problem Re-Examined." *Journal of the American Oriental Society* 82 (1962): 335–346.

Ding, J., Shi, Ch., and Weintrit, A. "An Important Waypoint on Passage of Navigation History: Zheng He's Sailing to West Ocean." *International Journal on Marine Navigation and Safety of Sea Transportation* 1 (2007): 285–293.

Djamil, Agus S. and Kartanegara, Mulyadhi. "The Philosophy of Oceanic Verses of the Quran and Its Relevance to Indonesian Context." *Analisa* 2 (2017): 103–121.

Djelloul, Néji. *Al-Ribāṭāt al-Baḥriyya bi-Ifrīqiya fī al-ʿAṣr al-Wasīṭ*. Tunis: Markaz al-Dirāsāt wa'l-Buḥūth al-Iqtiṣādiyya wa'l-Ijtimāʿiyya, 1999.

Dreyer, Edward L. *Zheng He: China and the Oceans in the Early Ming Dynasty, 1405–1433*. New York: Pearson Longman, 2007.

Drocourt, Nicholas. "Christian-Muslim Diplomatic Relations: An Overview of the Main Sources and Themes of Encounter (600–1000)." In *Christian-Muslim Relations: A Bibliographical History*. Edited by David Thomas and Alex Mallet. Leiden: E. J. Brill, 2010: 2:29–72.

Duggan, T. M. P. and Akçay, Aykan. "On the Missing Navigational Markers – Beacon Towers – Pharos of Antiquity – and Notice of Two Extant Small Marker Beacon Towers of the Roman Late 1st c. B.C. – Early 1st c. A.D. Anemorium." *Cedrus* 2 (2014): 377–442.

Ḍumayriyya, ʿUthmān J. *Usūl al-ʿAlāqāt al-Duwaliyya fī Fiqh al-Imām Muḥammad Ibn al-Ḥasan al-Shaybānī*. Amman: Dār al-Maʿālī, 1419/1999.

Al-Muʿāhadāt al-Duwaliyya fī Fiqh al-Imām Muḥammad Ibn al-Ḥasan al-Shaybānī: Dirāsa Muqārana. Mecca: Rābiṭat al-ʿĀlam al-Islāmī, 1417/1997.

Dunlop, Douglas M. "Baḥr al-Rūm." In *Encyclopaedia of Islam*, 2nd ed. Edited by P. Bearman, Th. Bianquis, C. E. Bosworth, E. van Donzel, and W. P. Heinrichs. Brill Online, 2012. http://brillonline.nl/entries/encyclopaedia-of-islam-2/bahr-al-rum-SIM_1065.

Duri, ʿAbd-ʿAzīz. "Notes on Taxation in Early Islam." *Journal of the Economic and Social History of the Orient* 17 (1974): 136–144.

Egberts, Arno. "The Chronology of 'The Report of Wenamun'." *Journal of Egyptian Archaeology* 77 (1991): 57–67.

Ehrenkreutz, Andrew S. "The Place of Saladin in the Naval History of the Mediterranean in the Middle Ages." *Journal of the American Oriental Society* 75 (1955): 100–116.

Emon, Anver M. "*Ḥuqūq Allāh* and *Ḥuqūq al-'Ibād*: A Legal Heuristic for a Natural Rights Regime." *Islamic Law and Society* 13 (2006): 325–391.

Fagan, Brian. *Beyond the Blue Horizon: How the Earliest Mariners Unlocked the Secrets of the Oceans*. London: Bloomsbury, 2012.

Fahmy, Aly M. *Muslim Naval Organisation in the Eastern Mediterranean from the Seventh to the Tenth Century A.D.* Cairo: National Publication and Printing House, 1966.

Muslim Sea-Power in the Eastern Mediterranean from the Seventh to the Tenth Century A.D. Cairo: National Publication and Printing House, 1966.

Fang, Liaw Y. *Undang-undang Melaka (The Laws of Melaka)*. The Hague: Martinus Nijhoff, 1976.

Fan, Ke. "Maritime Muslims and Hui Identity: A South Fujian Case." *Journal of Muslim Minority Affairs* 21 (2001): 309–332.

Fattal, Antoine. "How *Dhimmīs* were Judged in the Islamic World." In *Muslims and Others in Early Islamic Society*. Edited by Robert Hoyland. Burlington, VT: Ashgate, 2002: 83–102.

Fenn, Percy T. "Origins of the Theory of Territorial Waters." *American Journal of International Law* 20 (1926): 465–482.

"Justinian and the Freedom of the Sea." *American Journal of International Law* 19 (1925): 716–727.

Fierro, Maribel. "The *Qāḍī* as Ruler." In *Saber religioso y poder politico en el Islam: actas del Simposio Internacional (Granada, 15–18 octubre 1991)*. Madrid: Agencia Española de Cooperación Internacional, 1994: 71–116.

Finlay, Robert. "Portuguese and Chinese Maritime Imperialism: Camoes's Lusiads and Luo Maodeng's Voyage of the San Bao Eunuch." *Comparative Studies in Society and History* 34 (1992): 225–241.

"The Treasure-Ships of Zheng He: Chinese Maritime Imperialism in the Age of Discovery." *Terrae Incognitae* 23 (1991): 1–12.

Firestone, Reuven. *Jihad: The Origin of Holy War in Islam*. Berkeley: University of California Press, 2005.

Fischel, Walter J. "The Spice Trade in Mamlūk Egypt: A Contribution to the Economic History of Medieval Islam." *Journal of the Economic and Social History of the Orient* 2 (1958): 157–174.

Florsheim, Bowen L. "Territorial Sea – 3000 Year Old Question." *Journal of Air Law and Commerce* 36 (1970): 73–104.

Foucault, Michel. *Discipline and Punish: The Birth of the Prison*. Translated by Alan Sheridan. New York: Vintage Books, 1979.

Frantz-Murphy, Gladys. "Identity and Security in the Mediterranean World ca. AD 640 – ca. 1517." Proceedings of the Twenty-Fifth International Congress of Papyrology, Ann Arbor 2007, American Studies in Papyrology. Ann Arbor, 2010: 253–264.

Fredona, Robert. "Angelo degli Ubaldi and the Gulf of the Venetians: Custom, Commerce, and the Control of the Sea before Grotius." In *New Perspectives on the History of Political Economy*. Edited by Robert Fredona and Sophus A. Reinert. New York: Palgrave Macmillan, 2018: 29–73.

Friedell, Steven F. "Admiralty and the Sea of Jewish Law." *Journal of Maritime Law and Commerce* 27 (1996): 647–660.

Fuchs, Barbara and Liang, Yuen-Gen. "A Forgotten Empire: The Spanish-North African Borderlands." *Journal of Spanish Cultural Studies* 12 (2011): 261–273.

Fuess, Albrecht. "Rotting Ships and Razed Harbors: The Naval Policy of the Mamluks." *Mamlūk Studies Review* 5 (2001): 45–71.

Gari, Lutfallah. "A History of the *Ḥimā* Conservation System." *Environment and History* 12 (2006): 213–228.

George, Alain. "Direct Sea Trade between Early Islamic Iraq and Tang China: From the Exchange of Goods to the Transmission of Ideas." *Journal of the Royal Asiatic Society* 25 (2015): 579–624.

Ghāmidī, ʿAbd al-Laṭīf S. *Ḥuqūq al-Insān fī al-Islām*. Riyad: Naif Arab Academy for Security, 1421/2000.

Ghunaimi, Mohammad T. *The Muslim Conception of International Law and the Western Approach*. The Hague: Martinus Nijhoff, 1968.

Gormley, Paul W. "The Development and Subsequent Influence of the Roman Legal Norm of 'Freedom of the Seas'." *University of Detroit Law Journal* 40 (1963): 561–595.

Haider, Tazeem. "Universality in the Message of Qurʾān." *Journal of South Asian Studies* 4 (2016): 61–65.

Ḥajjī, ʿAbd al-Raḥmān ʿAlī. *Al-ʿAlāqāt al-Diblūmāsiyya al-Andalusiyya maʿ Urūbbā al-Gharbiyya khilāl al-Mudda al-Umawiyya (138–366/755–976): Dirāsa Tārīkhiyya*. Abu Dhabi: Al-Majmaʿ al-Thaqāfī, 1424/2004.

Andalusian Diplomatic Relations with Western Europe during the Umayyad Period (A.H. 138–366/A.D. 755–976): An Historical Survey. Beirut: Dār al-Irshād, 1970.

"Andalusian Diplomatic Relations with the Franks during the Umayyad Period." *Islamic Studies* 30 (1991): 241–262.

Hall, Kenneth R. *A History of Early Southeast Asia: Maritime Trade and Societal Development, 100–1500*. Lanham: Rowman and Littlefield Publishers, 2011.

"Local and International Trade and Traders in the Straits of Melaka Region: 600–1500." *Journal of the Economic and Social History of the Orient* 47 (2004): 213–260.

Hallaq, Wael B. *An Introduction to Islamic Law*. Cambridge: Cambridge University Press, 2009.

The Origins and Evolution of Islamic Law. Cambridge: Cambridge University Press, 2005.

Authority, Continuity and Change in Islamic Law. Cambridge: Cambridge University Press, 2004.

A History of Islamic Legal Theories. Cambridge: Cambridge University Press, 1997.

Hamadani, Abbas. "An Islamic Background to the Voyages of Discovery." In *The Legacy of Muslim Spain*. Edited by Salma K. Jayyusi. Leiden: E. J. Brill, 1992: 273–304.

Hamid, Ismail. "Islamic Influence on Malay Culture in Malaysia and Indonesia." *Islamic Culture* 56 (1982): 275–282.

Hanapi, Mohd Sh. "Development Actors in the Conventional Development Theory: Analysis based on Development Actors According to the Qur'ānic Worldwide." *International Journal of Academic Research in Business and Social Sciences* 7 (2017): 781–791.

Haq, Nomanul. "Islam and Ecology: Toward Retrieval and Reconstruction." *Daedalus* 130 (2001): 141–177.

Ḥasan, Aḥmad A. *Qānūn al-Biḥār wa'l-Anhār al-Duwaliyya fī al-Islām*. Cairo: Ma'had al-Buḥūth wa'l-Dirāsāt al-'Arabiyya, 1988.

Haykal, Muḥammad Kh. *Al-Jihād wa'l-Qitāl fī al-Siyāsa al-Shar'iyyah*. 3 vols. Beirut: Dār al-Bayāriq, 1417/1997.

Heidarizad, Mohammad, Kabiri, Sayyedtaghi, and Azarpanah, Mohammad. "Security from Qur'ān Perspective." *Advances in Environmental Biology* 7 (2013): 3383–3387.

Hendrickson, Jocelyn N. "Muslim Legal Responses to Portuguese Occupation in Late Fifteenth-Century North Africa." *Journal of Spanish Cultural Studies* 12 (2011): 309–325.

Heng, Derek. "State Formation and the Evolution of Naval Strategies in the Melaka Straits, c. 500–1500 C.E." *Journal of Southeast Asian Studies* 44 (2013): 380–399.

Herrera-Casais, Mónica. "The Nautical Atlases of 'Alī al-Sharafī." *Suhayl* 8 (2008): 223–263.

"The 1413–14 Sea Chart of Aḥmad al-Ṭanjī." In *A Shared Legacy: Islamic Science East and West – Homage to Prof. J. M. Millàs Vallicrosa*. Edited by Emilia Calvo, Mercè Comes, Roser Puig, and Mònica Rius. Barcelona: Universitat de Barcelona, 2008: 283–307.

Hessbruegge, Jan A. "The Historical Development of the Doctrines of Attribution and Due Diligence in International Law." *International Law and Politics* 36 (2004): 265–306.

Heuser, Beatrice. "*Regina Maris* and the Command of the Sea: The Sixteenth Century Origins of Modern Maritime Strategy." *Journal of Strategic Studies* 40 (2017): 225–262.

Hodgins, Thomas. "Ancient Law of Nations Respecting the Sea and Sea-Shore." *Canadian Law Times* 13 (1893): 14–21.

Hoenerbach, Wilhelm. *La Marina Arabe del Mar Mediterráneo en Tiempos de Mu'āwiya*. Tetuan: Instituto Muley el-Hasan, 1954.

Hollerich, Michael. "The Alexandrian Bishops and the Grain Trade: Ecclesiastical Commerce in Late Roman Egypt." *Journal of the Economic and Social History of the Orient* 25 (1982): 187–207.

Houben, Vincent J. H. "Southeast Asia and Islam." *Annals of the American Academy of Political and Social Science* 588 (2003): 149–170.

Hourani, George F. *Arab Seafaring in the Indian Ocean in Ancient and Early Times*. 3rd ed. Princeton: Princeton University Press, 1995.

Hunter, William A. *A Systematic and Historical Exposition of Roman Law*. London: William Maxwell and Son, 1885.

Hussain, Jamila. "More than One Law for All: Legal Pluralism in Southeast Asia." *Democracy and Security* 7 (2011): 374–389.

Ḥussein, Muḥsin M. *Al-Jaysh al-Ayyūbī fI 'Ahd Ṣalāḥ al-Dīn*. Erbil: Dār Tārās lil-Ṭibā'a, 2002.

Ibn Fāyi', 'Abd al-Raḥmān ibn Aḥmad. *Aḥkām al-Baḥr fī al-Fiqh al-Islāmī*. Jeddah: Dār Ibn Ḥazm, 1421/2000.

Idris, Hady R. "Commerce maritime et *kirāḍ* en berberie orientale d'après un recueil inédit *fatwās* médievales." *Journal of the Economic and Social History of the Orient* 4 (1961): 223–239.

Ilias, M. H. "Mappila Muslims and the Cultural Content of Trading Arab Diaspora on the Malabar Coast." *Asian Journal of Social Science* 35 (2007): 434–456.

Inalcik, Halil. "The Status of the Greek Orthodox Patriarch under the Ottomans." *Turcica* 21–23 (1991): 407–435.

Jack, Sybil. "Piracy: An Elemental Way of Life." *Arts: The Journal of the Sydney University Arts Association* 18 (1996): 109–123.

Jackson, Sherman A. "Domestic Terrorism in the Islamic Legal Tradition." *Muslim World* 91 (2001): 293–310.

Jacoby, David. "Foreigners and the Urban Economy in Thessalonike, ca. 1150–ca. 1450." *Dumbarton Oaks Papers* 57 (2003): 85–132.

Jados, Stanley S. *Consulate of the Sea and Related Documents*. Tuscaloosa: University of Alabama Press, 1975.

Johari, Fuadah. "The Dynamism in the Implementation of al-Kharaj during the Islamic Rule 634–785." *Sharī'ah Journal* 18 (2010), 629–688.

Johnston, Douglas M. *The Theory and History of Ocean Boundary-Making*. Kingston: McGill-Queen's University Press, 1988.

Jokisch, Benjamin. *Islamic Imperial Law: Harun al-Rashid's Codification Project*. Berlin: Walter de Gruyter, 2007.

Jones, A. H. M. "*Capitatio* and *Iugatio*." *Journal of Roman Studies* 47 (1957): 88–94.

Juraywī, Muḥammad. *Al-Sijn wa-Mūjibātuhu fī al-Sharī'ah al-Islāmiyya: Muqāranan bi-Niẓām al-Sijn wa'l-Tawqīf fī al-Mamlaka al-'Arabiyya al-Sa 'ūdiyya*. Riyad: Idārat al-Thaqāfa wa'l-Nashr, 1990.

Kaegi, Walter E. *Byzantium and the Early Islamic Conquests*. Cambridge: Cambridge University Press, 1992.

Kahlaoui, Tarek. "The Maghrib's Medieval Mariners and Sea Maps: The *Muqaddimah* as a Primary Source." *Journal of Historical Sociology* 30 (2017): 43–56.

Kamal, Mohd H. "International Legal Personality of Prophet Muhammad." *The Sixth Oceanic Conference on International Studies*, University of Melbourne, July 9–11, 2014: www.ocis.org.au/files/pdf/full-papers/ocis14final00103.pdf.

Kamali, Mohammad H. *Principles of Islamic Jurisprudence*. Cambridge: Islamic Texts Society, 1997.

"Islam and Sustainable Development." *Islam and Civilisational Renewal* 7 (2016): 8–26.

"Environmental Care in Islamic Teaching." *Islam and Civilisational Renewal* 3 (2011): 261–283.

"Citizenship: An Islamic Perspective." *Journal of Islamic Law and Culture* 11 (2009): 121–153.

"The Right to Personal Safety and the Principle of Legality in the *Sharīʿah*." *Islamic Studies* 39 (2000): 249–289.

Karmi, Hasan. "The Prophet Muḥammad and the Spirit of Compromise." *Islamic Quarterly* 8 (1964): 84–94.

Katele, Irene B. "Piracy and the Venetian State: The Dilemma of Maritime Defense in the Fourteenth Century." *Speculum* 63 (1988): 865–889.

Kauz, Ralph and Ptak, Roderich. "Hormuz in Yuan and Ming Sources." *Bulletin de l'Ecole française d'Extrême-Orient* 88 (2001): 27–75.

Kelsay, John. "Al-Shaybani and the Islamic Law of War." *Journal of Military Ethics* 2 (2003): 63–75.

Khadduri, Majid. *The Islamic Law of Nations: Shaybānī's Siyar*. Baltimore: Johns Hopkins University Press, 1966.

"Islam and the Modern Law of Nations." *American Journal of International Law* 50 (1956): 358–372.

War and Peace in the Law of Islam. Baltimore: Johns Hopkins University Press, 1955.

"Nature and Sources of Islamic Law." *George Washington Law Review* 22 (1953): 3–23.

"Human Rights in Islam." *American Academy of Political and Social Science* 243 (1946): 77–81.

The Law of War and Peace in Islam. London: Luzac and Co., 1941.

Khādim, Samīr ʿA. *Al-Sharq al-Islāmī wa'l-Gharb al-Masīḥī ʿabr al-ʿAlāqāt bayna al-Mudun al-Īṭāliyya wa-Sharqiyy al-Baḥr al-Mutawassiṭ 1450–1517*. Beirut: Muʾassasat al-Rīḥānī, 1989.

Khalaf, Iman N. and Yusoff, Zulkifli M. "The *Qur'ān*: Limits of Translatability." *International Journal of Quranic Research* 2 (2012): 73–85.

Khalilieh, Hassan S. *Admiralty and Maritime Laws in the Mediterranean (ca. 800–1050): The Kitāb Akriyat al-Sufun vis-à-vis the Nomos Rhodion Nautikos*. Leiden: E. J. Brill, 2006.

Islamic Maritime Law: An Introduction. Leiden: E. J. Brill, 1998.

"An Overview of the Slaves' Juridical Status in Roman, Byzantine, and Islamic Admiralty Laws." In *Histories of the Middle East: Studies in Middle Eastern Society, Economy, and Law in Honor of A. L. Udovitch*. Edited by Roxani Margariti, Adam Sabra, and Petra Sijpesteijn. Leiden: E. J. Brill, 2011: 73–100.

"*Amān*." In *The Encyclopaedia of Islam*. 3rd ed. Leiden: E. J. Brill, 2007: 1:111–113.

"Legal Aspects from a Cairo Geniza *Responsum* on the Islamic Law of the Sea." *Jewish Quarterly Review* 96 (2006): 180–202.

"Women at Sea: Modesty, Privacy, and Sexual Misconduct of Passengers and Sailors Aboard Islamic Ships." *Al-Qantara* 37 (2006): 137–153.

"Security Protection and Naval Escort during the 10th and 12th Centuries in the Islamic Mediterranean." *Graeco-Arabica* 7–8 (2000): 221–232.

"The *Ribāṭ* System and Its Role in Coastal Navigation." *Journal of the Economic and Social History of the Orient* 42 (1999): 212–225.

Khan, Khizr. "Juristic Classification of Islamic Law." *Houston Journal of International Law* 6 (1983–1984): 23–35.

Khoury, Ibrahim. *As-Sufāliyya: The Poem of Sofala: Arabic Navigation along the East African Coast in the 15th Century*. Coimbra: Junta de Investigações Científicas do Ultramar, 1983.

Khoury, Ibrāhīm and Tadmurī, Aḥmad J. *Salṭanat Hormuz al-ʿArabiyya*. 2 vols. Ras al-Khaimah: Documentaries and Studies Center, 1421/2000.

Kooria, Mahmood. "An Abode of Islam under a Hindu King: Circuitous Imagination of Kingdoms among Muslims of Sixteenth-Century Malabar." *Journal of Indian Ocean World Studies* (2017): 89–109.

Kulsrud, Carl J. *Maritime Neutrality to 1780: A History of the Main Principles Governing Neutrality and Belligerency to 1780*. Boston: Little, Brown, and Company, 1936.

Kuran, Timur. "The Economic Ascent of the Middle East's Religious Minorities: The Role of Islamic Legal Pluralism." *Journal of Legal Studies* 33 (2004): 475–515.

Kurup K. M. and Mathew, K. M. *Native Resistance against the Portuguese: The Saga of Kunjali Marakkars*. Calicut: Calicut University Press, 2000.

Labīb, Ṣubḥī. "Al-Tujār al-Kārimiyya wa-Tijārat Miṣr fī al-ʿUṣūr al-Wusṭā." *Al-Majalla al-Tārīkhiyya al-Miṣriyya* 4 (1952): 5–63

Laiou, Angeliki E. "Byzantine Trade with Christian and Muslims and Crusades." In *The Crusades from the Perspective of Byzantium and the Muslim World*. Edited by Angeliki E. Laiou and Roy P. Mottahedeh. Washington DC: Dumbarton Oaks Research Library, 2001: 157–196.

Lane, Edward W. *An Arabic–English Lexicon*. 2 vols. Cambridge: Islamic Texts Society Trust, 1984.

Lane, Frederic C. *Venice: A Maritime Republic*. Baltimore: Johns Hopkins University Press, 1973.

"Pepper Prices before Da Gama." *Journal of Economic History* 28 (1968): 590–597.

Leben, Charles. "Hebrew Sources in the Doctrine of the Law of Nature and Nations in Early Modern Europe." *European Journal of International Law* 27 (2016): 79–106.

Leder, Stefen. *Die arabische Ecloga*. Frankfurt: Forschungen zur byzantinischen Rechtsgeschichte, 1985.

Lee, Hee-Soo. "The Spread of Islamic Culture to the East Asia before the Era of Modern European Hegemony." *Islām Araştirmalari Dergisi* 7 (2002): 57–74.

Leiser, Gary L. "The Crusader Raid in the Red Sea in 578/1182–83." *Journal of the American Center in Egypt* 14 (1977): 87–100.

Letsios, Dimitrios G. "Sea Trade as Illustrated in the 'Rhodian Sea Law' with Special Reference to the Reception of Its Norms in the Arabic *Ecloga*." *Graeco-Arabica* 6 (1995): 209–225.

Levathes, Louise. *When China Ruled the Seas: The Treasure Fleet of the Dragon Throne, 1405–1433*. New York and Oxford: Oxford University Press, 1994.

Levi-Provençal, Évariste (ed.). *Thalāth Rasāʾil Andalusiyya fī Ādāb al-Ḥisba wa'l-Muḥtasib*. Cairo: L'Institut Français d'archéologie orientale, 1955.

(ed.). "Un nouveau texte d'histoire mérinide, le Musnad d'Ibn Marzūq." *Hespéris* 5 (1925): 1–82.

Levy-Rubin, Milka. *Non-Muslims in the Early Islamic Empire: From Surrender to Coexistence*. Cambridge: Cambridge University Press, 2011.

"*Shurūṭ ʿUmar* and Its Alternatives: The Legal Debate on the Status of the *Dhimmīs*." *Jerusalem Studies in Arabic and Islam* 30 (2005): 170–206.

Lewicki, T. "Les voies maritimes de la Méditerranée dans le haut Moyen Âge d'aprè le sources arabes." In *La navigazione mediterranea nell'alto medioevo*. Spoleto: Presso la sede del Centro, 1978: 439–469.

Lewis, Archibald. *Naval Power and Trade in the Mediterranean A.D. 500–1100*. Princeton: Princeton University Press, 1951.

Lewis, Bernard. "Legal and Historical Reflections on the Position of Muslim Populations under non-Muslim Rule." *Journal of Muslim Minority Affairs* 13 (1992): 1–16.

Libson, Gideon. "On the Development of Custom as a Source of Law in Islamic Law." *Islamic Law and Society* 4 (1997): 131–155.

Liebesny, Herbert J. "Comparative Legal History: Its Role in the Analysis of Islamic and Modern Near Eastern Legal Institutions." *American Journal of Comparative Law* 20 (1972): 38–52.

"Religious Law and Westernization in the Moslem Near East." *American Journal of Comparative Law* 2 (1953): 492–504.

Lirola Delgado, Jorge. *El poder naval de Al-Andalus en la época del Califato Omeya*. Granada: Universidad de Granada, 1993.

Lobato, Manuel. "'Melaka Is Like a Cropping Field': Trade Management in the Strait of Melaka during the Sultanate and the Portuguese Period." *Journal of Asian History* 46 (2012): 225–251.

Lockard, Craig A. "'The Sea Common to All': Maritime Frontiers, Port Cities, and Chinese Traders in the Southeast Asian Age of Commerce, ca. 1400–1750." *Journal of World History* 21 (2010): 219–247.

"Integrating Southeast Asia into the Framework of World History: The Period before 1500." *History Teacher* 29 (1995): 7–35.

Lodhi, Abdulaziz. "Muslims in Eastern Africa: Their Past and Present." *Nordic Journal of African Studies* 3 (1994): 88–98.

Lopez, Robert S. "Byzantine Law in the Seventh Century and Its Reception by the Germans and the Arabs." *Byzantion* 16 (1942–1943): 445–461.

Lourie, Elena. "Free Moslems in the Balearics under Christian Rule in the Thirteenth Century." *Speculum* 45 (1970): 624–649.

Lumbard, Joseph E. B. "Covenant and Covenants in the Qurʾan." *Journal of Qurʾanic Studies* 17 (2015): 1–23.

Lynch, Ryan J. "Cyprus and Its Legal and Historiographical Significance in Early Islamic History." *Journal of the American Oriental Society* 136 (2016): 535–550.

Lytle, Ephraim. "'Η θάλασσακοινή: Fishermen, the Sea, and the Limits of Ancient Greek Regulatory Reach." *Classical Antiquity* 31 (2012): 1–55.

MacLean, Derryl N. *Religion and Society in Arab Sind*. Leiden: E. J. Brill, 1989.

Madden, M. Stuart. "Paths of Western Law after Justinian." *London Law Review* 1 (2005): 368–433.

Maghen, Ze'ev. "'They Shall Not Draw Nigh': The Access of Unbelievers to Sacred Space in Islamic and Jewish Law." *Journal of Arabic and Islamic Studies* 7 (2007): 103–131.

Mahdihassan, S. "Chinese Words in the Holy Koran: Qirtas, Meaning Paper, and Its Synonym, Kagaz." *Journal of the University of Bombay* 24 (1955): 148–162.

Maḥmaṣṣānī, Ṣobḥī. *Al-Qānūn wa'l-'Alāqāt al-Duwaliyya fī al-Islām*. Beirut: Dār al-'Ilm lil-Malāyīn, 1392/1972.

Ma, Jianzhao. "The Role of Islam in the Formation of the Culture and Economy of the Hui Community in Guangzhou." *Journal of Muslim Minority Affairs* 16 (1996): 31–39.

Majumdar, Ramesh C. "The Overseas Expeditions of King Rājendra Cola." *Artibus Asiae* 24 (1961): 338–342.

Malekandathil, Pius. *Portuguese Cochin and the Maritime Trade of India, 1500–1663*. New Delhi: Manohar, 2001.

Mallett, Michael E. "The Sea Consuls of Florence in the Fifteenth-Century." *Papers of the British School at Rome* 27 (1959): 156–168.

Mancke, Elizabeth. "Early Modern Expansion and Politicization of Oceanic Space." *Geographical Review* 89 (1999): 225–236.

Magdalino, Paul. "The Maritime Neighborhoods of Constantinople: Commercial and Residential Functions, Sixth to Twelfth Centuries." *Dumbarton Oaks Papers* 54 (2000): 209–226.

Margariti, Roxani E. *Aden and the Indian Ocean Trade: 150 Years in the Life of Medieval Arabian Port*. Chapel Hill: University of North Carolina Press, 2007.

"Mercantile Networks, Port Cities, and 'Pirate' States: Conflict and Competition in the Indian Ocean World of Trade before the Sixteenth Century." *Journal of the Economic and Social History of the Orient* 51 (2008): 543–577.

Marsham, Andrew. "Public Execution in the Umayyad Period: Early Islamic Punitive Practice and Its Late Antique Context." *Journal of Arabic and Islamic Studies* 11 (2011): 101–136.

Marzano, Annalisa. *Harvesting the Sea: The Exploitation of Marine Resources in the Roman Mediterranean*. Oxford: Oxford University Press, 2013.

Masud, Muhammad K. "Being Muslim in a non-Muslim Polity: Three Alternate Models." *Journal of Muslim Minority Affairs* 10 (1989): 118–128.

Mathew, Kuzhippalli S. "Trade in the Indian Ocean and the Portuguese System of Cartazes." In *The First Portuguese Colonial Empire*. Edited by Malyn D. Newitt. Exeter: University of Exeter Press, 1986: 69–84.

Matvejević, Predrag. *Mediterranean: A Cultural Landscape*. Translated by Michael Heim. Berkeley: University of California Press, 1999.

Mayerson, Philip. "The First Muslim Attacks on Southern Palestine (A.D. 633–634)." Transactions and Proceedings of the American Philological Association 95 (1964): 155–199.

McCormick, Michael. *Origins of the European Economy: Communications and Commerce A.D. 300–900*. Cambridge: Cambridge University Press, 2001.

McPherson, Kenneth. "Cultural Exchange in the Indian Ocean Region." *Westerly* 4 (1984): 1–16.

"Processes of Cultural Interchange in the Indian Ocean Region: An Historical Perspective." *Great Circle* 6 (1984): 78–92.

Meijer, Fik. *A History of Seafaring in the Classical World*. London: Croom Helm, 1986.

Meloy, John L. *Imperial Power and Maritime Trade: Mecca and Cairo in the Later Middle Ages*. Chicago: University of Chicago, 2010.

Menache, Sophia. "Papal Attempts at a Commercial Boycott of the Muslims in the Crusader Period." *Journal of Ecclesiastical History* 63 (2012): 236–259.

Meyerson, Mark D. *The Muslims of Valencia in the Age of Fernando and Isabel: Between co-Existence and Crusade*. Berkeley: University of California Press, 1991.

Miceli, Augusto P. "Forum Juridicum: Bartolus of Sassoferrato." *Louisiana Law Review* 37 (1977): 1027–1036.

Miller, Dean A. "The Logothete of the Drome in the Middle Byzantine Period." *Byzantion* 36 (1966): 438–470.

Miller, Kathryn A. "Muslim Minorities and the Obligation to Emigrate to Islamic Territory: Two Fatwās from Fifteenth-Century Granada." *Islamic Law and Society* 7 (2000): 256–288.

Mills, John V. "Arab and Chinese Navigators in Malaysian Waters in about A.D. 1500." *Journal of the Malaysian Branch of the Royal Asiatic Society* 47 (1974): 1–82.

Mirza, Sarah. "*Dhimma* Agreements and Sanctuary Systems at Islamic Origins." *Journal of Near Eastern Studies* 77 (2018): 99–117.

Mi, Shoujiang and You, Jia. *Islam in China*. Translated by Min Chang. Beijing: China Intercontinental Press, 2005.

Mizuguchi, Akira. "From Ancient to Modern Times: A Retrospective of Japan's Relationship with the Middle East." *Asia-Pacific Review* 9 (2002): 93–103.

Mohammed, Khaleel. "Assessing English Translations of the Qurʾān." *Middle East Quarterly* 12 (2005): 58–71.

Molénat, Jean-Pierre. "Le problème de la permanence des musulmans dans les territoires conquis par les chrétiens, dupoint de vue de la loi islamique." *Arabica* 48 (2001): 392–400.

Mones, Hussain. *Tārīkh al-Muslimīn fī al-Baḥr al-Mutawassiṭ: Al-Awḍāʿ al-Siy āsiyya, wa'l-Iqtiṣādiyya, wa'l-Ijtimāʿiyya*. Cairo: Al-Dār al-Miṣriyya al-Lubn āniyya, 1413/1993.

Monks, George R. "The Church of Alexandria and the City's Economic Life in the Sixth Century." *Speculum* 28 (1953): 349–362.

Moore, John B. *A Digest of International Law as Embodied in Diplomatic Discussions, Treaties and Other International Agreements, International Awards, Decisions of Municipal Courts and the Writings of Jurists*. 8 vols. Washington DC: Government Printing Office, 1906.

Morgan, David O. and Reid, Anthony. "Introduction: Islam in a Plural Asia." In The New Cambridge History of Islam. Edited by David O. Morgan and Anthony Reid. Cambridge: Cambridge University Press, 2010: 3:1–17.

Mottahedeh, Roy P. and al-Sayyid, Ridwan. "The Idea of the *Jihād* in Islam before the Crusades." In *The Crusades from the Perspective of Byzantium and the Muslim World*. Edited by Angeliki E. Laiou and Roy P. Mottahedeh. Washington DC: Dumbarton Oaks Research Library and Collection, 2001: 23–29.

Mourison, Robert G. "The Portrayal of Nature in a Medieval Qur'ān Commentary." *Studia Islamica* 94 (2002): 115–137.

Muhammad, Munir. "The Concept of Treaty in Relation to War and Peace in Islam." Fikro Nazar Urdu Journal 47 (2009). Available at SSRN: http://ssrn.com/abstract=1813024.

Mujani, Wan K. "Some Notes on the Portuguese and Frankish Pirates during the Mamluk Period (872–922 A.H./1468–1517 A.D.)." *Jurnal Pengajian Umum Asia Tenggara* (*SEA Journal of General Studies*) 8 (2007): 17–30.

Mukherjee, Anup. "Calicut." In *Encyclopedia of World Trade from Ancient Times to the Present*. 4 vols. Edited by Cynthia C. Northrup. London: Taylor and Francis, 2015: 1:137–139.

Munt, Harry. "'No Two Religions': Non-Muslims in the Early Islamic Ḥijāz." *Bulletin of the School of Oriental and African Studies* 78 (2015): 249–269.

Muraikhi, Saif Sh. "Al-Qarṣana fī al-Khalīj al-ʿArabī wa'l-Baḥr al-Aḥmar wa'l-Muḥīṭ al-Hindī fī al-ʿUṣūr al-Islāmiyya al-'Ūlā min Qiyām al-Dawla al-ʿArabiyya al-Islāmiyya wa-ḥatā Muntaṣaf al-Qarn al-Thālith al-Hijrī." *Bulletin of the Faculty of Arts* [University of Alexandria] 58 (2008): 151–173.

"Imārat al-Baḥr fī ʿAṣr al-Khulafā' al-Rāshidīn wa'l-Umawiyyīn (11–131/632–748)." *Majallat Kulliyyat al-Insāniyyāt wa'l-ʿUlūm al-Ijtimāʿiyya* 23 (2000): 13–58.

Nājī, ʿAbd al-Jabbār. "Dirāsa Muqārana lil-Aḥwāl al-Tijāriyya li-Mawāni' al-Khalīj al-ʿArabī wa'l-Jazīra al-ʿArabiyya fī al-Qarn al-Rābiʿ al-Hijrī." *Majallat Dirāsāt al-Khalīj wa'l-Jazīra al-ʿArabiyya* 14 (1988): 173–198.

Nadavi, Sayyed S. "Arab Navigation." *Islamic Culture* 15.4 (1941): 435–448; 16.1 (1942): 72–86, 182–198, and 404–422.

Naqvi, Ali R. "Laws of War in Islam." *Islamic Studies* 13 (1974): 25–43.

Narayanan, Muttayil G. S. *Cultural Symbiosis in Kerala*. Trivandrum: Kerala Historical Society, 1972.

Nashshār, Muḥammad M. *ʿAlāqat Mamlakatay Qishtāla wa-Aragon bi-Salṭanat al-Mamālīk* (658–741/1260–1341). Cairo: ʿEin for Human and Social Studies, 1997.

Nasr, Seyyed H. "Islam, the Contemporary Islamic World, and the Environmental Crisis." In *Islam and Ecology: A Bestowed Trust*. Edited by Richard C. Foltz. Cambridge MA: Harvard University Press, 2003: 85–105.

Nazmi, Ahmad. "The Nile River in Islamic Geographical Sources." *Studia Arabistyczne i Islamistyczne* 12 (2004): 28–54.

Needham, Joseph. *Science and Civilisation in China*. 7 vols. Cambridge: Cambridge University Press, 1954–1998.

Needham, Joseph and Ronan, Colin A. *The Shorter Science and Civilisation in China*. Vol. 3. Cambridge: Cambridge University Press, 1986.

Newbold, Douglas. "The Crusaders in the Red Sea and the Sudan." *Sudan Notes and Records* 26 (1945): 213–227.

Newitt, Malyn. *A History of Portuguese Overseas Expansion*. New York: Routledge, 2005.

Nor, Mohd, Abdullah, Ahmad, and Ali, Abdul Karim. "From *Undang-undang Melaka* to Federal Constitution: The Dynamics of Multicultural Malaysia." *SpringerPlus* 5:1683 (2016): 1–8.

Nordin, Mardiana. "Undang-undang Laut Melaka: A Note on Malay Maritime Law in the 15th Century." In *Memory and Knowledge of the Sea in Southeast Asia*. Edited by Danny Wong Tze Ken. Institute of Ocean and Earth Sciences Monograph Series 3. Kuala Lumpur: University of Malaya Press, 2008: 15–21.

O'Callaghan, Joseph F. "Castile, Portugal, and the Canary Islands: Claims and Counterclaims, 1344–1479." *Viator* 24 (1993): 287–309.

Odeke, Ademun. "Somali Piracy – Effects on Oceanborne Commerce and Regional Security and Challenges to International Law and World Order." *Australian and New Zealand Maritime Law Journal* 25 (2011): 134–160.

Ormerod, Henry A. *Piracy in the Ancient World*. Liverpool; Liverpool University Press, 1924.

Oxman, Bernard H. "Human Rights and the United Nations Convention on the Law of the Sea." *Columbia Journal of Transnational Law* 36 (1998): 398–429.

Park, Hyunhee. *Mapping the Chinese and Islamic Worlds: Cross-Cultural Exchange in Pre-modern Asia*. Cambridge: Cambridge University Press, 2012.

Parray, Tauseef A. "The Legal Methodology of 'Fiqh al-Aqalliyyat' and Its Critics: An Analytical Study." *Journal of Muslim Minority Affairs* 32 (2012): 88–107.

Parvin, Manoucher and Sommer, Maurie. "Dar al-Islam: The Evolution of Muslim Territoriality and Its Implications for Conflict Resolution in the Middle East." *International Journal of Middle East Studies* 11 (1980): 1–21.

Passamaneck, Stephen M. "A Particular Analysis of General Average." *Journal of Jewish Studies* 25 (1974): 155–168.

"Two Aspects of Rabbinical Maritime Law." *Journal of Jewish Studies* 22 (1971): 53–67.

"Traces of Rabbinical Maritime Law and Custom." *Revue d'Histoire du Droit* 34 (1966): 525–551.

Patai, Raphael. "Ancient Jewish Seafaring and Riverfaring Laws." In *By Study and Also by Faith: Essays in Honor of Hugh W. Nibley*. Edited by John M. Lundquist and Stephen D. Ricks. Salt Lake City: Desert Book Company, 1990: 389–416.

Pearson, Michael N. *The Indian Ocean*. London: Routledge, 2003.

Merchants and Rulers in Gujarat: The Response to the Portuguese in the Sixteenth Century. Berkeley: University of California Press, 1976.

"Islamic Trade, Shipping, Port-States and Merchant Communities in the Indian Ocean, Seventh to Sixteenth Centuries." In *The New Cambridge History of Islam: The Eastern Islamic World – Eleventh to Eighteenth Centuries*. Edited by David O. Morgan and Anthony Reid. Cambridge: Cambridge University Press, 2010: 3:317–365.

"Brokers in Western Indian Port Cities: Their Role in Serving Foreign Merchants." *Modern Asian Studies* 22 (1988): 455–472.

Pedani, Maria P. *The Ottoman–Venetian Border (15th–18th Centuries)*. Venice: Università Ca' Foscari Venezia, 2017.

"Beyond the Frontier: The Ottoman–Venetian Border in the Adriatic Context from the Sixteenth to the Eighteenth Centuries." In *Zones of Fracture in Modern Europe: The Baltic Countries, the Balkans, and Northern Italy*. Edited by Almut Bues. Wiesbaden: Harrassowitz, 2005: 45–60.

Pellat, Ch., Imber, C. H., and Kelly, J. B. "Ḳurṣān." In *Encyclopaedia of Islam*. 2nd ed. Edited by P. Bearman, Th. Bianquis, C. E. Bosworth, E. van Donzel, and W. P. Heinrichs. Brill Online, 2012: http://referenceworks.brillonline.com/entries/encyclopaedia-of-islam-2/kursan-COM_0546.

Perruso, Richard. "The Development of the Doctrine of *Res Communes* in Medieval and Early Modern Europe." *Tijdschrift voor Rechtsgeschiedenis* 70 (2002): 69–93.

Peters, Francis E. *Muhammad and the Origins of Islam*. Albany: State University of New York, 1994.

Peters, Rudolph. *Crime and Punishment in Islamic Law: Theory and Practice from the Sixteenth to the Twenty-First Century*. Cambridge: Cambridge University Press, 2005.

Peterson, Andrew. *The Towns of Palestine under Muslim Rule AD 600–1600*. Oxford: Archaeopress, 2005.

Peterson, Barbara B. "The Ming Voyages of Cheng Ho (Zheng He), 1371–1433." *Great Circle* 16 (1994): 43–51.

Picard, Christophe. *Sea of the Caliphs: The Mediterranean in the Medieval Islamic World*. Cambridge MA: Harvard University Press, 2018.

La mer des califes: Une histoire de la Méditerranée musulmane (VIIe-XIIe siècle). Paris: Seuil, 2015.

La mer et les musulmans d'Occident au Moyen Âge. Paris: Presses Universitaires de France, 1997.

Pinto, Karen C. "In God's Eyes: The Sacrality of the Seas in the Islamic Cartographic Vision." *Espacio Tiempo y Forma* 5 (2017): 55–79.

"Ṣūrat Baḥr al-Rūm [Picture of the Sea of Byzantium]: Possible Meanings Underlying the Forms." In *Eastern Mediterranean Cartographies*. Edited by George Tolias and Dimitris Loupis. Proceedings of the 18th International Conference on the History of Cartography, Athens, July 11–16, 1999. Athens: Institute for Neohellenic Research, 2004: 223–241.

Pita, Victor O. "Commercial Litigation across Religious Borders: Rendering Justice for Valencian Merchants in Fifteenth-Century North Africa and Granada." *Comparative Legal History* 5 (2017): 88–106.

Plant, Glen. "Navigation Regime in the Turkish Straits for Merchant Ships in Peacetime: Safety, Environmental Protection and High Politics." *Marine Policy* 20 (1995): 15–27.

Potter, Pitman B. *The Freedom of the Seas in History, Law, and Politics*. New York: Longmans, Green and Co., 1924.

Potts, Daniel T. "Persian Gulf: Kish Island." *Circle of Ancient Iranian Studies*. www.cais-soas.com/CAIS/Geography/persian.gulf/kish_island.htm.

Pouwels, Randall L. "Eastern Africa and the Indian Ocean to 1800: Reviewing Relations in Historical Perspective." *International Journal of African Historical Studies* 35 (2002): 385–425.

Powers, David. "On Judicial Review in Islamic Law." *Law and Society Review* 26 (1992): 315–342.

Prange, Sebastian R. "The Contested Sea: Regimes of Maritime Violence in the Pre-Modern Indian Ocean." *Journal of Early Modern History* 17 (2013): 9–33.

"A Trade of No Dishonor: Piracy, Commerce, and Community in the Western Indian Ocean – Twelfth to Sixteenth Century." *American Historical Review* 116 (2011): 1269–1293.

"Scholars and the Sea: A Historiography of the Indian Ocean." *History Compass* 6/5 (2008): 1382–1393.

Puente, Julius I. "Functions and Powers of the Foreign Consulate: A Study in Medieval Legal History." *New York University Law Quarterly Review* 20 (1944): 57–100.

"The Nature of the Consular Establishment." *University of Pennsylvania Law Review and American Law Register* 78 (1930): 321–345.

Purcell, Nicholas. "The Boundless Sea of Unlikeness? On Defining the Mediterranean." *Mediterranean Historical Review* 18 (2010): 9–29.

Qannūjī, Ṣiddīq ibn Ḥasan. *Abjad al-ʿUlūm: Al-Washy al-Marqūm fī Bayān Aḥwāl al-ʿUlūm*. 3 vols. Damascus: Wizārat al-Thaqāfa wa'l-Irshād al-Qawmī, 1978.

Qarḍāwī, Yūsuf. *Fiqh al-Jihād: Dirāsa Muqārana li-Aḥkāmihi wa-Falsafatihi fī Ḍawʾ al-Qurʾān wa'l-Sunnah*. 2 vols. Cairo: Maktabat Wahba, 1430/ 2009.

Qāsim, ʿAwn al-Sharīf. *Nashʾat al-Dawla al-Islāmiyya ʿalā ʿAhd Rasūl Allāh*. 3rd ed. Beirut: Dār al-Jīl, 1411/1991.

Raffles, Sir Stamford. "The Maritime Code of the Malays." *Journal of the Straits Branch of the Royal Asiatic Society* 3 (1879): 62–84.

Rahim, Abdur. *The Principles of Muhammadan Jurisprudence According to the Hanafi, Maliki, Shafiʿi and Hanbali Schools*. London: Luzac and Co., 1911.

Rajab, Muṣṭafā M. *Al-Qānūn al-Baḥrī al-Islāmī ka-Maṣdar li-Qawāʿid al-Qānūn al-Baḥrī al-Muʿāṣir*. Alexandria: Al-Maktab al-ʿArabī al-Ḥadīth, 1990.

Ramadan, Hisham. "Larceny Offenses in Islamic Law." *Michigan State Law Review* 1609 (2006): 1610–1640.

Rathbone, Dominic. "Egypt, Augustus and Roman Taxation." *Cahiers du Centre Gustave Glotz* 4 (1993): 81–112.

Ray, Haraprasad. "An Analysis of the Chinese Maritime Voyages into the Indian Ocean during Early Ming Dynasty and Their *raison d'etre*." *China Report* 23 (1987): 65–87.

Ray, Himanshu P. "Writings on the Maritime History of Ancient India." In *Approaches to History: Essays in Indian Historiography*. Edited by

Sabyasachi Bhattacharya. New Delhi: Indian Council of Historical Research, 2011: 27–54.

Reeves, Jesse S. "The Codification of the Law of Territorial Waters." *American Journal of International Law* 24 (1930): 486–499.

"Two Conceptions of the Freedom of the Seas." *American Historical Review* 22 (1917): 535–543.

Reid, Anthony. "Hybrid Identities in the Fifteenth-Century Straits of Malacca." *Asia Research Institute Working Paper No. 67*. Singapore: Asia Research Institute, National University of Singapore, 2006: 1–31.

"Flows and Seepages in the Long-Term Chinese Interaction with Southeast Asia." In *Sojourners and Settlers: Histories of Southeast Asia and Chinese in Honour of Jennifer Cushman*. Edited by Anthony Reid. St Leonards, NSW: Allen and Unwin, 1996: 15–49.

Reinert, Stephen W. "The Muslim Presence in Constantinople, 9th–15th Centuries: Some Preliminary Observations." In *Studies on the Internal Diaspora of the Byzantine Empire*. Edited by Hélène Ahrweiler and Angeliki E. Laiou. Washington DC: Dumbarton Oaks Research Library and Collection, 1998: 125–150.

Reppy, Alison. "The Grotian Doctrine of the Freedom of the Sea Reappraised." *Fordham Law Review* 19 (1950): 243–285.

Resink, Gertrudes J. *Indonesia's History between the Myths: Essays in Legal and Historical Theory*. Amsterdam: Royal Tropical Institute, 1968.

Revere, Robert B. "'No Man's Coast': Ports of Trade in the Eastern Mediterranean." In *Trade and Market in the Early Empires: Economies in History and Theory*. Edited by Karl Polanyi, Conrad Arensberg, and Harry Pearson. Glencoe, IL: Free Press, 1957: 38–63.

Reyerson, Kathryn. "Identity in the Medieval Mediterranean World of Merchants and Pirates." *Mediterranean Studies* 20 (2012): 129–146.

Ricks, Thomas M. "Persian Gulf Seafaring and East Africa: Ninth–Twelfth Centuries." *African Historical Studies* 3 (1970): 339–357.

Risso, Patricia. *Merchants and Faith: Muslim Commerce and Culture in the Indian Ocean*. Boulder, CO: Westview Press, 1995.

Rivers, P. J. "Monsoon Rhythms and Trade Patterns: Ancient Times East of Suez." *Journal of the Malaysian Branch of the Royal Asiatic Society* 77 (2004): 59–93.

Rodger, Nicholas M. "The Naval Service of the Cinque Ports." *English Historical Review* 111 (1996): 636–651.

Roest-Crollius, Ary A. *The Word in the Experience of Revelation in Qur'ān and Hindu Scriptures*. Rome: Universitá Gregoriana Editrice, 1974.

Rose, Carol M. "Romans, Roads, and Romantic Creators: Traditions of Public Property in the Information Age." *Law and Contemporary Problems* 66 (2003): 89–110.

Rose, Richard R. "Islam and the Development of Personal Status Laws among Christian Dhimmis: Motives, Sources, Consequences." *Muslim World* 72 (1982): 159–179.

Ross, Edward D. "The Portuguese in India and Arabia between 1507 and 1517." *Journal of the Royal Asiatic Society of Great Britain and Ireland* 4 (1921): 545–562.

"The Portuguese in India and Arabia between 1517 and 1538." *Journal of the Royal Asiatic Society of Great Britain and Ireland* 4 (1922): 1–18.

Roxas-Lim, Aurora. "Historical and Cultural Significance of Admiral Zheng He's Ocean Voyages." *Asian Studies Journal* 39 (2003): 31–62.

Rubin, Alfred P. "The Concept of Neutrality in International Law." *Denver Journal of International Law and Policy* 16 (1987–1988): 353–375.

"The Law of Piracy." *Denver Journal of International Law and Policy* 15 (1986–1987): 173–233.

Ruddy, F. S. "*Res Nullius* and Occupation in Roman and International Law." *University of Missouri (Kansas City) Law Review* 36 (1968): 274–287.

Runciman, Steven. *The Great Church in Captivity: A Study of the Patriarchate of Constantinople*. Cambridge: Cambridge University Press, 1968.

Rutter, Eldon. "The Hejaz." *Geographical Journal* 77 (1931): 97–108.

Said, Abdul-Aziz. "Precept and Practice of Human Rights in Islam." *Universal Human Rights* 1 (1979): 63–79.

Salam, Nawaf A. "The Emergence of Citizenship in Islamdom." *Arab Law Quarterly* 12 (1997): 125–147.

Saleem, Muhammad T. "The English Translations of the Holy Qurʾan: A Critique." *Al-Idah* 27 (2013): 77–98.

Salerno, Mariarosaria. "Relations, Politics, and Economic Choices in the Mediterranean: The Kingdom of Naples and Tunisia between the Thirteenth and the Fourteenth Centuries." In *People and Goods on the Move: Merchants, Networks and Communication Routes in the Medieval and Early Modern Mediterranean*. Edited by Özlem Çaykent and Luca Zavagno. Fisciano: ICSR Mediterranean Knowledge, 2016: 65–75.

Sālim, ʿAbd al-ʿAzīz. *Al-Baḥr al-Aḥmar fī al-Tārīkh al-Islāmī*. Alexandria: Muʾassasat Shabāb al-Jāmiʿa, 1990.

Sālim, ʿAbd al-ʿAzīz and ʿAbbādī, Aḥmad. *Tārīkh al-Baḥriyya al-Islāmiyya fī Miṣr wa'l-Shām*. Beirut: Dār al-Nahḍa al-ʿArabiyya, 1981.

Tārīkh al-Baḥriyya al-Islāmiyya fī al-Maghrib wa'l-Andalus. Beirut: Dār al-Nahḍa al-ʿArabiyya, 1969.

Salisu, Taiwo M. "*ʿUrf/ʿAdah* (Custom): An Ancillary Mechanism in *Shariʿah*." *Ilorin Journal of Religious Studies* 3 (2013): 133–148.

Salleh, Badriyyah H. "Undang-undang Laut (Melaka Maritime Laws/Code)." In *Southeast Asia: A Historical Encyclopedia from Angkor Wat to East Timor*. Edited by Ooi Keat Gin. Santa Barbara: ABC-CLIO, 2004: 1360–1361.

Salvatori, Enrica. "Corsairs' Crews and Cross-Cultural Interactions: The Case of the Pisan Trapelicinus in the Twelfth Century." *Medieval Encounter* 13 (2007): 32–55.

Samarrai, Alauddin. "Medieval Commerce and Diplomacy: Islam and Europe, A.D. 850–1300." *Canadian Journal of History* 15 (1980): 1–21.

Samour, Nahed. "Is There a Role for Islamic International Law in the History of International Law?" *European Journal of International Law* 25 (2014): 313–319.

Sanborn, Frederic R. *Origins of the Early English Maritime and Commercial Law*. New York: Century Co., 1930.

Sasson, Jack. "Canaanite Maritime Involvement in the Second Millennium B.C." *Journal of the American Oriental Society* 86 (1966): 126–138.

Sawers, Brian. "The Poll Tax before Jim Crow." *American Journal of Legal History* 57 (2017): 166–197.

Schacht, Joseph. *An Introduction to Islamic Law*. Reprint, Oxford: Oxford University Press, 1993.

Schachte, William L. "The History of the Territorial Sea from a National Security Perspective." *Territorial Sea Journal* 1 (1990): 143–168.

Schilling, Ruth. "Asserting the Boundaries: Defining the City and Its Territory by Political Ritual." In *Imagining the City*. Edited by Christian Emden and David Midgley. Bern: Peter Lang – International Academic Publisher, 2006: 87–106.

Schmidt, Gerhard. "Mediterranean Elements in the British Navigation Act." *Speculum* 22 (1947): 342–357.

Schmitt, Carl. *The Nomos of the Earth in the International Law of the Jus Publicum Europaeum*. 2nd ed. Translated by G. L. Ulmen. New York: Telos Press Publishing, 2006.

Schuman, Lein O. *Political History of the Yemen at the Beginning of the 16th Century*. Amsterdam: Djambatan, 1961.

Seland, Eivind H. "The Indian Ships at Moscha and the Indo-Arabian Trading Circuit." Proceedings of the Seminar for Arabian Studies 38 (2008): 283–287.

Semple, Ellen C. "Pirate Coasts of the Mediterranean Sea." *Geographical Review* 2 (1916): 134–151.

Sen, Tansen. "The Military Campaigns of Rajendra Chola and the Chola-Srivijaya-China Triangle." In *Nagapattinam to Suvarnadwipa: Reflections on the Chola Naval Expeditions to Southeast Asia*. Edited by Hermann Kulke, K. Kesavapany, and Vijay Sakhuja. Singapore: Institute of Southeast Asian Studies, 2009: 61–75.

"The Formation of Chinese Maritime Networks to Southern Asia, 1250–1450." *Journal of the Economic and Social History of the Orient* 49 (2006): 421–453.

Sengupta, R. "History of Oceanography of the Indian Ocean." In *New Trends in Indian Art and Archaeology*. Edited by B. U. Nayak and N. C. Ghosh. New Delhi: Aditya Prakashan, 1992: 398–408.

Şentürk, Recep. "Ādamiyyah ʿIsmah: The Contested Relationship between Humanity and Human Rights in Classical Islamic Law." *Islām Araştirmalari Dergisi* 8 (2002): 39–69.

Serjeant, Robert B. *The Portuguese off the South Arabian Coast: Ḥaḍramī Chronicles*. Oxford: Clarendon Press, 1963.

"Maritime Customary Law off the Arabian Coasts." In *Sociétés et compagnies de commerce en orient et dans l'océan indien*. Edited by Michel Mollat. Paris: S. E. V. P. E. N., 1970: 195–207

Setia, ʿAdī. "*Taskhīr*, Fine-Tuning, Intelligent Design, and the Scientific Appreciation of Nature." *Islam and Science* 2 (2004): 7–31.
Shabana, Ayman. *Custom in Islamic Law and Legal Theory*. New York: Palgrave Macmillan, 2010.
Shahīd, Irfān A. *Byzantium and the Arabs in the Sixth-Century*. 2 vols. Washington DC: Dumbarton Oaks Research Library, 2009.
Shaw, Brent D. "Bandits in the Roman Empire." *Past and Present* 105 (1984): 3–52.
Sheriff, Abdul. *Dhow Cultures of the Indian Ocean: Cosmopolitanism, Commerce, and Islam*. London: Hurst and Company, 2010.
Sherman, Charles P. "The Roman Administrative Marine." In *Studi in onore di Salvatore Riccobono nel XL anno del suo insegnamento*. Edited by Salvatore Riccobono and Giovanni Baviera. Palermo: Arti grafiche G. Castiglia, 1936: 2:65–76.
Shihāb, Ḥasan Ṣ. *Al-Nūniyya al-Kubrā maʿ Sitt Qaṣāʾid Ukhrā Naẓm Shihāb al-Dīn Aḥmad Ibn Mājid*. Muscat: Wizārat al-Turāth al-Qawmī wa'l-Thaqāfa, 1413/1993.
Shokoohy, Mehrdad. "The Town of Cochin and Its Muslim Heritage on the Malabar Coast, South India." *Journal of the Royal Asiatic Society of Great Britain and Ireland* 8 (1998): 351–394.
Shoukri, Arafat M. *Refugee Status in Islam: Concepts of Protection in Islamic Tradition and International Law*. London: I. B. Tauris, 2011.
Sicking, Louis. "Introduction: Maritime Conflict Management, Diplomacy and International Law, 1100–1800." *Comparative Legal History* 5 (2017): 2–15.
Simonsohn, Shlomo. *The Jews in Sicily: 383–1300*. Leiden: E. J. Brill, 1997.
Simonsohn, Uriel. *A Common Justice: The Legal Allegiances of Christians and Jews under Early Islam*. Philadelphia: University of Pennsylvania Press, 2011.
"Communal Boundaries Reconsidered: Jews and Christians Appealing to Muslim Authorities in the Medieval Near East." *Jewish Studies Quarterly* 14 (2007): 328–363.
"Seeking Justice among the 'Outsiders': Christian Recourse to Non-Ecclesiastical Judicial Systems under Early Islam." *Church History and Religious Culture* 89 (2009): 191–216.
Sirks, Boudewijn. *Food for Rome: The Legal Structure of the Transportation and Processing of Supplies for the Imperial Distribution in Rome and Constantinople*. Amsterdam: J. C. Publishers, 1991.
Sī-Sālim, ʿIṣām S. *Juzur al-Andalus al-Mansiyya: Al-Tārīkh al-Islāmī li-Juzur al-Balyār 89–685/708–1287*. Beirut: Dār al-ʿIlm lil-Malāyīn, 1984.
Slessarev, Vsevolod. "Ecclesiae Mercatorum and the Rise of Merchant Colonies." *Business History Review* 41 (1967): 177–197.
Smith, Daniel J. "Heterogeneity and Exchange: Safe-Conducts in Medieval Spain." *Review of Australian Economics* 27 (2014): 183–197.
Smith, George P. "The Concept of Free Seas: Shaping Modern Maritime Policy within a Vector of Historical Influence." *International Lawyer* 11 (1977): 355–363.

Smith, Robert S. "The Early History of the Spanish Sea Consulate." *Politica* 3 (1935): 312–324.

Sobecki, Sebastian I. *The Sea and Medieval English Literature*. Cambridge: D. S. Brewer, 2008.

Soosa, Nasim M. "The Historical Interpretation of the Origin of the Capitulations in the Ottoman Empire." *Temple Law Quarterly* 4 (1929–1930): 358–371.

Sperber, Daniel. *Nautica Talmudica*. Leiden: E. J. Brill, 1986.

Stantchev, Stefan K. *Spiritual Rationality: Papal Embargo as Cultural Practice*. Oxford: Oxford University Press, 2014.

"The Medieval Origins of Embargo as a Policy Tool." *History of Political Thought* 33 (2012): 373–399.

Starr, Chester G. *The Roman Imperial Navy 31 B.C.–A.D. 324*. Chicago: Ares Publishers, 1993.

"Coastal Defense in the Roman World." *American Journal of Philology* 64 (1943): 56–70.

Steinberg, Philip E. *The Social Construction of the Ocean*. Cambridge: Cambridge University Press, 2001.

"Lines of Division, Lines of Connection: Stewardship in the World Ocean." *Geographical Review* 89 (1999): 254–264.

"Three Historical Systems of Ocean Governance: A Framework for Analyzing the Law of the Sea." *World Bulletin* 12 (1996): 1–19.

Stone, Jon R. *The Routledge Book of World Proverbs*. New York: Routledge, 2006.

Straumann, Benjamin. "Is Modern Liberty Ancient? Roman Remedies and Natural Rights in Hugo Grotius's Early Works on Natural Law." *Law and History Review* 27 (2009): 55–85.

"'Ancient Caesarian Lawyers' in a State of Nature: Roman Tradition and Natural Rights in Hugo Grotius's *De iure praedae*." *Political Theory* 34 (2006): 328–350.

Subramanian, Lakshmi. "Of Pirates and Potentates: Maritime Jurisdiction and the Trade Construction of Piracy in the Indian Ocean." In *Cultures of Trade: Indian Ocean Exchanges*. Edited by Devleena Ghosh and Stephen Muecke. Newcastle: Cambridge Scholars Publishing, 2007: 19–30.

Subrahmanyam, Sanjay. *The Political Economy of Commerce Southern India 1500–1650*. Cambridge: Cambridge University Press, 1990.

"Of Imārat and Tijārat: Asian Merchants and State Power in the Western Indian Ocean, 1400 to 1750." *Comparative Studies in Society and History* 37 (1995): 750–780.

Sutherland, Heather. "Geography as Destiny? The Role of Water in Southeast Asian History." In *A World of Water: Rain, Rivers and Seas in Southeast Asian Histories*. Edited by Peter Boomgaard. Leiden: KITLV Press, 2007: 27–70.

Tai, Emily S. "Piracy and Law in Medieval Genoa: The *Consilia* of Bartolomeo Bosco." *Medieval Encounters* 9 (2003): 256–282.

Takim, Liyakat. "Peace and War in the Qur'ān and Juridical Literature: A Comparative Perspective." *Journal of Sociology and Social Welfare* 38 (2011): 137–157.

Tammuz, Oded. "*Mare Clausum*: Sailing Seasons in the Mediterranean in Early Antiquity." *Mediterranean Historical Review* 20 (2005): 145–162.
Tan, Ta Sen. *Cheng Ho and Islam in Southeast Asia*. Singapore: Institute of Southeast Asian Studies, 2009.
Taubenschlag, Raphael. *The Law of Greco-Roman Egypt in the Light of the Papyri 332 B.C.–640 A.D.* 2 vols. New York: Herald Square Press, 1944–1948.
Taylor, Jean G. "The Chinese and the Early Centuries of Conversion to Islam in Indonesia." In *Chinese Indonesians: Remembering, Distorting, Forgetting*. Edited by Tim Lindsey and Helen Pausacker. Melbourne: Monash University Press, 2005: 148–164.
Taylor, Julie A. *Muslims in Medieval Italy: The Colony at Lucera*. Lanham: Lexington Books, 2003.
"Freedom and Bondage among Muslims in Southern Italy during the Thirteenth Century." *Journal of Muslim Minority Affairs* 27 (2007): 71–77.
Thayer, Lucius E. "The Capitulations of the Ottoman Empire and the Question of Their Abrogation as It Affects the United States." *American Journal of International Law* 17 (1923): 207–233.
Thomson, K. E. F. "Relations between the Fatimid and Byzantine Empires during the Reign of the Caliph al-Mustansir bi'llah, 1036–1094/427–487." *Byzantine and Modern Greek Studies*, 32 (2008): 50–62.
Thornton, Helen. "Hugo Grotius and the Freedom of the Seas." *International Journal of Maritime History* 16 (2004): 17–38.
Tibbetts, Gerald R. "The Role of Charts in Islamic Navigation in the Indian Ocean." In *The History of Cartography*. Edited by J. B. Harley and David Woodward. Chicago: University of Chicago Press, 1992: 2:256–262.
Arab Navigation in the Indian Ocean before the Coming of the Portuguese: Being a Translation of Kitāb al-Fawāʾid fī Uṣūl ʿIlm al-Baḥr waʾl-Qawāʿid of Aḥmad Ibn Mājid al-Najdī. London: Royal Asiatic Society of Great Britain and Ireland, 1971.
"Arab Navigation in the Red Sea." *Geographical Journal* 127 (1961): 322–334.
"Early Muslim Traders in South-East Asia." *Journal of the Malayan Branch of the Royal Asiatic Society* 30 (1957): 1–45.
"Pre-Islamic Arabia and South-East Asia." *Journal of the Malayan Branch of the Royal Asiatic Society* 29 (1956): 182–208.
Tlili, Sarra. *Animals in the Qurʾān*. Cambridge: Cambridge University Press, 2012.
Tolan, John. "Identité et statut minoritaire dans les traditions légales: Deux exemples (XIIe-XIIIe siècles)." In *Identitats Reunió Científica, XIX Curs d'Estiu Comtat d'Urgell*. Universitat de Lleida (2012): 99–106.
Tolmacheva, Marina. "The Indian Ocean in Arab Geography: Transmission of Knowledge between Formal and Informal Geographical Traditions." *Terra Brasilis* 6 (2015): 1–12.
Toorawa, Shawkat M. "Wāq al-Wāq: Fabulous, Fabular, Indian Ocean (?) Island(s) . . . ." *Emergences* 10 (2000): 387–402.

Treves, Tullio. "Human Rights and the Law of the Sea." *Berkeley Journal of International Law* 28 (2010): 1–14.

Tripati, Sila and Raut, L. N. "Monsoon Wind and Maritime Trade: A Case Study of Historical Evidence from Orissa, India." *Current Science* 90 (2006): 864–871.

Tritton, Arthur S. *The Caliphs and Their Non-Muslim Subjects: A Critical Study of the Covenant of 'Umar*. London: F. Cass, 1930.

Turki, Abdel-Magid. "Consultation juridique d'al-Imam al-Mazari sur le cas des musulmans vivant en Sicile sous l'autorité des Normands." *Mélanges de l'Université St-Joseph* 50 (1980): 691–704.

Udovitch, Abraham L. *Partnership and Profit in Medieval Islam*. Princeton: Princeton University Press, 1970.

"An Eleventh Century Islamic Treatise on the Law of the Sea." *Annales Islamologiques* 27 (1993): 37–54.

"Time, the Sea and Society: Duration of Commercial Voyages on the Southern Shores of the Mediterranean during the High Middle Ages." In *La navigazione mediterranea nell'alto medioevo*. Spoleto: Presso la sede del Centro, 1978: 503–563.

'Umarī, 'Abd al-'Azīz. *Rasūl Allāh wa-Khātam al-Nabiyyīn*. 5 vols. Riyad: Bīsān lil-Nashr wa'l-Tawzī', 1432/2011.

Ünlü, Nihan. *The Legal Regime of the Turkish Straits*. The Hague: Kluwer Law International, 2002.

'Uthmān, Muḥammad R. *Al-Ḥuqūq wa'l-Wājibāt wa'l-'Alāqāt al-Duwaliyya fī al-Islām*. Beirut: Dār Iqra', 1403/1982.

'Uthmān, Shawqī 'A. *Tijārat al-Muḥīṭ al-Hindī fī 'Aṣr al-Siyāda al-Islāmiyya* (41–904/661–1498). Kuwait: Al-Majlis al-Waṭanī lil-Thaqāfa, 1990.

Valérian, Dominique. "Ifrīqiyan Muslim Merchants in the Mediterranean at the End of the Middle Ages." *Mediterranean Historical Review* 14 (1999): 47–66.

Vallet, Eric. "Yemeni 'Oceanic Policy' at the End of the 13th Century." *Proceedings of the Seminar for Arabian Studies* 36 (2006): 289–296.

Vander Linden, H. "Alexander VI and the Demarcation of the Maritime and Colonial Domains of Spain and Portugal, 1493–1494." *American Historical Review* 22 (1916): 1–20.

Van Ittersum, Martine J. *Profit and Principle: Hugo Grotius, Natural Rights Theories and the Rise of Dutch Power in the East Indies*. Leiden: E. J. Brill, 2006.

Vergès, Françoise. "Writing on Water: Peripheries, Flows, Capital, and Struggles in the Indian Ocean." *Positions* 11 (2003): 241–257.

Vieira, Mónica B. "Mare Liberum *vs.* Mare Clausum: Grotius, Freitas, and Selden's Debate on Dominion over the Seas." *Journal of the History of Ideas* 64 (2003): 361–377.

Wade, Geoff. "Early Expansion in South East Asia, Eighth to Fifteenth Centuries." In *The New Cambridge History of Islam: The Eastern Islamic World – Eleventh to Eighteenth Centuries*. Edited by David O. Morgan and Anthony Reid. Cambridge: Cambridge University Press, 2010: 3:366–408.

"An Early Age of Commerce in Southeast Asia, 900–1300 CE." *Journal of Southeast Asian Studies* 40 (2009): 221–265.

"The Zheng He Voyages: A Reassessment." *Journal of the Malaysian Branch of the Royal Asiatic Society* 78 (2005): 37–58.

Wain, Alexander. "Chinese Muslims and the Conversion of Melaka to Islam." *International Proceedings of Economics Development and Research* 51 (2012): 35–40.

Waisberg, Tatiana. "The Treaty of Tordesillas and the (re)Invention of International Law in the Age of Discovery." *Journal of Global Studies* 47 (2017): 1–12.

Wake, Christopher H. "Malacca's Early Kings and the Reception of Islam." *Journal of Southeast Asian History* 5 (1964): 104–128.

Wang, Gungwu. "The First Three Rulers of Malacca." *Journal of the Malaysian Branch of the Royal Asiatic Society* 41 (1968): 11–22. An expanded version of this article by the same author appears in *Admiral Zheng He and Southeast Asia*. Edited by Leo Suryadinata. Singapore: Institute of Southeast Asian Studies, 2005: 26–41.

Ward, Kerry. *Networks of Empire: Forced Migration in the Dutch East India Company*. Cambridge: Cambridge University Press, 2009.

Washburn, Wilcomb E. "The Meaning of 'Discovery' in the Fifteenth and Sixteenth Centuries." *American Historical Review* 68 (1962): 1–21.

Whitehouse, David. "Maritime Trade in the Gulf: The 11th and 12th Centuries." *World Archaeology* 14 (1983): 328–334.

Wild, Stefan. "Muslim Translators and Translation of the Qur'an into English." *Journal of Qur'ānic Studies* 17 (2015): 158–182.

Wing, Patrick. "Indian Ocean Trade and Sultanic Authority: The *Nāẓir* of Jeddah and the Mamluk Political Economy." *Journal of the Economic and Social History of the Orient* 57 (2014): 55–75.

Wink, André. *Al-Hind: The Making of the Indo-Islamic World*. 3 vols. Leiden: E. J. Brill, 1991–2004.

"From the Mediterranean to the Indian Ocean: Medieval History in Geographic Perspective." *Comparative Studies in Society and History* 44 (2002): 416–445.

Winkel, Eric. "Three Relationships." *Islam and Civilisational Renewal* 2 (2010–2011): 222–223, 397–401.

Winstedt, Richard O. "The Date of the Malacca Legal Codes." *Journal of the Royal Asiatic Society of Great Britain and Ireland* 1–2 (1953): 31–33.

"The Malay Founder of Medieval Malacca." *Bulletin of the School of Oriental and African Studies* 12 (1948): 726–729.

"Old Malay Legal Digests and Malay Customary Law." *Journal of the Royal Asiatic Society of Great Britain and Ireland* 1 (1945): 17–29.

"Kedah Law." *Journal of the Malayan Branch of the Royal Asiatic Society* 6 (1928): 1–44.

Winstedt, Richard and De Josselin De Jong, P. E. "The Maritime Laws of Malacca." *Journal of the Malayan Branch of the Royal Asiatic Society* 29 (1956): 22–59.

Wohaibi, Abdullah. *The Northern Hijaz in the Writings of the Arab Geographers 800–1150*. Beirut: Al-Risalah, 1973.

Wolf, Robert. "Da Gama's Blundering: Trade Encounters in Africa and Asia during the European 'Age of Discovery,' 1450–1520." *The History Teacher* 31 (1998): 297–318.

Wright, R. F. "The High Seas and the Church in the Middle Ages." *Mariner's Mirror* 53 (1967): 3–31, 115–135.

Yajima, Hikoichi. "Maritime Activities of the Arab Gulf People and the Indian Ocean World in the Eleventh and Twelfth Centuries." *Journal of Asian and African Studies* 14 (1977): 195–208.

Yatim, Zakaria M. "The Development of the Law of the Sea in Relation to Malaysia." *Malaysian Management Journal* 1 (1992): 87–98.

Yousif, Ahmad. "Islam, Minorities, and Religious Freedom: A Challenge to Modern Theory of Pluralism." *Journal of Muslim Minority Affairs* 20 (2000): 29–41.

Zahid, Anowar and Shapiee, Rohimi. "Considering Custom in the Making of Siyar (Islamic International Law)." *Journal of East Asia and International Law* 3 (2010): 123–135.

"*Pacta Sunt Servanda*: Islamic Perception." *Journal of East Asia and International Law* 3 (2010): 375–385.

"Customs as a Source of *Siyar* and International Law: A Comparative of the Qualifying Criteria." *International Journal of Civil Society Law* 8 (2010): 36–55.

Zahoor, Akram. *Muslim History 570–1950 C.E.* Gaithersburg, MD: n.p., 2000.

Zayd, Ṣāliḥ ʿA. *Aḥkām ʿAqd al-Amān wa'l-Mustaʾminīn fī al-Islām*. Riyad: Al-Dār al-Waṭaniyya, 1406/1985.

Zaydān, ʿAbd al-Karīm. *Aḥkām al-Dhimmiyyīn wa'l-Mustaʾminīn fī Dār al-Isl ām*. Beirut: Muʾassasat al-Risālah, 1402/1982.

Ziskind, Jonathan. "The International Legal Status of the Sea in Antiquity." *Acta Orientalia* 35 (1973): 35–49.

"International Law and Ancient Sources: Grotius and Selden." *Review of Politics* 35 (1973): 537–559.

Zumayli, Zakaria I. and ʿIdwān, Kāʾināt M. "Al-Iʿjāz al-Tashrīʿī fī Ḥadday al-Sariqa wa'l-Ḥirāba." *Majallat al-Jāmiʿa al-Islāmiyya* 14 (2006): 75–121.

Žužul, Marina V. "The Law of the Sea in the Mediterranean throughout the History." *Miscellanea Hadriatica et Mediterranea* 4 (2017): 47–80.

UNPUBLISHED DISSERTATIONS AND THESES

Abdul Rahman, Hilmi M. "Just War, Peace, and Human Rights under Islamic and International Law." Master's thesis, Faculty of Graduate Studies, McGill University, 1997.

Abu Hamad, Omri. "The Sea and Marine Environment in the Qurʾān and the Ḥadīth and Their Reflections in the Classical Geographical and Astronomical Sources and Pilot-Books." PhD diss., Department of Maritime Civilizations, University of Haifa, 2014.

ʿĀmūdī, Abhara S. "Al-Arḍ fī Ḍaw' al-Qur'ān." Master's thesis, Islamic University, Gaza, 1427/2006.

Averbuch, Bryan D. "From Siraf to Sumatra: Seafaring and Spices in the Islamicate Indo-Pacific, Ninth–Eleventh Centuries C.E." PhD diss., Department of Near Eastern Languages and Civilizations, Harvard University, 2013.

Azmi, Ida M. "Intellectual Property Laws and Islam in Malaysia." PhD diss., Queen Mary and Westfield College, 1995.

Baaj, Amar S. "The Struggle for North Africa between Almohads, Ayyubids, and Banū Ghāniya (Late Twelfth to Early Thirteenth Centuries A.D.)." PhD diss., Department of Near Eastern Studies, University of Toronto, 2013.

Calafat, Guillaume. "Une mer jalousie: jurisdictions maritimes, ports francs et regulation du commerce en Méditerranée (1590–1740)." PhD diss., Université Paris 1 Panthéon-Sorbonne, 2013.

Clark, Patrick E. "Taxation and the Formation of the Late Roman Social Contract." PhD diss., Department of History, University of California Berkeley, 2017.

Cardoso, Elsa R. F. "Diplomacy and Oriental Influence in the Court of Cordoba (9th–10th Centuries)." Master's thesis, Department of History, University of Lisbon, 2015.

Davis, William M. "Analysis of the Strategy to Combat Maritime Piracy." Master's thesis, Fort Leavenworth, Kansas, 2009.

Denawy, Mahmood H. "A Reappraisal of Attitudes to the 'People of the Book' in the Qur'ān and *Ḥadīth*, with Particular Reference to Muslim Fiscal Policy and Covenant of ʿUmar." PhD diss., University of Durham, 2007.

Dick, Bryan D. "Framing 'Piracy': Restitution at Sea in the Later Middle Ages." PhD diss., Department of History, University of Glasgow, 2010.

El-Hadary, Tariq H. "Equivalence and Translatability of Qur'ānic Discourse: A Comparative and Analytical Evaluation." PhD diss., School of Modern Languages, University of Leeds, 2008.

Feakes, Michael J. "Formative Influences on the Evolution of International Law: A Case Study of Territorial Waters (1550–1650)." PhD diss., Law School, University of Hull, 1994.

Furtado, Michael A. "Islands of Castile: Artistic, Literary, and Legal Perception of the Sea in Castile-Leon, 1248–1450." PhD diss., Department of History, University of Oregon, 2011.

Ghirani, Muhammad M. "The Law of Charterparty with Particular Reference to Islamic Law." PhD diss., Glasgow College, 1990.

Greenwood, Ryan M. "Law and War in Late Medieval Italy: The *Jus Commune* on War and Its Application in Florence, c. 1150–1450." PhD diss., Department of History, University of Toronto, 2011.

Ḥajī-Ḥassan, ʿAbdullāh ʿA. "Sales and Contracts in Early Islamic Commercial Law." PhD diss., University of Edinburgh, 1986.

Harper, Alexander. "Patronage in the re-Christianized Landscape of Angevin Apulia: the Rebuilding of *Luceria sarracenorum* into *Civitas Sanctae Mariae*." PhD diss., Department of Art, University of Toronto, 2014.

Hemeidah, Ahmad S. Z. "Repentance as a Legal Concept." Master's thesis, Department of Near Eastern Studies, University of Arizona, 2011.

Hendrickson, Jocelyn N. "The Islamic Obligation to Emigrate: Al-Wansharīsī's *Asnā al-Matājir* Reconsidered." PhD diss., Graduate Division of Religion, Emory University, 2009.

Hosani, Naeem M. "Arab Wayfinding on Land and at Sea: An Historical Comparison of Traditional Navigation Techniques." Master's thesis, Department of Geography, University of Kansas, 2005.

Ismail, Muhammad-Basheer A. "Islamic Diplomatic Law and International Diplomatic Law: A Quest for Compatibility." PhD diss., University of Hull, 2012.

Kahlaoui, Tarek. "The Depiction of the Mediterranean in Islamic Cartography." PhD diss., History of Art, University of Pennsylvania, 2008.

Kanj, Sawsan G. "Aḥkām Mukhāṣamāt al-Musta'minīn fī al-Fiqh al-Islāmī." Master's thesis, Āl al-Bayt University, 2004.

Ledger, Jeremy F. "Mapping Mediterranean Geographies: Geographic and Cartographic Encounters between the Islamic World and Europe, c. 1100–1600." PhD diss., Department of History, University of Michigan, 2016.

Lee, Risha. "Constructing Community: Tamil Merchant Temples in India and China, 850–1281." PhD diss., Columbia University, 2012.

Masri, Ahmed M. "The Classical Conceptions of Treaty, Alliances, and Neutrality in Sunni Islam." PhD diss., Department of Politics, Newcastle University, 1998.

Merlino, Mark. "The Post-Byzantine Legal Tradition in Theory and Practice." Master's thesis, Institute of Economics and Social Sciences, Bilkent University, 2004.

Mikati, Rana M. "The Creation of Early Islamic Beirut: The Sea, Scholars, Jihad and the Sacred." PhD diss., Department of Near Eastern Languages and Civilizations, University of Chicago, 2013.

Mirza, Sarah Z. "Oral Tradition and Scribals Conventions in the Documents Attributed to the Prophet Muḥammad." PhD diss., Department of Near Eastern Studies, University of Michigan, 2010.

Noble, Deborah R. "The Principles of Islamic Maritime Law." PhD diss., Department of Law, School of Oriental and African Studies, University of London, 1988.

Omar, Abdallah M. "Towards the Conquest of Islamicjerusalem: The Three Main Practical Steps Taken by Prophet Muhammad." Master's thesis, University of Aberdeen, 2005.

Othman, Rana S. "Aḥkām al-Jinsiyya wa'l-Muwāṭana min Manẓūr Islāmī." Master's thesis, An-Najah National University, Nablus, Palestine, 2001.

Pitcaithly, William M. E. "Pirates, Robbers and other Malefactors: The Role Played by Violence at Sea in Relations between England and the Hanse Towns, 1385–1420." PhD diss., Department of History, University of Exeter, 2011.

Porter, Venetia-Ann. "The History and Monuments of the Tahirid Dynasty of the Yemen 858–923/1454–1517." PhD diss., Durham University, 1992. Available at E-Theses Online: http://etheses.dur.ac.uk/5867/.

Power, Timothy. "Red Sea Region during the 'Long' Late Antiquity (AD 500–1000)." PhD diss., Faculty of Oriental Studies, University of Oxford, 2010. https://ia600908.us.archive.org/33/items/redsea/Tim_Power__DPhil_Thesis_-_Red_Sea__AD_500–1000.pdf.

Qādirī, Muḥammad Ṭ. "Punishments in Islam: Their Classification and Philosophy." PhD diss., School of Law, Punjab University, Lahore, 1984.

Salman, Mohammed H. "Aspects of Portuguese Rule in the Arabian Gulf, 1521–1622." PhD diss., University of Hull, 2004.

Senior, Clive M. "An Investigation of the Activities and Importance of English Pirates 1603–40." PhD diss., University of Bristol, 1972.

Shafiq, Suhanna. "The Maritime Culture in the *Kitāb ʿAjāʾib al-Hind* (The Book of the Marvels of India) by Buzurg Ibn Shahriyār (d. 399/1009)." Master's thesis, University of Exeter, 2011.

Sharif, Mohd F. "The Concept of *Jihād* and *Baghy* in Islamic Law with Special Reference to Ibn Taymiyya." PhD diss., University of Edinburgh, 2006.

Shuayb, Fiazuddin. "Who's Better than God to Rule? An Inquiry into the Formation of the First Islamic State (622–32 C.E.)." PhD diss., UCLA International Institute, 2012.

Stantchev, Stefan K. "Embargo: The Origins on an Idea and the Implications of a Policy in Europe and the Mediterranean, ca 1100–ca. 1500." PhD diss., Department of History, University of Michigan, 2009.

Su, Chung-Jen, "The Expeditions of Cheng Ho to the Western Ocean." PhD diss., University of Hong Kong, 1964.

Sumaiti, Jamal. "The Contribution of Islamic Law to the Maritime Law." PhD diss., University of Wales, Lampeter, 2004.

Swarztrauber, Sayer A. "The Three-Mile Limit of Territorial Seas: A Brief History." PhD diss., School of International Services, American University, Washington DC, 1970.

Tai, Emily S. "Honor among Thieves: Piracy, Restitution, and Reprisal in Genoa, Venice, and the Crown of Catalonia-Aragon." PhD diss., Harvard University, 1996.

Thenayian, Mohammed Bin A. Rashed. "An Archaeological Study of the Yemeni Highland Pilgrim Route between Ṣanʿāʾ and Mecca." PhD diss., Durham University, 1993.

Thomas, Ross L. "Maritime Cultures of the Erythraean Sea." PhD diss., School of Humanities, University of Southampton, 2009.

Thurman, Aleksandra E. "The Justification of the Law of the Sea in Early Modern Europe." PhD diss., Department of Political Science, University of Michigan, 2010.

Wakil, Ahmed. "Searching for the Covenants: Identifying Authentic Documents of the Prophet based on Scribal Conventions and Textual Analysis." Master's thesis, College of Islamic Studies, Hamad bin Khalifa University, 2017.

Yakin, Ayang U. "Le droit musulman dans le monde insulindien du XIVe au XVIIe siècles." Paris: École des hautes études en sciences sociales, 2005.

Yaseen, Khaleda A. "Mawqif al-Rasūl min Yahūd al-Ḥijāz." Master's thesis, Department of History, An-Najah National University, Nablus, 2009.

Index

Other titles in the series

Agricultural Innovation in the Early Islamic World: The Diffusion of Crops and Farming Techniques, 700–1100, Andrew M. Watson

Muslim Tradition: Studies in Chronology, Provenance and Authorship of Early Hadith, G. H. A. Juynboll

Social History of Timbuktu: The Role of Muslim Scholars and Notables 1400–1900, Elias N. Saad

Sex and Society in Islam: Birth Control before the Nineteenth Century, B. F. Musallam

Towns and Townsmen of Ottoman Anatolia: Trade, Crafts and Food Production in an Urban Setting, 1520–1650, Suraiya Faroqhi

Unlawful Gain and Legitimate Profit in Islamic Law: Riba, Gharar and Islamic Banking, Nabil A. Saleh

Men of Modest Substance: House Owners and House Property in Seventeenth-Century Ankara and Kayseri, Suraiya Faroqhi

Roman, Provincial and Islamic Law: The Origins of the Islamic Patronate, Patricia Crone

Economic Life in Ottoman Jerusalem, Amnon Cohen

Mannerism in Arabic Poetry: A Structural Analysis of Selected Texts (3rd Century AH/9th Century AD – 5th Century AH/11th Century AD), Stefan Sperl

The Rise and Rule of Tamerlane, Beatrice Forbes Manz

Popular Culture in Medieval Cairo, Boaz Shoshan

Early Philosophical Shiism: The Ismaili Neoplatonism of Abu Ya'qub Al-Sijistani, Paul E. Walker

Indian Merchants and Eurasian Trade, 1600–1750, Stephen Frederic Dale

Palestinian Peasants and Ottoman Officials: Rural Administration around Sixteenth-Century Jerusalem, Amy Singer

Arabic Historical Thought in the Classical Period, Tarif Khalidi

Mongols and Mamluks: The Mamluk–Ilkhanid War, 1260–1281, Reuven Amitai-Preiss

Knowledge and Social Practice in Medieval Damascus, 1190–1350, Michael Chamberlain

The Politics of Households in Ottoman Egypt: The Rise of the Qazdağlis, Jane Hathaway

Hierarchy and Egalitarianism in Islamic Thought, Louise Marlow

Commodity and Exchange in the Mongol Empire: A Cultural History of Islamic Textiles, Thomas T. Allsen

State and Provincial Society in the Ottoman Empire: Mosul, 1540–1834, Dina Rizk Khoury

The Mamluks in Egyptian Politics and Society, Thomas Philipp and Ulrich Haarmann (eds.)

The Delhi Sultanate: A Political and Military History, Peter Jackson

European and Islamic Trade in the Early Ottoman State: The Merchants of Genoa and Turkey, Kate Fleet

The Ottoman City between East and West: Aleppo, Izmir, and Istanbul, Edhem Eldem, Daniel Goffman, and Bruce Masters

The Politics of Trade in Safavid Iran: Silk for Silver, 1600–1730, Rudolph P. Matthee

The Idea of Idolatry and the Emergence of Islam: From Polemic to History, G. R. Hawting
A Monetary History of the Ottoman Empire, Şevket Pamuk
Classical Arabic Biography: The Heirs of the Prophets in the Age of Al-Ma'mun, Michael Cooperson
Empire and Elites after the Muslim Conquest: The Transformation of Northern Mesopotamia, Chase F. Robinson
Poverty and Charity in Medieval Islam: Mamluk Egypt, 1250–1517, Adam Sabra
Culture and Conquest in Mongol Eurasia, Thomas T. Allsen
Christians and Jews in the Ottoman Arab World: The Roots of Sectarianism, Bruce Masters
Arabic Administration in Norman Sicily: The Royal Diwan, Jeremy Johns
Law, Society and Culture in the Maghrib, 1300–1500, David S. Powers
Revival and Reform in Islam: The Legacy of Muhammad al-Shawkani, Bernard Haykel
Tolerance and Coercion in Islam: Interfaith Relations in the Muslim Tradition, Yohanan Friedmann
Guns for the Sultan: Military Power and the Weapons Industry in the Ottoman Empire, Gábor Ágoston
Marriage, Money and Divorce in Medieval Islamic Society, Yossef Rapoport
The Empire of the Qara Khitai in Eurasian History: Between China and the Islamic World, Michal Biran
Domesticity and Power in the Early Mughal World, Ruby Lal
Power, Politics and Religion in Timurid Iran, Beatrice Forbes Manz
Postal Systems in the Pre-Modern Islamic World, Adam J. Silverstein
Kingship and Ideology in the Islamic and Mongol Worlds, Anne F. Broadbridge
Justice, Punishment and the Medieval Muslim Imagination, Christian Lange
The Shiites of Lebanon under Ottoman Rule, 1516–1788, Stefan Winter
Women and Slavery in the Late Ottoman Empire, Madeline Zilfi
The Second Ottoman Empire: Political and Social Transformation in the Early Modern World, Baki Tezcan
The Legendary Biographies of Tamerlane: Islam and Heroic Apocrypha in Central Asia, Ron Sela
Non-Muslims in the Early Islamic Empire: From Surrender to Coexistence, Milka Levy-Rubin
The Origins of the Shi'a: Identity, Ritual, and Sacred Space in Eighth-Century Kufa, Najam Haider
Politics, Law, and Community in Islamic Thought: The Taymiyyan Moment, Ovamir Anjum
The Power of Oratory in the Medieval Muslim World, Linda G. Jones
Animals in the Qur'an, Sarra Tlili
The Logic of Law Making in Islam: Women and Prayer in the Legal Tradition, Behnam Sadeghi
Empire and Power in the Reign of Süleyman: Narrating the Sixteenth-Century Ottoman World, Kaya Şahin
Law and Piety in Medieval Islam, Megan H. Reid
Women and the Transmission of Religious Knowledge in Islam, Asma Sayeed
The New Muslims of Post-Conquest Iran: Tradition, Memory, and Conversion, Sarah Bowen Savant

The Mamluk City in the Middle East: History, Culture, and the Urban Landscape, Nimrod Luz

Disability in the Ottoman Arab World, 1500–1800, Sara Scalenghe

The Holy City of Medina: Sacred Space in Early Islamic Arabia, Harry Munt

Muslim Midwives: The Craft of Birthing in the Premodern Middle East, Avner Giladi

Doubt in Islamic Law: A History of Legal Maxims, Interpretation, and Islamic Criminal Law, Intisar A. Rabb

The Second Formation of Islamic Law: The Hanafi School in the Early Modern Ottoman Empire, Guy Burak

Sexual Violation in Islamic Law: Substance, Evidence, and Procedure, Hina Azam

Gender Hierarchy in the Qur'an: Medieval Interpretations, Modern Responses, Karen Bauer

Intellectual Networks in Timurid Iran: Sharaf al-Din 'Ali Yazdi and the Islamicate Republic of Letters, Ilker Evrim Binbaş

Authority and Identity in Medieval Islamic Historiography: Persian Histories from the Peripheries, Mimi Hanaoka

The Economics of Ottoman Justice: Settlement and Trial in the Sharia Courts, Top of Form Metin Coşgel and Boğaç Ergene

The Mystics of al-Andalus: Ibn Barrajan and Islamic Thought in the Twelfth Century, Yousef Casewit

Muhammad's Heirs: The Rise of Muslim Scholarly Communities, 622–950, Jonathan E. Brockopp

The First of the Modern Ottomans: The Intellectual History of Ahmed Vasif, Ethan Menchinger

Non-Muslim Provinces under Early Islam: Islamic Rule and Iranian Legitimacy in Armenia and Caucasian Albania, Alison Vacca

Women and the Making of the Mongol Empire, Anne F. Broadbridge

Slavery and Empire in Central Asia, Jeff Eden

Christianity in Fifteenth-Century Iraq, Thomas A. Carlson

Child Custody in Islamic Law: Theory and Practice in Egypt since the Sixteenth Century, Ahmed Fekry Ibrahim

Ibadi Muslims of North Africa: Manuscripts, Mobilization and the Making of a Written Tradition, Paul M. Love Jr.

Islamic Law of the Sea: Freedom of Navigation and Passage Rights in Islamic Thought, Hassan S. Khalilieh